COLLECTED POETICAL WORKS

COLLECTED
POETICAL WORKS

BY

ALGERNON CHARLES SWINBURNE

VOLUME II

PUBLISHERS

HARPER AND BROTHERS

NEW YORK AND LONDON

CONTENTS

TRISTRAM OF LYONESSE

STUDIES IN SONG

CONTENTS

CONTENTS

SONNETS ON ENGLISH DRAMATIC POETS
1590-1650

THE HEPTALOGIA

CONTENTS

ASTROPHEL
AND OTHER POEMS

A CHANNEL PASSAGE
AND OTHER POEMS

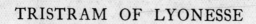

TRISTRAM OF LYONESSE

_25_

TO MY BEST FRIEND

THEODORE WATTS-DUNTON

VOL. II.   A

Spring speaks again, and all our woods are stirred,
  And all our wide glad wastes aflower around,
  That twice have heard keen April's clarion sound
Since here we first together saw and heard
Spring's light reverberate and reiterate word
  Shine forth and speak in season. Life stands crowned
  Here with the best one thing it ever found,
As of my soul's best birthdays dawns the third.

There is a friend that as the wise man saith
  Cleaves closer than a brother : nor to me
    Hath time not shown, through days like waves at strife,
This truth more sure than all things else but death,
  This pearl most perfect found in all the sea
    That washes toward your feet these waifs of life.

THE PINES : *April* 1882

PRELUDE

TRISTRAM AND ISEULT

Love, that is first and last of all things made,
The light that has the living world for shade,
The spirit that for temporal veil has on
The souls of all men woven in unison,
One fiery raiment with all lives inwrought
And lights of sunny and starry deed and thought,
And alway through new act and passion new
Shines the divine same body and beauty through,
The body spiritual of fire and light
That is to worldly noon as noon to night ;
Love, that is flesh upon the spirit of man
And spirit within the flesh whence breath began ;
Love, that keeps all the choir of lives in chime ;
Love, that is blood within the veins of time ;
That wrought the whole world without stroke of hand,
Shaping the breadth of sea, the length of land,
And with the pulse and motion of his breath
Through the great heart of the earth strikes life and
    death,
The sweet twain chords that make the sweet tune live
Through day and night of things alternative,
Through silence and through sound of stress and
    strife,
And ebb and flow of dying death and life :

Love, that sounds loud or light in all men's ears,
Whence all men's eyes take fire from sparks of tears,
That binds on all men's feet or chains or wings ;
Love, that is root and fruit of terrene things ;
Love, that the whole world's waters shall not drown,
The whole world's fiery forces not burn down ;
Love, that what time his own hands guard his head
The whole world's wrath and strength shall not strike
        dead ;
Love, that if once his own hands make his grave
The whole world's pity and sorrow shall not save ;
Love, that for very life shall not be sold,
Nor bought nor bound with iron nor with gold ;
So strong that heaven, could love bid heaven farewell,
Would turn to fruitless and unflowering hell ;
So sweet that hell, to hell could love be given,
Would turn to splendid and sonorous heaven ;
Love that is fire within thee and light above,
And lives by grace of nothing but of love ;
Through many and lovely thoughts and much desire
Led these twain to the life of tears and fire ;
Through many and lovely days and much delight
Led these twain to the lifeless life of night.
    Yea, but what then ? albeit all this were thus,
And soul smote soul and left it ruinous,
And love led love as eyeless men lead men,
Through chance by chance to deathward—Ah, what
        then ?
Hath love not likewise led them further yet,
Out through the years where memories rise and set,
Some large as suns, some moon-like warm and pale,
Some starry-sighted, some through clouds that sail
Seen as red flame through spectral float of fume,
Each with the blush of its own special bloom

On the fair face of its own coloured light,
Distinguishable in all the host of night,
Divisible from all the radiant rest
And separable in splendour?   Hath the best
Light of love's all, of all that burn and move,
A better heaven than heaven is ?   Hath not love
Made for all these their sweet particular air
To shine in, their own beams and names to bear,
Their ways to wander and their wards to keep,
Till story and song and glory and all things sleep?
Hath he not plucked from death of lovers dead
Their musical soft memories, and kept red
The rose of their remembrance in men's eyes,
The sunsets of their stories in his skies,
The blush of their dead blood in lips that speak
Of their dead lives, and in the listener's cheek
That trembles with the kindling pity lit
In gracious hearts for some sweet fever-fit,
A fiery pity enkindled of pure thought
By tales that make their honey out of nought,
The faithless faith that lives without belief
Its light life through, the griefless ghost of grief?
Yea, as warm night refashions the sere blood
In storm-struck petal or in sun-struck bud,
With tender hours and tempering dew to cure
The hunger and thirst of day's distemperature
And ravin of the dry discolouring hours,
Hath he not bid relume their flameless flowers
With summer fire and heat of lamping song,
And bid the short-lived things, long dead, live long,
And thought remake their wan funereal fames,
And the sweet shining signs of women's names
That mark the months out and the weeks anew
He moves in changeless change of seasons through

To fill the days up of his dateless year
Flame from Queen Helen to Queen Guenevere?
For first of all the sphery signs whereby
Love severs light from darkness, and most high,
In the white front of January there glows
The rose-red sign of Helen like a rose :
And gold-eyed as the shore-flower shelterless
Whereon the sharp-breathed sea blows bitterness,
A storm-star that the seafarers of love
Strain their wind-wearied eyes for glimpses of,
Shoots keen through February's grey frost and damp
The lamplike star of Hero for a lamp ;
The star that Marlowe sang into our skies
With mouth of gold, and morning in his eyes ;
And in clear March across the rough blue sea
The signal sapphire of Alcyone
Makes bright the blown brows of the wind-foot year ;
And shining like a sunbeam-smitten tear
Full ere it fall, the fair next sign in sight
Burns opal-wise with April-coloured light
When air is quick with song and rain and flame,
My birth-month star that in love's heaven hath name
Iseult, a light of blossom and beam and shower,
My singing sign that makes the song-tree flower ;
Next like a pale and burning pearl beyond
The rose-white sphere of flower-named Rosamond
Signs the sweet head of Maytime ; and for June
Flares like an angered and storm-reddening moon
Her signal sphere, whose Carthaginian pyre
Shadowed her traitor's flying sail with fire ;
Next, glittering as the wine-bright jacinth-stone,
A star south-risen that first to music shone,
The keen girl-star of golden Juliet bears
Light northward to the month whose forehead wears

Her name for flower upon it, and his trees
Mix their deep English song with Veronese;
And like an awful sovereign chrysolite
Burning, the supreme fire that blinds the night,
The hot gold head of Venus kissed by Mars,
A sun-flower among small sphered flowers of stars,
The light of Cleopatra fills and burns
The hollow of heaven whence ardent August yearns;
And fixed and shining as the sister-shed
Sweet tears for Phaethon disorbed and dead,
The pale bright autumn's amber-coloured sphere,
That through September sees the saddening year
As love sees change through sorrow, hath to name
Francesca's; and the star that watches flame
The embers of the harvest overgone
Is Thisbe's, slain of love in Babylon,
Set in the golden girdle of sweet signs
A blood-bright ruby; last save one light shines
An eastern wonder of sphery chrysopras,
The star that made men mad, Angelica's;
And latest named and lordliest, with a sound
Of swords and harps in heaven that ring it round,
Last love-light and last love-song of the year's,
Gleams like a glorious emerald Guenevere's.
These are the signs wherethrough the year sees
        move,
Full of the sun, the sun-god which is love,
A fiery body blood-red from the heart
Outward, with fire-white wings made wide apart,
That close not and unclose not, but upright
Steered without wind by their own light and might
Sweep through the flameless fire of air that rings
From heaven to heaven with thunder of wheels and
        wings

II.

A 2

And antiphones of motion-moulded rhyme
Through spaces out of space and timeless time.
  So shine above dead chance and conquered change
The spherèd signs, and leave without their range
Doubt and desire, and hope with fear for wife,
Pale pains, and pleasures long worn out of life.
Yea, even the shadows of them spiritless,
Through the dim door of sleep that seem to press,
Forms without form, a piteous people and blind,
Men and no men, whose lamentable kind
The shadow of death and shadow of life compel
Through semblances of heaven and false-faced hell,
Through dreams of light and dreams of darkness tost
On waves innavigable, are these so lost?
Shapes that wax pale and shift in swift strange wise,
Void faces with unspeculative eyes,
Dim things that gaze and glare, dead mouths that
    move,
Featureless heads discrowned of hate and love,
Mockeries and masks of motion and mute breath,
Leavings of life, the superflux of death—
If these things and no more than these things be
Left when man ends or changes, who can see?
Or who can say with what more subtle sense
Their subtler natures taste in air less dense
A life less thick and palpable than ours,
Warmed with faint fires and sweetened with dead
    flowers
And measured by low music? how time fares
In that wan time-forgotten world of theirs,
Their pale poor world too deep for sun or star
To live in, where the eyes of Helen are,
And hers who made as God's own eyes to shine
The eyes that met them of the Florentine,

Wherein the godhead thence transfigured lit
All time for all men with the shadow of it?
Ah, and these too felt on them as God's grace
The pity and glory of this man's breathing face;
For these too, these my lovers, these my twain,
Saw Dante, saw God visible by pain,
With lips that thundered and with feet that trod
Before men's eyes incognisable God;
Saw love and wrath and light and night and fire
Live with one life and at one mouth respire,
And in one golden sound their whole soul heard
Sounding, one sweet immitigable word.
   They have the night, who had like us the day;
We, whom day binds, shall have the night as they.
We, from the fetters of the light unbound,
Healed of our wound of living, shall sleep sound.
All gifts but one the jealous God may keep
From our soul's longing, one he cannot—sleep.
This, though he grudge all other grace to prayer,
This grace his closed hand cannot choose but spare.
This, though his ear be sealed to all that live,
Be it lightly given or lothly, God must give.
We, as the men whose name on earth is none,
We too shall surely pass out of the sun;
Out of the sound and eyeless light of things,
Wide as the stretch of life's time-wandering wings,
Wide as the naked world and shadowless,
And long-lived as the world's own weariness.
Us too, when all the fires of time are cold,
The heights shall hide us and the depths shall hold.
Us too, when all the tears of time are dry,
The night shall lighten from her tearless eye.
Blind is the day and eyeless all its light,
But the large unbewildered eye of night

Hath sense and speculation ; and the sheer
Limitless length of lifeless life and clear,
The timeless space wherein the brief worlds move
Clothed with light life and fruitful with light love,
With hopes that threaten, and with fears that cease,
Past fear and hope, hath in it only peace.
  Yet of these lives inlaid with hopes and fears,
Spun fine as fire and jewelled thick with tears,
These lives made out of loves that long since were,
Lives wrought as ours of earth and burning air,
Fugitive flame, and water of secret springs,
And clothed with joys and sorrows as with wings,
Some yet are good, if aught be good, to save
Some while from washing wreck and wrecking wave.
Was such not theirs, the twain I take, and give
Out of my life to make their dead life live
Some days of mine, and blow my living breath
Between dead lips forgotten even of death ?
So many and many of old have given my twain
Love and live song and honey-hearted pain,
Whose root is sweetness and whose fruit is sweet,
So many and with such joy have tracked their feet,
What should I do to follow ? yet I too,
I have the heart to follow, many or few
Be the feet gone before me ; for the way,
Rose-red with remnant roses of the day
Westward, and eastward white with stars that break,
Between the green and foam is fair to take
For any sail the sea-wind steers for me
From morning into morning, sea to sea.

I

THE SAILING OF THE SWALLOW

ABOUT the middle music of the spring
Came from the castled shore of Ireland's king
A fair ship stoutly sailing, eastward bound
And south by Wales and all its wonders round
To the loud rocks and ringing reaches home
That take the wild wrath of the Cornish foam,
Past Lyonesse unswallowed of the tides
And high Carlion that now the steep sea hides
To the wind-hollowed heights and gusty bays
Of sheer Tintagel, fair with famous days.
Above the stem a gilded swallow shone,
Wrought with straight wings and eyes of glittering
    stone
As flying sunward oversea, to bear
Green summer with it through the singing air.
And on the deck between the rowers at dawn,
As the bright sail with brightening wind was drawn,
Sat with full face against the strengthening light
Iseult, more fair than foam or dawn was white.
Her gaze was glad past love's own singing of,
And her face lovely past desire of love.
Past thought and speech her maiden motions were,
And a more golden sunrise was her hair.

The very veil of her bright flesh was made
As of light woven and moonbeam-coloured shade
More fine than moonbeams ; white her eyelids shone
As snow sun-stricken that endures the sun,
And through their curled and coloured clouds of deep
Luminous lashes thick as dreams in sleep
Shone as the sea's depth swallowing up the sky's
The springs of unimaginable eyes.
As the wave's subtler emerald is pierced through
With the utmost heaven's inextricable blue,
And both are woven and molten in one sleight
Of amorous colour and implicated light
Under the golden guard and gaze of noon,
So glowed their awless amorous plenilune,
Azure and gold and ardent grey, made strange
With fiery difference and deep interchange
Inexplicable of glories multiform ;
Now as the sullen sapphire swells toward storm
Foamless, their bitter beauty grew acold,
And now afire with ardour of fine gold.
Her flower-soft lips were meek and passionate,
For love upon them like a shadow sate
Patient, a foreseen vision of sweet things,
A dream with eyes fast shut and plumeless wings
That knew not what man's love or life should be,
Nor had it sight nor heart to hope or see
What thing should come, but childlike satisfied
Watched out its virgin vigil in soft pride
And unkissed expectation ; and the glad
Clear cheeks and throat and tender temples had
Such maiden heat as if a rose's blood
Beat in the live heart of a lily-bud.
Between the small round breasts a white way led
Heavenward, and from slight foot to slender head

The whole fair body flower-like swayed and shone
Moving, and what her light hand leant upon
Grew blossom-scented : her warm arms began
To round and ripen for delight of man
That they should clasp and circle : her fresh hands,
Like regent lilies of reflowering lands
Whose vassal firstlings, crown and star and plume,
Bow down to the empire of that sovereign bloom,
Shone sceptreless, and from her face there went
A silent light as of a God content ;
Save when, more swift and keen than love or shame,
Some flash of blood, light as the laugh of flame,
Broke it with sudden beam and shining speech,
As dream by dream shot through her eyes, and each
Outshone the last that lightened, and not one
Showed her such things as should be borne and
    done.
Though hard against her shone the sunlike face
That in all change and wreck of time and place
Should be the star of her sweet living soul.
Nor had love made it as his written scroll
For evil will and good to read in yet ;
But smooth and mighty, without scar or fret,
Fresh and high-lifted was the helmless brow
As the oak-tree flower that tops the topmost bough,
Ere it drop off before the perfect leaf ;
And nothing save his name he had of grief,
The name his mother, dying as he was born,
Made out of sorrow in very sorrow's scorn,
And set it on him smiling in her sight,
Tristram ; who now, clothed with sweet youth and
    might,
As a glad witness wore that bitter name,
The second symbol of the world for fame.

Famous and full of fortune was his youth
Ere the beard's bloom had left his cheek unsmooth,
And in his face a lordship of strong joy
And height of heart no chance could curb or cloy
Lightened, and all that warmed them at his eyes
Loved them as larks that kindle as they rise
Toward light they turn to music love the blue strong
    skies.
So like the morning through the morning moved
Tristram, a light to look on and be loved.
Song sprang between his lips and hands, and shone
Singing, and strengthened and sank down thereon
As a bird settles to the second flight,
Then from beneath his harping hands with might
Leapt, and made way and had its fill and died,
And all whose hearts were fed upon it sighed
Silent, and in them all the fire of tears
Burned as wine drunken not with lips but ears.
And gazing on his fervent hands that made
The might of music all their souls obeyed
With trembling strong subservience of delight
Full many a maid that had him once in sight
Thought in the secret rapture of her heart
In how dark onset had these hands borne part
How oft, and were so young and sweet of skill ;
And those red lips whereon the song burned still,
What words and cries of battle had they flung
Athwart the swing and shriek of swords, so young ;
And eyes as glad as summer, what strange youth
Fed them so full of happy heart and truth,
That had seen sway from side to sundering side
The steel flow of that terrible springtide
That the moon rules not, but the fire and light
Of men's hearts mixed in the mid mirth of fight.

Therefore the joy and love of him they had
Made thought more amorous in them and more
    glad
For his fame's sake remembered, and his youth
Gave his fame flowerlike fragrance and soft growth
As of a rose requickening, when he stood
Fair in their eye, a flower of faultless blood.
And that sad queen to whom his life was death,
A rose plucked forth of summer in mid breath,
A star fall'n out of season in mid throe
Of that life's joy that makes the star's life glow,
Made their love sadder toward him and more strong.
And in mid change of time and fight and song
Chance cast him westward on the low sweet strand
Where songs are sung of the old green Irish land,
And the sky loves it, and the sea loves best,
And as a bird is taken to man's breast
The sweet-souled land where sorrow sweetest sings
Is wrapt round with them as with hands and wings
And taken to the sea's heart as a flower.
There in the luck and light of his good hour
Came to the king's court like a noteless man
Tristram, and while some half a season ran
Abode before him harping in his hall,
And taught sweet craft of new things musical
To the dear maiden mouth and innocent hands
That for his sake are famous in all lands.
Yet was not love between them, for their fate
Lay wrapt in its appointed hour at wait,
And had no flower to show yet, and no sting.
But once being vexed with some past wound the
    king
Bade give him comfort of sweet baths, and then
Should Iseult watch him as his handmaiden,

For his more honour in men's sight, and ease
The hurts he had with holy remedies
Made by her mother's magic in strange hours
Out of live roots and life-compelling flowers.
And finding by the wound's shape in his side
This was the knight by whom their strength had died
And all their might in one man overthrown
Had left their shame in sight of all men shown,
She would have slain him swordless with his sword;
Yet seemed he to her so great and fair a lord
She heaved up hand and smote not; then said he,
Laughing—'What comfort shall this dead man be,
Damsel? what hurt is for my blood to heal?
But set your hand not near the toothèd steel
Lest the fang strike it.'—'Yea, the fang,' she said,
'Should it not sting the very serpent dead
That stung mine uncle? for his slayer art thou,
And half my mother's heart is bloodless now
Through thee, that mad'st the veins of all her kin
Bleed in his wounds whose veins through thee ran
    thin.'
Yet thought she how their hot chief's violent heart
Had flung the fierce word forth upon their part
Which bade to battle the best knight that stood
On Arthur's, and so dying of his wild mood
Had set upon his conqueror's flesh the seal
Of his mishallowed and anointed steel,
Whereof the venom and enchanted might
Made the sign burn here branded in her sight.
These things she stood recasting, and her soul
Subsiding till its wound of wrath were whole
Grew smooth again, as thought still softening stole
Through all its tempered passion; nor might hate
Keep high the fire against him lit of late;

But softly from his smiling sight she passed.
And peace thereafter made between them fast
Made peace between two kingdoms, when he went
Home with hands reconciled and heart content,
To bring fair truce 'twixt Cornwall's wild bright
    strand
And the long wrangling wars of that loud land.
And when full peace was struck betwixt them twain
Forth must he fare by those green straits again,
And bring back Iseult for a plighted bride
And set to reign at Mark his uncle's side.
So now with feast made and all triumphs done
They sailed between the moonfall and the sun
Under the spent stars eastward ; but the queen
Out of wise heart and subtle love had seen
Such things as might be, dark as in a glass,
And lest some doom of these should come to pass
Bethought her with her secret soul alone
To work some charm for marriage unison
And strike the heart of Iseult to her lord
With power compulsive more than stroke of sword.
Therefore with marvellous herbs and spells she
    wrought
To win the very wonder of her thought,
And brewed it with her secret hands and blest
And drew and gave out of her secret breast
To one her chosen and Iseult's handmaiden,
Brangwain, and bade her hide from sight of men
This marvel covered in a golden cup,
So covering in her heart the counsel up
As in the gold the wondrous wine lay close ;
And when the last shout with the last cup rose
About the bride and bridegroom bound to bed,
Then should this one word of her will be said

To her new-married maiden child, that she
Should drink with Mark this draught in unity,
And no lip touch it for her sake but theirs :
For with long love and consecrating prayers
The wine was hallowed for their mouths to pledge ;
And if a drop fell from the beaker's edge
That drop should Iseult hold as dear as blood
Shed from her mother's heart to do her good.
And having drunk they twain should be one heart
Who were one flesh till fleshly death should part—
Death, who parts all. So Brangwain swore, and
    kept
The hid thing by her while she waked or slept.
And now they sat to see the sun again
Whose light of eye had looked on no such twain
Since Galahault in the rose-time of the year
Brought Launcelot first to sight of Guenevere.
    And Tristram caught her changing eyes and said :
" As this day raises daylight from the dead
Might not this face the life of a dead man ? "
    And Iseult, gazing where the sea was wan
Out of the sun's way, said : " I pray you not
Praise me, but tell me there in Camelot,
Saving the queen, who hath most name of fair ?
I would I were a man and dwelling there,
That I might win me better praise than yours,
Even such as you have ; for your praise endures,
That with great deeds ye wring from mouths of
    men,
But ours—for shame, where is it ? Tell me then,
Since woman may not wear a better here,
Who of this praise hath most save Guenevere ? "
    And Tristram, lightening with a laugh held in—
" Surely a little praise is this to win,

A poor praise and a little ! but of these
Hapless, whom love serves only with bowed
    knees,
Of such poor women fairer face hath none
That lifts her eyes alive against the sun
Than Arthur's sister, whom the north seas call
Mistress of isles ; so yet majestical
Above the crowns on younger heads she moves,
Outlightening with her eyes our late-born loves."
    "Ah," said Iseult, " is she more tall than I ?
Look, I am tall ; " and struck the mast hard by,
With utmost upward reach of her bright hand ;
" And look, fair lord, now, when I rise and stand,
How high with feet unlifted I can touch
Standing straight up ; could this queen do thus
    much ?
Nay, over tall she must be then, like me ;
Less fair than lesser women. May this be,
That still she stands the second stateliest there,
So more than many so much younger fair,
She, born when yet the king your lord was not,
And has the third knight after Launcelot
And after you to serve her ? nay, sir, then
God made her for a godlike sign to men."
    " Ay," Tristram answered, " for a sign, a sign—
Would God it were not ! for no planets shine
With half such fearful forecast of men's fate
As a fair face so more unfortunate."
    Then with a smile that lit not on her brows
But moved upon her red mouth tremulous
Light as a sea-bird's motion oversea,
" Yea," quoth Iseult, " the happier hap for me,
With no such face to bring men no such fate.
Yet her might all we women born too late

Praise for good hap, who so enskied above
Not more in age excels us than man's love."
    There came a glooming light on Tristram's face
Answering : " God keep you better in his grace
Than to sit down beside her in men's sight.
For if men be not blind whom God gives light
And lie not in whose lips he bids truth live,
Great grief shall she be given, and greater give.
For Merlin witnessed of her years ago
That she should work woe and should suffer woe
Beyond the race of women : and in truth
Her face, a spell that knows nor age nor youth,
Like youth being soft, and subtler-eyed than age,
With lips that mock the doom her eyes presage,
Hath on it such a light of cloud and fire,
With charm and change of keen or dim desire,
And over all a fearless look of fear
Hung like a veil across its changing cheer,
Made up of fierce foreknowledge and sharp scorn,
That it were better she had not been born.
For not love's self can help a face which hath
Such insubmissive anguish of wan wrath,
Blind prescience and self-contemptuous hate
Of her own soul and heavy-footed fate,
Writ broad upon its beauty : none the less
Its fire of bright and burning bitterness
Takes with as quick a flame the sense of men
As any sunbeam, nor is quenched again
With any drop of dewfall ; yea, I think
No herb of force or blood-compelling drink
Would heal a heart that ever it made hot.
Ay, and men too that greatly love her not,
Seeing the great love of her and Lamoracke,
Make no great marvel, nor look strangely back

When with his gaze about her she goes by
Pale as a breathless and star-quickening sky
Between moonrise and sunset, and moves out
Clothed with the passion of his eyes about
As night with all her stars, yet night is black ;
And she, clothed warm with love of Lamoracke,
Girt with his worship as with girdling gold,
Seems all at heart anhungered and acold,
Seems sad at heart and loveless of the light,
As night, star-clothed or naked, is but night."

   And with her sweet eyes sunken, and the mirth
Dead in their look as earth lies dead in earth
That reigned on earth and triumphed, Iseult said:
" Is it her shame of something done and dead
Or fear of something to be born and done
That so in her soul's eye puts out the sun ? "

   And Tristram answered : "Surely, as I think,
This gives her soul such bitterness to drink,
The sin born blind, the sightless sin unknown,
Wrought when the summer in her blood was blown
But scarce aflower, and spring first flushed her will
With bloom of dreams no fruitage should fulfil,
When out of vision and desire was wrought
The sudden sin that from the living thought
Leaps a live deed and dies not : then there came
On that blind sin swift eyesight like a flame
Touching the dark to death, and made her mad
With helpless knowledge that too late forbade
What was before the bidding : and she knew
How sore a life dead love should lead her through
To what sure end how fearful ; and though yet
Nor with her blood nor tears her way be wet
And she look bravely with set face on fate,
Yet she knows well the serpent hour at wait

Somewhere to sting and spare not ; ay, and he,
Arthur "——
                    " The king," quoth Iseult suddenly,
" Doth the king too live so in sight of fear ?
They say sin touches not a man so near
As shame a woman ; yet he too should be
Part of the penance, being more deep than she
Set in the sin."
                    "Nay," Tristram said, " for thus
It fell by wicked hap and hazardous,
That wittingly he sinned no more than youth
May sin and be assoiled of God and truth,
Repenting ; since in his first year of reign
As he stood splendid with his foemen slain
And light of new-blown battles, flushed and hot
With hope and life, came greeting from King Lot
Out of his wind-worn islands oversea,
And homage to my king and fealty
Of those north seas wherein the strange shapes swim,
As from his man ; and Arthur greeted him
As his good lord and courteously, and bade
To his high feast ; who coming with him had
This Queen Morgause of Orkney, his fair wife,
In the green middle Maytime of her life,
And scarce in April was our king's as then,
And goodliest was he of all flowering men,
And of what graft as yet himself knew not ;
But cold as rains in autumn was King Lot
And grey-grown out of season : so there sprang
Swift love between them, and all spring through **sang**
Light in their joyous hearing ; for none knew
The bitter bond of blood between them two,
Twain fathers but one mother, till too late
The sacred mouth of Merlin set forth fate

And brake the secret seal on Arthur's birth,
And showed his ruin and his rule on earth
Inextricable, and light on lives to be.
For surely, though time slay us, yet shall we
Have such high name and lordship of good days
As shall sustain us living, and men's praise
Shall burn a beacon lit above us dead.
And of the king how shall not this be said
When any of us from any mouth has praise,
That such were men in only this king's days,
In Arthur's ? yea, come shine or shade, no less
His name shall be one name with knightliness,
His fame one light with sunlight.   Yet in sooth
His age shall bear the burdens of his youth
And bleed from his own bloodshed ; for indeed
Blind to him blind his sister brought forth seed,
And of the child between them shall be born
Destruction : so shall God not suffer scorn,
Nor in men's souls and lives his law lie dead."
    And as one moved and marvelling Iseult said :
" Great pity it is and strange it seems to me
God could not do them so much right as we,
Who slay not men for witless evil done ;
And these the noblest under God's glad sun
For sin they knew not he that knew shall slay,
And smite blind men for stumbling in fair day.
What good is it to God that such should die ?
Shall the sun's light grow sunnier in the sky
Because their light of spirit is clean put out ? "
    And sighing, she looked from wave to cloud about,
And even with that the full-grown feet of day
Sprang upright on the quivering water-way,
And his face burned against her meeting face
Most like a lover's thrilled with great love's grace

Whose glance takes fire and gives ; the quick sea
    shone
And shivered like spread wings of angels blown
By the sun's breath before him ; and a low
Sweet gale shook all the foam-flowers of thin snow
As into rainfall of sea-roses shed
Leaf by wild leaf on that green garden-bed
Which tempests till and sea-winds turn and plough:
For rosy and fiery round the running prow
Fluttered the flakes and feathers of the spray,
And bloomed like blossoms cast by God away
To waste on the ardent water ; swift the moon
Withered to westward as a face in swoon
Death-stricken by glad tidings : and the height
Throbbed and the centre quivered with delight
And the depth quailed with passion as of love,
Till like the heart of some new-mated dove
Air, light, and wave seemed full of burning rest,
With motion as of one God's beating breast.

    And her heart sprang in Iseult, and she drew
With all her spirit and life the sunrise through,
And through her lips the keen triumphant air
Sea-scented, sweeter than land-roses were,
And through her eyes the whole rejoicing east
Sun-satisfied, and all the heaven at feast
Spread for the morning ; and the imperious mirth
Of wind and light that moved upon the earth,
Making the spring, and all the fruitful might
And strong regeneration of delight
That swells the seedling leaf and sapling man,
Since the first life in the first world began
To burn and burgeon through void limbs and veins,
And the first love with sharp sweet procreant pains

To pierce and bring forth roses ; yea, she felt
Through her own soul the sovereign morning melt,
And all the sacred passion of the sun ;
And as the young clouds flamed and were undone
About him coming, touched and burnt away
In rosy ruin and yellow spoil of day,
The sweet veil of her body and corporal sense
Felt the dawn also cleave it, and incense
With light from inward and with effluent heat
The kindling soul through fleshly hands and feet.
And as the august great blossom of the dawn
Burst, and the full sun scarce from sea withdrawn
Seemed on the fiery water a flower afloat,
So as a fire the mighty morning smote
Throughout her, and incensed with the influent hour
Her whole soul's one great mystical red flower
Burst, and the bud of her sweet spirit broke
Rose-fashion, and the strong spring at a stroke
Thrilled, and was cloven, and from the full sheath
      came
The whole rose of the woman red as flame :
And all her Mayday blood as from a swoon
Flushed, and May rose up in her and was June.
So for a space her heart as heavenward burned :
Then with half summer in her eyes she turned,
And on her lips was April yet, and smiled,
As though the spirit and sense unreconciled
Shrank laughing back, and would not ere its hour
Let life put forth the irrevocable flower.
   And the soft speech between them grew again
With questionings and records of what men
Rose mightiest, and what names for love or fight
Shone starriest overhead of queen or knight.

There Tristram spake of many a noble thing,
High feast and storm of tournay round the king,
Strange quest by perilous lands of marsh and brake
And circling woods branch-knotted like a snake
And places pale with sins that they had seen,
Where was no life of red fruit or of green
But all was as a dead face wan and dun ;
And bowers of evil builders whence the sun
Turns silent, and the moon holds hardly light
Above them through the sick and star-crossed night ;
And of their hands through whom such holds lay
        waste,
And all their strengths dishevelled and defaced
Fell ruinous, and were not from north to south :
And of the might of Merlin's ancient mouth,
The son of no man's loins, begot by doom
In speechless sleep out of a spotless womb ;
For sleeping among graves where none had rest
And ominous houses of dead bones unblest
Among the grey grass rough as old rent hair
And wicked herbage whitening like despair
And blown upon with blasts of dolorous breath
From gaunt rare gaps and hollow doors of death,
A maid unspotted, senseless of the spell,
Felt not about her breathe some thing of hell
Whose child and hers was Merlin ; and to him
Great light from God gave sight of all things dim
And wisdom of all wondrous things, to say
What root should bear what fruit of night or day,
And sovereign speech and counsel higher than man ;
Wherefore his youth like age was wise and wan,
And his age sorrowful and fain to sleep ;
Yet should sleep never, neither laugh nor weep,

Till in some depth of deep sweet land or sea
The heavenly hands of holier Nimue,
That was the nurse of Launcelot, and most sweet
Of all that move with magical soft feet
Among us, being of lovelier blood and breath,
Should shut him in with sleep as kind as death :
For she could pass between the quick and dead :
And of her love toward Pelleas, for whose head
Love-wounded and world-wearied she had won
A place beyond all pain in Avalon ;
And of the fire that wasted afterward
The loveless eyes and bosom of Ettarde,
In whose false love his faultless heart had burned ;
And now being rapt from her, her lost heart
    yearned
To seek him, and passed hungering out of life :
And after all the thunder-hours of strife
That roared between King Claudas and King Ban
How Nimue's mighty nursling waxed to man,
And how from his first field such grace he got
That all men's hearts bowed down to Launcelot,
And how the high prince Galahault held him dear
And led him even to love of Guenevere
And to that kiss which made break forth as fire
The laugh that was the flower of his desire,
The laugh that lightened at her lips for bliss
To win from Love so great a lover's kiss :
And of the toil of Balen all his days
To reap but thorns for fruit and tears for praise,
Whose hap was evil as his heart was good,
And all his works and ways by wold and wood
Led through much pain to one last labouring day
When blood for tears washed grief with life away :

And of the kin of Arthur, and their might ;
The misborn head of Mordred, sad as night,
With cold waste cheeks and eyes as keen as pain,
And the close angry lips of Agravaine ;
And gracious Gawain, scattering words as flowers,
The kindliest head of worldly paramours ;
And the fair hand of Gareth, found in fight
Strong as a sea-beast's tushes and as white ;
And of the king's self, glorious yet and glad
For all the toil and doubt of doom he had,
Clothed with men's loves and full of kingly days.

    Then Iseult said : " Let each knight have his praise
And each good man good witness of his worth ;
But when men laud the second name on earth,
Whom would they praise to have no worldly peer
Save him whose love makes glorious Guenevere ? "

    " Nay," Tristram said, " such man as he is none."

    " What," said she, " there is none such under sun
Of all the large earth's living ? yet I deemed
Men spake of one—but maybe men that dreamed,
Fools and tongue-stricken, witless, babbler's breed —
That for all high things was his peer indeed
Save this one highest, to be so loved and love."

    And Tristram : " Little wit had these thereof ;
For there is none such in the world as this."

    " Ay, upon land," quoth Iseult, " none such is,
I doubt not, nor where fighting folk may be ;
But were there none such between sky and sea,
The world's whole worth were poorer than I wist."

    And Tristram took her flower-white hand and
    kissed,
Laughing ; and through his fair face as in shame
The light blood lightened. " Hear they no such
    name ? "

She said ; and he, " If there be such a word,
I wot the queen's poor harper hath not heard."
Then, as the fuller-feathered hours grew long,
He holp to speed their warm slow feet with song.

> " Love, is it morning risen or night deceased
> That makes the mirth of this triumphant east ?
>   Is it bliss given or bitterness put by
> That makes most glad men's hearts at love's high feast ?
>   Grief smiles, joy weeps, that day should live and die.

> " Is it with soul's thirst or with body's drouth
> That summer yearns out sunward to the south,
>   With all the flowers that when thy birth drew nigh
> Were molten in one rose to make thy mouth ?
>   O love, what care though day should live and die ?

> " Is the sun glad of all the love on earth,
> The spirit and sense and work of things and worth ?
>   Is the moon sad because the month must fly
> And bring her death that can but bring back birth ?
>   For all these things as day must live and die.

> " Love, is it day that makes thee thy delight
> Or thou that seest day made out of thy light ?
>   Love, as the sun and sea are thou and I,
> Sea without sun dark, sun without sea bright ;
>   The sun is one though day should live and die.

> " O which is elder, night or light, who knows ?
> And life or love, which first of these twain grows ?
>   For life is born of love to wail and cry,
> And love is born of life to heal his woes,
>   And light of night, that day should live and die.

> " O sun of heaven above the worldly sea,
> O very love, what light is this of thee !
>   My sea of soul is deep as thou art high,
> But all thy light is shed through all of me,
>   As love's through love, while day shall live and die.

" Nay," said Iseult, " your song is hard to read."
" Ay ? " said he : " or too light a song to heed,
Too slight to follow, it may be ?   Who shall sing
Of love but as a churl before a king
If by love's worth men rate his worthiness ?
Yet as the poor churl's worth to sing is less,
Surely the more shall be the great king's grace
To show for churlish love a kindlier face."
  " No churl," she said, " but one in soothsayer's
    wise
Who tells but truths that help no more than lies.
I have heard men sing of love a simpler way
Than these wrought riddles made of night and
    day,
Like jewelled reins whereon the rhyme-bells hang."
  And Tristram smiled and changed his song and
    sang.

> " The breath between my lips of lips not mine,
> Like spirit in sense that makes pure sense divine,
>   Is as life in them from the living sky
> That entering fills my heart with blood of thine
>   And thee with me, while day shall live and die.

> " Thy soul is shed into me with thy breath,
> And in my heart each heartbeat of thee saith
>   How in thy life the lifesprings of me lie,
> Even one life to be gathered of one death
>   In me and thee, though day may live and die.

> " Ah, who knows now if in my veins it be
> My blood that feels life sweet, or blood of thee,
>   And this thine eyesight kindled in mine eye
> That shows me in thy flesh the soul of me,
>   For thine made mine, while day may live and die ?

" Ah, who knows yet if one be twain or one,
And sunlight separable again from sun,
   And I from thee with all my lifesprings dry,
And thou from me with all thine heartbeats done,
   Dead separate souls while day shall live and die?

"I see my soul within thine eyes, and hear
My spirit in all thy pulses thrill with fear,
   And in my lips the passion of thee sigh,
And music of me made in mine own ear;
   Am I not thou while day shall live and die?

" Art thou not I as I thy love am thou?
So let all things pass from us; we are now,
   For all that was and will be, who knows why?
And all that is and is not, who knows how?
   Who knows? God knows why day should live and die."

And Iseult mused and spake no word, but sought
Through all the hushed ways of her tongueless
   thought
What face or covered likeness of a face
In what veiled hour or dream-determined place
She seeing might take for love's face, and believe
This was the spirit to whom all spirits cleave.
For that sweet wonder of the twain made one
And each one twain, incorporate sun with sun,
Star with star molten, soul with soul imbued,
And all the soul's works, all their multitude,
Made one thought and one vision and one song,
Love—this thing, this, laid hand on her so strong
She could not choose but yearn till she should see.
So went she musing down her thoughts; but he,
Sweet-hearted as a bird that takes the sun
With clear strong eyes and feels the glad god run

Bright through his blood and wide rejoicing wings,
And opens all himself to heaven and sings,
Made her mind light and full of noble mirth
With words and songs the gladdest grown on earth,
Till she was blithe and high of heart as he.
So swam the Swallow through the springing sea
   And while they sat at speech as at a feast,
Came a light wind fast hardening forth of the east
And blackening till its might had marred the skies ;
And the sea thrilled as with heart-sundering sighs
One after one drawn, with each breath it drew,
And the green hardened into iron blue,
And the soft light went out of all its face.
Then Tristram girt him for an oarsman's place
And took his oar and smote, and toiled with might
In the east wind's full face and the strong sea's spite
Labouring ; and all the rowers rowed hard, but he
More mightily than any wearier three.
And Iseult watched him rowing with sinless eyes
That loved him but in holy girlish wise
For noble joy in his fair manliness
And trust and tender wonder ; none the less
She thought if God had given her grace to be
Man, and make war on danger of earth and sea,
Even such a man she would be ; for his stroke
Was mightiest as the mightier water broke,
And in sheer measure like strong music drave
Clean through the wet weight of the wallowing
   wave ;
And as a tune before a great king played
For triumph was the tune their strong strokes made,
And sped the ship through with smooth strife of
   oars
Over the mid sea's grey foam-paven floors,

For all the loud breach of the waves at will.
So for an hour they fought the storm out still,
And the shorn foam spun from the blades, and high
The keel sprang from the wave-ridge, and the sky
Glared at them for a breath's space through the
    rain ;
Then the bows with a sharp shock plunged again
Down, and the sea clashed on them, and so rose
The bright stem like one panting from swift blows,
And as a swimmer's joyous beaten head
Rears itself laughing, so in that sharp stead
The light ship lifted her long quivering bows
As might the man his buffeted strong brows
Out of the wave-breach ; for with one stroke yet
Went all men's oars together, strongly set
As to loud music, and with hearts uplift
They smote their strong way through the drench and
    drift :
Till the keen hour had chafed itself to death
And the east wind fell fitfully, breath by breath,
Tired ; and across the thin and slackening rain
Sprang the face southward of the sun again.
Then all they rested and were eased at heart ;
And Iseult rose up where she sat apart,
And with her sweet soul deepening her deep eyes
Cast the furs from her and subtle embroideries
That wrapped her from the storming rain and
    spray,
And shining like all April in one day,
Hair, face, and throat dashed with the straying
    showers,
She stood the first of all the whole world's flowers,
And laughed on Tristram with her eyes, and said,
" I too have heart then, I was not afraid."

And answering some light courteous word of grace
He saw her clear face lighten on his face
Unwittingly, with unenamoured eyes.
For the last time.   A live man in such wise
Looks in the deadly face of his fixed hour
And laughs with lips wherein he hath no power
To keep the life yet some five minutes' space.
So Tristram looked on Iseult face to face
And knew not, and she knew not.   The last time—
The last that should be told in any rhyme
Heard anywhere on mouths of singing men
That ever should sing praise of them again ;
The last hour of their hurtless hearts at rest,
The last that peace should touch them, breast to
      breast,
The last that sorrow far from them should sit,
This last was with them, and they knew not it.
    For Tristram being athirst with toil now spake,
Saying, " Iseult, for all dear love's labour's sake
Give me to drink, and give me for a pledge
The touch of four lips on the beaker's edge."
And Iseult sought and would not wake Brangwain
Who slept as one half dead with fear and pain,
Being tender-natured ; so with hushed light feet
Went Iseult round her, with soft looks and sweet
Pitying her pain ; so sweet a spirited thing
She was, and daughter of a kindly king.
And spying what strange bright secret charge was
      kept
Fast in that maid's white bosom while she slept,
She sought and drew the gold cup forth and smiled
Marvelling, with such light wonder as a child
That hears of glad sad life in magic lands ;
And bare it back to Tristram with pure hands

Holding the love-draught that should be for flame
To burn out of them fear and faith and shame,
And lighten all their life up in men's sight,
And make them sad for ever.   Then the knight
Bowed toward her and craved whence had she this
    strange thing
That might be spoil of some dim Asian king,
By starlight stolen from some waste place of sands,
And a maid bore it here in harmless hands.
And Iseult, laughing—" Other lords that be
Feast, and their men feast after them ; but we,
Our men must keep the best wine back to feast
Till they be full and we of all men least
Feed after them and fain to fare so well :
So with mine handmaid and your squire it fell
That hid this bright thing from us in a wile : "
And with light lips yet full of their swift smile,
And hands that wist not though they dug a
    grave,
Undid the hasps of gold, and drank, and gave,
And he drank after, a deep glad kingly draught :
And all their life changed in them, for they quaffed
Death ; if it be death so to drink, and fare
As men who change and are what these twain
    were.
And shuddering with eyes full of fear and fire
And heart-stung with a serpentine desire
He turned and saw the terror in her eyes
That yearned upon him shining in such wise
As a star midway in the midnight fixed.
    Their Galahault was the cup, and she that
        mixed ;
Nor other hand there needed, nor sweet speech
To lure their lips together ; each on each

Hung with strange eyes and hovered as a bird
Wounded, and each mouth trembled for a word ;
Their heads neared, and their hands were drawn in
    one,
And they saw dark, though still the unsunken sun
Far through fine rain shot fire into the south ;
And their four lips became one burning mouth.

II

THE QUEEN'S PLEASANCE

Out of the night arose the second day,
And saw the ship's bows break the shoreward spray.
As the sun's boat of gold and fire began
To sail the sea of heaven unsailed of man,
And the soft waves of sacred air to break
Round the prow launched into the morning's lake,
They saw the sign of their sea-travel done.
    Ah, was not something seen of yester-sun,
When the sweet light that lightened all the skies
Saw nothing fairer than one maiden's eyes,
That whatsoever in all time's years may be
To-day's sun nor to-morrow's sun shall see?
Not while she lives, not when she comes to die,
Shall she look sunward with that sinless eye.
    Yet fairer now than song may show them stand
Tristram and Iseult, hand in amorous hand,
Soul-satisfied, their eyes made great and bright
With all the love of all the livelong night;
With all its hours yet singing in their ears
No mortal music made of thoughts and tears,
But such a song, past conscience of man's thought.
As hearing he grows god and knows it not.

Nought else they saw nor heard but what the
    night
Had left for seal upon their sense and sight,
Sound of past pulses beating, fire of amorous light
Enough, and overmuch, and never yet
Enough, though love still hungering feed and fret,
To fill the cup of night which dawn must overset.
For still their eyes were dimmer than with tears
And dizzier from diviner sounds their ears
Than though from choral thunders of the quiring
    spheres.
They heard not how the landward waters rang,
Nor saw where high into the morning sprang,
Riven from the shore and bastioned with the sea,
Toward summits where the north wind's nest might
    be,
A wave-walled palace with its eastern gate
Full of the sunrise now and wide at wait,
And on the mighty-moulded stairs that clomb
Sheer from the fierce lip of the lapping foam
The knights of Mark that stood before the wall.
So with loud joy and storm of festival
They brought the bride in up the towery way
That rose against the rising front of day,
Stair based on stair, between the rocks unhewn,
To those strange halls wherethrough the tidal tune
Rang loud or lower from soft or strengthening sea,
Tower shouldering tower, to windward and to lee,
With change of floors and stories, flight on flight,
That clomb and curled up to the crowning height
Whence men might see wide east and west in one
And on one sea waned moon and mounting sun.
And severed from the sea-rock's base, where stand
Some worn walls yet they saw the broken strand,

The beachless cliff that in the sheer sea dips,
The sleepless shore inexorable to ships,
And the straight causeway's bare gaunt spine between
The sea-spanned walls and naked mainland's green.
   On the mid stairs, between the light and dark,
Before the main tower's portal stood King Mark,
Crowned : and his face was as the face of one
Long time athirst and hungering for the sun
In barren thrall of bitter bonds, who now
Thinks here to feel its blessing on his brow.
A swart lean man, but kinglike, still of guise,
With black streaked beard and cold unquiet eyes,
Close-mouthed, gaunt-cheeked, wan as a morning
    moon,
Though hardly time on his worn hair had strewn
The thin first ashes from a sparing hand :
Yet little fire there burnt upon the brand,
And way-worn seemed he with life's wayfaring.
So between shade and sunlight stood the king,
And his face changed nor yearned not toward his
    bride ;
But fixed between mild hope and patient pride
Abode what gift of rare or lesser worth
This day might bring to all his days on earth.
But at the glory of her when she came
His heart endured not : very fear and shame
Smote him, to take her by the hand and kiss,
Till both were molten in the burning bliss,
And with a thin flame flushing his cold face
He led her silent to the bridal place.
There were they wed and hallowed of the priest ,
And all the loud time of the marriage feast
One thought within three hearts was as a fire,
Where craft and faith took counsel with desire.

For when the feast had made a glorious end
They gave the new queen for her maids to tend
At dawn of bride-night, and thereafter bring
With marriage music to the bridegroom king.
Then by device of craft between them laid
To him went Brangwain delicately, and prayed
That this thing even for love's sake might not be,
But without sound or light or eye to see
She might come in to bride-bed : and he laughed,
As one that wist not well of wise love's craft,
And bade all bridal things be as she would.
Yet of his gentleness he gat not good ;
For clothed and covered with the nuptial dark
Soft like a bride came Brangwain to King Mark,
And to the queen came Tristram ; and the night
Fled, and ere danger of detective light
From the king sleeping Brangwain slid away,
And where had lain her handmaid Iseult lay.
And the king waking saw beside his head
That face yet passion-coloured, amorous red
From lips not his, and all that strange hair shed
Across the tissued pillows, fold on fold,
Innumerable, incomparable, all gold,
To fire men's eyes with wonder, and with love
Men's hearts ; so shone its flowering crown above
The brows enwound with that imperial wreath,
And framed with fragrant radiance round the face
        beneath.
  And the king marvelled, seeing with sudden start
Her very glory, and said out of his heart ;
" What have I done of good for God to bless
That all this he should give me, tress on tress,
All this great wealth and wondrous ?   Was it this
That in mine arms I had all night to kiss,

And mix with me this beauty? this that seems
More fair than heaven doth in some tired saint's
    dreams,
Being part of that same heaven? yea, more, for he,
Though loved of God so, yet but seems to see,
But to me sinful such great grace is given
That in mine hands I hold this part of heaven,
Not to mine eyes lent merely. Doth God make
Such things so godlike for man's mortal sake?
Have I not sinned, that in this fleshly life
Have made of her a mere man's very wife?"
    So the king mused and murmured; and she
    heard
The faint sound trembling of each breathless word,
And laughed into the covering of her hair.
    And many a day for many a month as fair
Slid over them like music; and as bright
Burned with love's offerings many a secret night.
And many a dawn to many a fiery noon
Blew prelude, when the horn's heart-kindling tune
Lit the live woods with sovereign sound of mirth
Before the mightiest huntsman hailed on earth
Lord of its lordliest pleasure, where he rode
Hard by her rein whose peerless presence glowed
Not as that white queen's of the virgin hunt
Once, whose crown-crescent braves the night-wind's
    brunt,
But with the sun for frontlet of a queenlier front.
For where the flashing of her face was turned
As lightning was the fiery light that burned
From eyes and brows enkindled more with speed
And rapture of the rushing of her steed
Than once with only beauty; and her mouth
Was as a rose athirst that pants for drouth

Even while it laughs for pleasure of desire,
And all her heart was as a leaping fire.
Yet once more joy they took of woodland ways
Than came of all those flushed and fiery days
When the loud air was mad with life and sound,
Through many a dense green mile, of horn and hound
Before the king's hunt going along the wind,
And ere the timely leaves were changed or thinned,
Even in mid maze of summer.   For the knight
Forth was once ridden toward some frontier fight
Against the lewd folk of the Christless lands
That warred with wild and intermittent hands
Against the king's north border ; and there came
A knight unchristened yet of unknown name,
Swart Palamede, upon a secret quest,
To high Tintagel, and abode as guest
In likeness of a minstrel with the king.
Nor was there man could sound so sweet a string,
Save Tristram only, of all held best on earth.
And one loud eve, being full of wine and mirth,
Ere sunset left the walls and waters dark,
To that strange minstrel strongly swore King Mark,
By all that makes a knight's faith firm and strong,
That he for guerdon of his harp and song
Might crave and have his liking.   Straight there came
Up the swart cheek a flash of swarthier flame,
And the deep eyes fulfilled of glittering night
Laughed out in lightnings of triumphant light
As the grim harper spake : " O king, I crave
No gift of man that king may give to slave,
But this thy crowned queen only, this thy wife,
Whom yet unseen I loved, and set my life
On this poor chance to compass, even as here,
Being fairer famed than all save Guenevere."

Then as the noise of seaward storm that mocks
With roaring laughter from reverberate rocks
The cry from ships near shipwreck, harsh and high
Rose all the wrath and wonder in one cry
Through all the long roof's hollow depth and length
That hearts of strong men kindled in their strength
May speak in laughter lion-like, and cease,
Being wearied : only two men held their peace
And each glared hard on other : but King Mark
Spake first of these : " Man, though thy craft be dark
And thy mind evil that begat this thing,
Yet stands the word once plighted of a king
Fast : and albeit less evil it were for me
To give my life up than my wife, or be
A landless man crowned only with a curse,
Yet this in God's and all men's sight were worse,
To live soul-shamed, a man of broken troth,
Abhorred of men as I abhor mine oath
Which yet I may forswear not." And he bowed
His head, and wept : and all men wept aloud,
Save one, that heard him weeping : but the queen
Wept not : and statelier yet than eyes had seen
That ever looked upon her queenly state
She rose, and in her eyes her heart was great
And full of wrath seen manifest and scorn
More strong than anguish to go thence forlorn
Of all men's comfort and her natural right.
And they went forth into the dawn of night.
Long by wild ways and clouded light they rode,
Silent ; and fear less keen at heart abode
With Iseult than with Palamede : for awe
Constrained him, and the might of love's high law,
That can make lewd men loyal ; and his heart
Yearned on her, if perchance with amorous art

And soothfast skill of very love he might
For courtesy find favour in her sight
And comfort of her mercies : for he wist
More grace might come of that sweet mouth unkissed
Than joy for violence done it, that should make
His name abhorred for shame's disloyal sake.
And in the stormy starlight clouds were thinned
And thickened by short gusts of changing wind
That panted like a sick man's fitful breath :
And like a moan of lions hurt to death
Came the sea's hollow noise along the night.
But ere its gloom from aught but foam had light
They halted, being aweary : and the knight
As reverently forbore her where she lay
As one that watched his sister's sleep till day.
Nor durst he kiss or touch her hand or hair
For love and shamefast pity, seeing how fair
She slept, and fenceless from the fitful air.
And shame at heart stung nigh to death desire,
But grief at heart burned in him like a fire
For hers and his own sorrowing sake, that had
Such grace for guerdon as makes glad men sad,
To have their will and want it.   And the day
Sprang : and afar along the wild waste way
They heard the pulse and press of hurrying horse
    hoofs play :
And like the rushing of a ravenous flame
Whose wings make tempest of the darkness, came
Upon them headlong as in thunder borne
Forth of the darkness of the labouring morn
Tristram : and up forthright upon his steed
Leapt, as one blithe of battle, Palamede,
And mightily with shock of horse and man
They lashed together : and fair that fight began

As fair came up that sunrise : to and fro,
With knees nigh staggered and stout heads bent low
From each quick shock of spears on either side,
Reeled the strong steeds heavily, haggard-eyed
And heartened high with passion of their pride
As sheer the stout spears shocked again, and flew
Sharp-splintering : then, his sword as each knight
    drew,
They flashed and foined full royally, so long
That but to see so fair a strife and strong
A man might well have given out of his life
One year's void space forlorn of love or strife.
As when a bright north-easter, great of heart,
Scattering the strengths of squadrons, hurls apart
Ship from ship labouring violently, in such toil
As earns but ruin—with even so strong recoil
Back were the steeds hurled from the spear-shock,
    fain
And foiled of triumph : then with tightened rein
And stroke of spur, inveterate, either knight
Bore in again upon his foe with might,
Heart-hungry for the hot-mouthed feast of fight
And all athirst of mastery : but full soon
The jarring notes of that tempestuous tune
Fell, and its mighty music made of hands
Contending, clamorous through the loud waste lands,
Broke at once off ; and shattered from his steed
Fell, as a mainmast ruining, Palamede,
Stunned : and those lovers left him where he lay,
And lightly through green lawns they rode away.
    There was a bower beyond man's eye more fair
Than ever summer dews and sunniest air
Fed full with rest and radiance till the boughs
Had wrought a roof as for a holier house

Than aught save love might breathe in ; fairer far
Than keeps the sweet light back of moon and star
From high kings' chambers : there might love and sleep
Divide for joy the darkling hours, and keep
With amorous alternation of sweet strife
The soft and secret ways of death and life
Made smooth for pleasure's feet to rest and run
Even from the moondawn to the kindling sun,
Made bright for passion's feet to run and rest
Between the midnight's and the morning's breast,
Where hardly though her happy head lie down
It may forget the hour that wove its crown ;
Where hardly though her joyous limbs be laid
They may forget the mirth that midnight made.
And thither, ere sweet night had slain sweet day,
Iseult and Tristram took their wandering way,
And rested, and refreshed their hearts with cheer
In hunters' fashion of the woods ; and here
More sweet it seemed, while this might be, to dwell
And take of all world's weariness farewell
Than reign of all world's lordship queen and king.
Nor here would time for three moons' changes bring
Sorrow nor thought of sorrow ; but sweet earth
Fostered them like her babes of eldest birth,
Reared warm in pathless woods and cherished well.
And the sun sprang above the sea and fell,
And the stars rose and sank upon the sea ;
And outlaw-like, in forest wise and free,
The rising and the setting of their lights
Found those twain dwelling all those days and nights.
And under change of sun and star and moon
Flourished and fell the chaplets woven of June,
And fair through fervours of the deepening sky
Panted and passed the hours that lit July,

And each day blessed them out of heaven above,
And each night crowned them with the crown of love.
Nor till the might of August overhead
Weighed on the world was yet one roseleaf shed
Of all their joy's warm coronal, nor aught
Touched them in passing ever with a thought
That ever this might end on any day
Or any night not love them where they lay ;
But like a babbling tale of barren breath
Seemed all report and rumour held of death,
And a false bruit the legend tear-impearled
That such a thing as change was in the world.
And each bright song upon his lips that came,
Mocking the powers of change and death by name,
Blasphemed their bitter godhead, and defied
Time, though clothed round with ruin as kings with
      pride,
To blot the glad life out of love : and she
Drank lightly deep of his philosophy
In that warm wine of amorous words which is
Sweet with all truths of all philosophies.
For well he wist all subtle ways of song,
And in his soul the secret eye was strong
That burns in meditation, till bright words
Break flamelike forth as notes from fledgeling birds
That feel the soul speak through them of the spring.
So fared they night and day as queen and king
Crowned of a kingdom wide as day and night.
Nor ever cloudlet swept or swam in sight
Across the darkling depths of their delight
Whose stars no skill might number, nor man's art
Sound the deep stories of its heavenly heart.
Till, even for wonder that such life should live,
Desires and dreams of what death's self might give

Would touch with tears and laughter and wild speech
The lips and eyes of passion, fain to reach,
Beyond all bourne of time or trembling sense,
The verge of love's last possible eminence.
Out of the heaven that storm nor shadow mars,
Deep from the starry depth beyond the stars,
A yearning ardour without scope or name
Fell on them, and the bright night's breath of flame
Shot fire into their kisses ; and like fire
The lit dews lightened on the leaves, as higher
Night's heart beat on toward midnight. Far and fain
Somewhiles the soft rush of rejoicing rain
Solaced the darkness, and from steep to steep
Of heaven they saw the sweet sheet lightning leap
And laugh its heart out in a thousand smiles,
When the clear sea for miles on glimmering miles
Burned as though dawn were strewn abroad astray,
Or, showering out of heaven, all heaven's array
Had paven instead the waters : fain and far
Somewhiles the burning love of star for star
Spake words that love might wellnigh seem to hear
In such deep hours as turn delight to fear
Sweet as delight's self ever. So they lay
Tranced once, nor watched along the fiery bay
The shine of summer darkness palpitate and play.
She had nor sight nor voice ; her swooning eyes
Knew not if night or light were in the skies ;
Across her beauty sheer the moondawn shed
Its light as on a thing as white and dead ;
Only with stress of soft fierce hands she prest
Between the throbbing blossoms of her breast
His ardent face, and through his hair her breath
Went quivering as when life is hard on death ;
And with strong trembling fingers she strained fast
His head into her bosom ; till at last.

Satiate with sweetness of that burning bed,
His eyes afire with tears, he raised his head
And laughed into her lips; and all his heart
Filled hers; then face from face fell, and apart
Each hung on each with panting lips, and felt
Sense into sense and spirit in spirit melt.

  "Hast thou no sword? I would not live till day,
O love, this night and we must pass away,
It must die soon, and let not us die late."

  "Take then my sword and slay me; nay, but wait
Till day be risen; what, wouldst thou think to die
Before the light take hold upon the sky?"

  "Yea, love; for how shall we have twice, being
    twain,
This very night of love's most rapturous reign?
Live thou and have thy day, and year by year
Be great, but what shall I be? Slay me here;
Let me die not when love lies dead, but now
Strike through my heart: nay, sweet, what heart hast
    thou?
Is it so much I ask thee, and spend my breath
In asking? nay, thou knowest it is but death.
Hadst thou true heart to love me, thou wouldst give
This: but for hate's sake thou wilt let me live."

  Here he caught up her lips with his, and made
The wild prayer silent in her heart that prayed,
And strained her to him till all her faint breath
    sank
And her bright light limbs palpitated and shrank
And rose and fluctuated as flowers in rain
That bends them and they tremble and rise again
And heave and straighten and quiver all through with
    bliss
And turn afresh their mouths up for a kiss,

Amorous, athirst of that sweet influent love ;
So, hungering towards his hovering lips above,
Her red-rose mouth yearned silent, and her eyes
Closed, and flashed after, as through June's darkest
    skies
The divine heartbeats of the deep live light
Make open and shut the gates of the outer night.
    Long lay they still, subdued with love, nor knew
If cloud or light changed colour as it grew,
If star or moon beheld them ; if above
The heaven of night waxed fiery with their love,
Or earth beneath were moved at heart and root
To burn as they, to burn and bring forth fruit
Unseasonable for love's sake ; if tall trees
Bowed, and close flowers yearned open, and the
    breeze
Failed and fell silent as a flame that fails :
And all that hour unheard the nightingales
Clamoured, and all the woodland soul was stirred,
And depth and height were one great song unheard,
As though the world caught music and took fire
From the instant heart alone of their desire.
    So sped their night of nights between them : so,
For all fears past and shadows, shine and snow,
That one pure hour all-golden where they lay
Made their life perfect and their darkness day.
And warmer waved its harvest yet to reap,
Till in the lovely fight of love and sleep
At length had sleep the mastery ; and the dark
Was lit with soft live gleams they might not mark,
Fleet butterflies, each like a dead flower's ghost,
White, blue, and sere leaf-coloured ; but the most
White as the sparkle of snow-flowers in the sun
Ere with his breath they lie at noon undone

Whose kiss devours their tender beauty, and leaves
But raindrops on the grass and sere thin leaves
That were engraven with traceries of the snow
Flowerwise ere any flower of earth's would blow ;
So swift they sprang and sank, so sweet and light
They swam the deep dim breathless air of night.
Now on her rose-white amorous breast half bare,
Now on her slumberous love-dishevelled hair,
The white wings lit and vanished, and afresh
Lit soft as snow lights on her snow-soft flesh,
On hand or throat or shoulder ; and she stirred
Sleeping, and spake some tremulous bright word,
And laughed upon some dream too sweet for truth,
Yet not so sweet as very love and youth
That there had charmed her eyes to sleep at last.
Nor woke they till the perfect night was past,
And the soft sea thrilled with blind hope of light.
But ere the dusk had well the sun in sight
He turned and kissed her eyes awake and said,
Seeing earth and water neither quick nor dead
And twilight hungering toward the day to be,
"As the dawn loves the sunlight I love thee."
And even as rays with cloudlets in the skies
Confused in brief love's bright contentious wise,
Sleep strove with sense rekindling in her eyes ;
And as the flush of birth scarce overcame
The pale pure pearl of unborn light with flame
Soft as may touch the rose's heart with shame
To break not all reluctant out of bud,
Stole up her sleeping cheek her waking blood ;
And with the lovely laugh of love that takes
The whole soul prisoner ere the whole sense wakes,
Her lips for love's sake bade love's will be done.
And all the sea lay subject to the sun.

III

TRISTRAM IN BRITTANY

" ' As the dawn loves the sunlight I love thee ;
As men that shall be swallowed of the sea
Love the sea's lovely beauty ; as the night
That wanes before it loves the young sweet light,
And dies of loving ; as the worn-out noon
Loves twilight, and as twilight loves the moon
That on its grave a silver seal shall set—
We have loved and slain each other, and love yet.
Slain ; for we live not surely, being in twain :
In her I lived, and in me she is slain,
Who loved me that I brought her to her doom,
Who loved her that her love might be my tomb.
As all the streams on earth and all fresh springs
And sweetest waters, every brook that sings,
Each fountain where the young year dips its wings
First, and the first-fledged branches of it wave,
Even with one heart's love seek one bitter grave.
From hills that first see bared the morning's breast
And heights the sun last yearns to from the west,
All tend but toward the sea, all born most high
Strive downward, passing all things joyous by,
Seek to it and cast their lives in it and die.

So strive all lives for death which all lives win ;
So sought her soul to my soul, and therein
Was poured and perished : O my love, and mine
Sought to thee and died of thee and died as thine.
As the dawn loves the sunlight that must cease
Ere dawn again may rise and pass in peace ;
Must die that she being dead may live again,
To be by his new rising nearly slain.
So rolls the great wheel of the great world round,
And no change in it and no fault is found,
And no true life of perdurable breath,
And surely no irrevocable death.
Day after day night comes that day may break,
And day comes back for night's reiterate sake.
Each into each dies, each of each is born :
Day past is night, shall night past not be morn ?
Out of this moonless and faint-hearted night
That love yet lives in, shall there not be light ?
Light strong as love, that love may live in yet ?
Alas, but how shall foolish hope forget
How all these loving things that kill and die
Meet not but for a breath's space and pass by ?
Night is kissed once of dawn and dies, and day
But touches twilight and is rapt away.
So may my love and her love meet once more,
And meeting be divided as of yore.
Yea, surely as the day-star loves the sun
And when he hath risen is utterly undone,
So is my love of her and hers of me—
And its most sweetness bitter as the sea.
Would God yet dawn might see the sun and die ! "
    Three years had looked on earth and passed it by
Since Tristram looked on Iseult, when he stood
So communing with dreams of evil and good,

And let all sad thoughts through his spirit sweep
As leaves through air or tears through eyes that weep
Or snowflakes through dark weather : and his soul,
That had seen all those sightless seasons roll
One after one, wave over weary wave,
Was in him as a corpse is in its grave.
Yet, for his heart was mighty, and his might
Through all the world as a great sound and light,
The mood was rare upon him ; save that here
In the low sundawn of the lightening year
With all last year's toil and its triumph done
He could not choose but yearn for that set sun
Which at this season saw the firstborn kiss
That made his lady's mouth one fire with his.
Yet his great heart being greater than his grief
Kept all the summer of his strength in leaf
And all the rose of his sweet spirit in flower ;
Still his soul fed upon the sovereign hour
That had been or that should be ; and once more
He looked through drifted sea and drifting shore
That crumbled in the wave-breach, and again
Spake sad and deep within himself : "What pain
Should make a man's soul wholly break and die,
Sapped as weak sand by water ?   How shall I
Be less than all less things are that endure
And strive and yield when time is ?   Nay, full sure
All these and we are parts of one same end ;
And if through fire or water we twain tend
To that sure life where both must be made one,
If one we be, what matter ?   Thou, O sun,
The face of God, if God thou be not—nay,
What but God should I think thee, what should say,
Seeing thee rerisen, but very God ?—should I,
I fool, rebuke thee sovereign in thy sky,

The clouds dead round thee and the air alive,
The winds that lighten and the waves that strive
Toward this shore as to that beneath thy breath,
Because in me my thoughts bear all towards death?
O sun, that when we are dead wilt rise as bright,
Air deepening up toward heaven, and nameless light,
And heaven immeasurable, and faint clouds blown
Between us and the lowest aerial zone
And each least skirt of their imperial state—
Forgive us that we held ourselves so great!
What should I do to curse you?   I indeed
Am a thing meaner than this least wild weed
That my foot bruises and I know not—yet
Would not be mean enough for worms to fret
Before their time and mine was.

                  "Ah, and ye
Light washing weeds, blind waifs of dull blind sea,
Do ye so thirst and hunger and aspire,
Are ye so moved with such long strong desire
In the ebb and flow of your sad life, and strive
Still toward some end ye shall not see alive—
But at high noon ye know it by light and heat
Some half-hour, till ye feel the fresh tide beat
Up round you, and at night's most bitter noon
The ripples leave you naked to the moon?
And this dim dusty heather that I tread,
These half-born blossoms, born at once and dead,
Sere brown as funeral cloths, and purple as pall,
What if some life and grief be in them all?
  "Ay, what of these? but, O strong sun! O sea!
I bid not you, divine things! comfort me,
I stand not up to match you in your sight—
Who hath said ye have mercy toward us, ye who have
    might?

And though ye had mercy, I think I would not pray
That ye should change your counsel or your way
To make our life less bitter : if such power
Be given the stars on one deciduous hour,
And such might be in planets to destroy
Grief and rebuild, and break and build up joy,
What man would stretch forth hand on them to make
Fate mutable, God foolish, for his sake ?
For if in life or death be aught of trust,
And if some unseen just God or unjust
Put soul into the body of natural things
And in time's pauseless feet and worldwide wings
Some spirit of impulse and some sense of will
That steers them through the seas of good and ill
To some incognizable and actual end,
Be it just or unjust, foe to man or friend,
How should we make the stable spirit to swerve,
How teach the strong soul of the world to serve,
The imperious will in time and sense in space
That gives man life turn back to give man place—
The conscious law lose conscience of its way,
The rule and reason fail from night and day,
The streams flow back toward whence the springs
    began,
That less of thirst might sear the lips of man ?
Let that which is be, and sure strengths stand sure,
And evil or good and death or life endure,
Not alterable and rootless, but indeed
A very stem born of a very seed
That brings forth fruit in season : how should this
Die that was sown, and that not be which is,
And the old fruit change that came of the ancient
    root,
And he that planted bid it not bear fruit,

And he that watered smite his vine with drouth
Because its grapes are bitter in our mouth,
And he that kindled quench the sun with night
Because its beams are fire against our sight,
And he that tuned untune the sounding spheres
Because their song is thunder in our ears?
How should the skies change and the stars, and
    time
Break the large concord of the years that chime,
Answering, as wave to wave beneath the moon
That draws them shoreward, mar the whole tide's
    tune
For the instant foam's sake on one turning wave—
For man's sake that is grass upon a grave?
How should the law that knows not soon or late,
For whom no time nor space is—how should fate,
That is not good nor evil, wise nor mad,
Nor just nor unjust, neither glad nor sad—
How should the one thing that hath being, the one
That moves not as the stars move or the sun
Or any shadow or shape that lives or dies
In likeness of dead earth or living skies,
But its own darkness and its proper light
Clothe it with other names than day or night,
And its own soul of strength and spirit of breath
Feed it with other powers than life or death—
How should it turn from its great way to give
Man that must die a clearer space to live?
Why should the waters of the sea be cleft,
The hills be molten to his right and left,
That he from deep to deep might pass dry-shod,
Or look between the viewless heights on God?
Hath he such eyes as, when the shadows flee,
The sun looks out with to salute the sea?

Is his hand bounteous as the morning's hand?
Or where the night stands hath he feet to stand?
Will the storm cry not when he bids it cease?
Is it his voice that saith to the east wind, Peace?
Is his breath mightier than the west wind's breath?
Doth his heart know the things of life and death?
Can his face bring forth sunshine and give rain,
Or his weak will that dies and lives again
Make one thing certain or bind one thing fast,
That as he willed it shall be at the last?
How should the storms of heaven and kindled lights
And all the depths of things and topless heights
And air and earth and fire and water change
Their likeness, and the natural world grow strange,
And all the limits of their life undone
Lose count of time and conscience of the sun,
And that fall under which was fixed above,
That man might have a larger hour for love?"
   So musing with close lips and lifted eyes
That smiled with self-contempt to live so wise,
With silent heart so hungry now so long,
So late grown clear, so miserably made strong,
About the wolds a banished man he went,
The brown wolds bare and sad as banishment,
By wastes of fruitless flowerage, and grey downs
That felt the sea-wind shake their wild-flower
      crowns
As though fierce hands would pluck from some grey
      head
The spoils of majesty despised and dead,
And fill with crying and comfortless strange sound
Their hollow sides and heights of herbless ground.
Yet as he went fresh courage on him came,
Till dawn rose too within him as a flame;

The heart of the ancient hills and his were one ;
The winds took counsel with him, and the sun
Spake comfort ; in his ears the shout of birds
Was as the sound of clear sweet-spirited words,
The noise of streams as laughter from above
Of the old wild lands, and as a cry of love
Spring's trumpet-blast blown over moor and lea :
The skies were red as love is, and the sea
Was as the floor of heaven for love to tread.
So went he as with light about his head,
And in the joyous travail of the year
Grew April-hearted ; since nor grief nor fear
Can master so a young man's blood so long
That it shall move not to the mounting song
Of that sweet hour when earth replumes her wings
And with fair face and heart set heavenward sings
As an awakened angel unaware
That feels his sleep fall from him, and his hair
By some new breath of wind and music stirred,
Till like the sole song of one heavenly bird
Sounds all the singing of the host of heaven,
And all the glories of the sovereign Seven
Are as one face of one incorporate light.
And as that host of singers in God's sight
Might draw toward one that slumbered, and arouse
The lips requickened and rekindling brows,
So seemed the earthly host of all things born
In sight of spring and eyeshot of the morn,
All births of land or waifs of wind and sea,
To draw toward him that sorrowed, and set free
From presage and remembrance of all pains
The life that leapt and lightened in his veins.
So with no sense abashed nor sunless look,
But with exalted eyes and heart, he took

His part of sun or storm-wind, and was glad,
For all things lost, of these good things he had.
   And the spring loved him surely, being from birth
One made out of the better part of earth,
A man born as at sunrise ; one that saw
Not without reverence and sweet sense of awe
But wholly without fear or fitful breath
The face of life watched by the face of death ;
And living took his fill of rest and strife,
Of love and change, and fruit and seed of life,
And when his time to live in light was done
With unbent head would pass out of the sun :
A spirit as morning, fair and clear and strong,
Whose thought and work were as one harp and
     song
Heard through the world as in a strange king's hall
Some great guest's voice that sings of festival.
So seemed all things to love him, and his heart
In all their joy of life to take such part,
That with the live earth and the living sea
He was as one that communed mutually
With naked heart to heart of friend to friend :
And the star deepening at the sunset's end,
And the moon fallen before the gate of day
As one sore wearied with vain length of way,
And the winds wandering, and the streams and
     skies,
As faces of his fellows in his eyes.
Nor lacked there love where he was evermore
Of man and woman, friend of sea or shore,
Not measurable with weight of graven gold,
Free as the sun's gift of the world to hold
Given each day back to man's reconquering sight
That loses but its lordship for a night.

And now that after many a season spent
In barren ways and works of banishment,
Toil of strange fights and many a fruitless field,
Ventures of quest and vigils under shield,
He came back to the strait of sundering sea
That parts green Cornwall from grey Brittany,
Where dwelt the high king's daughter of the lands,
Iseult, named alway from her fair white hands,
She looked on him and loved him ; but being young
Made shamefastness a seal upon her tongue,
And on her heart, that none might hear its cry,
Set the sweet signet of humility.
Yet when he came a stranger in her sight,
A banished man and weary, no such knight
As when the Swallow dipped her bows in foam
Steered singing that imperial Iseult home,
This maiden with her sinless sixteen years
Full of sweet thoughts and hopes that played at
    fears
Cast her eyes on him but in courteous wise,
And lo, the man's face burned upon her eyes
As though she had turned them on the naked sun :
And through her limbs she felt sweet passion run
As fire that flowed down from her face, and beat
Soft through stirred veins on even to her hands and
    feet
As all her body were one heart on flame,
Athrob with love and wonder and sweet shame.
And when he spake there sounded in her ears
As 'twere a song out of the graves of years
Heard, and again forgotten, and again
Remembered with a rapturous pulse of pain.
But as the maiden mountain snow sublime
Takes the first sense of April's trembling time

Soft on a brow that burns not though it blush
To feel the sunrise hardly half aflush,
So took her soul the sense of change, nor thought
That more than maiden love was more than nought.
Her eyes went hardly after him, her cheek
Grew scarce a goodlier flower to hear him speak,
Her bright mouth no more trembled than a rose
May for the least wind's breathless sake that blows
Too soft to sue save for a sister's kiss,
And if she sighed in sleep she knew not this.
Yet in her heart hovered the thoughts of things
Past, that with lighter or with heavier wings
Beat round about her memory, till it burned
With grief that brightened and with hope that
    yearned,
Seeing him so great and sad, nor knowing what
    fate
Had bowed and crowned a head so sad and great.
Nor might she guess but little, first or last,
Though all her heart so hung upon his past,
Of what so bowed him for what sorrow's sake :
For scarce of aught at any time he spake
That from his own land oversea had sent
His lordly life to barren banishment.
Yet still or soft or keen remembrance clung
Close round her of the least word from his tongue
That fell by chance of courtesy, to greet
With grace of tender thanks her pity, sweet
As running straems to men's way-wearied feet.
And when between strange words her name would
    fall,
Suddenly straightway to that lure's recall
Back would his heart bound as the falconer's bird,
And tremble and bow down before the word.

' Iseult "—and all the cloudlike world grew flame,
And all his heart flashed lightning at her name ;
" Iseult "—and all the wan waste weary skies
Shone as his queen's own love-enkindled eyes.
And seeing the bright blood in his face leap up
As red wine mantling in a royal cup
To hear the sudden sweetness of the sound
Ring, but ere well his heart had time to bound
His cheek would change, and grief bow down his
          head,
" Haply," the girl's heart, though she spake not,
          said,
" This name of mine was worn of one long dead,
Some sister that he loved : " and therewithal
Would pity bring her heart more deep in thrall.
But once, when winds about the world made mirth,
And March held revel hard on April's birth
Till air and sea were jubilant as earth,
Delight and doubt in sense and soul began,
And yearning of the maiden toward the man,
Harping on high before her : for his word
Was fire that kindled in her heart that heard,
And alway through the rhymes reverberate came
The virginal soft burden of her name.
And ere the full song failed upon her ear
Joy strove within her till it cast out fear,
And all her heart was as his harp, and rang
Swift music, made of hope whose birthnote sprang
Bright in the blood that kindled as he sang.

> " Stars know not how we call them, nor may flowers
> Know by what happy name the hovering hours
>   Baptize their new-born heads with dew and flame :
> And Love, adored of all time as of ours,
>   Iseult, knew nought for ages of his name.

" With many tongues men called on him, but he
Wist not which word of all might worthiest be
      To sound for ever in his ear the same,
Till heart of man might hear and soul might see,
      Iseult, the radiance ringing from thy name.

" By many names men called him, as the night
By many a name calls many a starry light,
      Her several sovereigns of dividual fame ;
But day by one name only calls aright,
      Iseult, the sun that bids men praise his name.

" In many a name of man his name soared high
And song shone round it soaring, till the sky
      Rang rapture, and the world's fast-founded frame
Trembled with sense of triumph, even as I,
      Iseult, with sense of worship at thy name.

" In many a name of woman smiled his power
Incarnate, as all summer in a flower,
      Till winter bring forgetfulness or shame :
But thine, the keystone of his topless tower,
      Iseult, is one with Love's own lordliest name.

" Iseult my love, Iseult my queen twice crowned,
In thee my death, in thee my life lies bound :
      Names are there yet that all men's hearts acclaim,
But Love's own heart rings answer to the sound,
      Iseult, that bids it bow before thy name."

There ceased his voice yearning upon the word,
Struck with strong passion dumb : but she that
      heard
Quailed to the heart, and trembled ere her eyes
Durst let the loving light within them rise,
And yearn on his for answer : yet at last,
Albeit not all her fear was overpast,

Hope, kindling even the frost of fear apace
With sweet fleet bloom and breath of gradual grace,
Flushed in the changing roses of her face.
And ere the strife took truce of white with red,
Or joy for soft shame's sake durst lift up head,
Something she would and would not fain have said,
And wist not what the fluttering word would be,
But rose and reached forth to him her hand : and he,
Heart-stricken, bowed his head and dropped his knee,
And on her fragrant hand his lips were fire ;
And their two hearts were as one trembling lyre
Touched by the keen wind's kiss with brief desire
And music shuddering at its own delight.
So dawned the moonrise of their marriage night.

IV

THE MAIDEN MARRIAGE

Spring watched her last moon burn and fade with
    May
While the days deepened toward a bridal day.
And on her snowbright hand the ring was set
While in the maiden's ear the song's word yet
Hovered, that hailed as love's own queen by name
Iseult : and in her heart the word was flame ;
A pulse of light, a breath of tender fire,
Too dear for doubt, too driftless for desire.
Between her father's hand and brother's led
From hall to shrine, from shrine to marriage-bed,
She saw not how by hap at home-coming
Fell from her new lord's hand a royal ring,
Whereon he looked, and felt the pulse astart
Speak passion in his faith-forsaken heart.
For this was given him of the hand wherein
That heart's pledge lay for ever : so the sin
That should be done if truly he should take
This maid to wife for strange love's faithless sake
Struck all his mounting spirit abashed, and fear
Fell cold for shame's sake on his changing cheer.
Yea, shame's own fire that burned upon his brow
To bear the brand there of a broken vow

Was frozen again for very fear thereof
That wrung his heart with keener pangs than love
And all things rose upon him, all things past
Ere last they parted, cloven in twain at last,
Iseult from Tristram, Tristram from the queen ;
And how men found them in the wild woods green
Sleeping, but sundered by the sword between,
Dividing breast from amorous breast a span,
But scarce in heart the woman from the man
As far as hope from joy or sleep from truth,
And Mark that saw them held for sacred sooth
These were no fleshly lovers, by that sign
That severed them, still slumbering ; so divine
He deemed it : how at waking they beheld
The king's folk round the king, and uncompelled
Were fain to follow and fare among them home
Back to the towers washed round with rolling foam
And storied halls wherethrough sea-music rang :
And how report thereafter swelled and sprang,
A full-mouthed serpent, hissing in men's ears
Word of their loves : and one of all his peers
That most he trusted, being his kinsman born,
A man base-moulded for the stamp of scorn,
Whose heart with hate was keen and cold and dark,
Gave note by midnight whisper to King Mark
Where he might take them sleeping ; how ere day
Had seen the grim next morning all away
Fast bound they brought him down a weary way
With forty knights about him, and their chief
That traitor who for trust had given him grief,
To the old hoar chapel, like a strait stone tomb
Sheer on the sea-rocks, there to take his doom :
How, seeing he needs must die, he bade them yet
Bethink them if they durst for shame forget

What deeds for Cornwall had he done, and wrought
For all their sake what rescue, when he fought
Against the fierce foul Irish foe that came
To take of them for tribute in their shame
Three hundred heads of children ; whom in fight
His hand redeeming slew Moraunt the knight
That none durst lift his eyes against, not one
Had heart but he, who now had help of none,
To take the battle ; whence great shame it were
To knighthood, yea, foul shame on all men there,
To see him die so shamefully : nor durst
One man look up, nor one make answer first,
Save even the very traitor, who defied
And would have slain him naked in his pride,
But he, that saw the sword plucked forth to slay,
Looked on his hands, and wrenched their bonds away,
Haling those twain that he went bound between
Suddenly to him, and kindling in his mien
Shone lion-fashion forth with eyes alight,
And lion-wise leapt on that kinsman knight
And wrung forth of his felon hands with might
The sword that should have slain him weaponless,
And smote him sheer down : then came all the press
All raging in upon him ; but he wrought
So well for his deliverance as they fought
That ten strong knights rejoicingly he slew,
And took no wound, nor wearied : then the crew
Waxed greater, and their cry on him ; but he
Had won the chapel now above the sea
That chafed right under : then the heart in him
Sprang, seeing the low cliff clear to leap, and swim
Right out by the old blithe way the sea-mew takes
Across the bounding billow-belt that breaks
For ever, but the loud bright chain it makes

To bind the bridal bosom of the land
Time shall unlink not ever, till his hand
Fall by its own last blow dead : thence again
Might he win forth into the green great main
Far on beyond, and there yield up his breath
At least, with God's will, by no shameful death,
Or haply save himself, and come anew
Some long day later, ere sweet life were through.
And as the sea-gull hovers high, and turns
With eyes wherein the keen heart glittering yearns
Down toward the sweet green sea whereon the broad
    noon burns,
And suddenly, soul-stricken with delight,
Drops, and the glad wave gladdens, and the light
Sees wing and wave confuse their fluttering white,
So Tristram one brief breathing-space apart
Hung, and gazed down ; then with exulting heart
Plunged : and the fleet foam round a joyous head
Flashed, that shot under, and ere a shaft had sped
Rose again radiant, a rejoicing star,
And high along the water-ways afar
Triumphed : and all they deemed he needs must
    die ;
But Gouvernayle his squire, that watched hard by,
Sought where perchance a man might win ashore,
Striving, with strong limbs labouring long and sore,
And there abode an hour : till as from fight
Crowned with hard conquest won by mastering might.
Hardly, but happier for the imperious toil,
Swam the knight in forth of the close waves' coil,
Sea-satiate, bruised with buffets of the brine,
Laughing, and flushed as one afire with wine :
All this came hard upon him in a breath ;
And how he marvelled in his heart that death

Should be no bitterer than it seemed to be
There, in the strenuous impulse of the sea
Borne as to battle deathward : and at last
How all his after seasons overpast
Had brought him darkling to this dark sweet hour,
Where his foot faltered nigh the bridal bower.
And harder seemed the passage now to pass,
Though smoother-seeming than the still sea's glass,
More fit for very manhood's heart to fear,
Than all straits past of peril.   Hardly here
Might aught of all things hearten him save one,
Faith : and as men's eyes quail before the sun
So quailed his heart before the star whose light
Put out the torches of his bridal night,
So quailed and shrank with sense of faith's keen star
That burned as fire beheld by night afar
Deep in the darkness of his dreams ; for all
The bride-house now seemed hung with heavier pall
Than clothes the house of mourning.   Yet at last,
Soul-sick with trembling at the heart, he passed
Into the sweet light of the maiden bower
Where lay the lonely lily-featured flower
That, lying within his hand to gather, yet
Might not be gathered of it.   Fierce regret
And bitter loyalty strove hard at strife
With amorous pity toward the tender wife
That wife indeed might never be, to wear
The very crown of wedlock ; never bear
Children, to watch and worship her white hair
When time should change, with hand more soft than
      snow,
The fashion of its glory ; never know
The loveliness of laughing love that lives
On little lips of children : all that gives

Glory and grace and reverence and delight
To wedded woman by her bridal right,
All praise and pride that flowers too fair to fall,
Love that should give had stripped her of them all
And left her bare for ever.   So his thought
Consumed him, as a fire within that wrought
Visibly, ravening till its wrath were spent :
So pale he stood, so bowed and passion-rent,
Before the blithe-faced bride-folk, ere he went
Within the chamber, heavy-eyed : and there
Gleamed the white hands and glowed the glimmering
    hair
That might but move his memory more of one more
    fair,
More fair than all this beauty : but in sooth
So fair she too shone in her flower of youth
That scarcely might man's heart hold fast its
    truth,
Though strong, who gazed upon her : for her eyes
Were emerald-soft as evening-coloured skies,
And a smile in them like the light therein
Slept, or shone out in joy that knew not sin,
Clear as a child's own laughter : and her mouth,
Albeit no rose full-hearted from the south
And passion-coloured for the perfect kiss
That signs the soul for love and stamps it his,
Was soft and bright as any bud new-blown ;
And through her cheek the gentler lifebloom shone
Of mild wild roses nigh the northward sea.
So in her bride-bed lay the bride : and he
Drew nigh, and all the high sad heart in him
Yearned on her, seeing the twilight meek and dim
Through all the soft alcove tremblingly lit
With hovering silver, as a heart in it

II.   C 2

Beating, that burned from one deep lamp above,
Fainter than fire of torches, as the love
Within him fainter than a bridegroom's fire,
No marriage-torch red with the heart's desire,
But silver-soft, a flameless light that glowed
Starlike along night's dark and starry road
Wherein his soul was traveller. And he sighed,
Seeing, and with eyes set sadly toward his bride
Laid him down by her, and spake not : but within
His heart spake, saying how sore should be the sin
To break toward her, that of all womankind
Was faithfullest, faith plighted, or unbind
The bond first linked between them when they drank
The love-draught : and his quick blood sprang and
    sank,
Remembering in the pulse of all his veins
That red swift rapture, all its fiery pains
And all its fierier pleasures : and he spake
Aloud, one burning word for love's keen sake—
" Iseult ; " and full of love and lovelier fear
A virgin voice gave answer—" I am here."
And a pang rent his heart at root : but still,
For spirit and flesh were vassals to his will,
Strong faith held mastery on them : and the breath
Felt on his face did not his will to death,
Nor glance nor lute-like voice nor flower-soft touch
Might so prevail upon it overmuch
That constancy might less prevail than they,
For all he looked and loved her as she lay
Smiling ; and soft as bird alights on bough
He kissed her maiden mouth and blameless brow,
Once, and again his heart within him sighed :
But all his young blood's yearning toward his bride,

How hard soe'er it held his life awake
For passion, and sweet nature's unforbidden sake,
And will that strove unwillingly with will it might not
    break,
Fell silent as a wind abashed, whose breath
Dies out of heaven, suddenly done to death,
When in between them on the dumb dusk air
Floated the bright shade of a face more fair
Than hers that hard beside him shrank and smiled
And wist of all no more than might a child.
So had she all her heart's will, all she would,
For love's sake that sufficed her, glad and good,
All night safe sleeping in her maidenhood.

V

ISEULT AT TINTAGEL

But that same night in Cornwall oversea
Couched at Queen Iseult's hand, against her knee,
With keen kind eyes that read her whole heart's pain
Fast at wide watch lay Tristram's hound Hodain,
The goodliest and the mightiest born on earth,
That many a forest day of fiery mirth
Had plied his craft before them; and the queen
Cherished him, even for those dim years between,
More than of old in those bright months far flown
When ere a blast of Tristram's horn was blown
Each morning as the woods rekindled, ere
Day gat full empire of the glimmering air,
Delight of dawn would quicken him, and fire
Spring and pant in his breath with bright desire
To be among the dewy ways on quest:
But now perforce at restless-hearted rest
He chafed through days more barren than the sand,
Soothed hardly but soothed only with her hand,
Though fain to fawn thereon and follow, still
With all his heart and all his loving will
Desiring one divided from his sight,
For whose lost sake dawn was as dawn of night
And noon as night's noon in his eyes was dark.
But in the halls far under sat King Mark,

Feasting, and full of cheer, with heart uplift,
As on the night that harper gat his gift :
And music revelled on the fitful air,
And songs came floated up the festal stair,
And muffled roar of wassail, where the king
Took heart from wine-cups and the quiring string
Till all his cold thin veins rejoiced and ran
Strong as with lifeblood of a kinglier man.
But the queen shut from sound her wearied ears,
Shut her sad eyes from sense of aught save tears,
And wrung her hair with soft fierce hands, and
        prayed :
  " O God, God born of woman, of a maid,
Christ, once in flesh of thine own fashion clad ;
O very love, so glad in heaven and sad
On earth for earth's sake alway ; since thou art
Pure only, I only impure of spirit and heart,
Since thou for sin's sake and the bitter doom
Didst as a veil put on a virgin's womb,
I that am none, and cannot hear or see
Or shadow or likeness or a sound of thee
Far off, albeit with man's own speech and face
Thou shine yet and thou speak yet, showing forth
        grace—
Ah me ! grace only shed on souls that are
Lit and led forth of shadow by thy star—
Alas ! to these men only grace, to these,
Lord, whom thy love draws Godward, to thy knees—
I, can I draw thee me-ward, can I seek,
Who love thee not, to love me ? seeing how weak,
Lord, all this little love I bear thee is,
And how much is my strong love more than this,
My love that I love man with, that I bear
Him sinning through me sinning ? wilt thou care,

God, for this love, if love be any, alas,
In me to give thee, though long since there was,
How long, when I too, Lord, was clean, even I,
That now am unclean till the day I die—
Haply by burning, harlot-fashion, made
A horror in all hearts of wife and maid,
Hateful, not knowing if ever in these mine eyes
Shone any light of thine in any wise
Or this were love at all that I bore thee ? "
    And the night spake, and thundered on the sea,
Ravening aloud for ruin of lives : and all
The bastions of the main cliff's northward wall
Rang response out from all their deepening length,
As the east wind girded up his godlike strength
And hurled in hard against that high-towered hold
The fleeces of the flock that knows no fold,
The rent white shreds of shattering storm : but she
Heard not nor heeded wind or storming sea,
Knew not if night were mild or mad with wind.
    " Yea, though deep lips and tender hair be thinned,
Though cheek wither, brow fade, and bosom wane,
Shall I change also from this heart again
To maidenhood of heart and holiness ?
Shall I more love thee, Lord, or love him less—
Ah miserable ! though spirit and heart be rent,
Shall I repent, Lord God ? shall I repent ?
Nay, though thou slay me ! for herein I am blest,
That as I loved him yet I love him best—
More than mine own soul or thy love or thee,
Though thy love save and my love save not me.
Blest am I beyond women even herein,
That beyond all born women is my sin,
And perfect my transgression : that above
All offerings of all others is my love,

Who have chosen it only, and put away for this
Thee, and my soul's hope, Saviour, of the kiss
Wherewith thy lips make welcome all thine own
When in them life and death are overthrown ;
The sinless lips that seal the death of sin,
The kiss wherewith their dumb lips touched begin
Singing in heaven.
                    " Where we shall never, love,
Never stand up nor sing ! for God above
Knows us, how too much more than God to me
Thy sweet love is, my poor love is to thee !
Dear, dost thou see now, dost thou hear to-night,
Sleeping, my waste wild speech, my face worn
        white,
—Speech once heard soft by thee, face once kissed
        red !—
In such a dream as when men see their dead
And know not if they know if dead these be ?
Ah love, are thy days my days, and to thee
Are all nights like as my nights ? does the sun
Grieve thee ? art thou soul-sick till day be done,
And weary till day rises ? is thine heart
Full of dead things as mine is ?   Nay, thou art
Man, with man's strength and praise and pride of
        life,
No bondwoman, no queen, no loveless wife
That would be shamed albeit she had not sinned."
    And swordlike was the sound of the iron wind,
And as a breaking battle was the sea.
    " Nay, Lord, I pray thee let him love not me,
Love me not any more, nor like me die,
And be no more than such a thing as I.
Turn his heart from me, lest my love too lose
Thee as I lose thee, and his fair soul refuse

For my sake thy fair heaven, and as I fell
Fall, and be mixed with my soul and with hell.
Let me die rather, and only ; let me be
Hated of him so he be loved of thee,
Lord : for I would not have him with me there
Out of thy light and love in the unlit air,
Out of thy sight in the unseen hell where I
Go gladly, going alone, so thou on high
Lift up his soul and love him—Ah, Lord, Lord,
Shalt thou love as I love him ? she that poured
From the alabaster broken at thy feet
An ointment very precious, not so sweet
As that poured likewise forth before thee then
From the rehallowed heart of Magdalen,
From a heart broken, yearning like the dove,
An ointment very precious which is love—
Couldst thou being holy and God, and sinful she,
Love her indeed as surely she loved thee ?
Nay, but if not, then as we sinners can
Let us love still in the old sad wise of man.
For with less love than my love, having had
Mine, though God love him he shall not be glad
And with such love as my love, I wot well,
He shall not lie disconsolate in hell :
Sad only as souls for utter love's sake be
Here, and a little sad, perchance, for me—
Me happy, me more glad than God above,
In the utmost hell whose fires consume not love !
For in the waste ways emptied of the sun
He would say—' Dear, thy place is void, and one
Weeps among angels for thee, with his face
Veiled, saying, *O sister, how thy chosen place*
Stands desolate, that God made fair for thee ?
Is heaven not sweeter, and we thy brethren, we

Fairer than love on earth and life in hell ?'
And I—with me were all things then not well?
Should I not answer—'O love, be well content ;
Look on me, and behold if I repent.'
This were more to me than an angel's wings.
Yea, many men pray God for many things,
But I pray that this only thing may be."
   And as a full field charging was the sea,
And as the cry of slain men was the wind.
   "Yea, since I surely loved him, and he sinned
Surely, though not as my sin his be black,
God, give him to me—God, God, give him back !
For now how should we live in twain or die ?
I am he indeed, thou knowest, and he is I.
Not man and woman several as we were,
But one thing with one life and death to bear.
How should one love his own soul overmuch ?
And time is long since last I felt the touch,
The sweet touch of my lover, hand and breath,
In such delight as puts delight to death,
Burn my soul through, till spirit and soul and sense,
In the sharp grasp of the hour, with violence
Died, and again through pangs of violent birth
Lived, and laughed out with refluent might of mirth ;
Laughed each on other and shuddered into one,
As a cloud shuddering dies into the sun.
Ah, sense is that or spirit, soul or flesh,
That only love lulls or awakes afresh ?
Ah, sweet is that or bitter, evil or good,
That very love allays not as he would?
Nay, truth is this or vanity, that gives
No love assurance when love dies or lives ?
This that my spirit is wrung withal, and yet
No surelier knows if haply thine forget,

Thou that my spirit is wrung for, nor can say
Love is not in thee dead as yesterday?
Dost thou feel, thou, this heartbeat whence my heart
Would send thee word what life is mine apart,
And know by keen response what life is thine?
Dost thou not hear one cry of all of mine?
O Tristram's heart, have I no part in thee?"
    And all her soul was as the breaking sea,
And all her heart anhungered as the wind.
    " Dost thou repent thee of the sin we sinned?
Dost thou repent thee of the days and nights
That kindled and that quenched for us their lights,
The months that feasted us with all their hours,
The ways that breathed of us in all their flowers,
The dells that sang of us with all their doves?
Dost thou repent thee of the wildwood loves?
Is thine heart changed, and hallowed? art thou
        grown
God's, and not mine? Yet, though my heart make
        moan,
Fain would my soul give thanks for thine, if thou
Be saved—yea, fain praise God, and knows not how.
How should it know thanksgiving? nay, or learn
Aught of the love wherewith thine own should burn,
God's, that should cast out as an evil thing
Mine? yea, what hand of prayer have I to cling,
What heart to prophesy, what spirit of sight
To strain insensual eyes toward increate light,
Who look but back on life wherein I sinned?"
    And all their past came wailing in the wind,
And all their future thundered in the sea.
    " But if my soul might touch the time to be,
If hand might handle now or eye behold
My life and death ordained me from of old,

Life palpable, compact of blood and breath,
Visible, present, naked, very death,
Should I desire to know before the day
These that I know not, nor is man that may?
For haply, seeing, my heart would break for fear,
And my soul timeless cast its load off here,
Its load of life too bitter, love too sweet,
And fall down shamed and naked at thy feet,
God, who wouldst take no pity of it, nor give
One hour back, one of all its hours to live
Clothed with my mortal body, that once more,
Once, on this reach of barren beaten shore,
This stormy strand of life, ere sail were set,
Had haply felt love's arms about it yet—
Yea, ere death's bark put off to seaward, might
With many a grief have bought me one delight
That then should know me never.   Ah, what years
Would I endure not, filled up full with tears,
Bitter like blood and dark as dread of death,
To win one amorous hour of mingling breath,
One fire-eyed hour and sunnier than the sun,
    Or all these nights and days like nights but one?
One hour of heaven born once, a stormless birth,
For all these windy weary hours of earth?
One, but one hour from birth of joy to death,
For all these hungering hours of feverish breath?
And I should lose this, having died and sinned."

    And as man's anguish clamouring cried the wind,
And as God's anger answering rang the sea.

    " And yet what life—Lord God, what life for me
Has thy strong wrath made ready?   Dost thou think
How lips whose thirst hath only tears to drink
Grow grey for grief untimely?   Dost thou know,
O happy God, how men wax weary of woe—

Yea, for their wrong's sake that thine hand hath done
Come even to hate thy semblance in the sun ?
Turn back from dawn and noon and all thy light
To make their souls one with the soul of night ?
Christ, if thou hear yet or have eyes to see,
Thou that hadst pity, and hast no pity on me,
Know'st thou no more, as in this life's sharp span,
What pain thou hadst on earth, what pain hath man ?
Hast thou no care, that all we suffer yet ?
What help is ours of thee if thou forget ?
What profit have we though thy blood were given,
If we that sin bleed and be not forgiven ?
Not love but hate, thou bitter God and strange,
Whose heart as man's heart hath grown cold with
    change,
Not love but hate thou showest us that have sinned."
    And like a world's cry shuddering was the wind,
And like a God's voice threatening was the sea.
    " Nay, Lord, for thou wast gracious ; nay, in thee
No change can come with time or varying fate,
No tongue bid thine be less compassionate,
No sterner eye rebuke for mercy thine,
No sin put out thy pity—no, not mine.
Thou knowest us, Lord, thou knowest us, all we are,
He, and the soul that hath his soul for star :
Thou knowest as I know, Lord, how much more
    worth
Than all souls clad and clasped about with earth,
But most of all, God, how much more than I,
Is this man's soul that surely shall not die.
What righteousness, what judgment, Lord most
    high,
Were this, to bend a brow of doom as grim
As threats me, me the adulterous wife, on him ?

There lies none other nightly by his side :
He hath not sought, he shall not seek a bride.
Far as God sunders earth from heaven above,
So far was my love born beneath his love.
I loved him as the sea-wind loves the sea,
To rend and ruin it only and waste : but he,
As the sea loves a sea-bird loved he me,
To foster and uphold my tired life's wing,
And bounteously beneath me spread forth spring,
A springtide space whereon to float or fly,
A world of happy water, whence the sky
Glowed goodlier, lightening from so glad a glass,
Than with its own light only.   Now, alas !
Cloud hath come down and clothed it round with
    storm,
And gusts and fits of eddying winds deform
The feature of its glory.   Yet be thou,
God, merciful : nay, show but justice now,
And let the sin in him that scarce was his
Stand expiated with exile : and be this
The price for him, the atonement this, that I
With all the sin upon me live, and die
With all thy wrath on me that most have sinned."
   And like man's heart relenting sighed the wind,
And as God's wrath subsiding sank the sea.
   " But if such grace be possible—if it be
Not sin more strange than all sins past, and worse
Evil, that cries upon thee for a curse,
To pray such prayers from such a heart, do thou
Hear, and make wide thine hearing toward me now ;
Let not my soul and his for ever dwell
Sundered : though doom keep always heaven and hell
Irreconcilable, infinitely apart,
Keep not in twain for ever heart and heart

That once, albeit by not thy law, were one ;
Let this be not thy will, that this be done.
Let all else, all thou wilt of evil, be,
But no doom, none, dividing him and me."
   By this was heaven stirred eastward, and there came
Up the rough ripple a labouring light like flame ;
And dawn, sore trembling still and grey with fear,
Looked hardly forth, a face of heavier cheer
Than one which grief or dread yet half enshrouds,
Wild-eyed and wan, across the cleaving clouds.
And Iseult, worn with watch long held on pain.
Turned, and her eye lit on the hound Hodain,
And all her heart went out in tears : and he
Laid his kind head along her bended knee,
Till round his neck her arms went hard, and all
The night past from her as a chain might fall :
But yet the heart within her, half undone,
Wailed, and was loth to let her see the sun.
   And ere full day brought heaven and earth to
      flower,
Far thence, a maiden in a marriage bower,
That moment, hard by Tristram, oversea,
Woke with glad eyes Iseult of Brittany.

VI

JOYOUS GARD

A LITTLE time, O Love, a little light,
A little hour for ease before the night.
Sweet Love, that art so bitter ; foolish Love,
Whom wise men know for wiser, and thy dove
More subtle than the serpent ; for thy sake
These pray thee for a little beam to break,
A little grace to help them, lest men think
Thy servants have but hours like tears to drink.
O Love, a little comfort, lest they fear
To serve as these have served thee who stand here.
  For these are thine, thy servants these, that stand
Here nigh the limit of the wild north land,
At margin of the grey great eastern sea,
Dense-islanded with peaks and reefs, that see
No life but of the fleet wings fair and free
Which cleave the mist and sunlight all day long
With sleepless flight and cries more glad than song.
Strange ways of life have led them hither, here
To win fleet respite from desire and fear
With armistice from sorrow ; strange and sweet
Ways trodden by forlorn and casual feet
Till kindlier chance woke toward them kindly will
In happier hearts of lovers, and their ill

Found rest, as healing surely might it not,
By gift and kingly grace of Launcelot
At gracious bidding given of Guenevere.
For in the trembling twilight of this year
Ere April sprang from hope to certitude
Two hearts of friends fast linked had fallen at feud
As they rode forth on hawking, by the sign
Which gave his new bride's brother Ganhardine
To know the truth of Tristram's dealing, how
Faith kept of him against his marriage vow
Kept virginal his bride-bed night and morn ;
Whereat, as wroth his blood should suffer scorn,
Came Ganhardine to Tristram, saying, " Behold,
We have loved thee, and for love we have shown of
        old
Scorn hast thou shown us : wherefore is thy bride
Not thine indeed, a stranger at thy side,
Contemned ? what evil hath she done, to be
Mocked with mouth-marriage and despised of thee,
Shamed, set at nought, rejected ? " But there came
On Tristram's brow and eye the shadow and flame
Confused of wrath and wonder, ere he spake,
Saying, " Hath she bid thee for thy sister's sake
Plead with me, who believed of her in heart
More nobly than to deem such piteous part
Should find so fair a player ? or whence hast thou
Of us this knowledge ? " " Nay," said he, " but now,
Riding beneath these whitethorns overhead,
There fell a flower into her girdlestead
Which laughing she shook out, and smiling said—
' Lo, what large leave the wind hath given this stray,
To lie more near my heart than till this day
Aught ever since my mother lulled me lay

Or even my lord came ever ;' whence I wot
We are all thy scorn, a race regarded not
Nor held as worth communion of thine own,
Except in her be found some fault alone
To blemish our alliance." Then replied
Tristram, " Nor blame nor scorn may touch my bride,
Albeit unknown of love she live, and be
Worth a man worthier than her love thought me.
Faith only, faith withheld me, faith forbade
The blameless grace wherewith love's grace makes
      glad
All lives linked else in wedlock ; not that less
I loved the sweet light of her loveliness,
But that my love toward faith was more : and thou,
Albeit thine heart be keen against me now,
Couldst thou behold my very lady, then
No more of thee than of all other men
Should this my faith be held a faithless fault."
And ere that day their hawking came to halt,
Being sore of him entreated for a sign,
He sware to bring his brother Ganhardine
To sight of that strange Iseult : and thereon
Forth soon for Cornwall are these brethren gone,
Even to that royal pleasance where the hunt
Rang ever of old with Tristram s horn in front
Blithe as the queen's horse bounded at his side :
And first of all her dames forth pranced in pride
That day before them, with a ringing rein
All golden-glad, the king's false bride Brangwain,
The queen's true handmaid ever : and on her
Glancing, " Be called for all time truth-teller,
O Tristram, of all true men's tongues alive,"
Quoth Ganhardine ; " for may my soul so thrive

As yet mine eye drank never sight like this."
" Ay ? " Tristram said, " and she thou look'st on is
So great in grace of goodliness, that thou
Hast less thought left of wrath against me now,
Seeing but my lady's handmaid ? Nay, behold ;
See'st thou no light more golden than of gold
Shine where she moves in midst of all, above
All, past all price or praise or prayer of love ?
Lo, this is she."   But as one mazed with wine
Stood, stunned in spirit and stricken, Ganhardine,
And gazed out hard against them : and his heart
As with a sword was cloven, and rent apart
As with strong fangs of fire ; and scarce he spake,
Saying how his life for even a handmaid's sake
Was made a flame within him.   And the knight
Bade him, being known of none that stood in sight,
Bear to Brangwain his ring, that she unseen
Might give in token privily to the queen
And send swift word where under moon or sun
They twain might yet be no more twain but one.
And that same night, under the stars that rolled
Over their warm deep wildwood nights of old
Whose hours for grains of sand shed sparks of fire,
Such way was made anew for their desire
By secret wile of sickness feigned, to keep
The king far off her vigils or her sleep,
That in the queen's pavilion midway set
By glimmering moondawn were those lovers met,
And Ganhardine of Brangwain gat him grace.
And in some passionate soft interspace
Between two swells of passion, when their lips
Breathed, and made room for such brief speech as slips
From tongues athirst with draughts of amorous wine
That leaves them thirstier than the salt sea's brine,

Was counsel taken how to fly, and where
Find covert from the wild world's ravening air
That hunts with storm the feet of nights and days
Through strange thwart lines of life and flowerless
  ways.
Then said Iseult : " Lo, now the chance is here
Foreshown me late by word of Guenevere,
To give me comfort of thy rumoured wrong,
My traitor Tristram, when report was strong
Of me forsaken and thine heart estranged :
Nor should her sweet soul toward me yet be changed
Nor all her love lie barren, if mine hand
Crave harvest of it from the flowering land.
See therefore if this counsel please thee not,
That we take horse in haste for Camelot
And seek that friendship of her plighted troth
Which love shall be full fain to lend, nor loth
Shall my love be to take it." So next night
The multitudinous stars laughed round their flight,
Fulfilling far with laughter made of light
The encircling deeps of heaven : and in brief space
At Camelot their long love gat them grace
Of those fair twain whose heads men's praise im-
  pearled
As love's two lordliest lovers in the world :
And thence as guests for harbourage past they
  forth
To win this noblest hold of all the north.
Far by wild ways and many days they rode,
Till clear across June's kingliest sunset glowed
The great round girth of goodly wall that showed
Where for one clear sweet season's length should be
Their place of strength to rest in, fain and free,
By the utmost margin of the loud lone sea.

And now, O Love, what comfort ? God most
    high,
Whose life is as a flower's to live and die,
Whose light is everlasting : Lord, whose breath
Speaks music through the deathless lips of death
Whereto time's heart rings answer : Bard, whom
    time
Hears, and is vanquished with a wandering rhyme
That once thy lips made fragrant : Seer, whose
    sooth
Joy knows not well, but sorrow knows for truth,
Being priestess of thy soothsayings : Love, what
    grace
Shall these twain find at last before thy face ?
  This many a year they have served thee, and
    deserved,
If ever man might yet of all that served,
Since the first heartbeat bade the first man's knee
Bend, and his mouth take music, praising thee,
Some comfort ; and some honey indeed of thine
Thou hast mixed for these with life's most bitter
    wine,
Commending to their passionate lips a draught
No deadlier than thy chosen of old have quaffed
And blessed thine hand, their cupbearer's : for not
On all men comes the grace that seals their lot
As holier in thy sight, for all these feuds
That rend it, than the light-souled multitude's,
Nor thwarted of thine hand nor blessed ; but these
Shall see no twilight, Love, nor fade at ease,
Grey-grown and careless of desired delight,
But lie down tired and sleep before the night.
These shall not live till time or change may chill
Or doubt divide or shame subdue their will,

Or fear or slow repentance work them wrong,
Or love die first : these shall not live so long.
Death shall not take them drained of dear true life
Already, sick or stagnant from the strife,
Quenched : not with dry-drawn veins and lingering
    breath
Shall these through crumbling hours crouch down to
    death.
Swift, with one strong clean leap, ere life's pulse
    tire,
Most like the leap of lions or of fire,
Sheer death shall bound upon them : one pang past,
The first keen sense of him shall be their last,
Their last shall be no sense of any fear,
More than their life had sense of anguish here.
  Weeks and light months had fled at swallow's
    speed
Since here their first hour sowed for them the seed
Of many sweet as rest or hope could be ;
Since on the blown beach of a glad new sea
Wherein strange rocks like fighting men stand
    scarred
They saw the strength and help of Joyous Gard.
Within the full deep glorious tower that stands
Between the wild sea and the broad wild lands
Love led and gave them quiet : and they drew
Life like a God's life in each wind that blew,
And took their rest, and triumphed. Day by day
The mighty moorlands and the sea-walls grey,
The brown bright waters of green fells that sing
One song to rocks and flowers and birds on wing,
Beheld the joy and glory that they had,
Passing, and how the whole world made them
    glad,

And their great love was mixed with all things
    great,
As life being lovely, and yet being strong like fate.
For when the sun sprang on the sudden sea
Their eyes sprang eastward, and the day to be
Was lit in them untimely : such delight
They took yet of the clear cold breath and light
That goes before the morning, and such grace
Was deathless in them through their whole life's
    space
As dies in many with their dawn that dies
And leaves in pulseless hearts and flameless eyes
No light to lighten and no tear to weep
For youth's high joy that time has cast on sleep.
Yea, this old grace and height of joy they had,
To lose no jot of all that made them glad
And filled their springs of spirit with such fire
That all delight fed in them all desire ;
And no whit less than in their first keen prime
The spring's breath blew through all their summer
    time,
And in their skies would sunlike Love confuse
Clear April colours with hot August hues,
And in their hearts one light of sun and moon
Reigned, and the morning died not of the noon :
Such might of life was in them, and so high
Their heart of love rose higher than fate could fly.
And many a large delight of hawk and hound
The great glad land that knows no bourne or bound,
Save the wind's own and the outer sea-bank's, gave
Their days for comfort ; many a long blithe wave
Buoyed their blithe bark between the bare bald
    rocks,
Deep, steep, and still, save for the swift free flocks

Unshepherded, uncompassed, unconfined,
That when blown foam keeps all the loud air blind
Mix with the wind's their triumph, and partake
The joy of blasts that ravin, waves that break,
All round and all below their mustering wings,
A clanging cloud that round the cliff's edge clings
On each bleak bluff breaking the strenuous tides
That rings reverberate mirth when storm bestrides
The subject night in thunder : many a noon
They took the moorland's or the bright sea's boon
With all their hearts into their spirit of sense,
Rejoicing, where the sudden dells grew dense
With sharp thick flight of hillsie birds, or where
On some strait rock's ledge in the intense mute air
Erect against the cliff's sheer sunlit white
Blue as the clear north heaven, clothed warm with
    light,
Stood neck to bended neck and wing to wing
With heads fast hidden under, close as cling
Flowers on one flowering almond-branch in spring,
Three herons deep asleep against the sun,
Each with one bright foot downward poised, and
    one
Wing-hidden hard by the bright head, and all
Still as fair shapes fixed on some wondrous wall
Of minster-aisle or cloister-close or hall
To take even time's eye prisoner with delight.
Or, satisfied with joy of sound and sight,
They sat and communed of things past : what state
King Arthur, yet unwarred upon by fate,
Held high in hall at Camelot, like one
Whose lordly life was as the mounting sun
That climbs and pauses on the point of noon,
Sovereign : how royal rang the tourney's tune

Through Tristram's three days' triumph, spear to
    spear,
When Iseult shone enthroned by Guenevere,
Rose against rose, the highest adored on earth,
Imperial : yet with subtle notes of mirth
Would she bemock her praises, and bemoan
Her glory by that splendour overthrown
Which lightened from her sister's eyes elate ;
Saying how by night a little light seems great,
But less than least of all things, very nought,
When dawn undoes the web that darkness wrought ;
How like a tower of ivory well designed
By subtlest hand subserving subtlest mind,
Ivory with flower of rose incarnadined
And kindling with some God therein revealed,
A light for grief to look on and be healed,
Stood Guenevere : and all beholding her
Were heartstruck even as earth at midsummer
With burning wonder, hardly to be borne.
So was that amorous glorious lady born,
A fiery memory for all storied years :
Nor might men call her sisters crowned her peers,
Her sister queens, put all by her to scorn :
She had such eyes as are not made to mourn ;
But in her own a gleaming ghost of tears
Shone, and their glance was slower than Guenevere's,
And fitfuller with fancies grown of grief ;
Shamed as a Mayflower shames an autumn leaf
Full well she wist it could not choose but be
If in that other's eyeshot standing she
Should lift her looks up ever : wherewithal
Like fires whose light fills heaven with festival
Flamed her eyes full on Tristram's ; and he laughed
Answering, " What wile of sweet child-hearted craft

That children forge for children, to beguile
Eyes known of them not witless of the wile
But fain to seem for sport's sake self-deceived,
Wilt thou find out now not to be believed ?
Or how shall I trust more than ouphe or elf
Thy truth to me-ward, who beliest thyself ? "
" Nor elf nor ouphe or aught of airier kind,"
Quoth she, " though made of moonbeams moist and
        blind,
Is light if weighed with man's winged weightless
        mind.
Though thou keep somewise troth with me, God
        wot,
When thou didst wed, I doubt, thou thoughtest not
So charily to keep it."   " Nay," said he,
" Yet am not I rebukable by thee
As Launcelot, erring, held me ere he wist
No mouth save thine of mine was ever kissed
Save as a sister's only, since we twain
Drank first the draught assigned our lips to drain
That Fate and Love with darkling hands commixt
Poured, and no power to part them came betwixt,
But either's will, howbeit they seem at strife,
Was toward us one, as death itself and life
Are one sole doom toward all men, nor may one
Behold not darkness, who beholds the sun."
    " Ah, then," she said, " what word is this men hear
Of Merlin, how some doom too strange to fear
Was cast but late about him oversea,
Sweet recreant, in thy bridal Brittany ?
Is not his life sealed fast on him with sleep,
By witchcraft of his own and love's, to keep
Till earth be fire and ashes ? "
                                " Surely," said

Her lover, " not as one alive or dead
The great good wizard, well beloved and well
Predestinate of heaven that casts out hell
For guerdon gentler far than all men's fate,
Exempt alone of all predestinate,
Takes his strange rest at heart of slumberland,
More deep asleep in green Broceliande
Than shipwrecked sleepers in the soft·green sea
Beneath the weight of wandering waves : but he
Hath for those roofing waters overhead
Above him always all the summer spread
Or all the winter wailing : or the sweet
Late leaves marked red with autumn's burning
      feet,
Or withered with his weeping, round the seer
Rain, and he sees not, nor may heed or hear
The witness of the winter : but in spring
He hears above him all the winds on wing
Through the blue dawn between the brightening
      boughs,
And on shut eyes and slumber-smitten brows
Feels ambient change in the air and strengthening
      sun,
And knows the soul that was his soul at one
With the ardent world's, and in the spirit of earth
His spirit of life reborn to mightier birth
And mixed with things of elder life than ours ;
With cries of birds, and kindling lamps of flowers,
And sweep and song of winds, and fruitful light
Of sunbeams, and the far faint breath of night,
And waves and woods at morning : and in all,
Soft as at noon the slow sea's rise and fall,
He hears in spirit a song that none but he
Hears from the mystic mouth of Nimue

Shed like a consecration ; and his heart,
Hearing, is made for love's sake as a part
Of that far singing, and the life thereof
Part of that life that feeds the world with love :
Yea, heart in heart is molten, hers and his,
Into the world's heart and the soul that is
Beyond or sense or vision ; and their breath
Stirs the soft springs of deathless life and death,
Death that bears life, and change that brings forth
    seed
Of life to death and death to life indeed,
As blood recircling through the unsounded veins
Of earth and heaven with all their joys and pains.
Ah, that when love shall laugh no more nor weep
We too, we too might hear that song and sleep !"
    " Yea," said Iseult, " some joy it were to be
Lost in the sun's light and the all-girdling sea,
Mixed with the winds and woodlands, and to bear
Part in the large life of the quickening air,
And the sweet earth's, our mother : yet to pass
More fleet than mirrored faces from the glass
Out of all pain and all delight, so far
That love should seem but as the furthest star
Sunk deep in trembling heaven, scarce seen or
    known,
As a dead moon forgotten, once that shone
Where now the sun shines—nay, not all things yet,
Not all things always, dying, would I forget."
    And Tristram answered amorously, and said :
" O heart that here art mine, O heavenliest head
That ever took men's worship here, which art
Mine, how shall death put out the fire at heart,
Quench in men's eyes the head's remembered light,
That time shall set but higher in more men's sight ?

Think thou not much to die one earthly day,
Being made not in their mould who pass away
Nor who shall pass for ever."

                                   " Ah," she said,
" What shall it profit me, being praised and dead ?
What profit have the flowers of all men's praise ?
What pleasure of our pleasure have the days
That pour on us delight of life and mirth ?
What fruit of all our joy on earth has earth ?
Nor am I—nay, my lover, am I one
To take such part in heaven's enkindling sun
And in the inviolate air and sacred sea
As clothes with grace that wondrous Nimue ?
For all her works are bounties, all her deeds
Blessings ; her days are scrolls wherein **love**
     reads
The record of his mercies ; heaven above
Hath not more heavenly holiness of love
Than earth beneath, wherever pass or pause
Her feet that move not save by love's own laws,
In gentleness of godlike wayfaring
To heal men's hearts as earth is healed by spring
Of all such woes as winter : what am I,
Love, that have strength but to desire and die,
That have but grace to love and do thee wrong,
What am I that my name should live so long,
Save as the star that crossed thy star-struck lot,
With hers whose light was life to Launcelot ?
Life gave she him, and strength, and fame to be
For ever : I, what gift can I give thee ?
Peril and sleepless watches, fearful breath
Of dread more bitter for my sake than death
When death came nigh to call me by my name,
Exile, rebuke, remorse, and—O, not shame.

Shame only, this I gave thee not, whom none
May give that worst thing ever—no, not one.
Of all that hate, all hateful hearts that see
Darkness for light and hate where love should be,
None for my shame's sake may speak shame of thee."
    And Tristram answering ere he kissed her smiled:
" O very woman, god at once and child,
What ails thee to desire of me once more
The assurance that thou hadst in heart before?
For all this wild sweet waste of sweet vain breath,
Thou knowest I know thou hast given me life, not
    death.
The shadow of death, informed with shows of
    strife,
Was ere I won thee all I had of life.
Light war, light love, light living, dreams in sleep,
Joy slight and light, not glad enough to weep,
Filled up my foolish days with sound and shine,
Vision and gleam from strange men's cast on mine,
Reverberate light from eyes presaging thine
That shed but shadowy moonlight where thy face
Now sheds forth sunshine in the deep same place,
The deep live heart half dead and shallower then
Than summer fords which thwart not wandering
    men.
For how should I, signed sorrow's from my birth,
Kiss dumb the loud red laughing lips of mirth?
Or how, sealed thine to be, love less than heaven on
    earth?
My heart in me was held at restless rest,
Presageful of some prize beyond its quest,
Prophetic still with promise, fain to find the best.
For one was fond and one was blithe and one
Fairer than all save twain whose peers are none;

For third on earth is none that heaven hath seen
To stand with Guenevere beside my queen.
Not Nimue, girt with blessing as a guard :
Not the soft lures and laughters of Ettarde :
Not she, that splendour girdled round with gloom,
Crowned as with iron darkness of the tomb,
And clothed with clouding conscience of a monstrous
         doom,
Whose blind incestuous love brought forth a fire
To burn her ere it burn its darkling sire,
Her mother's son, King Arthur : yet but late
We saw pass by that fair live shadow of fate,
The queen Morgause of Orkney, like a dream
That scares the night when moon and starry beam
Sicken and swoon before some sorcerer's eyes
Whose wordless charms defile the saintly skies,
Bright still with fire and pulse of blood and breath,
Whom her own sons have doomed for shame to
         death."
    "Death—yea," quoth she, " there is not said or
         heard
So oft aloud on earth so sure a word.
Death, and again death, and for each that saith
Ten tongues chime answer to the sound of death.
Good end God send us ever—so men pray.
But I—this end God send me, would I say,
To die not of division and a heart
Rent or with sword of severance cloven apart,
But only when thou diest and only where thou art,
O thou my soul and spirit and breath to me,
O light, life, love ! yea, let this only be,
That dying I may praise God who gave me thee,
Let hap what will thereafter."
                              So that day

They communed, even till eyen was worn away,
Nor aught they said seemed strange or sad to say,
But sweet as night's dim dawn to weariness.
Nor loved they life or love for death's sake less,
Nor feared they death for love's or life's sake more
And on the sounding soft funereal shore
They, watching till the day should wholly die,
Saw the far sea sweep to the far grey sky,
Saw the long sands sweep to the long grey sea.
And night made one sweet mist of moor and lea,
And only far off shore the foam gave light.
And life in them sank silent as the night.

VII

THE WIFE'S VIGIL

But all that year in Brittany forlorn.
More sick at heart with wrath than fear of scorn
And less in love with love than grief, and less
With grief than pride of spirit and bitterness,
Till all the sweet life of her blood was changed
And all her soul from all her past estranged
And all her will with all itself at strife
And all her mind at war with all her life,
Dwelt the white-handed Iseult, maid and wife,
A mourner that for mourning robes had on
Anger and doubt and hate of things foregone.
For that sweet spirit of old which made her sweet
Was parched with blasts of thought as flowers with
    heat
And withered as with wind of evil will ;
Though slower than frosts or fires consume or kill
That bleak black wind vexed all her spirit still.
As ripples reddening in the roughening breath
Of the eager east when dawn does night to death,
So rose and stirred and kindled in her thought
Fierce barren fluctuant fires that lit not aught,
But scorched her soul with yearning keen as hate
And dreams that left her wrath disconsolate.

When change came first on that first heaven where all
Life's hours were flowers that dawn's light hand let
    fall,
The sun that smote her dewy cloud of days
Wrought from its showery folds his rainbow's rays,
For love the red, for hope the gentle green,
But yellow jealousy glared pale between.
Ere yet the sky grew heavier, and her head
Bent flowerwise, chill with change and fancies fled,
She saw but love arch all her heaven across with red,
A burning bloom that seemed to breathe and beat
And waver only as flame with rapturous heat
Wavers; and all the world therewith smelt sweet,
As incense kindling from the rose-red flame:
And when that full flush waned, and love became
Scarce fainter, though his fading horoscope
From certitude of sight receded, hope
Held yet her April-coloured light aloft
As though to lure back love, a lamp sublime and soft.
But soon that light paled as a leaf grows pale
And fluttered leaf-like in the gathering gale
And melted even as dew-flakes, whose brief sheen
The sun that gave despoils of glittering green;
Till harder shone 'twixt hope and love grown cold
A sallow light like withering autumn's gold,
The pale strong flame of jealous thought, that glows
More deep than hope's green bloom or love's
    enkindled rose:
As though the sunflower's faint fierce disk absorbed
The spirit and heart of starrier flowers disorbed.

    That same full hour of twilight's doors unbarred
To let bright night behold in Joyous Gard
The glad grave eyes of lovers far away
Watch with sweet thoughts of death the death of day

II.   D 2

Saw lonelier by the narrower opening sea
Sit fixed at watch Iseult of Brittany.
As darkness from deep valleys void and bleak
Climbs till it clothe with night the sunniest peak
Where only of all a mystic mountain-land
Day seems to cling yet with a trembling hand
And yielding heart reluctant to recede,
So, till her soul was clothed with night indeed,
Rose the slow cloud of envious will within
And hardening hate that held itself no sin,
Veiled heads of vision, eyes of evil gleam,
Dim thought on thought, and darkling dream on
    dream.
Far off she saw in spirit, and seeing abhorred,
The likeness wrought on darkness of her lord
Shine, and the imperial semblance at his side
Whose shadow from her seat cast down the bride,
Whose power and ghostly presence thrust her forth:
Beside that unknown other sea far north
She saw them, clearer than in present sight
Rose on her eyes the starry shadow of night;
And on her heart that heaved with gathering fate
Rose red with storm the starless shadow of hate;
And eyes and heart made one saw surge and swell
The fires of sunset like the fires of hell.
As though God's wrath would burn up sin with shame,
The incensed red gold of deepening heaven grew
    flame:
The sweet green spaces of the soft low sky
Faded, as fields that withering wind leaves dry:
The sea's was like a doomsman's blasting breath
From lips afoam with ravenous lust of death.
A night like desolation, sombre-starred,
Above the great walled girth of Joyous Gard

Spread forth its wide sad strength of shadow and
    gloom
Wherein those twain were compassed round with
    doom :
Hell from beneath called on them, and she heard
Reverberate judgment in the wild wind's word
Cry, till the sole sound of their names that rang
Clove all the sea-mist with a clarion's clang,
And clouds to clouds and flames to clustering flame
Beat back the dark noise of the direful names.
Fear and strong exultation caught her breath,
And triumph like the bitterness of death,
And rapture like the rage of hate allayed
With ruin and ravin that its might hath made ;
And her heart swelled and strained itself to hear
What may be heard of no man's hungering ear,
And as a soil that cleaves in twain for drouth
Thirsted for judgment given of God's own mouth
Against them, till the strength of dark desire
Was in her as a flame of hell's own fire.
Nor seemed the wrath which held her spirit in stress
Aught else or worse than passionate holiness,
Nor the ardent hate which called on judgment's rod
More hateful than the righteousness of God.

    " How long, till thou do justice, and my wrong
Stand expiate ?　O long-suffering judge, how long ?
Shalt thou not put him in mine hand one day
Whom I so loved, to spare not but to slay ?
Shalt thou not cast her down for me to tread,
Me, on the pale pride of her humbled head ?
Do I not well, being angry ? doth not hell
Require them ? yea, thou knowest that I do well.
Is not thy seal there set of bloodred light
For witness on the brows of day and night ?

Who shall unseal it? what shall melt away
Thy signet from the doors of night and day?
No man, nor strength of any spirit above,
Nor prayer, nor ardours of adulterous love.
Thou art God, the strong lord over body and soul :
Hast thou not in the terrors of thy scroll
All names of all men written as with fire?
Thine only breath bids time and space respire :
And are not all things evil in them done
More clear in thine eyes than in ours the sun?
Hast thou not sight stretched wide enough to see
These that offend it, these at once and me?
Is thine arm shortened or thine hand struck down
As palsied? have thy brows not strength to frown?
Are thine eyes blind with film of withering age?
Burns not thine heart with righteousness of rage
Yet, and the royal rancour toward thy foes
Retributive of ruin?   Time should close,
Thou said'st, and earth fade as a leaf grows grey,
Ere one word said of thine should pass away.
Was this then not thy word, thou God most high,
That sin shall surely bring forth death and die,
Seeing how these twain live and have joy of life,
His harlot and the man that made me wife?
For is it I, perchance, I that have sinned?
Me, peradventure, should thy wasting wind
Smite, and thy sun blast, and thy storms devour
Me with keen fangs of lightning? should thy power
Put forth on me the weight of its awakening hour?
Shall I that bear this burden bear that weight
Of judgment? is my sin against thee great,
If all my heart against them burn with all its hate?
Thine, and not mine, should hate be? nay, but me
They have spoiled and scoffed at, who can touch not
    thee.

Me, me, the fullness of their joy drains dry,
Their fruitfulness makes barren : thou, not I,
Lord, is it, whom their wrongdoing clothes with shame,
That all who speak shoot tongues out at thy name
As all who hear mock mine ?   Make me thy sword
At least, if even thou too be wronged, O Lord,
At all of these that wrong me : make mine hand
As lightning, or my tongue a fiery brand,
To burn or smite them with thy wrath : behold,
I have nought on earth save thee for hope or hold,
Fail me not thou : I have nought but this to crave,
Make me thy mean to give them to the grave,
Thy sign that all men seeing may speak thee just,
Thy word which turns the strengths of sin to dust,
Thy blast which burns up towers and thrones with
      fire.
Lord, is this gift, this grace that I require,
So great a gift, Lord, for thy grace to give.
And bid me bear thy part retributive ?
That I whom scorn makes mouths at, I might be
Thy witness if loud sin may mock at thee ?
For lo, my life is as a barren ear
Plucked from the sheaf : dark days drive past me here
Downtrodden, while joy's reapers pile their sheaves,
A thing more vile than autumn's weariest leaves,
For these the sun filled once with sap of life.
O thou my lord that hadst me to thy wife,
Dost thou not fear at all, remembering me,
The love that bowed my whole soul down to thee ?
Is this so wholly nought for man to dread,
Man, whose life walks between the quick and dead,
Naked, and warred about with wind and sea,
That one should love and hate as I do thee ?
That one should live in all the world his foe
So mortal as the hate that loves him so ?

Nought, is it nought, O husband, O my knight,
O strong man and indomitable in fight,
That one more weak than foam-bells on the sea
Should have in heart such thoughts as I of thee?
Thou art bound about with stately strengths for
     bands:
What strength shall keep thee from my strengthless
     hands?
Thou art girt about with goodly guards and great:
What fosse may fence thee round as deep as hate?
Thou art wise: will wisdom teach thee fear of me?
Thou art great of heart: shall this deliver thee?
What wall so massive, or what tower so high,
Shall be thy surety that thou shouldst not die,
If that which comes against thee be but I?
Who shall rise up of power to take thy part,
What skill find strength to save, what strength find
     art,
If that which wars against thee be my heart?
Not iron, nor the might of force afield,
Nor edge of sword, nor sheltering weight of shield,
Nor all thy fame since all thy praise began,
Nor all the love and laud thou hast of man,
Nor, though his noiseless hours with wool be shod,
Shall God's love keep thee from the wrath of God.
O son of sorrows, hast thou said at heart,
Haply, God loves thee, God shall take thy part,
Who hath all these years endured thee, since thy
     birth
From sorrow's womb bade sin be born on earth?
So long he hath cast his buckler over thee,
Shall he not surely guard thee even from me?
Yea, but if yet he give thee while I live
Into mine hands as he shall surely give,

Ere death at last bring darkness on thy face,
Call then on him, call not on me for grace,
Cast not away one prayer, one suppliant breath,
On me that commune all this while with death.
For I that was not and that was thy wife
Desire not but one hour of all thy life
Wherein to triumph till that hour be past ;
But this mine hour I look for is thy last."
   So mused she till the fire in sea and sky
Sank, and the northwest wind spake harsh on high,
And like the sea's heart waxed her heart that heard,
Strong, dark, and bitter, till the keen wind's word
Seemed of her own soul spoken, and the breath
All round her not of darkness, but of death.

·

VIII

THE LAST PILGRIMAGE

ENOUGH of ease, O Love, enough of light,
Enough of rest before the shadow of night.
Strong Love, whom death finds feebler ; kingly Love,
Whom time discrowns in season, seeing thy dove
Spell-stricken by the serpent ; for thy sake
These that saw light see night's dawn only break,
Night's cup filled up with slumber, whence men think
The draught more dread than thine was dire to drink.
O Love, thy day sets darkling : hope and fear
Fall from thee standing stern as death stands here.
   For what have these to do with fear or hope
On whom the gates of outer darkness ope,
On whom the door of life's desire is barred ?
Past like a cloud, their days in Joyous Gard
Gleam like a cloud the westering sun stains red
Till all the blood of day's blithe heart be bled
And all night's heart requickened ; in their eyes
So flame and fade those far memorial skies,
So shines the moorland, so revives the sea,
Whereon they gazing mused of things to be
And wist not more of them than waters know
What wind with next day's change of tide shall
      blow.

Dark roll the deepening days whose waves divide
Unseasonably, with storm-struck change of tide,
Tristram from Iseult : nor may sorrow say
If better wind shall blow than yesterday
With next day risen or any day to come.
For ere the songs of summer's death fell dumb,
And autumn bade the imperial moorlands change
Their purples, and the bracken's bloom grow strange
As hope's green blossom touched with time's harsh
    rust,
Was all their joy of life shaken to dust,
And all its fire made ashes : by the strand
Where late they strayed and communed hand from
    hand
For the last time fell separate, eyes of eyes
Took for the last time leave, and saw the skies
Dark with their deep division.   The last time—
The last that ever love's rekindling rhyme
Should keep for them life's days and nights in tune
With refluence of the morning and the moon
Alternative in music, and make one
The secrets of the stardawn and the sun
For these twain souls ere darkness held them fast ;
The last before the labour marked for last
And toil of utmost knighthood, till the wage
Of rest might crown his crowning pilgrimage
Whereon forth faring must he take farewell,
With spear for staff and sword for scallop-shell
And scrip wherein close memory hoarded yet
Things holier held than death might well forget ;
The last time ere the travel were begun
Whose goal is unbeholden of the sun,
The last wherewith love's eyes might yet be lit,
Came, and they could but dream they knew not it.

For Tristram parting from her wist at heart
How well she wist they might not choose but part,
And he pass forth a pilgrim, when there came
A sound of summons in the high king's name
For succour toward his vassal Triamour,
King in wild Wales, now spoiled of all his power,
As Tristram's father ere his fair son's birth,
By one the strongest of the sons of earth,
Urgan, an iron bulk of giant mould :
And Iseult in Tintagel as of old
Sat crowned with state and sorrow : for her lord
At Arthur's hand required her back restored,
And willingly compelled against her will
She yielded, saying within her own soul still
Some season yet of soft or stormier breath
Should haply give her life again or death :
For now nor quick nor dead nor bright nor dark
Were all her nights and days wherein King Mark
Held haggard watch upon her, and his eyes
Were cloudier than the gradual wintering skies
That closed about the wan wild land and sea.
And bitter toward him waxed her heart : but he
Was rent in twain betwixt harsh love and hate
With pain and passion half compassionate
That yearned and laboured to be quit of shame,
And could not : and his life grew smouldering flame.
And hers a cloud full-charged with storm and
        shower,
Though touched with trembling gleams of fire's bright
        flower
That flashed and faded on its fitful verge,
As hope would strive with darkness and emerge
And sink, a swimmer strangled by the swallowing
        surge.

But Tristram by dense hills and deepening vales
Rode through the wild glad wastes of glorious
    Wales,
High-hearted with desire of happy fight
And strong in soul with merrier sense of might
Than since the fair first years that hailed him
    knight :
For all his will was toward the war, so long
Had love repressed and wrought his glory wrong,
So far the triumph and so fair the praise
Seemed now that kindled all his April days.
And here in bright blown autumn, while his life
Was summer's yet for strength toward love or strife,
Blithe waxed his hope toward battle, and high desire
To pluck once more as out of circling fire
Fame, the broad flower whose breath makes death
    more sweet
Than roses crushed by love's receding feet.
But all the lovely land wherein he went
The blast of ruin and ravenous war had rent ;
And black with fire the fields where homesteads were,
And foul with festering dead the high soft air,
And loud with wail of women many a stream
Whose own live song was like love's deepening
    dream,
Spake all against the spoiler : wherefore still
Wrath waxed with pity, quickening all his will,
In Tristram's heart for every league he rode
Through the aching land so broad a curse bestrode
With so supreme a shadow : till one dawn
Above the green bloom of a gleaming lawn,
High on the strait steep windy bridge that spanned
A glen's deep mouth, he saw that shadow stand
Visible, sword on thigh and mace in hand

Vast as the mid bulk of a roof-tree's beam.
So, sheer above the wild wolf-haunted stream,
Dire as the face disfeatured of a dream,
Rose Urgan : and his eyes were night and flame ;
But like the fiery dawn were his that came
Against him, lit with more sublime desire
Than lifts toward heaven the leaping heart of fire :
And strong in vantage of his perilous place
The huge high presence, red as earth's first race,
Reared like a reed the might up of his mace,
And smote : but lightly Tristram swerved, and
    drove
Right in on him, whose void stroke only clove
Air, and fell wide, thundering athwart : and he
Sent forth a stormier cry than wind or sea
When midnight takes the tempest for her lord :
And all the glen's throat seemed as hell's that
    roared ;
But high like heaven's light over hell shone
    Tristram's sword,
Falling, and bright as storm shows God's bare
    brand
Flashed as it shore sheer off the huge right hand
Whose strength was as the shadow of death on all
    that land.
And like the trunk of some grim tree sawn through
Reeled Urgan, as his left hand grasped and drew
A steel by sorcerers tempered : and anew
Raged the red wind of fluctuant fight, till all
The cliffs were thrilled as by the clangorous call
Of storm's blown trumpets from the core of night,
Charging : and even as with the storm-wind's might
On Tristram's helm that sword crashed : and the
    knight

Fell, and his arms clashed, and a wide cry brake
From those far off that heard it, for his sake
Soul-stricken : and that bulk of monstrous birth
Sent forth again a cry more dire for mirth :
But ere the sunbright arms were soiled of earth
They flashed again, re-risen : and swift and loud
Rang the strokes out as from a circling cloud,
So dense the dust wrought over them its drifted
    shroud.
Strong strokes, within the mist their battle made,
Each hailed on other through the shifting shade
That clung about them hurtling as the swift fight
    swayed :
And each between the jointed corslet saw
Break forth his foe's bright blood at each grim flaw
Steel made in hammered iron : till again
The fiend put forth his might more strong for pain
And cleft the great knight's glittering shield in
    twain,
Laughing for very wrath and thirst to kill,
A beast's broad laugh of blind and wolfish will,
And smote again ere Tristram's lips drew breath
Panting, and swept as by the sense of death,
That surely should have touched and sealed them
    fast
Save that the sheer stroke shrilled aside, and passed
Frustrate : but answering Tristram smote anew,
And thrust the brute breast as with lightning through
Clean with one cleaving stroke of perfect might :
And violently the vast bulk leapt upright,
And plunged over the bridge, and fell : and all
The cliffs reverberate from his monstrous fall
Rang : and the land by Tristram's grace was free.
So with high laud and honour thence went he,

And southward set his sail again, and passed
The lone land's ending, first beheld and last
Of eyes that look on England from the sea:
And his heart mourned within him, knowing how
    she
Whose heart with his was fatefully made fast
Sat now fast bound, as though some charm were
    cast
About her, such a brief space eastward thence,
And yet might soul not break the bonds of sense
And bring her to him in very life and breath
More than had this been even the sea of death
That washed between them, and its wide sweet
    light
The dim strait's darkness of the narrowing night
That shuts about men dying whose souls put forth
To pierce its passage through: but south and north
Alike for him were other than they were:
For all the northward coast shone smooth and fair,
And off its iron cliffs the keen-edged air
Blew summer, kindling from her mute bright mouth;
But winter breathed out of the murmuring south,
Where, pale with wrathful watch on passing ships,
The lone wife lay in wait with wan dumb lips.
Yet, sailing where the shoreward ripple curled
Of the most wild sweet waves in all the world,
His soul took comfort even for joy to see
The strong deep joy of living sun and sea,
The large deep love of living sea and land,
As past the lonely lion-guarded strand
Where that huge warder lifts his couchant sides,
Asleep, above the sleepless lapse of tides,
The light sail swept, and past the unsounded caves
Unsearchable, wherein the pulse of waves

Throbs through perpetual darkness to and fro,
And the blind night swims heavily below
While heavily the strong noon broods above,
Even to the very bay whence very Love,
Strong daughter of the giant gods who wrought
Sun, earth, and sea out of their procreant thought,
Most meetly might have risen, and most divine
Beheld and heard things round her sound and shine
From floors of foam and gold to walls of serpentine.
For splendid as the limbs of that supreme
Incarnate beauty through men's visions gleam,
Whereof all fairest things are even but shadow or
    dream,
And lovely like as Love's own heavenliest face,
Gleams there and glows the presence and the grace
Even of the mother of all, in perfect pride of place.
For otherwhere beneath our world-wide sky
There may not be beheld of men that die
Aught else like this that dies not, nor may stress
Of ages that bow down men's works make less
The exultant awe that clothes with power its loveli-
    ness.
For who sets eye thereon soever knows
How since these rocks and waves first rolled and rose
The marvel of their many-coloured might
Hath borne this record sensible to sight,
The witness and the symbol of their own delight,
The gospel graven of life's most heavenly law,
Joy, brooding on its own still soul with awe,
A sense of godlike rest in godlike strife,
The sovereign conscience of the spirit of life.
Nor otherwhere on strand or mountain tower
Hath such fair beauty shining forth in flower
Put on the imperial robe of such imperious power.

For all the radiant rocks from depth to height
Burn with vast bloom of glories blossom-bright
As though the sun's own hand had thrilled them
     through with light
And stained them through with splendour : yet from
     thence
Such awe strikes rapture through the spirit of
     sense
From all the inaccessible sea-wall's girth,
That exultation, bright at heart as mirth,
Bows deeper down before the beauty of earth
Than fear may bow down ever : nor shall one
Who meets at Alpine dawn the mounting sun
On heights too high for many a wing to climb
Be touched with sense of aught seen more sublime
Than here smiles high and sweet in face of heaven
     and time.
For here the flower of fire, the soft hoar bloom
Of springtide olive-woods, the warm green gloom
Of clouded seas that swell and sound with dawn of
     doom,
The keen thwart lightning and the wan grey light
Of stormy sunrise crossed and vexed with night,
Flash, loom, and laugh with divers hues in one
From all the curved cliff's face, till day be done,
Against the sea's face and the gazing sun.
And whensoever a strong wave, high in hope,
Sweeps up some smooth slant breadth of stone
     aslope,
That glowed with duskier fire of hues less bright,
Swift as it sweeps back springs to sudden sight
The splendour of the moist rock's fervent light,
Fresh as from dew of birth when time was born
Out of the world-conceiving womb of morn.

All its quenched flames and darkling hues divine
Leap into lustrous life and laugh and shine
And darken into swift and dim decline
For one brief breath's space till the next wave run
Right up, and ripple down again, undone,
And leave it to be kissed and kindled of the sun.
And all these things, bright as they shone before
Man first set foot on earth or sail from shore,
Rose not less radiant than the sun sees now
When the autumn sea was cloven of Tristram's prow,
And strong in sorrow and hope and woful will
That hope might move not nor might sorrow kill
He held his way back toward the wild sad shore
Whence he should come to look on these no more,
Nor ever, save with sunless eyes shut fast,
Sail home to sleep in home-born earth at last.
　　And all these things fled fleet as light or breath
Past, and his heart waxed cold and dull as death,
Or swelled but as the tides of sorrow swell,
To sink with sullen sense of slow farewell.
So surely seemed the silence even to sigh
Assurance of inveterate prophecy,
" Thou shalt not come again home hither ere thou
　　die."
And the wind mourned and triumphed, and the sea
Wailed and took heart and trembled ; nor might he
Hear more of comfort in their speech, or see
More certitude in all the waste world's range
Than the only certitude of death and change.
And as the sense and semblance fluctuated
Of all things heard and seen alive or dead
That smote far off upon his ears or eyes
Or memory mixed with forecasts fain to rise
And fancies faint as ghostliest prophecies,

So seemed his own soul, changefully forlorn,
To shrink and triumph and mount up and mourn;
Yet all its fitful waters, clothed with night,
Lost heart not wholly, lacked not wholly light,
Seeing over life and death one star in sight
Where evening's gates as fair as morning's ope,
Whose name was memory, but whose flame was hope.
For all the tides of thought that rose and sank
Felt its fair strength wherefrom strong sorrow shrank
A mightier trust than time could change or cloy,
More strong than sorrow, more secure than joy.
So came he, nor content nor all unblest,
Back to the grey old land of Merlin's rest.

   But ere six paces forth on shore he trod
Before him stood a knight with feet unshod,
And kneeling called upon him, as on God
Might sick men call for pity, praying aloud
With hands held up and head made bare and bowed;
"Tristram, for God's love and thine own dear fame,
I Tristram that am one with thee in name
And one in heart with all that praise thee—I,
Most woful man of all that may not die
For heartbreak and the heavier scourge of shame,
By all thy glory done our woful name
Beseech thee, called of all men gentlest knight,
Be now not slow to do my sorrows right.
I charge thee for thy fame's sake through this land,
I pray thee by thine own wife's fair white hand,
Have pity of me whose love is borne away
By one that makes of poor men's lives his prey,
A felon masked with knighthood: at his side
Seven brethren hath he night or day to ride
With seven knights more that wait on all his will:
And here at hand, ere yet one day fulfil

Its flight through light and darkness, shall they fare
Forth, and my bride among them, whom they bear
Through these wild lands his prisoner ; and if now
I lose her, and my prayer be vain, and thou
Less fain to serve love's servants than of yore,
Then surely shall I see her face no more.
But if thou wilt, for love's sake of the bride
Who lay most loved of women at thy side,
Strike with me, straight then hence behoves us ride
And rest between the moorside and the sea
Where we may smite them passing : but for me,
Poor stranger, me not worthy scarce to touch
Thy kind strong hand, how shouldst thou do so much ?
For now lone left this long time waits thy wife
And lacks her lord and light of wedded life
Whilst thou far off art famous : yet thy fame,
If thou take pity on me that bear thy name
Unworthily, but by that name implore
Thy grace, how shall not even thy fame grow more ?
But be thy will as God's among us done,
Who art far in fame above us as the sun :
Yet only of him have all men help and grace."
    And all the lordly light of Tristram's face
Was softened as the sun's in kindly spring.
"Nay, then may God send me as evil a thing
When I give ear not to such prayers," he said,
" And make my place among the nameless dead
When I put back one hour the time to smite
And do the unrighteous griefs of good men right.
Behold, I will not enter in nor rest
Here in mine own halls till this piteous quest
Find end ere noon to-morrow : but do thou,
Whose sister's face I may not look on now,
Go, Ganhardine, with tiding of the vow

That bids me turn aside for one day's strife
Or live dishonoured all my days of life,
And greet for me in brother's wise my wife,
And crave her pardon that for knighthood's sake
And womanhood's, whose bands may no man break
And keep the bands of bounden honour fast,
I seek not her till two nights yet be past
And this my quest accomplished, so God please
By me to give this young man's anguish ease
And on his wrongdoer's head his wrong requite."
    And Tristram with that woful thankful knight
Rode by the seaside moorland wastes away
Between the quickening night and darkening day
Ere half the gathering stars had heart to shine.
And lightly toward his sister Ganhardine
Sped, where she sat and gazed alone afar
Above the grey sea for the sunset star,
And lightly kissed her hand and lightly spake
His tiding of that quest for knighthood's sake.
And the white-handed Iseult, bowing her head,
Gleamed on him with a glance athwart, and said,
"As God's on earth and far above the sun,
So toward his handmaid be my lord's will done."
And doubts too dim to question or divine
Touched as with shade the spirit of Ganhardine,
Hearing ; and scarce for half a doubtful breath
His bright light heart held half a thought of death
And knew not whence this darkling thought might be,
But surely not his sister's work : for she
Was ever sweet and good as summer air,
And soft as dew when all the night is fair,
And gracious as the golden maiden moon
When darkness craves her blessing : so full soon

His mind was light again as leaping waves,
Nor dreamed that hers was like a field of graves
Where no man's foot dares swerve to left or right,
Nor ear dares hearken, nor dares eye take sight
Of aught that moves and murmurs there at night.
    But by the sea-banks where at morn their foes
Might find them, lay those knightly name-fellows,
One sick with grief of heart and sleepless, one
With heart of hope triumphant as the sun
Dreaming asleep of love and fame and fight:
But sleep at last wrapped warm the wan young
    knight ;
And Tristram with the first pale windy light
Woke ere the sun spake summons, and his ear
Caught the sea's call that fired his heart to hear,
A noise of waking waters : for till dawn
The sea was silent as a mountain lawn
When the wind speaks not, and the pines are dumb,
And summer takes her fill ere autumn come
Of life more soft than slumber : but ere day
Rose, and the first beam smote the bounding bay,
Up sprang the strength of the dark East, and took
With its wide wings the waters as they shook,
And hurled them huddling on aheap, and cast
The full sea shoreward with a great glad blast,
Blown from the heart of morning : and with joy
Full-souled and perfect passion, as a boy
That leaps up light to wrestle with the sea
For pure heart's gladness and large ecstasy,
Up sprang the might of Tristram ; and his soul
Yearned for delight within him, and waxed whole
As a young child's with rapture of the hour
That brought his spirit and all the world to flower,

And all the bright blood in his veins beat time
To the wind's clarion and the water's chime
That called him and he followed it and stood
On the sand's verge before the grey great flood
Where the white hurtling heads of waves that met
Rose unsaluted of the sunrise yet.
And from his heart's root outward shot the sweet
Strong joy that thrilled him to the hands and feet,
Filling his limbs with pleasure and glad might,
And his soul drank the immeasurable delight
That earth drinks in with morning, and the free
Limitless love that lifts the stirring sea
When on her bare bright bosom as a bride
She takes the young sun, perfect in his pride,
Home to his place with passion : and the heart
Trembled for joy within the man whose part
Was here not least in living ; and his mind
Was rapt abroad beyond man's meaner kind
And pierced with love of all things and with mirth
Moved to make one with heaven and heavenlike earth
And with the light live water.   So awhile
He watched the dim sea with a deepening smile,
And felt the sound and savour and swift flight
Of waves that fled beneath the fading night
And died before the darkness, like a song
With harps between and trumpets blown along
Through the loud air of some triumphant day,
Sink through his spirit and purge all sense away
Save of the glorious gladness of his hour
And all the world about to break in flower
Before the sovereign laughter of the sun ;
And he, ere night's wide work lay all undone,
As earth from her bright body casts off night,
Cast off his raiment for a rapturous fight

And stood between the sea's edge and the sea
Naked, and godlike of his mould as he
Whose swift foot's sound shook all the towers of
    Troy ;
So clothed with might, so girt upon with joy
As, ere the knife had shorn to feed the fire
His glorious hair before the unkindled pyre
Whereon the half of his great heart was laid,
Stood, in the light of his live limbs arrayed,
Child of heroic earth and heavenly sea,
The flower of all men : scarce less bright than he,
If any of all men latter-born might stand,
Stood Tristram, silent, on the glimmering strand.
Not long : but with a cry of love that rang
As from a trumpet golden-mouthed, he sprang,
As toward a mother's where his head might rest
Her child rejoicing, toward the strong sea's breast
That none may gird nor measure : and his heart
Sent forth a shout that bade his lips not part,
But triumphed in him silent : no man's voice,
No song, no sound of clarions that rejoice,
Can set that glory forth which fills with fire
The body and soul that have their whole desire
Silent, and freer than birds or dreams are free
Take all their will of all the encountering sea.
And toward the foam he bent and forward smote,
Laughing, and launched his body like a boat
Full to the sea-breach, and against the tide
Struck strongly forth with amorous arms made
    wide
To take the bright breast of the wave to his
And on his lips the sharp sweet minute's kiss
Given of the wave's lip for a breath's space curled
And pure as at the daydawn of the world.

And round him all the bright rough shuddering sea
Kindled, as though the world were even as he,
Heart-stung with exultation of desire :
And all the life that moved him seemed to aspire,
As all the sea's life toward the sun : and still
Delight within him waxed with quickening will
More smooth and strong and perfect as a flame
That springs and spreads, till each glad limb became
A note of rapture in the tune of life,
Live music mild and keen as sleep and strife :
Till the sweet change that bids the sense grow sure
Of deeper depth and purity more pure
Wrapped him and lapped him round with clearer cold,
And all the rippling green grew royal gold
Between him and the far sun's rising rim.
And like the sun his heart rejoiced in him,
And brightened with a broadening flame of mirth :
And hardly seemed its life a part of earth,
But the life kindled of a fiery birth
And passion of a new-begotten son
Between the live sea and the living sun.
And mightier grew the joy to meet full-faced
Each wave, and mount with upward plunge, and taste
The rapture of its rolling strength, and cross
Its flickering crown of snows that flash and toss
Like plumes in battle's blithest charge, and thence
To match the next with yet more strenuous sense ;
Till on his eyes the light beat hard and bade
His face turn west and shoreward through the glad
Swift revel of the waters golden-clad,
And back with light reluctant heart he bore
Across the broad-backed rollers in to shore ;
Strong-spirited for the chance and cheer of fight,
And donned his arms again, and felt the might

In all his limbs rejoice for strength, and praised
God for such life as that whereon he gazed,
And wist not surely its joy was even as fleet
As that which laughed and lapsed against his feet,
The bright thin grey foam-blossom, glad and hoar,
That flings its flower along the flowerless shore
On sand or shingle, and still with sweet strange snows,
As where one great white storm-dishevelled rose
May rain her wild leaves on a windy land,
Strews for long leagues the sounding slope of strand,
And flower on flower falls flashing, and anew
A fresh light leaps up whence the last flash flew,
And casts its brief glad gleam of life away
To fade not flowerwise but as drops the day
Storm-smitten, when at once the dark devours
Heaven and the sea and earth with all their flowers ;
No star in heaven, on earth no rose to see,
But the white blown brief blossoms of the sea,
That make her green gloom starrier than the sky,
Dance yet before the tempest's tune, and die.
And all these things he glanced upon, and knew
How fair they shone, from earth's least flake of dew
To stretch of seas and imminence of skies,
Unwittingly, with unpresageful eyes,
For the last time.   The world's half heavenly face,
The music of the silence of the place,
The confluence and the refluence of the sea,
The wind's note ringing over wold and lea,
Smote once more through him keen as fire that smote,
Rang once more through him one reverberate note,
That faded as he turned again and went,
Fulfilled by strenuous joy with strong content,
To take his last delight of labour done
That yet should be beholden of the sun

Or ever give man comfort of his hand.
  Beside a wood's edge in the broken land
An hour at wait the twain together stood,
Till swift between the moorside and the wood
Flashed the spears forward of the coming train ;
And seeing beside the strong chief spoiler's rein
His wan love riding prisoner in the crew,
Forth with a cry the young man leapt, and flew
Right on that felon sudden as a flame ;
And hard at hand the mightier Tristram came,
Bright as the sun and terrible as fire :
And there had sword and spear their soul's desire,
And blood that quenched the spear's thirst as it poured
Slaked royally the hunger of the sword,
Till the fierce heart of steel could scarce fulfil
Its greed and ravin of insatiate will.
For three the fiery spear of Tristram drove
Down ere a point of theirs his harness clove
Or its own sheer mid shaft splintered in twain :
And his heart bounded in him, and was fain
As fire or wind that takes its fill by night
Of tempest and of triumph : so the knight
Rejoiced and ranged among them, great of hand,
Till seven lay slain upon the heathery sand
Or in the dense breadth of the woodside fern.
Nor did his heart not mightier in him burn
Seeing at his hand that young knight fallen, and high
The red sword reared again that bade him die.
But on the slayer exulting like the flame
Whose foot foreshines the thunder Tristram came
Raging, for piteous wrath had made him fire ;
And as a lion's look his face was dire
That flashed against his foeman ere the sword
Lightened and wrought the heart's will of its lord,

And clove through casque and crown the wrongdoer's
    head.
And right and left about their dark chief dead
Hurtled and hurled those felons to and fro,
Till as a storm-wind scatters leaves and snow
His right hand ravening scattered them ; but one
That fled with sidelong glance athwart the sun
Shot, and the shaft flew sure, and smote aright,
Full in the wound's print of his great first fight
When at his young strength's peril he made free
Cornwall, and slew beside its bordering sea
The fair land's foe, who yielding up his breath
Yet left him wounded nigh to dark slow death.
And hardly with long toil thence he won home
Between the grey moor and the glimmering foam,
And halting fared through his own gate, and fell,
Thirsting : for as the sleepless fire of hell
The fire within him of his wound again
Burned, and his face was dark as death for pain,
And blind the blithe light of his eyes : but they
Within that watched and wist not of the fray
Came forth and cried aloud on him for woe.
And scarce aloud his thanks fell faint and slow
As men reared up the strong man fallen and bore
Down the deep hall that looked along the shore,
And laid him soft abed, and sought in vain
If herb or hand of leech might heal his pain.
And the white-handed Iseult hearkening heard
All, and drew nigh, and spake no wifely word,
But gazed upon him doubtfully, with eyes
Clouded ; and he in kindly knightly wise
Spake with scant breath, and smiling : " Surely this
Is penance for discourteous lips to kiss

And feel the brand burn through them, here to lie
And lack the strength here to do more than sigh
And hope not hence for pardon." Then she bowed
Her head, still silent as a stooping cloud,
And laid her lips against his face; and he
Felt sink a shadow across him as the sea
Might feel a cloud stoop toward it: and his heart
Darkened as one that wastes by sorcerous art
And knows not whence it withers: and he turned
Back from her emerald eyes his own, and yearned
All night for eyes all golden: and the dark
Hung sleepless round him till the loud first lark
Rang record forth once more of darkness done,
And all things born took comfort from the sun.

IX

THE SAILING OF THE SWAN

FATE, that was born ere spirit and flesh were made,
The fire that fills man's life with light and shade ;
The power beyond all godhead which puts on
All forms of multitudinous unison,
A raiment of eternal change inwrought
With shapes and hues more subtly spun than thought,
Where all things old bear fruit of all things new
And one deep chord throbs all the music through,
The chord of change unchanging, shadow and light
Inseparable as reverberate day from night ;
Fate, that of all things save the soul of man
Is lord and God since body and soul began ;
Fate, that keeps all the tune of things in chime ;
Fate, that breathes power upon the lips of time ;
That smites and soothes with heavy and healing hand
All joys and sorrows born in life's dim land,
Till joy be found a shadow and sorrow a breath
And life no discord in the tune with death,
But all things fain alike to die and live
In pulse and lapse of tides alternative,
Through silence and through sound of peace and strife,
Till birth and death be one in sight of life ;
Fate, heard and seen of no man's eyes or ears,
To no man shown through light of smiles or tears,

And moved of no man's prayer to fold its wings ;
Fate, that is night and light on worldly things ;
Fate, that is fire to burn and sea to drown,
Strength to build up and thunder to cast down ;
Fate, shield and screen for each man's lifelong head,
And sword at last or dart that strikes it dead ;
Fate, higher than heaven and deeper than the grave,
That saves and spares not, spares and doth not save ;
Fate, that in gods' wise is not bought and sold
For prayer or price of penitence or gold ;
Whose law shall live when life bids earth farewell,
Whose justice hath for shadows heaven and hell ·
Whose judgment into no god's hand is given,
Nor is its doom not more than hell or heaven :
Fate, that is pure of love and clean of hate,
Being equal-eyed as nought may be but fate ;
Through many and weary days of foiled desire
Leads life to rest where tears no more take fire ;
Through many and weary dreams of quenched delight
Leads life through death past sense of day and night.
    Nor shall they feel or fear, whose date is done,
Aught that made once more dark the living sun
And bitterer in their breathing lips the breath
Than the dark dawn and bitter dust of death.
For all the light, with fragrance as of flowers,
That clothes the lithe live limbs of separate hours,
More sweet to savour and more clear to sight
Dawns on the soul death's undivided night.
No vigils has that perfect night to keep,
No fever-fits of vision shake that sleep.
Nor if they wake, and any place there be
Wherein the soul may feel her wings beat free
Through air too clear and still for sound or strife
If life were haply death, and death be life ;

If love with yet some lovelier laugh revive,
And song relume the light it bore alive,
And friendship, found of all earth's gifts most good,
Stand perfect in perpetual brotherhood ;
If aught indeed at all of all this be,
Though none might say nor any man might see,
Might he that sees the shade thereof not say
This dream were trustier than the truth of day.
Nor haply may not hope, with heart more clear,
Burn deathward, and the doubtful soul take cheer,
Seeing through the channelled darkness yearn a
    star
Whose eyebeams are not as the morning's are,
Transient, and subjugate of lordlier light,
But all unconquerable by noon or night,
Being kindled only of life's own inmost fire,
Truth, stablished and made sure by strong desire.
Fountain of all things living, source and seed,
Force that perforce transfigures dream to deed,
God that begets on time, the body of death,
Eternity : nor may man's darkening breath,
Albeit it stain, disfigure or destroy
The glass wherein the soul sees life and joy
Only, with strength renewed and spirit of youth,
And brighter than the sun's the body of Truth
Eternal, unimaginable of man,
Whose very face not Thought's own eyes may scan,
But see far off his radiant feet at least,
Trampling the head of Fear, the false high priest,
Whose broken chalice foams with blood no more,
And prostrate on that high priest's chancel floor,
Bruised, overthrown, blind, maimed, with bloodless
    rod,
The miscreation of his miscreant God.

That sovereign shadow cast of souls that dwell
In darkness and the prison-house of hell
Whose walls are built of deadly dread, and bound
The gates thereof with dreams as iron round,
And all the bars therein and stanchions wrought
Of shadow forged like steel and tempered thought
And words like swords and thunder-clouded creeds
And faiths more dire than sin's most direful deeds :
That shade accursed and worshipped, which hath
      made
The soul of man that brought it forth a shade
Black as the womb of darkness, void and vain,
A throne for fear, a pasturage for pain,
Impotent, abject, clothed upon with lies,
A foul blind fume of words and prayers that rise,
Aghast and harsh, abhorrent and abhorred,
Fierce as its God, blood-saturate as its Lord ;
With loves and mercies on its lips that hiss
Comfort, and kill compassion with a kiss,
And strike the world black with their blasting breath ;
That ghost whose core of life is very death
And all its light of heaven a shadow of hell,
Fades, falls, wanes, withers by none other spell
But theirs whose eyes and ears have seen and heard
Not the face naked, not the perfect word,
But the bright sound and feature felt from far
Of life which feeds the spirit and the star,
Thrills the live light of all the suns that roll,
And stirs the still sealed springs of every soul.
   Three dim days through, three slumberless nights
      long,
Perplexed at dawn, oppressed at evensong,
The strong man's soul now sealed indeed with pain
And all its springs half dried with drought, had lain

Prisoner within the fleshly dungeon-dress
Sore chafed and wasted with its weariness.
And fain it would have found the star, and fain
Made this funereal prison-house of pain
A watch-tower whence its eyes might sweep, and see
If any place for any hope might be
Beyond the hells and heavens of sleep and strife,
Or any light at all of any life
Beyond the dense false darkness woven above,
And could not, lacking grace to look on love,
And in the third night's dying hour he spake,
Seeing scarce the seals that bound the dayspring
        break
And scarce the daystar burn above the sea :
" O Ganhardine, my brother true to me,
I charge thee by those nights and days we knew
No great while since in England, by the dew
That bathed those nights with blessing, and the fire
That thrilled those days as music thrills a lyre,
Do now for me perchance the last good deed
That ever love may crave or life may need
Ere love lay life in ashes : take to thee
My ship that shows aloft against the sea
Carved on her stem the semblance of a swan,
And ere the waves at even again wax wan
Pass, if it may be, to my lady's land,
And give this ring into her secret hand,
And bid her think how hard on death I lie,
And fain would look upon her face and die.
But as a merchant's laden be the bark
With royal ware for fraughtage, that King Mark
May take for toll thereof some costly thing ;
And when this gift finds grace before the king,
Choose forth a cup, and put therein my ring

II.   E 2

Where sureliest only of one it may be seen,
And bid her handmaid bear it to the queen
For earnest of thine homage : then shall she
Fear, and take counsel privily with thee,
To know what errand there is thine from me
And what my need in secret of her sight.
But make thee two sails, one like sea-foam white
To spread for signal if thou bring her back,
And if she come not see the sail be black,
That I may know or ever thou take land
If these my lips may die upon her hand
Or hers may never more be mixed with mine."
    And his heart quailed for grief in Ganhardine,
Hearing ; and all his brother bade he swore
Surely to do, and straight fare forth from shore.
But the white-handed Iseult hearkening heard
All, and her heart waxed hot, and every word
Thereon seemed graven and printed in her thought
As lines with fire and molten iron wrought.
And hard within her heavy heart she cursed
Both, and her life was turned to fiery thirst,
And all her soul was hunger, and its breath
Of hope and life a blast of raging death.
For only in hope of evil was her life.
So bitter burned within the unchilded wife
A virgin lust for vengeance, and such hate
Wrought in her now the fervent work of fate.
    Then with a south-west wind the Swan set forth,
And over wintering waters bore to north,
And round the wild land's windy westward end
Up the blown channel bade her bright way bend
East on toward high Tintagel : where at dark
Landing, fair welcome found they of King Mark,

And Ganhardine with Brangwain as of old
Spake, and she took the cup of chiselled gold
Wherein lay secret Tristram's trothplight ring,
And bare it unbeholden of the king
Even to her lady's hand, which hardly took
A gift whereon a queen's eyes well might look,
With grace forlorn of weary gentleness.
But, seeing, her life leapt in her, keen to guess
The secret of the symbol : and her face
Flashed bright with blood whence all its grief-worn
    grace
Took fire and kindled to the quivering hair.
And in the dark soft hour of starriest air
Thrilled through with sense of midnight, when the
    world
Feels the wide wings of sleep about it furled,
Down stole the queen, deep-muffled to her war
Mute restless lips, and came where yet the Swan
Swung fast at anchor : whence by starlight she
Hoised snowbright sails, and took the glimmering
    sea.
  But all the long night long more keen and sore
His wound's grief waxed in Tristram evermore,
And heavier always hung his heart asway
Between dim fear and clouded hope of day.
And still with face and heart at silent strife
Beside him watched the maiden called his wife,
Patient, and spake not save when scarce he spake,
Murmuring with sense distraught and spirit awake
Speech bitterer than the words thereof were sweet:
And hatred thrilled her to the hands and feet,
Listening : for alway back reiterate came
The passionate faint burden of her name.

Nor ever through the labouring lips astir
Came any word of any thought of her.
But the soul wandering struggled and clung hard
Only to dreams of joy in Joyous Gard
Or wildwood nights beside the Cornish strand,
Or Merlin's holier sleep here hard at hand
Wrapped round with deep soft spells in dim Broce-
        liande.
And with such thirst as joy's drained wine-cup leaves
When fear to hope as hope to memory cleaves
His soul desired the dewy sense of leaves,
The soft green smell of thickets drenched with dawn.
The faint slot kindling on the fiery lawn
As day's first hour made keen the spirit again
That lured and spurred on quest his hound Hodain,
The breeze, the bloom, the splendour and the sound,
That stung like fire the hunter and the hound.
The pulse of wind, the passion of the sea,
The rapture of the woodland : then would he
Sigh, and as one that fain would all be dead
Heavily turn his heavy-laden head
Back, and close eyes for comfort, finding none.
And fain he would have died or seen the sun,
Being sick at heart of darkness : yet afresh
Began the long strong strife of spirit and flesh
And branching pangs of thought whose branches bear
The bloodred fruit whose core is black, despair.
And the wind slackened and again grew great,
Palpitant as men's pulses palpitate
Between the flowing and ebbing tides of fate
That wash their lifelong waifs of weal and woe
Through night and light and twilight to and fro
Now as a pulse of hope its heartbeat throbbed,
Now like one stricken shrank and sank and sobbed,

Then, yearning as with child of death, put forth
A wail that filled the night up south and north
With woful sound of waters : and he said,
" So might the wind wail if the world were dead
And its wings wandered over nought but sea.
I would I knew she would not come to me,
For surely she will come not : then should I,
Once knowing I shall not look upon her, die.
I knew not life could so long breathe such breath
As I do.   Nay, what grief were this, if death,
The sole sure friend of whom the whole world saith
He lies not, nor hath ever this been said,
That death would heal not grief—if death were dead
And all ways closed whence grief might pass with
    life ! "
  Then softly spake his watching virgin wife
Out of her heart, deep down below her breath :
" Fear not but death shall come—and after death
Judgment."   And he that heard not answered her,
Saying—" Ah, but one there was, if truth not err,
For true men's trustful tongues have said it—one
Whom these mine eyes knew living while the sun
Looked yet upon him, and mine own ears heard
The deep sweet sound once of his godlike word—
Who sleeps and dies not, but with soft live breath
Takes always all the deep delight of death,
Through love's gift of a woman : but for me
Love's hand is not the hand of Nimue,
Love's word no still smooth murmur of the dove,
No kiss of peace for me the kiss of love.
Nor, whatsoe'er thy life's love ever give,
Dear, shall it ever bid me sleep or live ;
Nor from thy brows and lips and living breast
As his from Nimue's shall my soul take rest ;

Not rest but unrest hath our long love given—
Unrest on earth that wins not rest in heaven.
What rest may we take ever? what have we
Had ever more of peace than has the sea?
Has not our life been as a wind that blows
Through lonelier lands than rear the wild white rose
That each year sees requickened, but for us
Time once and twice hath here or there done thus
And left the next year following empty and bare?
What rose hath our last year's rose left for heir,
What wine our last year's vintage? and to me
More were one fleet forbidden sense of thee,
One perfume of thy present grace, one thought
Made truth one hour, ere all mine hours be nought,
One very word, breath, look, sign, touch of hand,
Than all the green leaves in Broceliande
Full of sweet sound, full of sweet wind and sun;
O God, thou knowest I would no more but one,
I would no more but once more ere I die
Find thus much mercy.   Nay, but then were I
Happier than he whom there thy grace hath found,
For thine it must be, this that wraps him round,
Thine only, albeit a fiend's force gave him birth,
Thine that has given him heritage on earth
Of slumber-sweet eternity to keep
Fast in soft hold of everliving sleep.
Happier were I, more sinful man, than he,
Whom one love-worthier then than Nimue
Should with a breath make blest among the dead."
    And the wan wedded maiden answering said,
Soft as hate speaks within itself apart:
" Surely ye shall not, ye that rent mine heart,
Being one in sin, in punishment be twain."
    And the great knight that heard not spake again

And sighed, but sweet thought of sweet things gone
    by
Kindled with fire of joy the very sigh
And touched it through with rapture : " Ay, this
    were
How much more than the sun and sunbright air,
How much more than the springtide, how much more
Than sweet strong sea-wind quickening wave and
    shore
With one divine pulse of continuous breath,
If she might kiss me with the kiss of death,
And make the light of life by death's look dim ! "
    And the white wedded virgin answered him,
Inwardly, wan with hurt no herb makes whole :
" Yea surely, ye whose sin hath slain my soul,
Surely your own souls shall have peace in death
And pass with benediction in their breath
And blessing given of mine their sin hath slain."
    And Tristram with sore yearning spake again,
Saying : " Yea, might this thing once be, how
    should I,
With all my soul made one thanksgiving, die,
And pass before what judgment-seat may be,
And cry, ' Lord, now do all thou wilt with me,
Take all thy fill of justice, work thy will ;
Though all thy heart of wrath have all its fill,
My heart of suffering shall endure, and say,
For that thou gavest me living yesterday
I bless thee though thou curse me.'   Ay, and well
Might one cast down into the gulf of hell,
Remembering this, take heart and thank his fate—
That God, whose doom now scourges him with hate
Once, in the wild and whirling world above,
Bade mercy kiss his dying lips with love.

But if this come not, then he doth me wrong.
For what hath love done, all this long life long
That death should trample down his poor last prayer
Who prays not for forgiveness?   Though love were
Sin dark as hate, have we not here that sinned
Suffered? has that been less than wintry wind
Wherewith our love lies blasted?   O mine own,
O mine and no man's yet save mine alone,
Iseult! what ails thee that I lack so long
All of thee, all things thine for which I long?
For more than watersprings to shadeless sands,
More to me were the comfort of her hands
Touched once, and more than rays that set and rise
The glittering arrows of her glorious eyes,
More to my sense than fire to dead cold air
The wind and light and odour of her hair,
More to my soul than summer's to the south
The mute clear music of her amorous mouth,
And to my heart's heart more than heaven's great rest
The fullness of the fragrance of her breast.
Iseult, Iseult, what grace hath life to give
More than we twain have had of life, and live?
Iseult, Iseult, what grace may death not keep
As sweet for us to win of death, and sleep?
Come therefore, let us twain pass hence and try
If it be better not to live but die,
With love for lamp to light us out of life."

    And on that word his wedded maiden wife,
Pale as the moon in star-forsaken skies
Ere the sun fill them, rose with set strange eyes
And gazed on him that saw not: and her heart
Heaved as a man's death-smitten with a dart
That smites him sleeping, warm and full of life:
So toward her lord that was not looked his wife,

His wife that was not : and her heart within
Burnt bitter like an aftertaste of sin
To one whose memory drinks and loathes the lee
Of shame or sorrow deeper than the sea :
And no fear touched him of her eyes above
And ears that hoarded each poor word whence love
Made sweet the broken music of his breath.
" Iseult, my life that wast and art my death,
My life in life that hast been, and that art
Death in my death, sole wound that cleaves mine
      heart,
Mine heart that else, how spent soe'er, were whole,
Breath of my spirit and anguish of my soul,
How can this be that hence thou canst not hear,
Being but by space divided ?   One is here,
But one of twain I looked at once to see ;
Shall death keep time and thou not keep with me ? "
    And the white married maiden laughed at heart,
Hearing, and scarce with lips at all apart
Spake, and as fire between them was her breath ;
" Yea, now thou liest not : yea, for I am death."
    By this might eyes that watched without behold
Deep in the gulfs of aching air acold
The roses of the dawning heaven that strew
The low soft sun's way ere his power shine through
And burn them up with fire : but far to west
Had sunk the dead moon on the live sea's breast,
Slain as with bitter fear to see the sun :
And eastward was a strong bright wind begun
Between the clouds and waters : and he said,
Seeing hardly through dark dawn her doubtful head ;
" Iseult ? " and like a death-bell faint and clear
The virgin voice rang answer—" I am here."

And his heart sprang, and sank again : and she
Spake, saying, " What would my knightly lord with
    me ? "
And Tristram : " Hath my lady watched all night
Beside me, and I knew not ?   God requite
Her love for comfort shown a man nigh dead."
  " Yea, God shall surely guerdon it," she said,
" Who hath kept me all my days through to this
    hour."
  And Tristram : " God alone hath grace and power
To pay such grace toward one unworthier shown
Than ever durst, save only of God alone,
Crave pardon yet and comfort, as I would
Crave now for charity if my heart were good,
But as a coward's it fails me, even for shame."
  Then seemed her face a pale funereal flame
That burns down slow by midnight, as she said :
" Speak, and albeit thy bidding spake me dead,
God's love renounce me if it were not done."
  And Tristram : " When the sea-line takes the sun
That now should be not far off sight from far,
Look if there come not with the morning star
My ship bound hither from the northward back,
And if the sail be white thereof or black."
  And knowing the soothfast sense of his desire
So sore the heart within her raged like fire
She could not wring forth of her lips a word,
But bowing made sign how humbly had she heard.
And the sign given made light his heart ; and she
Set her face hard against the yearning sea
Now all athirst with trembling trust of hope
To see the sudden gates of sunrise ope ;
But thirstier yearned the heart whose fiery gate
Lay wide that vengeance might come in to hate.

And Tristram lay at thankful rest, and thought
Now surely life nor death could grieve him aught,
Since past was now life's anguish as a breath,
And surely past the bitterness of death.
For seeing he had found at these her hands this grace,
It could not be but yet some breathing-space
Might leave him life to look again on love's own face.
"Since if for death's sake," in his heart he said,
"Even she take pity upon me quick or dead,
How shall not even from God's hand be compassion
    shed?
For night bears dawn, how weak soe'er and wan,
And sweet ere death, men fable, sings the swan.
So seems the Swan my signal from the sea
To sound a song that sweetens death to me
Clasped round about with radiance from above
Of dawn, and closer clasped on earth by love.
Shall all things brighten, and this my sign be dark?"
    And high from heaven suddenly rang the lark,
Triumphant; and the far first refluent ray
Filled all the hollow darkness full with day.
And on the deep sky's verge a fluctuant light
Gleamed, grew, shone, strengthened into perfect
    sight,
As bowed and dipped and rose again the sail's clear
    white.
And swift and steadfast as a sea-mew's wing
It neared before the wind, as fain to bring
Comfort, and shorten yet its narrowing track.
And she that saw looked hardly toward him back,
Saying, "Ay, the ship comes surely; but her sail is
    black."
And fain he would have sprung upright, and seen,
And spoken: but strong death struck sheer between,

And darkness closed as iron round his head :
And smitten through the heart lay Tristram dead.
　　And scarce the word had flown abroad, and wail
Risen, ere to shoreward came the snowbright sail,
And lightly forth leapt Ganhardine on land,
And led from ship with swift and reverent hand
Iseult : and round them up from all the crowd
Broke the great wail for Tristram out aloud.
And ere her ear might hear her heart had heard,
Nor sought she sign for witness of the word ;
But came and stood above him newly dead,
And felt his death upon her : and her head
Bowed, as to reach the spring that slakes all
　　drouth ;
And their four lips became one silent mouth.

So came their hour on them that were in life
Tristram and Iseult : so from love and strife
The stroke of love's own hand felt last and best
Gave them deliverance to perpetual rest.
So, crownless of the wreaths that life had wound,
They slept, with flower of tenderer comfort crowned ;
From bondage and the fear of time set free,
And all the yoke of space on earth and sea
Cast as a curb for ever : nor might now
Fear and desire bid soar their souls or bow,
Lift up their hearts or break them : doubt nor grief
More now might move them, dread nor disbelief
Touch them with shadowy cold or fiery sting,
Nor sleepless languor with its weary wing,
Nor harsh estrangement, born of time's vain breath,
Nor change, a darkness deeper far than death.

And round the sleep that fell around them then
Earth lies not wrapped, nor records wrought of men
Rise up for timeless token : but their sleep
Hath round it like a raiment all the deep ;
No change or gleam or gloom of sun and rain,
But all time long the might of all the main
Spread round them as round earth soft heaven is
      spread,
And peace more strong than death round all the dead.
For death is of an hour, and after death
Peace : nor for aught that fear or fancy saith,
Nor even for very love's own sake, shall strife
Perplex again that perfect peace with life.
And if, as men that mourn may deem or dream,
Rest haply here than there might sweeter seem,
And sleep, that lays one hand on all, more good
By some sweet grave's grace given of wold or wood
Or clear high glen or sunbright wind-worn down
Than where life thunders through the trampling town
With daylong feet and nightlong overhead,
What grave may cast such grace round any dead,
What so sublime sweet sepulchre may be
For all that life leaves mortal, as the sea ?
And these, rapt forth perforce from earthly ground,
These twain the deep sea guards, and girdles round
Their sleep more deep than any sea's gulf lies,
Though changeless with the change in shifting skies,
Nor mutable with seasons : for the grave
That held them once, being weaker than a wave,
The waves long since have buried : though their tomb
Was royal that by ruth's relenting doom
Men gave them in Tintagel : for the word
Took wing which thrilled all piteous hearts that
      heard

The word wherethrough their lifelong lot stood
    shown,
And when the long sealed springs of fate were
    known,
The blind bright innocence of lips that quaffed
Love, and the marvel of the mastering draught,
And all the fraughtage of the fateful bark,
Loud like a child upon them wept King Mark,
Seeing round the sword's hilt which long since had
    fought
For Cornwall's love a scroll of writing wrought,
A scripture writ of Tristram's hand, wherein
Lay bare the sinless source of all their sin,
No choice of will, but chance and sorcerous art,
With prayer of him for pardon : and his heart
Was molten in him, wailing as he kissed
Each with the kiss of kinship—" Had I wist,
Ye had never sinned nor died thus, nor had I
Borne in this doom that bade you sin and die
So sore a part of sorrow."   And the king
Built for their tomb a chapel bright like spring
With flower-soft wealth of branching tracery made
Fair as the frondage each fleet year sees fade,
That should not fall till many a year were done.
There slept they wedded under moon and sun
And change of stars : and through the casements
    came
Midnight and noon girt round with shadow and
    flame
To illume their grave or veil it : till at last
On these things too was doom as darkness cast :
For the strong sea hath swallowed wall and tower,
And where their limbs were laid in woful hour

For many a fathom gleams and moves and moans
The tide that sweeps above their coffined bones
In the wrecked chancel by the shivered shrine :
Nor where they sleep shall moon or sunlight shine
Nor man look down for ever : none shall say,
Here once, or here, Tristram and Iseult lay :
But peace they have that none may gain who live,
And rest about them that no love can give,
And over them, while death and life shall be,
The light and sound and darkness of the sea.

THE TALE OF BALEN

DEDICATION

TO MY MOTHER

LOVE that holds life and death in fee,

Deep as the clear unsounded sea

And sweet as life or death can be,

Lays here my hope, my heart, and me

    Before you, silent, in a song.

Since the old wild tale, made new, found grace,

When half sung through, before your face,

It needs must live a springtide space,

    While April suns grow strong.

March 24, 1896.

I

In hawthorn-time the heart grows light,
The world is sweet in sound and sight,
Glad thoughts and birds take flower and flight,
The heather kindles toward the light,
    The whin is frankincense and flame.
And be it for strife or be it for love
The falcon quickens as the dove
When earth is touched from heaven above
    With joy that knows no name.

And glad in spirit and sad in soul
With dream and doubt of days that roll
As waves that race and find no goal
Rode on by bush and brake and bole
    A northern child of earth and sea.
The pride of life before him lay
Radiant : the heavens of night and day
Shone less than shone before his way
    His ways and days to be.

And all his life of blood and breath
Sang out within him : time and death
Were even as words a dreamer saith
When sleep within him slackeneth,
    And light and life and spring were one.

The steed between his knees that sprang,
The moors and woods that shone and sang,
The hours wherethrough the spring's breath rang,
    Seemed ageless as the sun.

But alway through the bounteous bloom
That earth gives thanks if heaven illume
His soul forefelt a shadow of doom,
His heart foreknew a gloomier gloom
    Than closes all men's equal ways.
Albeit the spirit of life's light spring
With pride of heart upheld him, king
And lord of hours like snakes that sting
    And nights that darken days.

And as the strong spring round him grew
Stronger, and all blithe winds that blew
Blither, and flowers that flowered anew
More glad of sun and air and dew,
    The shadow lightened on his soul
And brightened into death and died
Like winter, as the bloom waxed wide
From woodside on to riverside
    And southward goal to goal.

Along the wandering ways of Tyne,
By beech and birch and thorn that shine
And laugh when life's requickening wine
Makes night and noon and dawn divine
    And stirs in all the veins of spring,
And past the brightening banks of Tees,
He rode as one that breathes and sees
A sun more blithe, a merrier breeze,
    A life that hails him king.

And down the softening south that knows
No more how glad the heather glows,
Nor how, when winter's clarion blows
Across the bright Northumbrian snows,
    Sea-mists from east and westward meet,
Past Avon senseless yet of song
And Thames that bore but swans in throng
He rode elate in heart and strong
    In trust of days as sweet.

So came he through to Camelot,
Glad, though for shame his heart waxed hot,
For hope within it withered not
To see the shaft it dreamed of shot
    Fair toward the glimmering goal of fame.
And all King Arthur's knightliest there
Approved him knightly, swift to dare
And keen to bid their records bear
    Sir Balen's northern name.

Sir Balen of Northumberland
Gat grace before the king to stand
High as his heart was, and his hand
Wrought honour toward the strange north strand
    That sent him south so goodly a knight.
And envy, sick with sense of sin,
Began as poisonous herbs begin
To work in base men's blood, akin
    To men's of nobler might.

And even so fell it that his doom,
For all his bright life's kindling bloom
And light that took no thought for gloom,
Fell as a breath from the opening tomb
    Full on him ere he wist or thought.

For once a churl of royal seed,
King Arthur's kinsman, faint in deed
And loud in word that knew not heed,
    Spake shame where shame was nought.

" What doth one here in Camelot
Whose birth was northward ?   Wot we not
As all his brethren borderers wot
How blind of heart, how keen and hot,
    The wild north lives and hates the south ?
Men of the narrowing march that knows
Nought save the strength of storms and snows,
What would these carles where knighthood blows
    A trump of kinglike mouth ? "

Swift from his place leapt Balen, smote
The liar across his face, and wrote
His wrath in blood upon the bloat
Brute cheek that challenged shame for note
    How vile a king-born knave might be.
Forth sprang their swords, and Balen slew
The knave ere well one witness knew
Of all that round them stood or drew
    What sight was there to see.

Then spake the great king's wrathful will
A doom for six dark months to fill
Wherein close prison held him, still
And steadfast-souled for good or ill.
    But when those weary days lay dead
His lordliest knights and barons spake
Before the king for Balen's sake
Good speech and wise, of force to break
    The bonds that bowed his head.

II

In linden-time the heart is high
For pride of summer passing by
With lordly laughter in her eye ;
A heavy splendour in the sky
    Uplifts and bows it down again.
The spring had waned from wood and wold
Since Balen left his prison hold
And lowlier-hearted than of old
    Beheld it wax and wane.

Though humble heart and poor array
Kept not from spirit and sense away
Their noble nature, nor could slay
The pride they bade but pause and stay
    Till time should bring its trust to flower,
Yet even for noble shame's sake, born
Of hope that smiled on hate and scorn,
He held him still as earth ere morn
    Ring forth her rapturous hour.

But even as earth when dawn takes flight
And beats her wings of dewy light
Full in the faltering face of night,
His soul awoke to claim by right
    The life and death of deed and doom,

F

When once before the king there came
A maiden clad with grief and shame
And anguish burning her like flame
    That feeds on flowers in bloom.

Beneath a royal mantle, fair
With goodly work of lustrous vair,
Girt fast against her side she bare
A sword whose weight bade all men there
    Quail to behold her face again.
Save of a passing perfect knight
Not great alone in force and fight
It might not be for any might
    Drawn forth, and end her pain.

So said she : then King Arthur spake :
" Albeit indeed I dare not take
Such praise on me, for knighthood's sake
And love of ladies will I make
    Assay if better none may be."
By girdle and by sheath he caught
The sheathed and girded sword, and wrought
With strength whose force availed him nought
    To save and set her free.

Again she spake : " No need to set
The might that man has matched not yet
Against it ; he whose hand shall get
Grace to release the bonds that fret
    My bosom and my girdlestead
With little strain of strength or strife
Shall bring me as from death to life
And win to sister or to wife
    Fame that outlives men dead."

Then bade the king his knights assay
This mystery that before him lay
And mocked his might of manhood.   " Nay,"
Quoth she, " the man that takes away
    This burden laid on me must be
A knight of record clean and fair
As sunlight and the flowerful air,
By sire and mother born to bear
    A name to shame not me."

Then forth strode Launcelot, and laid
The mighty-moulded hand that made
Strong knights reel back like birds affrayed
By storm that smote them as they strayed
    Against the hilt that yielded not.
Then Tristram, bright and sad and kind
As one that bore in noble mind
Love that made light as darkness blind,
    Fared even as Launcelot.

Then Lamoracke, with hardier cheer,
As one that held all hope and fear
Wherethrough the spirit of man may steer
In life and death less dark or dear,
    Laid hand thereon, and fared as they.
With half a smile his hand he drew
Back from the spell-bound thing, and threw
With half a glance his heart anew
    Toward no such blameless may.

Between Iseult and Guenevere
Sat one of name as high to hear,
But darklier doomed than they whose cheer
Foreshowed not yet the deadlier year
    That bids the queenliest head bow down,

The queen Morgause of Orkney : they
With scarce a flash of the eye could say
The very word of dawn, when day
        Gives earth and heaven their crown.

But bright and dark as night or noon
And lowering as a storm-flushed moon
When clouds and thwarting winds distune
The music of the midnight, soon
        To die from darkening star to star
And leave a silence in the skies
That yearns till dawn find voice and rise,
Shone strange as fate Morgause, with eyes
        That dwelt on days afar.

A glance that shot on Lamoracke
As from a storm-cloud bright and black
Fire swift and blind as death's own track
Turned fleet as flame on Arthur back
        From him whose hand forsook the hilt :
And one in blood and one in sin
Their hearts caught fire of pain within
And knew no goal for them to win
        But death that guerdons guilt.

Then Gawain, sweet of soul and gay
As April ere he dreams of May,
Strove, and prevailed not ; then Sir Kay,
The snake-souled envier, vile as they
        That fawn and foam and lurk and lie,
Sire of the bastard band whose brood
Was alway found at servile feud
With honour, faint and false and lewd,
        Scarce grasped and put it by.

Then wept for woe the damsel bound
With iron and with anguish round,
That none to help her grief was found
Or loose the inextricably inwound
          Grim curse that girt her life with grief
And made a burden of her breath,
Harsh as the bitterness of death.
Then spake the king as one that saith
          Words bitterer even than brief.

" Methought the wide round world could bring
Before the face of queen or king
No knights more fit for fame to sing
Than fill this full Round Table's ring
          With honour higher than pride of place :
But now my heart is wrung to know,
Damsel, that none whom fame can show
Finds grace to heal or help thy woe :
          God gives them not the grace."

Then from the lowliest place thereby,
With heart-enkindled cheek and eye
Most like the star and kindling sky
That say the sundawn's hour is high
          When rapture trembles through the sea,
Strode Balen in his poor array
Forth, and took heart of grace to pray
The damsel suffer even him to assay
          His power to set her free.

Nay, how should he avail, she said,
Averse with scorn-averted head,
Where these availed not ? none had sped
Of all these mightier men that led
          The lists wherein he might not ride,

And how should less men speed ?   But he,
With lordlier pride of courtesy,
Put forth his hand and set her free
        From pain and humbled pride.

But on the sword he gazed elate
With hope set higher than fear or fate,
Or doubt of darkling days in wait ;
And when her thankful praise waxed great
        And craved of him the sword again,
He would not give it.   " Nay, for mine
It is till force may make it thine."
A smile that shone as death may shine
        Spake toward him bale and bane.

Strange lightning flickered from her eyes.
" Gentle and good in knightliest guise
And meet for quest of strange emprise
Thou hast here approved thee : yet not wise
        To keep the sword from me, I wis.
For with it thou shalt surely slay
Of all that look upon the day
The man best loved of thee, and lay
        Thine own life down for his."

" What chance God sends, that chance I take,"
He said.   Then soft and still she spake ;
" I would but for thine only sake
Have back the sword of thee, and break
        The links of doom that bind thee round.
But seeing thou wilt not have it so,
My heart for thine is wrung with woe."
" God's will," quoth he, " it is, we know,
        Wherewith our lives are bound."

"Repent it must thou soon," she said,
"Who wouldst not hear the rede I read
For thine and not for my sake, sped
In vain as waters heavenward shed
    From springs that falter and depart
Earthward. God bids not thee believe
Truth, and the web thy life must weave
For even this sword to close and cleave
    Hangs heavy round my heart."

So passed she mourning forth. But he,
With heart of springing hope set free
As birds that breast and brave the sea,
Bade horse and arms and armour be
    Made straightway ready toward the fray.
Nor even might Arthur's royal prayer
Withhold him, but with frank and fair
Thanksgiving and leave-taking there
    He turned him thence away.

III

As the east wind, when the morning's breast
Gleams like a bird's that leaves the nest,
A fledgeling halcyon's bound on quest,
Drives wave on wave on wave to west
    Till all the sea be life and light,
So time's mute breath, that brings to bloom
All flowers that strew the dead spring's tomb,
Drives day on day on day to doom
    Till all man's day be night.

Brief as the breaking of a wave
That hurls on man his thunderous grave
Ere fear find breath to cry or crave
Life that no chance may spare or save,
    The light of joy and glory shone
Even as in dreams where death seems dead
Round Balen's hope-exalted head,
Shone, passed, and lightened as it fled
    The shadow of doom thereon.

For as he bound him thence to fare,
Before the stately presence there
A lady like a windflower fair,
Girt on with raiment strange and rare
    That rippled whispering round her, came.

Her clear cold eyes, all glassy grey,
Seemed lit not with the light of day
But touched with gleams that waned away
 Of quelled and fading flame.

Before the king she bowed and spake :
" King, for thine old faith's plighted sake
To me the lady of the lake,
I come in trust of thee to take
 The guerdon of the gift I gave,
Thy sword Excalibur."   And he
Made answer : " Be it whate'er it be,
If mine to give, I give it thee,
 Nor need is thine to crave."

As when a gleam of wicked light
Turns half a low-lying water bright
That moans beneath the shivering night
With sense of evil sound and sight
 And whispering witchcraft's bated breath.
Her wan face quickened as she said :
" This knight that won the sword—his head
I crave or hers that brought it.   Dead,
 Let these be one in death."

" Not with mine honour this may be ;
Ask all save this thou wilt," quoth he,
" And have thy full desire."   But she
Made answer : " Nought will I of thee,
 Nought if not this."   Then Balen turned,
And saw the sorceress hard beside
By whose fell craft his mother died :
Three years he had sought her, and here espied
 His heart against her yearned.

II.   F 2

" Ill be thou met," he said, " whose ire
Would slake with blood thy soul's desire :
By thee my mother died in fire ;
Die thou by me a death less dire."
    Sharp flashed his sword forth, fleet as flame,
And shore away her sorcerous head.
" Alas for shame," the high king said,
" That one found once my friend lies dead ;
    Alas for all our shame !

" Thou shouldst have here forborne her ; yea,
Were all the wrongs that bid men slay
Thine, heaped too high for wrath to weigh,
Not here before my face to-day
    Was thine the right to wreak thy wrong."
Still stood he then as one that found
His rose of hope by storm discrowned,
And all the joy that girt him round
    Brief as a broken song.

Yet ere he passed he turned and spake :
" King, only for thy nobler sake
Than aught of power man's power may take
Or pride of place that pride may break
    I bid the lordlier man in thee,
That lives within the king, give ear.
This justice done before thee here
On one that hell's own heart holds dear,
    Needs might not this but be.

" Albeit, for all that pride would prove,
My heart be wrung to lose thy love,
It yet repents me not hereof :
So many an eagle and many a dove,
    So many a knight, so many a may,

This water-snake of poisonous tongue
To death by words and wiles hath stung,
That her their slayer, from hell's lake sprung,
    I did not ill to slay."

"Yea," said the king, "too high of heart
To stand before a king thou art ;
Yet irks it me to bid thee part
And take thy penance for thy part,
    That God may put upon thy pride."
Then Balen took the severed head
And toward his hostry turned and sped
As one that knew not quick from dead
    Nor good from evil tide.

He bade his squire before him stand
And take that sanguine spoil in hand
And bear it far by shore and strand
Till all in glad Northumberland
    That loved him, seeing it, all might know
His deadliest foe was dead, and hear
How free from prison as from fear
He dwelt in trust of the answering year
    To bring him weal for woe.

"And tell them, now I take my way
To meet in battle, if I may,
King Ryons of North Wales, and slay
That king of kernes whose fiery sway
    Doth all the marches dire despite
That serve King Arthur : so shall he
Again be gracious lord to me,
And I that leave thee meet with thee
    Once more in Arthur's sight."

So spake he ere they parted, nor
Took shame or fear to counsellor,
As one whom none laid ambush for ;
And wist not how Sir Launceor,
     The wild king's son of Ireland, hot
And high in wrath to know that one
Stood higher in fame before the sun,
Even Balen, since the sword was won,
     Drew nigh from Camelot.

For thence, in heat of hate and pride,
As one that man might bid not bide,
He craved the high king's grace to ride
On quest of Balen far and wide
     And wreak the wrong his wrath had wrought.
" Yea," Arthur said, " for such despite
Was done me never in my sight
As this thine hand shall now requite
     If trust avail us aught."

But ere he passed, in eager mood
To feed his hate with bitter food,
Before the king's face Merlin stood
And heard his tale of ill and good,
     Of Balen, and the sword achieved.
And whence it smote as heaven's red ire
That direful dame of doom as dire ;
And how the king's wrath turned to fire
     The grief wherewith he grieved.

And darkening as he gave it ear,
The still face of the sacred seer
Waxed wan with wrath and not with fear,
And ever changed its cloudier cheer
     Till all his face was very night.

" This damosel that brought the sword,"
He said, " before the king my lord,
And all these knights about his board,
  Hath done them all despite.

" The falsest damosel she is
That works men ill on earth, I wis,
And all her mind is toward but this,
To kill as with a lying kiss
  Truth, and the life of noble trust.
A brother hath she,—see but now
The flame of shame that brands her brow !—
A true man, pure as faith's own vow,
  Whose honour knows not rust.

" This good knight found within her bower
A felon and her paramour,
And slew him in his shameful hour,
As right gave might and righteous power
  To hands that wreaked so foul a wrong.
Then, for the hate her heart put on,
She sought by ways where death had gone
The lady Lyle of Avalon,
  Whose crafts are strange and strong.

" The sorceress, one with her in thought,
Gave her that sword of magic, wrought
By charms whereof sweet heaven sees nought,
That hither girt on her she brought
  To be by doom her brother's bane.
And grief it is to think how he
That won it, being of heart so free
And perfect found in chivalry,
  Shall by that sword lie slain.

" Great pity it is and strange despite
That one whose eyes are stars to light
Honour, and shine as heaven's own height,
Should perish, being the goodliest knight
  That even the all-glorious north has borne.
Nor shall my lord the king behold
A lordlier friend of mightier mould
Than Balen, though his tale be told
  Ere noon fulfil his morn."

IV

As morning hears before it run
The music of the mounting sun,
And laughs to watch his trophies won
From darkness, and her hosts undone,
    And all the night become a breath,
Nor dreams that fear should hear and flee
The summer menace of the sea,
So hears our hope what life may be,
    And knows it not for death.

Each day that slays its hours and dies
Weeps, laughs, and lightens on our eyes,
And sees and hears not : smiles and sighs
As flowers ephemeral fall and rise
    About its birth, about its way,
And pass as love and sorrow pass,
As shadows flashing down a glass,
As dew-flowers blowing in flowerless grass,
    As hope from yesterday.

The blossom of the sunny dew
That now the stronger sun strikes through
Fades off the blade whereon it blew
No fleetlier than the flowers that grew
    On hope's green stem in life's fierce light.

Nor might the glory soon to sit
Awhile on Balen's crest alit
Outshine the shadow of doom on it
    Or stay death's wings from flight.

Dawn on a golden moorland side
By holt and heath saw Balen ride
And Launceor after, pricked with pride
And stung with spurring envy : wide
    And far he had ridden athwart strange lands
And sought amiss the man he found
And cried on, till the stormy sound
Rang as a rallying trumpet round
    That fires men's hearts and hands.

Abide he bade him : nor was need
To bid when Balen wheeled his steed
Fiercely, less fain by word than deed
To bid his envier evil speed,
    And cried, " What wilt thou with me?" Loud
Rang Launceor's vehement answer : " Knight,
To avenge on thee the dire despite
Thou hast done us all in Arthur's sight
    I stand toward Arthur vowed."

" Ay ? " Balen said : " albeit I see
I needs must deal in strife with thee,
Light is the wyte thou layest on me ;
For her I slew and sinned not, she
    Was dire in all men's eyes as death,
Or none were lother found than I
By me to bid a woman die :
As lief were loyal men to lie,
    Or scorn what honour saith."

As the arched wave's weight against the reef
Hurls, and is hurled back like a leaf
Storm-shrivelled, and its rage of grief
Speaks all the loud broad sea in brief,
    And quells the hearkening hearts of men,
Or as the crash of overfalls
Down under blue smooth water brawls
Like jarring steel on ruining walls,
    So rang their meeting then.

As wave on wave shocks, and confounds
The bounding bulk whereon it bounds
And breaks and shattering seaward sounds
As crying of the old sea's wolves and hounds
    That moan and ravin and rage and wail,
So steed on steed encountering sheer
Shocked, and the strength of Launceor's spear
Shivered on Balen's shield, and fear
    Bade hope within him quail.

But Balen's spear through Launceor's shield
Clove as a ploughshare cleaves the field
And pierced the hauberk triple-steeled,
That horse with horseman stricken reeled,
    And as a storm-breached rock falls, fell,
And Balen turned his horse again
And wist not yet his foe lay slain,
And saw him dead that sought his bane
    And wrought and fared not well.

Suddenly, while he gazed and stood,
And mused in many-minded mood
If life or death were evil or good,
Forth of a covert of a wood
    That skirted half the moorland lea

Fast rode a maiden flower-like white
Full toward that fair wild place of fight,
Anhungered of the woful sight
    God gave her there to see.

And seeing the man there fallen and dead,
She cried against the sun that shed
Light on the living world, and said,
" O Balen, slayer whose hand is red,
    Two bodies and one heart thou hast slain,
Two hearts within one body : aye,
Two souls thou hast lost ; by thee they die,
Cast out of sight of earth and sky
    And all that made them fain."

And from the dead his sword she caught,
And fell in trance that wist of nought,
Swooning : but softly Balen sought
To win from her the sword she thought
    To die on, dying by Launceor's side.
Again her wakening wail outbroke
As wildly, sword in hand, she woke
And struck one swift and bitter stroke
    That healed her, and she died.

And sorrowing for their strange love's sake
Rode Balen forth by lawn and lake,
By moor and moss and briar and brake,
And in his heart their sorrow spake
    Whose lips were dumb as death, and said
Mute words of presage blind and vain
As rain-stars blurred and marred by rain
To wanderers on a moonless main
    Where night and day seem dead.

Then toward a sunbright wildwood side
He looked and saw beneath it ride
A knight whose arms afar espied
By note of name and proof of pride
    Bare witness of his brother born,
His brother Balan, hard at hand,
Twin flower of bright Northumberland,
Twin sea-bird of their loud sea-strand,
    Twin song-bird of their morn.

Ah then from Balen passed away
All dread of night, all doubt of day,
All care what life or death might say,
All thought of all worse months than May:
    Only the might of joy in love
Brake forth within him as a fire,
And deep delight in deep desire
Of far-flown days whose full-souled quire
    Rang round from the air above.

From choral earth and quiring air
Rang memories winged like songs that bear
Sweet gifts for spirit and sense to share :
For no man's life knows love more fair
    And fruitful of memorial things
Than this the deep dear love that breaks
With sense of life on life, and makes
The sundawn sunnier as it wakes
    Where morning round it rings.

" O brother, O my brother ! " cried
Each upon each, and cast aside
Their helms unbraced that might not hide
From sight of memory single-eyed
    The likeness graven of face and face,

And kissed and wept upon each other
For joy and pity of either brother,
And love engraffed by sire and mother,
    God's natural gift of grace.

And each with each took counsel meet
For comfort, making sorrow sweet,
And grief a goodly thing to greet:
And word from word leapt light and fleet
    Till all the venturous tale was told,
And how in Balen's hope it lay
To meet the wild Welsh king and slay,
And win from Arthur back for pay
    The grace he gave of old.

" And thither wilt not thou with me
And win as great a grace for thee ? "
" That will I well," quoth Balan : " we
Will cleave together, bound and free,
    As brethren should, being twain and one."
But ere they parted thence there came
A creature withered as with flame,
A dwarf mismade in nature's shame,
    Between them and the sun.

And riding fleet as fire may glide
He found the dead lie side by side,
And wailed and rent his hair and cried,
" Who hath done this deed ? "   And Balen eyed
    The strange thing loathfully, and said,
" The knight I slew, who found him fain
And keen to slay me : seeing him slain,
The maid I sought to save in vain,
    Self-stricken, here lies dead.

"Sore grief was mine to see her die,
And for her true faith's sake shall I
Love, and with love of heart more high,
All women better till I die."
    "Alas," the dwarf said, "ill for thee
In evil hour this deed was done:
For now the quest shall be begun
Against thee, from the dawning sun
    Even to the sunset sea.

"From shore to mountain, dawn to night,
The kinsfolk of this great dead knight
Will chase thee to thy death."   A light
Of swift blithe scorn flashed answer bright
    As fire from Balen's eye.   "For that,
Small fear shall fret my heart," quoth he:
"But that my lord the king should be
For this dead man's sake wroth with me,
    Weep might it well thereat."

Then murmuring passed the dwarf away,
And toward the knights in fair array
Came riding eastward up the way
From where the flower-soft lowlands lay
    A king whose name the sweet south-west
Held high in honour, and the land
That bowed beneath his gentle hand
Wore on its wild bright northern strand
    Tintagel for a crest.

And Balen hailed with homage due
King Mark of Cornwall, when he knew
The pennon that before him flew:
And for those lovers dead and true
    The king made moan to hear their doom;

And for their sorrow's sake he sware
To seek in all the marches there
The church that man might find most fair
    And build therein their tomb.

V

As thought from thought takes wing and flies,
As month on month with sunlit eyes
Tramples and triumphs in its rise,
As wave smites wave to death and dies,
    So chance on hurtling chance like steel
Strikes, flashes, and is quenched, ere fear
Can whisper hope, or hope can hear,
If sorrow or joy be far or near
    For time to hurt or heal.

Swift as a shadow and strange as light
That cleaves in twain the shadow of night
Before the wide-winged word takes flight
That thunder speaks to depth and height
    And quells the quiet hour with sound,
There came before King Mark and stood
Between the moorside and the wood
The man whose word God's will made good,
    Nor guile was in it found.

And Merlin said to Balen : "Lo,
Thou hast wrought thyself a grievous woe
To let this lady die, and know
Thou mightst have stayed her deadly blow."
    And Balen answered him and said,

" Nay, by my truth to faith, not I,
So fiercely fain she was to die ;
Ere well her sword had flashed on high,
    Self-slain she lay there dead."

Again and sadly Merlin spake :
" My heart is wrung for this deed's sake,
To know thee therefore doomed to take
Upon thine hand a curse, and make
    Three kingdoms pine through twelve years'
        change,
In want and woe : for thou shalt smite
The man most noble and truest knight
That looks upon the live world's light
    A dolorous stroke and strange.

" And not till years shall round their goal
May this man's wound thou hast given be whole."
And Balen, stricken through the soul
By dark-winged words of doom and dole,
    Made answer : " If I wist it were
No lie but sooth thou sayest of me,
Then even to make a liar of thee
Would I too slay myself, and see
    How death bids dead men fare."

And Merlin took his leave and passed
And was not : and the shadow as fast
Went with him that his word had cast,
Too fleet for thought thereof to last :
    And there those brethren bade King Mark
Farewell : but fain would Mark have known
The strong knight's name who had overthrown
The pride of Launceor, when it shone
    Bright as it now lay dark.

And Balan for his brother spake,
Saying : " Sir, albeit him list not break
The seal of secret time, nor shake
Night off him ere his morning wake,
    By these two swords he is girt withal
May men that praise him, knights and lords,
Call him the knight that bears two swords,
And all the praise his fame accords
    Make answer when they call."

So parted they toward eventide ;
And tender twilight, heavy-eyed,
Saw deep down glimmering woodlands ride
Balen and Balan side by side,
    Till where the leaves grew dense and dim
Again they spied from far draw near
The presence of the sacred seer,
But so disguised and strange of cheer
    That seeing they knew not him.

" Now whither ride ye," Merlin said,
" Through shadows that the sun strikes red,
Ere night be born or day be dead ? "
But they, for doubt half touched with dread,
    Would say not where their goal might lie.
" And thou," said Balen, " what art thou,
To walk with shrouded eye and brow ? "
He said : " Me lists not show thee now
    By name what man am I."

" Ill seen is this of thee," said they,
" That thou art true in word and way
Nor fain to fear the face of day,
Who wilt not as a true man say
    The name it shames not him to bear."

He answered : " Be it or be it not so,
Yet why ye ride this way I know,
To meet King Ryons as a foe,
    And how your hope shall fare.

" Well, if ye hearken toward my rede,
Ill, if ye hear not, shall ye speed."
" Ah, now," they cried, " thou art ours at need :
What Merlin saith we are fain to heed."
    " Great worship shall ye win," said he,
" And look that ye do knightly now,
For great shall be your need, I trow."
And Balen smiled : " By knighthood's vow,
    The best we may will we."

Then Merlin bade them turn and take
Rest, for their good steeds' weary sake,
Between the highway and the brake,
Till starry midnight bade them wake :
    Then " Rise," he said, " the king is nigh,
Who hath stolen from all his host away
With threescore horse in armed array,
The goodliest knights that bear his sway
    And hold his kingdom high.

" And twenty ride of them before
To bear his errand, ere the door
Turn of the night, sealed fast no more,
And sundawn bid the stars wax hoar ;
    For by the starshine of to-night
He seeks a leman where she waits
His coming, dark and swift as fate's,
And hearkens toward the unopening gates
    That yield not him to sight."

Then through the glimmering gloom around
A shadowy sense of light and sound
Made, ere the proof thereof were found,
The brave blithe hearts within them bound,
    And " Where," quoth Balen, " rides the king ? "
But softer spake the seer : " Abide,
Till hither toward your spears he ride,
Where all the narrowing woodland side
    Grows dense with boughs that cling."

There in that straitening way they met
The wild Welsh host against them set,
And smote their strong king down, ere yet
His hurrying horde of spears might get
    Fierce vantage of them.   Then the fight
Grew great and joyous as it grew,
For left and right those brethren slew,
Till all the lawn waxed red with dew
    More deep than dews of night.

And ere the full fierce tale was read
Full forty lay before them dead,
And fast the hurtling remnant fled
And wist not whither fear had led :
    And toward the king they went again,
And would have slain him : but he bowed
Before them, crying in fear aloud
For grace they gave him, seeing the proud
    Wild king brought lowest of men.

And ere the wildwood leaves were stirred
With song or wing of wakening bird,
In Camelot was Merlin's word
With joy in joyous wonder heard
    That told of Arthur's bitterest foe

Diskingdomed and discomfited.
"By whom?" the high king smiled and said,
He answered: "Ere the dawn wax red,
    To-morrow bids you know.

"Two knights whose heart and hope are one
And fain to win your grace have done
This work whereby if grace be won
Their hearts shall hail the enkindling sun
    With joy more keen and deep than day."
And ere the sundawn drank the dew
Those brethren with their prisoner drew
To the outer guard they gave him to
    And passed again away.

And Arthur came as toward his guest
To greet his foe, and bade him rest
As one returned from nobler quest
And welcome from the stormbright west,
    But by what chance he fain would hear.
"The chance was hard and strange, sir king,"
Quoth Ryons, bowed in thanksgiving.
"Who won you?" Arthur said: "the thing
    Is worth a warrior's ear."

The wild king flushed with pride and shame,
Answering: "I know not either name
Of those that there against us came
And withered all our strength like flame:
    The knight that bears two swords is one,
And one his brother: not on earth
May men meet men of knightlier worth
Nor mightier born of mortal birth
    That hail the sovereign sun."

And Arthur said: "I know them not;
But much am I for this, God wot,
Beholden to them: Launcelot
Nor Tristram, when the war waxed hot
    Along the marches east and west,
Wrought ever nobler work than this."
"Ah," Merlin said, "sore pity it is
And strange mischance of doom, I wis,
    That death should mar their quest.

"Balen, the perfect knight that won
The sword whose name is malison,
And made his deed his doom, is one:
Nor hath his brother Balan done
    Less royal service: not on earth
Lives there a nobler knight, more strong
Of soul to win men's praise in song,
Albeit the light abide not long
    That lightened round his birth.

"Yea, and of all sad things I know
The heaviest and the highest in woe
Is this, the doom whose date brings low
Too soon in timeless overthrow
    A head so high, a hope so sure.
The greatest moan for any knight
That ever won fair fame in fight
Shall be for Balen, seeing his might
    Must now not long endure."

"Alas," King Arthur said, "he hath shown
Such love to me-ward that the moan
Made of him should be mine alone
Above all other, knowing it known
    I have ill deserved it of him."   "Nay,"

Said Merlin, " he shall do for you
Much more, when time shall be anew,
Than time hath given him chance to do
      Or hope may think to say.

" But now must be your powers purveyed
To meet, ere noon of morn be made
To-morrow, all the host arrayed
Of this wild foe's wild brother, laid
      Around against you : see to it well,
For now I part from you."   And soon,
When sundawn slew the withering moon,
Two hosts were met to win the boon
      Whose tale is death's to tell.

A lordly tale of knights and lords
For death to tell by count of swords
When war's wild harp in all its chords
Rang royal triumph, and the hordes
      Of hurtling toemen rocked and reeled
As waves wind-thwarted on the sea,
Was told of all that there might be,
Till scarce might battle hear or see
      The fortune of the field.

And many a knight won fame that day
When even the serpent soul of Kay
Was kindled toward the fiery play
As might a lion's be for prey,
      And won him fame that might not die
With passing of his rancorous breath
But clung about his life and death
As fire that speaks in cloud, and saith
      What strong men hear and fly.

And glorious works were Arthur's there,
That lit the battle-darkened air :
But when they saw before them fare
Like stars of storm the knight that bare
    Two swords about him girt for fray,
Balen, and Balan with him, then
Strong wonder smote the souls of men
If heaven's own host or hell's deep den
    Had sent them forth to slay.

So keen they rode across the fight,
So sharp they smote to left and right,
And made of hurtling darkness light
With lightning of their swords, till flight
    And fear before them flew like flame,
That Arthur's self had never known,
He said, since first his blast was blown,
Such lords of war as these alone
    That whence he knew not came.

But while the fire of war waxed hot
The wild king hearkened, hearing not,
Through storm of spears and arrow-shot,
For succour toward him from King Lot
    And all his host of sea-born men,
Strong as the strong storm-baffling bird
Whose cry round Orkney's headlands heard
Is as the sea's own sovereign word
    That mocks our mortal ken.

For Merlin's craft of prophecy,
Who wist that one of twain must die,
Put might in him to say thereby
Which head should lose its crown, and lie
    Stricken, though loth he were to know

That either life should wane and fail ;
Yet most might Arthur's love avail,
And still with subtly tempered tale
          His wile held fast the foe.

With woven words of magic might
Wherein the subtle shadow and light
Changed hope and fear till fear took flight,
He stayed King Lot's fierce lust of fight
          Till all the wild Welsh war was driven
As foam before the wind that wakes
With the all-awakening sun, and breaks
Strong ships that rue the mirth it makes
          When grace to slay is given.

And ever hotter lit and higher,
As fire that meets encountering fire,
Waxed in King Lot his keen desire
To bid revenge within him tire
          On Arthur's ravaged fame and life :
Across the waves of war between
Floated and flashed, unseen and seen,
The lustrous likeness of the queen
          Whom shame had sealed his wife.

But when the woful word was brought
That while he tarried, doubting nought,
The hope was lost whose goal he sought
And all the fight he yearned for fought,
          His heart was rent for grief and shame,
And half his hope was set on flight
Till word was given him of a knight
Who said : " They are weary and worn with fight.
          And we more fresh than flame."

And bright and dark as night and day
Ere either find the unopening way
Clear, and forego the unaltering sway,
The sad king's face shone, frowning: " Yea,
 I would that every knight of mine
Would do his part as I shall do,"
He said, " till death or life anew
Shall judge between us as is due
 With wiser doom than thine."

Then thundered all the awakening field
With crash of hosts that clashed and reeled,
Banner to banner, shield to shield,
And spear to splintering spear-shaft, steeled
 As heart against high heart of man,
As hope against high hope of knight
To pluck the crest and crown of fight
From war's clenched hand by storm's wild light,
 For blessing given or ban.

All hearts of hearkening men that heard
The ban twin-born with blessing, stirred
Like springtide waters, knew the word
Whereby the steeds of storm are spurred
 With ravenous rapture to destroy,
And laughed for love of battle, pierced
With passion of tempestuous thirst
And hungering hope to assuage it first
 With draughts of stormy joy.

But sheer ahead of the iron tide
That rocked and roared from side to side
Rode as the lightning's lord might ride
King Lot, whose heart was set to abide
 All peril of the raging hour,

And all his host of warriors born
Where lands by warring seas are worn
Was only by his hands upborne
    Who gave them pride and power.

But as the sea's hand smites the shore
And shatters all the strengths that bore
The ravage earth may bear no more,
So smote the hand of Pellinore
    Charging, a knight of Arthur's chief,
And clove his strong steed's neck in twain,
And smote him sheer through brow and brain,
Falling : and there King Lot lay slain,
    And knew not wrath or grief.

And all the host of Orkney fled,
And many a mother's son lay dead :
But when they raised the stricken head
Whence pride and power and shame were fled
    And rage and anguish now cast out,
And bore it toward a kingly tomb,
The wife whose love had wrought his doom
Came thither, fair as morning's bloom
    And dark as twilight's doubt.

And there her four strong sons and his,
Gawain and Gareth, Gaherys
And Agravain, whose sword's sharp kiss
With sound of hell's own serpent's hiss
    Should one day turn her life to death,
Stood mourning with her : but by these
Seeing Mordred as a seer that sees,
Anguish of terror bent her knees
    And caught her shuddering breath.

The splendour of her sovereign eyes
Flashed darkness deeper than the skies
Feel or fear when the sunset dies
On his that felt as midnight rise
    Their doom upon them, there undone
By faith in fear ere thought could yield
A shadowy sense of days revealed,
The ravin of the final field,
    The terror of their son.

For Arthur's, as they caught the light
That sought and durst not seek his sight,
Darkened, and all his spirit's might
Withered within him even as night
    Withers when sunrise thrills the sea.
But Mordred's lightened as with fire
That smote his mother and his sire
With darkling doom and deep desire
    That bade its darkness be.

And heavier on their hearts the weight
Sank of the fear that brings forth fate,
The bitter doubt whose womb is great
With all the grief and love and hate
    That turn to fire men's days on earth.
And glorious was the funeral made,
And dark the deepening dread that swayed
Their darkening souls whose light grew shade
    With sense of death in birth.

VI

In autumn, when the wind and sea
Rejoice to live and laugh to be,
And scarce the blast that curbs the tree
And bids before it quail and flee
    The fiery foliage, where its brand
Is radiant as the seal of spring,
Sounds less delight, and waves a wing
Less lustrous, life's loud thanksgiving
    Puts life in sea and land.

High hope in Balen's heart alight
Laughed, as from all that clamorous fight
He passed and sought not Arthur's sight,
Who fain had found his kingliest knight
    And made amend for Balen's wrong.
But Merlin gave his soul to see
Fate, rising as a shoreward sea,
And all the sorrow that should be
    Ere hope or fear thought long.

" O where are they whose hands upbore
My battle," Arthur said, "before
The wild Welsh host's wide rage and roar?
Balen and Balan, Pellinore,
    Where are they?"   Merlin answered him :

" Balen shall be not long away
From sight of you, but night nor day
Shall bring his brother back to say
    If life burn bright or dim."

" Now, by my faith," said Arthur then,
" Two marvellous knights are they, whose ken
Toward battle makes the twain as ten,
And Balen most of all born men
    Passeth of prowess all I know
Or ever found or sought to see :
Would God he would abide with me
To face the times foretold of thee
    And all the latter woe."

For there had Merlin shown the king
The doom that songs unborn should sing,
The gifts that time should rise and bring
Of blithe and bitter days to spring
    As weeds and flowers against the sun.
And on the king for fear's sake fell
Sickness, and sorrow deep as hell,
Nor even might sleep bid fear farewell
    If grace to sleep were won.

Down in a meadow green and still
He bade the folk that wrought his will
Pitch his pavilion, where the chill
Soft night would let not rest fulfil
    His heart wherein dark fears lay deep.
And sharp against his hearing cast
Came a sound as of horsehoofs fast
Passing, that ere their sound were past
    Aroused him as from sleep.

And forth he looked along the grass
And saw before his portal pass
A knight that wailed aloud, " Alas
That life should find this dolorous pass
  And find no shield from doom and dole ! "
And hearing all his moan, " Abide,
Fair sir," the king arose and cried,
" And say what sorrow bids you ride
  So sorrowful of soul."

" My hurt may no man heal, God wot,
And help of man may speed me not,"
The sad knight said, " nor change my lot."
And toward the castle of Melyot
  Whose towers arose a league away
He passed forth sorrowing : and anon,
Ere well the woful sight were gone,
Came Balen down the meads that shone,
  Strong, bright, and brave as day.

And seeing the king there stand, the knight
Drew rein before his face to alight
In reverence made for love's sake bright
With joy that set his face alight
  As theirs who see, alive, above,
The sovereign of their souls, whose name
To them is even as love's own flame
To enkindle hope that heeds not fame
  And knows no lord but love.

And Arthur smiled on him, and said,
" Right welcome be thou : by my head,
I would not wish me better sped.
For even but now there came and fled
  Before me like a cloud that flies

A knight that made most heavy cheer,
I know not wherefore ; nor may fear
Or pity give my heart to hear
    Or lighten on mine eyes.

" But even for fear's and pity's sake
Fain were I thou shouldst overtake
And fetch again this knight that spake
No word of answering grace to make
    Reply to mine that hailed him : thou,
By force or by goodwill, shalt bring
His face before me."   " Yea, my king,"
Quoth Balen, "and a greater thing
    Were less than is my vow.

" I would the task required and heard
Were heavier than your sovereign word
Hath laid on me : " and thence he spurred
Elate at heart as youth, and stirred
    With hope as blithe as fires a boy :
And many a mile he rode, and found
Far in a forest's glimmering bound
The man he sought afar around
    And seeing took fire for joy.

And with him went a maiden, fair
As flowers aflush with April air.
And Balen bade him turn him there
To tell the king what woes they were
    That bowed him down so sore : and he
Made woful answer : " This should do
Great scathe to me, with nought for you
Of help that hope might hearken to
    For boot that may not be."

And Balen answered : "I were loth
To fight as one perforce made wroth
With one that owes by knighthood's oath
One love, one service, and one troth
    With me to him whose gracious hand
Holds fast the helm of knighthood here
Whereby man's hope and heart may steer :
I pray you let not sorrow or fear
    Against his bidding stand."

The strange knight gazed on him, and spake :
"Will you, for Arthur's royal sake,
Be warrant for me that I take
No scathe from strife that man may make ?
    Then will I go with you."   And he
Made joyous answer : "Yea, for I
Will be your warrant or will die."
And thence they rode with hearts as high
    As men's that search the sea.

And as by noon's large light the twain
Before the tented hall drew rein,
Suddenly fell the strange knight, slain
By one that came and went again
    And none might see him ; but his spear
Clove through the body, swift as fire,
The man whose doom, forefelt as dire,
Had darkened all his life's desire,
    As one that death held dear.

And dying he turned his face and said,
"Lo now thy warrant that my head
Should fall not, following forth where led
A knight whose pledge hath left me dead.
    This darkling manslayer hath to name

Garlon : take thou my goodlier steed,
Seeing thine is less of strength and speed,
And ride, if thou be knight indeed,
    Even thither whence we came.

" And as the maiden's fair behest
Shall bid you follow on my quest,
Follow : and when God's will sees best,
Revenge my death, and let me rest
    As one that lived and died a knight,
Unstained of shame alive or dead."
And Balen, wrung with sorrow, said,
" That shall I do : my hand and head
    I pledge to do you right."

And thence with sorrowing heart and cheer
He rode, in grief that cast out fear
Lest death in darkness yet were near,
And bore the truncheon of the spear
    Wherewith the woful knight lay slain
To her with whom he rode, and she
Still bare it with her, fain to see
What righteous doom of God's might be
    The darkling manslayer's bane.

And down a dim deep woodland way
They rode between the boughs asway
With flickering winds whose flash and play
Made sunlight sunnier where the day
    Laughed, leapt, and fluttered like a bird
Caught in a light loose leafy net
That earth for amorous heaven had set
To hold and see the sundawn yet
    And hear what morning heard.

II.   G 2

There in the sweet soft shifting light
Across their passage rode a knight
Flushed hot from hunting as from fight,
And seeing the sorrow-stricken sight
     Made question of them why they rode
As mourners sick at heart and sad,
When all alive about them bade
Sweet earth for heaven's sweet sake be glad
     As heaven for earth's love glowed.

"Me lists not tell you," Balen said.
The strange knight's face grew keen and red ;
"Now, might my hand but keep my head,
Even here should one of twain lie dead
     Were he no better armed than I."
And Balen spake with smiling speed,
Where scorn and courtesy kept heed
Of either : "That should little need :
     Not here shall either die."

And all the cause he told him through
As one that feared not though he knew
All : and the strange knight spake anew,
Saying : "I will part no more from you
     While life shall last me."   So they went
Where he might arm himself to ride,
And rode across wild ways and wide
To where against a churchyard side
     A hermit's harbour leant.

And there against them riding came
Fleet as the lightning's laugh and flame
The invisible evil, even the same
They sought and might not curse by name
     As hell's foul child on earth set free,

And smote the strange knight through, and fled,
And left the mourners by the dead.
" Alas, again," Sir Balen said,
    "This wrong he hath done to me."

And there they laid their dead to sleep
Royally, lying where wild winds keep
Keen watch and wail more soft and deep
Than where men's choirs bid music weep
    And song like incense heave and swell.
And forth again they rode, and found
Before them, dire in sight and sound,
A castle girt about and bound
    With sorrow like a spell.

Above it seemed the sun at noon
Sad as a wintry withering moon
That shudders while the waste wind's tune
Craves ever none may guess what boon,
    But all may know the boon for dire.
And evening on its darkness fell
More dark than very death's farewell,
And night about it hung like hell,
    Whose fume the dawn made fire.

And Balen lighted down and passed
Within the gateway, whence no blast
Rang as the sheer portcullis, cast
Suddenly down, fell, and made fast
    The gate behind him, whence he spied
A sudden rage of men without
And ravin of a murderous rout
That girt the maiden hard about
    With death on either side.

And seeing that shame and peril, fear
Bade wrath and grief awake and hear
What shame should say in fame's wide ear
If she, by sorrow sealed more dear
    Than joy might make her, so should die :
And up the tower's curled stair he sprang
As one that flies death's deadliest fang,
And leapt right out amid their gang
    As fire from heaven on high.

And they thereunder seeing the knight
Unhurt among their press alight
And bare his sword for chance of fight
Stood from him, loth to strive or smite,
    And bade him hear their woful word,
That not the maiden's death they sought ;
But there through years too dire for thought
Had lain their lady stricken, and nought
    Might heal her : and he heard.

For there a maiden clean and whole
In virgin body and virgin soul,
Whose name was writ on royal roll,
That would but stain a silver bowl
    With offering of her stainless blood,
Therewith might heal her : so they stayed
For hope's sad sake each blameless maid
There journeying in that dolorous shade
    Whose bloom was bright in bud.

No hurt nor harm to her it were
If she should yield a sister there
Some tribute of her blood, and fare
Forth with this joy at heart to bear,
    That all unhurt and unafraid

This grace she had here by God's grace wrought.
And kindling all with kindly thought
And love that saw save love's self nought,
     Shone, smiled, and spake the maid.

"Good knight of mine, good will have I
To help this healing though I die."
"Nay," Balen said, "but love may try
What help in living love may lie.
     —I will not lose the life of her
While my life lasteth."   So she gave
The tribute love was fain to crave,
But might not heal though fain to save,
     Were God's grace helpfuller.

Another maid in later Mays
Won with her life that woful praise,
And died.   But they, when surging day's
Deep tide fulfilled the dawn's wide ways,
     Rode forth, and found by day or night
No chance to cross their wayfaring
Till when they saw the fourth day spring
A knight's hall gave them harbouring
     Rich as a king's house might.

And while they sat at meat and spake
Words bright and kind as grace might make
Sweet for true knighthood's kindly sake,
They heard a cry beside them break
     The still-souled joy of blameless rest.
"What noise is this?" quoth Balen.   "Nay,"
His knightly host made answer, "may
Our grief not grieve you though I say
     How here I dwell unblest.

" Not many a day has lived and died
Since at a tournay late I tried
My strength to smite and turn and ride
Against a knight of kinglike pride,
        King Pellam's brother : twice I smote
The splendour of his strength to dust :
And he, fulfilled of hate's fierce lust,
Swore vengeance, pledged for hell to trust,
        And keen as hell's wide throat.

" Invisible as the spirit of night
That heaven and earth in depth and height
May see not by the mild moon's light
Nor even when stars would grant them sight,
        He walks and slays as plague's blind breath
Slays : and my son, whose anguish here
Makes moan perforce that mars our cheer,
He wounded, even ere love might fear
        That hate were strong as death.

" Nor may my son be whole till he
Whose stroke through him hath stricken me
Shall give again his blood to be
Our healing : yet may no man see
        This felon, clothed with darkness round
And keen as lightning's life."   Thereon
Spake Balen, and his presence shone
Even as the sun's when stars are gone
        That hear dawn's trumpet sound.

" That knight I know : two knights of mine,
Two comrades, sealed by faith's bright sign,
Whose eyes as ours that live should shine,
And drink the golden sunlight's wine
        With joy's thanksgiving that they live,

He hath slain in even the same blind wise :
Were all wide wealth beneath the skies
Mine, might I meet him, eyes on eyes,
    All would I laugh to give."

His host made answer, and his gaze
Grew bright with trust as dawn's moist maze
With fire : " Within these twenty days,
King Pellam, lord of Lystenayse,
    Holds feast through all this country cried,
And there before the knightly king
May no knight come except he bring
For witness of his wayfaring
    His paramour or bride.

" And there that day, so soon to shine,
This knight, your felon foe and mine,
Shall show, full-flushed with bloodred wine,
The fierce false face whereon we pine
    To wreak the wrong he hath wrought us, bare
As shame should see and brand it."   " Then,"
Said Balen, " shall he give again
His blood to heal your son, and men
    Shall see death blind him there."

" Forth will we fare to-morrow," said
His host : and forth, as sunrise led,
They rode ; and fifteen days were fled
Ere toward their goal their steeds had sped.
    And there alighting might they find
For Balen's host no place to rest,
Who came without a gentler guest
Beside him : and that household's hest
    Bade leave his sword behind.

" Nay," Balen said, " that do I not :
My country's custom stands, God wot,
That none whose lot is knighthood's lot,
To ride where chance as fire is hot
        With hope or promise given of fight,
Shall fail to keep, for knighthood's part,
His weapon with him as his heart ;
And as I came will I depart,
        Or hold herein my right."

Then gat he leave to wear his sword
Beside the strange king's festal board
Where feasted many a knight and lord
In seemliness of fair accord :
        And Balen asked of one beside,
" Is there not in this court, if fame
Keep faith, a knight that hath to name
Garlon ? " and saying that word of shame,
        He scanned that place of pride.

" Yonder he goeth against the light,
He with the face as swart as night,"
Quoth the other : " but he rides to fight
Hid round by charms from all men's sight,
        And many a noble knight he hath slain,
Being wrapt in darkness deep as hell
And silence dark as shame." " Ah, well,"
Said Balen, " is that he ? the spell
        May be the sorcerer's bane."

Then Balen gazed upon him long,
And thought, " If here I wreak my wrong,
Alive I may not scape, so strong
The felon's friends about him throng ;
        And if I leave him here alive,

This chance perchance may life not give
Again : much evil, if he live,
He needs must do, should fear forgive
  When wrongs bid strike and strive."

And Garlon, seeing how Balen's eye
Dwelt on him as his heart waxed high
With joy in wrath to see him nigh,
Rose wolf-like with a wolfish cry
  And crossed and smote him on the face,
Saying, " Knight, what wouldst thou with me ?
  Eat,
For shame, and gaze not : eat thy meat :
Do that thou art come for : stands thy seat
  Next ours of royal race ? "

" Well hast thou said : thy rede rings true ;
That which I came for will I do,"
Quoth Balen : forth his fleet sword flew,
And clove the head of Garlon through
  Clean to the shoulders. Then he cried
Loud to his lady, " Give me here
The truncheon of the shameful spear
Wherewith he slew your knight, when fear
  Bade hate in darkness ride."

And gladly, bright with grief made glad,
She gave the truncheon as he bade,
For still she bare it with her, sad
And strong in hopeless hope she had,
  Through all dark days of thwarting fear,
To see if doom should fall aright
And as God's fire-fraught thunder smite
That head, clothed round with hell-faced night,
  Bare now before her here.

And Balen smote therewith the dead
Dark felon's body through, and said
Aloud, " With even this truncheon, red
With baser blood than brave men bled
    Whom in thy shameful hand it slew,
Thou hast slain a nobler knight, and now
It clings and cleaves thy body : thou
Shalt cleave again no brave man's brow,
    Though hell would aid anew."

And toward his host he turned and spake ;
" Now for your son's long-suffering sake
Blood ye may fetch enough, and take
Wherewith to heal his hurt, and make
    Death warm as life."   Then rose a cry
Loud as the wind's when stormy spring
Makes all the woodland rage and ring :
" Thou hast slain my brother," said the king,
    " And here with him shalt die."

" Ay ? " Balen laughed him answer.   " Well,
Do it then thyself."   And the answer fell
Fierce as a blast of hate from hell,
" No man of mine that with me dwell
    Shall strike at thee but I their lord
For love of this my brother slain."
And Pellam caught and grasped amain
A grim great weapon, fierce and fain
    To feed his hungering sword.

And eagerly he smote, and sped
Not well : for Balen's blade, yet red
With lifeblood of the murderous dead,
Between the swordstroke and his head
    Shone, and the strength of the eager stroke

Shore it in sunder : then the knight,
Naked and weaponless for fight,
Ran seeking him a sword to smite
    As hope within him woke.

And so their flight for deathward fast
From chamber forth to chamber passed
Where lay no weapon, till the last
Whose doors made way for Balen cast
    Upon him as a sudden spell
Wonder that even as lightning leapt
Across his heart and eyes, and swept
As storm across his soul that kept
    Wild watch, and watched not well.

For there the deed he did, being near
Death's danger, breathless as the deer
Driven hard to bay, but void of fear,
Brought sorrow down for many a year
    On many a man in many a land.
All glorious shone that chamber, bright
As burns at sunrise heaven's own height :
With cloth of gold the bed was dight,
    That flamed on either hand.

And one he saw within it lie :
A table of all clear gold thereby
Stood stately, fair as morning's eye,
With four strong silver pillars, high
    And firm as faith and hope may be :
And on it shone the gift he sought,
A spear most marvellously wrought,
That when his eye and handgrip caught
    Small fear at heart had he.

Right on King Pellam then, as fire
Turns when the thwarting winds wax higher,
He turned, and smote him down.   So dire
The stroke was, when his heart's desire
        Struck, and had all its fill of hate,
That as the king fell swooning down
Fell the walls, rent from base to crown,
Prone as prone seas that break and drown
        Ships fraught with doom for freight.

And there for three days' silent space
Balen and Pellam face to face
Lay dead or deathlike, and the place
Was death's blind kingdom, till the grace
        That God had given the sacred seer
For counsel or for comfort led
His Merlin thither, and he said,
Standing between the quick and dead,
        " Rise up, and rest not here."

And Balen rose and set his eyes
Against the seer's as one that tries
His heart against the sea's and sky's
And fears not if he lives or dies,
        Saying, " I would have my damosel,
Ere I fare forth, to fare with me."
And sadly Merlin answered, " See
Where now she lies ; death knows if she
        Shall now fare ill or well.

" And in this world we meet no more,
Balen."   And Balen, sorrowing sore,
Though fearless yet the heart he bore
Beat toward the life that lay before,
        Rode forth through many a wild waste land

Where men cried out against him, mad
With grievous faith in fear that bade
Their wrath make moan for doubt they had
    Lest hell had armed his hand.

For in that chamber's wondrous shrine
Was part of Christ's own blood, the wine
Shed of the true triumphal vine
Whose growth bids earth's deep darkness shine
    As heaven's deep light through the air and sea ;
That mystery toward our northern shore
Arimathean Joseph bore
For healing of our sins of yore,
    That grace even there might be.

And with that spear there shrined apart
Was Christ's side smitten to the heart.
And fiercer than the lightning's dart
The stroke was, and the deathlike smart
    Wherewith, nigh drained of blood and breath,
The king lay stricken as one long dead :
And Joseph's was the blood there shed,
For near akin was he that bled,
    Near even as life to death.

And therefore fell on all that land
Sorrow : for still on either hand,
As Balen rode alone and scanned
Bright fields and cities built to stand
    Till time should break them, dead men lay ;
And loud and long from all their folk
Living, one cry that cursed him broke ;
Three countries had his dolorous stroke
    Slain, or should surely slay.

VII

In winter, when the year burns low
As fire wherein no firebrands glow,
And winds dishevel as they blow
The lovely stormy wings of snow,
 The hearts of northern men burn **bright**
With joy that mocks the joy of spring
To hear all heaven's keen clarions ring
Music that bids the spirit sing
 And day give thanks for night.

Aloud and dark as hell or hate
Round Balen's head the wind of fate
Blew storm and cloud from death's wide gate :
But joy as grief in him was great
 To face God's doom and live or die,
Sorrowing for ill wrought unaware,
Rejoicing in desire to dare
All ill that innocence might bear
 With changeless heart and eye.

Yet passing fain he was when past
Those lands and woes at length and last.
Eight times, as thence he fared forth fast,
Dawn rose and even was overcast
 With starry darkness dear as day,

Before his venturous quest might meet
Adventure, seeing within a sweet
Green low-lying forest, hushed in heat,
    A tower that barred his way.

Strong summer, dumb with rapture, bound
With golden calm the woodlands round
Wherethrough the knight forth faring found
A knight that on the greenwood ground
    Sat mourning : fair he was to see,
And moulded as for love or fight
A maiden's dreams might frame her knight ;
But sad in joy's far-flowering sight
    As grief's blind thrall might be.

" God save you," Balen softly said,
" What grief bows down your heart and head
Thus, as one sorrowing for his dead ?
Tell me, if haply I may stead
    In aught your sorrow, that I may."
" Sir knight," that other said, " thy word
Makes my grief heavier that I heard."
And pity and wonder inly stirred
    Drew Balen thence away.

And so withdrawn with silent speed
He saw the sad knight's stately steed,
A war-horse meet for warrior's need,
That none who passed might choose but heed,
    So strong he stood, so great, so fair,
With eyes afire for flight or fight,
A joy to look on, mild in might,
And swift and keen and kind as light,
    And all as clear of care.

And Balen, gazing on him, heard
Again his master's woful word
Sound sorrow through the calm unstirred
By fluttering wind or flickering bird,
　　Thus : " Ah, fair lady and faithless, why
Break thy pledged faith to meet me ? soon
An hour beyond thy trothplight noon
Shall strike my death-bell, and thy boon
　　Is this, that here I die.

" My curse for all thy gifts may be
Heavier than death or night on thee ;
For now this sword thou gavest me
Shall set me from thy bondage free."
　　And there the man had died self-slain,
But Balen leapt on him and caught
The blind fierce hand that fain had wrought
Self-murder, stung with fire of thought,
　　As rage makes anguish fain.

Then, mad for thwarted grief, " Let go
My hand," the fool of wrath and woe
Cried, " or I slay thee."　Scarce the glow
In Balen's cheek and eye might show,
　　As dawn shows day while seas lie chill,
He heard, though pity took not heed,
But smiled and spake, " That shall not need :
What man may do to bid you speed
　　I, so God speed me, will."

And the other craved his name, beguiled
By hope that made his madness mild.
Again Sir Balen spake and smiled :
" My name is Balen, called the Wild
　　By knights whom kings and courts make tame,

Because I ride alone afar
And follow but my soul for star."
" Ah, sir, I know the knight you are
        And all your fiery fame.

·" The knight that bears two swords I know,
Most praised of all men, friend and foe,
For prowess of your hands, that show
Dark war the way where balefires glow
        And kindle glory like the dawn's."
So spake the sorrowing knight, and stood
As one whose heart fresh hope made good :
And forth they rode by wold and wood
        And down the glimmering lawns.

And Balen craved his name who rode
Beside him, where the wild wood glowed
With joy to feel how noontide flowed
Through glade and glen and rough green road
        Till earth grew joyful as the sea.
" My name is Garnysshe of the Mount,
A poor man's son of none account,"
He said, " where springs of loftier fount
        Laugh loud with pride to be.

" But strength in weakness lives and stands
As rocks that rise through shifting sands ;
And for the prowess of my hands
One made me knight and gave me lands,
        Duke Hermel, lord from far to near,
Our prince ; and she that loved me—she
I love, and deemed she loved but me,
His daughter, pledged her faith to be
        Ere now beside me here."

And Balen, brief of speech as light
Whose word, beheld of depth and height,
Strikes silence through the stars of night,
Spake, and his face as dawn's grew bright,
    For hope to help a happier man,
" How far then lies she hence ? "   " By this,"
Her lover sighed and said, " I wis,
Not six fleet miles the passage is,
    And straight as thought could span."

So rode they swift and sure, and found
A castle walled and dyked around :
And Balen, as a warrior bound
On search where hope might fear to sound
    The darkness of the deeps of doubt,
Made entrance through the guardless gate
As life, while hope in life grows great,
Makes way between the doors of fate
    That death may pass thereout.

Through many a glorious chamber, wrought
For all delight that love's own thought
Might dream or dwell in, Balen sought
And found of all he looked for nought,
    For like a shining shell her bed
Shone void and vacant of her : thence
Through devious wonders bright and dense
He passed and saw with shame-struck sense
    Where shame and faith lay dead.

Down in a sweet small garden, fair
With flowerful joy in the ardent air,
He saw, and raged with loathing, where
She lay with love-dishevelled hair
    Beneath a broad bright laurel tree

And clasped in amorous arms a knight,
The unloveliest that his scornful sight
Had dwelt on yet ; a shame the bright
    Broad noon might shrink to see.

And thence in wrathful hope he turned,
Hot as the heart within him burned,
To meet the knight whose love, so spurned
And spat on and made nought of, yearned
    And dreamed and hoped and lived in vain,
And said, " I have found her sleeping fast,"
And led him where the shadows cast
From leaves wherethrough light winds ran past
    Screened her from sun and rain.

But Garnysshe, seeing, reeled as he stood
Like a tree, kingliest of the wood,
Half hewn through : and the burning blood
Through lips and nostrils burst aflood :
    And gathering back his rage and might
As broken breakers rally and roar
The loud wind down that drives off shore,
He smote their heads off : there no more
    Their life might shame the light.

Then turned he back toward Balen, mad
With grief, and said, " The grief I had
Was nought : ere this my life was glad :
Thou hast done this deed : I was but sad
    And fearful how my hope might fare :
I had lived my sorrow down, hadst thou
Not shown me what I saw but now."
The sorrow and scorn on Balen's brow
    Bade silence curb him there.

And Balen answered : " What I did
I did to hearten thee and bid
Thy courage know that shame should rid
A man's high heart of love that hid
      Blind shame within its core : God knows,
I did, to set a bondman free,
But as I would thou hadst done by me,
That seeing what love must die to see
      Love's end might well be woe's."

" Alas," the woful weakling said,
" I have slain what most I loved : I have shed
The blood most near my heart : the head
Lies cold as earth, defiled and dead,
      That all my life was lighted by,
That all my soul bowed down before,
And now may bear with life no more :
For now my sorrow that I bore
      Is twofold, and I die."

Then with his red wet sword he rove
His breast in sunder, where it clove
Life, and no pulse against it strove,
So sure and strong the deep stroke drove
      Deathward : and Balen, seeing him dead,
Rode thence, lest folk would say he had slain
Those three : and ere three days again
Had seen the sun's might wax and wane,
      Far forth he had spurred and sped.

And riding past a cross whereon
Broad golden letters written shone,
Saying, " No knight born may ride alone
Forth toward this castle," and all the stone
      Glowed in the sun's glare even as though

Blood stained it from the crucified
Dead burden of one that there had died,
An old hoar man he saw beside
    Whose face was wan as woe.

" Balen the Wild," he said, " this way
Thy way lies not : thou hast passed to-day
Thy bands : but turn again, and stay
Thy passage, while thy soul hath sway
    Within thee, and through God's good power
It will avail thee : " and anon
His likeness as a cloud was gone,
And Balen's heart within him shone
    Clear as the cloudless hour.

Nor fate nor fear might overcast
The soul now near its peace at last.
Suddenly, thence as forth he past,
A mighty and a deadly blast
    Blown of a hunting-horn he heard,
As when the chase hath nobly sped.
" That blast is blown for me," he said,
" The prize am I who am yet not dead,"
    And smiled upon the word.

As toward a royal hart's death rang
That note, whence all the loud wood sang
With winged and living sound that sprang
Like fire, and keen as fire's own fang
    Pierced the sweet silence that it slew.
But nought like death or strife was here :
Fair semblance and most goodly cheer
They made him, they whose troop drew near
    As death among them drew.

A hundred ladies well arrayed
And many a knight well weaponed made
That kindly show of cheer : the glade
Shone round them till its very shade
    Lightened and laughed from grove to **lawn**
To hear and see them : so they brought
Within a castle fair as thought
Could dream that wizard hands had wrought
    The guest among them drawn.

All manner of glorious joy was there :
Harping and dancing, loud and fair,
And minstrelsy that made of air
Fire, so like fire its raptures were.
    Then the chief lady spake on high :
" Knight with the two swords, one of two
Must help you here or fall from you :
For needs you now must have ado
    And joust with one hereby.

" A good knight guards an island here
Against all swords that chance brings near,
And there with stroke of sword and spear
Must all for whom these halls make cheer
    Fight, and redeem or yield up life."
" An evil custom," Balen said,
" Is this, that none whom chance hath led
Hither, if knighthood crown his head,
    May pass unstirred to strife."

" You shall not have ado to fight
Here save against one only knight,"
She said, and all her face grew bright
As hell-fire, lit with hungry light
    That wicked laughter touched with flame.

"Well, since I shall thereto," said he,
" I am ready at heart as death for me :
Fain would I be where death should be
    And life should lose its name.

" But travelling men whose goal afar
Shines as a cloud-constraining star
Are often weary, and wearier are
Their steeds that feel each fret and jar
    Wherewith the wild ways wound them : yet,
Albeit my horse be weary, still
My heart is nowise weary ; will
Sustains it even till death fulfil
    My trust upon him set."

" Sir," said a knight thereby that stood,
" Meseems your shield is now not good
But worn with warrior work, nor could
Sustain in strife the strokes it would :
    A larger will I lend you."   " Ay,
Thereof I thank you," Balen said,
Being single of heart as one that read
No face aright whence faith had fled,
    Nor dreamed that faith could fly.

And so he took that shield unknown
And left for treason's touch his own,
And toward that island rode alone,
Nor heard the blast against him blown
    Sound in the wind's and water's sound,
But hearkening toward the stream's edge heard
Nought save the soft stream's rippling word,
Glad with the gladness of a bird,
    That sang to the air around.

And there against the water-side
He saw, fast moored to rock and ride,
A fair great boat anear abide
Like one that waits the turning tide,
        Wherein embarked his horse and he
Passed over toward no kindly strand :
And where they stood again on land
There stood a maiden hard at hand
        Who seeing them wept to see.

And " O knight Balen," was her cry,
" Why have ye left your own shield ? why
Come hither out of time to die ?
For had ye kept your shield, thereby
        Ye had yet been known, and died not here.
Great pity it is of you this day
As ever was of knight, or may
Be ever, seeing in war's bright way
        Praise knows not Balen's peer."

And Balen said, " Thou hast heard my name
Right : it repenteth me, though shame
May tax me not with base men's blame,
That ever, hap what will, I came
        Within this country ; yet, being come,
For shame I may not turn again
Now, that myself and nobler men
May scorn me : now is more than then,
        And faith bids fear be dumb.

" Be it life or death, my chance I take,
Be it life's to build or death's to break :
And fall what may, me lists not make
Moan for sad life's or death's sad sake."
        Then looked he on his armour, glad

And high of heart, and found it strong :
And all his soul became a song
And soared in prayer that soared not long,
    For all the hope it had.

Then saw he whence against him came
A steed whose trappings shone like flame,
And he that rode him showed the same
Fierce colour, bright as fire or fame,
    But dark the visors were as night
That hid from Balen Balan's face,
And his from Balan : God's own grace
Forsook them for a shadowy space
    Where darkness cast out light.

The two swords girt that Balen bare
Gave Balan for a breath's while there
Pause, wondering if indeed it were
Balen his brother, bound to dare
    The chance of that unhappy quest :
But seeing not as he thought to see
His shield, he deemed it was not he,
And so, as fate bade sorrow be,
    They laid their spears in rest.

So mighty was the course they ran
With spear to spear so great of span,
Each fell back stricken, man by man,
Horse by horse, borne down : so the ban
    That wrought by doom against them wrought :
But Balen by his falling steed
Was bruised the sorer, being indeed
Way-weary, like a rain-bruised reed,
    With travel ere he fought.

And Balen rose again from swoon
First, and went toward him : all too soon
He too then rose, and the evil boon
Of strength came back, and the evil tune
    Of battle unnatural made again
Mad music as for death's wide ear
Listening and hungering toward the near
Last sigh that life or death might hear
    At last from dying men.

Balan smote Balen first, and clove
His lifted shield that rose and strove
In vain against the stroke that drove
Down : as the web that morning wove
    Of glimmering pearl from spray to spray
Dies when the strong sun strikes it, so
Shrank the steel, tempered thrice to show
Strength, as the mad might of the blow
    Shore Balen's helm away.

Then turning as a turning wave
Against the land-wind, blind and brave
In hope that dreams despair may save,
With even the unhappy sword that gave
    The gifts of fame and fate in one
He smote his brother, and there had nigh
Felled him : and while they breathed, his eye
Glanced up, and saw beneath the sky
    Sights fairer than the sun.

The towers of all the castle there
Stood full of ladies, blithe and fair
As the earth beneath and the amorous air
About them and above them were :
    So toward the blind and fateful fight

Again those brethren went, and sore
Were all the strokes they smote and bore,
And breathed again, and fell once more
  To battle in their sight.

With blood that either spilt and bled
Was all the ground they fought on red,
And each knight's hauberk hewn and shred
Left each unmailed and naked, shed
  From off them even as mantles cast :
And oft they breathed, and drew but breath
Brief as the word strong sorrow saith,
And poured and drank the draught of death,
  Till fate was full at last.

And Balan, younger born than he
Whom darkness bade him slay, and be
Slain, as in mist where none may see
If aught abide or fall or flee,
  Drew back a little and laid him down,
Dying : but Balen stood, and said,
As one between the quick and dead
Might stand and speak, " What good knight's head
  Hath won this mortal crown ?

" What knight art thou ? for never I
Who now beside thee dead shall die
Found yet the knight afar or nigh
That matched me."   Then his brother's eye
  Flashed pride and love ; he spake and smiled
And felt in death life's quickening flame,
And answered : " Balan is my name,
The good knight Balen's brother ; fame
  Calls and miscalls him wild."

The cry from Balen's lips that sprang
Sprang sharper than his sword's stroke rang.
More keen than death's or memory's fang,
Through sense and soul the shuddering pang
  Shivered : and scarce he had cried, " Alas
That ever I should see this day,"
When sorrow swooned from him away
As blindly back he fell, and lay
  Where sleep lets anguish pass.

But Balan rose on hands and knees
And crawled by childlike dim degrees
Up toward his brother, as a breeze
Creeps wingless over sluggard seas
  When all the wind's heart fails it : so
Beneath their mother's eyes had he,
A babe that laughed with joy to be,
Made toward him standing by her knee
  For love's sake long ago.

Then, gathering strength up for a space,
From off his brother's dying face
With dying hands that wrought apace
While death and life would grant them grace
  He loosed his helm and knew not him,
So scored with blood it was, and hewn
Athwart with darkening wounds : but soon
Life strove and shuddered through the swoon
  Wherein its light lay dim.

And sorrow set these chained words free :
" O Balan, O my brother ! me
Thou hast slain, and I, my brother, thee :
And now far hence, on shore and sea,
  Shall all the wide world speak of us."

" Alas," said Balan, " that I might
Not know you, seeing two swords were dight
About you ; now the unanswering sight
    Hath here found answer thus.

" Because you bore another shield
Than yours, that even ere youth could wield
Like arms with manhood's tried and steeled
Shone as my star of battle-field,
    I deemed it surely might not be
My brother." Then his brother spake
Fiercely : ' Would God, for thy sole sake,
I had my life again, to take
    Revenge for only thee !

" For all this deadly work was wrought
Of one false knight's false word and thought,
Whose mortal craft and counsel caught
And snared my faith who doubted nought,
    And made me put my shield away.
Ah, might I live, I would destroy
That castle for its customs : joy
There makes of grief a deadly toy,
    And death makes night of day."

" Well done were that, if aught were done
Well ever here beneath the sun,"
Said Balan : " better work were none :
For hither since I came and won
    A woful honour born of death,
When here my hap it was to slay
A knight who kept this island way,
I might not pass by night or day
    Hence, as this token saith.

" No more shouldst thou, for all the might
Of heart and hand that seals thee knight
Most noble of all that see the light,
Brother, hadst thou but slain in fight
        Me, and arisen unscathed and whole,
As would to God thou hadst risen ! though here
Light is as darkness, hope as fear,
And love as hate : and none draws near
        Save toward a mortal goal."

Then, fair as any poison-flower
Whose blossom blights the withering bower
Whereon its blasting breath has power,
Forth fared the lady of the tower
        With many a lady and many a knight,
And came across the water-way
Even where on death's dim border lay
Those brethren sent of her to slay
        And die in kindless fight.

And all those hard light hearts were swayed
With pity passing like a shade
That stays not, and may be not stayed,
To hear the mutual moan they made,
        Each to behold his brother die,
Saying, " Both we came out of one tomb,
One star-crossed mother's woful womb,
And so within one grave-pit's gloom
        Untimely shall we lie."

And Balan prayed, as God should bless
That lady for her gentleness,
That where the battle's mortal stress
Had made for them perforce to press
        The bed whence never man may rise

They twain, free now from hopes and fears,
Might sleep ; and she, as one that hears,
Bowed her bright head : and very tears
    Fell from her cold fierce eyes.

Then Balen prayed her send a priest
To housel them, that ere they ceased
The hansel of the heavenly feast
That fills with light from the answering east
    The sunset of the life of man
Might bless them, and their lips be kissed
With death's requickening eucharist,
And death's and life's dim sunlit mist
    Pass as a stream that ran.

And so their dying rites were done :
And Balen, seeing the death-struck sun
Sink, spake as he whose goal is won :
" Now, when our trophied tomb is one,
    And over us our tale is writ,
How two that loved each other, two
Born and begotten brethren, slew
Each other, none that reads anew
    Shall choose but weep for it.

" And no good knight and no good man
Whose eye shall ever come to scan
The record of the imperious ban
That made our life so sad a span
    Shall read or hear, who shall not pray
For us for ever." Then anon
Died Balan ; but the sun was gone,
And deep the stars of midnight shone,
    Ere Balen passed away.

And there low lying, as hour on hour
Fled, all his life in all its flower
Came back as in a sunlit shower
Of dreams, when sweet-souled sleep has power
    On life less sweet and glad to be.
He drank the draught of life's first wine
Again : he saw the moorland shine,
The rioting rapids of the Tyne,
    The woods, the cliffs, the sea.

The joy that lives at heart and home,
The joy to rest, the joy to roam,
The joy of crags and scaurs he clomb,
The rapture of the encountering foam
    Embraced and breasted of the boy,
The first good steed his knees bestrode,
The first wild sound of songs that flowed
Through ears that thrilled and heart that glowed,
    Fulfilled his death with joy.

So, dying not as a coward that dies
And dares not look in death's dim eyes
Straight as the stars on seas and skies
Whence moon and sun recoil and rise,
    He looked on life and death, and slept.
And there with morning Merlin came,
And on the tomb that told their fame
He wrote by Balan's Balen's name,
    And gazed thereon, and wept.

For all his heart within him yearned
With pity like as fire that burned.
The fate his fateful eye discerned
Far off now dimmed it, ere he turned
    His face toward Camelot, to tell

Arthur of all the storms that woke
Round Balen, and the dolorous stroke,
And how that last blind battle broke
    The consummated spell.

" Alas," King Arthur said, " this day
I have heard the worst that woe might say :
For in this world that wanes away
I know not two such knights as they."
    This is the tale that memory writes
Of men whose names like stars shall stand,
Balen and Balan, sure of hand,
Two brethren of Northumberland,
    In life and death good knights.

ATALANTA IN CALYDON

A TRAGEDY

Τοὺς ζῶντας εὖ δρᾶν · κατθανὼν δὲ πᾶς ἀνὴρ
Γῆ καὶ σκιά · τὸ μηδὲν εἰς οὐδὲν ῥέπει
                         EUR. *Fr. Mel.* 20 (537)

TO THE MEMORY

OF

WALTER SAVAGE LANDOR

I NOW DEDICATE, WITH EQUAL AFFECTION, REVERENCE, AND REGRET, A
POEM INSCRIBED TO HIM WHILE YET ALIVE IN WORDS WHICH ARE NOW
RETAINED BECAUSE THEY WERE LAID BEFORE HIM ; AND TO WHICH, RATHER
THAN CANCEL THEM, I HAVE ADDED SUCH OTHERS AS WERE EVOKED BY
THE NEWS OF HIS DEATH : THAT THOUGH LOSING THE PLEASURE I MAY
NOT LOSE THE HONOUR OF INSCRIBING IN FRONT OF MY WORK THE HIGHEST
OF CONTEMPORARY NAMES.

ᾤχεο δὴ Βορέηθεν ἀπότροπος· ἀλλά σε Νύμφαι
   ἤγαγον ἀσπασίαν ἡδύπνοοι καθ' ἅλα,
πληροῦσαι μέλιτος θεόθεν στόμα, μή τι Ποσειδῶν
   βλάψῃ, ἐν ὠσὶν ἔχων σὴν μελίγηρυν ὄπα.
τοῖος ἀοιδὸς ἔφυς· ἡμεῖς δ' ἔτι κλαίομεν, οἵ σου
   δευόμεθ' οἰχομένου, καί σε ποθοῦμεν ἀεί.
εἶπε δὲ Πιερίδων τις ἀναστρεφθεῖσα πρὸς ἄλλην·
   ἦλθεν, ἰδού, πάντων φίλτατος ἦλθε βροτῶν,
στέμματα δρεψάμενος νεοθηλέα χερσὶ γεραιαῖς,
   καὶ πολιὸν δάφναις ἀμφεκάλυψε κάρα,
ἡδύ τι Σικελικαῖς ἐπὶ πηκτίσιν, ἡδύ τι χόρδαις,
   ἀσόμενος· πολλὴν γὰρ μετέβαλλε λύραν,
πολλάκι δ' ἐν βήσσαισι καθήμενον εὗρεν Ἀπόλλων,
   ἄνθεσι δ' ἔστεψεν, τερπνὰ δ' ἔδωκε λέγειν,
Πᾶνά τ' ἀείμνηστόν τε Πίτυν Κόρυθόν τε δύσεδρον,
   ἥν τ' ἐφίλησε θεὰν θνητὸς Ἀμαδρυάδα·
πόντου δ' ἐν μεγάροισιν ἐκοίμισε Κυμοδάμειαν,
   τήν τ' Ἀγαμεμνονίαν παῖδ' ἀπέδωκε πατρί,
πρὸς δ' ἱεροὺς Δελφοὺς θεόπληκτον ἔπεμψεν Ὀρέστην·
   πειρόμενον στυγεραῖς ἔνθα καὶ ἔνθα θεαῖς.

ᾤχεο δὴ καὶ ἄνευθε φίλων καὶ ἄνευθεν ἀοιδῆς,
  δρεψόμενος μαλακῆς ἄνθεα Περσεφόνης.
ᾤχεο· κοὐκ ἔτ' ἔσει, κοὐκ αὖ ποτέ σοι παρεδοῦμαι
  ἀζόμενος, χειρῶν χερσὶ θιγὼν ὁσίαις·
νῦν δ' αὖ μνησάμενον γλυκύπικρος ὑπήλυθεν αἰδώς,
  οἷα τυχὼν οἵου πρὸς σέθεν οἷος ἔχω·
οὔποτε σοῖς, γέρον, ὄμμα φίλοις φίλον ὄμμασι τέρψω
  σῆς, γέρον, ἀψάμενος, φίλτατε, δεξιτερᾶς.
ἦ ψαφαρὰ κόνις, ἦ ψαφαρὸς βίος ἐστι· τί τούτων
  μεῖον ἐφημερίων; οὐ κόνις ἀλλὰ βίος.
ἀλλά μοι ἡδύτερός γε πέλεις πολὺ τῶν ἔτ' ἐόντων,
  ἔπλεο γάρ· σοὶ μὴν ταῦτα θανόντι φέρω,
παῦρα μὲν, ἀλλ' ἀπὸ κῆρος ἐτήτυμα· μηδ' ἀποτρεφθῇς,
  πρὸς δὲ βαλὼν ἔτι νῦν ἥσυχον ὄμμα δέχου.
οὐ γὰρ ἔχω, μέγα δή τι θέλων, σέθεν ἄξια δοῦναι,
  θαπτομένου περ ἀπών· οὐ γὰρ ἔνεστιν ἔμοι·
οὐδὲ μελικρήτου παρέχειν γάνος · εἰ γὰρ ἐνείη
  καί σε χεροῖν ψαύσαι καί σέ ποτ' αὖθις ἰδεῖν,
δάκρυσί τε σπονδαῖς τε κάρα φίλον ἀμφιπολεύειν
  ὀφθαλμούς θ' ἱεροὺς σοὺς ἱερόν τε δέμας.
εἴθ' ὄφελον· μάλα γὰρ τάδ' ἂν ἀμπαύσειε μερίμνης·
  νῦν δὲ πρόσωθεν ἄνευ σήματος οἶκτον ἄγω·
οὐδ' ἐπιτυμβίδιον θρηνῶ μέλος, ἀλλ' ἀπαμυνθεὶς,
  ἀλλ' ἀπάνευθεν ἔχων ἀμφιδάκρυτα πάθη.
ἀλλὰ σὺ χαῖρε θανών, καὶ ἔχων γέρας ἴσθι πρὸς ἀνδρῶν
  πρός τε θεῶν, ἐνέροις εἴ τις ἔπεστι θεός.
χαῖρε γέρον, φίλε χαῖρε πάτερ, πολὺ φέρτατ' ἀοιδῶν
  ὧν ἴδομεν, πολὺ δὴ φέρτατ' ἀεισομένων·
χαῖρε, καὶ ὄλβον ἔχοις, οἷόν γε θανόντες ἔχουσιν,
  ἡσυχίαν ἔχθρας καὶ φιλότητος ἄτερ.

σήματος οἰχομένου ὀοι μνήματ' ἐς ὕστερον ἔσται,
  σοί τε φίλη μνήμη μνήματος οἰχομένου·
ὃν Χάριτες κλαίουσι θεαί, κλαίει δ' Ἀφροδίτη
  καλλιχόροις Μουσῶν τερψαμένη στεφάνοις.
οὐ γὰρ ἅπαξ ἱερούς ποτε γῆρας ἔτριψεν ἀοιδούς·
  τήνδε τὸ σὸν φαίνει μνῆμα τόδ' ἀγλαΐαν.
ἦ φίλος ἦς μακάρεσσι βροτὸς, σοὶ δ' εἴ τινι Νύμφαι
  δῶρα ποθεινὰ νέμειν, ὕστατα δῶρ', ἔδοσαν.
τὰς νῦν χάλκεος ὕπνος ἔβη καὶ ἀνήνεμος αἰὼν,
  καὶ συνθαπτομέναι μοῖραν ἔχουσι μίαν.
εὕδεις καὶ σὺ, καλὸν καὶ ἀγάκλυτον ἐν χθονὶ κοίλῃ
  ὕπνον ἐφικόμενος, σῆς ἀπόνοσφι πάτρας,
τῆλε παρὰ ξανθοῦ Τυρσηνικὸν οἶδμα καθεύδεις
  νάματος, ἡ δ' ἔτι σὴ μαῖά σε γαῖα ποθεῖ,
ἀλλ' ἀπέχεις, καὶ πρόσθε φιλόπτολις ὤν περ ἀπεῖπας·
  εὗδε· μάκαρ δ' ἡμῖν οὐδ' ἀμέγαρτος ἔσει.
βαιὸς ἐπιχθονίων γε χρόνος καὶ μοῖρα κρατήσει,
  τοὺς δέ ποτ' εὐφροσύνη τοὺς δέ ποτ' ἄλγος ἔχει
πολλάκι δ' ἢ βλάπτει φάος ἢ σκότος ἀμφικαλύπτε
  μυρομένους, δάκνει δ' ὕπνος ἐγρηγορότας·
οὐδ' ἔθ' ὅτ' ἐν τύμβοισι κατέδραθεν ὄμμα θανόντων
  ἢ σκότος ἤ τι φάος δήξεται ἠελίου·
οὐδ' ὄναρ ἐννύχιον καὶ ἐνύπνιον οὐδ' ὕπαρ ἔσται
  ἤ ποτε τερπομένοις ἤ ποτ' ὀδυρομένοις·
ἀλλ' ἕνα πάντες ἀεὶ θᾶκον συνέχουσι καὶ ἕδραν
  ἀντὶ βροτῆς ἄβροτον, κάλλιον ἄντι κακῆς·

THE ARGUMENT

ALTHÆA, daughter of Thestius and Eurythemis, queen of Calydon, being with child of Meleager her first-born son, dreamed that she brought forth a brand burning; and upon his birth came the three Fates and prophesied of him three things, namely these; that he should have great strength of his hands, and good fortune in this life, and that he should live no longer when the brand then in the fire were consumed: wherefore his mother plucked it forth and kept it by her. And the child being a man grown sailed with Jason after the fleece of gold, and won himself great praise of all men living; and when the tribes of the north and west made war upon Ætolia, he fought against their army and scattered it. But Artemis, having at the first stirred up these tribes to war against Œneus king of Calydon, because he had offered sacrifice to all the gods saving her alone, but her he had forgotten to honour, was yet more wroth because of the destruction of this army, and sent upon the land of Calydon a wild boar which slew many and wasted all their increase, but him could none slay, and many went against him and perished. Then were all the chief men of Greece gathered together, and among them Atalanta daughter of Iasius the Arcadian, a virgin; for whose sake Artemis let slay the boar, seeing she favoured the

maiden greatly ; and Meleager having despatched it
gave the spoil thereof to Atalanta, as one beyond
measure enamoured of her ; but the brethren of
Althæa his mother, Toxeus and Plexippus, with such
others as misliked that she only should bear off the
praise whereas many had borne the labour, laid wait
for her to take away her spoil ; but Meleager fought
against them and slew them : whom when Althæa
their sister beheld and knew to be slain of her son,
she waxed for wrath and sorrow like as one mad,
and taking the brand whereby the measure of her
son's life was meted to him, she cast it upon a fire ;
and with the wasting thereof his life likewise wasted
away, that being brought back to his father's house
he died in a brief space ; and his mother also endured
not long after for very sorrow ; and this was his end,
and the end of that hunting.

THE PERSONS

CHIEF HUNTSMAN
CHORUS
ALTHÆA
MELEAGER
ŒNEUS
ATALANTA
TOXEUS
PLEXIPPUS
HERALD
MESSENGER
SECOND MESSENGER

ἴστω δ' ὅστις οὐχ ὑπόπτερος
φροντίσιν δαεὶς,
τὰν ἁ παιδολύμας τάλαινα Θεστιὰς μήσατο
πυρδαῆ τινα πρόνοιαν,
καταίθουσα παιδὸς δαφοινὸν
δαλὸν ἥλικ᾽, ἐπεὶ μολὼν
ματρόθεν κελάδησε ;
σύμμετρόν τε διαὶ βίου
μοιρόκραντον ἐς ἆμαρ.

ÆSCH. *Cho.* 602-612

ATALANTA IN CALYDON

CHIEF HUNTSMAN

MAIDEN, and mistress of the months and stars
Now folded in the flowerless fields of heaven,
Goddess whom all gods love with threefold heart,
Being treble in thy divided deity,
A light for dead men and dark hours, a foot
Swift on the hills as morning, and a hand
To all things fierce and fleet that roar and range
Mortal, with gentler shafts than snow or sleep ;
Hear now and help and lift no violent hand,
But favourable and fair as thine eye's beam
Hidden and shown in heaven ; for I all night
Amid the king's hounds and the hunting men
Have wrought and worshipped toward thee ; nor
    shall man
See goodlier hounds or deadlier edge of spears ;
But for the end, that lies unreached at yet
Between the hands and on the knees of gods.
O fair-faced sun, killing the stars and dews
And dreams and desolation of the night !
Rise up, shine, stretch thine hand out, with thy bow
Touch the most dimmest height of trembling heaven,
And burn and break the dark about thy ways,
Shot through and through with arrows ; let thine hair
Lighten as flame above that flameless shell
Which was the moon, and thine eyes fill the world

And thy lips kindle with swift beams ; let earth
Laugh, and the long sea fiery from thy feet
Through all the roar and ripple of streaming springs
And foam in reddening flakes and flying flowers
Shaken from hands and blown from lips of nymphs
Whose hair or breast divides the wandering wave
With salt close tresses cleaving lock to lock,
All gold, or shuddering and unfurrowed snow ;
And all the winds about thee with their wings,
And fountain-heads of all the watered world ;
Each horn of Acheloüs, and the green
Euenus, wedded with the straitening sea.
For in fair time thou comest ; come also thou,
Twin-born with him, and virgin, Artemis,
And give our spears their spoil, the wild boar's hide,
Sent in thine anger against us for sin done
And bloodless altars without wine or fire.
Him now consume thou ; for thy sacrifice
With sanguine-shining steam divides the dawn,
And one, the maiden rose of all thy maids,
Arcadian Atalanta, snowy-souled,
Fair as the snow and footed as the wind,
From Ladon and well-wooded Mænalus
Over the firm hills and the fleeting sea
Hast thou drawn hither, and many an armèd king,
Heroes, the crown of men, like gods in fight.
Moreover out of all the Ætolian land,
From the full-flowered Lelantian pasturage
To what of fruitful field the son of Zeus
Won from the roaring river and labouring sea
When the wild god shrank in his horn and fled
And foamed and lessened through his wrathful fords,
Leaving clear lands that steamed with sudden sun,
These virgins with the lightening of the day

Bring thee fresh wreaths and their own sweeter hair,
Luxurious locks and flower-like mixed with flowers,
Clean offering, and chaste hymns ; but me the time
Divides from these things ; whom do thou not less
Help and give honour, and to mine hounds good speed,
And edge to spears, and luck to each man's hand.

CHORUS

When the hounds of spring are on winter's traces,
　　The mother of months in meadow or plain
Fills the shadows and windy places
　　With lisp of leaves and ripple of rain ;
And the brown bright nightingale amorous
Is half assuaged for Itylus,
For the Thracian ships and the foreign faces,
　　The tongueless vigil, and all the pain.

Come with bows bent and with emptying of quivers,
　　Maiden most perfect, lady of light,
With a noise of winds and many rivers,
　　With a clamour of waters, and with might ;
Bind on thy sandals, O thou most fleet,
Over the splendour and speed of thy feet ;
For the faint east quickens, the wan west shivers,
　　Round the feet of the day and the feet of the night.

Where shall we find her, how shall we sing to her,
　　Fold our hands round her knees, and cling ?
O that man's heart were as fire and could spring to her,
　　Fire, or the strength of the streams that spring !
For the stars and the winds are unto her
As raiment, as songs of the harp-player ;
For the risen stars and the fallen cling to her,
　　And the southwest-wind and the west-wind sing.

For winter's rains and ruins are over,
   And all the season of snows and sins ;
The days dividing lover and lover,
   The light that loses, the night that wins ;
And time remembered is grief forgotten,
And frosts are slain and flowers begotten,
And in green underwood and cover
   Blossom by blossom the spring begins.

The full streams feed on flower of rushes,
   Ripe grasses trammel a travelling foot,
The faint fresh flame of the young year flushes
   From leaf to flower and flower to fruit ;
And fruit and leaf are as gold and fire,
And the oat is heard above the lyre,
And the hoofèd heel of a satyr crushes
   The chestnut-husk at the chestnut-root.

And Pan by noon and Bacchus by night,
   Fleeter of foot than the fleet-foot kid,
Follows with dancing and fills with delight
   The Mænad and the Bassarid ;
And soft as lips that laugh and hide
The laughing leaves of the trees divide,
And screen from seeing and leave in sight
   The god pursuing, the maiden hid.

The ivy falls with the Bacchanal's hair
   Over her eyebrows hiding her eyes ;
The wild vine slipping down leaves bare
   Her bright breast shortening into sighs ;
The wild vine slips with the weight of its leaves,
But the berried ivy catches and cleaves
To the limbs that glitter, the feet that scare
   The wolf that follows, the fawn that flies.

ALTHÆA

What do ye singing ? what is this ye sing ?

CHORUS

Flowers bring we, and pure lips that please the gods,
And raiment meet for service : lest the day
Turn sharp with all its honey in our lips.

ALTHÆA

Night, a black hound, follows the white fawn day,
Swifter than dreams the white flown feet of sleep ;
Will ye pray back the night with any prayers ?
And though the spring put back a little while
Winter, and snows that plague all men for sin,
And the iron time of cursing, yet I know
Spring shall be ruined with the rain, and storm
Eat up like fire the ashen autumn days.
I marvel what men do with prayers awake
Who dream and die with dreaming ; any god,
Yea the least god of all things called divine,
Is more than sleep and waking ; yet we say,
Perchance by praying a man shall match his god.
For if sleep have no mercy, and man's dreams
Bite to the blood and burn into the bone,
What shall this man do waking ?   By the gods,
He shall not pray to dream sweet things to-night,
Having dreamt once more bitter things than death.

CHORUS

Queen, but what is it that hath burnt thine heart ?
For thy speech flickers like a blown-out flame.

ALTHÆA

Look, ye say well, and know not what ye say;
For all my sleep is turned into a fire,
And all my dreams to stuff that kindles it.

CHORUS

Yet one doth well being patient of the gods.

ALTHÆA

Yea, lest they smite us with some four-foot plague.

CHORUS

But when time spreads find out some herb for it.

ALTHÆA

And with their healing herbs infect our blood.

CHORUS

What ails thee to be jealous of their ways?

ALTHÆA

What if they give us poisonous drinks for wine?

CHORUS

They have their will; much talking mends it not.

ALTHÆA

And gall for milk, and cursing for a prayer?

CHORUS

Have they not given life, and the end of life?

ALTHÆA

Lo, where they heal, they help not ; thus they do,
They mock us with a little piteousness,
And we say prayers, and weep ; but at the last,
Sparing awhile, they smite and spare no whit.

CHORUS

Small praise man gets dispraising the high gods :
What have they done that thou dishonourest them?

ALTHÆA

First Artemis for all this harried land
I praise not, and for wasting of the boar
That mars with tooth and tusk and fiery feet
Green pasturage and the grace of standing corn
And meadow and marsh with springs and unblown
    leaves,
Flocks and swift herds and all that bite sweet grass,
I praise her not ; what things are these to praise?

CHORUS

But when the king did sacrifice, and gave
Each god fair dues of wheat and blood and wine,
Her not with bloodshed nor burnt-offering
Revered he, nor with salt or cloven cake ;
Wherefore being wroth she plagued the land ; but
    now
Takes off from us fate and her heavy things.
Which deed of these twain were not good to praise?
For a just deed looks always either way
With blameless eyes, and mercy is no fault.

ALTHÆA

Yea, but a curse she hath sent above all these
To hurt us where she healed us ; and hath lit
Fire where the old fire went out, and where the wind
Slackened, hath blown on us with deadlier air.

CHORUS

What storm is this that tightens all our sail ?

ALTHÆA

Love, a thwart sea-wind full of rain and foam.

CHORUS

Whence blown, and born under what stormier star ?

ALTHÆA

Southward across Euenus from the sea.

CHORUS

Thy speech turns toward Arcadia like blown wind.

ALTHÆA

Sharp as the north sets when the snows are out.

CHORUS

Nay, for this maiden hath no touch of love.

ALTHÆA

I would she had sought in some cold gulf of sea
Love, or in dens where strange beasts lurk, or fire,
Or snows on the extreme hills, or iron land
Where no spring is; I would she had sought therein
And found, or ever love had found her here.

CHORUS

She is holier than all holy days or things,
The sprinkled water or fume of perfect fire ;
Chaste, dedicated to pure prayers, and filled
With higher thoughts than heaven ; a maiden clean,
Pure iron, fashioned for a sword ; and man
She loves not ; what should one such do with love ?

ALTHÆA

Look you, I speak not as one light of wit,
But as a queen speaks, being heart-vexed ; for oft
I hear my brothers wrangling in mid hall,
And am not moved ; and my son chiding them,
And these things nowise move me, but I know
Foolish and wise men must be to the end,
And feed myself with patience ; but this most,
This moves me, that for wise men as for fools
Love is one thing, an evil thing, and turns
Choice words and wisdom into fire and air.
And in the end shall no joy come, but grief,
Sharp words and soul's division and fresh tears
Flower-wise upon the old root of tears brought forth,
Fruit-wise upon the old flower of tears sprung up,
Pitiful sighs, and much regrafted pain.
These things are in my presage, and myself
Am part of them and know not ; but in dreams
The gods are heavy on me, and all the fates
Shed fire across my eyelids mixed with night,
And burn me blind, and disilluminate
My sense of seeing, and my perspicuous soul
Darken with vision ; seeing I see not, hear
And hearing am not holpen, but mine eyes
Stain many tender broideries in the bed

Drawn up about my face that I may weep
And the king wake not ; and my brows and lips
Tremble and sob in sleeping, like swift flames
That tremble, or water when it sobs with heat
Kindled from under ; and my tears fill my breast
And speck the fair dyed pillows round the king
With barren showers and salter than the sea,
Such dreams divide me dreaming ; for long since
I dreamed that out of this my womb had sprung
Fire and a firebrand ; this was ere my son,
Meleager, a goodly flower in fields of fight,
Felt the light touch him coming forth, and wailed
Childlike ; but yet he was not ; and in time
I bare him, and my heart was great ; for yet
So royally was never strong man born,
Nor queen so nobly bore as noble a thing
As this my son was : such a birth God sent
And such a grace to bear it.   Then came in
Three weaving women, and span each a thread,
Saying This for strength and That for luck, and one
Saying Till the brand upon the hearth burn down,
So long shall this man see good days and live.
And I with gathered raiment from the bed
Sprang, and drew forth the brand, and cast on it
Water, and trod the flame bare-foot, and crushed
With naked hand spark beaten out of spark
And blew against and quenched it ; for I said,
These are the most high Fates that dwell with us,
And we find favour a little in their sight,
A little, and more we miss of, and much time
Foils us ; howbeit they have pitied me, O son,
And thee most piteous, thee a tenderer thing
Than any flower of fleshly seed alive.
Wherefore I kissed and hid him with my hands,
And covered under arms and hair, and wept,

And feared to touch him with my tears, and laughed ;
So light a thing was this man, grown so great
Men cast their heads back, seeing against the sun
Blaze the armed man carven on his shield, and hear
The laughter of little bells along the brace
Ring, as birds singing or flutes blown, and watch,
High up, the cloven shadow of either plume
Divide the bright light of the brass, and make
His helmet as a windy and wintering moon
Seen through blown cloud and plume-like drift, when
     ships
Drive, and men strive with all the sea, and oars
Break, and the beaks dip under, drinking death ;
Yet was he then but a span long, and moaned
With inarticulate mouth inseparate words,
And with blind lips and fingers wrung my breast
Hard, and thrust out with foolish hands and feet,
Murmuring ; but those grey women with bound hair
Who fright the gods frighted not him ; he laughed
Seeing them, and pushed out hands to feel and haul
Distaff and thread, intangible ; but they
Passed, and I hid the brand, and in my heart
Laughed likewise, having all my will of heaven.
But now I know not if to left or right
The gods have drawn us hither ; for again
I dreamt, and saw the black brand burst on fire
As a branch bursts in flower, and saw the flame
Fade flower-wise, and Death came and with dry lips
Blew the charred ash into my breast ; and Love
Trampled the ember and crushed it with swift feet.
This I have also at heart ; that not for me,
Not for me only or son of mine, O girls,
The gods have wrought life, and desire of life,
Heart's love and heart's division ; but for all

There shines one sun and one wind blows till night.
And when night comes the wind sinks and the sun,
And there is no light after, and no storm,
But sleep and much forgetfulness of things.
In such wise I gat knowledge of the gods
Years hence, and heard high sayings of one most wise,
Eurythemis my mother, who beheld
With eyes alive and spake with lips of these
As one on earth disfleshed and disallied
From breath or blood corruptible ; such gifts
Time gave her, and an equal soul to these
And equal face to all things ; thus she said.
But whatsoever intolerable or glad
The swift hours weave and unweave, I go hence
Full of mine own soul, perfect of myself,
Toward mine and me sufficient ; and what chance
The gods cast lots for and shake out on us,
That shall we take, and that much bear withal.
And now, before these gather to the hunt,
I will go arm my son and bring him forth,
Lest love or some man's anger work him harm.

CHORUS

Before the beginning of years
    There came to the making of man
Time, with a gift of tears ;
    Grief, with a glass that ran ;
Pleasure, with pain for leaven ;
    Summer, with flowers that fell ;
Remembrance fallen from heaven,
    And madness risen from hell ;
Strength without hands to smite ;
    Love that endures for a breath :
Night, the shadow of light,
    And life, the shadow of death.

And the high gods took in hand
    Fire, and the falling of tears,
And a measure of sliding sand
    From under the feet of the years;
And froth and drift of the sea;
    And dust of the labouring earth;
And bodies of things to be
    In the houses of death and of birth;
And wrought with weeping and laughter,
    And fashioned with loathing and love
With life before and after
    And death beneath and above,
For a day and a night and a morrow,
    That his strength might endure for a span
With travail and heavy sorrow,
    The holy spirit of man.

From the winds of the north and the south
    They gathered as unto strife;
They breathed upon his mouth,
    They filled his body with life;
Eyesight and speech they wrought
    For the veils of the soul therein,
A time for labour and thought,
    A time to serve and to sin;
They gave him light in his ways,
    And love, and a space for delight,
And beauty and length of days,
    And night, and sleep in the night.
His speech is a burning fire;
    With his lips he travaileth;
In his heart is a blind desire,
    In his eyes foreknowledge of death;

He weaves, and is clothed with derision ;
    Sows, and he shall not reap ;
His life is a watch or a vision
    Between a sleep and a sleep.

MELEAGER

O sweet new heaven and air without a star,
Fair day, be fair and welcome, as to men
With deeds to do and praise to pluck from thee.
Come forth a child, born with clear sound and light,
With laughter and swift limbs and prosperous looks;
That this great hunt with heroes for the hounds
May leave thee memorable and us well sped.

ALTHÆA

Son, first I praise thy prayer, then bid thee speed ;
But the gods hear men's hands before their lips,
And heed beyond all crying and sacrifice
Light of things done and noise of labouring men.
But thou, being armed and perfect for the deed,
Abide ; for like rain-flakes in a wind they grow,
The men thy fellows, and the choice of the world,
Bound to root out the tuskèd plague, and leave
Thanks and safe days and peace in Calydon.

MELEAGER

For the whole city and all the low-lying land
Flames, and the soft air sounds with them that come ;
The gods give all these fruit of all their works.

ALTHÆA

Set thine eye thither and fix thy spirit and say
Whom there thou knowest ; for sharp mixed shadow
    and wind

Blown up between the morning and the mist,
With steam of steeds and flash of bridle or wheel,
And fire, and parcels of the broken dawn,
And dust divided by hard light, and spears
That shine and shift as the edge of wild beasts' eyes
Smite upon mine; so fiery their blind edge
Burns, and bright points break up and baffle day.

MELEAGER

The first, for many I know not, being far off,
Peleus the Larissæan, couched with whom
Sleeps the white sea-bred wife and silver-shod,
Fair as fled foam, a goddess; and their son
Most swift and splendid of men's children born,
Most like a god, full of the future fame.

ALTHÆA

Who are these shining like one sundered star?

MELEAGER

Thy sister's sons, a double flower of men.

ALTHÆA

O sweetest kin to me in all the world,
O twin-born blood of Leda, gracious heads
Like kindled lights in untempestuous heaven,
Fair flower-like stars on the iron foam of fight,
With what glad heart and kindliness of soul,
Even to the staining of both eyes with tears
And kindling of warm eyelids with desire,
A great way off I greet you, and rejoice
Seeing you so fair, and moulded like as gods.
Far off ye come, and least in years of these,
But lordliest, but worth love to look upon.

MELEAGER

Even such (for sailing hither I saw far hence,
And where Eurotas hollows his moist rock
Nigh Sparta with a strenuous-hearted stream)
Even such I saw their sisters ; one swan-white,
The little Helen, and less fair than she
Fair Clytæmnestra, grave as pasturing fawns
Who feed and fear some arrow ; but at whiles,
As one smitten with love or wrung with joy,
She laughs and lightens with her eyes, and then
Weeps ; whereat Helen, having laughed, weeps too,
And the other chides her, and she being chid speaks
    nought,
But cheeks and lips and eyelids kisses her,
Laughing ; so fare they, as in their bloomless bud
And full of unblown life, the blood of gods.

ALTHÆA

Sweet days befall them and good loves and lords,
And tender and temperate honours of the hearth,
Peace, and a perfect life and blameless bed.
But who shows next an eagle wrought in gold,
That flames and beats broad wings against the sun
And with void mouth gapes after emptier prey ?

MELEAGER

Know by that sign the reign of Telamon
Between the fierce mouths of the encountering brine
On the strait reefs of twice-washed Salamis.

ALTHÆA

For like one great of hand he bears himself,
Vine-chapleted, with savours of the sea,

Glittering as wine and moving as a wave.
But who girt round there roughly follows him?

MELEAGER

Ancæus, great of hand, an iron bulk,
Two-edged for fight as the axe against his arm,
Who drives against the surge of stormy spears
Full-sailed; him Cepheus follows, his twin-born,
Chief name next his of all Arcadian men.

ALTHÆA

Praise be with men abroad; chaste lives with us,
Home-keeping days and household reverences.

MELEAGER

Next by the left unsandalled foot know thou
The sail and oar of this Ætolian land,
Thy brethren, Toxeus and the violent-souled
Plexippus, over-swift with hand and tongue;
For hands are fruitful, but the ignorant mouth
Blows and corrupts their work with barren breath.

ALTHÆA

Speech too bears fruit, being worthy; and air blows
    down
Things poisonous, and high-seated violences,
And with charmed words and songs have men put
    out
Wild evil, and the fire of tyrannies.

MELEAGER

Yea, all things have they, save the gods and love.

ALTHÆA

Love thou the law and cleave to things ordained.

MELEAGER

Law lives upon their lips whom these applaud.

ALTHÆA

How sayest thou these ? what god applauds new
things ?

MELEAGER

Zeus, who hath fear and custom under foot.

ALTHÆA

But loves not laws thrown down and lives awry.

MELEAGER

Yet is not less himself than his own law.

ALTHÆA

Nor shifts and shuffles old things up and down.

MELEAGER

But what he will remoulds and discreates.

ALTHÆA

Much, but not this, that each thing live its life.

MELEAGER

Nor only live, but lighten and lift up higher.

ALTHÆA

Pride breaks itself, and too much gained is gone.

MELEAGER

Things gained are gone, but great things done
endure.

ALTHÆA

Child, if a man serve law through all his life
And with his whole heart worship, him all gods
Praise ; but who loves it only with his lips,
And not in heart and deed desiring it
Hides a perverse will with obsequious words,
Him heaven infatuates and his twin-born fate
Tracks, and gains on him, scenting sins far off,
And the swift hounds of violent death devour.
Be man at one with equal-minded gods,
So shall he prosper ; not through laws torn up,
Violated rule and a new face of things.
A woman armed makes war upon herself,
Unwomanlike, and treads down use and wont
And the sweet common honour that she hath,
Love, and the cry of children, and the hand
Trothplight and mutual mouth of marriages.
This doth she, being unloved ; whom if one love,
Not fire nor iron and the wide-mouthed wars
Are deadlier than her lips or braided hair.
For of the one comes poison, and a curse
Falls from the other and burns the lives of men.
But thou, son, be not filled with evil dreams,
Nor with desire of these things ; for with time
Blind love burns out ; but if one feed it full
Till some discolouring stain dyes all his life,
He shall keep nothing praiseworthy, nor die
The sweet wise death of old men honourable,
Who have lived out all the length of all their years
Blameless, and seen well-pleased the face of gods,
And without shame and without fear have wrought
Things memorable, and while their days held out
In sight of all men and the sun's great light

Have gat them glory and given of their own praise
To the earth that bare them and the day that bred,
Home friends and far-off hospitalities,
And filled with gracious and memorial fame
Lands loved of summer or washed by violent seas,
Towns populous and many unfooted ways,
And alien lips and native with their own.
But when white age and venerable death
Mow down the strength and life within their limbs,
Drain out the blood and darken their clear eyes,
Immortal honour is on them, having past
Through splendid life and death desirable
To the clear seat and remote throne of souls,
Lands indiscoverable in the unheard-of west,
Round which the strong stream of a sacred sea
Rolls without wind for ever, and the snow
There shows not her white wings and windy feet,
Nor thunder nor swift rain saith anything,
Nor the sun burns, but all things rest and thrive ;
And these, filled full of days, divine and dead,
Sages and singers fiery from the god,
And such as loved their land and all things good
And, best beloved of best men, liberty,
Free lives and lips, free hands of men free-born,
And whatsoever on earth was honourable
And whosoever of all the ephemeral seed,
Live there a life no liker to the gods
But nearer than their life of terrene days.
Love thou such life and look for such a death.
But from the light and fiery dreams of love
Spring heavy sorrows and a sleepless life,
Visions not dreams, whose lids no charm shall close
Nor song assuage them waking ; and swift death
Crushes with sterile feet the unripening ear,

Treads out the timeless vintage ; whom do thou
Eschewing embrace the luck of this thy life,
Not without honour ; and it shall bear to thee
Such fruit as men reap from spent hours and wear,
Few men, but happy ; of whom be thou, O son,
Happiest, if thou submit thy soul to fate,
And set thine eyes and heart on hopes high-born
And divine deeds and abstinence divine.
So shalt thou be toward all men all thy days
As light and might communicable, and burn
From heaven among the stars above the hours,
And break not as a man breaks nor burn down :
For to whom other of all heroic names
Have the gods given his life in hand as thine ?
And gloriously hast thou lived, and made thy life
To me that bare thee and to all men born
Thankworthy, a praise for ever ; and hast won fame
When wild wars broke all round thy father's house,
And the mad people of windy mountain ways
Laid spears against us like a sea, and all
Ætolia thundered with Thessalian hoofs ;
Yet these, as wind baffles the foam, and beats
Straight back the relaxed ripple, didst thou break
And loosen all their lances, till undone
And man from man they fell ; for ye twain stood
God against god, Ares and Artemis,
And thou the mightier ; wherefore she unleashed
A sharp-toothed curse thou too shalt overcome ;
For in the greener blossom of thy life
Ere the full blade caught flower, and when time
      gave
Respite, thou didst not slacken soul nor sleep,
But with great hand and heart seek praise of men
Out of sharp straits and many a grievous thing,

Seeing the strange foam of undivided seas
On channels never sailed in, and by shores
Where the old winds cease not blowing, and all the
    night
Thunders, and day is no delight to men.

CHORUS

Meleager, a noble wisdom and fair words
The gods have given this woman ; hear thou these.

MELEAGER

O mother, I am not fain to strive in speech
Nor set my mouth against thee, who art wise
Even as they say and full of sacred words.
But one thing I know surely, and cleave to this ;
That though I be not subtle of wit as thou
Nor womanlike to weave sweet words, and melt
Mutable minds of wise men as with fire,
I too, doing justly and reverencing the gods,
Shall not want wit to see what things be right.
For whom they love and whom reject, being gods,
There is no man but seeth, and in good time
Submits himself, refraining all his heart.
And I too as thou sayest have seen great things ;
Seen otherwhere, but chiefly when the sail
First caught between stretched ropes the roaring
    west,
And all our oars smote eastward, and the wind
First flung round faces of seafaring men
White splendid snow-flakes of the sundering foam,
And the first furrow in virginal green sea
Followed the plunging ploughshare of hewn pine,
And closed, as when deep sleep subdues man's breath
Lips close and heart subsides ; and closing, shone

Sunlike with many a Nereid's hair, and moved
Round many a trembling mouth of doubtful gods,
Risen out of sunless and sonorous gulfs
Through waning water and into shallow light,
That watched us ; and when flying the dove was
    snared
As with men's hands, but we shot after and sped
Clear through the irremeable Symplegades ;
And chiefliest when hoar beach and herbless cliff
Stood out ahead from Colchis, and we heard
Clefts hoarse with wind, and saw through narrowing
    reefs
The lightning of the intolerable wave
Flash, and the white wet flame of breakers burn
Far under a kindling south-wind, as a lamp
Burns and bends all its blowing flame one way ;
Wild heights untravelled of the wind, and vales
Cloven seaward by their violent streams, and white
With bitter flowers and bright salt scurf of brine ;
Heard sweep their sharp swift gales, and bowing
    birdwise
Shriek with birds' voices, and with furious feet
Tread loose the long skirts of a storm ; and saw
The whole white Euxine clash together and fall
Full-mouthed, and thunderous from a thousand
    throats :
Yet we drew thither and won the fleece and won
Medea, deadlier than the sea ; but there
Seeing many a wonder and fearful things to men
I saw not one thing like this one seen here,
Most fair and fearful, feminine, a god,
Faultless ; whom I that love not, being unlike,
Fear, and give honour, and choose from all the
    gods.

OENEUS

Lady, the daughter of Thestius, and thou, son,
Not ignorant of your strife nor light of wit,
Scared with vain dreams and fluttering like spent
    fire,
I come to judge between you, but a king
Full of past days and wise from years endured.
Nor thee I praise, who art fain to undo things done :
Nor thee, who art swift to esteem them overmuch.
For what the hours have given is given, and this
Changeless ; howbeit these change, and in good
    time
Devise new things and good, not one thing still.
Us have they sent now at our need for help
Among men armed a woman, foreign born,
Virgin, not like the natural flower of things
That grows and bears and brings forth fruit and
    dies ;
Unlovable, no light for a husband's house,
Espoused ; a glory among unwedded girls,
And chosen of gods who reverence maidenhood.
These too we honour in honouring her ; but thou,
Abstain thy feet from following, and thine eyes
From amorous touch ; nor set toward hers thine
    heart,
Son, lest hate bear no deadlier fruit than love.

ALTHÆA

O king, thou art wise, but wisdom halts ; and just,
But the gods love not justice more than fate,
And smite the righteous and the violent mouth,
And mix with insolent blood the reverent man's,
And bruise the holier as the lying lips.

Enough ; for wise words fail me, and my heart
Takes fire and trembles flamewise, O my son,
O child, for thine head's sake ; mine eyes wax thick,
Turning toward thee, so goodly a weaponed man,
So glorious ; and for love of thine own eyes
They are darkened, and tears burn them, fierce as
      fire,
And my lips pause and my soul sinks with love.
But by thine hand, by thy sweet life and eyes,
By thy great heart and these clasped knees, O son,
I pray thee that thou slay me not with thee.
For there was never a mother woman-born
Loved her sons better ; and never a queen of men
More perfect in her heart toward whom she loved.
For what lies light on many and they forget,
Small things and transitory as a wind o' the sea,
I forget never ; I have seen thee all thine years
A man in arms, strong and a joy to men
Seeing thine head glitter and thine hand burn its way
Through a heavy and iron furrow of sundering
      spears ;
But always also a flower of three suns old,
The small one thing that lying drew down my life
To lie with thee and feed thee ; a child and weak,
Mine, a delight to no man, sweet to me.
Who then sought to thee ? who gat help ? who knew
If thou wert goodly ? nay, no man at all.
Or what sea saw thee, or sounded with thine oar,
Child ? or what strange land shone with war through
      thee ?
But fair for me thou wert, O little life,
Fruitless, the fruit of mine own flesh, and blind,
More than much gold, ungrown, a foolish flower.
For silver nor bright snow nor feather of foam

Was whiter, and no gold yellower than thine hair,
O child, my child ; and now thou art lordlier grown,
Not lovelier, nor a new thing in mine eyes,
I charge thee by thy soul and this my breast,
Fear thou the gods and me and thine own heart,
Lest all these turn against thee ; for who knows
What wind upon what wave of altering time
Shall speak a storm and blow calamity ?
And there is nothing stabile in the world
But the gods break it ; yet not less, fair son,
If but one thing be stronger, if one endure,
Surely the bitter and the rooted love
That burns between us, going from me to thee,
Shall more endure than all things.   What dost thou,
Following strange loves ? why wilt thou kill mine
    heart ?
Lo, I talk wild and windy words, and fall
From my clear wits, and seem of mine own self
Dethroned, dispraised, disseated ; and my mind,
That was my crown, breaks, and mine heart is gone,
And I am naked of my soul, and stand
Ashamed, as a mean woman ; take thou thought :
Live if thou wilt, and if thou wilt not, look,
The gods have given thee life to lose or keep,
Thou shalt not die as men die, but thine end
Fallen upon thee shall break me unaware.

MELEAGER

Queen, my whole heart is molten with thy tears,
And my limbs yearn with pity of thee, and love
Compels with grief mine eyes and labouring breath ;
For what thou art I know thee, and this thy breast
And thy fair eyes I worship, and am bound
Toward thee in spirit and love thee in all my soul.

For there is nothing terribler to men
Than the sweet face of mothers, and the might.
But what shall be let be ; for us the day
Once only lives a little, and is not found.
Time and the fruitful hour are more than we,
And these lay hold upon us ; but thou, God,
Zeus, the sole steersman of the helm of things,
Father, be swift to see us, and as thou wilt
Help : or if adverse, as thou wilt, refrain.

CHORUS

We have seen thee, O Love, thou art fair ; thou art
    goodly, O Love ;
Thy wings make light in the air as the wings of a
    dove.
Thy feet are as winds that divide the stream of the
    sea ;
Earth is thy covering to hide thee, the garment of
    thee.
Thou art swift and subtle and blind as a flame of
    fire ;
Before thee the laughter, behind thee the tears of
    desire ;
And twain go forth beside thee, a man with a maid ;
Her eyes are the eyes of a bride whom delight makes
    afraid ;
As the breath in the buds that stir is her bridal
    breath :
But Fate is the name of her ; and his name is Death.

    For an evil blossom was born
      Of sea-foam and the frothing of blood,
        Blood-red and bitter of fruit,
          And the seed of it laughter and tears,

And the leaves of it madness and scorn ;
　A bitter flower from the bud,
　　Sprung of the sea without root,
　　　Sprung without graft from the years.

The weft of the world was untorn
　That is woven of the day on the night,
　The hair of the hours was not white
Nor the raiment of time overworn,
　When a wonder, a world's delight,
A perilous goddess was born ;
　And the waves of the sea as she came
Clove, and the foam at her feet,
　　Fawning, rejoiced to bring forth
A fleshly blossom, a flame
Filling the heavens with heat
　　To the cold white ends of the north.

And in air the clamorous birds,
　And men upon earth that hear
Sweet articulate words
　　Sweetly divided apart,
　And in shallow and channel and mere
The rapid and footless herds,
　　Rejoiced, being foolish of heart.

For all they said upon earth,
　She is fair, she is white like a dove,
　　And the life of the world in her breath
Breathes, and is born at her birth ;
　　For they knew thee for mother of love,
　　And knew thee not mother of death.

What hadst thou to do being born,
    Mother, when winds were at ease,
As a flower of the springtime of corn,
    A flower of the foam of the seas ?
For bitter thou wast from thy birth,
    Aphrodite, a mother of strife ;
For before thee some rest was on earth,
    A little respite from tears,
    A little pleasure of life ;
For life was not then as thou art,
    But as one that waxeth in years
Sweet-spoken, a fruitful wife ;
    Earth had no thorn, and desire
No sting, neither death any dart ;
    What hadst thou to do amongst these,
    Thou, clothed with a burning fire,
Thou, girt with sorrow of heart,
    Thou, sprung of the seed of the seas
As an ear from a seed of corn,
    As a brand plucked forth of a pyre,
As a ray shed forth of the morn,
    For division of soul and disease,
For a dart and a sting and a thorn ?
What ailed thee then to be born ?

Was there not evil enough,
    Mother, and anguish on earth
    Born with a man at his birth,
Wastes underfoot, and above
    Storm out of heaven, and dearth
Shaken down from the shining thereof,
    Wrecks from afar overseas
    And peril of shallow and firth,

And tears that spring and increase
In the barren places of mirth,
That thou, having wings as a dove,
Being girt with desire for a girth,
That thou must come after these,
That thou must lay on him love ?

Thou shouldst not so have been born :
But death should have risen with thee,
Mother, and visible fear,
Grief, and the wringing of hands,
And noise of many that mourn ;
The smitten bosom, the knee
Bowed, and in each man's ear
A cry as of perishing lands,
A moan as of people in prison,
A tumult of infinite griefs ;
And thunder of storm on the sands,
And wailing of wives on the shore ;
And under thee newly arisen
Loud shoals and shipwrecking reefs,
Fierce air and violent light ;
Sail rent and sundering oar,
Darkness, and noises of night ;
Clashing of streams in the sea,
Wave against wave as a sword,
Clamour of currents, and foam ;
Rains making ruin on earth,
Winds that wax ravenous and roam
As wolves in a wolfish horde ;
Fruits growing faint in the tree,
And blind things dead in their birth ;
Famine, and blighting of corn,
When thy time was come to be born.

All these we know of ; but thee
　　Who shall discern or declare ?
In the uttermost ends of the sea
　　The light of thine eyelids and hair,
　　　The light of thy bosom as fire
　　　　Between the wheel of the sun
　　And the flying flames of the air ?
　　　Wilt thou turn thee not yet nor have pity,
But abide with despair and desire
　　And the crying of armies undone,
　　　　Lamentation of one with another
　　　And breaking of city by city ;
　　The dividing of friend against friend,
　　　　The severing of brother and brother ;
　　Wilt thou utterly bring to an end ?
　　　Have mercy, mother !

For against all men from of old
　　Thou hast set thine hand as a curse,
　　　And cast out gods from their places.
　　　These things are spoken of thee.
Strong kings and goodly with gold
　　Thou hast found out arrows to pierce,
　　　And made their kingdoms and races
　　　As dust and surf of the sea.
All these, overburdened with woes
　　And with length of their days waxen weak,
　　　Thou slewest ; and sentest moreover
　　　Upon Tyro an evil thing,
Rent hair and a fetter and blows
　　Making bloody the flower of the cheek,
　　　Though she lay by a god as a lover,
　　　　Though fair, and the seed of a king.

For of old, being full of thy fire,
  She endured not longer to wear
    On her bosom a saffron vest,
      On her shoulder an ashwood quiver ;
Being mixed and made one through desire
  With Enipeus, and all her hair
    Made moist with his mouth, and her breast
      Filled full of the foam of the river.

ATALANTA

Sun, and clear light among green hills, and day
Late risen and long sought after, and you just gods
Whose hands divide anguish and recompense,
But first the sun's white sister, a maid in heaven,
On earth of all maids worshipped—hail, and hear,
And witness with me if not without sign sent,
Not without rule and reverence, I a maid
Hallowed, and huntress holy as whom I serve,
Here in your sight and eyeshot of these men
Stand, girt as they toward hunting, and my shafts
Drawn ; wherefore all ye stand up on my side,
If I be pure and all ye righteous gods,
Lest one revile me, a woman, yet no wife,
That bear a spear for spindle, and this bow strung
For a web woven ; and with pure lips salute
Heaven, and the face of all the gods, and dawn
Filling with maiden flames and maiden flowers
The starless fold o' the stars, and making sweet
The warm wan heights of the air, moon-trodden ways
And breathless gates and extreme hills of heaven.
Whom, having offered water and bloodless gifts,
Flowers, and a golden circlet of pure hair,
Next Artemis I bid be favourable
And make this day all golden, hers and ours,

Gracious and good and white to the unblamed end.
But thou, O well-beloved, of all my days
Bid it be fruitful, and a crown for all,
To bring forth leaves and bind round all my hair
With perfect chaplets woven for thine of thee.
For not without the word of thy chaste mouth,
For not without law given and clean command,
Across the white straits of the running sea
From Elis even to the Acheloïan horn,
I with clear winds came hither and gentle gods,
Far off my father's house, and left uncheered
Iasius, and uncheered the Arcadian hills
And all their green-haired waters, and all woods
Disconsolate, to hear no horn of mine
Blown, and behold no flash of swift white feet.

MELEAGER

For thy name's sake and awe toward thy chaste head,
O holiest Atalanta, no man dares
Praise thee, though fairer than whom all men praise,
And godlike for thy grace of hallowed hair
And holy habit of thine eyes, and feet
That make the blown foam neither swift nor white
Though the wind winnow and whirl it ; yet we praise
Gods, found because of thee adorable
And for thy sake praiseworthiest from all men :
Thee therefore we praise also, thee as these,
Pure, and a light lit at the hands of gods.

TOXEUS

How long will ye whet spears with eloquence,
Fight, and kill beasts dry-handed with sweet words ?
Cease, or talk still and slay thy boars at home.

PLEXIPPUS

Why, if she ride among us for a man,
Sit thou for her and spin ; a man grown girl
Is worth a woman weaponed ; sit thou here.

MELEAGER

Peace, and be wise ; no gods love idle speech.

PLEXIPPUS

Nor any man a man's mouth woman-tongued.

MELEAGER

For my lips bite not sharper than mine hands.

PLEXIPPUS

Nay, both bite soft, but no whit softly mine.

MELEAGER

Keep thine hands clean ; they have time enough to
    stain.

PLEXIPPUS

For thine shall rest and wax not red to-day.

MELEAGER

Have all thy will of words ; talk out thine heart.

ALTHÆA

Refrain your lips, O brethren, and my son,
Lest words turn snakes and bite you uttering them.

TOXEUS

Except she give her blood before the gods,
What profit shall a maid be among men ?

PLEXIPPUS

Let her come crowned and stretch her throat for a
     knife,
Bleat out her spirit and die, and so shall men
Through her too prosper and through prosperous
     gods,
But nowise through her living ; shall she live
A flower-bud of the flower-bed, or sweet fruit
For kisses and the honey-making mouth,
And play the shield for strong men and the spear ?
Then shall the heifer and her mate lock horns,
And the bride overbear the groom, and men ·
Gods ; for no less division sunders these ;
Since all things made are seasonable in time,
But if one alter unseasonable are all.
But thou, O Zeus, hear me that I may slay
This beast before thee and no man halve with me
Nor woman, lest these mock thee, though a god,
Who hast made men strong, and thou being wise be
     held
Foolish ; for wise is that thing which endures.

ATALANTA

Men, and the chosen of all this people, and thou,
King, I beseech you a little bear with me.
For if my life be shameful that I live,
Let the gods witness and their wrath ; but these
Cast no such word against me.   Thou, O mine,
O holy, O happy goddess, if I sin
Changing the words of women and the works
For spears and strange men's faces, hast not thou
One shaft of all thy sudden seven that pierced
Seven through the bosom or shining throat or side,

All couched about one mother's loosening knees,
All holy born, engraffed of Tantalus?
But if toward any of you I am overbold
That take thus much upon me, let him think
How I, for all my forest holiness,
Fame, and this armed and iron maidenhood,
Pay thus much also ; I shall have no man's love
For ever, and no face of children born
Or feeding lips upon me or fastening eyes
For ever, nor being dead shall kings my sons
Mourn me and bury, and tears on daughters' cheeks
Burn ; but a cold and sacred life, but strange,
But far from dances and the back-blowing torch,
Far off from flowers or any bed of man,
Shall my life be for ever : me the snows
That face the first o' the morning, and cold hills
Full of the land-wind and sea-travelling storms
And many a wandering wing of noisy nights
That know the thunder and hear the thickening
     wolves—
Me the utmost pine and footless frost of woods
That talk with many winds and gods, the hours
Re-risen, and white divisions of the dawn,
Springs thousand-tongued with the intermitting reed
And streams that murmur of the mother snow—
Me these allure, and know me ; but no man
Knows, and my goddess only. Lo now, see
If one of all you these things vex at all.
Would God that any of you had all the praise
And I no manner of memory when I die,
So might I show before her perfect eyes
Pure, whom I follow, a maiden to my death.
But for the rest let all have all they will ;
For is it a grief to you that I have part,

Being woman merely, in your male might and deeds
Done by main strength? yet in my body is throned
As great a heart, and in my spirit, O men,
I have not less of godlike. Evil it were
That one a coward should mix with you, one hand
Fearful, one eye abase itself; and these
Well might ye hate and well revile, not me.
For not the difference of the several flesh
Being vile or noble or beautiful or base
Makes praiseworthy, but purer spirit and heart
Higher than these meaner mouths and limbs, that
    feed,
Rise, rest, and are and are not; and for me,
What should I say? but by the gods of the world
And this my maiden body, by all oaths
That bind the tongue of men and the evil will,
I am not mighty-minded, nor desire
Crowns, nor the spoil of slain things nor the fame;
Feed ye on these, eat and wax fat; cry out,
Laugh, having eaten, and leap without a lyre,
Sing, mix the wind with clamour, smite and shake
Sonorous timbrels and tumultuous hair,
And fill the dance up with tempestuous feet,
For I will none; but having prayed my prayers
And made thank-offering for prosperities,
I shall go hence and no man see me more.
What thing is this for you to shout me down,
What, for a man to grudge me this my life
As it were envious of all yours, and I
A thief of reputations? nay, for now,
If there be any highest in heaven, a god
Above all thrones and thunders of the gods
Throned, and the wheel of the world roll under him,
Judge he between me and all of you, and see

If I transgress at all : but ye, refrain
Transgressing hands and reinless mouths, and keep
Silence, lest by much foam of violent words
And proper poison of your lips ye die.

OENEUS

O flower of Tegea, maiden, fleetest foot
And holiest head of women, have good cheer
Of thy good words : but ye, depart with her
In peace and reverence, each with blameless eye
Following his fate ; exalt your hands and hearts,
Strike, cease not, arrow on arrow and wound on
    wound,
And go with gods and with the gods return.

CHORUS

Who hath given man speech ? or who hath set
    therein
A thorn for peril and a snare for sin ?
For in the word his life is and his breath,
    And in the word his death,
That madness and the infatuate heart may breed
    From the word's womb the deed
And life bring one thing forth ere all pass by,
Even one thing which is ours yet cannot die—
Death.   Hast thou seen him ever anywhere,
Time's twin-born brother, imperishable as he
Is perishable and plaintive, clothed with care
    And mutable as sand,
But death is strong and full of blood and fair
And perdurable and like a lord of land ?
Nay, time thou seest not, death thou wilt not see
Till life's right hand be loosened from thine hand
    And thy life-days from thee.

For the gods very subtly fashion
   Madness with sadness upon earth :
Not knowing in any wise compassion,
   Nor holding pity of any worth ;
And many things they have given and taken,
   And wrought and ruined many things ;
The firm land have they loosed and shaken,
   And sealed the sea with all her springs ;
They have wearied time with heavy burdens
   And vexed the lips of life with breath :
Set men to labour and given them guerdons,
   Death, and great darkness after death :
Put moans into the bridal measure
   And on the bridal wools a stain ;
And circled pain about with pleasure,
   And girdled pleasure about with pain ;
And strewed one marriage-bed with tears and fire
For extreme loathing and supreme desire.

What shall be done with all these tears of ours ?
   Shall they make watersprings in the fair heaven
To bathe the brows of morning ? or like flowers
Be shed and shine before the starriest hours,
   Or made the raiment of the weeping Seven ?
Or rather, O our masters, shall they be
Food for the famine of the grievous sea,
   A great well-head of lamentation
Satiating the sad gods ? or fall and flow
Among the years and seasons to and fro,
   And wash their feet with tribulation
And fill them full with grieving ere they go ?
   Alas, our lords, and yet alas again,
Seeing all your iron heaven is gilt as gold
   But all we smite thereat in vain ;

Smite the gates barred with groanings manifold,
　　But all the floors are paven with our pain.
Yea, and with weariness of lips and eyes,
With breaking of the bosom, and with sighs,
　　We labour, and are clad and fed with grief
And filled with days we would not fain behold
And nights we would not hear of ; we wax old,
　　All we wax old and wither like a leaf.
We are outcast, strayed between bright sun and
　　　　moon ;
　　Our light and darkness are as leaves of flowers,
Black flowers and white, that perish ; and the noon
　　As midnight, and the night as daylight hours.
　　A little fruit a little while is ours,
　　　　And the worm finds it soon.

But up in heaven the high gods one by one
　　Lay hands upon the draught that quickeneth,
Fulfilled with all tears shed and all things done,
　　And stir with soft imperishable breath
　　The bubbling bitterness of life and death,
And hold it to our lips and laugh ; but they
Preserve their lips from tasting night or day,
　　Lest they too change and sleep, the fates that spun,
The lips that made us and the hands that slay ;
　　Lest all these change, and heaven bow down to
　　　　none,
Change and be subject to the secular sway
　　And terrene revolution of the sun.
Therefore they thrust it from them, putting time away.

I would the wine of time, made sharp and sweet
　　With multitudinous days and nights and tears
　　And many mixing savours of strange years,

Were no more trodden of them under feet,
   Cast out and spilt about their holy places :
That life were given them as a fruit to eat
And death to drink as water ; that the light
Might ebb, drawn backward from their eyes, and night
   Hide for one hour the imperishable faces.
That they might rise up sad in heaven, and know
Sorrow and sleep, one paler than young snow,
   One cold as blight of dew and ruinous rain ;
Rise up and rest and suffer a little, and be
Awhile as all things born with us and we,
   And grieve as men, and like slain men be slain.

For now we know not of them ; but one saith
   The gods are gracious, praising God ; and one,
When hast thou seen ? or hast thou felt his breath
   Touch, nor consume thine eyelids as the sun,
Nor fill thee to the lips with fiery death ?
   None hath beheld him, none
Seen above other gods and shapes of things,
Swift without feet and flying without wings,
Intolerable, not clad with death or life,
   Insatiable, not known of night or day,
The lord of love and loathing and of strife
   Who gives a star and takes a sun away ;
Who shapes the soul, and makes her a barren wife
   To the earthly body and grievous growth of clay ;
Who turns the large limbs to a little flame
   And binds the great sea with a little sand ;
Who makes desire, and slays desire with shame ;
   Who shakes the heaven as ashes in his hand ;
Who, seeing the light and shadow for the same,
   Bids day waste night as fire devours a brand,
Smites without sword, and scourges without rod ;
   The supreme evil, God.

Yea, with thine hate, O God, thou hast covered us,
   One saith, and hidden our eyes away from sight,
And made us transitory and hazardous,
   Light things and slight ;
Yet have men praised thee, saying, He hath made
      man thus,
   And he doeth right.
Thou hast kissed us, and hast smitten ; thou hast
      laid
Upon us with thy left hand life, and said,
Live : and again thou hast said, Yield up your
      breath,
And with thy right hand laid upon us death.
Thou hast sent us sleep, and stricken sleep with
      dreams,
   Saying, Joy is not, but love of joy shall be ;
Thou hast made sweet springs for all the pleasant
      streams,
   In the end thou hast made them bitter with the
      sea.
Thou hast fed one rose with dust of many men ;
   Thou hast marred one face with fire of many tears ;
Thou hast taken love, and given us sorrow again ;
   With pain thou hast filled us full to the eyes and
      ears.
Therefore because thou art strong, our father, and
      we
   Feeble ; and thou art against us, and thine hand
Constrains us in the shallows of the sea
   And breaks us at the limits of the land ;
Because thou hast bent thy lightnings as a bow,
   And loosed the hours like arrows ; and let fall
Sins and wild words and many a wingèd woe
   And wars among us, and one end of all ;

Because thou hast made the thunder, and thy feet
   Are as a rushing water when the skies
Break, but thy face as an exceeding heat
   And flames of fire the eyelids of thine eyes ;
Beeause thou art over all who are over us ;
   Because thy name is life and our name death ;
Because thou art cruel and men are piteous,
   And our hands labour and thine hand scattereth ;
Lo, with hearts rent and knees made tremulous,
    Lo, with ephemeral lips and casual breath,
      At least we witness of thee ere we die
That these things are not otherwise, but thus ;
    That each man in his heart sigheth, and saith,
      That all men even as I,
All we are against thee, against thee, O God most
    high.

   But ye, keep ye on earth
   Your lips from over-speech,
Loud words and longing are so little worth ;
   And the end is hard to reach.
For silence after grievous things is good,
   And reverence, and the fear that makes men whole,
And shame, and righteous governance of blood,
   And lordship of the soul.
But from sharp words and wits men pluck no fruit,
And gathering thorns they shake the tree at root ;
For words divide and rend ;
But silence is most noble till the end.

ALTHÆA

I heard within the house a cry of news
And came forth eastward hither, where the dawn
Cheers first these warder gods that face the sun

And next our eyes unrisen ; for unaware
Came clashes of swift hoofs and trampling feet
And through the windy pillared corridor
Light sharper than the frequent flames of day
That daily fill it from the fiery dawn ;
Gleams, and a thunder of people that cried out,
And dust and hurrying horsemen ; lo their chief,
That rode with Œneus rein by rein, returned.
What cheer, O herald of my lord the king ?

HERALD

Lady, good cheer and great ; the boar is slain.

CHORUS

Praised be all gods that look toward Calydon.

ALTHÆA

Good news and brief ; but by whose happier hand?

HERALD

A maiden's and a prophet's and thy son's.

ALTHÆA

Well fare the spear that severed him and life.

HERALD

Thine own, and not an alien, hast thou blest.

ALTHÆA

Twice be thou too for my sake blest and his.

HERALD

At the king's word I rode afoam for thine.

ALTHÆA

Thou sayest he tarrieth till they bring the spoil ?

HERALD

Hard by the quarry, where they breathe, O queen.

ALTHÆA

Speak thou their chance ; but some bring flowers and
   crown
These gods and all the lintel, and shed wine,
Fetch sacrifice and slay ; for heaven is good.

HERALD

Some furlongs northward where the brakes begin
West of that narrowing range of warrior hills
Whose brooks have bled with battle when thy son
Smote Acarnania, there all they made halt,
And with keen eye took note of spear and hound,
Royally ranked ; Laertes island-born,
The young Gerenian Nestor, Panopeus,
And Cepheus and Ancæus, mightiest thewed,
Arcadians ; next, and evil-eyed of these,
Arcadian Atalanta, with twain hounds
Lengthening the leash, and under nose and brow
Glittering with lipless tooth and fire-swift eye ;
But from her white braced shoulder the plumed shafts
Rang, and the bow shone from her side ; next her
Meleager, like a sun in spring that strikes
Branch into leaf and bloom into the world,
A glory among men meaner ; Iphicles,
And following him that slew the biform bull
Pirithous, and divine Eurytion,
And, bride-bound to the gods, Æacides.
Then Telamon his brother, and Argive-born
The seer and sayer of visions and of truth,
Amphiaraus ; and a four-fold strength,

Thine, even thy mother's and thy sister's sons.
And recent from the roar of foreign foam
Jason, and Dryas twin-begot with war,
A blossom of bright battle, sword and man
Shining ; and Idas, and the keenest eye
Of Lynceus, and Admetus twice-espoused,
And Hippasus and Hyleus, great in heart.
These having halted bade blow horns, and rode
Through woods and waste lands cleft by stormy
    streams,
Past yew-trees and the heavy hair of pines,
And where the dew is thickest under oaks,
This way and that ; but questing up and down
They saw no trail nor scented ; and one said,
Plexippus, Help, or help not, Artemis,
And we will flay thy boarskin with male hands ;
But saying, he ceased and said not that he would,
Seeing where the green ooze of a sun-struck marsh
Shook with a thousand reeds untunable,
And in their moist and multitudinous flower
Slept no soft sleep, with violent visions fed,
The blind bulk of the immeasurable beast.
And seeing, he shuddered with sharp lust of praise
Through all his limbs, and launched a double dart.
And missed ; for much desire divided him,
Too hot of spirit and feebler than his will,
That his hand failed, though fervent ; and the shaft,
Sundering the rushes, in a tamarisk stem
Shook, and stuck fast ; then all abode save one,
The Arcadian Atalanta ; from her side
Sprang her hounds, labouring at the leash, and
    slipped,
And plashed ear-deep with plunging feet ; but she
Saying, Speed it as I send it for thy sake,

Goddess, drew bow and loosed ; the sudden string
Rang, and sprang inward, and the waterish air
Hissed, and the moist plumes of the songless reeds
Moved as a wave which the wind moves no more.
But the boar heaved half out of ooze and slime
His tense flank trembling round the barbèd wound,
Hateful ; and fiery with invasive eyes
And bristling with intolerable hair
Plunged, and the hounds clung, and green flowers
          and white
Reddened and broke all round them where they
          came.
And charging with sheer tusk he drove, and smote
Hyleus ; and sharp death caught his sudden soul,
And violent sleep shed night upon his eyes.
Then Peleus, with strong strain of hand and heart,
Shot ; but the sidelong arrow slid, and slew
His comrade born and loving countryman,
Under the left arm smitten, as he no less
Poised a like arrow ; and bright blood brake afoam,
And falling, and weighed back by clamorous arms,
Sharp rang the dead limbs of Eurytion.
Then one shot happier, the Cadmean seer,
Amphiaraus ; for his sacred shaft
Pierced the red circlet of one ravening eye
Beneath the brute brows of the sanguine boar,
Now bloodier from one slain ; but he so galled
Sprang straight, and rearing cried no lesser cry
Than thunder and the roar of wintering streams
That mix their own foam with the yellower sea ;
And as a tower that falls by fire in fight
With ruin of walls and all its archery,
And breaks the iron flower of war beneath,
Crushing charred limbs and molten arms of men ;

So through crushed branches and the reddening
　　brake
Clamoured and crashed the fervour of his feet,
And trampled, springing sideways from the tusk,
Too tardy a moving mould of heavy strength,
Ancæus ; and as flakes of weak-winged snow
Break, all the hard thews of his heaving limbs
Broke, and rent flesh fell every way, and blood
Flew, and fierce fragments of no more a man.
Then all the heroes drew sharp breath, and gazed,
And smote not ; but Meleager, but thy son,
Right in the wild way of the coming curse
Rock-rooted, fair with fierce and fastened lips,
Clear eyes, and springing muscle and shortening
　　limb—
With chin aslant indrawn to a tightening throat,
Grave, and with gathered sinews, like a god,—
Aimed on the left side his well-handled spear
Grasped where the ash was knottiest hewn, and
　　smote,
And with no missile wound, the monstrous boar
Right in the hairiest hollow of his hide
Under the last rib, sheer through bulk and bone,
Deep in ; and deeply smitten, and to death,
The heavy horror with his hanging shafts
Leapt, and fell furiously, and from raging lips
Foamed out the latest wrath of all his life.
And all they praised the gods with mightier heart,
Zeus and all gods, but chiefliest Artemis,
Seeing ; but Meleager bade whet knives and flay,
Strip and stretch out the splendour of the spoil ;
And hot and horrid from the work all these
Sat, and drew breath and drank and made great
　　cheer

And washed the hard sweat off their calmer brows.
For much sweet grass grew higher than grew the
    reed,
And good for slumber, and every holier herb,
Narcissus, and the low-lying melilote,
And all of goodliest blade and bloom that springs
Where, hid by heavier hyacinth, violet buds
Blossom and burn ; and fire of yellower flowers
And light of crescent lilies, and such leaves
As fear the Faun's and know the Dryad's foot ;
Olive and ivy and poplar dedicate,
And many a well-spring overwatched of these.
There now they rest ; but me the king bade bear
Good tidings to rejoice this town and thee.
Wherefore be glad, and all ye give much thanks,
For fallen is all the trouble of Calydon.

ALTHÆA

Laud ye the gods ; for this they have given is
    good,
And what shall be they hide until their time.
Much good and somewhat grievous hast thou said,
And either well ; but let all sad things be,
Till all have made before the prosperous gods
Burnt-offering, and poured out the floral wine.
Look fair, O gods, and favourable ; for we
Praise you with no false heart or flattering mouth,
Being merciful, but with pure souls and prayer.

HERALD

Thou hast prayed well ; for whoso fears not these,
But once being prosperous waxes huge of heart,
Him shall some new thing unaware destroy.

CHORUS

O that I now, I too were
By deep wells and water-floods,
Streams of ancient hills, and where
All the wan green places bear
Blossoms cleaving to the sod,
Fruitless fruit, and grasses fair,
Or such darkest ivy-buds
As divide thy yellow hair,
Bacchus, and their leaves that nod
Round thy fawnskin brush the bare
Snow-soft shoulders of a god ;
There the year is sweet, and there
Earth is full of secret springs,
And the fervent rose-cheeked hours,
Those that marry dawn and noon,
There are sunless, there look pale
In dim leaves and hidden air,
Pale as grass or latter flowers
Or the wild vine's wan wet rings
Full of dew beneath the moon,
And all day the nightingale
Sleeps, and all night sings ;
There in cold remote recesses
That nor alien eyes assail,
Feet, nor imminence of wings,
Nor a wind nor any tune,
Thou, O queen and holiest,
Flower the whitest of all things,
With reluctant lengthening tresses
And with sudden splendid breast
Save of maidens unbeholden,
There art wont to enter, there

Thy divine swift limbs and golden
Maiden growth of unbound hair,
Bathed in waters white,
Shine, and many a maid's by thee
In moist woodland or the hilly
Flowerless brakes where wells abound
Out of all men's sight ;
Or in lower pools that see
All their marges clothed all round
With the innumerable lily,
Whence the golden-girdled bee
Flits through flowering rush to fret
White or duskier violet,
Fair as those that in far years
With their buds left luminous
And their little leaves made wet,
From the warmer dew of tears,
Mother's tears in extreme need,
Hid the limbs of Iamus,
Of thy brother's seed ;
For his heart was piteous
Toward him, even as thine heart now
Pitiful toward us ;
Thine, O goddess, turning hither
A benignant blameless brow ;
Seeing enough of evil done
And lives withered as leaves wither
In the blasting of the sun ;
Seeing enough of hunters dead,
Ruin enough of all our year,
Herds and harvests slain and shed,
Herdsmen stricken many an one,
Fruits and flocks consumed together,
And great length of deadly days.

Yet with reverent lips and fear
Turn we toward thee, turn and praise
For this lightening of clear weather
And prosperities begun.
For not seldom, when all air
As bright water without breath
Shines, and when men fear not, fate
Without thunder unaware
Breaks, and brings down death.
Joy with grief ye great gods give,
Good with bad, and overbear
All the pride of us that live,
All the high estate,
As ye long since overbore,
As in old time long before,
Many a strong man and a great,
All that were.
But do thou, sweet, otherwise,
Having heed of all our prayer,
Taking note of all our sighs ;
We beseech thee by thy light,
By thy bow, and thy sweet eyes,
And the kingdom of the night,
Be thou favourable and fair ;
By thine arrows and thy might
And Orion overthrown ;
By the maiden thy delight,
By the indissoluble zone
And the sacred hair.

MESSENGER

Maidens, if ye will sing now, shift your song,
Bow down, cry, wail for pity ; is this a time
For singing ? nay, for strewing of dust and ash,
Rent raiment, and for bruising of the breast.

CHORUS

What new thing wolf-like lurks behind thy words?
What snake's tongue in thy lips? what fire in the
eyes?

MESSENGER

Bring me before the queen and I will speak.

CHORUS

Lo, she comes forth as from thank-offering made.

MESSENGER

A barren offering for a bitter gift.

ALTHÆA

What are these borne on branches, and the face
Covered? no mean men living, but now slain
Such honour have they, if any dwell with death.

MESSENGER

Queen, thy twain brethren and thy mother's sons.

ALTHÆA

Lay down your dead till I behold their blood
If it be mine indeed, and I will weep.

MESSENGER

Weep if thou wilt, for these men shall no more.

ALTHÆA

O brethren, O my father's sons, of me
Well loved and well reputed, I should weep
Tears dearer than the dear blood drawn from you
But that I know you not uncomforted,
Sleeping no shameful sleep, however slain,
For my son surely hath avenged you dead.

MESSENGER

Nay, should thine own seed slay himself, O queen?

ALTHÆA

Thy double word brings forth a double death.

MESSENGER

Know this then singly, by one hand they fell.

ALTHÆA

What mutterest thou with thine ambiguous mouth?

MESSENGER

Slain by thy son's hand; is that saying so hard?

ALTHÆA

Our time is come upon us: it is here.

CHORUS

O miserable, and spoiled at thine own hand.

ALTHÆA

Wert thou not called Meleager from this womb?

CHORUS

A grievous huntsman hath it bred to thee.

ALTHÆA

Wert thou born fire, and shalt thou not devour?

CHORUS

The fire thou madest, will it consume even thee?

ALTHÆA

My dreams are fallen upon me; burn thou too.

CHORUS

Not without God are visions born and die.

ALTHÆA

The gods are many about me ; I am one.

CHORUS

She groans as men wrestling with heavier gods.

ALTHÆA

They rend me, they divide me, they destroy.

CHORUS

Or one labouring in travail of strange births.

ALTHÆA

They are strong, they are strong ; I am broken, and
    these prevail.

CHORUS

The god is great against her ; she will die.

ALTHÆA

Yea, but not now ; for my heart too is great.
I would I were not here in sight of the sun.
But thou, speak all thou sawest, and I will die.

MESSENGER

O queen, for queenlike hast thou borne thyself,
A little word may hold so great mischance.
For in division of the sanguine spoil
These men thy brethren wrangling bade yield up
The boar's head and the horror of the hide
That this might stand a wonder in Calydon,

Hallowed ; and some drew toward them ; but thy son
With great hands grasping all that weight of hair
Cast down the dead heap clanging and collapsed
At female feet, saying This thy spoil not mine,
Maiden, thine own hand for thyself hath reaped,
And all this praise God gives thee : she thereat
Laughed, as when dawn touches the sacred night
The sky sees laugh and redden and divide
Dim lips and eyelids virgin of the sun,
Hers, and the warm slow breasts of morning heave,
Fruitful, and flushed with flame from lamp-lit hours,
And maiden undulation of clear hair
Colour the clouds ; so laughed she from pure heart,
Lit with a low blush to the braided hair,
And rose-coloured and cold like very dawn,
Golden and godlike, chastely with chaste lips,
A faint grave laugh ; and all they held their peace,
And she passed by them.   Then one cried Lo now,
Shall not the Arcadian shoot out lips at us,
Saying all we were despoiled by this one girl ?
And all they rode against her violently
And cast the fresh crown from her hair, and now
They had rent her spoil away, dishonouring her,
Save that Meleager, as a tame lion chafed,
Bore on them, broke them, and as fire cleaves wood
So clove and drove them, smitten in twain ; but she
Smote not nor heaved up hand ; and this man first,
Plexippus, crying out This for love's sake, sweet,
Drove at Meleager, who with spear straightening
Pierced his cheek through ; then Toxeus made for
      him,
Dumb, but his spear spake ; vain and violent words.
Fruitless ; for him too stricken through both sides
The earth felt falling, and his horse's foam

Blanched thy son's face, his slayer; and these being
     slain,
None moved nor spake; but Œneus bade bear hence
These made of heaven infatuate in their deaths,
Foolish; for these would baffle fate, and fell.
And they passed on, and all men honoured her,
Being honourable, as one revered of heaven.

ALTHÆA

What say you, women? is all this not well done?

CHORUS

No man doth well but God hath part in him.

ALTHÆA

But no part here; for these my brethren born
Ye have no part in, these ye know not of
As I that was their sister, a sacrifice
Slain in their slaying.   I would I had died for these;
For this man dead walked with me, child by child,
And made a weak staff for my feebler feet
With his own tender wrist and hand, and held
And led me softly and shewed me gold and steel
And shining shapes of mirror and bright crown
And all things fair; and threw light spears, and
     brought
Young hounds to huddle at my feet and thrust
Tame heads against my little maiden breasts
And please me with great eyes; and those days went
And these are bitter and I a barren queen
And sister miserable, a grievous thing
And mother of many curses; and she too,
My sister Leda, sitting overseas
With fair fruits round her, and her faultless lord,

Shall curse me, saying A sorrow and not a son,
Sister, thou barest, even a burning fire,
A brand consuming thine own soul and me.
But ye now, sons of Thestius, make good cheer,
For ye shall have such wood to funeral fire
As no king hath ; and flame that once burnt down
Oil shall not quicken or breath relume or wine
Refresh again ; much costlier than fine gold,
And more than many lives of wandering men.

CHORUS

O queen, thou hast yet with thee love-worthy things,
Thine husband, and the great strength of thy son.

ALTHÆA

Who shall get brothers for me while I live ?
Who bear them ? who bring forth in lieu of these ?
Are not our fathers and our brethren one,
And no man like them ? are not mine here slain ?
Have we not hung together, he and I,
Flowerwise feeding as the feeding bees,
With mother-milk for honey ? and this man too,
Dead, with my son's spear thrust between his sides,
Hath he not seen us, later born than he,
Laugh with lips filled, and laughed again for love ?
There were no sons then in the world, nor spears,
Nor deadly births of women ; but the gods
Allowed us, and our days were clear of these.
I would I had died unwedded, and brought forth
No swords to vex the world ; for these that spake
Sweet words long since and loved me will not speak
Nor love nor look upon me ; and all my life
I shall not hear nor see them living men.
But I too living, how shall I now live ?

What life shall this be with my son, to know
What hath been and desire what will not be,
Look for dead eyes and listen for dead lips,
And kill mine own heart with remembering them,
And with those eyes that see their slayer alive
Weep, and wring hands that clasp him by the hand?
How shall I bear my dreams of them, to hear
False voices, feel the kisses of false mouths
And footless sound of perished feet, and then
Wake and hear only it may be their own hounds
Whine masterless in miserable sleep,
And see their boar-spears and their beds and seats
And all the gear and housings of their lives
And not the men? shall hounds and horses mourn,
Pine with strange eyes, and prick up hungry ears,
Famish and fail at heart for their dear lords,
And I not heed at all? and those blind things
Fall off from life for love's sake, and I live?
Surely some death is better than some life,
Better one death for him and these and me
For if the gods had slain them it may be
I had endured it ; if they had fallen by war
Or by the nets and knives of privy death
And by hired hands while sleeping, this thing too
I had set my soul to suffer ; or this hunt,
Had this despatched them, under tusk or tooth
Torn, sanguine, trodden, broken ; for all deaths
Or honourable or with facile feet avenged
And hands of swift gods following, all save this,
Are bearable ; but not for their sweet land
Fighting, but not a sacrifice, lo these
Dead ; for I had not then shed all mine heart
Out at mine eyes : then either with good speed,
Being just, I had slain their slayer atoningly,

Or strewn with flowers their fire and on their tombs
Hung crowns, and over them a song, and seen
Their praise outflame their ashes : for all men,
All maidens, had come thither, and from pure lips
Shed songs upon them, from heroic eyes
Tears ; and their death had been a deathless life ;
But now, by no man hired nor alien sword,
By their own kindred are they fallen, in peace,
After much peril, friendless among friends,
By hateful hands they loved ; and how shall mine
Touch these returning red and not from war,
These fatal from the vintage of men's veins,
Dead men my brethren ? how shall these wash off
No festal stains of undelightful wine,
How mix the blood, my blood on them, with me,
Holding mine hand ? or how shall I say, son,
That am no sister ? but by night and day
Shall we not sit and hate each other, and think
Things hate-worthy ? not live with shamefast eyes,
Brow-beaten, treading soft with fearful feet,
Each unupbraided, each without rebuke
Convicted, and without a word reviled
Each of another ? and I shall let thee live
And see thee strong and hear men for thy sake
Praise me, but these thou wouldest not let live
No man shall praise for ever ? these shall lie
Dead, unbeloved, unholpen, all through thee ?
Sweet were they toward me living, and mine heart
Desired them, but was then well satisfied,
That now is as men hungered ; and these dead
I shall want always to the day I die.
For all things else and all men may renew ;
Yea, son for son the gods may give and take,
But never a brother or sister any more.

CHORUS

Nay, for the son lies close about thine heart,
Full of thy milk, warm from thy womb, and drains
Life and the blood of life and all thy fruit,
Eats thee and drinks thee as who breaks bread and
    eats,
Treads wine and drinks, thyself, a sect of thee ;
And if he feed not, shall not thy flesh faint ?
Or drink not, are not thy lips dead for thirst ?
This thing moves more than all things, even thy son,
That thou cleave to him ; and he shall honour thee,
Thy womb that bare him and the breasts he knew,
Reverencing most for thy sake all his gods.

ALTHÆA

But these the gods too gave me, and these my son,
Not reverencing his gods nor mine own heart
Nor the old sweet years nor all venerable things,
But cruel, and in his ravin like a beast,
Hath taken away to slay them : yea, and she
She the strange woman, she the flower, the sword,
Red from spilt blood, a mortal flower to men,
Adorable, detestable—even she
Saw with strange eyes and with strange lips rejoiced,
Seeing these mine own slain of mine own, and me
Made miserable above all miseries made,
A grief among all women in the world,
A name to be washed out with all men's tears.

CHORUS

Strengthen thy spirit ; is this not also a god,
Chance, and the wheel of all necessities ?
Hard things have fallen upon us from harsh gods,
Whom lest worse hap rebuke we not for these.

ALTHÆA

My spirit is strong against itself, and I
For these things' sake cry out on mine own soul
That it endures outrage, and dolorous days,
And life, and this inexpiable impotence.
Weak am I, weak and shameful ; my breath drawn
Shames me, and monstrous things and violent gods.
What shall atone ? what heal me ? what bring back
Strength to the foot, light to the face ? what herb
Assuage me ? what restore me ? what release ?
What strange thing eaten or drunken, O great gods,
Make me as you or as the beasts that feed,
Slay and divide and cherish their own hearts ?
For these ye show us ; and we less than these
Have not wherewith to live as all these things
Which all their lives fare after their own kind
As who doth well rejoicing ; but we ill,
Weeping or laughing, we whom eyesight fails,
Knowledge and light of face and perfect heart,
And hands we lack, and wit ; and all our days
Sin, and have hunger, and die infatuated.
For madness have ye given us and not health,
And sins whereof we know not ; and for these
Death, and sudden destruction unaware.
What shall we say now ? what thing comes of us ?

CHORUS

Alas, for all this all men undergo.

ALTHÆA

Wherefore I will not that these twain, O gods,
Die as a dog dies, eaten of creeping things,
Abominable, a loathing ; but though dead
Shall they have honour and such funereal flame

As strews men's ashes in their enemies' face
And blinds their eyes who hate them : lest men say,
" Lo how they lie, and living had great kin,
And none of these hath pity of them, and none
Regards them lying, and none is wrung at heart,
None moved in spirit for them, naked and slain,
Abhorred, abased, and no tears comfort them : "
And in the dark this grieve Eurythemis,
Hearing how these her sons come down to her
Unburied, unavenged, as kinless men,
And had a queen their sister.   That were shame
Worse than this grief.   Yet how to atone at all
I know not ; seeing the love of my born son,
A new-made mother's new-born love, that grows
From the soft child to the strong man, now soft
Now strong as either, and still one sole same love,
Strives with me, no light thing to strive withal ;
This love is deep, and natural to man's blood,
And ineffaceable with many tears.
Yet shall not these rebuke me though I die,
Nor she in that waste world with all her dead,
My mother, among the pale flocks fallen as leaves,
Folds of dead people, and alien from the sun ;
Nor lack some bitter comfort, some poor praise,
Being queen, to have borne her daughter like a queen,
Righteous ; and though mine own fire burn me too,
She shall have honour and these her sons, though dead.
But all the gods will, all they do, and we
Not all we would, yet somewhat ; and one choice
We have, to live and do just deeds and die.

CHORUS

Terrible words she communes with, and turns
Swift fiery eyes in doubt against herself,
And murmurs as who talks in dreams with death.

ALTHÆA

For the unjust also dieth, and him all men
Hate, and himself abhors the unrighteousness,
And seeth his own dishonour intolerable.
But I being just, doing right upon myself,
Slay mine own soul, and no man born shames me.
For none constrains nor shall rebuke, being done,
What none compelled me doing ; thus these things
    fare.
Ah, ah, that such things should so fare ; ah me,
That I am found to do them and endure,
Chosen and constrained to choose, and bear myself
Mine own wound through mine own flesh to the heart
Violently stricken, a spoiler and a spoil,
A ruin ruinous, fallen on mine own son.
Ah, ah, for me too as for these ; alas,
For that is done that shall be, and mine hand
Full of the deed, and full of blood mine eyes,
That shall see never nor touch anything
Save blood unstanched and fire unquenchable.

CHORUS

What wilt thou do? what ails thee? for the house
Shakes ruinously ; wilt thou bring fire for it?

ALTHÆA

Fire in the roofs, and on the lintels fire.
Lo ye, who stand and weave, between the doors,
There ; and blood drips from hand and thread, and
    stains
Threshold and raiment and me passing in
Flecked with the sudden sanguine drops of death.

CHORUS

Alas that time is stronger than strong men,
Fate than all gods : and these are fallen on us.

ALTHÆA

A little since and I was glad ; and now
I never shall be glad or sad again.

CHORUS

Between two joys a grief grows unaware.

ALTHÆA

A little while and I shall laugh ; and then
I shall weep never and laugh not any more.

CHORUS

What shall be said? for words are thorns to grief.
Withhold thyself a little and fear the gods.

ALTHÆA

Fear died when these were slain ; and I am as dead,
And fear is of the living ; these fear none.

CHORUS

Have pity upon all people for their sake.

ALTHÆA

It is done now ; shall I put back my day?

CHORUS

An end is come, an end ; this is of God.

ALTHÆA

I am fire, and burn myself ; keep clear of fire.

CHORUS

The house is broken, is broken ; it shall not stand.

ALTHÆA

Woe, woe for him that breaketh ; and a rod
Smote it of old, and now the axe is here.

CHORUS

Not as with sundering of the earth
    Nor as with cleaving of the sea
Nor fierce foreshadowings of a birth
    Nor flying dreams of death to be
Nor loosening of the large world's girth
And quickening of the body of night,
    And sound of thunder in men's ears
And fire of lightning in men's sight,
    Fate, mother of desires and fears,
    Bore unto men the law of tears ;
But sudden, an unfathered flame,
    And broken out of night, she shone,
She, without body, without name,
    In days forgotten and foregone ;
And heaven rang round her as she came
Like smitten cymbals, and lay bare ;
    Clouds and great stars, thunders and snows,
The blue sad fields and folds of air,
    The life that breathes, the life that grows,
    All wind, all fire, that burns or blows,
Even all these knew her : for she is great ;
    The daughter of doom, the mother of death,
The sister of sorrow ; a lifelong weight
    That no man's finger lighteneth,
Nor any god can lighten fate ;

A landmark seen across the way
  Where one race treads as the other trod ;
An evil sceptre, an evil stay,
  Wrought for a staff, wrought for a rod,
    The bitter jealousy of God.

For death is deep as the sea,
  And fate as the waves thereof.
Shall the waves take pity on thee
  Or the southwind offer thee love ?
Wilt thou take the night for thy day
Or the darkness for light on thy way,
    Till thou say in thine heart Enough ?
Behold, thou art over fair, thou art over wise ;
The sweetness of spring in thine hair, and the light
    in thine eyes.
The light of the spring in thine eyes, and the sound
    in thine ears ;
Yet thine heart shall wax heavy with sighs and thine
    eyelids with tears.
Wilt thou cover thine hair with gold, and with silver
    thy feet ?
Hast thou taken the purple to fold thee, and made
    thy mouth sweet ?
Behold, when thy face is made bare, he that loved
    thee shall hate ;
Thy face shall be no more fair at the fall of thy fate.
For thy life shall fall as a leaf and be shed as the rain ;
And the veil of thine head shall be grief ; and the
    crown shall be pain.

ALTHÆA

Ho, ye that wail, and ye that sing, make way
Till I be come among you.   Hide your tears,

Ye little weepers, and your laughing lips,
Ye laughers for a little ; lo mine eyes
That outweep heaven at rainiest, and my mouth
That laughs as gods laugh at us. Fate's are we,
Yet fate is ours a breathing-space ; yea, mine,
Fate is made mine for ever ; he is my son,
My bedfellow, my brother. You strong gods,
Give place unto me ; I am as any of you,
To give life and to take life. Thou, old earth,
That hast made man and unmade ; thou whose mouth
Looks red from the eaten fruits of thine own womb ;
Behold me with what lips upon what food
I feed and fill my body ; even with flesh
Made of my body. Lo, the fire I lit
I burn with fire to quench it ; yea, with flame
I burn up even the dust and ash thereof.

CHORUS

Woman, what fire is this thou burnest with ?

ALTHÆA

Yea to the bone, yea to the blood and all.

CHORUS

For this thy face and hair are as one fire.

ALTHÆA

A tongue that licks and beats upon the dust.

CHORUS

And in thine eyes are hollow light and heat.

ALTHÆA

Of flame not fed with hand or frankincense.

CHORUS

I fear thee for the trembling of thine eyes,

ALTHÆA

Neither with love they tremble nor for fear.

CHORUS

And thy mouth shuddering like a shot bird.

ALTHÆA

Not as the bride's mouth when man kisses it.

CHORUS

Nay, but what thing is this thing thou hast done?

ALTHÆA

Look, I am silent, speak your eyes for me.

CHORUS

I see a faint fire lightening from the hall.

ALTHÆA

Gaze, stretch your eyes, strain till the lids drop off.

CHORUS

Flushed pillars down the flickering vestibule.

ALTHÆA

Stretch with your necks like birds : cry, chirp as
they.

CHORUS

And a long brand that blackens : and white dust.

ALTHÆA

O children, what is this ye see? your eyes
Are blinder than night's face at fall of moon.
That is my son, my flesh, my fruit of life,
My travail, and the year's weight of my womb.
Meleager, a fire enkindled of mine hands
And of mine hands extinguished; this is he.

CHORUS

O gods, what word has flown out at thy mouth?

ALTHÆA

I did this and I say this and I die.

CHORUS

Death stands upon the doorway of thy lips,
And in thy mouth has death set up his house.

ALTHÆA

O death, a little, a little while, sweet death,
Until I see the brand burnt down and die.

CHORUS

She reels as any reed under the wind,
And cleaves unto the ground with staggering feet.

ALTHÆA

Girls, one thing will I say and hold my peace.
I that did this will weep not nor cry out,
Cry ye and weep: I will not call on gods,
Call ye on them; I will not pity man,
Shew ye your pity. I know not if I live;
Save that I feel the fire upon my face
And on my cheek the burning of a brand.

Yea the smoke bites me, yea I drink the steam
With nostril and with eyelid and with lip
Insatiate and intolerant ; and mine hands
Burn, and fire feeds upon mine eyes ; I reel
As one made drunk with living, whence he draws
Drunken delight ; yet I, though mad for joy,
Loathe my long living and am waxen red
As with the shadow of shed blood ; behold,
I am kindled with the flames that fade in him,
I am swollen with subsiding of his veins,
I am flooded with his ebbing ; my lit eyes
Flame with the falling fire that leaves his lids
Bloodless ; my cheek is luminous with blood
Because his face is ashen. Yet, O child,
Son, first-born, fairest—O sweet mouth, sweet eyes,
That drew my life out through my suckling breast,
That shone and clove mine heart through—O soft
     knees
Clinging, O tender treadings of soft feet,
Cheeks warm with little kissings—O child, child,
What have we made each other ? Lo, I felt
Thy weight cleave to me, a burden of beauty, O son,
Thy cradled brows and loveliest loving lips,
The floral hair, the little lightening eyes,
And all thy goodly glory ; with mine hands
Delicately I fed thee, with my tongue
Tenderly spake, saying, Verily in God's time,
For all the little likeness of thy limbs,
Son, I shall make thee a kingly man to fight,
A lordly leader ; and hear before I die,
" She bore the goodliest sword of all the world."
Oh ! oh ! For all my life turns round on me ;
I am severed from myself, my name is gone,
My name that was a healing, it is changed,

My name is a consuming.   From this time,
Though mine eyes reach to the end of all these things,
My lips shall not unfasten till I die.

SEMICHORUS

She has filled with sighing the city,
    And the ways thereof with tears ;
She arose, she girdled her sides,
She set her face as a bride's ;
She wept, and she had no pity ;
    Trembled, and felt no fears.

SEMICHORUS

Her eyes were clear as the sun,
    Her brows were fresh as the day ;
She girdled herself with gold,
Her robes were manifold ;
But the days of her worship are done,
    Her praise is taken away.

SEMICHORUS

For she set her hand to the fire,
    With her mouth she kindled the same :
As the mouth of a flute-player,
So was the mouth of her ;
With the might of her strong desire
    She blew the breath of the flame.

SEMICHORUS

She set her hand to the wood,
    She took the fire in her hand ;
As one who is nigh to death,
She panted with strange breath ;
She opened her lips unto blood,
    She breathed and kindled the brand.

SEMICHORUS

As a wood-dove newly shot,
    She sobbed and lifted her breast;
She sighed and covered her eyes,
Filling her lips with sighs;
She sighed, she withdrew herself not,
    She refrained not, taking not rest;

SEMICHORUS

But as the wind which is drouth,
    And as the air which is death,
As storm that severeth ships,
Her breath severing her lips,
The breath came forth of her mouth
    And the fire came forth of her breath.

SECOND MESSENGER

Queen, and you maidens, there is come on us
A thing more deadly than the face of death;
Meleager the good lord is as one slain.

SEMICHORUS

Without sword, without sword is he stricken;
    Slain, and slain without hand.

SECOND MESSENGER

For as keen ice divided of the sun
His limbs divide, and as thawed snow the flesh
Thaws from off all his body to the hair.

SEMICHORUS

He wastes as the embers quicken;
    With the brand he fades as a brand.

SECOND MESSENGER

Even while they sang and all drew hither and he
Lifted both hands to crown the Arcadian's hair
And fix the looser leaves, both hands fell down.

SEMICHORUS

With rending of cheek and of hair
Lament ye, mourn for him, weep.

SECOND MESSENGER

Straightway the crown slid off and smote on earth,
First fallen ; and he, grasping his own hair, groaned
And cast his raiment round his face and fell.

SEMICHORUS

Alas for visions that were,
And soothsayings spoken in sleep.

SECOND MESSENGER

But the king twitched his reins in and leapt down
And caught him, crying out twice " O child " and
        thrice,
So that men's eyelids thickened with their tears.

SEMICHORUS

Lament with a long lamentation,
Cry, for an end is at hand.

SECOND MESSENGER

O son, he said, son, lift thine eyes, draw breath,
Pity me ; but Meleager with sharp lips
Gasped, and his face waxed like as sunburnt grass.

SEMICHORUS

Cry aloud, O thou kingdom, O nation,
   O stricken, a ruinous land.

SECOND MESSENGER

Whereat king Œneus, straightening feeble knees,
With feeble hands heaved up a lessening weight,
And laid him sadly in strange hands, and wept.

SEMICHORUS

Thou art smitten, her lord, her desire,
   Thy dear blood wasted as rain.

SECOND MESSENGER

And they with tears and rendings of the beard
Bear hither a breathing body, wept upon
And lightening at each footfall, sick to death.

SEMICHORUS

Thou madest thy sword as a fire,
   With fire for a sword thou art slain.

SECOND MESSENGER

And lo, the feast turned funeral, and the crowns
Fallen ; and the huntress and the hunter trapped ;
And weeping and changed faces and veiled hair.

MELEAGER

Let your hands meet
   Round the weight of my head ;
Lift ye my feet
   As the feet of the dead ;
For the flesh of my body is molten, the limbs of it
   molten as lead.

CHORUS

O thy luminous face.
   Thine imperious eyes !
O the grief, O the grace,
   As of day when it dies !
Who is this bending over thee, lord, with tears and
   suppression of sighs ?

MELEAGER

Is a bride so fair ?
   Is a maid so meek ?
With unchapleted hair,
   With unfilleted cheek,
Atalanta, the pure among women, whose name is as
   blessing to speak.

ATALANTA

I would that with feet
   Unsandalled, unshod,
Overbold, overfleet,
   I had swum not nor trod
From Arcadia to Calydon northward, a blast of the
   envy of God.

MELEAGER

Unto each man his fate ;
   Unto each as he saith
In whose fingers the weight
   Of the world is as breath ;
Yet I would that in clamour of battle mine hands had
   laid hold upon death.

CHORUS

Not with cleaving of shields
    And their clash in thine ear,
When the lord of fought fields
    Breaketh spearshaft from spear,
Thou art broken, our lord, thou art broken, with
    travail and labour and fear.

MELEAGER

Would God he had found me
    Beneath fresh boughs !
Would God he had bound me
    Unawares in mine house,
With light in mine eyes, and songs in my lips, and a
    crown on my brows !

CHORUS

Whence art thou sent from us ?
    Whither thy goal ?
How art thou rent from us,
    Thou that wert whole,
As with severing of eyelids and eyes, as with sunder-
    ing of body and soul !

MELEAGER

My heart is within me
    As an ash in the fire ;
Whosoever hath seen me,
    Without lute, without lyre,
Shall sing of me grievous things, even things that
    were ill to desire.

CHORUS

Who shall raise thee
    From the house of the dead?
Or what man praise thee
    That thy praise may be said?
Alas thy beauty! alas thy body! alas thine head!

MELEAGER

But thou, O mother,
    The dreamer of dreams,
Wilt thou bring forth another
    To feel the sun's beams
When I move among shadows a shadow, and wail
    by impassable streams?

ŒNEUS

What thing wilt thou leave me
    Now this thing is done?
A man wilt thou give me,
    A son for my son,
For the light of mine eyes, the desire of my life, the
    desirable one?

CHORUS

Thou wert glad above others,
    Yea, fair beyond word;
Thou wert glad among mothers;
    For each man that heard
Of thee, praise there was added unto thee, as wings
    to the feet of a bird.

ŒNEUS

Who shall give back
     Thy face of old years,
With travail made black,
     Grown grey among fears,
Mother of sorrow, mother of cursing, mother of
     tears?

MELEAGER

Though thou art as fire
     Fed with fuel in vain,
My delight, my desire,
     Is more chaste than the rain,
More pure than the dewfall, more holy than stars are
     that live without stain.

ATALANTA

I would that as water
     My life's blood had thawn,
Or as winter's wan daughter
     Leaves lowland and lawn
Spring-stricken, or ever mine eyes had beheld thee
     made dark in thy dawn.

CHORUS

When thou dravest the men
     Of the chosen of Thrace,
None turned him again
     Nor endured he thy face
Clothed round with the blush of the battle, with light
     from a terrible place.

CENEUS

Thou shouldst die as he dies
    For whom none sheddeth tears ;
Filling thine eyes
    And fulfilling thine ears
With the brilliance of battle, the bloom and the
beauty, the splendour of spears.

CHORUS

In the ears of the world
    It is sung, it is told,
And the light thereof hurled
    And the noise thereof rolled
From the Acroceraunian snow to the ford of the
fleece of gold.

MELEAGER

Would God ye could carry me
    Forth of all these ;
Heap sand and bury me
    By the Chersonese
Where the thundering Bosphorus answers the
thunder of Pontic seas.

CENEUS

Dost thou mock at our praise
    And the singing begun
And the men of strange days
    Praising my son
In the folds of the hills of home, high places of
Calydon ?

MELEAGER

For the dead man no home is ;
   Ah, better to be
What the flower of the foam is
   In fields of the sea,
That the sea-waves might be as my raiment, the
   gulf-stream a garment for me.

CHORUS

Who shall seek thee and bring
   And restore thee thy day,
When the dove dipt her wing
   And the oars won their way
Where the narrowing Symplegades whitened the
   straits of Propontis with spray ?

MELEAGER

Will ye crown me my tomb
   Or exalt me my name,
Now my spirits consume,
   Now my flesh is a flame ?
Let the sea slake it once, and men speak of me sleep-
   ing to praise me or shame.

CHORUS

Turn back now, turn thee,
   As who turns him to wake ;
Though the life in thee burn thee,
   Couldst thou bathe it and slake
Where the sea-ridge of Helle hangs heavier, and east
   upon west waters break ?

MELEAGER

Would the winds blow me back
Or the waves hurl me home?
Ah, to touch in the track
Where the pine learnt to roam
Cold girdles and crowns of the sea-gods, cool
blossoms of water and foam!

CHORUS

The gods may release
That they made fast;
Thy soul shall have ease
In thy limbs at the last;
But what shall they give thee for life, sweet life that
is overpast?

MELEAGER

Not the life of men's veins,
Not of flesh that conceives;
But the grace that remains,
The fair beauty that cleaves
To the life of the rains in the grasses, the life of the
dews on the leaves.

CHORUS

Thou wert helmsman and chief;
Wilt thou turn in an hour,
Thy limbs to the leaf,
Thy face to the flower,
Thy blood to the water, thy soul to the gods who
divide and devour?

MELEAGER

The years are hungry,
    They wail all their days ;
The gods wax angry
    And weary of praise ;
And who shall bridle their lips ? and who shall straiten
    their ways ?

CHORUS

The gods guard over us
    With sword and with rod ;
Weaving shadow to cover us,
    Heaping the sod,
That law may fulfil herself wholly, to darken man's
    face before God.

MELEAGER

O holy head of Œneus, lo thy son
Guiltless, yet red from alien guilt, yet foul
With kinship of contaminated lives,
Lo, for their blood I die ; and mine own blood
For bloodshedding of mine is mixed therewith,
That death may not discern me from my kin.
Yet with clean heart I die and faultless hand,
Not shamefully ; thou therefore of thy love
Salute me, and bid fare among the dead
Well, as the dead fare ; for the best man dead
Fares sadly ; nathless I now faring well
Pass without fear where nothing is to fear
Having thy love about me and thy goodwill,
O father, among dark places and men dead.

II.

L 2

OENEUS

Child, I salute thee with sad heart and tears,
And bid thee comfort, being a perfect man
In fight, and honourable in the house of peace.
The gods give thee fair wage and dues of death,
And me brief days and ways to come at thee.

MELEAGER

Pray thou thy days be long before thy death,
And full of ease and kingdom ; seeing in death
There is no comfort and none aftergrowth,
Nor shall one thence look up and see day's dawn
Nor light upon the land whither I go.
Live thou and take thy fill of days and die
When thy day comes ; and make not much of death
Lest ere thy day thou reap an evil thing.
Thou too, the bitter mother and mother-plague
Of this my weary body—thou too, queen,
The source and end, the sower and the scythe,
The rain that ripens and the drought that slays,
The sand that swallows and the spring that feeds,
To make me and unmake me—thou, I say,
Althæa, since my father's ploughshare, drawn
Through fatal seedland of a female field,
Furrowed thy body, whence a wheaten ear
Strong from the sun and fragrant from the rains
I sprang and cleft the closure of thy womb,
Mother, I dying with unforgetful tongue
Hail thee as holy and worship thee as just
Who art unjust and unholy ; and with my knees
Would worship, but thy fire and subtlety,
Dissundering them, devour me ; for these limbs
Are as light dust and crumblings from mine urn

Before the fire has touched them ; and my face
As a dead leaf or dead foot's mark on snow,
And all this body a broken barren tree
That was so strong, and all this flower of life
Disbranched and desecrated miserably,
And minished all that god-like muscle and might
And lesser than a man's : for all my veins
Fail me, and all mine ashen life burns down.
I would thou hadst let me live ; but gods averse,
But fortune, and the fiery feet of change,
And time, these would not, these tread out my life,
These and not thou ; me too thou hast loved, and I
Thee ; but this death was mixed with all my life,
Mine end with my beginning : and this law,
This only, slays me, and not my mother at all.
And let no brother or sister grieve too sore,
Nor melt their hearts out on me with their tears,
Since extreme love and sorrowing overmuch
Vex the great gods, and overloving men
Slay and are slain for love's sake ; and this house
Shall bear much better children ; why should these
Weep ? but in patience let them live their lives
And mine pass by forgotten : thou alone,
Mother, thou sole and only, thou not these,
Keep me in mind a little when I die
Because I was thy first-born ; let thy soul
Pity me, pity even me gone hence and dead,
Though thou wert wroth, and though thou bear again
Much happier sons, and all men later born
Exceedingly excel me ; yet do thou
Forget not, nor think shame ; I was thy son.
Time was I did not shame thee ; and time was
I thought to live and make thee honourable
With deeds as great as these men's ; but they live,

These, and I die ; and what thing should have been
Surely I know not ; yet I charge thee, seeing
I am dead already, love me not the less,
Me, O my mother ; I charge thee by these gods,
My father's, and that holier breast of thine,
By these that see me dying, and that which nursed,
Love me not less, thy first-born : though grief come,
Grief only, of me, and of all these great joy,
And shall come always to thee ; for thou knowest,
O mother, O breasts that bare me, for ye know,
O sweet head of my mother, sacred eyes,
Ye know my soul albeit I sinned, ye know
Albeit I kneel not neither touch thy knees,
But with my lips I kneel, and with my heart
I fall about thy feet and worship thee.
And ye farewell now, all my friends ; and ye,
Kinsmen, much younger and glorious more than I,
Sons of my mother's sister ; and all farewell
That were in Colchis with me, and bare down
The waves and wars that met us : and though times
Change, and though now I be not anything,
Forget not me among you, what I did
In my good time ; for even by all those days,
Those days and this, and your own living souls,
And by the light and luck of you that live,
And by this miserable spoil, and me
Dying, I beseech you, let my name not die.
But thou, dear, touch me with thy rose-like hands,
And fasten up mine eyelids with thy mouth,
A bitter kiss ; and grasp me with thine arms,
Printing with heavy lips my light waste flesh,
Made light and thin by heavy-handed fate,
And with thine holy maiden eyes drop dew,
Drop tears for dew upon me who am dead,

Me who have loved thee ; seeing without sin done
I am gone down to the empty weary house
Where no flesh is nor beauty nor swift eyes
Nor sound of mouth nor might of hands and feet.
But thou, dear, hide my body with thy veil,
And with thy raiment cover foot and head,
And stretch thyself upon me and touch hands
With hands and lips with lips : be pitiful
As thou art maiden perfect ; let no man
Defile me to despise me, saying, This man
Died woman-wise, a woman's offering, slain
Through female fingers in his woof of life,
Dishonourable ; for thou hast honoured me.
And now for God's sake kiss me once and twice
And let me go ; for the night gathers me,
And in the night shall no man gather fruit

ATALANTA

Hail thou : but I with heavy face and feet
Turn homeward and am gone out of thine eyes.

CHORUS

Who shall contend with his lords
    Or cross them or do them wrong ?
Who shall bind them as with cords ?
    Who shall tame them as with song ?
Who shall smite them as with swords ?
    For the hands of their kingdom are strong.

ERECHTHEUS

A TRAGEDY

ὦ ταὶ λιπαραὶ καὶ ἰοστέφανοι καὶ ἀοίδιμοι,
Ἑλλάδος ἔρεισμα, κλειναὶ Ἀθᾶναι, δαιμόνιον πτολίεθρον.

PIND. Fr. 47.

AT. τίς δὲ ποιμάνωρ ἔπεστι κἀπιδεσπόζει στρατοῦ;
XO. οὔτινος δοῦλοι κέκληνται φωτὸς οὐδ' ὑπήκοοι.

ÆSCH. Pers. 241-2.

TO

MY MOTHER

PERSONS

ERECHTHEUS.

CHORUS OF ATHENIAN ELDERS.

PRAXITHEA.

CHTHONIA.

HERALD OF EUMOLPUS.

MESSENGER.

ATHENIAN HERALD.

ATHENA.

ERECHTHEUS

ERECHTHEUS

MOTHER of life and death and all men's days,
Earth, whom I chief of all men born would bless,
And call thee with more loving lips than theirs
Mother, for of this very body of thine
And living blood I have my breath and live,
Behold me, even thy son, me crowned of men,
Me made thy child by that strong cunning God
Who fashions fire and iron, who begat
Me for a sword and beacon-fire on thee,
Me fosterling of Pallas, in her shade
Reared, that I first might pay the nursing debt,
Hallowing her fame with flower of third-year feasts,
And first bow down the bridled strength of steeds
To lose the wild wont of their birth, and bear
Clasp of man's knees and steerage of his hand
Or fourfold service of his fire-swift wheels
That whirl the four-yoked chariot ; me the king
Who stand before thee naked now, and cry,
O holy and general mother of all men born,
But mother most and motherliest of mine,
Earth, for I ask thee rather of all the Gods,
What have we done ? what word mistimed or work
Hath winged the wild feet of this timeless curse
To fall as fire upon us ? Lo, I stand

Here on this brow's crown of the city's head
That crowns its lovely body, till death's hour
Waste it ; but now the dew of dawn and birth
Is fresh upon it from thy womb, and we
Behold it born how beauteous ; one day more
I see the world's wheel of the circling sun
Roll up rejoicing to regard on earth
This one thing goodliest, fair as heaven or he,
Worth a God's gaze or strife of Gods ; but now
Would this day's ebb of their spent wave of strife
Sweep it to sea, wash it on wreck, and leave
A costless thing contemned ; and in our stead,
Where these walls were and sounding streets of men,
Make wide a waste for tongueless water-herds
And spoil of ravening fishes ; that no more
Should men say, Here was Athens. This shalt thou
Sustain not, nor thy son endure to see,
Nor thou to live and look on ; for the womb
Bare me not base that bare me miserable,
To hear this loud brood of the Thracian foam
Break its broad strength of billowy-beating war
Here, and upon it as a blast of death
Blowing, the keen wrath of a fire-souled king,
A strange growth grafted on our natural soil,
A root of Thrace in Eleusinian earth
Set for no comfort to the kindly land,
Son of the sea's lord and our first-born foe,
Eumolpus ; nothing sweet in ears of thine
The music of his making, nor a song
Toward hopes of ours auspicious ; for the note
Rings as for death oracular to thy sons
That goes before him on the sea-wind blown
Full of this charge laid on me, to put out
The brief light kindled of mine own child's life,

Or with this helmsman hand that steers the state
Run right on the under shoal and ridge of death
The populous ship with all its fraughtage gone
And sails that were to take the wind of time
Rent, and the tackling that should hold out fast
In confluent surge of loud calamities
Broken, with spars of rudders and lost oars
That were to row toward harbour and find rest
In some most glorious haven of all the world
And else may never near it : such a song
The Gods have set his lips on fire withal
Who threatens now in all their names to bring
Ruin ; but none of these, thou knowest, have I
Chid with my tongue or cursed at heart for grief,
Knowing how the soul runs reinless on sheer death
Whose grief or joy takes part against the Gods.
And what they will is more than our desire,
And their desire is more than what we will.
For no man's will and no desire of man's
Shall stand as doth a God's will.   Yet, O fair
Mother, that seest me how I cast no word
Against them, plead no reason, crave no cause,
Boast me not blameless, nor beweep me wronged,
By this fair wreath of towers we have decked thee
        with,
This chaplet that we give thee woven of walls,
This girdle of gate and temple and citadel
Drawn round beneath thy bosom, and fast linked
As to thine heart's root—this dear crown of thine.
This present light, this city—be not thou
Slow to take heed nor slack to strengthen her,
Fare we so short-lived howsoe'er, and pay
What price we may to ransom thee thy town,
Not me my life ; but thou that diest not, thou,

Though all our house die for this people's sake,
Keep thou for ours thy crown our city, guard
And give it life the lovelier that we died.

CHORUS.

Sun, that hast lightened and loosed by thy might
Ocean and Earth from the lordship of night,
Quickening with vision his eye that was veiled,
Freshening the force in her heart that had failed,
That sister fettered and blinded brother
Should have sight by thy grace and delight of each
     other,
    Behold now and see
  What profit is given them of thee ;
What wrath has enkindled with madness of mind
Her limbs that were bounden, his face that was blind,
To be locked as in wrestle together, and lighten
With fire that shall darken thy fire in the sky,
Body to body and eye against eye
    In a war against kind,
Till the bloom of her fields and her high hills whiten
  With the foam of his waves more high.
For the sea-marks set to divide of old
The kingdoms to Ocean and Earth assigned,
The hoar sea-fields from the cornfields' gold,
His wine-bright waves from her vineyards' fold,
    Frail forces we find
To bridle the spirit of Gods or bind
  Till the heat of their hearts wax cold.
But the peace that was stablished between them to
    stand
Is rent now in twain by the strength of his hand
Who stirs up the storm of his sons overbold
To pluck from fight what he lost of right,

By council and judgment of Gods that spake
And gave great Pallas the strife's fair stake,
The lordship and love of the lovely land,
The grace of the town that hath on it for crown
    But a headband to wear
  Of violets one-hued with her hair :
For the vales and the green high places of earth
    Hold nothing so fair,
And the depths of the sea bear no such birth
  Of the manifold births they bear.
Too well, too well was the great stake worth
A strife divine for the Gods to judge,
A crowned God's triumph, a foiled God's grudge,
Though the loser be strong and the victress wise
Who played long since for so large a prize,
The fruitful immortal anointed adored
Dear city of men without master or lord,
Fair fortress and fostress of sons born free,
Who stand in her sight and in thine, O sun,
Slaves of no man, subjects of none ;
A wonder enthroned on the hills and sea,
A maiden crowned with a fourfold glory
That none from the pride of her head may rend,
Violet and olive-leaf purple and hoary,
Song-wreath and story the fairest of fame,
Flowers that the winter can blast not or bend ;
A light upon earth as the sun's own flame,
    A name as his name,
  Athens, a praise without end.

A noise is arisen against us of waters,   [*Str.* 1.
  A sound as of battle come up from the sea.
Strange hunters are hard on us, hearts without pity;
They have staked their nets round the fair young city,

That the sons of her strength and her virgin
    daughters
  Should find not whither alive to flee.
And we know not yet of the word unwritten, [*Ant.* 1.
  The doom of the Pythian we have not heard;
From the navel of earth and the veiled mid altar
We wait for a token with hopes that falter,
With fears that hang on our hearts thought-smitten
  Lest her tongue be kindled with no good word.
O thou not born of the womb, nor bred   [*Str.* 2.
In the bride-night's warmth of a changed God's bed,
But thy life as a lightning was flashed from the light
    of thy father's head,
O chief God's child by a motherless birth,
If aught in thy sight we indeed be worth,
Keep death from us thou, that art none of the Gods
    of the dead under earth.
  Thou that hast power on us, save, if thou wilt; [*Ant.* 2.
  Let the blind wave breach not thy wall scarce
    built;
But bless us not so as by bloodshed, impute not for
    grace to us guilt,
  Nor by price of pollution of blood set us free;
  Let the hands be taintless that clasp thy knee,
Nor a maiden be slain to redeem for a maiden her
    shrine from the sea.
    O earth, O sun, turn back   [*Str.* 3.
    Full on his deadly track
Death, that would smite you black and mar your
  . creatures,
    And with one hand disroot
    All tender flower and fruit,
With one strike blind and mute the heaven's fair
    features.

Pluck out the eyes of morn, and make
Silence in the east and blackness whence the bright
   songs break.
     Help, earth, help, heaven, that hear   [*Ant.* 3.
     The song-notes of our fear,
Shrewd notes and shrill, not clear or joyful-sounding ;
     Hear, highest of Gods, and stay
     Death on his hunter's way,
Full on his forceless prey his beagles hounding ;
     Break thou his bow, make short his hand,
Maim his fleet foot whose passage kills the living
   land.
    Let a third wave smite not us, father,   [*Str.* 4.
     Long since sore smitten of twain,
       Lest the house of thy son's son perish
       And his name be barren on earth.
   Whose race wilt thou comfort rather
     If none to thy son remain ?
      Whose seed wilt thou choose to cherish
      If his be cut off in the birth ?
  For the first fair graft of his graffing   [*Ant.* 4.
    Was rent from its maiden root
     By the strong swift hand of a lover
     Who fills the night with his breath ;
On the lip of the stream low-laughing
   Her green soft virginal shoot
     Was plucked from the stream-side cover
     By the grasp of a love like death.
For a God's was the mouth that kissed her [*Str.* 5.
  Who speaks, and the leaves lie dead,
    When winter awakes as at warning
     To the sound of his foot from Thrace.
Nor happier the bed of her sister
   Though Love's self laid her abed

By a bridegroom beloved of the morning
    And fair as the dawn's own face.
For Procris, ensnared and ensnaring   [*Ant.* 5.
    By the fraud of a twofold wile,
        With the point of her own spear stricken
            By the gift of her own hand fell.
Oversubtle in doubts, overdaring
    In deeds and devices of guile,
        And strong to quench as to quicken,
            O Love, have we named thee well?
By thee was the spear's edge whetted   [*Str.* 6.
    That laid her dead in the dew,
        In the moist green glens of the midland
            By her dear lord slain and thee.
And him at the cliff's end fretted
    By the grey keen waves, him too,
        Thine hand from the white-browed headland
            Flung down for a spoil to the sea.
But enough now of griefs grey-growing   [*Ant.* 6.
    Have darkened the house divine,
        Have flowered on its boughs and faded,
            And green is the brave stock yet.
O father all seeing and all knowing,
    Let the last fruit fall not of thine
        From the tree with whose boughs we are
            shaded,
        From the stock that thy son's hand set.

ERECHTHEUS

O daughter of Cephisus, from all time
Wise have I found thee, wife and queen, of heart
Perfect ; nor in the days that knew not wind
Nor days when storm blew death upon our peace

Was thine heart swoln with seed of pride, or bowed
With blasts of bitter fear that break men's souls
Who lift too high their minds toward heaven, in
    thought
Too godlike grown for worship ; but of mood
Equal, in good time reverent of time bad,
And glad in ill days of the good that were.
Nor now too would I fear thee, now misdoubt
Lest fate should find thee lesser than thy doom,
Chosen if thou be to bear and to be great
Haply beyond all women ; and the word
Speaks thee divine, dear queen, that speaks thee dead,
Dead being alive, or quick and dead in one
Shall not men call thee living ? yet I fear
To slay thee timeless with my proper tongue,
With lips, thou knowest, that love thee ; and such
    work
Was never laid of Gods on men, such word
No mouth of man learnt ever, as from mine
Most loth to speak thine ear most loth shall take
And hold it hateful as the grave to hear.

PRAXITHEA

That word there is not in all speech of man,
King, that being spoken of the Gods and thee
I have not heart to honour, or dare hold
More than I hold thee or the Gods in hate
Hearing ; but if my heart abhor it heard
Being insubmissive, hold me not thy wife
But use me like a stranger, whom thine hand
Hath fed by chance and finding thence no thanks
Flung off for shame's sake to forgetfulness.

ERECHTHEUS

O, of what breath shall such a word be made,
Or from what heart find utterance? Would my
   tongue
Were rent forth rather from the quivering root
Than made as fire or poison thus for thee.

PRAXITHEA

But if thou speak of blood, and I that hear
Be chosen of all for this land's love to die
And save to thee thy city, know this well,
Happiest I hold me of her seed alive.

ERECHTHEUS

O sun that seest, what saying was this of thine,
God, that thy power has breathed into my lips?
For from no sunlit shrine darkling it came.

PRAXITHEA

What portent from the mid oracular place
Hath smitten thee so like a curse that flies
Wingless, to waste men with its plagues? yet speak.

ERECHTHEUS

Thy blood the Gods require not ; take this first.

PRAXITHEA

To me than thee more grievous this should sound.

ERECHTHEUS

That word rang truer and bitterer than it knew.

PRAXITHEA

This is not then thy grief, to see me die ?

ERECHTHEUS

Die shalt thou not, yet give thy blood to death.

PRAXITHEA

If this ring worse I know not ; strange it rang.

ERECHTHEUS

Alas, thou knowest not ; woe is me that know.

PRAXITHEA

And woe shall mine be, knowing ; yet halt not here.

ERECHTHEUS

Guiltless of blood this state may stand no more.

PRAXITHEA

Firm let it stand whatever bleed or fall.

ERECHTHEUS

O Gods, that I should say it shall and weep.

PRAXITHEA

Weep, and say this? no tears should bathe such words

ERECHTHEUS

Woe's me that I must weep upon them, woe.

PRAXITHEA

What stain is on them for thy tears to cleanse?

ERECHTHEUS

A stain of blood unpurgeable with tears.

PRAXITHEA

Whence? for thou sayest it is and is not mine.

ERECHTHEUS

Hear then and know why only of all men I
That bring such news as mine is, I alone
Must wash good words with weeping ; I and thou,
Woman, must wail to hear men sing, must groan
To see their joy who love us; all our friends
Save only we, and all save we that love
This holiness of Athens, in our sight
Shall lift their hearts up, in our hearing praise
Gods whom we may not ; for to these they give
Life of their children, flower of all their seed,
For all their travail fruit, for all their hopes
Harvest ; but we for all our good things, we
Have at their hands which fill all these folk full
Death, barrenness, child-slaughter, curses, cares,
Sea-leaguer and land-shipwreck ; which of these,
Which wilt thou first give thanks for ? all are thine.

PRAXITHEA

What first they give who give this city good,
For that first given to save it I give thanks
First, and thanks heartier from a happier tongue,
More than for any my peculiar grace
Shown me and not my country ; next for this
That none of all these but for all these I
Must bear my burden, and no eye but mine
Weep of all women's in this broad land born
Who see their land's deliverance ; but much more,
But most for this I thank them most of all,
That this their edge of doom is chosen to pierce
My heart and not my country's ; for the sword
Drawn to smite there and sharpened for such stroke
Should wound more deep than any turned on me.

CHORUS

Well fares the land that bears such fruit, and well
The spirit that breeds such thought and speech in man.

ERECHTHEUS

O woman, thou hast shamed my heart with thine,
To show so strong a patience ; take then all ;
For all shall break not nor bring down thy soul.
The word that journeying to the bright God's shrine
Who speaks askance and darkling, but his name
Hath in it slaying and ruin broad writ out,
I heard, hear thou : thus saith he ; There shall die
One soul for all this people ; from thy womb
Came forth the seed that here on dry bare ground
Death's hand must sow untimely, to bring forth
Nor blade nor shoot in season, being by name
To the under Gods made holy, who require
For this land's life her death and maiden blood
To save a maiden city.   Thus I heard,
And thus with all said leave thee ; for save this
No word is left us, and no hope alive.

CHORUS

He hath uttered too surely his wrath not obscurely,
          nor wrapt as in mists of his breath,   [Str.
The master that lightens not hearts he enlightens, but
          gives them foreknowledge of death.
     As a bolt from the cloud hath he sent it aloud and
          proclaimed it afar,
  From the darkness and height of the horror of night
          hath he shown us a star.
          Star may I name it and err not, or flame shall I say,
          Born of the womb that was born for the tomb
          of the day ?

O Night, whom other but thee for mother, and Death
      for the father, Night,   [*Ant.*
Snall we dream to discover, save thee and thy lover,
      to bring such a sorrow to sight?
    From the slumberless bed for thy bedfellow spread
      and his bride under earth
    Hast thou brought forth a wild and insatiable child,
      an unbearable birth.
      Fierce are the fangs of his wrath, and the pangs
        that they give;
      None is there, none that may bear them, not one
        that would live.

CHTHONIA

Forth of the fine-spun folds of veils that hide
My virgin chamber toward the full-faced sun
I set my foot not moved of mine own will,
Unmaidenlike, nor with unprompted speed
Turn eyes too broad or doglike unabashed
On reverend heads of men and thence on thine,
Mother, now covered from the light and bowed
As hers who mourns her brethren; but what grief
Bends thy blind head thus earthward, holds thus mute,
I know not till thy will be to lift up
Toward mine thy sorrow-muffled eyes and speak;
And till thy will be would I know this not.

PRAXITHEA

Old men and childless, or if sons ye have seen
And daughters, elder-born were these than mine,
Look on this child, how young of years, how sweet,
How scant of time and green of age her life
Puts forth its flower of girlhood; and her gait
How virginal, how soft her speech, her eyes

How seemly smiling ; wise should all ye be,
All honourable and kindly men of age ;
Now give me counsel and one word to say
That I may bear to speak, and hold my peace
Henceforth for all time even as all ye now.
Dumb are ye all, bowed eyes and tongueless mouths,
Unprofitable ; if this were wind that speaks,
As much its breath might move you.   Thou then,
  child,
Set thy sweet eyes on mine ; look through them well ;
Take note of all the writing of my face
As of a tablet or a tomb inscribed
That bears me record ; lifeless now, my life
Thereon that was think written ; brief to read,
Yet shall the scripture sear thine eyes as fire
And leave them dark as dead men's.   Nay, dear child,
Thou hast no skill, my maiden, and no sense
To take such knowledge ; sweet is all thy lore,
And all this bitter ; yet I charge thee learn
And love and lay this up within thine heart,
Even this my word ; less ill it were to die
Than live and look upon thy mother dead,
Thy mother-land that bare thee ; no man slain
But him who hath seen it shall men count unblest,
None blest as him who hath died and seen it not.

CHTHONIA

That sight some God keep from me though I die.

PRAXITHEA

A God from thee shall keep it ; fear not this.

CHTHONIA

Thanks all my life long shall he gain of mine.

PRAXITHEA

Short gain of all yet shall he get of thee.

CHTHONIA

Brief be my life, yet so long live my thanks.

PRAXITHEA

So long? so little; how long shall they live?

CHTHONIA

Even while I see the sunlight and thine eyes.

PRAXITHEA

Would mine might shut ere thine upon the sun.

CHTHONIA

For me thou prayest unkindly; change that prayer.

PRAXITHEA

Not well for me thou sayest, and ill for thee.

CHTHONIA

Nay, for me well, if thou shalt live, not I.

PRAXITHEA

How live, and lose these loving looks of thine?

CHTHONIA

It seems I too, thus praying, then, love thee not.

PRAXITHEA

Lov'st thou not life? what wouldst thou do to die?

CHTHONIA

Well, but not more than all things, love I life.

PRAXITHEA

And fain wouldst keep it as thine age allows?

CHTHONIA

Fain would I live, and fain not fear to die.

PRAXITHEA

That I might bid thee die not !   Peace ; no more.

CHORUS

A godlike race of grief the Gods have set
For these to run matched equal, heart with heart.

PRAXITHEA

Child of the chief of Gods, and maiden crowned,
Queen of these towers and fostress of their king,
Pallas, and thou my father's holiest head,
A living well of life nor stanched nor stained,
O God Cephisus, thee too charge I next,
Be to me judge and witness ; nor thine ear
Shall now my tongue invoke not, thou to me
Most hateful of things holy, mournfullest
Of all old sacred streams that wash the world,
Ilissus, on whose marge at flowery play
A whirlwind-footed bridegroom found my child
And rapt her northward where mine elder-born
Keeps now the Thracian bride-bed of a God
Intolerable to seamen, but this land
Finds him in hope for her sake favourable,
A gracious son by wedlock ; hear me then
Thou likewise, if with no faint heart or false
The word I say be said, the gift be given,
Which might I choose I had rather die than give
Or speak and die not.   Ere thy limbs were made

Or thine eyes lightened, strife, thou knowest, my
    child,
'Twixt God and God had risen, which heavenlier
    name
Should here stand hallowed, whose more liberal grace
Should win this city's worship, and our land
To which of these do reverence ; first the lord
Whose wheels make lightnings of the foam-flowered
    sea
Here on this rock, whose height brow-bound with
    dawn
Is head and heart of Athens, one sheer blow
Struck, and beneath the triple wound that shook
The stony sinews and stark roots of the earth
Sprang toward the sun a sharp salt fount, and sank
Where lying it lights the heart up of the hill,
A well of bright strange brine ; but she that reared
Thy father with her same chaste fostering hand
Set for a sign against it in our guard
The holy bloom of the olive, whose hoar leaf
High in the shadowy shrine of Pandrosus
Hath honour of us all ; and of this strife
The twelve most high Gods judging with one mouth
Acclaimed her victress ; wroth whereat, as wronged
That she should hold from him such prize and place,
The strong king of the tempest-rifted sea
Loosed reinless on the low Thriasian plain
The thunders of his chariots, swallowing stunned
Earth, beasts, and men, the whole blind foundering
    world
That was the sun's at morning, and ere noon
Death's ; nor this only prey fulfilled his mind ;
For with strange crook-toothed prows of Carian folk
Who snatch a sanguine life out of the sea,

Thieves keen to pluck their bloody fruit of spoil
From the grey fruitless waters, has their God
Furrowed our shores to waste them, as the fields
Were landward harried from the north with swords
Aonian, sickles of man-slaughtering edge
Ground for no hopeful harvest of live grain
Against us in Bœotia ; these being spent,
Now this third time his wind of wrath has blown
Right on this people a mightier wave of war,
Three times more huge a ruin ; such its ridge
Foam-rimmed and hollow like the womb of heaven,
But black for shining, and with death for life
Big now to birth and ripe with child, full-blown
With fear and fruit of havoc, takes the sun
Out of our eyes, darkening the day, and blinds
The fair sky's face unseasonably with change,
A cloud in one and billow of battle, a surge
High reared as heaven with monstrous surf of spears
That shake on us their shadow, till men's heads
Bend, and their hearts even with its forward wind
Wither, so blasts all seed in them of hope
Its breath and blight of presage ; yea, even now
The winter of this wind out of the deeps
Makes cold our trust in comfort of the Gods
And blind our eye toward outlook ; yet not here,
Here never shall the Thracian plant on high
For ours his father's symbol, nor with wreaths
A strange folk wreathe it upright set and crowned
Here where our natural people born behold
The golden Gorgon of the shield's defence
That screens their flowering olive, nor strange Gods
Be graced, and Pallas here have praise no more.
And if this be not I must give my child,
Thee, mine own very blood and spirit of mine,

Thee to be slain.   Turn from me, turn thine eyes
A little from me ; I can bear not yet
To see if still they smile on mine or no,
If fear make faint the light in them, or faith
Fix them as stars of safety.   Need have we,
Sore need of stars that set not in mid storm,
Lights that outlast the lightnings ; yet my heart
Endures not to make proof of thine or these,
Not yet to know thee whom I made, and bare
What manner of woman ; had I borne thee man,
I had made no question of thine eyes or heart,
Nor spared to read the scriptures in them writ,
Wert thou my son ; yet couldst thou then but die
Fallen in sheer fight by chance and charge of spears
And have no more of memory, fill no tomb
More famous than thy fellows in fair field,
Where many share the grave, many the praise ;
But one crown shall one only girl my child
Wear, dead for this dear city, and give back life
To him that gave her and to me that bare,
And save two sisters living ; and all this,
Is this not all good ?   I shall give thee, child,
Thee but by fleshly nature mine, to bleed
For dear land's love ; but if the city fall
What part is left me in my children then ?
But if it stand and thou for it lie dead,
Then hast thou in it a better part than we,
A holier portion than we all ; for each
Hath but the length of his own life to live,
And this most glorious mother-land on earth
To worship till that life have end ; but thine
Hath end no more than hers ; thou, dead, shalt live
Till Athens live not ; for the days and nights
Given of thy bare brief dark dividual life,

Shall she give thee half all her agelong own
And all its glory ; for thou givest her these ;
But with one hand she takes and gives again
More than I gave or she requires of thee.
Come therefore, I will make thee fit for death,
I that could give thee, dear, no gift at birth
Save of light life that breathes and bleeds, even I
Will help thee to this better gift than mine
And lead thee by this little living hand
That death shall make so strong, to that great end
Whence it shall lighten like a God's, and strike
Dead the strong heart of battle that would break
Athens ; but ye, pray for this land, old men,
That it may bring forth never child on earth
To love it less, for none may more, than we.

CHORUS

Out of the north wind grief came forth,   [*Str.* 1.
　And the shining of a sword out of the sea.
Yea, of old the first-blown blast blew the prelude
　　of this last,
　The blast of his trumpet upon Rhodope.
Out of the north skies full of his cloud,
With the clamour of his storms as of a crowd
At the wheels of a great king crying aloud,
At the axle of a strong king's car
That has girded on the girdle of war—
With hands that lightened the skies in sunder
And feet whose fall was followed of thunder,
　A God, a great God strange of name,
　With horse-yoke fleeter-hoofed than flame,
To the mountain bed of a maiden came,
Oreithyia, the bride mismated,

II.   M 2

Wofully wed in a snow-strewn bed
With a bridegroom that kisses the bride's mouth
    dead ;
Without garland, without glory, without song,
As a fawn by night on the hills belated,
Given over for a spoil unto the strong.
From lips how pale so keen a wail   [*Ant.* 1.
    At the grasp of a God's hand on her she gave,
When his breath that darkens air made a havoc
    of her hair,
    It rang from the mountain even to the wave ;
Rang with a cry, *Woe's me, woe is me !*
From the darkness upon Hæmus to the sea :
And with hands that clung to her new lord's knee,
As a virgin overborne with shame,
She besought him by her spouseless fame,
By the blameless breasts of a maid unmarried,
And locks unmaidenly rent and harried,
    And all her flower of body, born
    To match the maidenhood of morn,
With the might of the wind's wrath wrenched and
    torn.
Vain, all vain as a dead man's vision
Falling by night in his old friends' sight,
To be scattered with slumber and slain ere light ;
Such a breath of such a bridegroom in that hour
Of her prayers made mock, of her fears derision,
And a ravage of her youth as of a flower.
With a leap of his limbs as a lion's, a cry from his
            lips as of thunder,   [*Str.* 2.
In a storm of amorous godhead filled with fire,
From the height of the heaven that was rent with
            the roar of his coming in sunder,
    Sprang the strong God on the spoil of his desire.

And the pines of the hills were as green reeds
    shattered,
And their branches as buds of the soft spring
    scattered,
And the west wind and east, and the sound of the
    south,
Fell dumb at the blast of the north wind's mouth,
  At the cry of his coming out of heaven.
And the wild beasts quailed in the rifts and hollows
Where hound nor clarion of huntsman follows,
And the depths of the sea were aghast, and
    whitened,
And the crowns of their waves were as flame that
    lightened,
  And the heart of the floods thereof was riven.
But she knew not him coming for terror, she felt not
    her wrong that he wrought her,   [*Ant.* 2.
  When her locks as leaves were shed before his
    breath,
And she heard not for terror his prayer, though the
    cry was a God's that besought her,
  Blown from lips that strew the world-wide seas
    with death.
  For the heart was molten within her to hear,
  And her knees beneath her were loosened for
    fear,
  And her blood fast bound as a frost-bound water,
  And the soft new bloom of the green earth's
    daughter
    Wind-wasted as blossom of a tree ;
  As the wild God rapt her from earth's breast
    lifted,
  On the strength of the stream of his dark breath
    drifted,

From the bosom of earth as a bride from the
    mother,
With storm for bridesman and wreck for brother.
    As a cloud that he sheds upon the sea.

      Of this hoary-headed woe   [*Epode.*
      Song made memory long ago ;
      Now a younger grief to mourn
      Needs a new song younger born.
      Who shall teach our tongues to reach
      What strange height of saddest speech,
    For the new bride's sake that is given to be
    A stay to fetter the foot of the sea,
    Lest it quite spurn down and trample the town,
    Ere the violets be dead that were plucked for
      its crown,
      Or its olive-leaf whiten and wither ?
      Who shall say of the wind's way
      That he journeyed yesterday,
    Or the track of the storm that shall sound to-
      morrow,
    If the new be more than the grey-grown sorrow ?
    For the wind of the green first season was keen,
    And the blast shall be sharper than blew between
      That the breath of the sea blows hither.

HERALD OF EUMOLPUS

Old men, grey borderers on the march of death,
Tongue-fighters, tough of talk and sinewy speech,
Else nerveless, from no crew of such faint folk
Whose tongues are stouter than their hands come I
To bid not you to battle ; let them strike
Whose swords are sharper than your keen-tongued
    wail,

And ye, sit fast and sorrow ; but what man
Of all this land-folk and earth-labouring herd
For heart or hand seems foremost, him I call
If heart be his to hearken, him bid forth
To try if one be in the sun's sight born
Of all that grope and grovel on dry ground
That may join hands in battle grip for death
With them whose seed and strength is of the sea.

CHORUS

Know thou this much for all thy loud blast blown,
We lack not hands to speak with, swords to plead,
For proof of peril, not of boisterous breath,
Sea-wind and storm of barren mouths that foam
And rough rock's edge of menace ; and short space
May lesson thy large ignorance and inform
This insolence with knowledge if there live
Men earth-begotten of no tenderer thews
Than knit the great joints of the grim sea's brood
With hasps of steel together ; heaven to help,
One man shall break, even on their own flood's verge,
That iron bulk of battle ; but thine eye
That sees it now swell higher than sand or shore
Haply shall see not when thine host shall shrink

HERALD OF EUMOLPUS

Not haply, nay, but surely, shall not thine.

CHORUS

That lot shall no God give who fights for thee.

HERALD OF EUMOLPUS

Shall Gods bear bit and bridle, fool, of men ?

CHORUS

Nor them forbid we nor shalt thou constrain.

HERALD OF EUMOLPUS

Yet say'st thou none shall make the good lot mine ?

CHORUS

Of thy side none, nor moved for fear of thee.

HERALD OF EUMOLPUS

Gods hast thou then to baffle Gods of ours ?

CHORUS

Nor thine nor mine, but equal-souled are they.

HERALD OF EUMOLPUS

Toward good and ill, then, equal-eyed of soul ?

CHORUS

Nay, but swift-eyed to note where ill thoughts breed.

HERALD OF EUMOLPUS

Thy shaft word-feathered flies yet far of me.

CHORUS

Pride knows not, wounded, till the heart be cleft.

HERALD OF EUMOLPUS

No shaft wounds deep whose wing is plumed with words.

CHORUS

Lay that to heart, and bid thy tongue learn grace.

HERALD OF EUMOLPUS

Grace shall thine own crave soon too late of mine.

CHORUS

Boast thou till then, but I wage words no more.

ERECHTHEUS

Man, what shrill wind of speech and wrangling air
Blows in our ears a summons from thy lips
Winged with what message, or what gift or grace
Requiring ? none but what his hand may take
Here may the foe think hence to reap, nor this
Except some doom from Godward yield it him.

HERALD OF EUMOLPUS

King of this land-folk, by my mouth to thee
Thus saith the son of him that shakes thine earth,
Eumolpus ; now the stakes of war are set,
For land or sea to win by throw and wear ;
Choose therefore or to quit thy side and give
The palm unfought for to his bloodless hand,
Or by that father's sceptre, and the foot
Whose tramp far off makes tremble for pure fear
Thy soul-struck mother, piercing like a sword
The immortal womb that bare thee ; by the waves
That no man bridles and that bound thy world,
And by the winds and storms of all the sea,
He swears to raze from eyeshot of the sun
This city named not of his father's name,
And wash to deathward down one flood of doom
This whole fresh brood of earth yeaned naturally,
Green yet and faint in its first blade, unblown
With yellow hope of harvest ; so do thou,

Seeing whom thy time is come to meet, for fear
Yield, or gird up thy force to fight and die.

To fight then be it ; for if to die or live,
No man but only a God knows this much yet
Seeing us fare forth, who bear but in our hands
The weapons not the fortunes of our fight ;
For these now rest as lots that yet undrawn
Lie in the lap of the unknown hour ; but this
I know, not thou, whose hollow mouth of storm
Is but a warlike wind, a sharp salt breath
That bites and wounds not ; death nor life of mine
Shall give to death or lordship of strange kings
The soul of this live city, nor their heel
Bruise her dear brow discrowned, nor snaffle or goad
Wound her free mouth or stain her sanguine side
Yet masterless of man ; so bid thy lord
Learn ere he weep to learn it, and too late
Gnash teeth that could not fasten on her flesh,
And foam his life out in dark froth of blood
Vain as a wind's waif of the loud-mouthed sea
Torn from the wave's edge whitening. Tell him this ;
Though thrice his might were mustered for our
　　scathe
And thicker set with fence of thorn-edged spears
Than sands are whirled about the wintering beach
When storms have swoln the rivers, and their blasts
Have breached the broad sea-banks with stress of
　　sea,
That waves of inland and the main make war
As men that mix and grapple ; though his ranks
Were more to number than all wildwood leaves
The wind waves on the hills of all the world,

Yet should the heart not faint, the head not fall,
The breath not fail of Athens.   Say, the Gods
From lips that have no more on earth to say
Have told thee this the last good news or ill
That I shall speak in sight of earth and sun
Or he shall hear and see them : for the next
That ear of his from tongue of mine may take
Must be the first word spoken underground
From dead to dead in darkness.   Hence ;   make
        haste,
Lest war's fleet foot be swifter than thy tongue
And I that part not to return again
On him that comes not to depart away
Be fallen before thee ; for the time is full,
And with such mortal hope as knows not fear
I go this high last way to the end of all.

CHORUS

Who shall put a bridle in the mourner's lips to chasten
        them,   [*Str.* I.
    Or seal up the fountains of his tears for shame ?
Song nor prayer nor prophecy shall slacken tears nor
        hasten them,
        Till grief be within him as a burnt-out flame ;
            Till the passion be broken in his breast
            And the might thereof molten into rest,
            And the rain of eyes that weep be dry,
            And the breath be stilled of lips that sigh.
Death at last for all men is a harbour ; yet they flee
        from it,   [*Ant.* I.
    Set sails to the storm-wind and again to sea ;
Yet for all their labour no whit further shall they be
        from it,
    Nor longer but wearier shall their life's work be.

And with anguish of travail until night
Shall they steer into shipwreck out of sight,
And with oars that break and shrouds that strain
Shall they drive whence no ship steers again.

Bitter and strange is the word of the God most
high,   [*Str.* 2.
        And steep the strait of his way.

Through a pass rock-rimmed and narrow the light
    that gleams
On the faces of men falls faint as the dawn of dreams,
The dayspring of death as a star in an under sky
        Where night is the dead men's day.

As darkness and storm is his will that on earth is
    done,   [*Ant.* 2.
        As a cloud is the face of his strength.

King of kings, holiest of holies, and mightiest of
    might,
Lord of the lords of thine heaven that are humble in
    thy sight,
Hast thou set not an end for the path of the fires of
    the sun,
        To appoint him a rest at length ?

Hast thou told not by measure the waves of the
    waste wide sea,   [*Str.* 3.
And the ways of the wind their master and thrall to
    thee ?
        Hast thou filled not the furrows with fruit for
            the world's increase ?

Has thine ear not heard from of old or thine eye not
    read
The thought and the deed of us living, the doom of
    us dead ?
        Hast thou made not war upon earth, and again
            made peace ?

Therefore, O father, that seest us whose lives are a
   breath,   [*Ant.* 3.
Take off us thy burden, and give us not wholly to
   death.
     For lovely is life, and the law wherein all
       things live,
And gracious the season of each, and the hour of its
   kind,
And precious the seed of his life in a wise man's
   mind ;
     But all save life for his life will a base man
       give.
But a life that is given for the life of the whole live
   land,   [*Str.* 4.
From a heart unspotted a gift of a spotless hand,
Of pure will perfect and free, for the land's life's sake,
What man shall fear not to put forth his hand and
   take ?
For the fruit of a sweet life plucked in its pure green
   prime   [*Ant.* 4.
On his hand who plucks is as blood, on his soul as
   crime.
With cursing ye buy not blessing, nor peace with
   strife,
And the hand is hateful that chaffers with death for
   life.
     Hast thou heard, O my heart, and endurest [*Str.* 5.
       The word that is said,
      What a garland by sentence found surest
       Is wrought for what head ?
With what blossomless flowerage of sea-foam and
   blood-coloured foliage inwound
It shall crown as a heifer's for slaughter the forehead
   for marriage uncrowned ?

How the veils and the wreaths that should
     cover   [*Ant.* 5.
    The brows of the bride
Shall be shed by the breath of what lover
    And scattered aside?
With a blast of the mouth of what bridegroom the
    crowns shall be cast from her hair,
And her head by what altar made humble be left of
    them naked and bare?
At a shrine unbeloved of a God unbeholden a gift
    shall be given for the land,   [*Str.* 6.
That its ramparts though shaken with clamour and
    horror of manifold waters may stand :
That the crests of its citadels crowned and its turrets
    that thrust up their heads to the sun
May behold him unblinded with darkness of waves
    overmastering their bulwarks begun.
As a bride shall they bring her, a prey for the bride-
    groom, a flower for the couch of her lord ; [*Ant.* 6.
They shall muffle her mouth that she cry not or
    curse them, and cover her eyes from the sword.
They shall fasten her lips as with bit and with bridle,
    and darken the light of her face,
That the soul of the slayer may not falter, his heart
    be not molten, his hand give not grace.
  If she weep then, yet may none that hear take
      pity ;   [*Str.* 7.
    If she cry not, none should hearken though she
      cried.
  Shall a virgin shield thine head for love, O city,
    With a virgin's blood anointed as for pride?
  Yet we held thee dear and hallowed of her favour,
                    [*Ant.* 7.
    Dear of all men held thy people to her heart ;

Nought she loves the breath of blood, the sanguine
    savour,
   Who hath built with us her throne and chosen
      her part.
      Bloodless are her works, and sweet   [*Epode.*
      All the ways that feel her feet ;
      From the empire of her eyes
      Light takes life and darkness flies ;
      From the harvest of her hands
      Wealth strikes root in prosperous lands ;
      Wisdom of her word is made ;
      At her strength is strength afraid ;
      From the beam of her bright spear
      War's fleet foot goes back for fear ;
      In her shrine she reared the birth
      Fire-begotten on live earth ;
      Glory from her helm was shed
      On his olive-shadowed head ;
      By no hand but his shall she
      Scourge the storms back of the sea,
      To no fame but his shall give
      Grace, being dead, with hers to live,
      And in double name divine
      Half the godhead of their shrine.
But now with what word, with what woe may we
    meet
The timeless passage of piteous feet,
Hither that bend to the last way's end
    They shall walk upon earth ?
What song be rolled for a bride black-stoled
And the mother whose hand of her hand hath hold ?
For anguish of heart is my soul's strength broken
And the tongue sealed fast that would fain have
    spoken,

To behold thee, O child of so bitter a birth
    That we counted so sweet,
What way thy steps to what bride-feast tend,
What gift he must give that shall wed thee for
    token
    If the bridegroom be goodly to greet.

CHTHONIA

People, old men of my city, lordly wise and hoar of
    head,
I a spouseless bride and crownless but with garlands
    of the dead
From the fruitful light turn silent to my dark un-
    childed bed.

CHORUS

Wise of word was he too surely, but with deadlier
    wisdom wise,
First who gave thee name from under earth, no breath
    from upper skies,
When, foredoomed to this day's darkness, their first
    daylight filled thine eyes.

PRAXITHEA

Child, my child that wast and art but death's and now
    no more of mine,
Half my heart is cloven with anguish by the sword
    made sharp for thine,
Half exalts its wing for triumph, that I bare thee
    thus divine.

CHTHONIA

Though for me the sword's edge thirst that sets no
    point against thy breast,
Mother, O my mother, where I drank of life and fell
    on rest.
Thine, not mine, is all the grief that marks this hour
    accurst and blest.

CHORUS

Sweet thy sleep and sweet the bosom was that gave
    thee sleep and birth ;
Harder now the breast, and girded with no marriage-
    band for girth,
Where thine head shall sleep, the namechild of the
    lords of under earth.

PRAXITHEA

Dark the name and dark the gifts they gave thee,
    child, in childbirth were,
Sprung from him that rent the womb of earth, a
    bitter seed to bear,
Born with groanings of the ground that gave him
    way toward heaven's dear air.

CHTHONIA

Day to day makes answer, first to last, and life to
    death ; but I,
Born for death's sake, die for life's sake, if indeed this
    be to die,
This my doom that seals me deathless till the springs
    of time run dry.

CHORUS

Children shalt thou bear to memory, that to man
　　shalt bring forth none ;
Yea, the lordliest that lift eyes and hearts and songs
　　to meet the sun,
Names to fire men's ears like music till the round
　　world's race be run.

PRAXITHEA

I thy mother, named of Gods that wreak revenge and
　　brand with blame,
Now for thy love shall be loved as thou, and famous
　　with thy fame,
While this city's name on earth shall be for earth her
　　mightiest name.

CHTHONIA

That I may give this poor girl's blood of mine
Scarce yet sun-warmed with summer, this thin life
Still green with flowerless growth of seedling days,
To build again my city ; that no drop
Fallen of these innocent veins on the cold ground
But shall help knit the joints of her firm walls
To knead the stones together, and make sure
The band about her maiden girdlestead
Once fastened, and of all men's violent hands
Inviolable for ever ; these to me
Were no such gifts as crave no thanksgiving,
If with one blow dividing the sheer life
I might make end, and one pang wind up all
And seal mine eyes from sorrow ; for such end
The Gods give none they love not ; but my heart,
That leaps up lightened of all sloth or fear

To take the sword's point, yet with one thought's
    load
Flags, and falls back, broken of wing, that halts
Maimed in mid flight for thy sake and borne down,
Mother, that in the places where I played
An arm's length from thy bosom and no more
Shalt find me never, nor thine eye wax glad
To mix with mine its eyesight and for love
Laugh without word, filled with sweet light, and speak
Divine dumb things of the inward spirit and heart,
Moved silently ; nor hand or lip again
Touch hand or lip of either, but for mine
Shall thine meet only shadows of swift night,
Dreams and dead thoughts of dead things ; and the
    bed
Thou strewedst, a sterile place for all time, strewn
For my sleep only, with its void sad sheets
Shall vex thee, and the unfruitful coverlid
For empty days reproach me dead, that leave
No profit of my body, but am gone
As one not worth being born to bear no seed,
A sapless stock and branchless ; yet thy womb
Shall want not honour of me, that brought forth
For all this people freedom, and for earth
From the unborn city born out of my blood
To light the face of all men evermore
Glory ; but lay thou this to thy great heart
Whereunder in the dark of birth conceived
Mine unlit life lay girdled with the zone
That bound thy bridal bosom ; set this thought
Against all edge of evil as a sword
To beat back sorrow, that for all the world
Thou brought'st me forth a saviour, who shall save
Athens ; for none but I from none but thee

Shall take this death for garland ; and the men
Mine unknown children of unsounded years,
My sons unrisen shall rise up at thine hand,
Sown of thy seed to bring forth seed to thee,
And call thee most of all most fruitful found
Blessed ; but me too for my barren womb
More than my sisters for their children born
Shall these give honour, yea in scorn's own place
Shall men set love and bring for mockery praise
And thanks for curses ; for the dry wild vine
Scoffed at and cursed of all men that was I
Shall shed them wine to make the world's heart
　　warm,
That all eyes seeing may lighten, and all ears
Hear and be kindled ; such a draught to drink
Shall be the blood that bids this dust bring forth,
The chaliced life here spilt on this mine earth,
Mine, my great father's mother ; whom I pray
Take me now gently, tenderly take home,
And softly lay in his my cold chaste hand
Who is called of men by my name, being of Gods
Charged only and chosen to bring men under earth,
And now must lead and stay me with his staff
A silent soul led of a silent God,
Toward sightless things led sightless ; and on earth
I see now but the shadow of mine end,
And this last light of all for me in heaven.

PRAXITHEA

Farewell I bid thee ; so bid thou not me,
Lest the Gods hear and mock us ; yet on these
I lay the weight not of this grief, nor cast
Ill words for ill deeds back : for if one say

They have done men wrong, what hurt have they to
    hear,
Or he what help to have said it ? surely, child,
If one among men born might say it and live
Blameless, none more than I may, who being vexed
Hold yet my peace ; for now through tears enough
Mine eyes have seen the sun that from this day
Thine shall see never more ; and in the night
Enough has blown of evil, and mine ears
With wail enough the winds have filled, and brought
Too much of cloud from over the sharp sea
To mar for me the morning ; such a blast
Rent from these wide void arms and helpless breast
Long since one graft of me disbranched, and bore
Beyond the wild ways of the unwandered world
And loud wastes of the thunder-throated sea,
Springs of the night and openings of the heaven,
The old garden of the Sun ; whence never more
From west or east shall winds bring back that blow
From folds of opening heaven or founts of night
The flower of mine once ravished, born my child
To bear strange children ; nor on wings of theirs
Shall comfort come back to me, nor their sire
Breathe help upon my peril, nor his strength
Raise up my weakness ; but of Gods and men
I drift unsteered on ruin, and the wave
Darkens my head with imminent height, and hangs
Dumb, filled too full with thunder that shall leave
These ears death-deafened when the tide finds tongue
And all its wrath bears on them ; thee, O child.
I help not, nor am holpen ; fain, ah fain,
More than was ever mother born of man,
Were I to help thee ; fain beyond all prayer,
Beyond all thought fain to redeem thee, torn

More timeless from me sorrowing than the dream
That was thy sister ; so shalt thou be too,
Thou but a vision, shadow-shaped of sleep,
By grief made out of nothing ; now but once
I touch, but once more hold thee, one more kiss
This last time and none other ever more
Leave on thy lips and leave them.   Go ; thou wast
My heart, my heart's blood, life-blood of my life,
My child, my nursling : now this breast once thine
Shall rear again no children ; never now
Shall any mortal blossom born like thee
Lie there, nor ever with small silent mouth
Draw the sweet springs dry for an hour that feed
The blind blithe life that knows not ; never head
Rest here to make these cold veins warm, nor eye
Laugh itself open with the lips that reach
Lovingly toward a fount more loving ; these
Death makes as all good lesser things now dead,
And all the latter hopes that flowered from these
And fall as these fell fruitless ; no joy more
Shall man take of thy maidenhood, no tongue
Praise it ; no good shall eyes get more of thee
That lightened for thy love's sake.   Now, take note,
Give ear, O all ye people, that my word
May pierce your hearts through, and the stroke that
        cleaves
Be fruitful to them ; so shall all that hear
Grow great at heart with child of thought most high
And bring forth seed in season ; this my child,
This flower of this my body, this sweet life,
This fair live youth I give you, to be slain,
Spent, shed, poured out, and perish ; take my gift
And give it death and the under Gods who crave
So much for that they give ; for this is more.

Much more is this than all we ; for they give
Freedom, and for a blast, an air of breath,
A little soul that is not, they give back
Light for all eyes, cheer for all hearts, and life
That fills the world's width full of fame and praise
And mightier love than children's. This they give,
The grace to make thy country great, and wrest
From time and death power to take hold on her
And strength to scathe for ever ; and this gift,
Is this no more than man's love is or mine,
Mine and all mothers'? nay, where that seems more,
Where one loves life of child, wife, father, friend,
Son, husband, mother, more than this, even there
Are all these lives worth nothing, all loves else
With this love slain and buried, and their tomb
A thing for shame to spit on ; for what love
Hath a slave left to love with? or the heart
Base-born and bound in bondage fast to fear,
What should it do to love thee? what hath he,
The man that hath no country ? Gods nor men
Have such to friend, yoked beast-like to base life,
Vile, fruitless, grovelling at the foot of death,
Landless and kinless thralls of no man's blood,
Unchilded and unmothered, abject limbs
That breed things abject ; but who loves on earth
Not friend, wife, husband, father, mother, child,
Nor loves his own life for his own land's sake,
But only this thing most, more this than all,
He loves all well and well of all is loved,
And this love lives for ever. See now, friends,
My countrymen, my brothers, with what heart
I give you this that of your hands again
The Gods require for Athens ; as I give
So give ye to them what their hearts would have

Who shall give back things better ; yea, and these
I take for me to witness, all these Gods,
Were their great will more grievous than it is,
Not one but three, for this one thin-spun thread
A threefold band of children would I give
For this land's love's sake ; for whose love to-day
I bid thee, child, fare deathward and farewell.

CHORUS

O wofullest of women, yet of all
Happiest, thy word be hallowed ; in all time
Thy name shall blossom, and from strange new
    tongues
High things be spoken of thee ; for such grace
The Gods have dealt to no man, that on none
Have laid so heavy sorrow. From this day
Live thou assured of godhead in thy blood,
And in thy fate no lowlier than a God
In all good things and evil ; such a name
Shall be thy child this city's, and thine own
Next hers that called it Athens. Go now forth
Blest, and grace with thee to the doors of death.

CHTHONIA

O city, O glory of Athens, O crown of my father's
    land, farewell.

CHORUS

  For welfare is given her of thee.

CHTHONIA

O Goddess, be good to thy people, that in them
    dominion and freedom may dwell.

CHORUS

Turn from us the strengths of the sea.

CHTHONIA

Let glory's and theirs be one name in the mouths of
all nations made glad with the sun.

CHORUS

For the cloud is blown back with thy breath.

CHTHONIA

With the long last love of mine eyes I salute thee,
O land where my days now are done.

CHORUS

But her life shall be born of thy death.

CHTHONIA

I put on me the darkness thy shadow, my mother, and
symbol, O Earth, of my name.

CHORUS

For thine was her witness from birth.

CHTHONIA

In thy likeness I come to thee darkling, a daughter
whose dawn and her even are the same.

CHORUS

Be thine heart to her gracious, O Earth.

CHTHONIA

To thine own kind be kindly, for thy son's name's
sake.

CHORUS

That sons unborn may praise thee and thy first-
born son.

CHTHONIA

Give me thy sleep, who give thee all my life awake.

CHORUS

Too swift a sleep, ere half the web of day be spun.

CHTHONIA

Death brings the shears or ever life wind up the weft.

CHORUS

Their edge is ground and sharpened ; who shall
stay his hand ?

CHTHONIA

The woof is thin, a small short life, with no thread
left.

CHORUS

Yet hath it strength, stretched out, to shelter all
the land.

CHTHONIA

Too frail a tent for covering, and a screen too strait.

CHORUS

Yet broad enough for buckler shall thy sweet life be.

CHTHONIA

A little bolt to bar off battle from the gate.

CHORUS

A wide sea-wall, that shatters the besieging sea.

CHTHONIA

I lift up mine eyes from the skirts of the shadow, [*Str.*
  From the border of death to the limits of light ;
O streams and rivers of mountain and meadow
      That hallow the last of my sight,
      O father that wast of my mother
      Cephisus, O thou too his brother
      From the bloom of whose banks as a prey
      Winds harried my sister away,
      O crown on the world's head lying
          Too high for its waters to drown,
      Take yet this one word of me dying,
              O city, O crown.
Though land-wind and sea wind with mouths that
      blow slaughter   [*Ant.*
  Should gird them to battle against thee again,
New-born of the blood of a maiden thy daughter,
      The rage of their breath shall be vain.
      For their strength shall be quenched and made
          idle,
      And the foam of their mouths find a bridle,
      And the height of their heads bow down
      At the foot of the towers of the town.
      Be blest and beloved as I love thee
          Of all that shall draw from thee breath
      Be thy life as the sun's is above thee ;
              I go to my death.

CHORUS

  Many loves of many a mood and many a kind [*Str.* 1.
  Fill the life of man, and mould the secret mind ;
  Many days bring many dooms, to loose and bind ;

Sweet is each in season, good the gift it brings,
Sweet as change of night and day with altering
  wings,
Night that lulls world-weary day, day that comforts
  night,
Night that fills our eyes with sleep, day that fills with
  light.
  None of all is lovelier, loftier love is none,   [*Ant.* 1.
  Less is bride's for bridegroom, mother's less for
    son,
  Child, than this that crowns and binds up all in
    one ;
  Love of thy sweet light, thy fostering breast and
    hand,
  Mother Earth, and city chosen, and natural land ;
Hills that bring the strong streams forth, heights of
  heavenlier air,
Fields aflower with winds and suns, woods with
  shadowing hair.
But none of the nations of men shall they liken to
  thee,   [*Str.* 2.
Whose children true-born and the fruit of thy body
  are we.
The rest are thy sons but in figure, in word are thy
  seed ;
We only the flower of thy travail, thy children in-
  deed.
Of thy soil hast thou fashioned our limbs, of thy
  waters their blood,
And the life of thy springs everlasting is fount of our
  flood.
No wind oversea blew us hither adrift on thy shore,
None sowed us by land in thy womb that conceived
  us and bore.

But the stroke of the shaft of the sunlight that brought
us to birth
Pierced only and quickened thy furrows to bear us,
O Earth.
With the beams of his love wast thou cloven as with
iron or fire,
And the life in thee yearned for his life, and grew
great with desire.
And the hunger and thirst to be wounded and healed
with his dart
Made fruitful the love in thy veins and the depth of
thine heart.
And the showers out of heaven overflowing and liquid
with love
Fulfilled thee with child of his godhead as rain from
above.
Such desire had ye twain of each other, till molten
in one   [*Ant.* 2.
Ye might bear and beget of your bodies the fruits of
the sun.
And the trees in their season brought forth and were
kindled anew
By the warmth of the moisture of marriage, the child-
bearing dew.
And the firstlings were fair of the wedlock of heaven
and of earth ;
All countries were bounteous with blossom and
burgeon of birth.
Green pastures of grass for all cattle, and life-giving
corn ;
But here of thy bosom, here only, the man-child was
born.
All races but one are as aliens engrafted or
sown,

Strange children and changelings ; but we, O our
    mother, thine own.
Thy nurslings are others, and seedlings they know not
    of whom ;
For these hast thou fostered, but us thou hast borne
    in thy womb.
Who is he of us all, O beloved, that owe thee for birth,
Who would give not his blood for his birth's sake, O
    mother, O Earth ?
What landsman is he that was fostered and reared of
    thine hand
Who may vaunt him as we may in death though he
    died for the land ?

Well doth she therefore who gives thee in guerdon
    The bloom of the life of thy giving ;   [*Epode.*
And thy body was bowed by no fruitless burden,
    That bore such fruit of thee living.
        For her face was not darkened for fear,
        For her eyelids conceived not a tear,
          Nor a cry from her lips craved pity ;
        But her mouth was a fountain of song,
        And her heart as a citadel strong
          That guards the heart of the city.

MESSENGER

High things of strong-souled men that loved their land
On brass and stone are written, and their deeds
On high days chanted ; but none graven or sung
That ever set men's eyes or spirits on fire,
Athenians, has the sun's height seen, or earth
Heard in her depth reverberate as from heaven,
More worth men's praise and good report of Gods
Than here I bring for record in your ears.

For now being come to the altar, where as priest
Death ministering should meet her, and his hand
Seal her sweet eyes asleep, the maiden stood,
With light in all her face as of a bride
Smiling, or shine of festal flame by night
Far flung from towers of triumph ; and her lips
Trembled with pride in pleasure, that no fear
Blanched them nor death before his time drank dry
The blood whose bloom fulfilled them ; for her cheeks
Lightened, and brighter than a bridal veil
Her hair enrobed her bosom and enrolled
From face to feet the body's whole soft length
As with a cloud sun-saturate ; then she spake
With maiden tongue words manlike, but her eyes
Lit mildly like a maiden's : *Countrymen,*
With more goodwill and height of happier heart
I give me to you than my mother bare,
And go more gladly this great way to death
Than young men bound to battle. Then with face
Turned to the shadowiest part of all the shrine
And eyes fast set upon the further shade,
Take me, dear Gods ; and as some form had shone
From the deep hollow shadow, some God's tongue
Answered, *I bless you that your guardian grace*
Gives me to guard this country, takes my blood,
Your child's by name, to heal it. Then the priest
Set to the flower-sweet snow of her soft throat
The sheer knife's edge that severed it, and loosed
From the fair bondage of so spotless flesh
So strong a spirit ; and all that girt them round
Gazing, with souls that hung on that sad stroke,
Groaned, and kept silence after while a man
Might count how far the fresh blood crept, and bathed
How deep the dark robe and the bright shrine's base

Red-rounded with a running ring that grew
More large and duskier as the wells that fed
Were drained of that pure effluence : but the queen
Groaned not nor spake nor wept, but as a dream
Floats out of eyes awakening so past forth
Ghost-like, a shadow of sorrow, from all sight
To the inner court and chamber where she sits
Dumb, till word reach her of this whole day's end.

CHORUS

  More hapless born by far   [*Str.*
  Beneath some wintrier star,
 One sits in stone among high Lydian snows,
  The tomb of her own woes :
Yet happiest was once of the daughters of Gods, and
  divine by her sire and her lord,
Ere her tongue was a shaft for the hearts of her sons,
  for the heart of her husband a sword.

  For she, too great of mind,   [*Ant.*
  Grown through her good things blind,
 With godless lips and fire of her own breath
  Spake all her house to death ;
But thou, no mother unmothered, nor kindled in
  spirit with pride of thy seed,
Thou hast hallowed thy child for a blameless blood-
  offering, and ransomed thy race by thy deed.

MESSENGER

As flower is graffed on flower, so grief on grief
Engraffed brings forth new blossoms of strange tears,
Fresh buds and green fruits of an alien pain ;
For now flies rumour on a dark wide wing,

Murmuring of woes more than ye knew, most like
Hers whom ye hailed most wretched ; for the twain
Last left of all this house that wore last night
A threefold crown of maidens, and to-day
Should let but one fall dead out of the wreath,
If mad with grief we know not and sore love
For this their sister, or with shame soul-stung
To outlive her dead or doubt lest their lives too
The Gods require to seal their country safe
And bring the oracular doom to perfect end,
Have slain themselves, and fallen at the altar-foot
Lie by their own hands done to death ; and fear
Shakes all the city as winds a wintering tree,
And as dead leaves are men's hearts blown about
And shrunken with ill thoughts, and flowerless hopes
Parched up with presage, lest the piteous blood
Shed of these maidens guiltless fall and fix
On this land's forehead like a curse that cleaves
To the unclean soul's inexpiate hunted head
Whom his own crime tracks hotlier than a hound
To life's veiled end unsleeping ; and this hour
Now blackens toward the battle that must close
All gates of hope and fear on all their hearts
Who tremble toward its issue, knowing not yet
If blood may buy them surety, cleanse or soil
The helpless hands men raise and reach no stay.

CHORUS

Ill thoughts breed fear, and fear ill words ; but these
The Gods turn from us that have kept their law.
 Let us lift up the strength of our hearts in song, [*Str.* I.
  And our souls to the height of the darkling day.
  If the wind in our eyes blow blood for spray,

Be the spirit that breathes in us life more strong,
Though the prow reel round and the helm point
      wrong,
   And sharp reefs whiten the shoreward way.
For the steersman time sits hidden astern,   [*Ant.* 1.
   With dark hand plying the rudder of doom,
   And the surf-smoke under it flies like fume
As the blast shears off and the oar-blades
      churn
The foam of our lives that to death return,
   Blown back as they break to the gulfing gloom.
What cloud upon heaven is arisen, what shadow,
      what sound,   [*Str.* 2.
   From the world beyond earth, from the night
      underground,
That scatters from wings unbeholden the weight of
   its darkness around ?
For the sense of my spirit is broken, and blinded
      its eye,   [*Ant.* 2.
   As the soul of a sick man ready to die,
With fear of the hour that is on me, with dread if an
   end be not nigh.
O Earth, O Gods of the land, have ye heart now to
      see and to hear   [*Str.* 3.
   What slays with terror mine eyesight and seals
      mine ear ?
O fountains of streams everlasting, are all ye not
   shrunk up and withered for fear ?
Lo, night is arisen on the noon, and her hounds
      are in quest by day,   [*Ant.* 3.
   And the world is fulfilled of the noise of them
      crying for their prey,
And the sun's self stricken in heaven, and cast out of
   his course as a blind man astray.

From east to west of the south sea-line   [*Str.* 4.
  Glitters the lightning of spears that shine ;
As a storm-cloud swoln that comes up from the skirts
      of the sea
  By the wind for helmsman to shoreward ferried,
  So black behind them the live storm serried
Shakes earth with the tramp of its foot, and the
      terror to be.

  Shall the sea give death whom the land gave
      birth ?   [*Ant.* 4.
  O Earth, fair mother, O sweet live Earth,
Hide us again in thy womb from the waves of it,
      help us or hide.
  As a sword is the heart of the God thy
      brother,
  But thine as the heart of a new-made mother,
To deliver thy sons from his ravin, and rage of his
      tide.

  O strong north wind, the pilot of cloud and rain,
          [*Str.* 5.

  For the gift we gave thee what gift hast thou given
      us again ?
O God dark-winged, deep-throated, a terror to forth-
      faring ships by night,
  What bride-song is this that is blown on the blast
      of thy breath ?
  A gift but of grief to thy kinsmen, a song but of
      death,
For the bride's folk weeping, and woe for her father,
      who finds thee against him in fight.

  Turn back from us, turn thy battle, take heed of
      our cry ;   [*Ant.* 5.
  Let thy dread breath sound, and the waters of war
      be dry ;

II.   N 2

Let thy strong wrath shatter the strength of our foe-
    men, the sword of their strength and the shield ;
  As vapours in heaven, or as waves or the wrecks
    of ships,
  So break thou the ranks of their spears with the
    breath of thy lips,
Till their corpses have covered and clothed as with
    raiment the face of the sword-ploughed field.
  O son of the rose-red morning, O God twin-born
    with the day,   [*Str.* 6.
  O wind with the young sun waking, and winged
    for the same wide way,
Give up not the house of thy kin to the host thou
    hast marshalled from northward for prey.
  From the cold of thy cradle in Thrace, from the
    mists of the fountains of night,   [*Ant.* 6.
  From the bride-bed of dawn whence day leaps
    laughing, on fire for his flight,
Come down with their doom in thine hand on the
    ships thou hast brought up against us to fight.
For now not in word but in deed is the harvest of
    spears begun,   [*Str.* 7.
And its clamour outbellows the thunder, its lightning
    outlightens the sun.
From the springs of the morning it thunders and
    lightens across and afar
To the wave where the moonset ends and the fall of
    the last low star.
With a trampling of drenched red hoofs and an earth
    quake of men that meet,
Strong war sets hand to the scythe, and the furrows
    take fire from his feet.
Earth groans from her great rent heart, and the
    hollows of rocks are afraid,

And the mountains are moved, and the valleys as
  waves in a storm-wind swayed.
From the roots of the hills to the plain's dim verge
  and the dark loud shore,
Air shudders with shrill spears crossing, and hurtling
  of wheels that roar.
As the grinding of teeth in the jaws of a lion that
  foam as they gnash
Is the shriek of the axles that loosen, the shock of the
  poles that crash.
The dense manes darken and glitter, the mouths of
  the mad steeds champ,
Their heads flash blind through the battle, and death's
  foot rings in their tramp.
For a fourfold host upon earth and in heaven is
  arrayed for the fight,
Clouds ruining in thunder and armies encountering
  as clouds in the night.
Mine ears are amazed with the terror of trumpets,
  with darkness mine eyes,
At the sound of the sea's host charging that deafens
  the roar of the sky's.
White frontlet is dashed upon frontlet, and horse
  against horse reels hurled,
And the gorge of the gulfs of the battle is wide for
  the spoil of the world.
And the meadows are cumbered with shipwreck of
  chariots that founder on land,   [*Ant.* 7.
And the horsemen are broken with breach as of
  breakers, and scattered as sand.
Through the roar and recoil of the charges that
  mingle their cries and confound,
Like fire are the notes of the trumpets that flash
  through the darkness of sound.

As the swing of the sea churned yellow that sways
    with the wind as it swells
Is the lift and relapse of the wave of the chargers
    that clash with their bells;
And the clang of the sharp shrill brass through the
    burst of the wave as it shocks
Rings clean as the clear wind's cry through the roar
    of the surge on the rocks:
And the heads of the steeds in their headgear of war,
    and their corsleted breasts,
Gleam broad as the brows of the billows that brighten
    the storm with their crests,
Gleam dread as their bosoms that heave to the ship-
    wrecking wind as they rise,
Filled full of the terror and thunder of water, that
    slays as it dies.
So dire is the glare of their foreheads, so fearful the
    fire of their breath,
And the light of their eyeballs enkindled so bright
    with the lightnings of death;
And the foam of their mouths as the sea's when the
    jaws of its gulf are as graves,
And the ridge of their necks as the wind-shaken mane
    on the ridges of waves:
And their fetlocks afire as they rear drip thick with a
    dewfall of blood
As the lips of the rearing breaker with froth of the
    manslaying flood.
And the whole plain reels and resounds as the fields
    of the sea by night
When the stroke of the wind falls darkling, and death
    is the seafarer's light.

But thou, fair beauty of heaven, dear face of the day
    nigh dead,   [*Epode.*

What horror hath hidden thy glory, what hand hath
muffled thine head?

O sun, with what song shall we call thee, or ward off
thy wrath by what name,

With what prayer shall we seek to thee, soothe with
what incense, assuage with what gift,

If thy light be such only as lightens to deathward
the seaman adrift

With the fire of his house for a beacon, that foemen
have wasted with flame?

Arise now, lift up thy light; give ear to us, put forth
thine hand,

Reach toward us thy torch of deliverance, a lamp for
the night of the land.

Thine eye is the light of the living, no lamp for the
dead;

O, lift up the light of thine eye on the dark of our
dread.

Who hath blinded thee? who hath prevailed on
thee? who hath ensnared?

Who hath broken thy bow, and the shafts for thy
battle prepared?

Have they found out a fetter to bind thee, a chain for
thine arm that was bared?

Be the name of thy conqueror set forth, and the might
of thy master declared.

O God, fair God of the morning, O glory of
day,

What ails thee to cast from thy forehead its
garland away?

To pluck from thy temples their chaplet enwreathed
of the light,

And bind on the brows of thy godhead a frontlet
of night?

Thou hast loosened the necks of thine horses, and
    goaded their flanks with affright,
To the race of a course that we know not on ways
    that are hid from our sight.
  As a wind through the darkness the wheels of their
    chariot are whirled,
  And the light of its passage is night on the face of
    the world.
  And there falls from the wings of thy glory no help
    from on high,
  But a shadow that smites us with fear and desire of
    thine eye.
For our hearts are as reeds that a wind on the water
    bows down and goes by,
To behold not thy comfort in heaven that hath left us
    untimely to die.
  But what light is it now leaps forth on the land
  Enkindling the waters and ways of the air
        From thy forehead made bare,
      From the gleam of thy bow-bearing hand ?
  Hast thou set not thy right hand again to the string,
  With the back-bowed horns bent sharp for a spring
        And the barbed shaft drawn,
  Till the shrill steel sing and the tense nerve ring
  That pierces the heart of the dark with dawn,
        O huntsman, O king,
  When the flame of thy face hath twilight in chase
      As a hound hath a blood-mottled fawn ?
  He has glanced into golden the grey sea-strands,
  And the clouds are shot through with the fires of
    his hands,
  And the height of the hollow of heaven that he fills
  As the heart of a strong man is quickened and
    thrills ;

High over the folds of the low-lying lands,
   On the shadowless hills
  As a guard on his watchtower he stands.
All earth and all ocean, all depth and all height,
At the flash of an eyebeam are filled with his might :
The sea roars backward, the storm drops dumb,
And silence as dew on the fire of the fight
Falls kind in our ears as his face in our sight
   With presage of peace to come.
Fresh hope in my heart from the ashes of dread
Leaps clear as a flame from the pyres of the dead,
    That joy out of woe
May arise as the spring out of tempest and snow,
With the flower-feasted month in her hands rose-
   red
Borne soft as a babe from the bearing-bed.
Yet it knows not indeed if a God be friend,
If rescue may be from the rage of the sea,
   Or the wrath of its lord have end.
For the season is full now of death or of birth,
To bring forth life, or an end of all ;
And we know not if anything stand or fall
That is girdled about with the round sea's girth
   As a town with its wall ;
But thou that art highest of the Gods most high,
That art lord if we live, that art lord though we die,
Have heed of the tongues of our terror that cry
   For a grace to the children of Earth.

ATHENIAN HERALD

Sons of Athens, heavy-laden with the holy weight of
   years,
Be your hearts as young men's lightened of their
   loathlier load of fears ;

For the wave is sunk whose thunder shoreward shook
    the shuddering lands,
And unbreached of warring waters Athens like a sea-
    rock stands.

CHORUS

Well thy word has cheered us, well thy face and
    glittering eyes, that spake
Ere thy tongue spake words of comfort: yet no
    pause behoves it make
Till the whole good hap find utterance that the Gods
    have given at length.

ATHENIAN HERALD

All is this, that yet the city stands unforced by
    stranger strength.

CHORUS

Sweeter sound might no mouth utter in man's ear
    than this thy word.

ATHENIAN HERALD

Feed thy soul then full of sweetness till some bitterer
    note be heard.

CHORUS

None, if this ring sure, can mar the music fallen from
    heaven as rain.

ATHENIAN HERALD

If no fire of sun or star untimely sear the tender
    grain.

CHORUS

Fresh the dewfall of thy tidings on our hopes re-
    flowering lies.

ATHENIAN HERALD

Till a joyless shower and fruitless blight them, raining from thine eyes.

CHORUS

Bitter springs have barren issues ; these bedew grief's arid sands.

ATHENIAN HERALD

Such thank-offerings ask such altars as expect thy suppliant hands.

CHORUS

Tears for triumph, wail for welfare, what strange godhead's shrine requires ?

ATHENIAN HERALD

Death's or victory's be it, a funeral torch feeds all its festal fires.

CHORUS

Like a star should burn the beacon flaming from our city's head.

ATHENIAN HERALD

Like a balefire should the flame go up that says the king is dead.

CHORUS

Out of heaven, a wild-haired meteor, shoots this new sign, scattering fear.

ATHENIAN HERALD

Yea, the word has wings of fire that hovered, loth to burn thine ear.

CHORUS

From thy lips it leapt forth loosened on a shrill and
    shadowy wing.

ATHENIAN HERALD

Long they faltered, fain to hide it deep as death that
    hides the king.

CHORUS

Dead with him blind hope lies blasted by the light-
    ning of one sword.

ATHENIAN HERALD

On thy tongue truth wars with error ; no man's edge
    hath touched thy lord.

CHORUS

False was thine then, jangling menace like a war-
    steed's brow-bound bell ?

ATHENIAN HERALD

False it rang not joy nor sorrow ; but by no man's
    hand he fell.

CHORUS

Vainly then good news and evil through so faint a
    trumpet spake.

ATHENIAN HERALD

All too long thy soul yet labours, as who sleeping
    fain would wake,
Waking, fain would fall on sleep again ; the woe
    thou knowest not yet,
When thou knowest, shall make thy memory thirst
    and hunger to forget.

CHORUS

Long my heart has hearkened, hanging on thy
    clamorous ominous cry,
Fain yet fearful of the knowledge whence it looks to
    live or die ;
Now to take the perfect presage of thy dark and side-
    long flight
Comes a surer soothsayer sorrowing, sable-stoled as
    birds of night.

PRAXITHEA

Man, what thy mother bare thee born to say
Speak ; for no word yet wavering on thy lip
Can wound me worse than thought forestalls or fear.

ATHENIAN HERALD

I have no will to weave too fine or far,
O queen, the weft of sweet with bitter speech,
Bright words with darkling ; but the brief truth
    shown
Shall plead my pardon for a lingering tongue,
Loth yet to strike hope through the heart and slay.
The sun's light still was lordly housed in heaven
When the twain fronts of war encountering smote
First fire out of the battle ; but not long
Had the fresh wave of windy fight begun
Heaving, and all the surge of swords to sway,
When timeless night laid hold of heaven, and took
With its great gorge the noon as in a gulf,
Strangled ; and thicker than the shrill-winged shafts
Flew the fleet lightnings, held in chase through heaven
By headlong heat of thunders on their trail
Loosed as on quest of quarry ; that our host
Smit with sick presage of some wrathful God

Quailed, but the foe as from one iron throat
With one great sheer sole thousand-throated cry
Shook earth, heart-staggered from their shout, and
    clove
The eyeless hollow of heaven ; and breached there-
    with
As with an onset of strength-shattering sound
The rent vault of the roaring noon of night
From her throned seat of usurpation rang
Reverberate answer ; such response there pealed
As though the tide's charge of a storming sea
Had burst the sky's wall, and made broad a breach
In the ambient girth and bastion flanked with stars
Guarding the fortress of the Gods, and all
Crashed now together on ruin ; and through that cry
And higher above it ceasing one man's note
Tore its way like a trumpet : *Charge, make end,*
Charge, halt not, strike, rend up their strength by the
    roots,
Strike, break them, make your birthright's promise
    sure,
Show your hearts hardier than the fenced land breeds
And souls breathed in you from no spirit of earth,
Sons of the sea's waves ; and all ears that heard
Rang with that fiery cry, that the fine air
Thereat was fired, and kindling filled the plain
Full of that fierce and trumpet-quenching breath
That spake the clarions silent ; no glad song
For folk to hear that wist how dire a God
Begat this peril to them, what strong race
Fathered the sea-born tongue that sang them death,
Threatening ; so raged through the red foam of fight
Poseidon's son Eumolpus ; and the war
Quailed round him coming, and our side bore back,

As a stream thwarted by the wind and sea
That meet it midway mouth to mouth, and beat
The flood back of its issue ; but the king
Shouted against them, crying, *O Father-God,*
Source of the God my father, from thine hand
Send me what end seems good now in thy sight,
But death from mine to this man ; and the word
Quick on his lips yet like a blast of fire
Blew them together ; and round its lords that met
Paused all the reeling battle ; two main waves
Meeting, one hurled sheer from the sea-wall back
That shocks it sideways, one right in from sea
Charging, that full in face takes at one blow
That whole recoil and ruin, with less fear
Startle men's eyes late shipwrecked ; for a breath,
Crest fronting crest hung, wave to wave rose poised,
Then clashed, breaker to breaker ; cloud with cloud
In heaven, chariot with chariot closed on earth,
One fourfold flash and thunder ; yet a breath,
And with the king's spear through his red heart's
      root
Driven, like a rock split from its hill-side, fell
Hurled under his own horsehoofs dead on earth
The sea-beast that made war on earth from sea,
Dumb, with no shrill note left of storming song,
Eumolpus ; and his whole host with one stroke
Spear-stricken through its dense deep iron heart
Fell hurtling from us, and in fierce recoil
Drew seaward as with one wide wail of waves,
Resorbed with reluctation ; such a groan
Rose from the fluctuant refluence of its ranks,
Sucked sullen back and strengthless ; but scarce yet
The steeds had sprung and wheels had bruised their
      lord

Fallen, when from highest height of the sundering
    heaven
The Father for his brother's son's sake slain
Sent a sheer shaft of lightning writhen and smote
Right on his son's son's forehead, that unhelmed
Shone like the star that shines down storm, and gave
Light to men's eyes that saw thy lord their king
Stand and take breath from battle ; then too soon
Saw sink down as a sunset in sea-mist
The high bright head that here in van of the earth
Rose like a headland, and through storm and night
Took all the sea's wrath on it ; and now dead
They bring thee back by war-forsaken ways
The strength called once thy husband, the great
    guard
That was of all men, stay of all men's lives,
They bear him slain of no man but a God,
Godlike ; and toward him dead the city's gates
Fling their arms open mother-like, through him
Saved ; and the whole clear land is purged of war
What wilt thou say now of this weal and woe ?

PRAXITHEA

I praise the Gods for Athens.   O sweet Earth,
Mother, what joy thy soul has of thy son,
Thy life of my dead lord, mine own soul knows
That knows thee godlike ; and what grief should mine,
What sorrow should my heart have, who behold
Thee made so heavenlike happy ?   This alone
I only of all these blessed, all thy kind,
Crave this for blessing to me, that in theirs
Have but a part thus bitter ; give me too
Death, and the sight of eyes that meet not mine.
And thee too from no godless heart or tongue

Reproachful, thee too by thy living name,
Father divine, merciful God, I call,
Spring of my life-springs, fountain of my stream,
Pure and poured forth to one great end with thine,
Sweet head sublime of triumph and these tears,
Cephisus, if thou seest as gladly shed
Thy blood in mine as thine own waves are given
To do this great land good, to give for love
The same lips drink and comfort the same hearts,
Do thou then, O my father, white-souled God,
To thy most pure earth-hallowing heart eterne
Take what thou gavest to be given for these,
Take thy child to thee ; for her time is full,
For all she hath borne she hath given, seen all she
    had
Flow from her, from her eyes and breasts and hands
Flow forth to feed this people ; but be thou,
Dear God and gracious to all souls alive,
Good to thine own seed also ; let me sleep,
Father ; my sleepless darkling day is done,
My day of life like night, but slumberless :
For all my fresh fair springs, and his that ran
In one stream's bed with mine, are all run out
Into the deep of death.   The Gods have saved
Athens ; my blood has bought her at their hand,
And ye sit safe ; be glorious and be glad
As now for all time always, countrymen,
And love my dead for ever ; but me, me,
What shall man give for these so good as death ?

CHORUS

From the cup of my heart I pour **through** my lips
    along   [*Str.* I.
The mingled wine of a joyful and sorrowful song ;

Wine sweeter than honey and bitterer than blood that
     is poured
From the chalice of gold, from the point of the two-
     edged sword.
For the city redeemed should joy flow forth as a flood,
And a dirge make moan for the city polluted with
     blood.
Great praise should the Gods have surely, my
     country, of thee,   [*Ant.* 1.
Were thy brow but as white as of old for thy sons to
     see,
Were thy hands as bloodless, as blameless thy cheek
     divine ;
But a stain on it stands of the life-blood offered for
     thine.
What thanks shall we give that are mixed not and
     marred with dread
For the price that has ransomed thine own with thine
     own child's head ?
     For a taint there cleaves to the people redeemed
          with blood,   [*Str.* 2.
     And a plague to the blood-red hand.
     The rain shall not cleanse it, the dew nor the
          sacred flood
     That blesses the glad live land.
     In the darkness of earth beneath, in the world with-
          out sun,   [*Ant.* 2.
     The shadows of past things reign ;
     And a cry goes up from the ghost of an ill deed done,
          And a curse for a virgin slain.

ATHENA

Hear, men that mourn, and woman without mate,
Hearken ; ye sick of soul with fear, and thou

Dumb-stricken for thy children ; hear ye too,
Earth, and the glory of heaven, and winds of the air,
And the most holy heart of the deep sea,
Late wrath, now full of quiet ; hear thou, sun,
Rolled round with the upper fire of rolling heaven
And all the stars returning ; hills and streams,
Springs and fresh fountains, day that seest these deeds,
Night that shalt hide not ; and thou child of mine,
Child of a maiden, by a maid redeemed,
Blood-guiltless, though bought back with innocent
    blood,
City mine own ; I Pallas bring thee word,
I virgin daughter of the most high God
Give all you charge and lay command on all
The word I bring be wasted not ; for this
The Gods have stablished and his soul hath sworn,
That time nor earth nor changing sons of man
Nor waves of generations, nor the winds
Of ages risen and fallen that steer their tides
Through light and dark of birth and lovelier death
From storm toward haven inviolable, shall see
So great a light alive beneath the sun
As the awless eye of Athens ; all fame else
Shall be to her fame as a shadow in sleep
To this wide noon at waking ; men most praised
In lands most happy for their children found
Shall hold as highest of honours given of God
To be but likened to the least of thine,
Thy least of all, my city ; thine shall be
The crown of all songs sung, of all deeds done
Thine the full flower for all time ; in thine hand
Shall time be like a sceptre, and thine head
Wear worship for a garland ; nor one leaf
Shall change or winter cast out of thy crown

Till all flowers wither in the world ; thine eyes
Shall first in man's flash lightning liberty,
Thy tongue shall first say freedom ; thy first hand
Shall loose the thunder terror as a hound
To hunt from sunset to the springs of the sun
Kings that rose up out of the populous east
To make their quarry of thee, and shall strew
With multitudinous limbs of myriad herds
The foodless pastures of the sea, and make
With wrecks immeasurable and unsummed defeat.
One ruin of all their many-folded flocks
Ill shepherded from Asia ; by thy side
Shall fight thy son the north wind, and the sea
That was thine enemy shall be sworn thy friend
And hand be struck in hand of his and thine
To hold faith fast for aye ; with thee, though each
Make war on other, wind and sea shall keep
Peace, and take truce as brethren for thy sake
Leagued with one spirit and single-hearted strength
To break thy foes in pieces, who shall meet
The wind's whole soul and might of the main sea
Full in their face of battle, and become
A laughter to thee ; like a shower of leaves
Shall their long galleys rank by staggering rank
Be dashed adrift on ruin, and in thy sight
The sea deride them, and that lord of the air
Who took by violent hand thy child to wife
With his loud lips bemock them, by his breath
Swept out of sight of being ; so great a grace
Shall this day give thee, that makes one in heart
With mine the deep sea's godhead, and his son
With him that was thine helmsman, king with king,
Dead man with dead ; such only names as these
Shalt thou call royal, take none else or less

To hold of men in honour ; but with me
Shall these be worshipped as one God, and mix
With mine the might of their mysterious names
In one same shrine served singly, thence to keep
Perpetual guard on Athens ; time and change,
Masters and lords of all men, shall be made
To thee that knowest no master and no lord
Servants ; the days that lighten heaven and nights
That darken shall be ministers of thine
To attend upon thy glory, the great years
As light-engraven letters of thy name
Writ by the sun's hand on the front of the earth
For world-beholden witness ; such a gift
For one fair chaplet of three lives enwreathed
To hang for ever from thy storied shrine,
And this thy steersman fallen with tiller in hand
To stand for ever at thy ship's helm seen,
Shall he that bade their threefold flower be shorn
And laid him low that planted, give thee back
In sign of sweet land reconciled with sea
And heavenlike earth with heaven ; such promise-
    pledge
I daughter without mother born of God
To the most woful mother born of man
Plight for continual comfort.   Hail, and live
Beyond all human hap of mortal doom
Happy ; for so my sire hath sworn and I.

PRAXITHEA

O queen Athena, from a heart made whole
Take as thou givest us blessing ; never tear
Shall stain for shame nor groan untune the song
That as a bird shall spread and fold its wings
Here in thy praise for ever, and fulfil

The whole world's crowning city crowned with thee
As the sun's eye fulfils and crowns with sight
The circling crown of heaven.   There is no grief
Great as the joy to be made one in will
With him that is the heart and rule of life
And thee, God born of God ; thy name is ours,
And thy large grace more great than our desire.

CHORUS

From the depth of the springs of my spirit a fountain
        is poured of thanksgiving,
    My country, my mother, for thee,
That thy dead for their death shall have life in thy
        sight and a name everliving
    At heart of thy people to be
In the darkness of change on the waters of time they
        shall turn from afar
To the beam of this dawn for a beacon, the light of
        these pyres for a star.
They shall see thee who love and take comfort, who
        hate thee shall see and take warning,
    Our mother that makest us free ;
And the sons of thine earth shall have help of the
        Waves that made war on their morning,
    And friendship and fame of the sea.

NOTES

v. 497–503. Cf. Eurip. Fr. *Erechtheus*, 46–48.

v. 522–530. Id. 32–40.

v. 778. Æsch. *Supp.* 524–6.

v. 983. Soph. Fr. (*Oreithyia*) 555.

>   ὑπέρ τε πόντον πάντ' ἐπ' ἔσχατα χθονὸς
>   νυκτός τε πηγὰς οὐρανοῦ τ' ἀναπ°°υγὰς,
>   Φοίβου παλαιὸν κῆπον.

v. 1163. Æsch. Fr. (*Danaides*) 38.

>   ὄμβρος δ' ἀπ' εὐνάεντος οὐρανοῦ πεσὼι
>   ἔκυσε γαῖαν.

v. 1168. Id.

>   δενδρῶτις ὥρα δ' ἐκ νοτίζοντος γάμου
>   τέλειός ἐστι.

v. 1749. ' *God born of God.*' Soph. *Ant.* 834 θεός τοι καὶ θεογεννης.

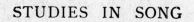

STUDIES IN SONG

SONG FOR THE CENTENARY

OF

WALTER SAVAGE LANDOR

BORN JANUARY 30TH, 1775

DIED SEPTEMBER 17TH, 1864

There is delight in singing, though none hear
Beside the singer : and there is delight
In praising, though the praiser sit alone
And see the praised far off him, far above.

LANDOR.

DEDICATION

TO MRS. LYNN LINTON

DAUGHTER in spirit elect and consecrate
  By love and reverence of the Olympian sire
Whom I too loved and worshipped, seeing so great,
  And found so gracious toward my long desire
To bid that love in song before his gate
  Sound, and my lute be loyal to his lyre,
To none save one it now may dedicate
  Song's new burnt-offering on a century's pyre.
    And though the gift be light
    As ashes in men's sight,
  Left by the flame of no ethereal fire,
    Yet, for his worthier sake
    Than words are worthless, take
  This wreath of words ere yet their hour expire :
    So, haply, from some heaven above,
He, seeing, may set next yours my sacrifice of love.

May 24, 1880.

SONG FOR THE CENTENARY OF
WALTER SAVAGE LANDOR

I

FIVE years beyond an hundred years have seen
   Their winters, white as faith's and age's hue,
Melt, smiling through brief tears that broke between,
   And hope's young conquering colours reared anew,
Since, on the day whose edge for kings made keen
   Smote sharper once than ever storm-wind blew,
A head predestined for the girdling green
   That laughs at lightning all the seasons through,
      Nor frost or change can sunder
      Its crown untouched of thunder,
   Leaf from least leaf of all its leaves that grew
      Alone for brows too bold
      For storm to sear of old,
   Elect to shine in time's eternal view,
      Rose on the verge of radiant life
Between the winds and sunbeams mingling love with
      strife.

2

The darkling day that gave its bloodred birth
   To Milton's white republic undefiled
That might endure so few fleet years on earth
   Bore in him likewise as divine a child;

But born not less for crowns of love and mirth,
  Of palm and myrtle passionate and mild,
The leaf that girds about with gentler girth
  The brow steel-bound in battle, and the wild
        Soft spray that flowers above
        The flower-soft hair of love ;
  And the white lips of wayworn winter smiled
        And grew serene as spring's
        When with stretched clouds like wings
  Or wings like drift of snow-clouds massed and
      piled
    The godlike giant, softening, spread
A shadow of stormy shelter round the new-born
    head.

3

And o'er it brightening bowed the wild-haired hour,
  And touched his tongue with honey and with fire,
And breathed between his lips the note of power
  That makes of all the winds of heaven a lyre
Whose strings are stretched from topmost peaks that
    tower
  To softest springs of waters that suspire,
With sounds too dim to shake the lowliest flower
  Breathless with hope and dauntless with desire :
        And bright before his face
        That Hour became a Grace,
    As in the light of their Athenian quire
        When the Hours before the sun
        And Graces were made one,
  Called by sweet Love down from the aerial gyre
      By one dear name of natural joy,
To bear on her bright breast from heaven a heaven-
    born boy.

4

Ere light could kiss the little lids in sunder
  Or love could lift them for the sun to smite,
His fiery birth-star as a sign of wonder
  Had risen, perplexing the presageful night
With shadow and glory around her sphere and
      under
  And portents prophesying by sound and sight ;
And half the sound was song and half was thunder,
  And half his life of lightning, half of light :
        And in the soft clenched hand
        Shone like a burning brand
  A shadowy sword for swordless fields of fight,
        Wrought only for such lord
        As so may wield the sword
  That all things ill be put to fear and flight
    Even at the flash and sweep and gleam
Of one swift stroke beheld but in a shuddering
      dream.

5

Like the sun's rays that blind the night's wild beasts
  The sword of song shines as the swordsman
      sings ;
From the west wind's verge even to the arduous
      east's
  The splendour of the shadow that it flings
Makes fire and storm in heaven above the feasts
  Of men fulfilled with food of evil things ;
Strikes dumb the lying and hungering lips of priests,
  Smites dead the slaying and ravening hands of
      kings ;

Turns dark the lamp's hot light,
And turns the darkness bright.
As with the shadow of dawn's reverberate wings ;
　　And far before its way
　　Heaven, yearning toward the day,
Shines with its thunder and round its lightning
　　rings ;
　　And never hand yet earlier played
With that keen sword whose hilt is cloud, and fire
　　its blade.

6

As dropping flakes of honey-heavy dew
　　More soft than slumber's, fell the first note's
　　　　sound
From strings the swift young hand strayed lightlier
　　　　through
　　Than leaves through calm air wheeling toward the
　　　　ground
Stray down the drifting wind when skies are blue
　　Nor yet the wings of latter winds unbound,
Ere winter loosen all the Æolian crew
　　With storm unleashèd behind them like a hound.
　　　　As lightly rose and sank
　　　　Beside a green-flowered bank
　　The clear first notes his burning boyhood found
　　　　To sing her sacred praise
　　　　Who rode her city's ways
Clothed with bright hair and with high purpose
　　crowned ;
　　A song of soft presageful breath,
Prefiguring all his love and faith in life and death ;

7

Who should love two things only and only praise
  More than all else for ever : even the glory
Of goodly beauty in women, whence all days
  Take light whereby death's self seems transitory ;
And loftier love than loveliest eyes can raise,
  Love that wipes off the miry stains and gory
From Time's worn feet, besmirched on bloodred
      ways,
  And lightens with his light the night of story ;
     Love that lifts up from dust
     Life, and makes darkness just,
  And purges as with fire of purgatory
     The dense disastrous air,
     To burn old falsehood bare
  And give the wind its ashes heaped and hoary ;
   Love, that with eyes of ageless youth
Sees on the breast of Freedom borne her nursling
    Truth.

8

For at his birth the sistering stars were one
  That flamed upon it as one fiery star ;
Freedom, whose light makes pale the mounting sun,
  And Song, whose fires are quenched when Free-
    dom's are.
Of all that love not liberty let none
  Love her that fills our lips with fire from far
To mix with winds and seas in unison
  And sound athwart life's tideless harbour-bar
     Out where our songs fly free
     Across time's bounded sea,

A boundless flight beyond the dim sun's car,
    Till all the spheres of night
      Chime concord round their flight
Too loud for blasts of warring change to mar,
    From stars that sang for Homer's birth
To these that gave our Landor welcome back from
    earth.

9

Shine, as above his cradle, on his grave,
    Stars of our worship, lights of our desire !
For never man that heard the world's wind rave
    To you was truer in trust of heart and lyre :
Nor Greece nor England on a brow more brave
    Beheld your flame against the wind burn higher :
Nor all the gusts that blanch life's worldly wave
    With surf and surge could quench its flawless fire :
      No blast of all that blow
      Might bid the torch burn low
That lightens on us yet as o'er his pyre,
      Indomitable of storm,
      That now no flaws deform
Nor thwart winds baffle ere it all aspire,
    One light of godlike breath and flame,
To write on heaven with man's most glorious names
    his name.

10

The very dawn was dashed with stormy dew
    And freaked with fire as when God's hand would
    mar
Palaces reared of tyrants, and the blue
    Deep heaven was kindled round her thunderous car,

That saw how swift a gathering glory grew
  About him risen, ere clouds could blind or bar
A splendour strong to burn and burst them through
  And mix in one sheer light things near and far.
      First flew before his path
      Light shafts of love and wrath,
  But winged and edged as elder warriors' are ;
      Then rose a light that showed
      Across the midsea road
  From radiant Calpe to revealed Masar
    The way of war and love and fate
Between the goals of fear and fortune, hope and hate.

II

Mine own twice banished fathers' harbour-land,
  Their nursing-mother France, the well-beloved,
By the arduous blast of sanguine sunrise fanned,
  Flamed on him, and his burning lips were moved
As that live statue's throned on Lybian sand
  When morning moves it, ere her light faith roved
From promise, and her tyrant's poisonous hand
      Fed hope with Corsic honey till she proved
      More deadly than despair
      And falser even than fair,
  Though fairer than all elder hopes removed
      As landmarks by the crime
      Of inundating time ;
  Light faith by grief too loud too long reproved :
    For even as in some darkling dance
Wronged love changed hands with hate, and turned
    his heart from France.

12

But past the snows and summits Pyrenean
    Love stronger-winged held more prevailing flight
That o'er Tyrrhene, Iberian, and Ægean
    Shores lightened with one storm of sound and
        light.
From earliest even to hoariest years one pæan
    Rang rapture through the fluctuant roar of fight,
From Nestor's tongue in accents Achillean
    On death's blind verge dominant over night.
        For voice as hand and hand
        As voice for one fair land
    Rose radiant, smote sonorous, past the height
        Where darkling pines enrobe
        The steel-cold Lake of Gaube,
  Deep as dark death and keen as death to smite,
    To where on peak or moor or plain
His heart and song and sword were one to strike for
    Spain.

13

Resurgent at his lifted voice and hand
    Pale in the light of war or treacherous fate
Song bade before him all their shadows stand
    For whom his will unbarred their funeral grate.
The father by whose wrong revenged his land
    Was given for sword and fire to desolate
Rose fire-encircled as a burning brand,
    Great as the woes he wrought and bore were great.
        Fair as she smiled and died,
        Death's crowned and breathless bride
Smiled as one living even on craft and hate :

And pity, a star unrisen,
  Scarce lit Ferrante's prison
Ere night unnatural closed the natural gate
  That gave their life and love and light
To those fair eyes despoiled by fratricide of sight.

14

Tears bright and sweet as fire and incense fell
  In perfect notes of music-measured pain
On veiled sweet heads that heard not love's farewell
  Sob through the song that bade them rise again ;
Rise in the light of living song, to dwell
  With memories crowned of memory : so the strain
Made soft as heaven the stream that girdles hell
  And sweet the darkness of the breathless plain,
      And with Elysian flowers
      Recrowned the wreathless hours
  That mused and mourned upon their works in vain ;
      For all their works of death
      Song filled with light and breath,
  And listening grief relaxed her lightening chain ;
    For sweet as all the wide sweet south
She found the song like honey from the lion's mouth.

15

High from his throne in heaven Simonides,
  Crowned with mild aureole of memorial tears
That the everlasting sun of all time sees
  All golden, molten from the forge of years,
Smiled, as the gift was laid upon his knees
  Of songs that hang like pearls in mourners' ears
Mild as the murmuring of Hymettian bees
  And honied as their harvest, that endears

The toil of flowery days;
And smiling perfect praise
Hailed his one brother mateless else of peers:
Whom we that hear not him
For length of date grown dim
Hear, and the heart grows glad of grief that hears;
And harshest heights of sorrowing hours,
Like snows of Alpine April, melt from tears to
flowers.

10

Therefore to him the shadow of death was none,
The darkness was not, nor the temporal tomb:
And multitudinous time for him was one,
Who bade before his equal seat of doom
Rise and stand up for judgment in the sun
The weavers of the world's large-historied loom,
By their own works of light or darkness done
Clothed round with light or girt about with gloom
In speech of purer gold
Than even they spake of old
He bade the breath of Sidney's lips relume
The fire of thought and love
That made his bright life move
Through fair brief seasons of benignant bloom
To blameless music ever, strong
As death and sweet as death-annihilating song.

17

Thought gave his wings the width of time to roam,
Love gave his thought strength equal to release
From bonds of old forgetful years, like foam
Vanished, the fame of memories that decrease;

So strongly faith had fledged for flight from home
  The soul's large pinions till her strife should cease :
And through the trumpet of a child of Rome
  Rang the pure music of the flutes of Greece.
      As though some northern hand
      Reft from the Latin land
  A spoil more costly than the Colchian fleece
      To clothe with golden sound
      Of old joy newly found
  And rapture as of penetrating peace
    The naked north-wind's cloudiest clime,
And give its darkness light of the old Sicilian time.

18

He saw the brand that fired the towers of Troy
  Fade, and the darkness at Œnone's prayer
Close upon her that closed upon her boy,
  For all the curse of godhead that she bare ;
And the Apollonian serpent gleam and toy
  With scathless maiden limbs and shuddering hair ;
And his love smitten in their dawn of joy
  Leave Pan the pine-leaf of her change to wear ;
      And one in flowery coils
      Caught as in fiery toils
  Smite Calydon with mourning unaware ;
      And where her low turf shrine
      Showed Modesty divine
  The fairest mother's daughter far more fair
    Hide on her breast the heavenly shame
That kindled once with love should kindle Troy with
    flame.

19

Nor less the light of story than of song
  With graver glories girt his godlike head,
Reverted alway from the temporal throng
  Of lives that live not toward the living dead.
The shadows and the splendours of their throng
  Made bright and dark about his board and bed
The lines of life and vision, sweet or strong
  With sound of lutes or trumpets blown, that led
      Forth of the ghostly gate
      Opening in spite of fate
  Shapes of majestic or tumultuous tread,
      Divine and direful things,
      These foul as priests or kings,
  Those fair as heaven or love or freedom, red
    With blood and green with palms and white
With raiment woven of deeds divine and words of
    light.

20

The thunder-fire of Cromwell, and the ray
  That keeps the place of Phocion's name serene
And clears the cloud from Kosciusko's day,
  Alternate as dark hours with bright between,
Met in the heaven of his high thought, which lay
  For all stars open that all eyes had seen
Rise on the night or twilight of the way
  Where feet of human hopes and fears had been.
      Again the sovereign word
      On Milton's lips was heard
  Living : again the tender three days' queen

Drew bright and gentle breath
On the sharp edge of death :
And, staged again to show of mortal scene,
Tiberius, ere his name grew dire,
Wept, stainless yet of empire, tears of blood and fire.

21

Most ardent and most awful and most fond,
The fervour of his Apollonian eye
Yearned upon Hellas, yet enthralled in bond
Of time whose years beheld her and past by
Silent and shameful, till she rose and donned
The casque again of Pallas ; for her cry
Forth of the past and future, depths beyond
This where the present and its tyrants lie,
As one great voice of twain
For him had pealed again,
Heard but of hearts high as her own was high,
High as her own and his
And pure as love's heart is,
That lives though hope at once and memory die :
And with her breath his clarion's blast
Was filled as cloud with fire or future souls with past.

22

As a wave only obsequious to the wind
Leaps to the lifting breeze that bids it leap,
Large-hearted, and its thickening mane be thinned
By the strong god's breath moving on the deep
From utmost Atlas even to extremest Ind
That shakes the plain where no men sow nor reap,

So, moved with wrath toward men that ruled and
    sinned
  And pity toward all tears he saw men weep,
        Arose to take man's part
        His loving lion heart,
  Kind as the sun's that has in charge to keep
        Earth and the seed thereof
        Safe in his lordly love,
  Strong as sheer truth and soft as very sleep ;
    The mightiest heart since Milton's leapt,
The gentlest since the gentlest heart of Shakespeare
    slept.

23

Like the wind's own on her divided sea
  His song arose on Corinth, and aloud
Recalled her Isthmian song and strife when she
  Was thronged with glories as with gods in crowd
And as the wind's own spirit her breath was free
  And as the heaven's own heart her soul was proud,
But freer and prouder stood no son than he
  Of all she bare before her heart was bowed ;
      None higher than he who heard
      Medea's keen last word
Transpierce her traitor, and like a rushing cloud
      That sundering shows a star
      Saw pass her thunderous car
And a face whiter and deadlier than a shroud
    That lightened from it, and the brand
Of tender blood that falling seared his suppliant hand.

24

More fair than all things born and slain of fate,
　More glorious than all births of days and nights.
He bade the spirit of man regenerate,
　Rekindling, rise and reassume the rights
That in high seasons of his old estate
　Clothed him and armed with majesties and mights
Heroic, when the times and hearts were great
　And in the depths of ages rose the heights
　　　Radiant of high deeds done
　　　And souls that matched the sun
For splendour with the lightnings of their lights
　　　Whence even their uttered names
　　　Burn like the strong twin flames
Of song that shakes a throne and steel that smites ;
　　As on Thermopylæ when shone
Leonidas, on Syracuse Timoleon.

25

Or, sweeter than the breathless buds when spring
　With smiles and tears and kisses bids them breathe,
Fell with its music from his quiring string
　Fragrance of pine-leaves and odorous heath
Twined round the lute whereto he sighed to sing
　Of the oak that screened and showed its maid
　　beneath,
Who seeing her bee crawl back with broken wing
　Faded, a fairer flower than all her wreath,
　　　And paler, though her oak
　　　Stood scathless of the stroke
More sharp than edge of axe or wolfish teeth,

That mixed with mortals dead
Her own half heavenly head
And life incorporate with a sylvan sheath,
And left the wild rose and the dove
A secret place and sacred from all guests but Love.

26

But in the sweet clear fields beyond the river
Dividing pain from peace and man from shade
He saw the wings that there no longer quiver
Sink of the hours whose parting footfalls fade
On ears which hear the rustling amaranth shiver
With sweeter sound of wind than ever made
Music on earth : departing, they deliver
The soul that shame or wrath or sorrow swayed ;
And round the king of men
Clash the clear arms again,
Clear of all soil and bright as laurel braid,
That rang less high for joy
Through the gates fallen of Troy
Than here to hail the sacrificial maid,
Iphigeneia, when the ford
Fast-flowing of sorrows brought her father and their
lord.

27

And in the clear gulf of the hollow sea
He saw light glimmering through the grave green
gloom
That hardly gave the sun's eye leave to see
Cymodameia ; but nor tower nor tomb,
No tower on earth, no tomb of waves may be,
That may not sometime by diviner doom

Be plain and pervious to the poet ; he
   Bids time stand back from him and fate make room
      For passage of his feet,
      Strong as their own are fleet,
  And yield the prey no years may reassume
      Through all their clamorous track,
      Nor night nor day win back
  Nor give to darkness what his eyes illume
    And his lips bless for ever : he
Knows what earth knows not, sings truth sung not
    of the sea.

28

Before the sentence of a curule chair
  More sacred than the Roman, rose and stood
To take their several doom the imperial pair
  Diversely born of Venus, and in mood
Diverse as their one mother, and as fair,
  Though like two stars contrasted, and as good,
Though different as dark eyes from golden hair ;
  One as that iron planet red like blood
     That bears among the stars
     Fierce witness of her Mars
  In bitter fire by her sweet light subdued ;
     One in the gentler skies
     Sweet as her amorous eyes :
  One proud of worlds and seas and darkness rude
    Composed and conquered ; one content
With lightnings from loved eyes of lovers lightly
    sent.

29

And where Alpheus and where Ladon ran
  Radiant, by many a rushy and rippling cove
More known to glance of god than wandering man,
  He sang the strife of strengths divine that strove,
Unequal, one with other, for a span,
  Who should be friends for ever in heaven above
And here on pastoral earth : Arcadian Pan,
    And the awless lord of kings and shepherds, Love :
        All the sweet strife and strange
        With fervid counterchange
  Till one fierce wail through many a glade and grove
        Rang, and its breath made shiver
        The reeds of many a river,
  And the warm airs waxed wintry that it clove,
      Keen-edged as ice-retempered brand ;
Nor might god's hurt find healing save of godlike
        hand.

30

As when the jarring gates of thunder ope
  Like earthquake felt in heaven, so dire a cry,
So fearful and so fierce—" Give the sword scope ! "—
  Rang from a daughter's lips, darkening the sky
To the extreme azure of all its cloudless cope
  With starless horror : nor the God's own eye
Whose doom bade smite, whose ordinance bade
        hope,
    Might well endure to see the adulteress die,
        The husband-slayer fordone
        By swordstroke of her son,
  Unutterable, unimaginable on high,

On earth abhorrent, fell
   Beyond all scourge of hell,
Yet righteous as redemption : Love stood nigh,
  Mute, sister-like, and closer clung
Than all fierce forms of threatening coil and madden-
    ing tongue.

31

All these things heard and seen and sung of old,
  He heard and saw and sang them.   Once again
Might foot of man tread, eye of man behold
  Things unbeholden save of ancient men,
Ways save by gods untrodden.   In his hold
  The staff that stayed through some Ætnean glen
The steps of the most highest, most awful-souled
  And mightiest-mouthed of singers, even as then
    Became a prophet's rod,
    A lyre on fire of God,
  Being still the staff of exile : yea, as when
    The voice poured forth on us
    Was even of Æschylus,
  And his one word great as the crying of ten,
   Crying in men's ears of wrath toward wrong,
Of love toward right immortal, sanctified with song.

32

Him too whom none save one before him ever
  Beheld, nor since hath man again beholden,
Whom Dante seeing him saw not, nor the giver
  Of all gifts back to man by time withholden,
Shakespeare—him too, whom sea-like ages sever,
  As waves divide men's eyes from lights upholden

To landward, from our songs that find him never,
    Seeking, though memory fire and hope embolden—
            Him too this one song found,
            And raised at its sole sound
    Up from the dust of darkling dreams and olden
            Legends forlorn of breath,
            Up from the deeps of death,
    Ulysses : him whose name turns all songs golden,
        The wise divine strong soul, whom fate
Could make no less than change and chance beheld
    him great.

                    33

Nor stands the seer who raised him less august
    Before us, nor in judgment frail and rathe,
Less constant or less loving or less just,
    But fruitful-ripe and full of tender faith,
Holding all high and gentle names in trust
    Of time for honour ; so his quickening breath
Called from the darkness of their martyred dust
        Our sweet Saints Alice and Elizabeth,
            Revived and reinspired
            With speech from heavenward fired
    By love to say what Love the Archangel saith
            Only, nor may such word
            Save by such ears be heard
    As hear the tongues of angels after death
        Descending on them like a dove
Has taken all earthly sense of thought away but
    love.

34

All sweet, all sacred, all heroic things,
  All generous names and loyal, and all wise,
With all his heart in all its wayfarings
  He sought, and worshipped, seeing them with his
    eyes
In very present glory, clothed with wings
  Of words and deeds and dreams immortal, rise
Visible more than living slaves and kings,
  Audible more than actual vows and lies :
      These, with scorn's fieriest rod,
      These and the Lord their God,
The Lord their likeness, tyrant of the skies
      As they Lord Gods of earth,
      These with a rage of mirth
He mocked and scourged and spat on, in such wise
  That none might stand before his rod,
  And these being slain the Spirit alone be lord or
    God.

35

For of all souls for all time glorious none
  Loved Freedom better, of all who have loved her
    best,
Than he who wrote that scripture of the sun
  Writ as with fire and light on heaven's own crest,
Of all words heard on earth the noblest one
  That ever spake for souls and left them blest :
GLADLY WE SHOULD REST EVER, HAD WE WON
  FREEDOM : WE HAVE LOST, AND VERY GLADLY REST.
      O poet hero, lord
      And father, we record
Deep in the burning tablets of the breast

Thankfully those divine
And living words of thine
For faith and comfort in our hearts imprest
With strokes engraven past hurt of years
And lines inured with fire of immemorial tears.

36

But who being less than thou shall sing of thee
    Words worthy of more than pity or less than scorn ?
Who sing the golden garland woven of three,
    Thy daughters, Graces mightier than the morn,
More godlike than the graven gods men see
    Made all but all immortal, human born
And heavenly natured ?   With the first came He,
    Led by the living hand, who left forlorn
            Life by his death, and time
            More by his life sublime
    Than by the lives of all whom all men mourn,
            And even for mourning praise
            Heaven, as for all those days
    These dead men's lives clothed round with glories
        worn
        By memory till all time lie dead,
And higher than all behold the bay round Shake-
        speare's head.

37

Then, fairer than the fairest Grace of ours,
    Came girt with Grecian gold the second Grace,
And verier daughter of his most perfect hours
    Than any of latter time or alien place
Named, or with hair inwoven of English flowers
    Only, nor wearing on her statelier face

The lordlier light of Athens.   All the Powers
  That graced and guarded round that holiest race,
      That heavenliest and most high
      Time hath seen live and die,
Poured all their power upon him to retrace
      The erased immortal roll
      Of Love's most sovereign scroll
And Wisdom's warm from Freedom's wide embrace,
  The scroll that on Aspasia's knees
Laid once made manifest the Olympian Pericles.

38

Clothed on with tenderest weft of Tuscan air,
  Came laughing like Etrurian spring the third,
With green Valdelsa's hill-flowers in her hair
  Deep-drenched with May-dews, in her voice the
     bird
Whose voice hath night and morning in it ; fair
  As the ambient gold of wall-flowers that engird
The walls engirdling with a circling stair
    My sweet San Gimignano : nor a word
      Fell from her flowerlike mouth
      Not sweet with all the south ;
  As though the dust shrined in Certaldo stirred
      And spake, as o'er it shone
      That bright Pentameron,
And his own vines again and chestnuts heard
    Boccaccio : nor swift Elsa's chime
Mixed not her golden babble with Petrarca's rhyme.

39

No lovelier laughed the garden which receives
    Yet, and yet hides not from our following eyes
With soft rose-laurels and low strawberry-leaves,
    Ternissa, sweet as April-coloured skies,
Bowed like a flowering reed when May's wind heaves
    The reed-bed that the stream kisses and sighs,
In love that shrinks and murmurs and believes
    What yet the wisest of the starriest wise
        Whom Greece might ever hear
        Speaks in the gentlest ear
That ever heard love's lips philosophize
        With such deep-reasoning words
        As blossoms use and birds,
Nor heeds Leontion lingering till they rise
    Far off, in no wise over far,
Beneath a heaven all amorous of its first-born star.

40

What sound, what storm and splendour of what fire,
    Darkening the light of heaven, lightening the night,
Rings, rages, flashes round what ravening pyre
    That makes time's face pale with its reflex light
And leaves on earth, who seeing might scarce respire,
    A shadow of red remembrance? Right nor might
Alternating wore ever shapes more dire
    Nor manifest in all men's awful sight
        In form and face that wore
        Heaven's light and likeness more
Than these, or held suspense men s hearts at
    height

More fearful, since man first
    Slaked with man's blood his thirst,
Than when Rome clashed with Hannibal in fight,
    Till tower on ruining tower was hurled
Where Scipio stood, and Carthage was not in the
    world.

41

Nor lacked there power of purpose in his hand
    Who carved their several praise in words of gold
To bare the brows of conquerors and to brand,
    Made shelterless of laurels bought and sold
For price of blood or incense, dust or sand,
    Triumph or terror.   He that sought of old
His father Ammon in a stranger's land,
    And shrank before the serpentining fold,
        Stood in our seer's wide eye
        No higher than man most high,
    And lowest in heart when highest in hope to hold
        Fast as a scripture furled
        The scroll of all the world
    Sealed with his signet : nor the blind and bold
        First thief of empire, round whose head
Swarmed carrion flies for bees, on flesh for violets fed.[1]

42

As fire that kisses, killing with a kiss,
    He saw the light of death, riotous and red,
Flame round the bent brows of Semiramis
    Re-risen, and mightier, from the Assyrian dead,

---

[1] Thy lifelong works, Napoleon, who shall write?
    Time, in his children's blood who takes delight.
             From the Greek of Landor.

Kindling, as dawn a frost-bound precipice,
  The steely snows of Russia, for the tread
Of feet that felt before them crawl and hiss
  The snaky lines of blood violently shed
        Like living creeping things
        That writhe but have no stings
  To scare adulterers from the imperial bed
        Bowed with its load of lust,
        Or chill the ravenous gust
  That made her body a fire from heel to head ;
    Or change her high bright spirit and clear,
For all its mortal stains, from taint of fraud or fear.

43

As light that blesses, hallowing with a look,
  He saw the godhead in Vittoria's face
Shine soft on Buonarroti's, till he took,
  Albeit himself God, a more godlike grace,
A strength more heavenly to confront and brook
  All ill things coiled about his worldly race,
From the bright scripture of that present book
  Wherein his tired grand eyes got power to trace
        Comfort more sweet than youth,
        And hope whose child was truth,
  And love that brought forth sorrow for a space,
        Only that she might bear
        Joy : these things, written there,
  Made even his soul's high heaven a heavenliei
      place,
    Perused with eyes whose glory and glow
Had in their fires the spirit of Michael Angelo.

44

With balms and dews of blessing he consoled
    The fair fame wounded by the black priest's fang,
Giovanna's, and washed off her blithe and bold
    Boy-bridegroom's blood, that seemed so long to
        hang
On her fair hand, even till the stain of old
    Was cleansed with healing song, that after sang
Sharp truth by sweetest singers' lips untold
    Of pale Beatrice, though her death-note rang
            From other strings divine
            Ere his rekindling line
    With yet more piteous and intolerant pang
            Pierced all men's hearts anew
            That heard her passion through
    Till fierce from throes of fiery pity sprang
        Wrath, armed for chase of monstrous beasts,
Strong to lay waste the kingdom of the seed of
        priests.

45

He knew the high-souled humbleness, the mirth
    And majesty of meanest men born free,
That made with Luther's or with Hofer's birth
    The whole world worthier of the sun to see :
The wealth of spirit among the snows, the dearth
    Wherein souls festered by the servile sea
That saw the lowest of even crowned heads on earth
    Thronged round with worship in Parthenope.
            His hand bade Justice guide
            Her child Tyrannicide,
    Light winged by fire that brings the dawn to be ;

And pierced with Tyrrel's dart
Again the riotous heart
That mocked at mercy's tongue and manhood's
knee :
And oped the cell where kinglike death
Hung o'er her brows discrowned who bare Elizabeth.

46

Toward Spenser or toward Bacon proud or kind
He bared the heart of Essex, twain and one,
For the base heart that soiled the starry mind
Stern, for the father in his child undone
Soft as his own toward children, stamped and signed
With their sweet image visibly set on
As by God's hand, clear as his own designed
The likeness radiant out of ages gone
That none may now destroy
Of that high Roman boy
Whom Julius and Cleopatra saw their son
True-born of sovereign seed,
Foredoomed even thence to bleed,
The stately grace of bright Cæsarion,
The head unbent, the heart unbowed,
That not the shadow of death could make less clear
and proud.

47

With gracious gods he communed, honouring thus
At once by service and similitude,
Service devout and worship emulous
Of the same golden Muses once they wooed,
The names and shades adored of all of us,
The nurslings of the brave world's earlier brood,

Grown gods for us themselves: Theocritus
  First, and more dear Catullus, names bedewed
      With blessings bright like tears
      From the old memorial years,
  And loves and lovely laughters, every mood
      Sweet as the drops that fell
      Of their own œnomel
  From living lips to cheer the multitude
    That feeds on words divine, and grows
More worthy, seeing their world reblossom like a
    rose.

48

Peace, the soft seal of long life's closing story,
  The silent music that no strange note jars,
Crowned not with gentler hand the years that glory
  Crowned, but could hide not all the spiritual scars
Time writes on the inward strengths of warriors
    hoary
  With much long warfare, and with gradual bars
Blindly pent in : but these, being transitory,
  Broke, and the power came back that passion
    mars :
      And at the lovely last
      Above all anguish past
  Before his own the sightless eyes like stars
      Arose that watched arise
      Like stars in other skies
  Above the strife of ships and hurtling cars
    The Dioscurian songs divine
That lighten all the world with lightning of their
    line.

49

He sang the last of Homer, having sung
   The last of his Ulysses.   Bright and wide
For him time's dark strait ways, like clouds that
    clung
   About the day-star, doubtful to divide,
Waxed in his spiritual eyeshot, and his tongue
   Spake as his soul bore witness, that descried,
Like those twin towering lights in darkness hung,
   Homer, and grey Laertes at his side
        Kingly as kings are none
        Beneath a later sun,
  And the sweet maiden ministering in pride
      To sovereign and to sage
      In their more sweet old age :
These things he sang, himself as old, and died.
    And if death be not, if life be,
As Homer and as Milton are in heaven is he.

50

Poet whose large-eyed loyalty of love
   Was pure toward all high poets, all their kind
And all bright words and all sweet works thereof ;
   Strong like the sun, and like the sunlight kind ;
Heart that no fear but every grief might move
   Wherewith men's hearts were bound of powers
    that bind ;
The purest soul that ever proof could prove
   From taint of tortuous or of envious mind ;
        Whose eyes elate and clear
        Nor shame nor ever fear
But only pity or glorious wrath could blind ;

Name set for love apart,
Held lifelong in my heart,
Face like a father's toward my face inclined ;
No gifts like thine are mine to give,
Who by thine own words only bid thee hail, and
live.

NOTES

"J'en passe, et des meilleurs." But who can enumerate all or half our obligations to the illimitable and inexhaustible genius of the great man whose life and whose labour lasted even from the generation of our fathers' fathers to our own ? Hardly any reader can feel, I think, so deeply as I feel the inadequacy of my poor praise and too imperfect gratitude to the majestic subject of their attempted expression ; but "such as I had have I given him."

GRAND CHORUS OF BIRDS

FROM

ARISTOPHANES

Attempted in English verse after the original metre

I WAS allured into the audacity of this experiment by consideration of a fact which hitherto does not seem to have been taken into consideration by any translator of the half divine humourist in whose incomparable genius the highest qualities of Rabelais were fused and harmonized with the supremest gifts of Shelley : namely, that his marvellous metrical invention of the anapæstic heptameter was almost exactly reproducible in a language to which all variations and combinations of anapæstic, iambic, or trochaic metre are as natural and pliable as all dactylic and spondaic forms of verse are unnatural and abhorrent. As it happens, this highest central interlude of a most adorable masterpiece is as easy to detach from its dramatic setting, and even from its lyrical context, as it was easy to give line for line of it in English. In two metrical points only does my version vary from the verbal pattern of the original. I have of course added rhymes, and double rhymes, as necessary makeweights for the imperfection of an otherwise inadequate language ; and equally of course I have not attempted the impossible and undesirable task of reproducing the rare exceptional effect of a line overcharged on purpose with a preponderance of heavy-footed spondees : and this for the obvious reason that even if such a line—which I doubt—could be exactly represented, foot by foot and pause for pause, in English, this English line would no more be a verse in any proper sense of the word than is the line I am writing at this moment. And my main intention, or at least my main desire, in the undertaking of this brief adventure, was to renew as far as possible for English ears the music of this resonant and triumphant metre, which goes ringing at full gallop as of horses who

> "dance as 'twere to the music
> Their own hoofs make."

I would not seem over curious in search of an apt or inapt quotation : but nothing can be fitter than a verse of Shakespeare's to praise at once and to describe the most typical verse of Aristophanes.

THE BIRDS

(685-723)

COME on then, ye dwellers by nature in darkness, and
      like to the leaves' generations,
That are little of might, that are moulded of mire,
      unenduring and shadowlike nations,
Poor plumeless ephemerals, comfortless mortals, as
      visions of creatures fast fleeing,
Lift up your mind unto us that are deathless, and
      dateless the date of our being :
Us, children of heaven, us, ageless for aye, us, all of
      whose thoughts are eternal ;
That ye may from henceforth, having heard of us all
      things aright as to matters supernal,
Of the being of birds and beginning of gods, and of
      streams, and the dark beyond reaching,
Truthfully knowing aright, in my name bid Prodicus
      pack with his preaching.

It was Chaos and Night at the first, and the black-
      ness of darkness, and hell's broad border,
Earth was not, nor air, neither heaven ; when in
      depths of the womb of the dark without order
First thing first-born of the black-plumed Night was
      a wind-egg hatched in her bosom,
Whence timely with seasons revolving again sweet
      Love burst out as a blossom,

Gold wings glittering forth of his back, like whirl-
      winds gustily turning.
He, after his wedlock with Chaos, whose wings are
      of darkness, in hell broad-burning,
For his nestlings begat him the race of us first, and
      upraised us to light new-lighted.
And before this was not the race of the gods, until
      all things by Love were united ;
And of kind united with kind in communion of nature
      the sky and the sea are
Brought forth, and the earth, and the race of the
      gods everlasting and blest.   So that we are
Far away the most ancient of all things blest.   And
      that we are of Love's generation
There are manifest manifold signs.   We have wings,
      and with us have the Loves habitation ;
And manifold fair young folk that forswore love once,
      ere the bloom of them ended,
Have the men that pursued and desired them sub-
      dued, by the help of us only befriended,
With such baits as a quail, a flamingo, a goose, or
      a cock's comb staring and splendid.

All best good things that befall men come from us
      birds, as is plain to all reason :
For first we proclaim and make known to them
      spring, and the winter and autumn in season ;
Bid sow, when the crane starts clanging for Afric, in
      shrill-voiced emigrant number,
And calls to the pilot to hang up his rudder again for
      the season, and slumber ;
And then weave cloak for Orestes the thief, lest he
      strip men of theirs if it freezes.
And again thereafter the kite reappearing announces
      a change in the breezes,

And that here is the season for shearing your sheep
    of their spring wool.   Then does the swallow
Give you notice to sell your greatcoat, and provide
    something light for the heat that's to follow.
Thus are we as Ammon or Delphi unto you, Dodona,
    nay, Phœbus Apollo.
For, as first ye come all to get auguries of birds, even
    such is in all things your carriage,
Be the matter a matter of trade, or of earning your
    bread, or of any one's marriage.
And all things ye lay to the charge of a bird that
    belong to discerning prediction :
Winged fame is a bird, as you reckon : you sneeze,
    and the sign's as a bird for conviction :
All tokens are " birds " with you—sounds too, and
    lackeys, and donkeys.   Then must it not follow
That we ARE to you all as the manifest godhead that
    speaks in prophetic Apollo ?

October 19, 1880.

OFF SHORE

WHEN the might of the summer
　　Is most on the sea ;
When the days overcome her
　　With joy but to be,
With rapture of royal enchantment, and sorcery that
　　sets her not free,

　　But for hours upon hours
　　　　As a thrall she remains
　　Spell-bound as with flowers
　　　　And content in their chains,
And her loud steeds fret not, and lift not a lock of
　　their deep white manes ;

　　Then only, far under
　　　　In the depths of her hold,
　　Some gleam of its wonder
　　　　Man's eye may behold,
Its wild-weed forests of crimson and russet and olive
　　and gold.

　　Still deeper and dimmer
　　　　And goodlier they glow
　　For the eyes of the swimmer
　　　　Who scans them below
As he crosses the zone of their flowerage that knows
　　not of sunshine and snow.

Soft blossomless frondage
And foliage that gleams
As to prisoners in bondage
The light of their dreams,
The desire of a dawn unbeholden, with hope on the
wings of its beams.

Not as prisoners entombed
Waxen haggard and wizen,
But consoled and illumed
In the depths of their prison
With delight of the light everlasting and vision of
dawn on them risen,

From the banks and the beds
Of the waters divine
They lift up their heads
And the flowers of them shine
Through the splendour of darkness that clothes them
of water that glimmers like wine.

Bright bank over bank
Making glorious the gloom,
Soft rank upon rank,
Strange bloom after bloom,
They kindle the liquid low twilight, the dusk of the
dim sea's womb.

Through the subtle and tangible
Gloom without form,
Their branches, infrangible
Ever of storm,
Spread softer their sprays than the shoots of the
woodland when April is warm.

As the flight of the thunder, full
    Charged with its word,
Dividing the wonderful
    Depths like a bird,
Speaks wrath and delight to the heart of the night
    that exults to have heard,

So swiftly, though soundless
    In silence's ear,
Light, winged from the boundless
    Blue depths full of cheer,
Speaks joy to the heart of the waters that part not
    before him, but hear.

Light, perfect and visible
    Godhead of God,
God indivisible,
    Lifts but his rod,
And the shadows are scattered in sunder, and dark-
    ness is light at his nod.

At the touch of his wand,
    At the nod of his head
From the spaces beyond
    Where the dawn hath her bed,
Earth, water, and air are transfigured, and rise as
    one risen from the dead.

He puts forth his hand,
    And the mountains are thrilled
To the heart as they stand
    In his presence, fulfilled
With his glory that utters his grace upon earth, and
    her sorrows are stilled.

The moan of her travail
　　That groans for the light
Till dayspring unravel
　　The weft of the night,
At the sound of the strings of the music of morning,
　　falls dumb with delight.

He gives forth his word,
　　And the word that he saith,
Ere well it be heard,
　　Strikes darkness to death ;
For the thought of his heart is the sunrise, and dawn
　　as the sound of his breath.

And the strength of its pulses
　　That passion makes proud
Confounds and convulses
　　The depths of the cloud
Of the darkness that heaven was engirt with, divided
　　and rent as a shroud,

As the veil of the shrine
　　Of the temple of old
When darkness divine
　　Over noonday was rolled ;
So the heart of the night by the pulse of the light is
　　convulsed and controlled.

And the sea's heart, groaning
　　For glories withdrawn,
And the waves' mouths, moaning
　　All night for the dawn,
Are uplift as the hearts and the mouths of the singers
　　on leaside and lawn.

And the sound of the quiring
    Of all these as one,
Desired and desiring
    Till dawn's will be done,
Fills full with delight of them heaven till it burns as
    the heart of the sun.

Till the waves too inherit
    And waters take part
In the sense of the spirit
    That breathes from his heart,
And are kindled with music as fire when the lips of
    the morning part,

With music unheard
    In the light of her lips,
In the life-giving word
    Of the dewfall that drips
On the grasses of earth, and the wind that enkindles
    the wings of the ships.

White glories of wings
    As of seafaring birds
That flock from the springs
    Of the sunrise in herds
With the wind for a herdsman, and hasten or halt at
    the change of his words.

At the watchword's change
    When the wind's note shifts,
And the skies grow strange,
    And the white squall drifts
Up sharp from the sea-line, vexing the sea till the
    low cloud lifts.

At the charge of his word
    Bidding pause, bidding haste,
When the ranks are stirred
    And the lines displaced,
They scatter as wild swans parting adrift on the wan
    green waste.

At the hush of his word
    In a pause of his breath
When the waters have heard
    His will that he saith,
They stand as a flock penned close in its fold for
    division of death.

As a flock by division
    Of death to be thinned,
As the shades in a vision
    Of spirits that sinned ;
So glimmer their shrouds and their sheetings as
    clouds on the stream of the wind.

But the sun stands fast,
    And the sea burns bright,
And the flight of them past
    Is no more than the flight
Of the snow-soft swarm of serene wings poised and
    afloat in the light.

Like flowers upon flowers
    In a festival way
When hours after hours
    Shed grace on the day,
White blossomlike butterflies hover and gleam
    through the snows of the spray.

Like snow-coloured petals
Of blossoms that flee
From storm that unsettles
The flower as the tree
They flutter, a legion of flowers on the wing, through
the field of the sea.

Through the furrowless field
Where the foam-blossoms blow
And the secrets are sealed
Of their harvest below
They float in the path of the sunbeams, as flakes or
as blossoms of snow.

Till the sea's ways darken,
And the God, withdrawn,
Give ear not or hearken
If prayer on him fawn,
And the sun's self seem but a shadow, the noon as a
ghost of the dawn.

No shadow, but rather
God, father of song,
Show grace to me, Father
God, loved of me long,
That I lose not the light of thy face, that my trust in
thee work me not wrong.

While yet I make forward
With face toward thee
Not turned yet in shoreward,
Be thine upon me ;
Be thy light on my forehead or ever I turn it again
from the sea.

As a kiss on my brow
    Be the light of thy grace,
Be thy glance on me now
    From the pride of thy place :
As the sign of a sire to a son be the light on my face
    of thy face.

Thou wast father of olden
    Times hailed and adored,
And the sense of thy golden
    Great harp's monochord
Was the joy in the soul of the singers that hailed
    thee for master and lord.

Fair father of all
    In thy ways that have trod,
That have risen at thy call,
    That have thrilled at thy nod,
Arise, shine, lighten upon me, O sun that we see to
    be God.

As my soul has been dutiful
    Only to thee,
O God most beautiful,
    Lighten thou me,
As I swim through the dim long rollers, with eyelids
    uplift from the sea.

Be praised and adored of us
    All in accord,
Father and lord of us
    Alway adored,
The slayer and the stayer and the harper, the light
    of us all and our lord.

At the sound of thy lyre,
    At the touch of thy rod,
Air quickens to fire
    By the foot of thee trod,
The saviour and healer and singer, the living and
    visible God.

The years are before thee
    As shadows of thee,
    As men that adore thee,
    As cloudlets that flee :
But thou art the God, and thy kingdom is heaven,
    and thy shrine is the sea.

AFTER NINE YEARS

TO JOSEPH MAZZINI

Primâ dicte mihi, summâ dicende Camenâ

I

THE shadows fallen of years are nine
Since heaven grew seven times more divine
With thy soul entering, and the dearth
Of souls on earth
Grew sevenfold sadder, wanting One
Whose light of life, quenched here and done,
Burns there eternal as the sun.

2

Beyond all word, beyond all deed,
Beyond all thought beloved, what need
Has death or love that speech should be,
Hast thou of me?
I had no word, no prayer, no cry,
To praise or hail or mourn thee by,
As when thou too wast man as I.

3

Nay, never, nor as any born
Save one whose name priests turn to scorn,
Who haply, though we know not now,
Was man as thou,
A wanderer branded with men's blame,
Loved past man's utterance : yea, the same,
Perchance, and as his name thy name.

4

Thou wast as very Christ—not he
Degraded into Deity,
And priest-polluted by such prayer
As poisons air,
Tongue-worship of the tongue that slays,
False faith and parricidal praise :
But the man crowned with suffering days.

5

God only, being of all mankind
Most manlike, of most equal mind
And heart most perfect, more than can
Be heart of man
Once in ten ages, born to be
As haply Christ was, and as we
Knew surely, seeing, and worshipped thee.

6

To know thee—this at least was ours,
God, clothed upon with human hours,
O face beloved, O spirit adored,
Saviour and lord !

That wast not only for thine own
Redeemer—not of these alone
But all to whom thy word was known.

7

Ten years have wrought their will with me
Since last my words took wing for thee
Who then wast even as now above
Me, and my love.
As then thou knewest not scorn, so now
With that beloved benignant brow
Take these of him whose light wast thou.

FOR A PORTRAIT OF FELICE ORSINI

STEADFAST as sorrow, fiery sad, and sweet
   With underthoughts of love and faith, more
      strong
   Than doubt and hate and all ill thoughts which
      throng,
Haply, round hope's or fear's world-wandering feet
That find no rest from wandering till they meet
   Death, bearing palms in hand and crowns of song ;
   His face, who thought to vanquish wrong with
      wrong,
Erring, and make rage and redemption greet,
Havoc and freedom ; weaving in one weft
Good with his right hand, evil with his left ;
   But all a hero lived and erred and died ;
Looked thus upon the living world he left
   So bravely that with pity less than pride
   Men hail him Patriot and Tyrannicide.

EVENING ON THE BROADS

OVER two shadowless waters, adrift as a pinnace in
        peril,
  Hangs as in heavy suspense, charged with irresolute
        light,
Softly the soul of the sunset upholden awhile on the
        sterile
  Waves and wastes of the land, half repossessed by
        the night.
Inland glimmer the shallows asleep and afar in the
        breathless
  Twilight : yonder the depths darken afar and
        asleep.
Slowly the semblance of death out of heaven descends
        on the deathless
  Waters : hardly the light lives on the face of the
        deep—
Hardly, but here for awhile. All over the grey soft
        shallow
  Hover the colours and clouds of the twilight, void
        of a star.
As a bird unfledged is the broad-winged night, whose
        winglets are callow
  Yet, but soon with their plumes will she cover her
        brood from afar,

Cover the brood of her worlds that cumber the skies
    with their blossom
  Thick as the darkness of leaf-shadowed spring is
    encumbered with flowers.
World upon world is enwound in the bountiful girth
    of her bosom,
  Warm and lustrous with life lovely to look on as
    ours.
Still is the sunset adrift as a spirit in doubt that dis-
    sembles
  Still with itself, being sick of division and dimmed
    by dismay—
Nay, not so; but with love and delight beyond
    passion it trembles,
  Fearful and fain of the night, lovely with love of
    the day:
Fain and fearful of rest that is like unto death, and
    begotten
  Out of the womb of the tomb, born of the seed of
    the grave:
Lovely with shadows of loves that are only not
    wholly forgotten,
  Only not wholly suppressed by the dark as a wreck
    by the wave.
Still there linger the loves of the morning and noon,
    in a vision
  Blindly beheld, but in vain: ghosts that are tired,
    and would rest.
But the glories beloved of the night rise all too dense
    for division,
  Deep in the depth of her breast sheltered as doves
    in a nest.
Fainter the beams of the loves of the daylight season
    enkindled

Wane, and the memories of hours that were fair
    with the love of them fade :
Loftier, aloft of the lights of the sunset stricken and
    dwindled,
    Gather the signs of the love at the heart of the
        night new-made.
New-made night, new-born of the sunset, immeasur-
    able, endless,
    Opens the secret of love hid from of old in her heart,
In the deep sweet heart full-charged with faultless
    love of the friendless
    Spirits of men that are eased when the wheels of
        the sun depart.
Still is the sunset afloat as a ship on the waters
    upholden
    Full-sailed, wide-winged, poised softly for ever
        asway—
Nay, not so, but at least for a little, awhile at the
    golden
    Limit of arching air fain for an hour to delay.
Here on the bar of the sand-bank, steep yet aslope
    to the gleaming
    Waste of the water without, waste of the water
        within,
Lights overhead and lights underneath seem doubt-
    fully dreaming
    Whether the day be done, whether the night may
        begin.
Far and afar and farther again they falter and hover,
    Warm on the water and deep in the sky and pale
        on the cloud :
Colder again and slowly remoter, afraid to recover
    Breath, yet fain to revive, as it seems, from the
        skirt of the shroud.

Faintly the heartbeats shorten and pause of the light
    in the westward
      Heaven, as eastward quicken the paces of star
        upon star
Hurried and eager of life as a child that strains to
    the breast-ward
      Eagerly, yearning forth of the deeps where the
        ways of them are,
Glad of the glory of the gift of their life and the
    wealth of its wonder,
      Fain of the night and the sea and the sweet wan
        face of the earth.
Over them air grows deeper, intense with delight in
    them : under
      Things are thrilled in their sleep as with sense of
        a sure new birth.
But here by the sand-bank watching, with eyes on
    the sea-line, stranger
      Grows to me also the weight of the sea-ridge
        gazed on of me,
Heavily heaped up, changefully changeless, void
    though of danger
      Void not of menace, but full of the might of the
        dense dull sea.
Like as the wave is before me, behind is the bank
    deep-drifted ;
      Yellow and thick as the bank is behind me in front
        is the wave.
As the wall of a prison imprisoning the mere is the
    girth of it lifted :
      But the rampire of water in front is erect as the
        wall of a grave.
And the crests of it crumble and topple and change,
    but the wall is not broken :

Standing still dry-shod, I see it as higher than my
    head,
Moving inland alway again, reared up as in token
    Still of impending wrath still in the foam of it shed.
And even in the pauses between them, dividing the
    rollers in sunder,
    High overhead seems ever the sea-line fixed as a
        mark,
And the shore where I stand as a valley beholden of
    hills whence thunder
    Cloud and torrent and storm, darkening the depths
        of the dark.
Up to the sea, not upon it or over it, upward from
    under
    Seems he to gaze, whose eyes yearn after it here
        from the shore :
A wall of turbid water, aslope to the wide sky's
    wonder
    Of colour and cloud, it climbs, or spreads as a
        slanted floor.
And the large lights change on the face of the mere
    like things that were living,
    Winged and wonderful, beams like as birds are
        that pass and are free :
But the light is dense as darkness, a gift withheld in
    the giving,
    That lies as dead on the fierce dull face of the land-
        ward sea.
Stained and stifled and soiled, made earthier than
    earth is and duller,
    Grimly she puts back light as rejected, a thing put
        away :
No transparent rapture, a molten music of colour ;
    No translucent love taken and given of the day.

Fettered and marred and begrimed is the light's live
    self on her falling,
    As the light of a man's life lighted the fume of a
        dungeon mars :
Only she knows of the wind, when her wrath gives
    ear to him calling ;
    The delight of the light she knows not, nor answers
        the sun or the stars.
Love she hath none to return for the luminous love
    of their giving :
    None to reflect from the bitter and shallow response
        of her heart.
Yearly she feeds on her dead, yet herself seems dead
    and not living,
    Or confused as a soul heavy-laden with trouble
        that will not depart.
In the sound of her speech to the darkness the moan
    of her evil remorse is,
    Haply, for strong ships gnawed by the dog-toothed
        sea-bank's fang
And trampled to death by the rage of the feet of her
    foam-lipped horses
    Whose manes are yellow as plague, and as ensigns
        of pestilence hang,
That wave in the foul faint air of the breath of a
    death-stricken city ;
    So menacing heaves she the manes of her rollers
        knotted with sand,
Discoloured, opaque, suspended in sign as of strength
    without pity,
    That shake with flameless thunder the low long
        length of the strand.
Here, far off in the farther extreme of the shore as it
    lengthens

Northward, lonely for miles, ere ever a village begin,

On the lapsing land that recedes as the growth of the strong sea strengthens

Shoreward, thrusting further and further its outworks in,

Here in Shakespeare's vision, a flower of her kin forsaken,

Lay in her golden raiment alone on the wild wave's edge,

Surely by no shore else, but here on the bank storm-shaken,

Perdita, bright as a dew-drop engilt of the sun on the sedge.

Here on a shore unbeheld of his eyes in a dream he beheld her

Outcast, fair as a fairy, the child of a far-off king :

And over the babe-flower gently the head of a pastoral elder

Bowed, compassionate, hoar as the hawthorn-blossom in spring,

And kind as harvest in autumn : a shelter of shade on the lonely

Shelterless unknown shore scourged of implacable waves :

Here, where the wind walks royal, alone in his kingdom, and only

Sounds to the sedges a wail as of triumph that conquers and craves.

All these waters and wastes are his empire of old, and awaken

From barren and stagnant slumber at only the sound of his breath :

Yet the hunger is eased not that aches in his heart,
    nor the goal overtaken
  That his wide wings yearn for and labour as hearts
    that yearn after death.
All the solitude sighs and expects with a blind ex-
    pectation
  Somewhat unknown of its own sad heart, grown
    heartsick of strife :
Till sometime its wild heart maddens, and moans,
    and the vast ululation
  Takes wing with the clouds on the waters, and
    wails to be quit of its life.
For the spirit and soul of the waste is the wind, and
    his wings with their waving
  Darken and lighten the darkness and light of it
    thickened or thinned ;
But the heart that impels them is even as a conqueror's
    insatiably craving
  That victory can fill not, as power cannot satiate
    the want of the wind.
All these moorlands and marshes are full of his might,
    and oppose not
  Aught of defence nor of barrier, of forest or preci-
    pice piled :
But the will of the wind works ever as his that desires
    what he knows not,
  And the wail of his want unfulfilled is as one
    making moan for her child.
And the cry of his triumph is even as the crying of
    hunger that maddens
  The heart of a strong man aching in vain as the
    wind's heart aches
And the sadness itself of the land for its infinite
    solitude saddens

More for the sound than the silence athirst for the
    sound that slakes.
And the sunset at last and the twilight are dead :
    and the darkness is breathless
    With fear of the wind's breath rising that seems
      and seems not to sleep :
But a sense of the sound of it alway, a spirit un-
    sleeping and deathless,
    Ghost or God, evermore moves on the face of the
      deep.

THE EMPEROR'S PROGRESS

A STUDY IN THREE STAGES

(On the Busts of Nero in the Uffizj.)

I

A CHILD of brighter than the morning's birth
　　And lovelier than all smiles that may be smiled
　　Save only of little children undefiled,
Sweet, perfect, witless of their own dear worth,
Live rose of love, mute melody of mirth,
　　Glad as a bird is when the woods are mild,
　　Adorable as is nothing save a child,
Hails with wide eyes and lips his life on earth,
His lovely life with all its heaven to be.
　　And whoso reads the name inscribed or hears
　　Feels his own heart a frozen well of tears,
Child, for deep dread and fearful pity of thee
Whom God would not let rather die than see
　　The incumbent horror of impending years.

II

Man, that wast godlike being a child, and now,
　　No less than kinglike, art no more in sooth
　　For all thy grace and lordliness of youth,
The crown that bids men's branded foreheads bow

Much more has branded and bowed down thy brow
  And gnawn upon it as with fire or tooth
  Of steel or snake so sorely, that the truth
Seems here to bear false witness.   Is it thou,
Child? and is all the summer of all thy spring
  This? are the smiles that drew men's kisses down
  All faded and transfigured to the frown
That grieves thy face?   Art thou this weary thing?
  Then is no slave's load heavier than a crown
And such a thrall no bondman as a king.

III

Misery, beyond all men's most miserable,
  Absolute, whole, defiant of defence,
  Inevitable, inexplacable, intense,
More vast than heaven is high, more deep than hell,
Past cure or charm of solace or of spell,
  Possesses and pervades the spirit and sense
  Whereto the expanse of the earth pays tribute;
    whence
Breeds evil only, and broods on fumes that swell
Rank from the blood of brother and mother and
    wife.
  "Misery of miseries, all is misery," saith
The heavy fair-faced hateful head, at strife
  With its own lusts that burn with feverous breath
Lips which the loathsome bitterness of life
  Leaves fearful of the bitterness of death.

THE RESURRECTION OF ALCILIA

(Gratefully inscribed to Dr. A. B. Grosart.)

SWEET song-flower of the Mayspring of our song,
  Be welcome to us, with loving thanks and praise
  To his good hand who travelling on strange ways
Found thee forlorn and fragrant, lain along
Beneath dead leaves that many a winter's wrong
    Had rained and heaped through nigh three centuries'
    maze
  Above thy Maybloom, hiding from our gaze
The life that in thy leaves lay sweet and strong.
For thine have life, while many above thine head
Piled by the wind lie blossomless and dead.
  So now disburdened of such load above
That lay as death's own dust upon thee shed
  By days too deaf to hear thee like a dove
    Murmuring, we hear thee. bird and flower of love.

THE FOURTEENTH OF JULY

(On the refusal by the French Senate of the plenary amnesty de-
manded by Victor Hugo, in his speech of July 3rd, for the
surviving exiles of the Commune.)

THOU shouldst have risen as never dawn yet rose,
   Day of the sunrise of the soul of France,
   Dawn of the whole world's morning, when the
      trance
Of all the world had end, and all its woes
Respite, prophetic of their perfect close.
   Light of all tribes of men, all names and clans,
   Dawn of the whole world's morning and of man's,
Flower of the heart of morning's mystic rose,
Dawn of the very dawn of very day,
   When the sun brighter breaks night's ruinous
      prison,
   Thou shouldst have risen as yet no dawn has risen,
Evoked of him whose word puts night away,
   Our father, at the music of whose word
   Exile had ended, and the world had heard.

   July 5, 1880.

THE LAUNCH OF THE LIVADIA

Malâ soluta navis exit alite.

                    HOR.

Rigged with curses dark.

                    MILTON.

THE LAUNCH OF THE LIVADIA

I

GOLD, and fair marbles, and again more gold,
 And space of halls afloat that glance and gleam
 Like the green heights of sunset heaven, or seem
The golden steeps of sunrise red and cold
On deserts where dark exile keeps the fold
 Fast of the flocks of torment, where no beam
 Falls of kind light or comfort save in dream,
These we far off behold not, who behold
The cordage woven of curses, and the decks
 With mortal hate and mortal peril paven ;
 From stem to stern the lines of doom engraven
That mark for sure inevitable wrecks
Those sails predestinate, though no storm vex,
 To miss on earth and find in hell their haven.

II

All curses be about her, and all ill
 Go with her ; heaven be dark above her way,
 The gulf beneath her glad and sure of prey,
And, wheresoe'er her prow be pointed, still
The winds of heaven have all one evil will
 Conspirant even as hearts of kings to slay
 With mouths of kings to lie and smile and pray,
And chiefliest his whose wintrier breath makes chill

II.   Q 2

With more than winter's and more poisonous cold
　　The horror of his kingdom toward the north,
　　　The deserts of his kingdom toward the east.
And though death hide not in her direful hold
　　Be all stars adverse toward her that come forth
　　　Nightly, by day all hours till all have ceased:

III

Till all have ceased for ever, and the sum
　　Be summed of all the sumless curses told
　　Out on his head by all dark seasons rolled
Over its cursed and crowned existence, dumb
And blind and stark as though the snows made numb
　　All sense within it, and all conscience cold,
　　That hangs round hearts of less imperial mould
Like a snake feeding till their doomsday come.
O heart fast bound of frozen poison, be
All nature's as all true men's hearts to thee,
　　A two-edged sword of judgment; hope be far
And fear at hand for pilot oversea
　　With death for compass and despair for star,
　　And the white foam a shroud for the White Czar.

September 30, 1880.

SIX YEARS OLD

To H. W. M.

Between the springs of six and seven,
  Two fresh years' fountains, clear
Of all but golden sand for leaven,
  Child, midway passing here,
As earth for love's sake dares bless heaven,
  So dare I bless you, dear.

Between two bright well-heads, that brighten
  With every breath that blows
Too loud to lull, too low to frighten,
  But fain to rock, the rose,
Your feet stand fast, your lit smiles lighten,
  That might rear flowers from snows.

You came when winds unleashed were snarling
  Behind the frost-bound hours,
A snow-bird sturdier than the starling,
  A storm-bird fledged for showers,
That spring might smile to find you, darling,
  First born of all the flowers.

Could love make worthy things of worthless,
    My song were worth an ear :
Its note should make the days most mirthless
    The merriest of the year,
And wake to birth all buds yet birthless
    To keep your birthday, dear.

But where your birthday brightens heaven
    No need has earth, God knows,
Of light or warmth to melt or leaven
    The frost or fog that glows
With sevenfold heavenly lights of seven
    Sweet springs that cleave the snows.

Could love make worthy music of you,
    And match my Master's powers,
Had even my love less heart to love you,
    A better song were ours ;
With all the rhymes like stars above you,
    And all the words like flowers.

September 30, 1880.

A PARTING SONG

(To a friend leaving England for a year's residence in Australia.)

THESE winds and suns of spring
That warm with breath and wing
The trembling sleep of earth, till half awake
She laughs and blushes ere her slumber break,
For all good gifts they bring
Require one better thing,
For all the loans of joy they lend us, borrow
One sharper dole of sorrow,
To sunder soon by half a world of sea
Her son from England and my friend from me.

Nor hope nor love nor fear
May speed or stay one year,
Nor song nor prayer may bid, as mine would fain,
The seasons perish and be born again,
Restoring all we lend,
Reluctant, of a friend,
The voice, the hand, the presence and the sight
That lend their life and light
To present gladness and heart-strengthening cheer,
Now lent again for one reluctant year.

So much we lend indeed,
Perforce, by force of need,
So much we must ; even these things and no more
The far sea sundering and the sundered shore,
A world apart from ours,
So much the imperious hours,
Exact, and spare not ; but no more than these
All earth and all her seas
From thought and faith of trust and truth can
borrow,
Not memory from desire, nor hope from sorrow.

Through bright and dark and bright
Returns of day and night
I bid the swift year speed and change and give
His breath of life to make the next year live
With sunnier suns for us
A life more prosperous,
And laugh with flowers more fragrant, that shall see
A merrier March for me,
A rosier-girdled race of night with day,
A goodlier April and a tenderer May.

For him the inverted year
Shall mark our seasons here
With alien alternation, and revive
This withered winter, slaying the spring alive
With darts more sharply drawn
As nearer draws the dawn
In heaven transfigured over earth transformed
And with our winters warmed
And wasted with our summers, till the beams
Rise on his face that rose on Dante's dreams.

Till fourfold morning rise
Of starshine on his eyes,
Dawn of the spheres that brand steep heaven across
At height of night with semblance of a cross
Whose grace and ghostly glory
Poured heaven on purgatory,
Seeing with their flamelets risen all heaven grow
glad
For love thereof it had
And lovely joy of loving ; so may these
Make bright with welcome now their southern seas.

O happy stars, whose mirth
The saddest soul on earth
That ever soared and sang found strong to bless,
Lightening his life's harsh load of heaviness
With comfort sown like seed
In dream though not in deed
On sprinkled wastes of darkling thought divine,
Let all your lights now shine
With all as glorious gladness on his eyes
For whom indeed and not in dream they rise.

As those great twins of air
Hailed once with oldworld prayer
Of all folk alway faring forth by sea,
So now may these for grace and guidance be,
To guard his sail and bring
Again to brighten spring
The face we look for and the hand we lack
Still, till they light him back,
As welcome as to first discovering eyes
Their light rose ever, soon on his to rise.

As parting now he goes
From snow-time back to snows,
So back to spring from summer may next year
Restore him, and our hearts receive him here
The best good gift that spring
Had ever grace to bring
At fortune's happiest hour of star-blest birth
Back to love's homebright earth,
To eyes with eyes that commune, hand with hand
And the old warm bosom of all our mother-land.

Earth and sea-wind and sea
And stars and sunlight be
Alike all prosperous for him, and all hours
Have all one heart, and all that heart as ours.
All things as good as strange
Crown all the seasons' change
With changing flower and compensating fruit
From one year's ripening root;
Till next year bring us, roused at spring's recall,
A heartier flower and goodlier fruit than all.

March 26, 1880.

BY THE NORTH SEA

TO WALTER THEODORE WATTS

"We are what suns and winds and waters make us."—LANDOR.

SEA, wind, and sun, with light and sound and breath
    The spirit of man fulfilling—these create
    That joy wherewith man's life grown passionate
Gains heart to hear and sense to read and faith
To know the secret word our Mother saith
    In silence, and to see, though doubt wax great,
    Death as the shadow cast by life on fate,
Passing, whose shade we call the shadow of death.

Brother, to whom our Mother as to me
    Is dearer than all dreams of days undone,
This song I give you of the sovereign three
    That are as life and sleep and death are, one :
A song the sea-wind gave me from the sea,
    Where nought of man's endures before the sun.

BY THE NORTH SEA

I

1

A LAND that is lonelier than ruin ;
  A sea that is stranger than death :
Far fields that a rose never blew in,
  Wan waste where the winds lack breath ;
Waste endless and boundless and flowerless
  But of marsh-blossoms fruitless as free :
Where earth lies exhausted, as powerless
      To strive with the sea.

2

Far flickers the flight of the swallows,
  Far flutters the weft of the grass
Spun dense over desolate hollows
  More pale than the clouds as they pass :
Thick woven as the weft of a witch is
  Round the heart of a thrall that hath sinned,
Whose youth and the wrecks of its riches
      Are waifs on the wind.

3

The pastures are herdless and sheepless,
　　No pasture or shelter for herds :
The wind is relentless and sleepless,
　　And restless and songless the birds ;
Their cries from afar fall breathless,
　　Their wings are as lightnings that flee ;
For the land has two lords that are deathless :
　　　　Death's self, and the sea.

4

These twain, as a king with his fellow,
　　Hold converse of desolate speech :
And her waters are haggard and yellow
　　And crass with the scurf of the beach :
And his garments are grey as the hoary
　　Wan sky where the day lies dim ;
And his power is to her, and his glory,
　　　　As hers unto him.

5

In the pride of his power she rejoices,
　　In her glory he glows and is glad :
In her darkness the sound of his voice is,
　　With his breath she dilates and is mad :
" If thou slay me, O death, and outlive me,
　　Yet thy love hath fulfilled me of thee."
" Shall I give thee not back if thou give me,
　　　　O sister, O sea ? "

6

And year upon year dawns living,
   And age upon age drops dead :
And his hand is not weary of giving,
   And the thirst of her heart is not fed :
And the hunger that moans in her passion,
   And the rage in her hunger that roars,
As a wolf's that the winter lays lash on,
      Still calls and implores.

7

Her walls have no granite for girder,
   No fortalice fronting her stands :
But reefs the bloodguiltiest of murder
   Are less than the banks of her sands :
These number their slain by the thousand ;
   For the ship hath no surety to be,
When the bank is abreast of her bows and
      Aflush with the sea.

8

No surety to stand, and no shelter
   To dawn out of darkness but one,
Out of waters that hurtle and welter
   No succour to dawn with the sun,
But a rest from the wind as it passes,
   Where, hardly redeemed from the waves,
Lie thick as the blades of the grasses
      The dead in their graves.

9

A multitude noteless of numbers,
   As wild weeds cast on an heap :
And sounder than sleep are their slumbers,
   And softer than song is their sleep ;
And sweeter than all things and stranger
   The sense, if perchance it may be,
That the wind is divested of danger
      And scatheless the sea.

10

That the roar of the banks they breasted
   Is hurtless as bellowing of herds,
And the strength of his wings that invested
   The wind, as the strength of a bird's ;
As the sea-mew's might or the swallow's
   That cry to him back if he cries,
As over the graves and their hollows
      Days darken and rise.

11

As the souls of the dead men disburdened
   And clean of the sins that they sinned,
With a lovelier than man's life guerdoned
   And delight as a wave's in the wind,
And delight as the wind's in the billow,
   Birds pass, and deride with their glee
The flesh that has dust for its pillow
      As wrecks have the sea.

12

When the ways of the sun wax dimmer,
  Wings flash through the dusk like beams ;
As the clouds in the lit sky glimmer,
  The bird in the graveyard gleams ;
As the cloud at its wing's edge whitens
  When the clarions of sunrise are heard,
The graves that the bird's note brightens
  Grow bright for the bird.

13

As the waves of the numberless waters
  That the wind cannot number who guides
Are the sons of the shore and the daughters
  Here lulled by the chime of the tides :
And here in the press of them standing
  We know not if these or if we
Live truliest, or anchored to landing
  Or drifted to sea.

14

In the valley he named of decision
  No denser were multitudes met
When the soul of the seer in her vision
  Saw nations for doom of them set ;
Saw darkness in dawn, and the splendour
  Of judgment, the sword and the rod ;
But the doom here of death is more tender
  And gentler the god.

15

And gentler the wind from the dreary
    Sea-banks by the waves overlapped,
Being weary, speaks peace to the weary
    From slopes that the tide-stream hath **sapped ;**
And sweeter than all that we call so
    The seal of their slumber shall be
Till the graves that embosom them also
      Be sapped of the sea.

II

1

For the heart of the waters is cruel,
    And the kisses are dire of their lips,
And their waves are as fire is to fuel
    To the strength of the sea-faring ships,
Though the sea's eye gleam as a jewel
    To the sun's eye back as he dips.

2

Though the sun's eye flash to the sea's
    Live light of delight and of laughter,
And her lips breathe back to the breeze
    The kiss that the wind's lips waft her
From the sun that subsides, and sees
    No gleam of the storm's dawn after.

3

And the wastes of the wild sea-marches
    Where the borderers are matched in their might—
Bleak fens that the sun's weight parches,
    Dense waves that reject his light—
Change under the change-coloured arches
    Of changeless morning and night.

4

The waves are as ranks enrolled
    Too close for the storm to sever :
The fens lie naked and cold,
    But their heart fails utterly never :
The lists are set from of old,
    And the warfare endureth for ever.

III

1

Miles, and miles, and miles of desolation!
   Leagues on leagues on leagues without a change!
Sign or token of some eldest nation
   Here would make the strange land not so strange.
Time-forgotten, yea since time's creation,
   Seem these borders where the sea-birds range.

2

Slowly, gladly, full of peace and wonder
   Grows his heart who journeys here alone.
Earth and all its thoughts of earth sink under
   Deep as deep in water sinks a stone.
Hardly knows it if the rollers thunder,
   Hardly whence the lonely wind is blown.

3

Tall the plumage of the rush-flower tosses,
   Sharp and soft in many a curve and line
Gleam and glow the sea-coloured marsh-mosses
   Salt and splendid from the circling brine.
Streak on streak of glimmering seashine crosses
   All the land sea-saturate as with wine.

4

Far, and far between, in divers orders,
    Clear grey steeples cleave the low grey sky;
Fast and firm as time-unshaken warders,
    Hearts made sure by faith, by hope made high.
These alone in all the wild sea-borders
    Fear no blast of days and nights that die.

5

All the land is like as one man's face is,
    Pale and troubled still with change of cares.
Doubt and death pervade her clouded spaces:
    Strength and length of life and peace are theirs;
Theirs alone amid these weary places,
    Seeing not how the wild world frets and fares.

6

Firm and fast where all is cloud that changes
    Cloud-clogged sunlight, cloud by sunlight thinned,
Stern and sweet, above the sand-hill ranges
    Watch the towers and tombs of men that sinned
Once, now calm as earth whose only change is
    Wind, and light, and wind, and cloud, and wind.

7

Out and in and out the sharp straits wander,
    In and out and in the wild way strives,
Starred and paved and lined with flowers that
        squander
    Gold as golden as the gold of hives,
Salt and moist and multiform: but yonder
    See, what sign of life or death survives?

8

Seen then only when the songs of olden
    Harps were young whose echoes yet endure,
Hymned of Homer when his years were golden,
    Known of only when the world was pure,
Here is Hades, manifest, beholden,
    Surely, surely here, if aught be sure !

9

Where the border-line was crossed, that, sundering
    Death from life, keeps weariness from rest,
None can tell, who fares here forward wondering ;
    None may doubt but here might end his quest.
Here life's lightning joys and woes once thundering
    Sea-like round him cease like storm suppressed.

10

Here the wise wave-wandering steadfast-hearted
    Guest of many a lord of many a land
Saw the shape or shade of years departed,
    Saw the semblance risen and hard at hand,
Saw the mother long from love's reach parted,
    Anticleia, like a statue stand.

11

Statue ? nay, nor tissued image woven
    Fair on hangings in his father's hall ;
Nay, too fast her faith of heart was proven,
    Far too firm her loveliest love of all ;
Love wherethrough the loving heart was cloven,
    Love that hears not when the loud Fates call.

12

Love that lives and stands up re-created
    Then when life has ebbed and anguish fled ;
Love more strong than death or all things fated,
    Child's and mother's, lit by love and led ;
Love that found what life so long awaited
    Here, when life came down among the dead.

13

Here, where never came alive another,
    Came her son across the sundering tide
Crossed before by many a warrior brother
    Once that warred on Ilion at his side ;
Here spread forth vain hands to clasp the mother
    Dead, that sorrowing for his love's sake died.

14

Parted, though by narrowest of divisions,
    Clasp he might not, only might implore,
Sundered yet by bitterest of derisions,
    Son, and mother from the son she bore—
Here ?   But all dispeopled here of visions
    Lies, forlorn of shadows even, the shore.

15

All too sweet such men's Hellenic speech is,
    All too fain they lived of light to see,
Once to see the darkness of these beaches,
    Once to sing this Hades found of me
Ghostless, all its gulfs and creeks and reaches,
    Sky, and shore, and cloud, and waste, and sea.

IV

1

But aloft and afront of me faring
   Far forward as folk in a dream
That strive, between doubting and daring,
   Right on till the goal for them gleam,
Full forth till their goal on them lighten,
   The harbour where fain they would be,
What headlands there darken and brighten?
     What change in the sea?

2

What houses and woodlands that nestle
   Safe inland to lee of the hill
As it slopes from the headlands that wrestle
   And succumb to the strong sea's will?
Truce is not, nor respite, nor pity,
   For the battle is waged not of hands
Where over the grave of a city
     The ghost of it stands.

3

Where the wings of the sea-wind slacken,
   Green lawns to the landward thrive,
Fields brighten and pine-woods blacken,
   And the heat in their heart is alive;

They blossom and warble and murmur,
    For the sense of their spirit is free :
But harder to shoreward and firmer
    The grasp of the sea.

4

Like ashes the low cliffs crumble,
    The banks drop down into dust,
The heights of the hills are made humble,
    As a reed's is the strength of their trust :
As a city's that armies environ,
    The strength of their stay is of sand :
But the grasp of the sea is as iron,
    Laid hard on the land.

5

A land that is thirstier than ruin ;
    A sea that is hungrier than death ;
Heaped hills that a tree never grew in ;
    Wide sands where the wave draws breath ;
All solace is here for the spirit
    That ever for ever may be
For the soul of thy son to inherit,
    My mother, my sea.

6

O delight of the headlands and beaches !
    O desire of the wind on the wold,
More glad than a man's when it reaches
    That end which it sought from of old

And the palm of possession is dreary
  To the sense that in search of it sinned ;
But nor satisfied ever nor weary
  Is ever the wind.

7

The delight that he takes but in living
  Is more than of all things that live :
For the world that has all things for giving
  Has nothing so goodly to give :
But more than delight his desire is,
  For the goal where his pinions would be
Is immortal as air or as fire is,
  Immense as the sea.

8

Though hence come the moan that he borrows
  From darkness and depth of the night,
Though hence be the spring of his sorrows,
  Hence too is the joy of his might ;
The delight that his doom is for ever
  To seek and desire and rejoice,
And the sense that eternity never
  Shall silence his voice.

9

That satiety never may stifle
  Nor weariness ever estrange
Nor time be so strong as to rifle
  Nor change be so great as to change

His gift that renews in the giving,
 The joy that exalts him to be
Alone of all elements living
  The lord of the sea.

10

What is fire, that its flame should consume her?
 More fierce than all fires are her waves :
What is earth, that its gulfs should entomb her?
 More deep are her own than their graves.
Life shrinks from his pinions that cover
 The darkness by thunders bedinned :
But she knows him, her lord and her lover
  The godhead of wind.

11

For a season his wings are about her,
 His breath on her lips for a space ;
Such rapture he wins not without her
 In the width of his worldwide race.
Though the forests bow down, and the mountains
 Wax dark, and the tribes of them flee,
His delight is more deep in the fountains
  And springs of the sea.

12

There are those too of mortals that love him,
 There are souls that desire and require,
Be the glories of midnight above him
 Or beneath him the daysprings of fire :
And their hearts are as harps that approve him
 And praise him as chords of a lyre

That were fain with their music to move him
        To meet their desire

13

To descend through the darkness to grace them,
    Till darkness were lovelier than light :
To encompass and grasp and embrace them,
    Till their weakness were one with his might :
With the strength of his wings to caress them,
    With the blast of his breath to set free ;
With the mouths of his thunders to bless them
        For sons of the sea.

14

For these have the toil and the guerdon
    That the wind has eternally : these
Have part in the boon and the burden
    Of the sleepless unsatisfied breeze,
That finds not, but seeking rejoices
    That possession can work him no wrong :
And the voice at the heart of their voice is
        The sense of his song.

15

For the wind's is their doom and their blessing ;
    To desire, and have always above
A possession beyond their possessing,
    A love beyond reach of their love.
Green earth has her sons and her daughters,
    And these have their guerdons ; but we
Are the wind's and the sun's and the water's,
        Elect of the sea.

V

1

For the sea too seeks and rejoices,
　　Gains and loses and gains,
And the joy of her heart's own choice is
　　As ours, and as ours are her pains :
As the thoughts of our hearts are her voices,
　　And as hers is the pulse of our veins.

2

Her fields that know not of dearth
　　Nor lie for their fruit's sake fallow
Laugh large in the depth of their mirth :
　　But inshore here in the shallow,
Embroiled with encumbrance of earth,
　　Their skirts are turbid and yellow.

3

The grime of her greed is upon her,
　　The sign of her deed is her soil ;
As the earth's is her own dishonour,
　　And corruption the crown of her toil :
She hath spoiled and devoured, and her honour
　　Is this, to be shamed by her spoil.

4

But afar where pollution is none,
  Nor ensign of strife nor endeavour,
Where her heart and the sun's are one,
  And the soil of her sin comes never,
She is pure as the wind and the sun,
  And her sweetness endureth for ever.

VI

1

Death, and change, and darkness everlasting,
    Deaf, that hears not what the daystar saith,
Blind, past all remembrance and forecasting,
    Dead, past memory that it once drew breath;
These, above the washing tides and wasting,
    Reign, and rule this land of utter death.

2

Change of change, darkness of darkness, hidden,
    Very death of very death, begun
When none knows,—the knowledge is forbidden—
    Self-begotten, self-proceeding, one,
Born, not made—abhorred, unchained, unchidden,
    Night stands here defiant of the sun.

3

Change of change, and death of death begotten,
    Darkness born of darkness, one and three,
Ghostly godhead of a world forgotten,
    Crowned with heaven, enthroned on land and sea,
Here, where earth with dead men's bones is rotten,
    God of Time, thy likeness worships thee.

4

Lo, thy likeness of thy desolation,
  Shape and figure of thy might, O Lord,
Formless form, incarnate miscreation,
  Served of all things living and abhorred ;
Earth herself is here thine incarnation,
  Time, of all things born on earth adored.

5

All that worship thee are fearful of thee ;
  No man may not worship thee for fear :
Prayers nor curses prove not nor disprove thee,
  Move nor change thee with our change of cheer :
All at last, though all abhorred thee, love thee,
  God, the sceptre of whose throne is here.

6

Here thy throne and sceptre of thy station,
  Here the palace paven for thy feet ;
Here thy sign from nation unto nation
  Passed as watchword for thy guards to greet,
Guards that go before thine exaltation,
  Ages, clothed with bitter years and sweet.

7

Here, where sharp the sea-bird shrills his ditty,
  Flickering flame-wise through the clear live calm,
Rose triumphal, crowning all a city,
  Roofs exalted once with prayer and psalm,
Built of holy hands for holy pity,
  Frank and fruitful as a sheltering palm.

8

Church and hospice wrought in faultless fashion,
    Hall and chancel bounteous and sublime,
Wide and sweet and glorious as compassion,
    Filled and thrilled with force of choral chime,
Filled with spirit of prayer and thrilled with passion,
    Hailed a God more merciful than Time.

9

Ah, less mighty, less than Time prevailing,
    Shrunk, expelled, made nothing at his nod,
Less than clouds across the sea-line sailing,
    Lies he, stricken by his master's rod.
" Where is man ? " the cloister murmurs wailing ;
    Back the mute shrine thunders—" Where is God ? "

10

Here is all the end of all his glory—
    Dust, and grass, and barren silent stones.
Dead, like him, one hollow tower and hoary
    Naked in the sea-wind stands and moans,
Filled and thrilled with its perpetual story :
    Here, where earth is dense with dead men's bones.

11

Low and loud and long, a voice for ever,
    Sounds the wind's clear story like a song.
Tomb from tomb the waves devouring sever,
    Dust from dust as years relapse along ;
Graves where men made sure to rest, and never
    Lie dismantled by the seasons' wrong.

12

Now displaced, devoured and desecrated,
  Now by Time's hands darkly disinterred,
These poor dead that sleeping here awaited
  Long the archangel's re-creating word,
Closed about with roofs and walls high-gated
  Till the blast of judgment should be heard,

13

Naked, shamed, cast out of consecration,
  Corpse and coffin, yea the very graves,
Scoffed at, scattered, shaken from their station,
  Spurned and scourged of wind and sea like slaves,
Desolate beyond man's desolation,
  Shrink and sink into the waste of waves.

14

Tombs, with bare white piteous bones protruded,
  Shroudless, down the loose collapsing banks,
Crumble, from their constant place detruded,
  That the sea devours and gives not thanks.
Graves where hope and prayer and sorrow brooded
  Gape and slide and perish, ranks on ranks.

15

Rows on rows and line by line they crumble,
  They that thought for all time through to be.
Scarce a stone whereon a child might stumble
  Breaks the grim field paced alone of me.
Earth, and man, and all their gods wax humble
  Here, where Time brings pasture to the sea.

II.   R 2

VII

1

But afar on the headland exalted,
  But beyond in the curl of the bay,
From the depth of his dome deep-vaulted
  Our father is lord of the day.
Our father and lord that we follow,
  For deathless and ageless is he ;
And his robe is the whole sky's hollow,
  His sandal the sea.

2

Where the horn of the headland is sharper,
  And her green floor glitters with fire,
The sea has the sun for a harper,
  The sun has the sea for a lyre.
The waves are a pavement of amber,
  By the feet of the sea-winds trod
To receive in a god's presence-chamber
  Our father, the God.

3

Time, haggard and changeful and hoary,
  Is master and God of the land :
But the air is fulfilled of the glory
  That is shed from our lord's right hand.

O father of all of us ever,
  All glory be only to thee
From heaven, that is void of thee never,
  And earth, and the sea.

4

O Sun, whereof all is beholden,
  Behold now the shadow of this death,
This place of the sepulchres, olden
  And emptied and vain as a breath.
The bloom of the bountiful heather
  Laughs broadly beyond in thy light
As dawn, with her glories to gather,
  At darkness and night.

5

Though the Gods of the night lie rotten
  And their honour be taken away
And the noise of their names forgotten,
  Thou, Lord, art God of the day.
Thou art father and saviour and spirit,
  O Sun, of the soul that is free
And hath grace of thy grace to inherit
  Thine earth and thy sea.

6

The hills and the sands and the beaches,
  The waters adrift and afar,
The banks and the creeks and the reaches,
  How glad of thee all these are !

The flowers, overflowing, overcrowded,
　　Are drunk with the mad wind's mirth :
The delight of thy coming unclouded
　　Makes music of earth.

7

I, last least voice of her voices,
　　Give thanks that were mute in me long
To the soul in my soul that rejoices
　　For the song that is over my song.
Time gives what he gains for the giving
　　Or takes for his tribute of me ;
My dreams to the wind everliving,
　　My song to the sea.

A CENTURY OF ROUNDELS

DEDICATION

TO

CHRISTINA G. ROSSETTI

SONGS light as these may sound, though deep and strong
The heart spake through them, scarce should hope to please
Ears tuned to strains of loftier thoughts than throng
      Songs light as these.

Yet grace may set their sometime doubt at ease,
Nor need their too rash reverence fear to wrong
The shrine it serves at and the hope it sees.

For childlike loves and laughters thence prolong
Notes that bid enter, fearless as the breeze,
Even to the shrine of holiest-hearted song,
      Songs light as these.

IN HARBOUR

I

GOODNIGHT and goodbye to the life whose signs
    denote us
As mourners clothed with regret for the life gone by ;
To the waters of gloom whence winds of the day-
    spring float us
        Goodnight and goodbye.

A time is for mourning, a season for grief to sigh ;
But were we not fools and blind, by day to devote us
As thralls to the darkness, unseen of the sundawn's
    eye ?

We have drunken of Lethe at length, we have eaten
    of lotus ;
What hurts it us here that sorrows are born and die ?
We have said to the dream that caressed and the
    dread that smote us
        Goodnight and goodbye.

II

Outside of the port ye are moored in, lying
Close from the wind and at ease from the tide,
What sounds come swelling, what notes fall dying
    Outside ?

They will not cease, they will not abide :
Voices of presage in darkness crying
Pass and return and relapse aside.

Ye see not, but hear ye not wild wings flying
To the future that wakes from the past that died ?
Is grief still sleeping, is joy not sighing
    Outside ?

THE WAY OF THE WIND

The wind's way in the deep sky's hollow
None may measure, as none can say
How the heart in her shows the swallow
    The wind's way.

Hope nor fear can avail to stay
Waves that whiten on wrecks that wallow,
Times and seasons that wane and slay.

Life and love, till the strong night swallow
Thought and hope and the red last ray,
Swim the waters of years that follow
    The wind's way.

" HAD I WIST "

HAD I wist, when life was like a warm wind playing
Light and loud through sundawn and the dew's
   bright mist,
How the time should come for hearts to sigh in
   saying
      " Had I wist "—

Surely not the roses, laughing as they kissed,
Not the lovelier laugh of seas in sunshine swaying,
Should have lured my soul to look thereon and list.

Now the wind is like a soul cast out and praying
Vainly, prayers that pierce not ears when hearts
   resist :
Now mine own soul sighs, adrift as wind and
   straying,
      " Had I wist."

RECOLLECTIONS

Years upon years, as a course of clouds that thicken,
Thronging the ways of the wind that shifts and
    veers,
Pass, and the flames of remembered fires requicken
        Years upon years.

Surely the thought in a man's heart hopes or fears
Now that forgetfulness needs must here have stricken
Anguish, and sweetened the sealed-up springs of
    tears.

Ah, but the strength of regrets that strain and sicken,
Yearning for love that the veil of death endears,
Slackens not wing for the wings of years that
    quicken—
        Years upon years.

II

Years upon years, and the flame of love's high altar
Trembles and sinks, and the sense of listening ears
Heeds not the sound that it heard of love's blithe
    psalter
        Years upon years.

Only the sense of a heart that hearkens hears,
Louder than dreams that assail and doubts that
　　　palter,
Sorrow that slept and that wakes ere sundawn peers.

Wakes, that the heart may behold, and yet not falter,
Faces of children as stars unknown of, spheres
Seen but of love, that endures though all things alter,
　　　Years upon years.

III

Years upon years, as a watch by night that passes,
Pass, and the light of their eyes is fire that sears
Slowly the hopes of the fruit that life amasses
　　　Years upon years.

Pale as the glimmer of stars on moorland meres
Lighten the shadows reverberate from the glasses
Held in their hands as they pass among their peers.

Lights that are shadows, as ghosts on graveyard
　　　grasses,
Moving on paths that the moon of memory cheers,
Show but as mists over cloudy mountain passes
　　　Years upon years.

TIME AND LIFE

I

Time, thy name is sorrow, says the stricken
Heart of life, laid waste with wasting flame
Ere the change of things and thoughts requicken,
    Time, thy name.

Girt about with shadow, blind and lame,
Ghosts of things that smite and thoughts that sicken
Hunt and hound thee down to death and shame.

Eyes of hours whose paces halt or quicken
Read in bloodred lines of loss and blame,
Writ where cloud and darkness round it thicken,
    Time, thy name.

II

Nay, but rest is born of me for healing,
—So might haply time, with voice represt,
Speak : is grief the last gift of my dealing?
    Nay, but rest.

All the world is wearied, east and west,
Tired with toil to watch the slow sun wheeling,
Twelve loud hours of life's laborious quest.

Eyes forspent with vigil, faint and reeling,
Find at last my comfort, and are blest,
Not with rapturous light of life's revealing—
　　　Nay, but rest.

A DIALOGUE

I

DEATH, if thou wilt, fain would I plead with thee :
Canst thou not spare, of all our hopes have built,
One shelter where our spirits fain would be,
    Death, if thou wilt ?

No dome with suns and dews impearled and gilt,
Imperial : but some roof of wildwood tree,
Too mean for sceptre's heft or swordblade's hilt.

Some low sweet roof where love might live, set free
From change and fear and dreams of grief or guilt ;
Canst thou not leave life even thus much to see,
    Death, if thou wilt ?

II

Man, what art thou to speak and plead with me ?
What knowest thou of my workings, where and how
What things I fashion ?   Nay, behold and see,
    Man, what art thou ?

Thy fruits of life, and blossoms of thy bough,
What are they but my seedlings ?   Earth and sea
Bear nought but when I breathe on it must bow.

Bow thou too down before me : though thou be
Great, all the pride shall fade from off thy brow,
When Time and strong Oblivion ask of thee.
    Man, what art thou ?

III

Death, if thou be or be not, as was said,
Immortal ; if thou make us nought, or we
Survive : thy power is made but of our dread,
    Death, if thou be.

Thy might is made out of our fear of thee :
Who fears thee not, hath plucked from off thine head
The crown of cloud that darkens earth and sea.

Earth, sea, and sky, as rain or vapour shed,
Shall vanish ; all the shows of them shall flee :
Then shall we know full surely, quick or dead,
    Death, if thou be.

PLUS ULTRA

Far beyond the sunrise and the sunset rises
Heaven, with worlds on worlds that lighten and
    respond :
Thought can see not thence the goal of hope's sur-
    mises
       Far beyond.

Night and day have made an everlasting bond
Each with each to hide in yet more deep disguises
Truth, till souls of men that thirst for truth despond.

All that man in pride of spirit slights or prizes,
All the dreams that make him fearful, fain, or fond,
Fade at forethought's touch of life's unknown
    surprises
       Far beyond.

A DEAD FRIEND

I

Gone, O gentle heart and true,
  Friend of hopes foregone,
Hopes and hopeful days with you
  Gone?

  Days of old that shone
Saw what none shall see anew,
  When we gazed thereon.

Soul as clear as sunlit dew,
  Why so soon pass on,
Forth from all we loved and knew
  Gone?

II

Friend of many a season fled,
  What may sorrow send
Toward thee now from lips that said
  "Friend"?

  Sighs and songs to blend
Praise with pain uncomforted
  Though the praise ascend?

Darkness hides no dearer head :
  Why should darkness end
Day so soon, O dear and dead
  Friend?

III

Dear in death, thou hast thy part
  Yet in life, to cheer
Hearts that held thy gentle heart
  Dear.

Time and chance may sear
Hope with grief, and death may part
  Hand from hand's clasp here :

Memory, blind with tears that start,
  Sees through every tear
All that made thee, as thou art,
  Dear.

IV

True and tender, single-souled,
  What should memory do
Weeping o'er the trust we hold
  True ?

Known and loved of few,
But of these, though small their fold,
  Loved how well were you !

Change, that makes of new things old,
  Leaves one old thing new ;
Love which promised truth, and told
  True.

V

Kind as heaven, while earth's control
  Still had leave to bind
Thee, thy heart was toward man's whole
  Kind.

  Thee no shadows blind
Now : the change of hours that roll
  Leaves thy sleep behind.

Love, that hears thy death-bell toll
  Yet, may call to mind
Scarce a soul as thy sweet soul
  Kind.

VI

How should life, O friend, forget
  Death, whose guest art thou ?
Faith responds to love's regret,
  How ?

  Still, for us that bow
Sorrowing, still, though life be set,
  Shines thy bright mild brow.

Yea, though death and thou be met,
  Love may find thee now
Still, albeit we know not yet
  How.

VII

Past as music fades, that shone
    While its life might last ;
As a song-bird's shadow flown
    Past !

Death's reverberate blast
Now for music's lord has blown
    Whom thy love held fast.

Dead thy king, and void his throne ·
    Yet for grief at last
Love makes music of his own
    Past.

PAST DAYS

I

Dead and gone, the days we had together,
Shadow-stricken all the lights that shone
Round them, flown as flies the blown foam's feather,
       Dead and gone.

Where we went, we twain, in time foregone,
Forth by land and sea, and cared not whether,
If I go again, I go alone.

Bound am I with time as with a tether ;
Thee perchance death leads enfranchised on,
Far from deathlike life and changeful weather,
       Dead and gone.

II

Above the sea and sea-washed town we dwelt,
We twain together, two brief summers, free
From heed of hours as light as clouds that melt
       Above the sea.

Free from all heed of aught at all were we,
Save chance of change that clouds or sunbeams dealt
And gleam of heaven to windward or to lee.

The Norman downs with bright grey waves for belt
Were more for us than inland ways might be ;
A clearer sense of nearer heaven was felt
    Above the sea.

III

Cliffs and downs and headlands which the forward-
    hasting
Flight of dawn and eve empurples and embrowns,
Wings of wild sea-winds and stormy seasons wasting
    Cliffs and downs,

These, or ever man was, were : the same sky frowns,
Laughs, and lightens, as before his soul, forecasting
Times to be, conceived such hopes as time discrowns.

These we loved of old : but now for me the blasting
Breath of death makes dull the bright small seaward
    towns,
Clothes with human change these all but everlasting
    Cliffs and downs.

AUTUMN AND WINTER

I

THREE months bade wane and wax the wintering
    moon
Between two dates of death, while men were fain
Yet of the living light that all too soon
      Three months bade wane.

Cold autumn, wan with wrath of wind and rain,
Saw pass a soul sweet as the sovereign tune
That death smote silent when he smote again.

First went my friend, in life's mid light of noon,
Who loved the lord of music : then the strain
Whence earth was kindled like as heaven in June
      Three months bade wane.

II

A herald soul before its master's flying
Touched by some few moons first the darkling goal
Where shades rose up to greet the shade, espying
      A herald soul ;

Shades of dead lords of music, who control
Men living by the might of men undying,
With strength of strains that make delight of dole.

The deep dense dust on death's dim threshold lying
Trembled with sense of kindling sound that stole
Through darkness, and the night gave ear, descrying
    A herald soul.

III

One went before, one after, but so fast
They seem gone hence together, from the shore
Whence we now gaze : yet ere the mightier passed
    One went before ;

One whose whole heart of love, being set of yore
On that high joy which music lends us, cast
Light round him forth of music's radiant store.

Then went, while earth on winter glared aghast,
The mortal god he worshipped, through the door
Wherethrough so late, his lover to the last,
    One went before.

IV

A star had set an hour before the sun
Sank from the skies wherethrough his heart's pulse
    yet
Thrills audibly : but few took heed, or none,
    A star had set.

All heaven rings back, sonorous with regret,
The deep dirge of the sunset : how should one
Soft star be missed in all the concourse met ?

But, O sweet single heart whose work is done,
Whose songs are silent, how should I forget
That ere the sunset's fiery goal was won
      A star had set ?

THE DEATH OF RICHARD WAGNER

I

MOURNING on earth, as when dark hours descend,
Wide-winged with plagues, from heaven ; when hope
    and mirth
Wane, and no lips rebuke or reprehend
      Mourning on earth.

The soul wherein her songs of death and birth,
Darkness and light, were wont to sound and blend,
Now silent, leaves the whole world less in worth.

Winds that make moan and triumph, skies that bend,
Thunders, and sound of tides in gulf and firth,
Spake through his spirit of speech, whose death
    should send
      Mourning on earth.

II

The world's great heart, whence all things strange
    and rare
Take form and sound, that each inseparate part
May bear its burden in all tuned thoughts that share
      The world's great heart—

The fountain forces, whence like steeds that start
Leap forth the powers of earth and fire and air,
Seas that revolve and rivers that depart—

Spake, and were turned to song : yea, all they were,
With all their works, found in his mastering art
Speech as of powers whose uttered word laid bare
    The world's great heart.

III

From the depths of the sea, from the wellsprings of
    earth, from the wastes of the midmost night,
From the fountains of darkness and tempest and
    thunder, from heights where the soul would be,
The spell of the mage of music evoked their sense,
    as an unknown light
      From the depths of the sea.

As a vision of heaven from the hollows of ocean, that
    none but a god might see,
Rose out of the silence of things unknown of a
    presence, a form, a might,
And we heard as a prophet that hears God's message
    against him, and may not flee.

Eye might not endure it, but ear and heart with
    a rapture of dark delight,
With a terror and wonder whose core was joy, and a
    passion of thought set free,
Felt inly the rising of doom divine as a sundawn risen
    to sight
      From the depths of the sea.

TWO PRELUDES

I

LOHENGRIN

Love, out of the depth of things,
As a dewfall felt from above,
From the heaven whence only springs
    Love,

Love, heard from the heights thereof,
The clouds and the watersprings,
Draws close as the clouds remove.

And the soul in it speaks and sings,
A swan sweet-souled as a dove,
An echo that only rings
    Love.

II

TRISTAN UND ISOLDE

Fate, out of the deep sea's gloom,
When a man's heart's pride grows **great,**
And nought seems now to foredoom
    Fate.

Fate, laden with fears in wait,
Draws close through the clouds that loom,
Till the soul see, all too late,

More dark than a dead world's tomb,
More high than the sheer dawn's gate,
More deep than the wide sea's womb,
    Fate.

THE LUTE AND THE LYRE

Deep desire, that pierces heart and spirit to the root,
Finds reluctant voice in verse that yearns like soaring
    fire,
Takes exultant voice when music holds in high
    pursuit
        Deep desire.

Keen as burns the passion of the rose whose buds
    respire,
Strong as grows the yearning of the blossom toward
    the fruit,
Sounds the secret half unspoken ere the deep tones
    tire.

Slow subsides the rapture that possessed love's
    flower-soft lute,
Slow the palpitation of the triumph of the lyre :
Still the soul feels burn, a flame unslaked though
    these be mute,
        Deep desire.

PLUS INTRA

SOUL within sense, immeasurable, obscure,
Insepulchred and deathless, through the dense
Deep elements may scarce be felt as pure
    Soul within sense.

From depth and height by measurers left immense,
Through sound and shape and colour, comes the unsure
Vague utterance, fitful with supreme suspense.

All that may pass, and all that must endure,
Song speaks not, painting shows not : more intense
And keen than these, art wakes with music's lure
    Soul within sense.

CHANGE

But now life's face beholden
  Seemed bright as heaven's bare brow
With hope of gifts withholden
  But now.

  From time's full-flowering bough
Each bud spake bloom to embolden
  Love's heart, and seal his vow.

Joy's eyes grew deep with olden
  Dreams, born he wist not how;
Thought's meanest garb was golden;
  But now!

A BABY'S DEATH

A LITTLE soul scarce fledged for earth
Takes wing with heaven again for goal
Even while we hailed as fresh from birth
    A little soul.

Our thoughts ring sad as bells that toll,
Not knowing beyond this blind world's girth
What things are writ in heaven's full scroll.

Our fruitfulness is there but dearth,
And all things held in time's control
Seem there, perchance, ill dreams, not worth
    A little soul.

II

The little feet that never trod
Earth, never strayed in field or street,
What hand leads upward back to God
    The little feet?

A rose in June's most honied heat,
When life makes keen the kindling sod,
Was not so soft and warm and sweet.

Their pilgrimage's period
A few swift moons have seen complete
Since mother's hands first clasped and shod
    The little feet.

III

The little hands that never sought
Earth's prizes, worthless all as sands,
What gift has death, God's servant, brought
    The little hands?

We ask: but love's self silent stands,
Love, that lends eyes and wings to thought
To search where death's dim heaven expands.

Ere this, perchance, though love know nought,
Flowers fill them, grown in lovelier lands,
Where hands of guiding angels caught
    The little hands.

IV

The little eyes that never knew
Light other than of dawning skies,
What new life now lights up anew
    The little eyes?

Who knows but on their sleep may rise
Such light as never heaven let through
To lighten earth from Paradise?

No storm, we know, may change the blue
Soft heaven that haply death descries;
No tears, like these in ours, bedew
    The little eyes.

V

Was life so strange, so sad the sky,
    So strait the wide world's range,
He would not stay to wonder why
    Was life so strange?

Was earth's fair house a joyless grange
    Beside that house on high
Whence Time that bore him failed to estrange?

That here at once his soul put by
    All gifts of time and change,
And left us heavier hearts to sigh
    "Was life so strange?"

VI

Angel by name love called him, seeing so fair
    The sweet small frame;
Meet to be called, if ever man's child were,
    Angel by name.

Rose-bright and warm from heaven's own heart he
            came,
    And might not bear
The cloud that covers earth's wan face with shame.

His little light of life was all too rare
    And soft a flame:
Heaven yearned for him till angels hailed him there
    Angel by name.

VII

The song that smiled upon his birthday here
Weeps on the grave that holds him undefiled
Whose loss makes bitterer than a soundless tear
    The song that smiled.

His name crowned once the mightiest ever styled
Sovereign of arts, and angel : fate and fear
Knew then their master, and were reconciled.

But we saw born beneath some tenderer sphere
Michael, an angel and a little child,
Whose loss bows down to weep upon his bier
    The song that smiled.

ONE OF TWAIN

I

One of twain, twin-born with flowers that waken,
Now hath passed from sense of sun and rain :
Wind from off the flower-crowned branch hath shaken
    One of twain.

One twin flower must pass, and one remain :
One, the word said soothly, shall be taken,
And another left : can death refrain ?

Two years since was love's light song mistaken,
Blessing then both blossoms, half in vain ?
Night outspeeding light hath overtaken
    One of twain.

II

Night and light ? O thou of heart unwary,
Love, what knowest thou here at all aright,
Lured, abused, misled as men by fairy
    Night and light ?

Haply, where thine eyes behold but night,
Soft as o'er her babe the smile of Mary
Light breaks flowerwise into new-born sight.

What though night of light to thee be chary?
What though stars of hope like flowers take flight?
Seest thou all things here, where all see vary
    Night and light?

DEATH AND BIRTH

Death and birth should dwell not near together :
Wealth keeps house not, even for shame, with
 dearth :
Fate doth ill to link in one brief tether
   Death and birth.

Harsh the yoke that binds them, strange the girth
Seems that girds them each with each : yet whether
Death be best, who knows, or life on earth ?

Ill the rose-red and the sable feather
Blend in one crown's plume, as grief with mirth :
Ill met still are warm and wintry weather,
   Death and birth.

BIRTH AND DEATH

BIRTH and death, twin-sister and twin-brother,
Night and day, on all things that draw breath,
Reign, while time keeps friends with one another
     Birth and death.

Each brow-bound with flowers diverse of wreath,
Heaven they hail as father, earth as mother,
Faithful found above them and beneath.

Smiles may lighten tears, and tears may smother
Smiles, for all that joy or sorrow saith:
Joy nor sorrow knows not from each other
     Birth and death.

BENEDICTION

BLEST in death and life beyond man's guessing
Little children live and die, possest
Still of grace that keeps them past expressing
  Blest.

Each least chirp that rings from every nest,
Each least touch of flower-soft fingers pressing
Aught that yearns and trembles to be prest,

Each least glance, gives gift of grace, redressing
Grief's worst wrongs : each mother's nurturing breast
Feeds a flower of bliss, beyond all blessing
  Blest.

ETUDE RÉALISTE

A BABY's feet, like sea-shells pink,
  Might tempt, should heaven see meet,
An angel's lips to kiss, we think,
  A baby's feet.

Like rose-hued sea-flowers toward the heat
  They stretch and spread and wink
Their ten soft buds that part and meet.

No flower-bells that expand and shrink
  Gleam half so heavenly sweet
As shine on life's untrodden brink
  A baby's feet.

II

A baby's hands, like rosebuds furled
  Whence yet no leaf expands,
Ope if you touch, though close upcurled,
  A baby's hands.

Then, fast as warriors grip their brands
  When battle's bolt is hurled,
They close, clenched hard like tightening bands.

No rosebuds yet by dawn impearled
   Match, even in loveliest lands,
The sweetest flowers in all the world—
   A baby's hands.

III

A baby's eyes, ere speech begin,
   Ere lips learn words or sighs,
Bless all things bright enough to win
   A baby's eyes.

Love, while the sweet thing laughs and lies,
   And sleep flows out and in,
Sees perfect in them Paradise.

Their glance might cast out pain and sin,
   Their speech make dumb the wise,
By mute glad godhead felt within
   A baby's eyes.

BABYHOOD

I

A baby shines as bright
If winter or if May be
On eyes that keep in sight
    A baby.

Though dark the skies or grey be
It fills our eyes with light,
If midnight or midday be.

Love hails it, day and night,
The sweetest thing that may be,
Yet cannot praise aright
    A baby.

II

All heaven, in every baby born,
All absolute of earthly leaven,
Reveals itself, though man may scorn
    All heaven.

Yet man might feel all sin forgiven,
All grief appeased, all pain outworn,
By this one revelation given.

Soul, now forget thy burdens borne :
Heart, be thy joys now seven times seven :
Love shows in light more bright than morn
    All heaven.

III

What likeness may define, and stray not
   From truth's exactest way,
A baby's beauty?   Love can say not
   What likeness may.

The Mayflower loveliest held in May
   Of all that shine and stay not
Laughs not in rosier disarray.

Sleek satin, swansdown, buds that play not
   As yet with winds that play,
Would fain be matched with this, and may not :
   What likeness may?

IV

   Rose, round whose bed
   Dawn's cloudlets close,
   Earth's brightest-bred
     Rose !

   No song, love knows,
   May praise the head
   Your curtain shows.

   Ere sleep has fled,
   The whole child glows
   One sweet live red
     Rose.

FIRST FOOTSTEPS

A LITTLE way, more soft and sweet
  Than fields aflower with May,
A babe's feet, venturing, scarce complete
  A little way.

  Eyes full of dawning day
Look up for mother's eyes to meet,
  Too blithe for song to say.

Glad as the golden spring to greet
  Its first live leaflet's play,
Love, laughing, leads the little feet
  A little way.

A NINTH BIRTHDAY

February 4, 1883.

I

THREE times thrice hath winter's rough white wing
Crossed and curdled wells and streams with ice
Since his birth whose praises love would sing
      Three times thrice.

Earth nor sea bears flower nor pearl of price
Fit to crown the forehead of my king,
Honey meet to please him, balm, nor spice.

Love can think of nought but love to bring
Fit to serve or do him sacrifice
Ere his eyes have looked upon the spring
      Three times thrice.

II

Three times thrice the world has fallen on slumber,
Shone and waned and withered in a trice,
Frost has fettered Thames and Tyne and Humber
      Three times thrice,

Fogs have swoln too thick for steel to slice,
Cloud and mud have soiled with grime and umber
Earth and heaven, defaced as souls with vice,

Winds have risen to wreck, snows fallen to cumber,
Ships and chariots, trapped like rats or mice,
Since my king first smiled, whose years now number
　　　Three times thrice.

III

Three times thrice, in wine of song full-flowing,
Pledge, my heart, the child whose eyes suffice,
Once beheld, to set thy joy-bells going
　　　Three times thrice.

Not the lands of palm and date and rice
Glow more bright when summer leaves them glowing,
Laugh more light when suns and winds entice.

Noon and eve and midnight and cock-crowing,
Child whose love makes life as paradise,
Love should sound your praise with clarions blowing
　　　Three times thrice.

NOT A CHILD

I

" Not a child : I call myself a boy,"
Says my king, with accent stern yet mild,
Now nine years have brought him change of joy ;
    " Not a child."

How could reason be so far beguiled,
Err so far from sense's safe employ,
Stray so wide of truth, or run so wild?

Seeing his face bent over book or toy,
Child I called him, smiling : but he smiled
Back, as one too high for vain annoy—
    Not a child.

II

Not a child? alack the year !
What should ail an undefiled
Heart, that he would fain appear
    Not a child?

Men, with years and memories piled
Each on other, far and near,
Fain again would so be styled :

Fain would cast off hope and fear,
Rest, forget, be reconciled :
Why would you so fain be, dear,
    Not a child ?

III

Child or boy, my darling, which you will,
Still your praise finds heart and song employ,
Heart and song both yearning toward you still,
    Child or boy.

All joys else might sooner pall or cloy
Love than this which inly takes its fill,
Dear, of sight of your more perfect joy.

Nay, be aught you please, let all fulfil
All your pleasure ; be your world your toy :
Mild or wild we love you, loud or still,
    Child or boy.

TO DORA DORIAN

CHILD of two strong nations, heir
Born of high-souled hope that smiled,
Seeing for each brought forth a fair
     Child,

By thy gracious brows, and wild
Golden-clouded heaven of hair,
By thine eyes elate and mild,

Hope would fain take heart to swear
Men should yet be reconciled,
Seeing the sign she bids thee bear,
     Child.

THE ROUNDEL

A ROUNDEL is wrought as a ring or a starbright
     sphere,
With craft of delight and with cunning of sound
     unsought,
That the heart of the hearer may smile if to pleasure
     his ear
          A roundel is wrought.

Its jewel of music is carven of all or of aught—
Love, laughter, or mourning—remembrance of
     rapture or fear—
That fancy may fashion to hang in the ear of
     thought.

As a bird's quick song runs round, and the hearts in
     us hear
Pause answer to pause, and again the same strain
     caught,
So moves the device whence, round as a pearl or
     tear,
          A roundel is wrought.

AT SEA

" Farewell and adieu " was the burden prevailing
Long since in the chant of a home-faring crew ;
And the heart in us echoes, with laughing or wailing,
      Farewell and adieu.

Each year that we live shall we sing it anew,
With a water untravelled before us for sailing
And a water behind us that wrecks may bestrew.

The stars of the past and the beacons are paling,
The heavens and the waters are hoarier of hue :
But the heart in us chants not an all unavailing
      Farewell and adieu.

WASTED LOVE

WHAT shall be done for sorrow
  With love whose race is run?
Where help is none to borrow,
  What shall be done?

In vain his hands have spun
  The web, or drawn the furrow:
No rest their toil hath won.

His task is all gone thorough
  And fruit thereof is none:
And who dare say to-morrow
  What shall be done?

BEFORE SUNSET

Love's twilight wanes in heaven above,
  On earth ere twilight reigns :
Ere fear may feel the chill thereof,
  Love's twilight wanes.

Ere yet the insatiate heart complains
  "Too much, and scarce enough,"
The lip so late athirst refrains.

Soft on the neck of either dove
  Love's hands let slip the reins :
And while we look for light of love
  Love's twilight wanes.

A SINGING LESSON

FAR-FETCHED and dear-bought, as the proverb re-
     hearses,
Is good, or was held so, for ladies : but nought
In a song can be good if the turn of the verse is
          Far-fetched and dear-bought.

As the turn of a wave should it sound, and the
     thought
Ring smooth, and as light as the spray that disperses
Be the gleam of the words for the garb thereof
     wrought.

Let the soul in it shine through the sound as it pierces
Men's hearts with possession of music unsought ;
For the bounties of song are no jealous god's mercies,
          Far-fetched and dear-bought.

FLOWER-PIECES

I

LOVE LIES BLEEDING

Love lies bleeding in the bed whereover
Roses lean with smiling mouths or pleading :
Earth lies laughing where the sun's dart clove her :
    Love lies bleeding.

Stately shine his purple plumes, exceeding
Pride of princes : nor shall maid or lover
Find on earth a fairer sign worth heeding.

Yet may love, sore wounded, scarce recover
Strength and spirit again, with life receding :
Hope and joy, wind-winged, about him hover :
    Love lies bleeding.

II

LOVE IN A MIST

Light love in a mist, by the midsummer moon mis-
    guided,
Scarce seen in the twilight garden if gloom insist,
Seems vainly to seek for a star whose gleam has
    derided
        Light love in a mist.

All day in the sun, when the breezes do all they list,
His soft blue raiment of cloudlike blossom abided
Unrent and unwithered of winds and of rays that
kissed.

Blithe-hearted or sad, as the cloud or the sun subsided,
Love smiled in the flower with a meaning whereof
none wist
Save two that beheld, as a gleam that before them
glided,
Light love in a mist.

THREE FACES

I

VENTIMIGLIA

The sky and sea glared hard and bright and blank :
Down the one steep street, with slow steps firm and
    free,
A tall girl paced, with eyes too proud to thank
      The sky and sea.

One dead flat sapphire, void of wrath or glee,
Through bay on bay shone blind from bank to bank
The weary Mediterranean, drear to see.

More deep, more living, shone her eyes that drank
The breathless light and shed again on me,
Till pale before their splendour waned and shrank
      The sky and sea.

II

GENOA

Again the same strange might of eyes, that saw
In heaven and earth nought fairer, overcame
My sight with rapture of reiterate awe,
    Again the same.

The self-same pulse of wonder shook like flame
The spirit of sense within me : what strange law
Had bid this be, for blessing or for blame ?

To what veiled end that fate or chance foresaw
Came forth this second sister face, that came
Absolute, perfect, fair without a flaw,
    Again the same ?

III

VENICE

Out of the dark pure twilight, where the stream
Flows glimmering, streaked by many a birdlike bark
That skims the gloom whence towers and bridges
    gleam
    Out of the dark.

Once more a face no glance might choose but mark
Shone pale and bright, with eyes whose deep slow
    beam
Made quick the twilight, lifeless else and stark.

The same it seemed, or mystery made it seem,
As those before beholden ; but St. Mark
Ruled here the ways that showed it like a dream
    Out of the dark.

EROS

I

Eros, from rest in isles far-famed,
With rising Anthesterion rose,
And all Hellenic heights acclaimed
    Eros.

The sea one pearl, the shore one rose,
All round him all the flower-month flamed
And lightened, laughing off repose.

Earth's heart, sublime and unashamed,
Knew, even perchance as man's heart knows,
The thirst of all men's nature named
    Eros.

II

Eros, a fire of heart untamed,
A light of spirit in sense that glows,
Flamed heavenward still ere earth defamed
    Eros.

Nor fear nor shame durst curb or close
His golden godhead, marred and maimed,
Fast round with bonds that burnt and froze.

Ere evil faith struck blind and lamed
Love, pure as fire or flowers or snows,
Earth hailed as blameless and unblamed
    Eros.

III

Eros, with shafts by thousands aimed
At laughing lovers round in rows,
Fades from their sight whose tongues proclaimed
    Eros.

But higher than transient shapes or shows
The light of love in life inflamed
Springs, toward no goal that these disclose.

Above those heavens which passion claimed
Shines, veiled by change that ebbs and flows,
The soul in all things born or framed,
    Eros.

SORROW

Sorrow, on wing through the world for ever,
Here and there for awhile would borrow
Rest, if rest might haply deliver
    Sorrow.

One thought lies close in her heart gnawn thorough
With pain, a weed in a dried-up river,
A rust-red share in an empty furrow.

Hearts that strain at her chain would sever
The link where yesterday frets to-morrow:
All things pass in the world, but never
    Sorrow.

SLEEP

SLEEP, when a soul that her own clouds cover
Wails that sorrow should always keep
Watch, nor see in the gloom above her
       Sleep,

Down, through darkness naked and steep,
Sinks, and the gifts of his grace recover
Soon the soul, though her wound be deep.

God beloved of us, all men's lover,
All most weary that smile or weep
Feel thee afar or anear them hover,
       Sleep.

ON AN OLD ROUNDEL

Translated by D. G. Rossetti from the French of Villon.

I

DEATH, from thy rigour a voice appealed,
And men still hear what the sweet cry saith,
Crying aloud in thine ears fast sealed,
    Death.

As a voice in a vision that vanisheth,
Through the grave's gate barred and the portal
    steeled
The sound of the wail of it travelleth.

Wailing aloud from a heart unhealed,
It woke response of melodious breath
From lips now too by thy kiss congealed,
    Death.

II

Ages ago, from the lips of a sad glad poet
Whose soul was a wild dove lost in the whirling snow,
The soft keen plaint of his pain took voice to show it
    Ages ago.

So clear, so deep, the divine drear accents flow,
No soul that listens may choose but thrill to know it,
Pierced and wrung by the passionate music's throe.

For us there murmurs a nearer voice below it,
Known once of ears that never again shall know,
Now mute as the mouth which felt death's wave
     o'erflow it
          Ages ago.

A LANDSCAPE BY COURBET

Low lies the mere beneath the moorside, still
And glad of silence : down the wood sweeps clear
To the utmost verge where fed with many a rill
    Low lies the mere.

The wind speaks only summer : eye nor ear
Sees aught at all of dark, hears aught of shrill,
From sound or shadow felt or fancied here.

Strange, as we praise the dead man's might and skill,
Strange that harsh thoughts should make such heavy
    cheer,
While, clothed with peace by heaven's most gentle will,
    Low lies the mere.

A FLOWER-PIECE BY FANTIN

HEART'S EASE or pansy, pleasure or thought
Which would the picture give us of these?
Surely the heart that conceived it sought
      Heart's ease.

Surely by glad and divine degrees
The heart impelling the hand that wrought
Wrought comfort here for a soul's disease.

Deep flowers, with lustre and darkness fraught,
From glass that gleams as the chill still seas
Lean and lend for a heart distraught
      Heart's ease.

A NIGHT-PIECE BY MILLET

WIND and sea and cloud and cloud-forsaking
Mirth of moonlight where the storm leaves free
Heaven awhile, for all the wrath of waking
      Wind and sea.

Bright with glad mad rapture, fierce with glee,
Laughs the moon, borne on past cloud's o'er-
    taking
Fast, it seems, as wind or sail can flee.

One blown sail beneath her, hardly making
Forth, wild-winged for harbourage yet to be,
Strives and leaps and pants beneath the breaking
      Wind and sea.

"MARZO PAZZO"

MAD March with the wind in his wings wide-spread,
Leaps from heaven, and the deep dawn's arch
Hails re-risen again from the dead
        Mad March.

Soft small flames on rowan and larch
Break forth as laughter on lips that said
Nought till the pulse in them beat love's march.

But the heartbeat now in the lips rose-red
Speaks life to the world, and the winds that parch
Bring April forth as a bride to wed
        Mad March.

DEAD LOVE

DEAD love, by treason slain, lies stark,
White as a dead stark-stricken dove :
None that pass by him pause to mark
    Dead love.

His heart, that strained and yearned and strove
As toward the sundawn strives the lark,
Is cold as all the old joy thereof.

Dead men, re-risen from dust, may hark
When rings the trumpet blown above :
It will not raise from out the dark
    Dead love.

DISCORD

UNRECONCILED by life's fleet years, that fled
With changeful clang of pinions wide and wild,
Though two great spirits had lived, and hence had
    sped
            Unreconciled ;

Though time and change, harsh time's imperious
    child,
That wed strange hands together, might not wed
High hearts by hope's misprision once beguiled ;

Faith, by the light from either's memory shed,
Sees, radiant as their ends were undefiled,
One goal for each—not twain among the dead
            Unreconciled.

CONCORD

RECONCILED by death's mild hand, that giving
Peace gives wisdom, not more strong than mild,
Love beholds them, each without misgiving
           Reconciled.

Each on earth alike of earth reviled,
Hated, feared, derided, and forgiving,
Each alike had heaven at heart, and smiled.

Both bright names, clothed round with man's thanks-
      giving,
Shine, twin stars above the storm-drifts piled,
Dead and deathless, whom we saw not living
           Reconciled.

MOURNING

ALAS my brother! the cry of the mourners of old
        That cried on each other,
All crying aloud on the dead as the death-note rolled,
        Alas my brother!

As flashes of dawn that mists from an east wind
    smother
        With fold upon fold,
The past years gleam that linked us one with another.

Time sunders hearts as of brethren whose eyes
    behold
        No more their mother:
But a cry sounds yet from the shrine whose fires wax
    cold,
        Alas my brother!

APEROTOS EROS

STRONG as death, and cruel as the grave,
Clothed with cloud and tempest's blackening breath,
Known of death's dread self, whom none outbrave,
    Strong as death,

Love, brow-bound with anguish for a wreath,
Fierce with pain, a tyrant-hearted slave,
Burns above a world that groans beneath

Hath not pity power on thee to save,
Love ? hath power no pity ?   Nought he saith,
Answering : blind he walks as wind or wave,
    Strong as death.

TO CATULLUS

My brother, my Valerius, dearest head
Of all whose crowning bay-leaves crown their mother
Rome, in the notes first heard of thine I read
    My brother.

No dust that death or time can strew may smother
Love and the sense of kinship inly bred
From loves and hates at one with one another.

To thee was Cæsar's self nor dear nor dread,
Song and the sea were sweeter each than other :
How should I living fear to call thee dead,
    My brother?

"INSULARUM OCELLE"

SARK, fairer than aught in the world that the lit skies
    cover,
Laughs inly behind her cliffs, and the seafarers mark
As a shrine where the sunlight serves, though the
    blown clouds hover,
        Sark.

We mourn, for love of a song that outsang the lark,
That nought so lovely beholden of Sirmio's lover
Made glad in Propontis the flight of his Pontic bark.

Here earth lies lordly, triumphal as heaven is above
    her,
And splendid and strange as the sea that upbears as
    an ark,
As a sign for the rapture of storm-spent eyes to
    discover,
        Sark.

IN SARK

ABREAST and ahead of the sea is a crag's front cloven
 asunder
With strong sea-breach and with wasting of winds
 whence terror is shed
As a shadow of death from the wings of the darkness
 on waters that thunder
 Abreast and ahead.

At its edge is a sepulchre hollowed and hewn for a
 lone man's bed,
Propped open with rock and agape on the sky and
 the sea thereunder,
But roofed and walled in well from the wrath of them
 slept its dead.

Here might not a man drink rapture of rest, or
 delight above wonder,
Beholding, a soul disembodied, the days and the
 nights that fled,
With splendour and sound of the tempest around and
 above him and under,
 Abreast and ahead?

IN GUERNSEY

TO THEODORE WATTS

I

THE heavenly bay, ringed round with cliffs and moors,
Storm-stained ravines, and crags that lawns inlay,
Soothes as with love the rocks whose guard secures
    The heavenly bay.

O friend, shall time take ever this away,
This blessing given of beauty that endures,
This glory shown us, not to pass but stay?

Though sight be changed for memory, love ensures
What memory, changed by love to sight, would say—
The word that seals for ever mine and yours
    The heavenly bay.

II

My mother sea, my fostress, what new strand,
What new delight of waters, may this be,
The fairest found since time's first breezes fanned
    My mother sea?

Once more I give me body and soul to thee,
Who hast my soul for ever : cliff and sand
Recede, and heart to heart once more are we.

My heart springs first and plunges, ere my hand
Strike out from shore : more close it brings to me,
More near and dear than seems my fatherland,
        My mother sea.

III

Across and along, as the bay's breadth opens, and
        o'er us
Wild autumn exults in the wind, swift rapture and
        strong
Impels us, and broader the wide waves brighten
        before us
        Across and along.

The whole world's heart is uplifted, and knows not
        wrong ;
The whole world's life is a chant to the sea-tide's
        chorus ;
Are we not as waves of the water, as notes of the
        song ?

Like children unworn of the passions and toils that
        wore us,
We breast for a season the breadth of the seas that
        throng,
Rejoicing as they, to be borne as of old they bore us
        Across and along.

IV

On Dante's track by some funereal spell
Drawn down through desperate ways that lead not
     back
We seem to move, bound forth past flood and fell
     On Dante's track.

The grey path ends : the gaunt rocks gape : the
     black
Deep hollow tortuous night, a soundless shell,
Glares darkness : are the fires of old grown slack?

Nay, then, what flames are these that leap and swell
As 'twere to show, where earth's foundations crack,
The secrets of the sepulchres of hell
     On Dante's track?

V

By mere men's hands the flame was lit, we know,
From heaps of dry waste whin and casual brands :
Yet, knowing, we scarce believe it kindled so
     By mere men's hands.

Above, around, high-vaulted hell expands,
Steep, dense, a labyrinth walled and roofed with woe,
Whose mysteries even itself not understands.

The scorn in Farinata's eyes aglow
Seems visible in this flame : there Geryon stands :
No stage of earth's is here, set forth to show
     By mere men's hands.

VI

Night, in utmost noon forlorn and strong, with heart
    athirst and fasting,
Hungers here, barred up for ever, whence as one
    whom dreams affright
Day recoils before the low-browed lintel threatening
    doom and casting Night.

All the reefs and islands, all the lawns and highlands,
    clothed with light,
Laugh for love's sake in their sleep outside : but here
    the night speaks, blasting
Day with silent speech and scorn of all things known
    from depth to height.

Lower than dive the thoughts of spirit-stricken fear in
    souls forecasting
Hell, the deep void seems to yawn beyond fear's
    reach, and higher than sight
Rise the walls and roofs that compass it about with
    everlasting Night.

VII

The house accurst, with cursing sealed and signed,
Heeds not what storms about it burn and burst :
No fear more fearful than its own may find
    The house accurst.

Barren as crime, anhungered and athirst,
Blank miles of moor sweep inland, sere and blind,
Where summer's best rebukes not winter's worst.

The low bleak tower with nought save wastes behind
Stares down the abyss whereon chance reared and
    nursed
This type and likeness of the accurst man's mind,
        The house accurst.

VIII

Beloved and blest, lit warm with love and fame,
The house that had the light of the eartn for guest
Hears for his name's sake all men hail its name
        Beloved and blest.

This eyrie was the homeless eagle's nest
When storm laid waste his eyrie : hence he came
Again, when storm smote sore his mother's breast.

Bow down men bade us, or be clothed with blame
And mocked for madness : worst, they sware, was
    best :
But grief shone here, while joy was one with shame.
        Beloved and blest.

ENVOI

FLY, white butterflies, out to sea,
Frail pale wings for the winds to try,
Small white wings that we scarce can see
  Fly.

Here and there may a chance-caught eye
Note in a score of you twain or three
Brighter or darker of tinge or dye.

Some fly light as a laugh of glee,
Some fly soft as a low long sigh :
All to the haven where each would be
  Fly.

ATHENS: AN ODE

U

ATHENS

AN ODE

ERE from under earth again like fire the violet
   kindle,   [*Str.* 1.
   Ere the holy buds and hoar on olive-branches
      bloom,
Ere the crescent of the last pale month of winter
      dwindle,
   Shrink, and fall as falls a dead leaf on the dead
      month's tomb,
Round the hills whose heights the first-born olive-
      blossom brightened,
   Round the city brow-bound once with violets like
      a bride,
Up from under earth again a light that long since
      lightened
   Breaks, whence all the world took comfort as all
      time takes pride.
Pride have all men in their fathers that were free
      before them,
   In the warriors that begat us free-born pride have
      we :
But the fathers of their spirits, how may men adore
      them,
   With what rapture may we praise, who bade our
      souls be free ?

Sons of Athens born in spirit and truth are all born
    free men ;
    Most of all, we, nurtured where the north wind
        holds his reign :
Children all we sea-folk of the Salaminian seamen,
    Sons of them that beat back Persia they that beat
        back Spain.
Since the songs of Greece fell silent, none like ours
    have risen ;
    Since the sails of Greece fell slack, no ships have
        sailed like ours ;
How should we lament not, if her spirit sit in
    prison ?
    How should we rejoice not, if her wreaths renew
        their flowers ?
All the world is sweeter, if the Athenian violet
    quicken :
    All the world is brighter, if the Athenian sun
        return :
All things foul on earth wax fainter, by that sun's
    light stricken :
    All ill growths are withered, where those fragrant
        flower-lights burn.
All the wandering waves of seas with all their warring
    waters
    Roll the record on for ever of the sea-fight there,
When the capes were battle's lists, and all the straits
    were slaughter's,
    And the myriad Medes as foam-flakes on the
        scattering air.
Ours the lightning was that cleared the north and lit
    the nations,
    But the light that gave the whole world light of
        old was she :

Ours an age or twain, but hers are endless genera-
    tions :
  All the world is hers at heart, and most of all are
    we.

Ye that bear the name about you of her glory, [*Ant.* 1.
  Men that wear the sign of Greeks upon you sealed,
Yours is yet the choice to write yourselves in story
  Sons of them that fought the Marathonian field.
Slaves of no man were ye, said your warrior poet,
  Neither subject unto man as underlings :
Yours is now the season here wherein to show it,
  If the seed ye be of them that knew not kings.
If ye be not, swords nor words alike found brittle
  From the dust of death to raise you shall prevail :
Subject swords and dead men's words may stead you
    little,
  If their old king-hating heart within you fail.
If your spirit of old, and not your bonds, be broken,
  If the kingless heart be molten in your breasts,
By what signs and wonders, by what word or token,
  Shall ye drive the vultures from your eagles' nests ?
All the gains of tyrants Freedom counts for losses ;
  Nought of all the work done holds she worth the
    work,
When the slaves whose faith is set on crowns and
    crosses
  Drive the Cossack bear against the tiger Turk.
Neither cross nor crown nor crescent shall ye bow to,
  Nought of Araby nor Jewry, priest nor king :
As your watchword was of old, so be it now too :
  As from lips long stilled, from yours let healing
    spring.

Through the fights of old, your battle-cry was healing,
  And the Saviour that ye called on was the Sun :
Dawn by dawn behold in heaven your God, revealing
  Light from darkness as when Marathon was won.
Gods were yours yet strange to Turk or Galilean,
  Light and Wisdom only then as gods adored :
Pallas was your shield, your comforter was Pæan,
  From your bright world's navel spake the Sun your
      Lord.

Though the names be lost, and changed the signs
    of Light and Wisdom be,   [*Ep.* 1.
By these only shall men conquer, by these only be set
    free :
When the whole world's eye was Athens, these were
    yours, and theirs were ye.
Light was given you of your wisdom, light ye gave
    the world again :
As the sun whose godhead lightened on her soul was
    Hellas then :
Yea, the least of all her children as the chosen of
    other men.
Change your hearts not with your garments, nor your
    faith with creeds that change :
Truth was yours, the truth which time and chance
    transform not nor estrange :
Purer truth nor higher abides not in the reach of
    time's whole range.
Gods are they in all men's memories and for all time's
    periods,
They that hurled the host back seaward which had
    scourged the sea with rods :
Gods for us are all your fathers, even the least of
    these as gods.

In the dark of days the thought of them is with us,
    strong to save,
They that had no lord, and made the Great King
    lesser than a slave ;
They that rolled all Asia back on Asia, broken like a
    wave.
No man's men were they, no master's and no God's
    but these their own :
Gods not loved in vain nor served amiss, nor all yet
    overthrown :
Love of country, Freedom, Wisdom, Light, and none
    save these alone.
King by king came up against them, sire and son,
    and turned to flee :
Host on host roared westward, mightier each than
    each, if more might be :
Field to field made answer, clamorous like as wave
    to wave at sea.
Strife to strife responded, loud as rocks to clangorous
    rocks respond
Where the deep rings wreck to seamen held in tem-
    pest's thrall and bond,
Till when war's bright work was perfect peace as
    radiant rose beyond :
Peace made bright with fruit of battle, stronger made
    for storm gone down,
With the flower of song held heavenward for the
    violet of her crown
Woven about the fragrant forehead of the fostress
    maiden's town.
Gods arose alive on earth from under stroke of human
    hands :
As the hands that wrought them, these are dead, and
    mixed with time's dead sands :

But the godhead of supernal song, though these now
  stand not, stands.
Pallas is not, Phœbus breathes no more in breathing
  brass or gold :
Clytæmnestra towers, Cassandra wails, for ever :
  Time is bold,
But nor heart nor hand hath he to unwrite the scrip-
  tures writ of old.
Dead the great chryselephantine God, as dew last
  evening shed :
Dust of earth or foam of ocean is the symbol of his
  head :
Earth and ocean shall be shadows when Prometheus
  shall be dead.

Fame around her warriors living rang through Greece
        and lightened,   [*Str.* 2.
  Moving equal with their stature, stately with their
    strength :
Thebes and Lacedæmon at their breathing presence
    brightened,
    Sense or sound of them filled all the live land's
      breadth and length.
All the lesser tribes put on the pure Athenian fashion,
    One Hellenic heart was from the mountains to the
      sea :
Sparta's bitter self grew sweet with high half-human
      passion,
    And her dry thorns flushed aflower in strait Ther-
      mopylæ.
Fruitless yet the flowers had fallen, and all the deeds
      died fruitless,
    Save that tongues of after men, the children of her
      peace,

Took the tale up of her glories, transient else and
    rootless,
    And in ears and hearts of all men left the praise of
        Greece.
Fair the war-time was when still, as beacon answering
    beacon,
    Sea to land flashed fight, and thundered note of
        wrath or cheer ;
But the strength of noonday night hath power to
    waste and weaken,
    Nor may light be passed from hand to hand of
        year to year
If the dying deed be saved not, ere it die for ever,
    By the hands and lips of men more wise than years
        are strong ;
If the soul of man take heed not that the deed die
    never,
    Clothed about with purple and gold of story,
        crowned with song.
Still the burning heart of boy and man alike re-
    joices,
    Hearing words which made it seem of old for all
        who sang
That their heaven of heavens waxed happier when
    from free men's voices
    Well-beloved Harmodius and Aristogeiton rang.
Never fell such fragrance from the flower-month's
    rose-red kirtle
    As from chaplets on the bright friends' brows who
        slew their lord :
Greener grew the leaf and balmier blew the flower of
    myrtle
    When its blossom sheathed the sheer tyrannicidal
        sword.

None so glorious garland crowned the feast Pan-
    athenæan
  As this wreath too frail to fetter fast the Cyprian
    dove :
None so fiery song sprang sunwards annual as the
    pæan
  Praising perfect love of friends and perfect country's
    love.

Higher than highest of all those heavens wherefrom
    the starry   [*Ant.* 2.
  Song of Homer shone above the rolling fight,
Gleams like spring's green bloom on boughs all gaunt
    and gnarry
  Soft live splendour as of flowers of foam in flight,
Glows a glory of mild-winged maidens upward mount-
    ing
  Sheer through air made shrill with strokes of smooth
    swift wings
Round the rocks beyond foot's reach, past eyesight's
    counting,
  Up the cleft where iron wind of winter rings
Round a God fast clenched in iron jaws of fetters,
  Him who culled for man the fruitful flower of fire,
Bared the darkling scriptures writ in dazzling letters,
  Taught the truth of dreams deceiving men's desire,
Gave their water-wandering chariot-seats of ocean
  Wings, and bade the rage of war-steeds champ the
    rein,
Showed the symbols of the wild birds' wheeling
    motion,
  Waged for man's sake war with God and all his
    train.

Earth, whose name was also Righteousness, a
    mother
  Many-named and single-natured, gave him breath
Whence God's wrath could wring but this word and
    none other—
He may smite me, yet he shall not do to death.
Him the tongue that sang triumphant while tor-
    mented
  Sang as loud the sevenfold storm that roared ere-
    while
Round the towers of Thebes till wrath might rest
    contented :
  Sang the flight from smooth soft-sanded banks of
    Nile,
When like mateless doves that fly from snare or
    tether
  Came the suppliants landwards trembling as they
    trod,
And the prayer took wing from all their tongues
    together—
King of kings, most holy of holies, blessed God.
But what mouth may chant again, what heart may
    know it,
  All the rapture that all hearts of men put on
When of Salamis the time-transcending poet
  Sang, whose hand had chased the Mede at Mara-
    thon ?

Darker dawned the song with stormier wings above
    the watch-fire spread   *[Ep.* 2.
Whence from Ida toward the hill of Hermes leapt the
    light that said

Troy was fallen, a torch funereal for the king's triumphal head.

Dire indeed the birth of Leda's womb that had God's
self to sire

Bloomed, a flower of love that stung the soul with
fangs that gnaw like fire :

But the twin-born human-fathered sister-flower bore
fruit more dire.

Scarce the cry that called on airy heaven and all swift
winds on wing,

Wells of river-heads, and countless laugh of waves
past reckoning,

Earth which brought forth all, and the orbèd sun that
looks on everything,

Scarce that cry fills yet men's hearts more full of
heart-devouring dread

Than the murderous word said mocking, how the
child whose blood he shed

Might clasp fast and kiss her father where the dead
salute the dead.

But the latter note of anguish from the lips that
mocked her lord,

When her son's hand bared against the breast that
suckled him his sword,

How might man endure, O Æschylus, to hear it and
record ?

How might man endure, being mortal yet, O thou
most highest, to hear ?

How record, being born of woman ? Surely not thy
Furies near,

Surely this beheld, this only, blasted hearts to death
with fear.

Not the hissing hair, nor flakes of blood that oozed
from eyes of fire,

Nor the snort of savage sleep that snuffed the hunger-
    ing heart's desire
Where the hunted prey found hardly space and har-
    bour to respire ;
She whose likeness called them—" Sleep ye, ho ?
    what need of you that sleep ? "
(Ah, what need indeed, where she was, of all shapes
    that night may keep
Hidden dark as death and deeper than men's dreams
    of hell are deep ?)
She the murderess of her husband, she the huntress
    of her son,
More than ye was she, the shadow that no God with-
    stands but one,
Wisdom equal-eyed and stronger and more splendid
    than the sun.
Yea, no God may stand betwixt us and the shadows
    of our deeds,
Nor the light of dreams that lighten darkness, nor the
    prayer that pleads,
But the wisdom equal-souled with heaven, the light
    alone that leads.
Light whose law bids home those childless children
    of eternal night,
Soothed and reconciled and mastered and transmuted
    in men's sight
Who behold their own souls, clothed with darkness
    once, now clothed with light.
King of kings and father crowned of all our fathers
    crowned of yore,
Lord of all the lords of song, whose head all heads
    bow down before,
Glory be to thee from all thy sons in all tongues ever-
    more.

Rose and vine and olive and deep ivy-bloom en-
            twining   [*Str.* 3.
  Close the goodliest grave that e'er they closeliest
            might entwine
Keep the wind from wasting and the sun from too
            strong shining
  Where the sound and light of sweetest songs still
            float and shine.
Here the music seems to illume the shade, the light
            to whisper
  Song, the flowers to put not odours only forth, but
            words
Sweeter far than fragrance: here the wandering
            wreaths twine crisper
  Far, and louder far exults the note of all wild
            birds.
Thoughts that change us, joys that crown and sorrows
            that enthrone us,
  Passions that enrobe us with a clearer air than
            ours,
Move and breathe as living things beheld round white
            Colonus,
  Audibler than melodies and visibler than flowers.
Love, in fight unconquered, Love, with spoils of great
            men laden,
  Never sang so sweet from throat of woman or of
            dove :
Love, whose bed by night is in the soft cheeks of a
            maiden,
  And his march is over seas, and low roofs lack not
            Love ;
Nor may one of all that live, ephemeral or eternal,
  Fly nor hide from Love ; but whoso clasps him
            fast goes mad.

Never since the first-born year with flowers first-born
      grew vernal
  Such a song made listening hearts of lovers glad or
     sad.
Never sounded note so radiant at the rayless portal
  Opening wide on the all-concealing lowland of the
     dead
As the music mingling, when her doomsday marked
      her mortal,
  From her own and old men's voices round the
     bride's way shed,
Round the grave her bride-house, hewn for endless
      habitation,
  Where, shut out from sunshine, with no bridegroom
     by, she slept ;
But beloved of all her dark and fateful generation,
  But with all time's tears and praise besprinkled
     and bewept :
Well-beloved of outcast father and self-slaughtered
      mother,
  Born, yet unpolluted, of their blind incestuous
     bed ;
Best-beloved of him for whose dead sake she died,
      her brother,
  Hallowing by her own life's gift her own born
     brother's head ;

Not with wine or oil nor any less libation   [*Ant.* 3.
  Hallowed, nor made sweet with humbler perfume's
     breath ;
Not with only these redeemed from desecration,
  But with blood and spirit of life poured forth to
     death ;

Blood unspotted, spirit unsullied, life devoted,
 Sister too supreme to make the bride's hope
  good,
Daughter too divine as woman to be noted,
 Spouse of only death in mateless maidenhood.
Yea, in her was all the prayer fulfilled, the saying
 All accomplished—*Would that' fate would let me
  wear*

Hallowed innocence of words and all deeds, weighing
 Well the laws thereof, begot on holier air,
Far on high sublimely stablished, whereof only
 Heaven is father ; nor did birth of mortal mould
Bring them forth, nor shall oblivion lull to lonely
 Slumber.   Great in these is God, and grows not old.
Therefore even that inner darkness where she
  perished
 Surely seems as holy and lovely, seen aright,
As desirable and as dearly to be cherished,
 As the haunt closed in with laurels from the light,
Deep inwound with olive and wild vine inwoven,
 Where a godhead known and unknown makes men
  pale,
But the darkness of the twilight noon is cloven
 Still with shrill sweet moan of many a nightingale.
Closer clustering there they make sweet noise to-
  gether,
 Where the fearful gods look gentler than our fear,
And the grove thronged through with birds of holiest
  feather
 Grows nor pale nor dumb with sense of dark things
  near.
There her father, called upon with signs of wonder,
 Passed with tenderest words away by ways un-
  known,

Not by sea-storm stricken down, nor touched of
    thunder,
  To the dark benign deep underworld, alone.

Third of three that ruled in Athens, kings with
    sceptral song for staff,   [*Ep.* 3.
Gladdest heart that God gave ever milk and wine of
    thought to quaff,
Clearest eye that lightened ever to the broad lip's
    lordliest laugh,
Praise be thine as theirs whose tragic brows the
    loftier leaf engirds
For the live and lyric lightning of thy honey-hearted
    words,
Soft like sunny dewy wings of clouds and bright as
    crying of birds ;
Full of all sweet rays and notes that make of earth
    and air and sea
One great light and sound of laughter from one great
    God's heart, to be
Sign and semblance of the gladness of man's life
    where men breathe free
With no Loxian sound obscure God uttered once, and
    all time heard,
All the soul of Athens, all the soul of England, in
    that word :
Rome arose the second child of freedom : northward
    rose the third.
Ere her Boreal dawn came kindling seas afoam and
    fields of snow,
Yet again, while Europe groaned and grovelled, shone
    like suns aglow
Doria splendid over Genoa, Venice bright with Dan-
    dolo.

Dead was Hellas, but Ausonia by the light of dead
men's deeds

Rose and walked awhile alive, though mocked as
whom the fen-fire leads

By the creed-wrought faith of faithless souls that
mock their doubts with creeds.

Dead are these, and man is risen again : and haply
now the three

Yet coequal and triune may stand in story, marked
as free

By the token of the washing of the waters of the
sea.

Athens first of all earth's kindred many-tongued and
many-kinned

Had the sea to friend and comfort, and for kinsman
had the wind :

She that bare Columbus next : then she that made
her spoil of Ind.

She that hears not what man's rage but only what
the sea-wind saith :

She that turned Spain's ships to cloud-wrack at the
blasting of her breath,

By her strengths of strong-souled children and of
strong winds done to death.

North and south the Great King's galleons went in
Persian wise : and here

She, with Æschylean music on her lips that laughed
back fear,

In the face of Time's grey godhead shook the splendour of her spear.

Fair as Athens then with foot upon her foeman's
front, and strong

Even as Athens for redemption of the world from
sovereign wrong,

Like as Athens crowned she stood before the sun
    with crowning song.
All the world is theirs with whom is freedom : first
    of all the free,
Blest are they whom song has crowned and clothed
    with blessing : these as we,
These alone have part in spirit with the sun that
    crowns the sea.

April 1881.

THE STATUE OF VICTOR HUGO

1

SINCE in Athens God stood plain for adoration,
　　Since the sun beheld his likeness reared in stone,
Since the bronze or gold of human consecration
　　Gave to Greece her guardian's form and feature
　　　　shown,
Never hand of sculptor, never heart of nation,
　　Found so glorious aim in all these ages flown
As is theirs who rear for all time's acclamation
　　Here the likeness of our mightiest and their own.

2

Theirs and ours and all men's living who behold him
　　Crowned with garlands multiform and manifold ;
Praise and thanksgiving of all mankind enfold him
　　Who for all men casts abroad his gifts of gold.
With the gods of song have all men's tongues enrolled
　　　　him,
　　With the helpful gods have all men's hearts
　　　　enrolled :
Ours he is who love him, ours whose hearts' hearts
　　　　hold him
　　Fast as his the trust that hearts like his may hold.

3

He, the heart most high, the spirit on earth most
    blameless,
  Takes in charge all spirits, holds all hearts in
    trust :
As the sea-wind's on the sea his ways are tameless,
  As the laws that steer the world his works are just.
All most noble feel him nobler, all most shameless
  Feel his wrath and scorn make pale their pride and
    lust :
All most poor and lowliest, all whose wrongs were
    nameless,
  Feel his word of comfort raise them from the dust.

4

Pride of place and lust of empire bloody-fruited
  Knew the blasting of his breath on leaf and fruit :
Now the hand that smote the death-tree now dis-
    rooted
  Plants the refuge-tree that has man's hope for root.
Ah, but we by whom his darkness was saluted,
  How shall now all we that see his day salute ?
How should love not seem by love's own speech
    confuted,
  Song before the sovereign singer not be mute ?

5

With what worship, by what blessing, in what
    measure,
  May we sing of him, salute him, or adore,
With what hymn for praise, what thanksgiving for
    pleasure,
  Who had given us more than heaven, and gives us
    more ?

Heaven's whole treasury, filled up full with night's
    whole treasure,
  Holds not so divine or deep a starry store
As the soul supreme that deals forth worlds at leisure
  Clothed with light and darkness, dense with flower
    and ore.

6

Song had touched the bourn : fresh verses over-
    flow it,
  Loud and radiant, waves on waves on waves that
    throng ;
Still the tide grows, and the sea-mark still below it
  Sinks and shifts and rises, changed and swept
    along.
Rose it like a rock ? the waters overthrow it,
  And another stands beyond them sheer and strong :
Goal by goal pays down its prize, and yields its poet
  Tribute claimed of triumph, palm achieved of song.

7

Since his hand that holds the keys of fear and wonder
  Opened on the high priest's dreaming eyes a door
Whence the lights of heaven and hell above and
    under
  Shone, and smote the face that men bow down
    before,
Thrice again one singer's note had cloven in sunder
  Night, who blows again not one blast now but
    four,
And the fourfold heaven is kindled with his thunder,
  And the stars about his forehead are fourscore.

8

From the deep soul's depths where alway love
    abounded
  First had risen a song with healing on its wings
Whence the dews of mercy raining balms unbounded
  Shed their last compassion even on sceptred things.[1]
Even on heads that like a curse the crown surrounded
  Fell his crowning pity, soft as cleansing springs ;
And the sweet last note his wrath relenting sounded
    Bade men's hearts be melted not for slaves but
    kings.

9

Next, that faith might strengthen fear and love
    embolden,
  On the creeds of priests a scourge of sunbeams fell :
And its flash made bare the deeps of heaven, beholden
    Not of men that cry, Lord, Lord, from church or
    cell.[2]
Hope as young as dawn from night obscure and olden
  Rose again, such power abides in truth's one spell :
Night, if dawn it be that touches her, grows golden ;
  Tears, if such as angels weep, extinguish hell.

10

Through the blind loud mills of barren blear-eyed
    learning
  Where in dust and darkness children's foreheads
  bow,
While men's labour, vain as wind or water turning
  Wheels and sails of dreams, makes life a leafless
    bough,

[1] *La Pitié Suprême.*   1879.
[2] *Religions et Religion.*   1880.

Fell the light of scorn and pity touched with yearning,
  Next, from words that shone as heaven's own kind-
      ling brow.[1]
Stars were these as watch-fires on the world's waste
      burning,
  Stars that fade not in the fourfold sunrise now.[2]

11

Now the voice that faints not till all wrongs be
      wroken
  Sounds as might the sun's song from the morning's
      breast,
All the seals of silence sealed of night are broken,
  All the winds that bear the fourfold word are blest.
All the keen fierce east flames forth one fiery token ;
  All the north is loud with life that knows not rest,
All the south with song as though the stars had
      spoken ;
  All the judgment-fire of sunset scathes the west.

12

Sound of pæan, roll of chanted panegyric,
  Though by Pindar's mouth song's trumpet spake
      forth praise,
March of warrior songs in Pythian mood or Pyrrhic,
  Though the blast were blown by lips of ancient
      days,

---

[1] *L'Ane.* 1880.
[2] *Les Quatre Vents de l'Esprit.* I. *Le Livre satirique.*
II. *Le Livre dramatique.* III. *Le Livre lyrique.* IV. *Le
Livre épique.* 1881.

Ring not clearer than the clarion of satiric
    Song whose breath sweeps bare the plague-infected
       ways
Till the world be pure as heaven is for the lyric
    Sun to rise up clothed with radiant sounds as rays.

13

Clear across the cloud-rack fluctuant and erratic
    As the strong star smiles that lets no mourner
       mourn,
Hymned alike from lips of Lesbian choirs or Attic
    Once at evensong and morning newly born,
Clear and sure above the changes of dramatic
    Tide and current, soft with love and keen with
       scorn,
Smiles the strong sweet soul of maidenhood, ecstatic
    And inviolate as the red glad mouth of morn.

14

Pure and passionate as dawn, whose apparition
    Thrills with fire from heaven the wheels of hours
       that whirl,
Rose and passed her radiance in serene transition
    From his eyes who sought a grain and found a
       pearl.
But the food by cunning hope for vain fruition
    Lightly stolen away from keeping of a churl
Left the bitterness of death and hope's perdition
    On the lip that scorn was wont for shame to curl.[1]

---

[1] *Les Deux Trouvailles de Gallus.* I. *Margarita, comédie.*
II. *Esca, drame.*

15

Over waves that darken round the wave-worn rover
  Rang his clarion higher than winds cried round
    the ship,
Rose a pageant of set suns and storms blown over,
  Hands that held life's guerdons fast or let them
    slip.
But no tongue may tell, no thanksgiving discover,
  Half the heaven of blessing, soft with clouds that
    drip,
Keen with beams that kindle, dear as love to lover,
  Opening by the spell's strength on his lyric lip.

16

By that spell the soul transfigured and dilated
  Puts forth wings that widen, breathes a brightening
    air,
Feeds on light and drinks of music, whence elated
  All her sense grows godlike, seeing all depths made
    bare,
All the mists wherein before she sat belated
  Shrink, till now the sunlight knows not if they
    were ;
All this earth transformed is Eden recreated,
  With the breath of heaven remurmuring in her hair.

17

Sweeter far than aught of sweet that April nurses
  Deep in dew-dropt woodland folded fast and furled
Breathes the fragrant song whose burning dawn
    disperses
  Darkness, like the surge of armies backward hurled,

Even as though the touch of spring's own hand, that
    pierces
  Earth with life's delight, had hidden in the im-
    pearled
Golden bells and buds and petals of his verses
  All the breath of all the flowers in all the world.

18

But the soul therein, the light that our souls follow,
  Fires and fills the song with more of prophet's
    pride,
More of life than all the gulfs of death may swallow,
  More of flame than all the might of night may hide.
Though the whole dark age were loud and void and
    hollow,
  Strength of trust were here, and help for all souls
    tried,
And a token from the flight of that strange swallow[1]
  Whose migration still is toward the wintry side

19

Never came such token for divine solution
  From the oraculous live darkness whence of yore
Ancient faith sought word of help and retribution,
  Truth to lighten doubt, a sign to go before.
Never so baptismal waters of ablution
  Bathed the brows of exile on so stern a shore,
Where the lightnings of the sea of revolution
  Flashed across them ere its thunders yet might
    roar.

[1] Je suis une hirondelle étrange, car j'émigre
    Du côté de l'hiver.

Le Livre Lyrique, liii.

20

By the lightning's light of present revelation
  Shown, with epic thunder as from skies that frown,
Clothed in darkness as of darkling expiation,
  Rose a vision of dead stars and suns gone down,
Whence of old fierce fire devoured the star-struck
      nation,
  Till its wrath and woe lit red the raging town,
Now made glorious with his statue's crowning station,
  Where may never gleam again a viler crown.

21

King, with time for throne and all the years for pages,
  He shall reign though all thrones else be over-
      hurled,
Served of souls that have his living words for wages,
  Crowned of heaven each dawn that leaves his brows
      impearled ;
Girt about with robes unrent of storm that rages,
  Robes not wrought with hands, from no loom's
      weft unfurled ;
All the praise of all earth's tongues in all earth's ages,
  All the love of all men's hearts in all the world.

22

Yet what hand shall carve the soul or cast the spirit,
  Mould the face of fame, bid glory's feature glow ?
Who bequeath for eyes of ages hence to inherit
  Him, the Master, whom love knows not if it know ?
Scarcely perfect praise of men man's work might
      merit,
  Scarcely bid such aim to perfect stature grow,
Were his hand the hand of Phidias who shall rear it, ·
  And his soul the very soul of Angelo.

23

Michael, awful angel of the world's last session,
  Once on earth, like him, with fire of suffering tried,
Thine it were, if man's it were, without transgression,
  Thine alone, to take this toil upon thy pride.
Thine, whose heart was great against the world's
    oppression,
  Even as his whose word is lamp and staff and guide :
Advocate for man, untired of intercession,
  Pleads his voice for slaves whose lords his voice
    defied.

24

Earth, with all the kings and thralls on earth, below it,
  Heaven alone, with all the worlds in heaven, above,
Let his likeness rise for suns and stars to know it,
  High for men to worship, plain for men to love :
Brow that braved the tides which fain would over-
    flow it,
  Lip that gave the challenge, hand that flung the
    glove ;
Comforter and prophet, Paraclete and poet,
  Soul whose emblems are an eagle and a dove.

25

Sun, that hast not seen a loftier head wax hoary,
  Earth, which hast not shown the sun a nobler birth,
Time, that hast not on thy scroll defiled and gory
  One man's name writ brighter in its whole wide
    girth,
Witness, till the final years fulfil their story,
  Till the stars break off the music of their mirth,
What among the sons of men was this man's glory,
  What the vesture of his soul revealed on earth.

SONNETS

HOPE AND FEAR

BENEATH the shadow of dawn's aerial cope,
   With eyes enkindled as the sun's own sphere,
   Hope from the front of youth in godlike cheer
Looks Godward, past the shades where blind men
      grope
Round the dark door that prayers nor dreams can
      ope,
   And makes for joy the very darkness dear
   That gives her wide wings play ; nor dreams that
      fear
At noon may rise and pierce the heart of hope.
Then, when the soul leaves off to dream and yearn,
May truth first purge her eyesight to discern
   What once being known leaves time no power to
      appal ;
Till youth at last, ere yet youth be not, learn
   The kind wise word that falls from years that
      fall—
   " Hope thou not much, and fear thou not at all."

AFTER SUNSET

"Si quis piorum Manibus locus."

I

STRAIGHT from the sun's grave in the deep clear
      west
  A sweet strong wind blows, glad of life : and I,
    Under the soft keen stardawn whence the sky
Takes life renewed, and all night's godlike breast
Palpitates, gradually revealed at rest
  By growth and change of ardours felt on high,
    Make onward, till the last flame fall and die
And all the world by night's broad hand lie blest.
Haply, meseems, as from that edge of death,
Whereon the day lies dark, a brightening breath
  Blows more of benediction than the morn,
So from the graves whereon grief gazing saith
    That half our heart of life there lies forlorn
    May light or breath at least of hope be born.

II

The wind was soft before the sunset fled :
  Now, while the cloud-enshrouded corpse of day
  Is lowered along a red funereal way
Down to the dark that knows not white from red,

A clear sheer breeze against the night makes head,
   Serene, but sure of life as ere a ray
   Springs, or the dusk of dawn knows red from
      grey,
Being as a soul that knows not quick from dead.
From far beyond the sunset, far above,
   Full toward the starry soundless east it blows
   Bright as a child's breath breathing on a rose,
Smooth to the sense as plume of any dove ;
   Till more and more as darkness grows and glows
Silence and night seem likest life and love.

III

If light of life outlive the set of sun
   That men call death and end of all things, then
   How should not that which life held best for men
And proved most precious, though it seem undone
By force of death and woful victory won,
   Be first and surest of revival, when
   Death shall bow down to life arisen again ?
So shall the soul seen be the self-same one
That looked and spake with even such lips and eyes
As love shall doubt not then to recognise,
   And all bright thoughts and smiles of all time
      past
Revive, transfigured, but in spirit and sense
None other than we knew, for evidence
   That love's last mortal word was not his last.

A STUDY FROM MEMORY

IF that be yet a living soul which here
　　Seemed brighter for the growth of numbered
　　　　springs
　　And clothed by Time and Pain with goodlier
　　　　things
Each year it saw fulfilled a fresh fleet year,
Death can have changed not aught that made it
　　　　dear ;
　　Half humorous goodness, grave-eyed mirth on
　　　　wings
　　Bright-balanced, blither-voiced than quiring
　　　　strings ;
Most radiant patience, crowned with conquering
　　　　cheer ;
A spirit inviolable that smiled and sang
　　By might of nature and heroic need
　　More sweet and strong than loftiest dream or
　　　　deed ;
A song that shone, a light whence music rang
　　High as the sunniest heights of kindliest thought ;
　　All these must be, or all she was be nought.

TO DR. JOHN BROWN

BEYOND the north wind lay the land of old
    Where men dwelt blithe and blameless, clothed
        and fed
    With joy's bright raiment and with love's sweet
        bread,
The whitest flock of earth's maternal fold.
None there might wear about his brows enrolled
    A light of lovelier fame than rings your head,
    Whose lovesome love of children and the dead
All men give thanks for : I far off behold
A dear dead hand that links us, and a light
The blithest and benignest of the night,
    The night of death's sweet sleep, wherein may be
A star to show your spirit in present sight
    Some happier island in the Elysian sea
    Where Rab may lick the hand of Marjorie.

March 1882.

TO WILLIAM BELL SCOTT

THE larks are loud above our leagues of whin
   Now the sun's perfume fills their glorious gold
   With odour like the colour : all the wold
Is only light and song and wind wherein
These twain are blent in one with shining din.
   And now your gift, a giver's kingly-souled,
   Dear old fast friend whose honours grow not old,
Bids memory's note as loud and sweet begin.
Though all but we from life be now gone forth
Of that bright household in our joyous north
Where I, scarce clear of boyhood just at end,
   First met your hand ; yet under life's clear dome,
Now seventy strenuous years have crowned my friend,
   Shines no less bright his full-sheaved harvest-
      home.

April 20, 1882.

A DEATH ON EASTER DAY

THE strong spring sun rejoicingly may rise,
  Rise and make revel, as of old men said,
  Like dancing hearts of lovers newly wed :
A light more bright than ever bathed the skies
Departs for all time out of all men's eyes.
  The crowns that girt last night a living head
  Shine only now, though deathless, on the dead :
Art that mocks death, and Song that never dies.
Albeit the bright sweet mothlike wings be furled,
  Hope sees, past all division and defection,
    And higher than swims the mist of human
      breath,
The soul most radiant once in all the world
  Requickened to regenerate resurrection
    Out of the likeness of the shadow of death.

April 1882.

ON THE DEATHS OF THOMAS CARLYLE
AND GEORGE ELIOT

Two souls diverse out of our human sight
  Pass, followed one with love and each with
    wonder :
  The stormy sophist with his mouth of thunder,
Clothed with loud words and mantled in the might
Of darkness and magnificence of night ;
  And one whose eye could smite the night in
    sunder,
  Searching if light or no light were thereunder,
And found in love of loving-kindness light.
Duty divine and Thought with eyes of fire
Still following Righteousness with deep desire
  Shone sole and stern before her and above,
Sure stars and sole to steer by ; but more sweet
Shone lower the loveliest lamp for earthly feet,
  The light of little children, and their love.

AFTER LOOKING INTO CARLYLE'S
REMINISCENCES

I

THREE men lived yet when this dead man was young
   Whose names and words endure for ever : one
   Whose eyes grew dim with straining toward the
      sun,
And his wings weakened, and his angel's tongue
Lost half the sweetest song was ever sung,
   But like the strain half uttered earth hears none,
   Nor shall man hear till all men's songs are done :
One whose clear spirit like an eagle hung
Between the mountains hallowed by his love
And the sky stainless as his soul above :
   And one the sweetest heart that ever spake
The brightest words wherein sweet wisdom smiled.
These deathless names by this dead snake defiled
   Bid memory spit upon him for their sake.

II

Sweet heart, forgive me for thine own sweet sake,
   Whose kind blithe soul such seas of sorrow swam,
   And for my love's sake, powerless as I am
For love to praise thee, or like thee to make

II.   X 2

Music of mirth where hearts less pure would break,
  Less pure than thine, our life-unspotted Lamb.
  Things hatefullest thou hadst not heart to damn,
Nor wouldst have set thine heel on this dead snake.
Let worms consume its memory with its tongue,
The fang that stabbed fair Truth, the lip that stung
  Men's memories uncorroded with its breath.
Forgive me, that with bitter words like his
I mix the gentlest English name that is,
  The tenderest held of all that know not death.

A LAST LOOK

Sick of self-love, Malvolio, like an owl
  That hoots the sun rerisen where starlight sank,
  With German garters crossed athwart thy frank
Stout Scottish legs, men watched thee snarl and
    scowl,
And boys responsive with reverberate howl
  Shrilled, hearing how to thee the springtime stank
  And as thine own soul all the world smelt rank
And as thine own thoughts Liberty seemed foul.
Now, for all ill thoughts nursed and ill words given
Not all condemned, not utterly forgiven,
  Son of the storm and darkness, pass in peace.
Peace upon earth thou knewest not : now, being
    dead,
Rest, with nor curse nor blessing on thine head,
  Where high-strung hate and strenuous envy cease.

DICKENS

CHIEF in thy generation born of men
  Whom English praise acclaimed as English-born,
  With eyes that matched the worldwide eyes of
      morn
For gleam of tears or laughter, tenderest then
When thoughts of children warmed their light, or
      when
  Reverence of age with love and labour worn,
  Or godlike pity fired with godlike scorn,
Shot through them flame that winged thy swift live
      pen :
Where stars and suns that we behold not burn,
  Higher even than here, though highest was here
      thy place,
    Love sees thy spirit laugh and speak and shine
With Shakespeare and the soft bright soul of Sterne
  And Fielding's kindliest might and Goldsmith's
      grace ;
    Scarce one more loved or worthier love than thine.

ON LAMB'S SPECIMENS OF DRAMATIC POETS

I

IF all the flowers of all the fields on earth
  By wonder-working summer were made one,
  Its fragrance were not sweeter in the sun,
Its treasure-house of leaves were not more worth
Than those wherefrom thy light of musing mirth
  Shone, till each leaf whereon thy pen would run
  Breathed life, and all its breath was benison.
Beloved beyond all names of English birth,
More dear than mightier memories ; gentlest name
That ever clothed itself with flower-sweet fame,
Or linked itself with loftiest names of old
  By right and might of loving ; I, that am
Less than the least of those within thy fold,
  Give only thanks for them to thee, Charles Lamb.

II

So many a year had borne its own bright bees
  And slain them since thy honey-bees were hived,
  John Day, in cells of flower-sweet verse contrived
So well with craft of moulding melodies,

Thy soul perchance in amaranth fields at ease
  Thought not to hear the sound on earth revived
  Of summer music from the spring derived
When thy song sucked the flower of flowering trees.
But thine was not the chance of every day :
  Time, after many a darkling hour, grew sunny,
    And light between the clouds ere sunset swam,
Laughing, and kissed their darkness all away,
  When, touched and tasted and approved, thy honey
    Took subtler sweetness from the lips of Lamb.

TO JOHN NICHOL

I

FRIEND of the dead, and friend of all my days
 Even since they cast off boyhood, I salute
 The song saluting friends whose songs are mute
With full burnt-offerings of clear-spirited praise.
That since our old young years our several ways
 Have led through fields diverse of flower and fruit,
 Yet no cross wind has once relaxed the root
We set long since beneath the sundawn's rays,
The root of trust whence towered the trusty tree,
 Friendship—this only and duly might impel
  My song to salutation of your own ;
More even than praise of one unseen of me
 And loved—the starry spirit of Dobell,
  To mine by light and music only known.

II

But more than this what moves me most of all
 To leave not all unworded and unsped
 The whole heart's greeting of my thanks unsaid
Scarce needs this sign, that from my tongue should
  fall

His name whom sorrow and reverent love recall,
   The sign to friends on earth of that dear head
   Alive, which now long since untimely dead
The wan grey waters covered for a pall.
Their trustless reaches dense with tangling stems
   Took never life more taintless of rebuke,
     More pure and perfect, more serene and kind,
Than when those clear eyes closed beneath the
      Thames,
    And made the now more hallowed name of Luke
    Memorial to us of morning left behind.

May 1881

DYSTHANATOS

Ad generem Cereris sine cæde et vulnere pauci
Descendunt reges, aut siccâ morte tyranni.

By no dry death another king goes down
  The way of kings.   Yet may no free man's voice,
  For stern compassion and deep awe, rejoice
That one sign more is given against the crown,
That one more head those dark red waters drown
    Which rise round thrones whose trembling equi-
       poise
  Is propped on sand and bloodshed and such toys
As human hearts that shrink at human frown.
The name writ red on Polish earth, the star
That was to outshine our England's in the far
  East heaven of empire—where is one that saith
Proud words now, prophesying of this White Czar?
    "In bloodless pangs few kings yield up their
      breath,
    Few tyrants perish by no violent death."

March 14, 1881.

658

EUONYMOS

εὖ μὴν ᾗ τιμὴν ἐδίδου νικηφόρος ἀλκὴ
ἐκ νίκης ὄνομ' ἔσχε φόβου κέαρ αἰὲν ἄθικτος.

A YEAR ago red wrath and keen despair
  Spake, and the sole word from their darkness sent
  Laid low the lord not all omnipotent
Who stood most like a god of all that were
As gods for pride of power, till fire and air
  Made earth of all his godhead. Lightning rent
  The heart of empire's lurid firmament,
And laid the mortal core of manhood bare.
But when the calm crowned head that all revere
For valour higher than that which casts out fear,
  Since fear came near it never, comes near death,
Blind murder cowers before it, knowing that here
  No braver soul drew bright and queenly breath
  Since England wept upon Elizabeth.

March 8, 1882.

ON THE RUSSIAN PERSECUTION OF
THE JEWS

O son of man, by lying tongues adored,
  By slaughterous hands of slaves with feet red-shod
  In carnage deep as ever Christian trod
Profaned with prayer and sacrifice abhorred
And incense from the trembling tyrant's horde,
  Brute worshippers or wielders of the rod,
  Most murderous even of all that call thee God,
Most treacherous even that ever called thee Lord ;
Face loved of little children long ago,
  Head hated of the priests and rulers then,
    If thou see this, or hear these hounds of thine
    Run ravening as the Gadarean swine,
Say, was not this thy Passion, to foreknow
  In death's worst hour the works of Christian men ?

January 23, 1882.

BISMARCK AT CANOSSA

Not all disgraced, in that Italian town,
  The imperial German cowered beneath thine hand,
  Alone indeed imperial Hildebrand,
And felt thy foot and Rome's, and felt her frown
And thine, more strong and sovereign than his crown,
  Though iron forged its blood-encrusted band.
  But now the princely wielder of his land,
For hatred's sake toward freedom, so bows down,
No strength is in the foot to spurn : its tread
Can bruise not now the proud submitted head :
  But how much more abased, much lower brought
    low,
And more intolerably humiliated,
  The neck submissive of the prosperous foe,
  Than his whom scorn saw shuddering in the snow !

December 31, 1881.

QUIA NOMINOR LEO

I

WHAT part is left thee, lion? Ravenous beast,
  Which hadst the world for pasture, and for scope
  And compass of thine homicidal hope
The kingdom of the spirit of man, the feast
Of souls subdued from west to sunless east,
  From blackening north to bloodred south aslope,
  All servile ; earth for footcloth of the pope,
And heaven for chancel-ceiling of the priest ;
Thou that hadst earth by right of rack and rod,
Thou that hadst Rome because thy name was God,
  And by thy creed's gift heaven wherein to dwell ;
Heaven laughs with all his light and might above
That earth has cast thee out of faith and love ;
  Thy part is but the hollow dream of hell.

II

The light of life has faded from thy cause,
  High priest of heaven and hell and purgatory :
  Thy lips are loud with strains of oldworld story,
But the red prey was rent out of thy paws

Long since : and they that dying brake down thy laws
   Have with the fires of death-enkindled glory
   Put out the flame that faltered on thy hoary
High altars, waning with the world's applause.
This Italy was Dante's : Bruno died
Here : Campanella, too sublime for pride,
   Endured thy God's worst here, and hence went home.
And what art thou, that time's full tide should shrink
For thy sake downward ?   What art thou, to think
   Thy God shall give thee back for birthright Rome ?

January 1882.

THE CHANNEL TUNNEL

Not for less love, all glorious France, to thee,
 " Sweet enemy " called in days long since at end,
 Now found and hailed of England sweeter friend,
Bright sister of our freedom now, being free ;
Not for less love or faith in friendship we
 Whose love burnt ever toward thee reprehend
 The vile vain greed whose pursy dreams portend
Between our shores suppression of the sea.
Not by dull toil of blind mechanic art
Shall these be linked for no man's force to part
 Nor length of years and changes to divide,
But union only of trust and loving heart
 And perfect faith in freedom strong to abide
 And spirit at one with spirit on either side.

April 3, 1882.

SIR WILLIAM GOMM

I

At threescore years and five aroused anew
  To rule in India, forth a soldier went
  On whose bright-fronted youth fierce war had spent
Its iron stress of storm, till glory grew
Full as the red sun waned on Waterloo.
  Landing, he met the word from England sent
  Which bade him yield up rule : and he, content,
Resigned it, as a mightier warrior's due ;
And wrote as one rejoicing to record
That " from the first " his royal heart was lord
  Of its own pride or pain ; that thought was none
Therein save this, that in her perilous strait
England, whose womb brings forth her sons so great,
  Should choose to serve her first her mightiest son.

II

Glory beyond all flight of warlike fame
  Go with the warrior's memory who preferred
  To praise of men whereby men's hearts are stirred,
And acclamation of his own proud name

With blare of trumpet-blasts and sound and flame
  Of pageant honour, and the titular word
  That only wins men worship of the herd,
His country's sovereign good ; who overcame
Pride, wrath, and hope of all high chance on earth,
For this land's love that gave his great heart birth.
  O nursling of the sea-winds and the sea,
Immortal England, goddess ocean-born,
What shall thy children fear, what strengths not scorn,
  While children of such mould are born to thee ?

EUTHANATOS

In memory of Mrs. Thellusson

Forth of our ways and woes,
Forth of the winds and snows,
A white soul soaring goes,
   Winged like a dove :
So sweet, so pure, so clear,
So heavenly tempered here,
Love need not hope or fear her changed above

Ere dawned her day to die,
So heavenly, that on high
Change could not glorify
   Nor death refine her :
Pure gold of perfect love,
On earth like heaven's own dove,
She cannot wear, above, a smile diviner.

Her voice in heaven's own quire
Can sound no heavenlier lyre
Than here : no purer fire
   Her soul can soar :
No sweeter stars her eyes
In unimagined skies
Beyond our sight can rise than here before.

Hardly long years had shed
Their shadows on her head :
Hardly we think her dead,
  Who hardly thought her
Old : hardly can believe
The grief our hearts receive
And wonder while they grieve, as wrong were wrought
      her.

But though strong grief be strong
No word or thought of wrong
May stain the trembling song,
  Wring the bruised heart,
That sounds or sighs its faint
Low note of love, nor taint
Grief for so sweet a saint, when such depart.

A saint whose perfect soul,
With perfect love for goal,
Faith hardly might control,
  Creeds might not harden :
A flower more splendid far
Than the most radiant star
Seen here of all that are in God's own garden.

Surely the stars we see
Rise and relapse as we,
And change and set, may be
  But shadows too :
But spirits that man's lot
Could neither mar nor spot
Like these false lights are not, being heavenly true.

Not like these dying lights
Of worlds whose glory smites
The passage of the nights
   Through heaven's blind prison :
Not like their souls who see,
If thought fly far and free,
No heavenlier heaven to be for souls rerisen.

A soul wherein love shone
Even like the sun, alone,
With fervour of its own
   And splendour fed,
Made by no creeds less kind
Toward souls by none confined,
Could Death's self quench or blind, Love's self were
   dead.

February 4, 1881.

FIRST AND LAST

Upon the borderlands of being,
  Where life draws hardly breath
Between the lights and shadows fleeing
  Fast as a word one saith,
Two flowers rejoice our eyesight, seeing
  The dawns of birth and death.

Behind the babe his dawn is lying
  Half risen with notes of mirth
From all the winds about it flying
  Through new-born heaven and earth :
Before bright age his day for dying
  Dawns equal-eyed with birth.

Equal the dews of even and dawn,
  Equal the sun's eye seen
A hand's breadth risen and half withdrawn :
  But no bright hour between
Brings aught so bright by stream or lawn
  To noonday growths of green.

Which flower of life may smell the sweeter
  To love's insensual sense,
Which fragrance move with offering meeter
  His soothed omnipotence,
Being chosen as fairer or as fleeter,
  Borne hither or borne hence,

Love's foiled omniscience knows not : this
   Were more than all he knows
With all his lore of bale and bliss,
   The choice of rose and rose,
One red as lips that touch with his,
   One white as moonlit snows.

No hope is half so sweet and good,
   No dream of saint or sage
So fair as these are : no dark mood
   But these might best assuage ;
The sweet red rose of babyhood,
   The white sweet rose of age.

LINES ON THE DEATH OF EDWARD JOHN TRELAWNY

LAST high star of the years whose thunder
　　Still men's listening remembrance hears,
　　Last light left of our fathers' years,
Watched with honour and hailed with wonder
Thee too then have the years borne under.
　　Thou too then hast regained thy peers.

Wings that warred with the winds of morning,
　　Storm-winds rocking the red great dawn,
　　Close at last, and a film is drawn
Over the eyes of the storm-bird, scorning
Now no longer the loud wind's warning,
　　Waves that threaten or waves that fawn.

Peers were none of thee left us living,
　　Peers of theirs we shall see no more.
　　Eight years over the full fourscore
Knew thee : now shalt thou sleep, forgiving
All griefs past of the wild world's giving,
　　Moored at last on the stormless shore.

Worldwide liberty's lifelong lover,
　　Lover no less of the strength of song,
　　Sea-king, swordsman, hater of wrong,
Over thy dust that the dust shall cover
Comes my song as a bird to hover,
　　Borne of its will as of wings along.

Cherished of thee were this brief song's brothers
  Now that follows them, cherishing thee.
  Over the tides and the tideless sea
Soft as a smile of the earth our mother's
Flies it faster than all those others,
  First of the troop at thy tomb to be.

Memories of Greece and the mountain's hollow
  Guarded alone of thy loyal sword
  Hold thy name for our hearts in ward :
Yet more fain are our hearts to follow
One way now with the southward swallow
  Back to the grave of the man their lord.

Heart of hearts, art thou moved not, hearing
  Surely, if hearts of the dead may hear,
  Whose true heart it is now draws near ?
Surely the sense of it thrills thee, cheering
Darkness and death with the news now nearing—
  Shelley, Trelawny rejoins thee here.

ADIEUX À MARIE STUART

I

QUEEN, for whose house my fathers fought,
  With hopes that rose and fell,
Red star of boyhood's fiery thought,
  Farewell.

They gave their lives, and I, my queen,
  Have given you of my life,
Seeing your brave star burn high between
  Men's strife.

The strife that lightened round their spears
  Long since fell still : so long
Hardly may hope to last in years
  My song.

But still through strife of time and thought
  Your light on me too fell :
Queen, in whose name we sang or fought,
  Farewell.

II

There beats no heart on either border
  Wherethrough the north blasts blow
But keeps your memory as a warder
  His beacon-fire aglow.

Long since it fired with love and wonder
    Mine, for whose April age
Blithe midsummer made banquet under
    The shade of Hermitage.

Soft sang the burn's blithe notes, that gather
    Strength to ring true :
And air and trees and sun and heather
    Remembered you.

Old border ghosts of fight or fairy
    Or love or teen,
These they forgot, remembering Mary
    The Queen.

III

Queen once of Scots and ever of ours
    Whose sires brought forth for you
Their lives to strew your way like flowers,
    Adieu.

Dead is full many a dead man's name
    Who died for you this long
Time past : shall this too fare the same,
    My song ?

But surely, though it die or live,
    Your face was worth
All that a man may think to give
    On earth.

No darkness cast of years between
    Can darken you :
Man's love will never bid my queen
    Adieu.

IV

Love hangs like light about your name
  As music round the shell :
No heart can take of you a tame
    Farewell.

Yet, when your very face was seen,
  Ill gifts were yours for giving :
Love gat strange guerdons of my queen
    When living.

O diamond heart unflawed and clear,
  The whole world's crowning jewel !
Was ever heart so deadly dear
    So cruel ?

Yet none for you of all that bled
  Grudged once one drop that fell :
Not one to life reluctant said
    Farewell.

V

Strange love they have given you, love disloyal,
  Who mock with praise your name,
To leave a head so rare and royal
    Too low for praise or blame.

You could not love nor hate, they tell us,
  You had nor sense nor sting :
In God's name, then, what plague befell us
    To fight for such a thing ?

" Some faults the gods will give," to fetter
    Man's highest intent :
But surely you were something better
    Than innocent !

No maid that strays with steps unwary
    Through snares unseen,
But one to live and die for ; Mary,
    The Queen.

VI

Forgive them all their praise, who blot
    Your fame with praise of you :
Then love may say, and falter not,
    Adieu.

Yet some you hardly would forgive
    Who did you much less wrong
Once : but resentment should not live
    Too long.

They never saw your lip's bright bow,
    Your swordbright eyes,
The bluest of heavenly things below
    The skies.

Clear eyes that love's self finds most like
    A swordblade's blue,
A swordblade's ever keen to strike,
    Adieu.

VII

Though all things breathe or sound of fight
    That yet make up your spell,
To bid you were to bid the light
    Farewell.

Farewell the song says only, being
    A star whose race is run :
Farewell the soul says never, seeing
    The sun.

Yet, wellnigh as with flash of tears,
    The song must say but so
That took your praise up twenty years
    Ago.

More bright than stars or moons that vary,
    Sun kindling heaven and hell,
Here, after all these years, Queen Mary,
    Farewell.

HERSE

WHEN grace is given us ever to behold
    A child some sweet months old,
Love, laying across our lips his finger, saith,
    Smiling, with bated breath,
Hush! for the holiest thing that lives is here,
    And heaven's own heart how near!
How dare we, that may gaze not on the sun,
    Gaze on this verier one?
Heart, hold thy peace; eyes, be cast down for
       shame;
    Lips, breathe not yet its name.
In heaven they know what name to call it; we,
    How should we know? For, see!
The adorable sweet living marvellous
    Strange light that lightens us
Who gaze, desertless of such glorious grace,
    Full in a babe's warm face!
All roses that the morning rears are nought,
    All stars not worth a thought,
Set this one star against them, or suppose
    As rival this one rose.
What price could pay with earth's whole weight of
       gold
    One least flushed roseleaf's fold
Of all this dimpling store of smiles that shine
    From each warm curve and line,

Each charm of flower-sweet flesh, to reillume
 The dappled rose-red bloom
Of all its dainty body, honey-sweet
 Clenched hands and curled-up feet,
That on the roses of the dawn have trod
 As they came down from God,
And keep the flush and colour that the sky
 Takes when the sun comes nigh,
And keep the likeness of the smile their grace
 Evoked on God's own face
When, seeing this work of his most heavenly mood,
 He saw that it was good?
For all its warm sweet body seems one smile,
 And mere men's love too vile
To meet it, or with eyes that worship dims
 Read o'er the little limbs,
Read all the book of all their beauties o'er,
 Rejoice, revere, adore,
Bow down and worship each delight in turn,
 Laugh, wonder, yield, and yearn.
But when our trembling kisses dare, yet dread,
 Even to draw nigh its head,
And touch, and scarce with touch or breath surprise
 Its mild miraculous eyes
Out of their viewless vision—O, what then,
 What may be said of men?
What speech may name a new-born child? what
  word
 Earth ever spake or heard?
The best men's tongue that ever glory knew
 Called that a drop of dew
Which from the breathing creature's kindly womb
 Came forth in blameless bloom.
We have no word, as had those men most high,
 To call a baby by.

Rose, ruby, lily, pearl of stormless seas—
    A better word than these,
A better sign it was than flower or gem
    That love revealed to them :
They knew that whence comes light or quickening
      flame,
    Thence only this thing came,
And only might be likened of our love
    To somewhat born above,
Not even to sweetest things dropped else on earth,
    Only to dew's own birth.
Nor doubt we but their sense was heavenly true,
    Babe, when we gaze on you,
A dew-drop out of heaven whose colours are
    More bright than sun or star,
As now, ere watching love dare fear or hope,
    Lips, hands, and eyelids ope,
And all your life is mixed with earthly leaven.
    O child, what news from heaven ?

TWINS

AFFECTIONATELY INSCRIBED TO W. M. R. AND L. R.

APRIL, on whose wings
Ride all gracious things,
Like the star that brings
   All things good to man,
Ere his light, that yet
Makes the month shine, set,
And fair May forget
   Whence her birth began,

Brings, as heart would choose,
Sound of golden news,
Bright as kindling dews
   When the dawn begins;
Tidings clear as mirth,
Sweet as air and earth
Now that hail the birth,
   Twice thus blest, of twins.

In the lovely land
Where with hand in hand
Lovers wedded stand
   Other joys before
Made your mixed life sweet:
Now, as Time sees meet,
Three glad blossoms greet
   Two glad blossoms more.

Fed with sun and dew,
While your joys were new,
First arose and grew
　　One bright olive-shoot :
Then a fair and fine
Slip of warm-haired pine
Felt the sweet sun shine
　　On its leaf and fruit.

And it wore for mark
Graven on the dark
Beauty of its bark
　　That the noblest name
Worn in song of old
By the king whose bold
Hand had fast in hold
　　All the flower of fame.

Then, with southern skies
Flattered in her eyes,
Which, in lovelier wise
　　Yet, reflect their blue
Brightened more, being bright
Here with life's delight,
And with love's live light
　　Glorified anew,

Came, as fair as came
One who bore her name
(She that broke as flame
　　From the swan-shell white),
Crowned with tender hair
Only, but more fair
Than all queens that were
　　Themes of oldworld fight,

Of your flowers the third
Bud, or new-fledged bird
In your hearts' nest heard
   Murmuring like a dove
Bright as those that drew
Over waves where blew
No loud wind the blue
   Heaven-hued car of love.

Not the glorious grace
Even of that one face
Potent to displace
   All the towers of Troy
Surely shone more clear
Once with childlike cheer
Than this child's face here
   Now with living joy.

After these again
Here in April's train
Breaks the bloom of twain
   Blossoms in one birth
For a crown of May
On the front of day
When he takes his way
   Over heaven and earth

Half a heavenly thing
Given from heaven to Spring
By the sun her king,
   Half a tender toy,
Seems a child of curl
Yet too soft to twirl ;
Seems the flower-sweet girl
   By the flower-bright boy.

All the kind gods' grace,
All their love, embrace
Ever either face,
    Ever brood above them:
All soft wings of hours
Screen them as with flowers
From all beams and showers:
    All life's seasons love them.

When the dews of sleep
Falling lightliest keep
Eyes too close to peep
    Forth and laugh off rest,
Joy from face to feet
Fill them, as is meet:
Life to them be sweet
    As their mother's breast.

When those dews are dry,
And in day's bright eye
Looking full they lie
    Bright as rose and pearl,
All returns of joy
Pure of time's alloy
Bless the rose-red boy,
    Guard the rose-white girl.

POSTSCRIPT

Friends, if I could take
Half a note from Blake
Or but one verse make
    Of the Conqueror's mine,

Better than my best
Song above your nest
I would sing : the quest
  Now seems too divine.

April 28, 1881.

THE SALT OF THE EARTH

If childhood were not in the world,
  But only men and women grown ;
No baby-locks in tendrils curled,
  No baby-blossoms blown ;

Though men were stronger, women fairer,
  And nearer all delights in reach,
And verse and music uttered rarer
  Tones of more godlike speech ;

Though the utmost life of life's best hours
  Found, as it cannot now find, words ;
Though desert sands were sweet as flowers
  And flowers could sing like birds,

But children never heard them, never
  They felt a child's foot leap and run
This were a drearier star than ever
  Yet looked upon the sun.

SEVEN YEARS OLD

I

SEVEN white roses on one tree,
  Seven white loaves of blameless leaven,
Seven white sails on one soft sea,
Seven white swans on one lake's lee,
  Seven white flowerlike stars in heaven,
All are types unmeet to be
  For a birthday's crown of seven.

II

Not the radiance of the roses,
  Not the blessing of the bread,
Not the breeze that ere day grows is
Fresh for sails and swans, and closes
  Wings above the sun's grave spread,
When the starshine on the snows is
  Sweet as sleep on sorrow shed,

III

Nothing sweetest, nothing best,
  Holds so good and sweet a treasure
As the love wherewith once blest
Joy grows holy, grief takes rest,
  Life, half tired with hours to measure,
Fills his eyes and lips and breast
  With most light and breath of pleasure ;

IV

As the rapture unpolluted,
   As the passion undefiled,
By whose force all pains heart-rooted
Are transfigured and transmuted,
   Recompensed and reconciled,
Through the imperial, undisputed,
   Present godhead of a child.

V

Brown bright eyes and fair bright head,
   Worth a worthier crown than this is,
Worth a worthier song instead,
Sweet grave wise round mouth, full fed
   With the joy of love, whose bliss is
More than mortal wine and bread,
   Lips whose words are sweet as kisses.

VI

Little hands so glad of giving,
   Little heart so glad of love,
Little soul so glad of living,
While the strong swift hours are weaving
   Light with darkness woven above,
Time for mirth and time for grieving,
   Plume of raven and plume of dove,

VII

I can give you but a word
   Warm with love therein for leaven,
But a song that falls unheard
Yet on ears of sense unstirred
   Yet by song so far from heaven,
Whence you came the brightest bird,
   Seven years since, of seven times seven.

EIGHT YEARS OLD

I

Sun, whom the faltering snow-cloud fears,
  Rise, let the time of year be May,
Speak now the word that April hears,
  Let March have all his royal way;
Bid all spring raise in winter's ears
  All tunes her children hear or play,
Because the crown of eight glad years
  On one bright head is set to-day.

II

What matters cloud or sun to-day
  To him who wears the wreath of years
So many, and all like flowers at play
  With wind and sunshine, while his ears
Hear only song on every way?
  More sweet than spring triumphant hears
Ring through the revel-rout of May
  Are these, the notes that winter fears.

III

Strong-hearted winter knows and fears
  The music made of love at play,
Or haply loves the tune he hears
  From hearts fulfilled with flowering May,

Whose molten music thaws his ears
 Late frozen, deaf but yesterday
To sounds of dying and dawning years,
 Now quickened on his deathward way.

IV

For deathward now lies winter's way
 Down the green vestibule of years
That each year brightens day by day
 With flower and shower till hope scarce fears
And fear grows wholly hope of May.
 But we—the music in our ears
Made of love's pulses as they play
 The heart alone that makes it hears.

V

The heart it is that plays and hears
 High salutation of to-day.
Tongue falters, hand shrinks back, song fears
 Its own unworthiness to play
Fit music for those eight sweet years,
 Or sing their blithe accomplished way.
No song quite worth a young child's ears
 Broke ever even from birds in May.

VI

There beats not in the heart of May,
 When summer hopes and springtide fears,
There falls not from the height of day,
 When sunlight speaks and silence hears,

So sweet a psalm as children play
   And sing, each hour of all their years,
Each moment of their lovely way,
   And know not how it thrills our ears.

VII

Ah child, what are we, that our ears
   Should hear you singing on your way,
Should have this happiness?   The years
   Whose hurrying wings about us play
Are not like yours, whose flower-time fears
   Nought worse than sunlit showers in May,
Being sinless as the spring, that hears
   Her own heart praise her every day.

VIII

Yet we too triumph in the day
   That bare, to entrance our eyes and ears,
To lighten daylight, and to play
   Such notes as darkness knows and fears,
The child whose face illumes our way,
   Whose voice lifts up the heart that hears,
Whose hand is as the hand of May
   To bring us flowers from eight full years.

February 4, 1882.

COMPARISONS

CHILD, when they say that others
   Have been or are like you,
Babes fit to be your brotners,
   Sweet human drops of dew,
Bright fruit of mortal motners,
   What should one say or ao?

We know the thought is treason,
   We feel the dream absurd ;
A claim rebuked of reason,
   That withers at a word :
For never shone the season
   That bore so blithe a bird.

Some smiles may seem as merry,
   Some glances gleam as wise,
From lips as like a cherry
   And scarce less gracious eyes ;
Eyes browner than a berry,
   Lips red as morning's rise.

But never yet rang laughter
   So sweet in gladdened ears
Through wall and floor and rafter
   As all this household hears
And rings response thereafter
   Till cloudiest weather clears.

When those your chosen of all men,
　Whose honey never cloys,
Two lights whose smiles enthrall men,
　Were called at your age boys,
Those mighty men, while small men,
　Could make no merrier noise.

Our Shakespeare, surely, daffed not
　More lightly pain aside
From radiant lips that quaffed not
　Of forethought's tragic tide :
Our Dickens, doubtless, laughed not
　More loud with life's first pride.

The dawn were not more cheerless
　With neither light nor dew
Than we without the fearless
　Clear laugh that thrills us through :
If ever child stood peerless,
　Love knows that child is you.

WHAT IS DEATH?

Looking on a page where stood
Graven of old on old-world wood
Death, and by the grave's edge grim,
Pale, the young man facing him,
Asked my well-beloved of me
Once what strange thing this might be,
    Gaunt and great of limb.

Death, I told him : and, surprise
Deepening more his wildwood eyes
(Like some sweet fleet thing's whose breath
Speaks all spring though nought it saith),
Up he turned his rosebright face
Glorious with its seven years' grace,
    Asking—What is death?

A CHILD'S PITY

No sweeter thing than children's ways and wiles,
   Surely, we say, can gladden eyes and ears :
Yet sometime sweeter than their words or smiles
   Are even their tears.

To one for once a piteous tale was read,
   How, when the murderous mother crocodile
Was slain, her fierce brood famished, and lay dead,
   Starved, by the Nile.

In vast green reed-beds on the vast grey slime
   Those monsters motherless and helpless lay,
Perishing only for the parent's crime
   Whose seed were they.

Hours after, toward the dusk, our blithe small bird
   Of Paradise, who has our hearts in keeping,
Was heard or seen, but hardly seen or heard,
   For pity weeping.

He was so sorry, sitting still apart,
   For the poor little crocodiles, he said.
Six years had given him, for an angel's heart,
   A child's instead.

Feigned tears the false beasts shed for murderous
    ends,
  We know from travellers' tales of crocodiles :
But these tears wept upon them of my friend's   .
  Outshine his smiles.

What heavenliest angels of what heavenly city
  Could match the heavenly heart in children here ?
The heart that hallowing all things with its pity
  Casts out all fear ?

So lovely, so divine, so dear their laughter
  Seems to us, we know not what could be more
    dear :
But lovelier yet we see the sign thereafter
  Of such a tear.

With sense of love half laughing and half weeping
  We met your tears, our small sweet-spirited
    friend :
Let your love have us in its heavenly keeping
  To life's last end.

A CHILD'S LAUGHTER

ALL the bells of heaven may ring,
All the birds of heaven may sing,
All the wells on earth may spring,
All the winds on earth may bring
　All sweet sounds together ;
Sweeter far than all things heard,
Hand of harper, tone of bird,
Sound of woods at sundawn stirred,
Welling water's winsome word,
　Wind in warm wan weather,

One thing yet there is, that none
Hearing ere its chime be done
Knows not well the sweetest one
Heard of man beneath the sun,
　Hoped in heaven hereafter ;
Soft and strong and loud and light,
Very sound of very light
Heard from morning's rosiest height,
When the soul of all delight
　Fills a child's clear laughter.

Golden bells of welcome rolled
Never forth such notes, nor told
Hours so blithe in tones so bold,
As the radiant mouth of gold
    Here that rings forth heaven.
If the golden-crested wren
Were a nightingale—why, then,
Something seen and heard of men
Might be half as sweet as when
    Laughs a child of seven.

A CHILD'S THANKS

How low soe'er men rank us,
  How high soe'er we win,
The children far above us
Dwell, and they deign to love us,
With lovelier love than ours,
And smiles more sweet than flowers ;
As though the sun should thank us
  For letting light come in.

With too divine complaisance,
  Whose grace misleads them thus,
Being, in heavenly blindness
They call our worship kindness,
Our pebble-gift a gem :
They think us good to them,
Whose glance, whose breath, whose presence,
  Are gifts too good for us.

The poet high and hoary
  Of meres that mountains bind
Felt his great heart more often
Yearn, and its proud strength soften
From stern to tenderer mood,
At thought of gratitude
Shown than of song or story
  He heard of hearts unkind.

But with what words for token
  And what adoring tears
Of reverence risen to passion,
In what glad prostrate fashion
Of spirit and soul subdued,
May man show gratitude
For thanks of children spoken
  That hover in his ears ?

The angels laugh, your brothers,
  Child, hearing you thank me,
With eyes whence night grows sunny,
And touch of lips like honey,
And words like honey-dew :
But how shall I thank you ?
For gifts above all others
  What guerdon-gift may be ?

What wealth of words caressing,
  What choice of songs found best,
Would seem not as derision,
Found vain beside the vision
And glory from above
Shown in a child's heart's love ?
His part in life is blessing ;
  Ours, only to be blest.

A CHILD'S BATTLES

πὺξ ἀρετὰν εὑρών.—PINDAR.

PRAISE of the knights of old
May sleep : their tale is told,
    And no man cares :
The praise which fires our lips is
A knight's whose fame eclipses
      All of theirs.

The ruddiest light in heaven
Blazed as his birth-star seven
    Long years ago :
All glory crown that old year
Which brought our stout small soldier
      With the snow !

Each baby born has one
Star, for his friends a sun,
    The first of stars :
And we, the more we scan it,
The more grow sure your planet,
      Child, was Mars.

For each one flower, perchance,
Blooms as his cognizance :
    The snowdrop chill,

The violet unbeholden,
For some : for you the golden
        Daffodil.

Erect, a fighting flower,
It breasts the breeziest hour
        That ever blew.
And bent or broke things brittle
Or frail, unlike a little
        Knight like you.

Its flower is firm and fresh
And stout like sturdiest flesh
        Of children : all
The strenuous blast that parches
Spring hurts it not till March is
        Near his fall.

If winds that prate and fret
Remark, rebuke, regret,
        Lament, or blame
The brave plant's martial passion,
It keeps its own free fashion
        All the same.

We that would fain seem wise
Assume grave mouths and eyes
        Whose looks reprove
Too much delight in battle :
But your great heart our prattle
        Cannot move.

We say, small children should
Be placid, mildly good
        And blandly meek :

Whereat the broad smile rushes
Full on your lips, and flushes
    All your cheek.

If all the stars that are
Laughed out, and every star
    Could here be heard,
Such peals of golden laughter
We should not hear, as after
    Such a word.

For all the storm saith, still,
Stout stands the daffodil :
    For all we say,
Howe'er he look demurely,
Our martialist will surely
    Have his way.

We may not bind with bands
Those large and liberal hands,
    Nor stay from fight,
Nor hold them back from giving :
No lean mean laws of living
    Bind a knight.

And always here of old
Such gentle hearts and bold
    Our land has bred :
How durst her eye rest else on
The glory shed from Nelson
    Quick and dead ?

Shame were it, if but one
Such once were born her son,
    That one to have borne,

And brought him ne'er a brother :
His praise should bring his mother
  Shame and scorn.

A child high-souled as he
Whose manhood shook the sea
  Smiles haply here :
His face, where love lies basking,
With bright shut mouth seems asking,
  What is fear ?

The sunshine-coloured fists
Beyond his dimpling wrists
  Were never closed
For saving or for sparing—
For only deeds of daring
  Predisposed.

Unclenched, the gracious hands
Let slip their gifts like sands
  Made rich with ore
That tongues of beggars ravish
From small stout hands so lavish
  Of their store.

Sweet hardy kindly hands
Like these were his that stands
  With heel on gorge
Seen trampling down the dragon
On sign or flask or flagon,
  Sweet Saint George.

Some tournament, perchance,
Of hands that couch no lance,
  Might mark this spot

Your lists, if here some pleasant
Small Guenevere were present,
        Launcelot.

My brave bright flower, you need
No foolish song, nor heed
        It more than spring
The sighs of winter stricken
Dead when your haunts requicken
        Here, my king.

Yet O, how hardly may
The wheels of singing stay
        That whirl along
Bright paths whence echo raises
The phantom of your praises,
        Child, my song !

Beyond all other things
That give my words fleet wings,
        Fleet wings and strong,
You set their jesses ringing
Till hardly can I, singing,
        Stint my song.

But all things better, friend,
And worse must find an end :
        And, right or wrong,
'Tis time, lest rhyme should baffle,
I doubt, to put a snaffle
        On my song.

And never may your ear
Aught harsher hear or fear,
        Nor wolfish night

Nor dog-toothed winter snarling
Behind your steps, my darling
　　My delight !

For all the gifts you give
Me, dear, each day you live,
　　Of thanks above
All thanks that could be spoken
Take not my song in token,
　　Take my love。

A CHILD'S FUTURE

What will it please you, my darling, hereafter to be?
Fame upon land will you look for, or glory by sea?
Gallant your life will be always, and all of it free.

Free as the wind when the heart of the twilight is
stirred
Eastward, and sounds from the springs of the sunrise
are heard :
Free—and we know not another as infinite word.

Darkness or twilight or sunlight may compass us
round,
Hate may arise up against us, or hope may confound ;
Love may forsake us ; yet may not the spirit be bound.

Free in oppression of grief as in ardour of joy
Still may the soul be, and each to her strength as a
toy :
Free in the glance of the man as the smile of the boy.

Freedom alone is the salt and the spirit that gives
Life, and without her is nothing that verily lives :
Death cannot slay her : she laughs upon death and
forgives.

Brightest and hardiest of roses anear and afar
Glitters the blithe little face of you, round as a star :
Liberty bless you and keep you to be as you are.

England and liberty bless you and keep you to be
Worthy the name of their child and the sight of their
    sea :
Fear not at all ; for a slave, if he fears not, is free.

SONNETS

ON

ENGLISH DRAMATIC POETS

(1590–1650)

I

CHRISTOPHER MARLOWE

CROWNED, girdled, garbed and shod with light and fire,
  Son first-born of the morning, sovereign star !
  Soul nearest ours of all, that wert most far,
Most far off in the abysm of time, thy lyre
Hung highest above the dawn-enkindled quire
  Where all ye sang together, all that are,
  And all the starry songs behind thy car
Rang sequence, all our souls acclaim thee sire.

" If all the pens that ever poets held
  Had fed the feeling of their masters' thoughts,"
  And as with rush of hurtling chariots
The flight of all their spirits were impelled
  Toward one great end, thy glory—nay, not then,
  Not yet might'st thou be praised enough of men.

II

WILLIAM SHAKESPEARE

Not if men's tongues and angels' all in one
  Spake, might the word be said that might speak
    Thee.
  Streams, winds, woods, flowers, fields, mountains,
    yea, the sea,
What power is in them all to praise the sun?
His praise is this,—he can be praised of none.
  Man, woman, child, praise God for him; but he
  Exults not to be worshipped, but to be.
He is; and, being, beholds his work well done.
All joy, all glory, all sorrow, all strength, all mirth,
Are his: without him, day were night on earth.
  Time knows not his from time's own period.
All lutes, all harps, all viols, all flutes, all lyres,
Fall dumb before him ere one string suspires.
  All stars are angels; but the sun is God.

III

BEN JONSON

BROAD-BASED, broad-fronted, bounteous, multiform,
  With many a valley impleached with ivy and vine,
  Wherein the springs of all the streams run wine,
And many a crag full-faced against the storm,
The mountain where thy Muse's feet made warm
  Those lawns that revelled with her dance divine
  Shines yet with fire as it was wont to shine
From tossing torches round the dance aswarm.

Nor less, high-stationed on the grey grave heights,
High-thoughted seers with heaven's heart-kindling
        lights
  Hold converse : and the herd of meaner things
Knows or by fiery scourge or fiery shaft
When wrath on thy broad brows has risen, and
        laughed
  Darkening thy soul with shadow of thunderous
        wings.

IV

BEAUMONT AND FLETCHER

AN hour ere sudden sunset fired the west,
  Arose two stars upon the pale deep east.
  The hall of heaven was clear for night's high feast,
Yet was not yet day's fiery heart at rest.
Love leapt up from his mother's burning breast
  To see those warm twin lights, as day decreased,
  Wax wider, till when all the sun had ceased
As suns they shone from evening's kindled crest.
Across them and between, a quickening fire,
Flamed Venus, laughing with appeased desire.
  Their dawn, scarce lovelier for the gleam of tears,
Filled half the hollow shell 'twixt heaven and earth
With sound like moonlight, mingling moan and mirth,
  Which rings and glitters down the darkling years.

V

PHILIP MASSINGER

CLOUDS here and there arisen an hour past noon
   Chequered our English heaven with lengthening
      bars
   And shadow and sound of wheel-winged thunder-
      cars
Assembling strength to put forth tempest soon,
When the clear still warm concord of thy tune
   Rose under skies unscared by reddening Mars
   Yet, like a sound of silver speech of stars,
With full mild flame as of the mellowing moon.
Grave and great-hearted Massinger, thy face
High melancholy lights with loftier grace
   Than gilds the brows of revel : sad and wise,
The spirit of thought that moved thy deeper song,
Sorrow serene in soft calm scorn of wrong,
   Speaks patience yet from thy majestic eyes.

VI

JOHN FORD

HEW hard the marble from the mountain's heart
  Where hardest night holds fast in iron gloom
  Gems brighter than an April dawn in bloom,
That his Memnonian likeness thence may start
Revealed, whose hand with high funereal art
  Carved night, and chiselled shadow : be the tomb
  That speaks him famous graven with signs of doom
Intrenched inevitably in lines athwart,
As on some thunder-blasted Titan's brow
  His record of rebellion.   Not the day
    Shall strike forth music from so stern a chord,
Touching this marble : darkness, none knows how,
  And stars impenetrable of midnight, may.
    So looms the likeness of thy soul, John Ford.

VII

JOHN WEBSTER

THUNDER : the flesh quails, and the soul bows down.
  Night: east, west, south, and northward, very night.
  Star upon struggling star strives into sight,
Star after shuddering star the deep storms drown.
The very throne of night, her very crown,
  A man lays hand on, and usurps her right.
  Song from the highest of heaven's imperious height
Shoots, as a fire to smite some towering town.
Rage, anguish, harrowing fear, heart-crazing crime,
Make monstrous all the murderous face of Time
  Shown in the spheral orbit of a glass
Revolving. Earth cries out from all her graves.
Frail, on frail rafts, across wide-wallowing waves,
  Shapes here and there of child and mother pass.

VIII

THOMAS DECKER

Out of the depths of darkling life where sin
   Laughs piteously that sorrow should not know
   Her own ill name, nor woe be counted woe ;
Where hate and craft and lust make drearier din
Than sounds through dreams that grief holds revel in ;
   What charm of joy-bells ringing, streams that flow,
   Winds that blow healing in each note they blow,
Is this that the outer darkness hears begin ?

O sweetest heart of all thy time save one,
Star seen for love's sake nearest to the sun,
   Hung lamplike o'er a dense and doleful city,
Not Shakespeare's very spirit, howe'er more great,
Than thine toward man was more compassionate,
   Nor gave Christ praise from lips more sweet with
      pity.

IX

THOMAS MIDDLETON

A WILD moon riding high from cloud to cloud,
  That sees and sees not, glimmering far beneath,
  Hell's children revel along the shuddering heath
With dirge-like mirth and raiment like a shroud :
A worse fair face than witchcraft's, passion-proud,
  With brows blood-flecked behind their bridal
    wreath
  And lips that bade the assassin's sword find sheath
Deep in the heart whereto love's heart was vowed :
A game of close contentious crafts and creeds
  Played till white England bring black Spain to
    shame :
A son's bright sword and brighter soul, whose deeds
  High conscience lights for mother's love and fame ·
Pure gipsy flowers, and poisonous courtly weeds :
  Such tokens and such trophies crown thy name.

X

THOMAS HEYWOOD

Tom, if they loved thee best who called thee Tom,
  What else may all men call thee, seeing thus bright
  Even yet the laughing and the weeping light
That still thy kind old eyes are kindled from?
Small care was thine to assail and overcome
  Time and his child Oblivion : yet of right
  Thy name has part with names of lordlier might
For English love and homely sense of home,
Whose fragrance keeps thy small sweet bayleaf
      young
  And gives it place aloft among thy peers
    Whence many a wreath once higher strong Time
      has hurled :
And this thy praise is sweet on Shakespeare's
      tongue—
  " O good old man, how well in thee appears
    The constant service of the antique world ! "

XI

GEORGE CHAPMAN

HIGH priest of Homer, not elect in vain,
  Deep trumpets blow before thee, shawms behind
  Mix music with the rolling wheels that wind
Slow through the labouring triumph of thy train :
Fierce history, molten in thy forging brain,
  Takes form and fire and fashion from thy mind,
  Tormented and transmuted out of kind :
But howsoe'er thou shift thy strenuous strain,
Like Tailor [1] smooth, like Fisher [2] swollen, and now
  Grim Yarrington [3] scarce bloodier marked than
    thou,
  Then bluff as Mayne's [4] or broad-mouthed Barry's [5]
    glee ;
Proud still with hoar predominance of brow
  And beard like foam swept off the broad blown sea,
  Where'er thou go, men's reverence goes with thee.

[1] Author of *The Hog hath lost his Pearl.*
[2] Author of *Fuimus Troes, or the True Trojans.*
[3] Author of *Two Tragedies in One.*
[4] Author of *The City Match.*
[5] Author of *Ram-Alley, or Merry Tricks.*

XII

JOHN MARSTON

The bitterness of death and bitterer scorn
    Breathes from the broad-leafed aloe-plant whence
      thou
    Wast fain to gather for thy bended brow
A chaplet by no gentler forehead worn.
Grief deep as hell, wrath hardly to be borne,
    Ploughed up thy soul till round the furrowing
      plough
    The strange black soil foamed, as a black beaked
      prow
Bids night-black waves foam where its track has
    torn.
Too faint the phrase for thee that only saith
Scorn bitterer than the bitterness of death
    Pervades the sullen splendour of thy soul,
Where hate and pain make war on force and fraud
And all the strengths of tyrants ; whence unflawed
    It keeps this noble heart of hatred whole.

XIII

JOHN DAY

Day was a full-blown flower in heaven, alive
  With murmuring joy of bees and birds aswarm,
  When in the skies of song yet flushed and warm
With music where all passion seems to strive
For utterance, all things bright and fierce to drive
  Struggling along the splendour of the storm,
  Day for an hour put off his fiery form,
And golden murmurs from a golden hive
Across the strong bright summer wind were heard,
  And laughter soft as smiles from girls at play
  And loud from lips of boys brow-bound with May
Our mightiest age let fall its gentlest word,
When Song, in semblance of a sweet small bird,
  Lit fluttering on the light swift hand of Day.

XIV

JAMES SHIRLEY

THE dusk of day's decline was hard on dark
   When evening trembled round thy glowworm lamp
   That shone across her shades and dewy damp
A small clear beacon whose benignant spark
Was gracious yet for loiterers' eyes to mark,
   Though changed the watchword of our English
      camp
   Since the outposts rang round Marlowe's lion
      ramp,
When thy steed's pace went ambling round Hyde
      Park.

And in the thickening twilight under thee
Walks Davenant, pensive in the paths where he,
The blithest throat that ever carolled love
   In music made of morning's merriest heart,
Glad Suckling, stumbled from his seat above
   And reeled on slippery roads of alien art.

XV

THE TRIBE OF BENJAMIN

Sons born of many a loyal Muse to Ben,
  All true-begotten, warm with wine or ale,
  Bright from the broad light of its presence, hail!
Prince Randolph, nighest his throne of all his men,
Being highest in spirit and heart who hailed him
    then
  King, nor might other spread so blithe a sail :
  Cartwright, a soul pent in with narrower pale,
Praised of thy sire for manful might of pen :
Marmion, whose verse keeps alway keen and fine
The perfume of their Apollonian wine
  Who shared with that stout sire of all and thee
The exuberant chalice of his echoing shrine :
  Is not your praise writ broad in gold which he
  Inscribed, that all who praise his name should see ?

XVI

ANONYMOUS PLAYS:

"ARDEN OF FEVERSHAM"

MOTHER whose womb brought forth our man of men,
  Mother of Shakespeare, whom all time acclaims
  Queen therefore, sovereign queen of English dames,
Throned higher than sat thy sonless empress then,
Was it thy son's young passion-guided pen
  Which drew, reflected from encircling flames,
  A figure marked by the earlier of thy names
Wife, and from all her wedded kinswomen
Marked by the sign of murderess?   Pale and great,
  Great in her grief and sin, but in her death
  And anguish of her penitential breath
Greater than all her sin or sin-born fate,
  She stands, the holocaust of dark desire,
  Clothed round with song for ever as with fire.

XVII

ANONYMOUS PLAYS

YE too, dim watchfires of some darkling hour,
  Whose fame forlorn time saves not nor proclaims
  For ever, but forgetfulness defames
And darkness and the shadow of death devour,
Lift up ye too your light, put forth your power,
  Let the far twilight feel your soft small flames
  And smile, albeit night name not even their names,
Ghost by ghost passing, flower blown down on flower:
That sweet-tongued shadow, like a star's that passed
Singing, and light was from its darkness cast
  To paint the face of Painting fair with praise:[1]
And that wherein forefigured smiles the pure
Fraternal face of Wordsworth's Elidure
  Between two child-faced masks of merrier days.[2]

[1] *Doctor Dodypol.*　　　[2] *Nobody and Somebody.*

XVIII

ANONYMOUS PLAYS

MORE yet and more, and yet we mark not all
　　The Warning fain to bid fair women heed
　　Its hard brief note of deadly doom and deed ; [1]
The verse that strewed too thick with flowers the hall
Whence Nero watched his fiery festival ; [2]
　　That iron page wherein men's eyes who read
　　See, bruised and marred between two babes that
　　　bleed,
A mad red-handed husband's martyr fall ; [3]
The scene which crossed and streaked with mirth the
　　　strife
Of Henry with his sons and witchlike wife ; [4]
And that sweet pageant of the kindly fiend,
　　Who, seeing three friends in spirit and heart made
　　　one,
Crowned with good hap the true-love wiles he screened
　　In the pleached lanes of pleasant Edmonton. [5]

[1] *A Warning for Fair Women.*
[2] *The Tragedy of Nero.*
[3] *A Yorkshire Tragedy.*
[4] *Look about you.*
[5] *The Merry Devil of Edmonton.*

XIX

THE MANY

I

GREENE, garlanded with February's few flowers,
   Ere March came in with Marlowe's rapturous rage:
   Peele, from whose hand the sweet white locks of age
Took the mild chaplet woven of honoured hours :
Nash, laughing hard : Lodge, flushed from lyric
      bowers :
   And Lilly, a goldfinch in a twisted cage
   Fed by some gay great lady's pettish page
Till short sweet songs gush clear like short spring
      showers :
Kid, whose grim sport still gambolled over graves :
   And Chettle, in whose fresh funereal verse
   Weeps Marian yet on Robin's wildwood hearse :
Cooke, whose light boat of song one soft breath saves,
   Sighed from a maiden's amorous mouth averse :
Live likewise ye : Time takes not you for slaves.

XX

THE MANY

II

HAUGHTON, whose mirth gave woman all her will :
  Field, bright and loud with laughing flower and
    bird
  And keen alternate notes of laud and gird :
Barnes, darkening once with Borgia's deeds the quill
Which tuned the passion of Parthenophil :
  Blithe burly Porter, broad and bold of word :
  Wilkins, a voice with strenuous pity stirred :
Turk Mason : Brewer, whose tongue drops honey
    still :
Rough Rowley, handling song with Esau's hand :
  Light Nabbes : lean Sharpham, rank and raw by
    turns,
  But fragrant with a forethought once of Burns :
Soft Davenport, sad-robed, but blithe and bland :
  Brome, gipsy-led across the woodland ferns :
Praise be with all, and place among our band.

XXI

EPILOGUE

Our mother, which wast twice, as history saith,
　　Found first among the nations : once, when she
　　Who bore thine ensign saw the God in thee
Smite Spain, and bring forth Shakespeare : once,
　　when death
Shrank, and Rome's bloodhounds cowered, at
　　Milton's breath :
　　More than thy place, then first among the free
　　More than that sovereign lordship of the sea
Bequeathed to Cromwell from Elizabeth,
More than thy fiery guiding-star, which Drake
Hailed, and the deep saw lit again for Blake,
　　More than all deeds wrought of thy strong right
　　　　hand,
This praise keeps most thy fame's memorial strong
That thou wast head of all these streams of song,
　　And time bows down to thee as Shakespeare's land.

A DARK MONTH

"La maison sans enfants!"—VICTOR HUGO.

I

A MONTH without sight of the sun
 Rising or reigning or setting
Through days without use of the day,
Who calls it the month of May?
The sense of the name is undone
 And the sound of it fit for forgetting.

We shall not feel if the sun rise,
 We shall not care when it sets:
If a nightingale make night's air
As noontide, why should we care?
Till a light of delight that is done rise,
 Extinguishing grey regrets;

Till a child's face lighten again
 On the twilight of older faces;
Till a child's voice fall as the dew
On furrows with heat parched through
And all but hopeless of grain,
 Refreshing the desolate places—

Fall clear on the ears of us hearkening
 And hungering for food of the sound
And thirsting for joy of his voice:
Till the hearts in us hear and rejoice,
And the thoughts of them doubting and
  darkening
 Rejoice with a glad thing found.

When the heart of our gladness is gone,
 What comfort is left with us after?
When the light of our eyes is away,
What glory remains upon May,
What blessing of song is thereon
 If we drink not the light of his laughter?

No small sweet face with the daytime
 To welcome, warmer than noon!
No sweet small voice as a bird's
To bring us the day's first words!
Mid May for us here is not Maytime:
 No summer begins with June.

A whole dead month in the dark,
 A dawn in the mists that o'ercome hei
Stifled and smothered and sad—
Swift speed to it, barren and bad!
And return to us, voice of the lark,
 And remain with us, sunlight of summer.

II

Alas, what right has the dawn to glimmer,
  What right has the wind to do aught but
    moan?
All the day should be dimmer
  Because we are left alone.

Yestermorn like a sunbeam present
  Hither and thither a light step smiled,
And made each place for us pleasant
  With the sense or the sight of a child.

But the leaves persist as before, and after
  Our parting the dull day still bears flowers;
And songs less bright than his laughter
  Deride us from birds in the bowers.

Birds, and blossoms, and sunlight only,
  As though such folly sufficed for spring!
As though the house were not lonely
  For want of the child its king!

III

Asleep and afar to-night my darling
    Lies, and heeds not the night,
If winds be stirring or storms be snarling··
    For his sleep is its own sweet light.

I sit where he sat beside me quaffing
    The wine of story and song
Poured forth of immortal cups, and laughing
    When mirth in the draught grew strong.

I broke the gold of the words, to melt it
    For hands but seven years old,
And they caught the tale as a bird, and felt it
    More bright than visible gold.

And he drank down deep, with his eyes broad
        beaming,
    Here in this room where I am,
The golden vintage of Shakespeare, gleaming
    In the silver vessels of Lamb.

Here by my hearth where he was I listen
    For the shade of the sound of a word,
Athirst for the birdlike eyes to glisten,
    For the tongue to chirp like a bird.

At the blast of battle, how broad they brightened,
   Like fire in the spheres of stars,
And clung to the pictured page, and lightened
   As keen as the heart of Mars !

At the touch of laughter, how swift it twittered
   The shrillest music on earth ;
How the lithe limbs laughed and the whole child
     glittered
   With radiant riot of mirth !

Our Shakespeare now, as a man dumb-stricken,
   Stands silent there on the shelf :
And my thoughts, that had song in the heart of
     them, sicken,
   And relish not Shakespeare's self.

And my mood grows moodier than Hamlet's **even,**
   And man delights not me,
But only the face that morn and even
   My heart leapt only to see.

That my heart made merry within me seeing,
   And sang as his laugh kept time :
But song finds now no pleasure in being,
   And love no reason in rhyme.

IV

MILD May-blossom and proud sweet bay-flower,
  What, for shame, would you have with us here?
It is not the month of the May-flower
  This, but the fall of the year.

Flowers open only their lips in derision,
  Leaves are as fingers that point in scorn ·
The shows we see are a vision ;
  Spring is not verily born.

Yet boughs turn supple and buds grow sappy,
  As though the sun were indeed the sun :
And all our woods are happy
  With all their birds save one.

But spring is over, but summer is over,
  But autumn is over, and winter stands
With his feet sunk deep in the clover
  And cowslips cold in his hands.

His hoar grim head has a hawthorn bonnet,
  His gnarled gaunt hand has a gay green staff
With new-blown rose-blossom on it :
  But his laugh is a dead man's laugh.

The laugh of spring that the heart seeks after,
  The hand that the whole world yearns to kiss,
It rings not here in his laughter,
  The sign of it is not this.

There is not strength in it left to splinter
  Tall oaks, nor frost in his breath to sting :
Yet it is but a breath as of winter,
  And it is not the hand of spring.

V

Thirty-one pale maidens, clad
    All in mourning dresses,
Pass, with lips and eyes more sad
That it seems they should be glad,
Heads discrowned of crowns they had,
    Grey for golden tresses.

Grey their girdles too for green,
    And their veils dishevelled :
None would say, to see their mien,
That the least of these had been
Born no baser than a queen,
    Reared where flower-fays revelled.

Dreams that strive to seem awake,
    Ghosts that walk by daytime,
Weary winds the way they take,
Since, for one child's absent sake,
May knows well, whate'er things make
    Sport, it is not Maytime.

VI

A HAND at the door taps light
As the hand of my heart's delight :
  It is but a full-grown hand,
Yet the stroke of it seems to start
Hope like a bird in my heart,
  Too feeble to soar or to stand.

To start light hope from her cover
Is to raise but a kite for a plover
  If her wings be not fledged to soar.
Desire, but in dreams, cannot ope
The door that was shut upon hope
  When love went out at the door.

Well were it if vision could keep
The lids of desire as in sleep
  Fast locked, and over his eyes
A dream with the dark soft key
In her hand might hover, and be
  Their keeper till morning rise ;

The morning that brings after many
Days fled with no light upon any
  The small face back which is gone ;
When the loved little hands once more
Shall struggle and strain at the door
  They beat their summons upon.

VII

IF a soul for but seven days were cast out of heaven
  and its mirth,
They would seem to her fears like as seventy years
  upon earth.

Even and morrow should seem to her sorrow as long
As the passage of numberless ages in slumberless
  song.

Dawn, roused by the lark, would be surely as dark in
  her sight
As her measureless measure of shadowless pleasure
  was bright.

Noon, gilt but with glory of gold, would be hoary
  and grey
In her eyes that had gazed on the depths, unamazed
  with the day.

Night hardly would seem to make darker her dream
  never done,
When it could but withhold what a man may behold
  of the sun.

For dreams would perplex, were the days that should
    vex her but seven,
The sight of her vision, made dark with division from
    heaven.

Till the light on my lonely way lighten that only now
    gleams,
I too am divided from heaven and derided of dreams.

VIII

A TWILIGHT fire-fly may suggest
　　How flames the fire that feeds the sun :
" A crooked figure may attest
　　In little space a million."

But this faint-figured verse, that dresses
　　With flowers the bones of one bare month,
Of all it would say scarce expresses
　　In crooked ways a millionth.

A fire-fly tenders to the father
　　Of fires a tribute something worth :
My verse, a shard-borne beetle rather,
　　Drones over scarce-illumined earth.

Some inches round me though it brighten
　　With light of music-making thought,
The dark indeed it may not lighten,
　　The silence moves not, hearing nought.

Only my heart is eased with hearing,
　　Only mine eyes are soothed with seeing,
A face brought nigh, a footfall nearing,
　　Till hopes take form and dreams have being.

IX

As a poor man hungering stands with insatiate eyes
  and hands
            Void of bread
Right in sight of men that feast while his famine with
  no least
            Crumb is fed,

Here across the garden-wall can I hear strange children call,
            Watch them play,
From the windowed seat above, whence the goodlier
  child I love
            Is away.

Here the sights we saw together moved his fancy like
  a feather
            To and fro,
Now to wonder, and thereafter to the sunny storm of
  laughter
            Loud and low—

Sights engraven on storied pages where man's tale of
  seven swift ages
            All was told—
Seen of eyes yet bright from heaven—for the lips that
  laughed were seven
            Sweet years old.

X

Why should May remember
    March, if March forget
The days that began with December
    The nights that a frost could fret?

All their griefs are done with
    Now the bright months bless
Fit souls to rejoice in the sun with,
    Fit heads for the wind's caress ;

Souls of children quickening
    With the whole world's mirth,
Heads closelier than field-flowers thickening
    That crowd and illuminate earth,

Now that May's call musters
    Files of baby bands
To marshal in joyfuller clusters
    Than the flowers that encumber their hands.

Yet morose November
    Found them no less gay,
With nought to forget or remember
    Less bright than a branch of may.

All the seasons moving
  Move their minds alike
Applauding, acclaiming, approving
  All hours of the year that strike.

So my heart may fret not,
  Wondering if my friend
Remember me not or forget not
  Or ever the month find end.

Not that love sows lighter
  Seed in children sown,
But that life being lit in them brighter
  Moves fleeter than even our own.

May nor yet September
  Binds their hearts, that yet
Remember, forget, and remember,
  Forget, and recall, and forget.

XI

As light on a lake's face moving
 Between a cloud and a cloud
Till night reclaim it, reproving
 The heart that exults too loud,

The heart that watching rejoices
 When soft it swims into signt
Applauded of all the voices
 And stars of the windy night.

So brief and unsure, but sweeter
 Than ever a moondawn smiled,
Moves, measured of no tune's metre,
 The song in the soul of a child ;

The song that the sweet soul singing
 Half listens, and hardly hears,
Though sweeter than joy-bells ringing
 And brighter than joy's own tears ;

The song that remembrance of pleasure
 Begins, and forgetfulness ends
With a soft swift change in the measure
 That rings in remembrance of friends

As the moon on the lake's face flashes,
  So haply may gleam at whiles
A dream through the dear deep lashes
  Whereunder a child's eye smiles,

And the least of us all that love him
  May take for a moment part
With angels around and above him,
  And I find place in his heart.

XII

CHILD, were you kinless and lonely—
    Dear, were you kin to me—
My love were compassionate only
    Or such as it needs would be.

But eyes of father and mother
    Like sunlight shed on you shine :
What need you have heed of another
    Such new strange love as is mine?

It is not meet if unruly
    Hands take of the children's bread
And cast it to dogs ; but truly
    The dogs after all would be fed.

On crumbs from the children's table
    That crumble, dropped from above,
My heart feeds, fed with unstable
    Loose waifs of a child's light love.

Though love in your heart were brittle
    As glass that breaks with a touch,
You haply would lend him a little
    Who surely would give you much.

XIII

HERE is a rough
   Rude sketch of my friend,
Faint-coloured enough
   And unworthily penned.

Fearlessly fair
   And triumphant he stands,
And holds unaware
   Friends' hearts in his hands ;

Stalwart and straight
   As an oak that should bring
Forth gallant and great
   Fresh roses in spring.

On the paths of his pleasure
   All graces that wait
What metre shall measure
   What rhyme shall relate

Each action, each motion,
   Each feature, each limb,
Demands a devotion
   In honour of him :

Head that the hand
　　Of a god might have blest,
Laid lustrous and bland
　　On the curve of its crest :

Mouth sweeter than cherries,
　　Keen eyes as of Mars,
Browner than berries
　　And brighter than stars.

Nor colour nor wordy
　　Weak song can declare
The stature how sturdy,
　　How stalwart his air.

As a king in his bright
　　Presence-chamber may be,
So seems he in height—
　　Twice higher than your knee.

As a warrior sedate
　　With reserve of his power,
So seems he in state—
　　As tall as a flower :

As a rose overtowering
　　The ranks of the rest
That beneath it lie cowering,
　　Less bright than their best.

And his hands are as sunny
　　As ruddy ripe corn
Or the browner-hued honey
　　From heather-bells borne.

When summer sits proudest,
  Fulfilled with its mirth,
And rapture is loudest
  In air and on earth,

The suns of all hours
  That have ripened the roots
Bring forth not such flowers
  And beget not such fruits.

And well though I know it,
  As fain would I write,
Child, never a poet
  Could praise you aright.

I bless you? the blessing
  Were less than a jest
Too poor for expressing;
  I come to be blest,

With humble and dutiful
  Heart, from above:
Bless me, O my beautiful
  Innocent love!

This rhyme in your praise
  With a smile was begun;
But the goal of his ways
  Is uncovered to none,

Nor pervious till after
  The limit impend;
It is not in laughter
  These rhymes of you end.

XIV

SPRING, and fall, and summer, and winter,
  Which may Earth love least of them all,
Whose arms embrace as their signs imprint her,
  Summer, or winter, or spring, or fall?

The clear-eyed spring with the wood-birds mating,
  The rose-red summer with eyes aglow,
The yellow fall with serene eyes waiting,
  The wild-eyed winter with hair all snow?

Spring's eyes are soft, but if frosts benumb her
  As winter's own will her shrewd breath sting:
Storms may rend the raiment of summer,
  And fall grow bitter as harsh-lipped spring.

One sign for summer and winter guides me,
  One for spring, and the like for fall:
Whichever from sight of my friend divides me,
  That is the worst ill season of all.

XV

Worse than winter is spring
If I come not to sight of my king :
But then what a spring will it be
When my king takes homage of me !

I send his grace from afar
Homage, as though to a star ;
As a shepherd whose flock takes flight
May worship a star by night.

As a flock that a wolf is upon
My songs take flight and are gone :
No heart is in any to sing
Aught but the praise of my king.

Fain would I once and again
Sing deeds and passions of men :
But ever a child's head gleams
Between my work and my dreams.

Between my hand and my eyes
The lines of a small face rise,
And the lines I trace and retrace
Are none but those of the face.

XVI

TILL the tale of all this flock of days alike
    All be done,
Weary days of waiting till the month's hand strike
    Thirty-one,
Till the clock's hand of the month break off, and end
    With the clock,
Till the last and whitest sheep at last be penned
    Of the flock,
I their shepherd keep the count of night and day
    With my song,
Though my song be, like this month which once was
      May,
    All too long.

XVII

THE incarnate sun, a tall strong youth,
  On old Greek eyes in sculpture smiled :
But trulier had it given the truth
  To shape him like a child.

No face full-grown of all our dearest
  So lightens all our darkness, none
Most loved of all our hearts hold nearest
  To far outshines the sun.

As when with sly shy smiles that feign
  Doubt if the hour be clear, the time
Fit to break off my work again
  Or sport of prose or rhyme,

My friend peers in on me with merry
  Wise face, and though the sky stay dim
The very light of day, the very
  Sun's self comes in with him.

XVIII

OUT of sight,
   Out of mind !
Could the light
   Prove unkind ?

Can the sun
   Quite forget
What was done
   Ere he set ?

Does the moon
   When she wanes
Leave no tune
   That remains

In the void
   Shell of night
Overcloyed
   With her light ?

Must the shore
   At low tide
Feel no more
   Hope or pride,

No intense
   Joy to be,
In the sense
   Of the sea—

In the pulses
  Of her shocks
It repulses,
  When its rocks

Thrill and ring
  As with glee ?
Has my king
  Cast off me,

Whom no bird
  Flying south
Brings one word
  From his mouth ?

Not the ghost
  Of a word
Riding post
  Have I heard,

Since the day
  When my king
Took away
  With him spring,

And the cup
  Of each flower
Shrivelled up
  That same hour,

With no light
  Left behind.
Out of sight,
  Out of mind !

XIX

BECAUSE I adore you
    And fall
On the knees of my spirit before you—
    After all,

You need not insult,
    My king,
With neglect, though your spirit exult
    In the spring,

Even me, though not worth,
    God knows,
One word of you sent me in mirth,
    Or one rose

Out of all in your garden
    That grow
Where the frost and the wind never harden
    Flakes of snow,

Nor ever is rain
    At all,
But the roses rejoice to remain
    Fair and tall—

The roses of love,
  More sweet
Than blossoms that rain from above
  Round our feet,

When under high bowers
  We pass,
Where the west wind freckles with flowers
  All the grass.

But a child's thoughts bear
  More bright
Sweet visions by day, and more fair
  Dreams by night,

Than summer's whole treasure
  Can be :
What am I that his thought should take pleasure,
  Then, in me ?

I am only my love's
  True lover,
With a nestful of songs, like doves
  Under cover,

That I bring in my cap
  Fresh caught,
To be laid on my small king's lap—
  Worth just nought.

Yet it haply may hap
  That he,
When the mirth in his veins is as sap
  In a tree,

Will remember me too
 Some day
Ere the transit be thoroughly through
 Of this May—

Or perchance, if such grace
 May be,
Some night when I dream of his face
 Dream of me.

Or if this be too high
 A hope
For me to prefigure in my
 Horoscope,

He may dream of the place
 Where we
Basked once in the light of his face,
 Who now see

Nought brighter, not one
 Thing bright,
Than the stars and the moon and the sun,
 Day nor night.

XX

Day by darkling day,
  Overpassing, bears away
Somewhat of the burden of this weary May.

  Night by numbered night,
    Waning, brings more near in sight
Hope that grows to vision of my heart's delight.

  Nearer seems to burn
    In the dawn's rekindling urn
Flame of fragrant incense, hailing his return.

  Louder seems each bird
    In the brightening branches heard
Still to speak some ever more delightful word.

  All the mists that swim
    Round the dawns that grow less dim
Still wax brighter and more bright with hope of him.

  All the suns that rise
    Bring that day more near our eyes
When the sight of him shall clear our clouded skies.

  All the winds that roam
    Fruitful fields or fruitless foam
Blow the bright hour near that brings his bright face
      home.

XXI

I HEAR of two far hence
  In a garden met,
And the fragrance blown from thence
  Fades not yet.

The one is seven years old,
  And my friend is he :
But the years of the other have told
  Eighty-three.

To hear these twain converse
  Or to see them greet
Were sweeter than softest verse
  May be sweet.

The hoar old gardener there
  With an eye more mild
Perchance than his mild white hair
  Meets the child.

I had rather hear the words
  That the twain exchange
Than the songs of all the birds
  There that range,

Call, chirp, and twitter there
   Through the garden-beds
Where the sun alike sees fair
   Those two heads,

And which may holier be
   Held in heaven of those
Or more worth heart's thanks to see
   No man knows.

XXII

OF such is the kingdom of heaven,
　　No glory that ever was shed
From the crowning star of the seven
　　That crown the north world's head,

No word that ever was spoken
　　Of human or godlike tongue,
Gave ever such godlike token
　　Since human harps were strung.

No sign that ever was given
　　To faithful or faithless eyes
Showed ever beyond clouds riven
　　So clear a Paradise.

Earth's creeds may be seventy times seven
　　And blood have defiled each creed :
If of such be the kingdom of heaven,
　　It must be heaven indeed.

XXIII

THE wind on the downs is bright
  As though from the sea :
And morning and night
  Take comfort again with me.

He is nearer to-day,
  Each night to each morning saith,
Whose return shall revive dead May
  With the balm of his breath.

The sunset says to the moon,
  He is nearer to-night
Whose coming in June
  Is looked for more than the light.

Bird answers to bird,
  Hour passes the sign on to hour,
And for joy of the bright news heard
  Flower murmurs to flower.

The ways that were glad of his feet
  In the woods that he knew
Grow softer to meet
  The sense of his footfall anew.

He is near now as day,
  Says hope to the new-born light :
He is near now as June is to May,
  Says love to the night.

XXIV

Good things I keep to console me
  For lack of the best of all,
A child to command and control me,
  Bid come and remain at his call.

Sun, wind, and woodland and highland,
  Give all that ever they gave :
But my world is a cultureless island,
  My spirit a masterless slave.

And friends are about me, and better
  At summons of no man stand :
But I pine for the touch of a fetter,
  The curb of a strong king's hand.

Each hour of the day in her season
  Is mine to be served as I will :
And for no more exquisite reason
  Are all served idly and ill.

By slavery my sense is corrupted,
  My soul not fit to be free :
I would fain be controlled, interrupted,
  Compelled as a thrall may be.

For fault of spur and of bridle
  I tire of my stall to death :
My sail flaps joyless and idle
  For want of a small child's breath.

XXV

WHITER and whiter
  The dark lines grow,
And broader opens and brighter
  The sense of the text below.

Nightfall and morrow
  Bring nigher the boy
Whom wanting we want not sorrow,
  Whom having we want no joy.

Clearer and clearer
  The sweet sense grows
Of the word which hath summer for hearer,
  The word on the lips of the rose.

Duskily dwindles
  Each deathlike day,
Till June rearising rekindles
  The depth of the darkness of May.

XXVI

" In his bright radiance and collateral light
Must I be comforted, not in his sphere."

STARS in heaven are many,
  Suns in heaven but one :
Nor for man may any
  Star supplant the sun.

Many a child as joyous
  As our far-off king
Meets as though to annoy us
  In the paths of spring.

Sure as spring gives warning,
  All things dance in tune :
Sun on Easter morning,
  Cloud and windy moon,

Stars between the tossing
  Boughs of tuneful trees,
Sails of ships recrossing
  Leagues of dancing seas ;

Best, in all this playtime,
  Best of all in tune,
Girls more glad than Maytime,
  Boys more bright than June ;

Mixed with all those dances,
   Far through field and street
Sing their silent glances,
   Ring their radiant feet.

Flowers wherewith May crowned us
   Fall ere June be crowned :
Children blossom round us
   All the whole year round.

Is the garland worthless
   For one rose the less,
And the feast made mirthless ?
   Love, at least, says yes.

Strange it were, with many
   Stars enkindling air,
Should but one find any
   Welcome : strange it were,

Had one star alone won
   Praise for light from far :
Nay, love needs his own one
   Bright particular star.

Hope and recollection
   Only lead him right
In its bright reflection
   And collateral light.

Find as yet we may not
   Comfort in its sphere :
Yet these days will weigh not
   When it warms us here :

When full-orbed it rises,
   Now divined afar :
None in all the skies is
   Half so good a star ;

None that seers importune
   Till a sign be won :
Star of our good fortune,
   Rise and reign, our sun !

XXVII

I PASS by the small room now forlorn
 Where once each night as I passed I knew
A child's bright sleep from even to morn
 Made sweet the whole night through.

As a soundless shell, as a songless nest,
 Seems now the room that was radiant then
And fragrant with his happier rest
 Than that of slumbering men.

The day therein is less than the day,
 The night is indeed night now therein :
Heavier the dark seems there to weigh,
 And slower the dawns begin.

As a nest fulfilled with birds, as a shell
 Fulfilled with breath of a god's own hymn,
Again shall be this bare blank cell,
 Made sweet again with him.

XXVIII

SPRING darkens before us,
  A flame going down,
With chant from the chorus
  Of days without crown—
Cloud, rain, and sonorous
  Soft wind on the down.

She is wearier not of us
  Than we of the dream
That spring was to love us
  And joy was to gleam
Through the shadows above us
  That shift as they stream.

Half dark and half hoary,
  Float far on the loud
Mild wind, as a glory
  Half pale and half proud
From the twilight of story,
  Her tresses of cloud ;

Like phantoms that glimmer
  Of glories of old
With ever yet dimmer
  Pale circlets of gold
As darkness grows grimmer
  And memory more cold.

A DARK MONTH

Like hope growing clearer
  With wane of the moon,
Shines toward us the nearer
  Gold frontlet of June,
And a face with it dearer
  Than midsummer moon.

XXIX

You send me your love in a letter,
  I send you my love in a song :
Ah child, your gift is the better,
  Mine does you but wrong.

No fame, were the best less brittle,
  No praise, were it wide as earth,
Is worth so much as a little
  Child's love may be worth.

We see the children above us
  As they might angels above :
Come back to us, child, if you love us,
  And bring us your love.

XXX

No time for books or for letters :
   What time should there be ?
No room for tasks and their fetters :
   Full room to be free.

The wind and the sun and the Maytime
   Had never a guest
More worthy the most that his playtime
   Could give of its best.

If rain should come on, peradventure,
   (But sunshine forbid !)
Vain hope in us haply might venture
   To dream as it did.

But never may come, of all comers
   Least welcome, the rain,
To mix with his servant the summer's
   Rose-garlanded train !

He would write, but his hours are as busy
   As bees in the sun,
And the jubilant whirl of their dizzy
   Dance never is done.

The message is more than a letter,
   Let love understand,
And the thought of his joys even better
   Than sight of his hand.

XXXI

WIND, high-souled, full-hearted
　　South-west wind of the spring !
Ere April and earth had parted,
　　Skies, bright with thy forward wing,
Grew dark in an hour with the shadow behind it, that
　　bade not a bird dare sing.

Wind whose feet are sunny,
　　Wind whose wings are cloud,
With lips more sweet than honey
　　Still, speak they low or loud,
Rejoice now again in the strength of thine heart: let
　　the depth of thy soul wax proud.

We hear thee singing or sighing,
　　Just not given to sight,
All but visibly flying
　　Between the clouds and the light,
And the light in our hearts is enkindled, the shadow
　　therein of the clouds put to flight.

From the gift of thine hands we gather
　　The core of the flowers therein,
Keen glad heart of heather,
　　Hot sweet heart of whin,
Twin breaths in thy godlike breath close blended of
　　wild spring's wildest of kin.

All but visibly beating
    We feel thy wings in the far
Clear waste, and the plumes of them fleeting,
    Soft as swan's plumes are,
And strong as a wild swan's pinions, and swift as the
    flash of the flight of a star.

As the flight of a planet enkindled
    Seems thy far soft flight
Now May's reign has dwindled
    And the crescent of June takes light
And the presence of summer is here, and the hope of
    a welcomer presence in sight.

Wind, sweet-souled, great-hearted
    Southwest wind on the wold!
From us is a glory departed
    That now shall return as of old,
Borne back on thy wings as an eagle's expanding, and
    crowned with the sundawn's gold.

There is not a flower but rejoices,
    There is not a leaf but has heard:
All the fields find voices,
    All the woods are stirred:
There is not a nest but is brighter because of the
    coming of one bright bird.

Out of dawn and morning,
    Noon and afternoon,
The sun to the world gives warning
    Of news that brightens the moon;
And the stars all night exult with us, hearing of joy
    that shall come with June.

SUNRISE

If the wind and the sunlight of April and August had
    mingled the past and hereafter
In a single adorable season whose life were a rapture
    of love and of laughter,
And the blithest of singers were back with a song ; if
    again from his tomb as from prison,
If again from the night or the twilight of ages Aristo-
    phanes had arisen,
With the gold-feathered wings of a bird that were
    also a god upon earth at his shoulders,
And the gold-flowing laugh of the manhood of old at
    his lips, for a joy to beholders,
He alone unrebuked of presumption were able to set
    to some adequate measure
The delight of our eyes in the dawn that restores
    them the sun of their sense and the pleasure.
For the days of the darkness of spirit are over for all
    of us here, and the season
When desire was a longing, and absence a thorn, and
    rejoicing a word without reason.
For the roof overhead of the pines is astir with delight
    as of jubilant voices,
And the floor underfoot of the bracken and heather
    alive as a heart that rejoices.

For the house that was childless awhile, and the light
    of it darkened, the pulse of it dwindled,
Rings radiant again with a child's bright feet, with
    the light of his face is rekindled.
And the ways of the meadows that knew him, the
    sweep of the down that the sky's belt closes,
Grow gladder at heart than the soft wind made them
    whose feet were but fragrant with roses,
Though the fall of the year be upon us, who trusted
    in June and by June were defrauded,
And the summer that brought us not back the desire
    of our eyes be gone hence unapplauded.
For July came joyless among us, and August went
    out from us arid and sterile,
And the hope of our hearts, as it seemed, was no
    more than a flower that the seasons imperil,
And the joy of our hearts, as it seemed, than a thought
    which regret had not heart to remember,
Till four dark months overpast were atoned for, and
    summer began in September.
Hark, April again as a bird in the house with a child's
    voice hither and thither :
See, May in the garden again with a child's face
    cheering the woods ere they wither.
June laughs in the light of his eyes, and July on the
    sunbright cheeks of him slumbers,
And August glows in a smile more sweet than the
    cadence of gold-mouthed numbers.
In the morning the sight of him brightens the sun,
    and the noon with delight in him flushes,
And the silence of nightfall is music about him as
    soft as the sleep that it hushes.
We awake with a sense of a sunrise that is not a gift
    of the sundawn's giving,

And a voice that salutes us is sweeter than all sounds
    else in the world of the living,
And a presence that warms us is brighter than all in
    the world of our visions beholden,
Though the dreams of our sleep were as those that
    the light of a world without grief makes golden.
For the best that the best of us ever devised as a
    likeness of heaven and its glory,
What was it of old, or what is it and will be for ever,
    in song or in story,
Or in shape or in colour of carven or painted resem-
    blance, adored of all ages,
But a vision recorded of children alive in the pictures
    of old or the pages ?
Where children are not, heaven is not, and heaven if
    they come not again shall be never :
But the face and the voice of a child are assurance of
    heaven and its promise for ever.

SPECIMENS OF MODERN POETS

THE HEPTALOGIA

OR

THE SEVEN AGAINST SENSE

A CAP WITH SEVEN BELLS

THE HIGHER PANTHEISM
IN A NUTSHELL

ONE, who is not, we see : but one, whom we see not,
 is :
Surely this is not that : but that is assuredly this.

What, and wherefore, and whence ? for under is over
 and under :
If thunder could be without lightning, lightning could
 be without thunder.

Doubt is faith in the main : but faith, on the whole,
 is doubt :
We cannot believe by proof : but could we believe
 without ?

Why, and whither, and how ? for barley and rye are
 not clover :
Neither are straight lines curves : yet over is under
 and over.

Two and two may be four : but four and four are not
 eight :
Fate and God may be twain : but God is the same
 thing as fate.

Ask a man what he thinks, and get from a man what
    he feels :
God, once caught in the fact, shows you a fair pair
    of heels.

Body and spirit are twins : God only knows which is
    which :
The soul squats down in the flesh, like a tinker drunk
    in a ditch.

More is the whole than a part : but half is more than
    the whole :
Clearly, the soul is the body : but is not the body the
    soul ?

One and two are not one : but one and nothing is
    two :
Truth can hardly be false, if falsehood cannot be
    true.

Once the mastodon was : pterodactyls were common
    as cocks :
Then the mammoth was God : now is He a prize ox.

Parallels all things are : yet many of these are askew
You are certainly I : but certainly I am not you.

Springs the rock from the plain, shoots the stream
    from the rock :
Cocks exist for the hen : but hens exist for the cock.

God, whom we see not, is : and God, who is not, we
    see :
Fiddle, we know, is diddle : and diddle, we take it,
    is dee.

JOHN JONES'S WIFE

I

AT THE PIANO

I

Love me and leave me; what love bids retrieve me?
    can June's fist grasp May?
Leave me and love me; hopes eyed once above me
    like spring's sprouts decay;
Fall as the snow falls, when summer leaves grow
    false—cards packed for storm's play!

II

Nay, say Decay's self be but last May's elf, wing
    shifted, eye sheathed—
Changeling in April's crib rocked, who lets 'scape
    rills locked fast since frost breathed—
Skin cast (think!) adder-like, now bloom bursts
    bladder-like,—bloom frost bequeathed?

III

Ah, how can fear sit and hear as love hears it grief's
    heart's cracked grate's screech?
Chance lets the gate sway that opens on hate's way
    and shews on shame's beach
Crouched like an imp sly change watch sweet love's
    shrimps lie, a toothful in each.

IV

Time feels his tooth slip on husks wet from Truth's
    lip, which drops them and grins—
Shells where no throb stirs of life left in lobsters
    since joy thrilled their fins—
Hues of the prawn's tail or comb that makes dawn
    stale, so red for our sins !

V

Years blind and deaf use the soul's joys as refuse,
    heart's peace as manure,
Reared whence, next June's rose shall bloom where
    our moons rose last year, just as pure :
Moons' ends match roses' ends : men by beasts'
    noses' ends mete sin's stink's cure.

VI

Leaves love last year smelt now feel dead love's tears
    melt—flies caught in time's mesh !
Salt are the dews in which new time breeds new sin,
    brews blood and stews flesh ;
Next year may see dead more germs than this weeded
    and reared them afresh.

VII

Old times left perish, there's new time to cherish ;
    life just shifts its tune ;
As, when the day dies, earth, half afraid, eyes the
    growth of the moon ;
Love me and save me, take me or waive me ; death
    takes one so soon !

II

BY THE CLIFF

I

Is it daytime (guess),
   You that feed my soul
      To excess
With that light in those eyes
   And those curls drawn like a scroll
In that round grave guise?
      No or yes?

II

Oh, the end, I'd say!
   Such a foolish thing
      (Pure girls' play!)
As a mere mute heart,
   Was it worth a kiss, a ring,
This? for two must part—
      Not to-day.

III

Look, the whole sand crawls,
   Hums, a heaving hive,
      Scrapes and scrawls—

Such a buzz and burst!
  Here just one thing's not alive,
One that was at first—
    But life palls.

IV

Yes, my heart, I know,
  Just my heart's stone dead—
    Yes, just so.
Sick with heat, those worms
  Drop down scorched and overfed—
No more need of germs!
    Let them go.

V

Yes, but you now, look,
  You, the rouged stage female
    With a crook,
Chalked Arcadian sham,
  You that made my soul's sleep's dream
    ail—
Your soul fit to damn?
    Shut the book.

III

ON THE SANDS

I

THERE was nothing at all in the case (conceive)
  But love ; being love, it was not (understand)
Such a thing as the years let fall (believe)
  Like the rope's coil dropt from a fisherman's hand
When the boat's hauled up—" by your leave ! "

II

So—well ! How that crab writhes--leg after leg
  Drawn, as a worm draws ring upon ring
Gradually, not gladly ! Chicken or egg,
  Is it more than the ransom (say) of a king
(Take my meaning at least) that I beg ?

III

Not so ! You were ready to learn, I think,
  What the world said ! "He loves you too well
  (suppose)
For such leanings ! These poets, their love's mere
  ink—
  Like a flower, their flame flashes—a rosebud,
  blows—
Then it all drops down at a wink !

IV

" Ah, the instance !   A curl of a blossomless vine
    The vinedresser passing it sickens to see
And mutters ' Much hope (under God) of His wine
    From the branch and the bark of a barren tree
Spring reared not, and winter lets pine—

V

" ' His wine that should glorify (saith He) the cup
    That a man beholding (not tasting) might say
" Pour out life at a draught, drain it dry, drink it up,
    Give this one thing, and huddle the rest away—
Save the bitch, and be hanged to the pup ! "

VI

" ' Let it rot then ! ' which saying, he leaves it—we'll
        guess,
    Feels (if the sap move at all) thus much—
Yearns, and would blossom, would quicken no less,
    Bud at an eye's glance, flower at a touch—
' Die, perhaps, would you not, for her ? '—' Yes ! '

VII

" Note the hitch there !   That's piteous—so much
        being done,
    (He'll think some day, your lover) so little to do !
Such infinite days to wear out, once begun !
    Since the hand its glove holds, and the footsole its
        shoe—
Overhead too there's always the sun ! "

VIII

Oh, no doubt they had said so, your friends—been
  profuse
  Of good counsel, wise hints—"where the trap
  lurks, walk warily—
Squeeze the fruit to the core ere you count on the
  juice!
  For the graft may fail, shift, wax, change colour,
  wane, vary, lie—"
You were cautious, God knows—to what use?

IX

This crab's wiser, it strikes me—no twist but implies
  life—
  Not a curl but's so fit you could find none fitter—
For the brute from its brutehood looks up thus and
  eyes life—
  Stoop your soul down and listen, you'll hear it
  twitter,
Laughing lightly,—my crab's life's the wise life!

X

Those who've read S. T. Coleridge remember how
  Sammy sighs
  To his pensive (I think he says) Sara—"most
  soothing-sweet"—
Crab's bulk's less (look!) than man's—yet (quoth
  Cancer) I am my size,
  And my bulk's girth contents me! Man's maw
  (see?) craves two things—wheat
And flesh likewise—man's gluttonous—damn his
  eyes!

XI

Crab's content with crab's provender : crab's love, if
    soothing,
  Is no sweeter than pincers are soft—and a new
    sickle
Cuts no sharper than crab's claws nip, keen as boar's
    toothing !
  Yet crab's love's no less fervent than bard's, if less
    musical—
'Tis a new thing I'd lilt—but a true thing.

XII

Old songs tell us, of all drinks for Englishmen
    fighting, ale's
  Out and out best : salt water contents crab, it
    seems to me,
Though pugnacious as sailors, and skilled to steer
    right in gales
  That craze pilots, if slow to sing—" Sleep'st thou ?
    thou dream'st o' me ! "
In such love-strains as mine—or a nightingale's.

XIII

Ah, now, look you—tail foremost, the beast sets sea-
    ward—
  The sea draws it, sand sucks it—he's wise, my
    crab !
From the napkin out jumps his one talent—good
    steward,
  Just judge ! So a man shirks the smile or the
    stab,
And sets his sail duly to leeward !

XIV

Trust me? Hardly! I bid you not lean (remark)
  On my spirit, your spirit—my flesh, your flesh—
Hold my hand, and tread safe through the horrible
      dark—
  Quench my soul as with sprinklings of snow, then
    refresh
With some blast of new bellows the spark!

XV

By no means! This were easy (men tell me) to
      say—
  "Give her all, throw your chance up, fall back on
    her heart!"
(Say my friends) "she must change! after night
    follows day—"
  No such fool! I am safe set in hell, for my
    part—
So let heaven do the worst now he may!

XVI

What they bid me? Well, this, nothing more—
    "Tell her this—
  'You are mine, I yours, though the whole world
    fail—
Though things are not, I know there is one thing
    which is—
  Though the oars break, there's hope for us yet—
    hoist the sail!
Oh, your heart! what's the heart? but your kiss!'

XVII

"Then she breaks, she drops down, she lies flat at
    your feet—
  Take her then!" Well, I knew it—what fools are
    men!
Take the bee by her horns, will your honey prove
    sweet?
  Sweet is grass—will you pasture your cows in a
    fen?
Oh, if contraries could but once meet!

XVIII

Love you call it? Some twitch in the moon's face
    (observe),
  Wet blink of her eyelid, tear dropt about dewfall,
Cheek flushed or obscured—does it make the sky
    swerve?
  Fetch the test, work the question to rags, bring to
    proof all—
Find what souls want and bodies deserve!

XIX

Ah, we know you! Your soul works to infinite
    ends,
  Frets, uses life up for death's sake, takes pains,
Flings down love's self—"but you, bear me witness,
    my friends!
  Have I lost spring? count up (see) the winter's
    fresh gains!
Is the shrub spoilt? the pine's hair impends!"

XX

What, you'd say—" Mark how God works ! Years
          crowd, time wears thin,
     Earth keeps good yet, the sun goes on, stars hold
          their own,
And you'll change, climb past sight of the world, shift
          your skin,
     Never heeding how life moans—' more flesh now,
          less bone !'
For that cheek's worn waste outline (death's grin)

XXI

" Pleads with time still—' what good if I lose this?
          but see—'"
     (There's the crab gone !) "' I said, " Though earth
          sinks,"'" (you perceive ?
Ah, true, back there !) your soul now—"'" yet some
          vein might be
     (Could one find it alive in the heart's core's pulse,
          cleave
Through the life-springs where "you" melts in
          "me")—

XXII

"'" Some true vein of the absolute soul, which sur-
          vives
     All that flesh runs to waste through "—and lo, this
          fails !
Here's death close on us ! One life ? a million of
          lives !
     Why choose one sail to watch of these infinite
          sails ?
Time's a tennis-play ? thank you, no, fives !

XXIII

" ' Stop life's ball then ! ' Such folly ! melt earth
    down for that,
  Till the pure ore eludes you and leaves you raw
    scoriæ ?
Pish, the vein's wrong !"   But you, friends—come,
    what were you at
  When God spat you out suddenly ? what was the
    story He
Cut short thus, the growth He laid flat ?

XXIV

Wait ! the crab's twice alive, mark !   Oh, worthy,
    your soul,
  Of strange ends, great results, novel labours !
    Take note,
I reject this for one ! (ay, now, straight to the hole !
  Safe in sand there—your skirts smooth out all as
    they float !)
I, shirk drinking through flaws in the bowl ?

XXV

Or suppose now that rock's cleft—grim, scored to the
    quick,
  As a man's face kept fighting all life through gets
    scored,
Mossed and marked with grey purulent leprosies,
    sick,
  Flat and foul as man's life here (be swift with your
    sword—
Cut the soul out, stuck fast where thorns prick !)

XXVI

—Say it let the rock's heart out, its meaning, the
    thing
  All was made for, devised, ruled out gradually,
    planned—
Ah, that sea-shell, perhaps—since it lies, such a ring
  Of pure colour, a cup full of sunbeams, to stand
(Say, in Lent) at the priest's hand—(no king !)

XXVII

Blame the cleft then ? Praise rather ! So—just a
    chance gone !
  Had you said—" Save the seed and secure souls
    in flower "—
Ah, how time laughs, years palpitate, pro grapples
    con,
  Till one day you shrug shoulders—" Well, gone,
    the good hour ! "
Till one night—" Is God off now ? or on ? "

IV

UP THE SPOUT

I

Hi! Just you drop that! Stop, I say!
   Shirk work, think slink off, twist friend's wrist?
Where that spined sand's lined band's the bay—
   Lined blind with true sea's blue, as due—
Promising—not to pay?

II

For the sea's debt leaves wet the sand;
   Burst worst fate's weights in one burst gun?
A man's own yacht, blown—What? off land?
   Tack back, or veer round here, then—queer!
Reef points, though—understand?

III

I'm blest if I do. Sigh? be blowed!
   Love's doves make break life's ropes, eh? Tropes!
Faith's brig, baulked, sides caulked, rides at road;
   Hope's gropes befogged, storm-dogged and
     bogged—
Clogged, water-logged, her load!

IV

Stowed, by Jove, right and tight, away!
  No show now how best plough sea's brow,
Wrinkling—breeze quick, tease thick, ere day,
  Clear sheer wave's sheen of green, I mean,
With twinkling wrinkles—eh?

V

Sea sprinkles winkles, tinkles light
  Shells' bells—boy's joys that hap to snap!
It's just sea's fun, breeze done, to spite
  God's rods that scourge her surge, I'd urge—
Not proper, is it—quite?

VI

See, fore and aft, life's craft undone!
  Crank plank, split spritsail—mark, sea's lark!
That grey cold sea's old sprees, begun
  When men lay dark i' the ark, no spark,
All water—just God's fun!

VII

Not bright, at best, his jest to these
  Seemed—screamed, shrieked, wreaked on kin for
    sin!
When for mirth's yell earth's knell seemed please
  Some dumb new grim great whim in him
Made Jews take chalk for cheese.

VIII

Could God's rods bruise God's Jews?   Their jowls
   Bobbed, sobbed, gaped, aped the plaice in face:
None heard, 'tis odds, his—God's—folk's howls.
   Now, how must I apply, to try
This hookiest-beaked of owls?

IX

Well, I suppose God knows—I don't.
   Time's crimes mark dark men's types, in stripes
Broad as fen's lands men's hands were wont
   Leave grieve unploughed, though proud and loud
With birds' words—No! he won't!

X

One never should think good impossible.
   Eh? say I'd hide this Jew's oil's cruse—
His shop might hold bright gold, engrossible
   By spy—spring's air takes there no care
To wave the heath-flower's glossy bell!

XI

But gold bells chime in time there, coined—
   Gold!   Old Sphinx winks there—"Read my
     screed!"
Doctrine Jews learn, use, burn for, joined
   (Through new craft's stealth) with health and
     wealth—
At once all three purloined!

XII

I rose with dawn, to pawn, no doubt,
  (Miss this chance, glance untried aside?)
John's shirt, my—no! Ay, so—the lout!
  Let yet the door gape, store on floor
And not a soul about?

XIII

Such men lay traps, perhaps—and I'm
  Weak—meek—mild—child of woe, you know!
But theft, I doubt, my lout calls crime.
  Shrink? Think! Love's dawn in pawn—you
    spawn
Of Jewry! Just in time!

V

OFF THE PIER

I

ONE last glance at these sands and stones !
 Time goes past men, and lives to his liking,
Steals, and ruins, and sometimes atones.
  Why should he be king, though, and why not
  I king ?
There now, that wind, like a swarm of sick drones !

II

Is it heaven or mere earth (come !) that moves so and
  moans ?
  Oh, I knew, when you loved me, my soul was in
  flowerage—
Now the frost comes ; from prime, though, I watched
  through to nones,
  Read love's litanies over—his age was not our
  age !
No more flutes in this world for me now, dear ! trombones.

III

All that youth once denied and made mouths at, age
  owns.
  Facts put fangs out and bite us; life stings and
    grows viperous;
And time's fugues are a hubbub of meaningless tones.
  Once we followed the piper; now why not the piper
    us?
Love, grown grey, plays mere solos; we want anti-
  phones.

IV

And we sharpen our wits up with passions for hones,
  Melt down loadstars for magnets, use women for
    whetstones,
Learn to bear with dead calms by remembering
  cyclones,
  Snap strings short with sharp thumbnails, till
    silence begets tones,
Burn our souls out, shift spirits, turn skins and change
  zones;

V

Then the heart, when all's done with, wakes,
  whimpers, intones
  Some lost fragment of tune it thought sweet ere it
    grew sick;
(Is it life that disclaims this, or death that disowns?)
  Mere dead metal, scrawled bars—ah, one touch,
    you make music!
Love's worth saving, youth doubts, but experience
  depones.

VI

In the darkness (right Dickens) of Tom-All-Alone's
　　Or the Morgue out in Paris, where tragedy
　　　centuples
Life's effects by Death's algebra, Shakespeare
　　(Malone's)
　　Might have said sleep was murdered—new
　　　scholiasts have sent you pills
To purge text of him! Bread? give me—Scottice—
　　scones!

VII

Think, what use, when youth's saddle galls bay's
　　　back or roan's,
　　To seek chords on love's keys to strike, other than
　　　his chords?
There's an error joy winks at and grief half condones,
　　Or life's counterpoint grates the C major of
　　　discords—
'Tis man's choice 'twixt sluts rose-crowned and
　　queens age dethrones.

VIII

I for instance might groan as a bag-pipe groans,
　　Give the flesh of my heart for sharp sorrows to
　　　flagellate,
Grief might grind my cheeks down, age make sticks
　　of my bones,
　　(Though a queen drowned in tears must be worth
　　　more than Madge elate)[1]
Rose might turn burdock, and pine-apples cones;

[1] First edition :—
And my face bear his brand—mine, that once bore Love's badge
　elate!

IX

My skin might change to a pitiful crone's,
   My lips to a lizard's, my hair to weed,
My features, in fact, to a series of loans;
   Thus much is conceded; now, you, concede
You would hardly salute me by choice, John Jones?

THE POET AND THE WOODLOUSE

SAID a poet to a woodlouse—" Thou art certainly my
    brother ;
  I discern in thee the markings of the fingers of the
    Whole ;
And I recognize, in spite of all the terrene smut and
    smother,
  In the colours shaded off thee, the suggestions of a
    soul.

" Yea," the poet said, " I smell thee by some passive
    divination,
  I am satisfied with insight of the measure of thine
    house ;
What had happened I conjecture, in a blank and
    rhythmic passion,
  Had the æons thought of making thee a man, and
    me a louse.

" The broad lives of upper planets, their absorption
    and digestion,
  Food and famine, health and sickness, I can
    scrutinize and test ;
Through a shiver of the senses comes a resonance of
    question,
  And by proof of balanced answer I decide that I am
    best.

" Man, the fleshly marvel, alway feels a certain kind
  of awe stick
    To the skirts of contemplation, cramped with
      nympholeptic weight :
Feels his faint sense charred and branded by the
  touch of solar caustic,
    On the forehead of his spirit feels the footprint of
      a Fate."

" Notwithstanding which, O poet," spake the woodlouse, very blandly,
    " I am likewise the created,—I the equipoise of
      thee ;
I the particle, the atom, I behold on either hand
  lie
    The inane of measured ages that were embryos
      of me.

" I am fed with intimations, I am clothed with conse-
  quences,
    And the air I breathe is coloured with apocalyptic
      blush :
Ripest-budded odours blossom out of dim chaotic
  stenches,
    And the Soul plants spirit-lilies in sick leagues of
      human slush.

" I am thrilled half cosmically through by crypto-
  phantic surgings,
    Till the rhythmic hills roar silent through a
      spongious kind of blee :
And earth's soul yawns disembowelled of her pan-
  creatic organs,
    Like a madrepore if mesmerized, in rapt catalepsy.

" And I sacrifice, a Levite—and I palpitate, a poet ;—
    Can I close dead ears against the rush and resonance
        of things ?
Symbols in me breathe and flicker up the heights of
        the heroic ;
    Earth's worst spawn, you said, and cursed me ?
        look ! approve me ! I have wings.

" Ah, men's poets ! men's conventions crust you round
        and swathe you mist-like,
    And the world's wheels grind your spirits down the
        dust ye overtrod :
We stand sinlessly stark-naked in effulgence of the
        Christlight,
    And our polecat chokes not cherubs ; and our skunk
        smells sweet to God.

" For He grasps the pale Created by some thousand
        vital handles,
    Till a Godshine, bluely winnowed through the sieve
        of thunderstorms,
Shimmers up the non-existent round the churning feet
        of angels ;
    And the atoms of that glory may be seraphs, being
        worms.

" Friends, your nature underlies us and your pulses
        overplay us ;
    Ye, with social sores unbandaged, can ye sing right
        and steer wrong ?
For the transient cosmic, rooted in imperishable chaos,
    Must be kneaded into drastics as material for a
        song.

" Eyes once purged from homebred vapours through
   humanitarian passion
   See that monochrome a despot through a democratic
   prism ;
Hands that rip the soul up, reeking from divine evis-
   ceration,
   Not with priestlike oil anoint him, but a stronger-
   smelling chrism.

"Pass, O poet, retransfigured ! God, the psychometric
   rhapsode,
   Fills with fiery rhythms the silence, stings the dark
   with stars that blink ;
All eternities hang round him like an old man's clothes
   collapsèd,
   While he makes his mundane music—AND HE WILL
   NOT STOP, I THINK '

THE PERSON OF THE HOUSE

IDYL CCCLXVI

THE ACCOMPANIMENTS

1. THE MONTHLY NURSE
2. THE CAUDLE
3. THE SENTENCES

THE KID

1. THE MONTHLY NURSE

THE sickly airs had died of damp ;
  Through huddling leaves the holy chime
Flagged ; I, expecting Mrs. Gamp,
  Thought—" Will the woman come in time ? "
Upstairs I knew the matron bed
  Held her whose name confirms all joy
To me ; and tremblingly I said,
  " Ah ! will it be a girl or boy ? "
And, soothed, my fluttering doubts began
  To sift the pleasantness of things ;
Developing the unshapen man,
  An eagle baffled of his wings ;
Considering, next, how fair the state
  And large the license that sublimes
A nineteenth-century female fate—
  Sweet cause that thralls my liberal rhymes !

And Chastities and colder Shames,
   Decorums mute and marvellous,
And fair Behaviour that reclaims
   All fancies grown erroneous,
Moved round me musing, till my choice
   Faltered.   A female in a wig
Stood by me, and a drouthy voice
   Announced her—Mrs. Betsy Prig.

2. THE CAUDLE

Sweet Love that sways the reeling years,
   The crown and chief of certitudes,
For whose calm eyes and modest ears
   Time writes the rule and text of prudes—
That, surpliced, stoops a nuptial head,
   Nor chooses to live blindly free,
But, with all pulses quieted,
   Plays tunes of domesticity—
That Love I sing of and have sung
   And mean to sing till Death yawn sheer,
He rules the music of my tongue,
   Stills it or quickens, there or here.
I say but this : as we went up
   I heard the Monthly give a sniff
And " *if* the big dog makes the pup—"
   She murmured—then repeated "if ! "
The caudle on a slab was placed ;
   She snuffed it, snorting loud and long ;
I fled—I would not stop to taste—
   And dreamed all night of things gone wrong.

3. THE SENTENCES

I

Abortive Love is half a sin ;
　But Love's abortions dearer far
Than wheels without an axle-pin
　Or life without a married star.

II

My rules are hard to understand
　For him whom sensual rules depress ;
A bandbox in a midwife's hand
　May hold a costlier bridal dress.

III

" I like her not ; in fact I loathe ;
　Bugs hath she brought from London beds."
Friend ! wouldst thou rather bear their growth
　Or have a baby with two heads ?

IDYL CCCLXVI

THE KID

MY spirit, in the doorway's pause,
   Fluttered with fancies in my breast;
Obsequious to all decent laws,
   I felt exceedingly distressed.
I knew it rude to enter there
   With Mrs. V. in such a state;
And, 'neath a magisterial air,
   Felt actually indelicate.
I knew the nurse began to grin;
   I turned to greet my Love.   Said she—
" Confound your modesty, come in!
   —What shall we call the darling, V.?"
(There are so many charming names!
   Girls'—Peg, Moll, Doll, Fan, Kate, Blanche,
      Bab:
Boys'—Mahershahal-hashbaz, James,
   Luke, Nick, Dick, Mark, Aminadab.)

Lo, as the acorn to the oak,
   As well-heads to the river's height,
As to the chicken the moist yolk,
   As to high noon the day's first white—
Such is the baby to the man.
   There, straddling one red arm and leg,
Lay my last work, in length a span,
   Half hatched, and conscious of the egg.

A creditable child, I hoped ;
   And half a score of joys to be
Through sunny lengths of prospect sloped
   Smooth to the bland futurity.
O, fate surpassing other dooms,
   O, hope above all wrecks of time !
O, light that fills all vanquished glooms,
   O, silent song o'ermastering rhyme !
I covered either little foot,
   I drew the strings about its waist ;
Pink as the unshell'd inner fruit,
   But barely decent, hardly chaste,
Its nudity had startled me ;
   But when the petticoats were on,
" I know," I said ; " its name shall be
   Paul Cyril Athanasius John."
" Why," said my wife, " the child's a girl."
   My brain swooned, sick with failing sense ;
With all perception in a whirl,
   How could I tell the difference ?
" Nay," smiled the nurse, " the child's a boy."
   And all my soul was soothed to hear
That so it was : then startled Joy
   Mocked Sorrow with a doubtful tear.
And I was glad as one who sees
   For sensual optics things unmeet :
As purity makes passion freeze,
   So faith warns science off her beat.
Blessed are they that have not seen,
   And yet, not seeing, have believed :
To walk by faith, as preached the Dean,
   And not by sight, have I achieved.
Let love, that does not look, believe ;
   Let knowledge, that believes not, look :

Truth pins her trust on falsehood's sleeve,
  While reason blunders by the book.
Then Mrs. Prig addressed me thus ;
  " Sir, if you'll be advised by me,
You'll leave the blessed babe to us ;
  It's my belief he wants his tea."

LAST WORDS OF A SEVENTH-RATE POET

BILL, I feel far from quite right—if not further:
  already the pill
Seems, if I may say so, to bubble inside me.   A poet's
  heart, Bill,
Is a sort of a thing that is made of the tenderest young
  bloom on a fruit.
You may pass me the mixture at once, if you please—
  and I'll thank you to boot
For that poem—and then for the julep.   This really
  is damnable stuff !
(Not the poem, of course.) Do you snivel, old
  friend ? well, it's nasty enough,
But I think I can stand it—I think so—ay, Bill, and
  I could were it worse.
But I'll tell you a thing that I can't and I won't.
  'Tis the old, old curse—
The gall of the gold-fruited Eden, the lure of the
  angels that fell.
'Tis the core of the fruit snake-spotted in the hush of
  the shadows of hell,
Where a lost man sits with his head drawn down,
  and a weight on his eyes.
You know what I mean, Bill—the tender and delicate
  mother of lies,

Woman, the devil's first cousin—no doubt by the
    female side.

The breath of her mouth still moves in my hair, and
    I know that she lied,

And I feel her, Bill, sir, inside me—she operates there
    like a drug.

Were it better to live like a beetle, to wear the cast
    clothes of a slug,

Be the louse in the locks of the hangman, the mote
    in the eye of the bat,

Than to live and believe in a woman, who must one
    day grow aged and fat?

You must see it's preposterous, Bill, sir. And yet,
    how the thought of it clings!

I have lived out my time—I have prigged lots of
    verse—I have kissed (ah, that stings!)

Lips that swore I had cribbed every line that I wrote
    on them—cribbed—honour bright!

Then I loathed her ; but now I forgive her ; perhaps
    after all she was right.

Yet I swear it was shameful—unwomanly, Bill, sir—
    to say that I fibbed.

Why, the poems were mine, for I bought them in
    print.   Cribbed? of course they were cribbed.

Yet I wouldn't say, cribbed from the French—Lady
    Bathsheba thought it was vulgar—

But picked up on the banks of the Don, from the lips
    of a highly intelligent Bulgar.

I'm aware, Bill, that's out of all metre—I can't help
    it—I'm none of your sort

Who set metres, by Jove, above morals—not exactly.
    They don't go to Court—

As I mentioned one night to that cowslip-faced pet,
    Lady Rahab Redrabbit

(Whom the Marquis calls Drabby for short). Well,
    I say, if you want a thing, grab it—

That's what I did, at least, when I took that *danseuse*
    to a swell *cabaret*,

Where expense was no consideration. A poet, you
    see, now and then must be gay.

(I declined to give more, I remember, than fifty
    centeems to the waiter ;

For I asked him if that was enough ; and the
    jackanapes answered—*Peut-être.*

Ah, it isn't in you to draw up a *menu* such as ours
    was, though humble :

When I told Lady Shoreditch, she thought it a
    regular *grand tout ensemble.*)

She danced the heart out of my body—I can see in
    the glare of the lights,

I can see her again as I saw her that evening, in
    spangles and tights.

When I spoke to her first, her eye flashed so,
    I heard—as I fancied—the spark whiz

From her eyelid—I said so next day to that jealous
    old fool of a Marquis.

She reminded me, Bill, of a lovely volcano, whose
    entrails are lava—

Or (you know my *penchant* for original types) of the
    upas in Java.

In the curve of her sensitive nose was a singular
    species of dimple,

Where the flush was the mark of an angel's creased
    kiss—if it wasn't a pimple.

Now I'm none of your bashful John Bulls who don't
    know a pilau from a puggaree

Nor a chili, by George, from a chopstick. So, sir,
    I marched into her snuggery,

And proposed a light supper by way of a finish.
    I treated her, Bill,
To six *entrées* of ortolans, sprats, maraschino, and
    oysters. It made her quite ill.
Of which moment of sickness I took some advantage.
    I held her like this,
And availed myself, sir, of her sneezing, to shut up
    her lips with a kiss.
The waiters, I saw, were quite struck ; and I felt,
    I may say, *entre nous,*
Like Don Juan, Lauzun, Almaviva, Lord Byron, and
    old Richelieu.
(You'll observe, Bill, that rhyme's quite Parisian ; a
    Londoner, sir, would have cited old Q.
People tell me the French in my verses recalls that
    of Jeames or John Thomas : I
Must maintain it's as good as the average accent of
    British diplomacy.)
These are moments that thrill the whole spirit with
    spasms that excite and exalt.
I stood more than the peer of the great Casanova—
    you know—de Seingalt.
She was worth, sir, I say it without hesitation, two
    brace of her sisters.
Ah, why should all honey turn rhubarb—all cherries
    grow onions—all kisses leave blisters?
Oh, and why should I ask myself questions? I've
    heard such before—once or twice.
Ah, I can't understand it—but, O, I imagine it strikes
    me as nice.
There's a deity shapes us our ends, sir, rough-hew
    them, my boy, how we will—
As I stated myself in a poem I published last year,
    you know, Bill—

Where I mentioned that that was the question—to be,
or, by Jove, not to be.

Ah, it's something—you'll think so hereafter—to wait
on a poet like me.

Had I written no more than those verses on that
Countess I used to call Pussy—

Yes, Minette or Manon—and—you'll hardly believe
it—she said they were all out of Musset.

Now I don't say they weren't—but what then? and
I don't say they were—I'll bet pounds against
pennies on

The subject—I wish I may never die Laureate, if
some of them weren't out of Tennyson.

And I think—I don't like to be certain, with Death,
so to speak, by me, frowning—

But I think there were some—say a dozen, perhaps,
or a score—out of Browning.

And—though God knows his poems are not (as all
mine are, sir) perfumed with orris—

Or at least with patchouli—I wouldn't be sworn there
were none out of Morris.

And it's possible—only the legend of Circe is quite an
old yarn—old

As the hills—that I might have been thinking, perhaps,
of a poem by Arnold

When I sang how Ulysses—Odysseus I mean—would
have yearned to dishevel her

Bright hair with his kisses, and painted myself at her
feet—a Strayed Reveller.

As for poets who go on a contrary tack to what I go
and you go—

You remember my lyrics *translated*—like " sweet
bully Bottom "—from Hugo ?

Though I will say it's curious that simply on just
    that account there should be
Men so bold as to say that not one of my poems was
    written by me.
It would stir the political bile or the physical spleen
    of a drab or a Tory
To hear critics disputing my claim to Empedocles,
    Maud, and the Laboratory.
Yes, it's singular—nay, I can't think of a parallel
    (ain't it a high lark?
As that Countess would say)—there are few men
    believe it was I wrote the Ode to a Skylark.
And it often has given myself and Lord Albert no end
    of diversion
To hear fellows maintain to my face it was Words-
    worth who wrote the Excursion,
When they know that whole reams of the verses
    recur in my authorized works
Here and there, up and down! Why, such readers
    are infidels—heretics—Turks.
And the pitiful critics who think in their paltry pre-
    sumption to pay me a
Pretty compliment, pairing me off, sir, with Keats—
    as if *he* could write Lamia!
While I never produced a more characteristic and
    exquisite book,
One that gave me more real satisfaction, than did, on
    the whole, Lalla Rookh.
Was it there that I called on all debtors, being
    pestered myself by a creditor, (he
Isn't paid yet) to rise, by the proud appellation of
    bondsmen—hereditary?
Yes—I think so. And yet, on my word, I can't think
    why I think it was so.

It more probably was in the poem I made a few seasons
    ago

On that Duchess—her name now ? ah, thus one out-
    lives a whole cycle of joys !

Fair supplants black and brown succeeds golden.
    The poem made rather a noise.

And indeed I have seen worse verses ; but as for the
    woman, my friend—

Though his neck had been never so stiff, she'd have
    made a philosopher bend.

As the broken heart of a sunset that bleeds pure
    purple and gold

In the shudder and swoon of the sickness of colour,
    the agonies old

That engirdle the brows of the day when he sinks
    with a spasm into rest

And the splash of his kingly blood is dashed on the
    skirts of the west,

Even such was my own, when I felt how much sharper
    than any snake's tooth

Was the passion that made me mistake Lady Eve for
    her niece Lady Ruth.

The whole world, colourless, lapsed. Earth fled from
    my feet like a dream,

And the whirl of the walls of Space was about me,
    and moved as a stream

Flowing and ebbing and flowing all night to a weary
    tune

(" Such as that of my verses " ? Get out !) in the
    face of a sick-souled moon.

The keen stars kindled and faded and fled, and the
    wind in my ears

Was the wail of a poet for failure—you needn't come
    snivelling tears

And spoiling the mixture, confound you, with dropping
    your tears into that !
I know I'm pathetic—I must be—and you soft-
    hearted and fat,
And I'm grateful of course for your kindness—there,
    don't come hugging me, now—
But because a fellow's pathetic, you needn't low like
    a cow.

    I should like—on my soul, I should like—to re-
    member—but somehow I can't—
If the lady whose love has reduced me to this was
    the niece or the aunt.
But whichever it was, I feel sure, when I published
    my lays of last year
(You remember their title—The Tramp—only seven-
    and-sixpence—not dear),
I sent her a copy (perhaps her tears fell on the title-
    page—yes—
I should like to imagine she wept)—and the Bride of
    Bulgaria (MS.)
I forwarded with it.   The lyrics, no doubt, she found
    bitter—and sweet ;
But the Bride she rejected, you know, with expressions
    I will not repeat.
Well—she did no more than all publishers did.
    Though my prospects were marred,
I can pity and pardon them.   Blindness, mere blind-
    ness !   And yet it was hard.
For a poet, Bill, is a blossom—a bird—a billow—a
    breeze—
A kind of creature that moves among men as a wind
    among trees.

And a bard who is also the pet of patricians and
    dowagers doubly can

Express his contempt for canaille in his fables where
    beasts are republican.

Yet with all my disdainful forgiveness for men so
    deficient in *ton*

I cannot but feel it was cruel—I cannot but think it
    was wrong.

I with the heat of my heart still burning against all
    bars

As the fire of the dawn, so to speak, in the blanched
    blank brows of the stars—

I with my tremulous lips made pale by musical
    breath—

I with the shade in my eyes that was left by the kisses
    of Death—

(For Death came near me in youth, and touched my
    face with his face,

And put in my lips the songs that belong to a desolate
    place—

Desolate truly, my heart and my lips, till her kiss
    filled them up!)

I with my soul like wine poured out with my flesh for
    the cup—

It was hard for me—it was hard—Bill, Bill, you great
    owl, was it not?

For the day creeps in like a Fate : and I think my
    grand passion is rot :

And I dreamily seem to perceive, by the light of a
    life's dream done,

The lotion at six, and the mixture at ten, and the
    draught before one.

Yes—I feel rather better.   Man's life is a mull, at
the best ;

And the patent perturbator pills are like bullets of
lead in my chest.

When a man's whole spirit is like the lost Pleiad, a
blown-out star,

Is there comfort in Holloway, Bill? is there hope of
salvation in Parr?

True, most things work to their end—and an end
that the shroud overlaps.

Under lace, under silk, under gold, sir, the skirt of
a winding-sheet flaps—

Which explains, if you think of it, Bill, why I can't,
though my soul thereon broodeth,

Quite make out if I loved Lady Tamar as much as
I loved Lady Judith.

Yet her dress was of violet velvet, her hair was
. hyacinth-hued,

And her ankles—no matter.   A face where the music
of every mood

Was touched by the tremulous fingers of passionate
feeling, and made

Strange melodies, scornful, but sweeter than strings
whereon sorrow has played

To enrapture the hearing of mirth when his garland
of blossom and green

Turns to lead on the anguished forehead—"you don't
understand what I mean"?

Well, of course I knew you were stupid—you always
were stupid at school—

Now don't say you weren't—but I'm hanged if I
thought you were quite such a fool !

You don't see the point of all this?   I was talking of
sickness and death—

In that poem I made years ago, I said this—" Love,
    the flower-time whose breath

Smells sweet through a summer of kisses and
    perfumes an autumn of tears

Is sadder at root than a winter—its hopes heavy-
    hearted like fears.

Though I love your Grace more than I love little
    Letty, the maid of the mill,

Yet the heat of your lips when I kiss them " (you see
    we were intimate, Bill)

" And the beat of the delicate blood in your eyelids
    of azure and white

Leave the taste of the grave in my mouth and the
    shadow of death on my sight.

Fill the cup—twine the chaplet—come into the garden
    —get out of the house—

Drink to *me* with your eyes—there's a banquet behind,
    where worms only carouse !

As I said to sweet Katie, who lived by the brook on
    the land Philip farmed—

Worms shall graze where my kisses found pasture ! "
    The Duchess, I may say, was charmed.

It was read to the Duke, and he cried like a child.
    If you'll give me a pill,

I'll go on till past midnight.   That poem was said to
    be—Somebody's, Bill.

But you see you can always be sure of my hand as
    the mother that bore me

By the fact that I never write verse which has never
    been written before me.

Other poets—I blush for them, Bill—may adore and
    repudiate in turn a

Libitina, perhaps, or Pandemos ; my Venus, you
    know, is Laverna.

Nay, that epic of mine which begins from foundations
    the Bible is built on—
" Of man's *first* disobedience "—I've heard it at-
    tributed, dammy, to Milton.
Well, it's lucky for them that it's not worth my while,
    as I may say, to break spears
With the hirelings, forsooth, of the press who assert
    that Othello was Shakespeare's.
When he that can run, sir, may read—if he borrows
    the book, or goes on tick—
In my poems the bit that describes how the Hellespont
    joins the Propontic.
There are men, I believe, who will tell you that Gray
    wrote the whole of The Bard—
Or that I didn't write half the Elegy, Bill, in a
    Country Churchyard.
When you know that my poem, The Poet, begins—
    " Ruin seize thee ! " and ends
With recapitulations of horrors the poet invokes on
    his friends.
And I'll swear, if you look at the dirge on my relatives
    under the turf, you
Will perceive it winds up with some lines on myself—
    and begins with the curfew.
Now you'll grant it's more probable, Bill—as a man
    of the world, if you please—
That all these should have prigged from myself than
    that I should have prigged from all these.
I could cry when I think of it, friend, if such tears
    would comport with my dignity,
That the author of Christabel ever should smart from
    such vulgar malignity.
(You remember perhaps that was one of the first little
    things that I carolled

After finishing Marmion, the Princess, the Song of
the Shirt, and Childe Harold.)

Oh, doubtless it always has been so—Ah, doubtless
it always will be—

There are men who would say that myself is a
different person from me.

Better the porridge of patience a poor man snuffs in
his plate

Than the water of poisonous laurels distilled by the
fingers of hate.

'Tis a dark-purple sort of a moonlighted kind of a
midnight, I know ;

You remember those verses I wrote on Irene, from
Edgar A. Poe ?

It was Lady Aholibah Levison, daughter of old Lord
St. Giles,

Who inspired those delectable strains, and rewarded
her bard with her smiles.

There are tasters who've sipped of Castalia, who don't
look on *my* brew as *the* brew :

There are fools who can't think why the names of my
heroines of title should always be Hebrew.

'Twas my comrade, Sir Alister Knox, said, " Noo,
dinna ye fash wi' Apollo, mon ;

Gang to Jewry for wives and for concubines, lad—
look at David and Solomon.

And it gives an erotico-scriptural twang," said that
high-born young man, "—tickles

The lug " (he meant ear) " of the reader—to throw in
a touch of the Canticles."

So I versified half of The Preacher—it took me a
week, working slowly.   Bah !

You don't half know the sex, Bill—they like it.   And
    what if her name was Aholibah?

I recited her charms, in conjunction with those of a
    girl at the *café*,

In a poem I published in collaboration with Templeton
    (Taffy).

There are prudes in a world full of envy—and some
    of them thought it too strong

To compare an earl's daughter by name with a girl
    at a French *restaurant.*

I regarded her, though, with the chivalrous eyes of
    a knight-errant on quest ;

I may say I don't know that I ever felt prouder, old
    friend, of a conquest.

And when *I*'ve been made happy, I never have cared
    a brass farthing who knew it ; I

Thank my stars I'm as free from mock-modesty,
    friend, as from vulgar fatuity.

I can't say if my spirit retains—for the subject appears
    to me misty—any tie

To such associations as Poesy weaves round the
    records of Christianity.

There are bards—I may be one myself—who delight
    in their skill to unlock a lip's

Rosy secrets by kisses and whispers of texts from the
    charming Apocalypse.

It was thus that I won, by such biblical pills of
    poetical manna,

From two elders—Sir Seth and Lord Isaac—the liking
    of Lady Susanna.

But I left her—a woman to me is no more than a
    match, sir, at tennis is—

When I heard she'd gone off with my valet, and
    burnt my rhymed version of Genesis.

You may see by my shortness of speech that my
    time's almost up : I perceive
That my new-fangled brevity strikes you : but don't
    —though the public will—grieve.
As it's sometimes my whim to be vulgar, it's some-
    times my whim to be brief ;
As when once I observed, after Heine, that " she was
    a harlot, and I " (which is true) " was a thief."
(Though you hardly should cite this particular line,
    by the way, as an instance of absolute brevity :
I'm aware, man, of that ; so you needn't disgrace
    yourself, sir, by such grossly mistimed and
    impertinent levity.)
I don't like to break off, any more than you wish me
    to stop : but my fate is
Not to vent half a million such rhymes without block-
    heads exclaiming—

JAM SATIS.

Specimen from the speaker's original poems.

Come into the orchard, Anne,
    For the dark owl, Night, has fled,
And Phosphor slumbers, as well as he can
    With a daffodil sky for a bed :
And the musk of the roses perplexes a man,
    And the pimpernel muddles his head.

SONNET FOR A PICTURE

THAT nose is out of drawing. With a gasp,
   She pants upon the passionate lips that ache
   With the red drain of her own mouth, and make
A monochord of colour. Like an asp,
One lithe lock wriggles in his rutilant grasp.
   Her bosom is an oven of myrrh, to bake
   Love's white warm shewbread to a browner cake.
The lock his fingers clench has burst its hasp.
The legs are absolutely abominable.
   Ah! what keen overgust of wild-eyed woes
   Flags in that bosom, flushes in that nose?
Nay! Death sets riddles for desire to spell,
   Responsive. What red hem earth's passion sews,
But may be ravenously unripped in hell?

NEPHELIDIA

From the depth of the dreamy decline of the dawn
  through a notable nimbus of nebulous noonshine,
  Pallid and pink as the palm of the flag-flower that
    flickers with fear of the flies as they float,
Are they looks of our lovers that lustrously lean from
  a marvel of mystic miraculous moonshine,
  These that we feel in the blood of our blushes that
    thicken and threaten with throbs through the
    throat?
Thicken and thrill as a theatre thronged at appeal of
  an actor's appalled agitation,
  Fainter with fear of the fires of the future than pale
    with the promise of pride in the past;
Flushed with the famishing fullness of fever that
  reddens with radiance of rathe recreation,
  Gaunt as the ghastliest of glimpses that gleam
    through the gloom of the gloaming when ghosts
    go aghast?
Nay, for the nick of the tick of the time is a tremulous
  touch on the temples of terror,
  Strained as the sinews yet strenuous with strife of
    the dead who is dumb as the dust-heaps of death:
Surely no soul is it, sweet as the spasm of erotic emo-
  tional exquisite error,
  Bathed in the balms of beatified bliss, beatific itself
    by beatitude's breath.

Surely no spirit or sense of a soul that was soft to the
    spirit and soul of our senses
  Sweetens the stress of suspiring suspicion that sobs
    in the semblance and sound of a sigh ;
Only this oracle opens Olympian, in mystical moods
    and triangular tenses—
  " Life is the lust of a lamp for the light that is dark
    till the dawn of the day when we die."
Mild is the mirk and monotonous music of memory,
    melodiously mute as it may be,
  While the hope in the heart of a hero is bruised by
    the breach of men's rapiers, resigned to the rod ;
Made meek as a mother whose bosom-beats bound
    with the bliss-bringing bulk of a balm-breathing
    baby,
  As they grope through the grave-yard of creeds,
    under skies growing green at a groan for the
    grimness of God.
Blank is the book of his bounty beholden of old, and
    its binding is blacker than bluer :
  Out of blue into black is the scheme of the skies,
    and their dews are the wine of the bloodshed of
    things ;
Till the darkling desire of delight shall be free as a
    fawn that is freed from the fangs that pursue her,
  Till the heart-beats of hell shall be hushed by a
    hymn from the hunt that has harried the kennel
    of kings.

A

MIDSUMMER HOLIDAY

AND OTHER POEMS

A MIDSUMMER HOLIDAY

To Theodore Watts

]

THE SEABOARD

THE sea is at ebb, and the sound of her utmost word
Is soft as the least wave's lapse in a still small reach.
From bay into bay, on quest of a goal deferred,
From headland ever to headland and breach to
    breach
Where earth gives ear to the message that all days
    preach
With changes of gladness and sadness that cheer and
    chide,
The lone way lures me along by a chance untried
That haply, if hope dissolve not and faith be whole,
Not all for nought shall I seek, with a dream for
    guide,
The goal that is not, and ever again the goal.

The trackless ways are untravelled of sail or bird ,
The hoar wave hardly recedes from the soundless
    beach.
The silence of instant noon goes nigh to be heard,
The viewless void to be visible : all and each,
A closure of calm no clamour of storm can breach
Concludes and confines and absorbs them on either
    side,
All forces of light and of life and the live world's
    pride.

Sands hardly ruffled of ripples that hardly roll
Seem ever to show as in reach of a swift brief stride
The goal that is not, and ever again the goal.

The waves are a joy to the seamew, the meads to the
    herd,
And a joy to the heart is a goal that it may not reach.
No sense that for ever the limits of sense engird,
No hearing or sight that is vassal to form or speech,
Learns ever the secret that shadow and silence teach,
Hears ever the notes that or ever they swell subside,
Sees ever the light that lights not the loud world's
    tide,
Clasps ever the cause of the lifelong scheme's control
Wherethrough we pursue, till the waters of life be
    dried,
The goal that is not, and ever again the goal.

Friend, what have we sought or seek we, whate'er
    betide,
Though the seaboard shift its mark from afar
    descried,
But aims whence ever anew shall arise the soul?
Love, thought, song, life, but show for a glimpse and
    hide
The goal that is not, and ever again the goal.

II

A HAVEN

East and north a waste of waters, south and west
Lonelier lands than dreams in sleep would feign
    to be,
When the soul goes forth on travel, and is prest
Round and compassed in with clouds that flash and
    flee.
Dells without a streamlet, downs without a tree,
Cirques of hollow cliff that crumble, give their guest
Little hope, till hard at hand he pause, to see
Where the small town smiles, a warm still sea-side
    nest.

Many a lone long mile, by many a headland's crest,
Down by many a garden dear to bird and bee,
Up by many a sea-down's bare and breezy breast,
Winds the sandy strait of road where flowers run
    free.
Here along the deep steep lanes by field and lea
Knights have carolled, pilgrims chanted, on their
    quest,
Haply, ere a roof rose toward the bleak strand's lee,
Where the small town smiles, a warm still sea-side
    nest.

Are the wild lands cursed perchance of time, or blest,
Sad with fear or glad with comfort of the sea?
Are the ruinous towers of churches fallen on rest
Watched of wanderers woful now, glad once as we,
When the night has all men's eyes and hearts in fee,
When the soul bows down dethroned and dispossest?
Yet must peace keep guard, by day's and night's
    decree,
Where the small town smiles, a warm still sea-side
    nest.

Friend, the lonely land is bright for you and me
All its wild ways through : but this methinks is best,
Here to watch how kindly time and change agree
Where the small town smiles, a warm still sea-side
    nest.

III

ON A COUNTRY ROAD

ALONG these low pleached lanes, on such a day,
So soft a day as this, through shade and sun,
With glad grave eyes that scanned the glad wild
    way,
And heart still hovering o'er a song begun,
And smile that warmed the world with benison,
Our father, lord long since of lordly rhyme,
Long since hath haply ridden, when the lime
Bloomed broad above him, flowering where he came.
Because thy passage once made warm this clime,
Our father Chaucer, here we praise thy name.

Each year that England clothes herself with May,
She takes thy likeness on her.   Time hath spun
Fresh raiment all in vain and strange array
For earth and man's new spirit, fain to shun
Things past for dreams of better to be won,
Through many a century since thy funeral chime
Rang, and men deemed it death's most direful crime
To have spared not thee for very love or shame ;
And yet, while mists round last year's memories
    climb,
Our father Chaucer, here we praise thy name.

Each turn of the old wild road whereon we stray,
Meseems, might bring us face to face with one
Whom seeing we could not but give thanks, and pray
For England's love our father and her son
To speak with us as once in days long done
With all men, sage and churl and monk and mime,
Who knew not as we know the soul sublime
That sang for song's love more than lust of fame.
Yet, though this be not, yet, in happy time,
Our father Chaucer, here we praise thy name.

Friend, even as bees about the flowering thyme,
Years crowd on years, till hoar decay begrime
Names once beloved ; but, seeing the sun the same,
As birds of autumn fain to praise the prime,
Our father Chaucer, here we praise thy name.

IV

THE MILL GARDEN

STATELY stand the sunflowers, glowing down the
    garden-side,
Ranged in royal rank arow along the warm grey
    wall,
Whence their deep disks burn at rich midnoon afire
    with pride,
Even as though their beams indeed were sunbeams,
    and the tall
Sceptral stems bore stars whose reign endures, not
    flowers that fall.

Lowlier laughs and basks the kindlier flower of
    homelier fame,
Held by love the sweeter that it blooms in Shake-
    speare's name,
Fragrant yet as though his hand had touched and
    made it thrill,
Like the whole world's heart, with warm new life
    and gladdening flame.
Fair befall the fair green close that lies below the
    mill !

Softlier here the flower-soft feet of refluent seasons
    glide,
Lightlier breathes the long low note of change's
    gentler call.

Wind and storm and landslip feed the lone sea's
    gulf outside,
Half a seamew's first flight hence ; but scarce may
    these appal
Peace, whose perfect seal is set for signet here on all.
Steep and deep and sterile, under fields no plough
    can tame,
Dip the cliffs full-fledged with poppies red as love or
    shame,
Wide wan daisies bleak and bold, or herbage harsh
    and chill ;
Here the full clove pinks and wallflowers crown the
    love they claim.
Fair befall the fair green close that lies below the
    mill !

All the place breathes low, but not for fear lest ill
    betide,
Soft as roses answering roses, or a dove's recall.
Little heeds it how the seaward banks may stoop and
    slide,
How the winds and years may hold all outer things
    in thrall,
How their wrath may work on hoar church tower
    and boundary wall.
Far and wide the waste and ravin of their rule pro-
    claim
Change alone the changeless lord of things, alone
    the same :
Here a flower is stronger than the winds that work
    their will,
Or the years that wing their way through darkness
    toward their aim.
Fair befall the fair green close that lies below the
    mill !

Friend, the home that smiled us welcome hither when
    we came,
When we pass again with summer, surely should
    reclaim
Somewhat given of heart's thanksgiving more than
    words fulfil—
More than song, were song more sweet than all but
    love, might frame.
Fair befall the fair green close that lies below the
    mill !

V

A SEA-MARK

RAINS have left the sea-banks ill to climb :
Waveward sinks the loosening seaboard's floor :
Half the sliding cliffs are mire and slime.
Earth, a fruit rain-rotted to the core,
Drops dissolving down in flakes, that pour
Dense as gouts from eaves grown foul with grime.
One sole rock which years that scathe not score
Stands a sea-mark in the tides of time.

Time were even as even the rainiest clime,
Life were even as even this lapsing shore,
Might not aught outlive their trustless prime :
Vainly fear would wail or hope implore,
Vainly grief revile or love adore
Seasons clothed in sunshine, rain, or rime.
Now for me one comfort held in store
Stands a sea-mark in the tides of time.

Once, by fate's default or chance's crime,
Each apart, our burdens each we bore ;
Heard, in monotones like bells that chime,
Chime the sounds of sorrows, float and soar

Joy's full carols, near or far before ;
Heard not yet across the alternate rhyme
Time's tongue tell what sign set fast of yore
Stands a sea-mark in the tides of time.

Friend, the sign we knew not heretofore
Towers in sight here present and sublime.
Faith in faith established evermore
Stands a sea-mark in the tides of time.

VI

THE CLIFFSIDE PATH

SEAWARD goes the sun, and homeward by the down
We, before the night upon his grave be sealed.
Low behind us lies the bright steep murmuring
    town,
High before us heaves the steep rough silent field.
Breach by ghastlier breach, the cliffs collapsing
    yield :
Half the path is broken, half the banks divide ;
Flawed and crumbled, riven and rent, they cleave
    and slide
Toward the ridged and wrinkled waste of girdling
    sand
Deep beneath, whose furrows tell how far and wide
Wind is lord and change is sovereign of the strand.

Star by star on the unsunned waters twiring down.
Golden spear-points glance against a silver shield.
Over banks and bents, across the headland's crown,
As by pulse of gradual plumes through twilight
    wheeled,
Soft as sleep, the waking wind awakes the weald.
Moor and copse and fallow, near or far descried,
Feel the mild wings move, and gladden where they
    glide :

Silence, uttering love that all things understand,
Bids the quiet fields forget that hard beside
Wind is lord and change is sovereign of the strand.

Yet may sight, ere all the hoar soft shade grow
        brown,
Hardly reckon half the rifts and rents unhealed
Where the scarred cliffs downward sundering drive
        and drown,
Hewn as if with stroke of swords in tempest steeled,
Wielded as the night's will and the wind's may
        wield.
Crowned and zoned in vain with flowers of autumn-
        tide,
Soon the blasts shall break them, soon the waters
        hide ;
Soon, where late we stood, shall no man ever stand.
Life and love seek harbourage on the landward side :
Wind is lord and change is sovereign of the strand.

Friend, though man be less than these, for all his
        pride,
Yet, for all his weakness, shall not hope abide ?
Wind and change can wreck but life and waste but
        land :
Truth and trust are sure, though here till all subside
Wind is lord and change is sovereign of the strand.

VII

IN THE WATER

THE sea is awake, and the sound of the song of the
  joy of her waking is rolled
From afar to the star that recedes, from anear to the
  wastes of the wild wide shore.
Her call is a trumpet compelling us homeward: if
  dawn in her east be acold,
From the sea shall we crave not her grace to rekindle
  the life that it kindled before,
Her breath to requicken, her bosom to rock us, her
  kisses to bless as of yore?
For the wind, with his wings half open, at pause in
  the sky, neither fettered nor free,
Leans waveward and flutters the ripple to laughter :
  and fain would the twain of us be
Where lightly the wave yearns forward from under
  the curve of the deep dawn's dome,
And, full of the morning and fired with the pride of
  the glory thereof and the glee,
Strike out from the shore as the heart in us bids and
  beseeches, athirst for the foam.

Life holds not an hour that is better to live in : the
  past is a tale that is told,
The future a sun-flecked shadow, alive and asleep,
  with a blessing in store.

As we give us again to the waters, the rapture of
   limbs that the waters enfold
Is less than the rapture of spirit whereby, though the
   burden it quits were sore,
Our souls and the bodies they wield at their will are
   absorbed in the life they adore—
In the life that endures no burden, and bows not the
   forehead, and bends not the knee—
In the life everlasting of earth and of heaven, in the
   laws that atone and agree,
In the measureless music of things, in the fervour of
   forces that rest or that roam,
That cross and return and reissue, as I after you and
   as you after me
Strike out from the shore as the heart in us bids and
   beseeches, athirst for the foam.

For, albeit he were less than the least of them, haply
   the heart of a man may be bold
To rejoice in the word of the sea as a mother's that
   saith to the son she bore,
Child, was not the life in thee mine, and my spirit
   the breath in thy lips from of old?
Have I let not thy weakness exult in my strength,
   and thy foolishness learn of my lore?
Have I helped not or healed not thine anguish, or
   made not the might of thy gladness more?
And surely his heart should answer, The light of the
   love of my life is in thee.
She is fairer than earth, and the sun is not fairer,
   the wind is not blither than she :
From my youth hath she shown me the joy of her
   bays that I crossed, of her cliffs that I clomb,

Till now that the twain of us here, in desire of the
    dawn and in trust of the sea,
Strike out from the shore as the heart in us bids and
    beseeches, athirst for the foam.

Friend, earth is a harbour of refuge for winter, a
    covert whereunder to flee
When day is the vassal of night, and the strength of
    the hosts of her mightier than he ;
But here is the presence adored of me, here my desire
    is at rest and at home.
There are cliffs to be climbed upon land, there are
    ways to be trodden and ridden : but we
Strike out from the shore as the heart in us bids and
    beseeches, athirst for the foam.

VIII

THE SUNBOWS

Spray of song that springs in April, light of love that
    laughs through May,
Live and die and live for ever : nought of all things
    far less fair
Keeps a surer life than these that seem to pass like
    fire away.

In the souls they live which are but all the brighter
    that they were ;
In the hearts that kindle, thinking what delight of old
    was there.

Wind that shapes and lifts and shifts them bids
    perpetual memory play
Over dreams and in and out of deeds and thoughts
    which seem to wear
Light that leaps and runs and revels through the
    springing flames of spray.

Dawn is wild upon the waters where we drink of
    dawn to-day :
Wide, from wave to wave rekindling in rebound
    through radiant air,
Flash the fires unwoven and woven again of wind
    that works in play,
Working wonders more than heart may note or sight
    may wellnigh dare,

Wefts of rarer light than colours rain from heaven,
  though this be rare.
Arch on arch unbuilt in building, reared and ruined
  ray by ray,
Breaks and brightens, laughs and lessens, even till
  eyes may hardly bear
Light that leaps and runs and revels through the
  springing flames of spray.

Year on year sheds light and music rolled and flashed
  from bay to bay
Round the summer capes of time and winter head
  lands keen and bare
Whence the soul keeps watch, and bids her vassal
  memory watch and pray,
If perchance the dawn may quicken, or perchance the
  midnight spare.
Silence quells not music, darkness takes not sunlight
  in her snare ;
Shall not joys endure that perish ?   Yea, saith dawn,
  though night say nay :
Life on life goes out, but very life enkindles everywhere
Light that leaps and runs and revels through the
  springing flames of spray.

Friend, were life no more than this is, well would yet
  the living fare.
All aflower and all afire and all flung heavenward,
  who shall say
Such a flash of life were worthless ? This is worth
  a world of care—
Light that leaps and runs and revels through the
  springing flames of spray.

IX

ON THE VERGE

Here begins the sea that ends not till the world's
    end.   Where we stand,
Could we know the next high sea-mark set beyond
    these waves that gleam,
We should know what never man hath known, nor
    eye of man hath scanned.
Nought beyond these coiling clouds that melt like
    fume of shrines that steam
Breaks or stays the strength of waters till they pass
    our bounds of dream.
Where the waste Land's End leans westward, all the
    seas it watches roll
Find their border fixed beyond them, and a world-
    wide shore's control :
These whereby we stand no shore beyond us limits :
    these are free.
Gazing hence, we see the water that grows iron
    round the Pole,
From the shore that hath no shore beyond it set in
    all the sea.

Sail on sail along the sea-line fades and flashes ; here
    on land
Flash and fade the wheeling wings on wings of mews
    that plunge and scream.

Hour on hour along the line of life and time's evasive
 strand
Shines and darkens, wanes and waxes, slays and
 dies : and scarce they seem
More than motes that thronged and trembled in the
 brief noon's breath and beam.
Some with crying and wailing, some with notes like
 sound of bells that toll,
Some with sighing and laughing, some with words
 that blessed and made us whole,
Passed, and left us, and we know not what they were,
 nor what were we.
Would we know, being mortal ? Never breath of
 answering whisper stole
From the shore that hath no shore beyond it set in
 all the sea.

Shadows, would we question darkness ? Ere our
 eyes and brows be fanned
Round with airs of twilight, washed with dews from
 sleep's eternal stream,
Would we know sleep's guarded secret ? Ere the fire
 consume the brand,
Would it know if yet its ashes may requicken ? yet
 we deem
Surely man may know, or ever night unyoke her
 starry team,
What the dawn shall be, or if the dawn shall be not :
 yea, the scroll
Would we read of sleep's dark scripture, pledge of
 peace or doom of dole.
Ah, but here man's heart leaps, yearning toward the
 gloom with venturous glee,

Though his pilot eye behold nor bay nor harbour, rock
    nor shoal,
From the shore that hath no shore beyond it set in
    all the sea.

Friend, who knows if death indeed have life or life
    have death for goal ?
Day nor night can tell us, nor may seas declare nor
    skies unroll
What has been from everlasting, or if aught shall
    alway be.
Silence answering only strikes response reverberate
    on the soul
From the shore that hath no shore beyond it set in
    all the sea.

A NEW-YEAR ODE

To Victor Hugo

I

TWICE twelve times have the springs of years refilled
 Their fountains from the river-head of time
Since by the green sea's marge, ere autumn chilled
 Waters and woods with sense of changing clime,
A great light rose upon my soul, and thrilled
 My spirit of sense with sense of spheres in chime,
Sound as of song wherewith a God would build
 Towers that no force of conquering war might climb.
  Wind shook the glimmering sea
  Even as my soul in me
Was stirred with breath of mastery more sublime,
  Uplift and borne along
  More thunderous tides of song,
 Where wave rang back to wave more rapturous
  rhyme
 And world on world flashed lordlier light
Than ever lit the wandering ways of ships by night.

II

The spirit of God, whose breath of life is song,
 Moved, though his word was human, on the face
Of those deep waters of the soul, too long
 Dumb, dark, and cold, that waited for the grace
Wherewith day kindles heaven : and as some throng
 Of quiring wings fills full some lone chill place
With sudden rush of life and joy, more strong
 Than death or sorrow or all night's darkling race,

So was my heart, that heard
All heaven in each deep word,
Filled full with light of thought, and waxed apace
Itself more wide and deep,
To take that gift and keep
And cherish while my days fulfilled their space
A record wide as earth and sea,
The Legend writ of Ages past and yet to be.

III

As high the chant of Paradise and Hell
Rose, when the soul of Milton gave it wings ;
As wide the sweep of Shakespeare's empire fell,
When life had bared for him her secret springs ;
But not his various soul might range and dwell
Amid the mysteries of the founts of things ;
Nor Milton's range of rule so far might swell
Across the kingdoms of forgotten kings.
Men, centuries, nations, time,
Life, death, love, trust, and crime,
Rang record through the change of smitten strings
That felt an exile's hand
Sound hope for every land
More loud than storm's cloud-sundering trumpet
rings,
And bid strong death for judgment rise,
And life bow down for judgment of his awless eyes

IV

And death, soul-stricken in his strength, resigned
The keeping of the sepulchres to song ;
And life was humbled, and his height of mind
Brought lower than lies a grave-stone fallen along ;

And like a ghost and like a God mankind
 Rose clad with light and darkness ; weak and
  strong,
Clean and unclean, with eyes afire and blind,
 Wounded and whole, fast bound with cord and
  thong,
   Free ; fair and foul, sin-stained,
   And sinless ; crowned and chained ;
 Fleet-limbed, and halting all his lifetime long ;
   Glad of deep shame, and sad
   For shame's sake ; wise, and mad ;
 Girt round with love and hate of right and wrong ;
  Armed and disarmed for sleep and strife ;
Proud, and sore fear made havoc of his pride of life.

      v

Shadows and shapes of fable and storied sooth
 Rose glorious as with gleam of gold unpriced ;
Eve, clothed with heavenly nakedness and youth
 That matched the morning's ; Cain, self-sacrificed
On crime's first altar : legends wise as truth,
 And truth in legends deep embalmed and spiced ;
The stars that saw the starlike eyes of Ruth,
 The grave that heard the clarion call of Christ.
   And higher than sorrow and mirth
   The heavenly song of earth
 Sprang, in such notes as might have well sufficed
   To still the storms of time
   And sin's contentious clime
With peace renewed of life reparadised :
  Earth, scarred not yet with temporal scars ;
Goddess of gods, our mother, chosen among the
 stars.

VI

Earth fair as heaven, ere change and time set odds
  Between them, light and darkness know not when,
And fear, grown strong through panic periods,
  Crouched, a crowned worm, in faith's Lernean fen,
And love lay bound, and hope was scourged with
    rods,
  And death cried out from desert and from den,
Seeing all the heaven above him dark with gods
  And all the world about him marred of men.
      Cities that nought might purge
      Save the sea's whelming surge
  From all the pent pollutions in their pen
      Deep death drank down, and wrought,
      With wreck of all things, nought,
  That none might live of all their names again,
      Nor aught of all whose life is breath
Serve any God whose likeness was not like to death.

VII

Till by the lips and eyes of one live nation
  The blind mute world found grace to see and
    speak,
And light watched rise a more divine creation
  At that more godlike utterance of the Greek,
Let there be freedom. Kings whose orient station
  Made pale the morn, and all her presage bleak,
Girt each with strengths of all his generation,
  Dim tribes of shamefaced soul and sun-swart cheek,
      Twice, urged with one desire,
      Son following hard on sire,
  With all the wrath of all a world to wreak,

And all the rage of night
Afire against the light
Whose weakness makes her strong-winged empire
    weak,
Stood up to unsay that saying, and fell
Too far for song, though song were thousand-tongued,
    to tell.

VIII

From those deep echoes of the loud Ægean
  That rolled response whereat false fear was chid
By songs of joy sublime and Sophoclean,
  Fresh notes reverberate westward rose to bid
All wearier times take comfort from the pæan
  That tells the night what deeds the sunrise did,
Even till the lawns and torrents Pyrenean
  Ring answer from the records of the Cid.
      But never force of fountains
      From sunniest hearts of mountains
  Wherein the soul of hidden June was hid
      Poured forth so pure and strong
      Springs of reiterate song,
  Loud as the streams his fame was reared amid,
    More sweet than flowers they feed, and fair
With grace of lordlier sunshine and more lambent
    air.

IX

A star more prosperous than the storm-clothed east's
  Clothed all the warm south-west with light like
    spring's,
When hands of strong men spread the wolves their
    feasts
  And from snake-spirited princes plucked the stings;

Ere earth, grown all one den of hurtling beasts,
 Had for her sunshine and her watersprings
The fire of hell that warmed the hearts of priests,
 The wells of blood that slaked the lips of kings.
  The shadow of night made stone
  Stood populous and alone,
 Dense with its dead and loathed of living things
  That draw not life from death,
  And as with hell's own breath
And clangour of immitigable wings
  Vexed the fair face of Paris, made
Foul in its murderous imminence of sound and shade.

x

And all these things were parcels of the vision
 That moved a cloud before his eyes, or stood
A tower half shattered by the strong collision
 Of spirit and spirit, of evil gods with good ;
A ruinous wall rent through with grim division,
 Where time had marked his every monstrous mood
Of scorn and strength and pride and self-derision :
  The Tower of Things, that felt upon it brood
   Night, and about it cast
   The storm of all the past
 Now mute and forceless as a fire subdued :
   Yet through the rifted years
   And centuries veiled with tears
 And ages as with very death imbrued
  Freedom, whence hope and faith grow strong,
Smiles, and firm love sustains the indissoluble song.

XI

Above the cloudy coil of days deceased,
  Its might of flight, with mists and storms beset,
Burns heavenward, as with heart and hope increased,
  For all the change of tempests, all the fret
Of frost or fire, keen fraud or force released,
  Wherewith the world once wasted knows not yet
If evil or good lit all the darkling east
    From the ardent moon of sovereign Mahomet.
      Sublime in work and will
      The song sublimer still
Salutes him, ere the splendour shrink and set ;
      Then with imperious eye
      And wing that sounds the sky
Soars and sees risen as ghosts in concourse met
    The old world's seven elder wonders, firm
As dust and fixed as shadows, weaker than the worm.

XII

High witness borne of knights high-souled and hoary
  Before death's face and empire's rings and glows
Even from the dust their life poured forth left gory,
  As the eagle's cry rings after from the snows
Supreme rebuke of shame clothed round with glory
  And hosts whose track the false crowned eagle
    shows ;
More loud than sounds through stormiest song and
    story
  The laugh of slayers whose names the sea-wind
    knows ;
      More loud than peals on land
      In many a red wet hand
  The clash of gold and cymbals as they close ;

Loud as the blast that meets
   The might of marshalled fleets
And sheds it into shipwreck, like a rose
    Blown from a child's light grasp in sign
That earth's high lords are lords not over breeze and
   brine.

XIII

Above the dust and mire of man's dejection
   The wide-winged spirit of song resurgent sees
His wingless and long-labouring resurrection
   Up the arduous heaven, by sore and strange degrees,
Mount, and with splendour of the soul's reflection
   Strike heaven's dark sovereign down upon his
    knees,
Pale in the light of orient insurrection,
   And dumb before the almightier lord's decrees
     Who bade him be of yore,
     Who bids him be no more :
   And all earth's heart is quickened as the sea's,
     Even as when sunrise burns
     The very sea's heart yearns
   That heard not on the midnight-walking breeze
     The wail that woke with evensong
From hearts of poor folk watching all the darkness
   long.

XIV

Dawn and the beams of sunbright song illume
   Love, with strange children at her piteous breast,
By grace of weakness from the grave-mouthed gloom
   Plucked, and by mercy lulled to living rest,
Soft as the nursling's nigh the grandsire's tomb
   That fell on sleep, a bird of rifled nest ;

Soft as the lips whose smile unsaid the doom
  That gave their sire to violent death's arrest.
        Even for such love's sake strong,
        Wrath fires the inveterate song
  That bids hell gape for one whose bland mouth
    blest
        All slayers and liars that sighed
        Prayer as they slew and lied
  Till blood had clothed his priesthood as a vest,
      And hears, though darkness yet be dumb,
The silence of the trumpet of the wrath to come.

                    XV

Nor lacked these lights of constellated age
  A star among them fed with life more dire,
Lit with his bloodred fame, whose withering rage
  Made earth for heaven's sake one funereal pyre
And life in faith's name one appointed stage
  For death to purge the souls of men with fire.
Heaven, earth, and hell on one thrice tragic page
  Mixed all their light and darkness : one man's lyre
        Gave all their echoes voice ;
        Bade rose-cheeked love rejoice,
  And cold-lipped craft with ravenous fear conspire,
        And fire-eyed faith smite hope
        Dead, seeing enthroned as Pope
  And crowned of heaven on earth at hell's desire
      Sin, called by death's incestuous name
Borgia : the world that heard it flushed and quailed
    with shame.

XVI

Another year, and hope triumphant heard
  The consummating sound of song that spake
Conclusion to the multitudinous word
  Whose expectation held her spirit awake
Till full delight for twice twelve years deferred
  Bade all souls entering eat and drink, and take
A third time comfort given them, that the third
  Might heap the measure up of twain, and make
      The sinking year sublime
      Among all sons of time
  And fair in all men's memories for his sake.
      Each thought of ours became
      Fire, kindling from his flame,
  And music widening in his wide song's wake.
      Yea, and the world bore witness here
How great a light was risen upon this darkening year.

XVII

It was the dawn of winter : sword in sheath,
  Change, veiled and mild, came down the gradual air
With cold slow smiles that hid the doom beneath.
  Five days to die in yet were autumn's, ere
The last leaf withered from his flowerless wreath.
  South, east, and north, our skies were all blown bare,
But westward over glimmering holt and heath
  Cloud, wind, and light had made a heaven more
      fair
      Than ever dream or truth
      Showed earth in time's keen youth
  When men with angels communed unaware.

Above the sun's head, now
Veiled even to the ardent brow,
Rose two sheer wings of sundering cloud, that were
As a bird's poised for vehement flight,
Full-fledged with plumes of tawny fire and hoar grey
light.

XVIII

As midnight black, as twilight brown, they spread,
But feathered thick with flame that streaked and
lined
Their living darkness, ominous else of dread,
From south to northmost verge of heaven inclined
Most like some giant angel's, whose bent head
Bowed earthward, as with message for mankind
Of doom or benediction to be shed
From passage of his presence. Far behind,
Even while they seemed to close,
Stoop, and take flight, arose
Above them, higher than heavenliest thought may
find
In light or night supreme
Of vision or of dream,
Immeasurable of men's eyes or mounting mind,
Heaven, manifest in manifold
Light of pure pallid amber, cheered with fire of gold.

XIX

And where the fine gold faded all the sky
Shone green as the outer sea when April glows,
Inlaid with flakes and feathers fledged to fly
Of clouds suspense in rapture and repose,
With large live petals, broad as love bids lie
Full open when the sun salutes the rose,

And small rent sprays wherewith the heavens most
   high
  Were strewn as autumn strews the garden-close
      With ruinous roseleaves whirled
      About their wan chill world,
  Through wind-worn bowers that now no music
    knows,
      Spoil of the dim dusk year
      Whose utter night is near,
  And near the flower of dawn beyond it blows ;
      Till east and west were fire and light,
As though the dawn to come had flushed the coming
   night.

XX

The highways paced of men that toil or play,
  The byways known of none but lonely feet,
Were paven of purple woven of night and day
  With hands that met as hands of friends might
    meet—
As though night's were not lifted up to slay
  And day's had waxed not weaker. Peace more
    sweet
Than music, light more soft than shadow, lay
  On downs and moorlands wan with day's defeat,
      That watched afar above
      Life's very rose of love
  Let all its lustrous leaves fall, fade, and fleet,
      And fill all heaven and earth
      Full as with fires of birth
  Whence time should feed his years with light and
    heat :
      Nay, not life's, but a flower more strong
Than life or time or death, love's very rose of song.

XXI

Song visible, whence all men's eyes were lit
  With love and loving wonder : song that glowed
Through cloud and change on souls that knew not it
  And hearts that wist not whence their comfort
      flowed,
Whence fear was lightened of her fever-fit,
  Whence anguish of her life-compelling load.
Yea, no man's head whereon the fire alit,
  Of all that passed along that sunset road
      Westward, no brow so drear,
      No eye so dull of cheer,
  No face so mean whereon that light abode,
      But as with alien pride
      Strange godhead glorified
  Each feature flushed from heaven with fire that
      showed
    The likeness of its own life wrought
By strong transfiguration as of living thought.

XXII

Nor only clouds of the everlasting sky,
  Nor only men that paced that sunward way
To the utter bourne of evening, passed not by
  Unblest or unillumined : none might say,
Of all things visible in the wide world's eye,
  That all too low for all that grace it lay :
The lowliest lakelets of the moorland nigh,
  The narrowest pools where shallowest wavelets
      play,
      Were filled from heaven above
      With light like fire of love,

With flames and colours like a dawn in May,
  As hearts that lowlier live
  With light of thoughts that give
Light from the depth of souls more deep than they
  Through song's or story's kindling scroll,
The splendour of the shadow that reveals the soul.

XXIII

For, when such light is in the world, we share,
  All of us, all the rays thereof that shine :
Its presence is alive in the unseen air,
  Its fire within our veins as quickening wine ;
A spirit is shed on all men everywhere,
  Known or not known of all men for divine.
Yea, as the sun makes heaven, that light makes fair
  All souls of ours, all lesser souls than thine,
    Priest, prophet, seer and sage,
    Lord of a subject age
  That bears thy seal upon it for a sign ;
    Whose name shall be thy name,
    Whose light thy light of fame,
  The light of love that makes thy soul a shrine
    Whose record through all years to be
Shall bear this witness written—that its womb bare
  thee.

XXIV

O mystery, whence to one man's hand was given
  Power upon all things of the spirit, and might
Whereby the veil of all the years was riven
  And naked stood the secret soul of night !
O marvel, hailed of eyes whence cloud is driven,
  That shows at last wrong reconciled with right

By death divine of evil and sin forgiven !
  O light of song, whose fire is perfect light ;
    No speech, no voice, no thought,
    No love, avails us aught
  For service of thanksgiving in his sight
      Who hath given us all for ever
      Such gifts that man gave never
  So many and great since first Time's wings took
    flight.
    Man may not praise a spirit above
Man's : life and death shall praise him : we can only
  love.

XXV

Life, everlasting while the worlds endure,
  Death, self-abased before a power more high,
Shall bear one witness, and their word stand sure,
  That not till time be dead shall this man die.
Love, like a bird, comes loyal to his lure ;
  Fame flies before him, wingless else to fly.
A child's heart toward his kind is not more pure,
  An eagle's toward the sun no lordlier eye.
      Awe sweet as love and proud
      As fame, though hushed and bowed,
  Yearns toward him silent as his face goes by :
      All crowns before his crown
      Triumphantly bow down,
  For pride that one more great than all draws nigh
    All souls applaud, all hearts acclaim,
One heart benign, one soul supreme, one conquering
  name.

NOTES

LINES ON THE MONUMENT OF GIUSEPPE MAZZINI.

ITALIA, mother of the souls of men,
    Mother divine,
Of all that served thee best with sword or pen,
    All sons of thine,

Thou knowest that here the likeness of the best
    Before thee stands ;
The head most high, the heart found faithfullest,
    The purest hands.

Above the fume and foam of time that flits,
    The soul, we know,
Now sits on high where Alighieri sits
    With Angelo.

Not his own heavenly tongue hath heavenly speech
    Enough to say
What this man was, whose praise no thought may
    reach,
    No words can weigh.

Since man's first mother brought to mortal birth
    Her first-born son,
Such grace befell not ever man on earth
    As crowns this one.

Of God nor man was ever this thing said,
    That he could give
Life back to her who gave him, whence his dead
    Mother might live.

But this man found his mother dead and slain,
    With fast sealed eyes,
And bade the dead rise up and live again,
    And she did rise.

And all the world was bright with her through
    him :
    But dark with strife,
Like heaven's own sun that storming clouds bedim,
    Was all his life.

Life and the clouds are vanished : hate and fear
    Have had their span
Of time to hurt, and are not : he is here,
    The sunlike man.

City superb that hadst Columbus first
    For sovereign son,
Be prouder that thy breast hath later nurst
    This mightier one.

Glory be his for ever, while his land
    Lives and is free,
As with controlling breath and sovereign hand
    He bade her be.

Earth shows to heaven the names by thousands told
    That crown her fame,
But highest of all that heaven and earth behold
    Mazzini's name.

LES CASQUETS.

FROM the depths of the waters that lighten and darken
  With change everlasting of life and of death,
Where hardly by noon if the lulled ear hearken
  It hears the sea's as a tired child's breath,
Where hardly by night if an eye dare scan it
  The storm lets shipwreck be seen or heard,
As the reefs to the waves and the foam to the granite
    Respond one merciless word,

Sheer seen and far, in the sea's live heaven,
  A seamew's flight from the wild sweet land,
White-plumed with foam if the wind wake, seven
  Black helms as of warriors that stir not stand.
From the depths that abide and the waves that environ
  Seven rocks rear heads that the midnight masks ;
And the strokes of the swords of the storm are as iron
    On the steel of the wave-worn casques.

Be night's dark word as the word of a wizard,
  Be the word of dawn as a god's glad word,
Like heads of the spirits of darkness visored
  That see not for ever, nor ever have heard,
These basnets, plumed as for fight or plumeless,
  Crowned of the storm and by storm discrowned,
Keep ward of the lists where the dead lie tombless
    And the tale of them is not found.

Nor eye may number nor hand may reckon
  The tithes that are taken of life by the dark,
Or the ways of the path, if doom's hand beckon,
  For the soul to fare as a helmless bark—
Fare forth on a way that no sign showeth,
  Nor aught of its goal or of aught between
A path for her flight which no fowl knoweth,
    Which the vulture's eye hath not seen.

Here still, though the wave and the wind seem
    lovers
  Lulled half asleep by their own soft words,
A dream as of death in the sun's light hovers,
  And a sign in the motions and cries of the birds.
Dark auguries and keen from the sweet sea-swallows
  Strike noon with a sense as of midnight's breath,
And the wing that flees and the wing that follows
    Are as types of the wings of death.

For here, when the night roars round, and under
  The white sea lightens and leaps like fire,
Acclaimed of storm and applauded in thunder,
  Sits death on the throne of his crowned desire.
Yea, hardly the hand of the god might fashion
  A seat more strong for his strength to take,
For the might of his heart and the pride of his
    passion
    To rejoice in the wars they make.

When the heart in him brightens with blitheness of
    battle
  And the depth of its thirst is fulfilled with strife,
And his ear with the ravage of bolts that rattle,
  And the soul of death with the pride of life,

Till the darkness is loud with his dark thanksgiving
And wind and cloud are as chords of his hymn,
There is nought save death in the deep night living,
And the whole night worships him.

Heaven's height bows down to him, signed with his
token,
And the sea's depth, moved as a heart that yearns,
Heaves up to him, strong as a heart half broken,
A heart that breaks in a prayer that burns.
Of cloud is the shrine of his worship moulded,
But the altar therein is of sea-shaped stone,
Whereon, with the strength of his wide wings folded,
Sits death in the dark, alone.

He hears the word of his servant spoken,
The word that the wind his servant saith ;
Storm writes on the front of the night his token,
That the skies may seem to bow down to death.
But the clouds that stoop and the storms that minister
Serve but as thralls that fulfil their tasks ;
And his seal is not set save here on the sinister
Crests reared of the crownless casques.

Nor flame nor plume of the storm that crowned them
Gilds or quickens their stark black strength.
Life lightens and murmurs and laughs right round
them,
At peace with the noon's whole breadth and length,
At one with the heart of the soft-souled heaven,
At one with the life of the kind wild land :
But its touch may unbrace not the strengths of the
seven
Casques hewn of the storm-wind's hand.

No touch may loosen the black braced helmets
    For the wild elves' heads of the wild waves
        wrought.
As flowers on the sea are her small green realmlets,
    Like heavens made out of a child's heart's thought ;
But these as thorns of her desolate places,
    Strong fangs that fasten and hold lives fast :
And the vizors are framed as for formless faces
        That a dark dream sees go past.

Of fear and of fate are the frontlets fashioned,
    And the heads behind them are dire and dumb.
When the heart of the darkness is scarce impassioned,
    Thrilled scarce with sense of the wrath to come,
They bear the sign from of old engraven,
    Though peace be round them and strife seem far,
That here is none but the night-wind's haven,
        With death for the harbour bar.

Of the iron of doom are the casquets carven,
    That never the rivets thereof should burst.
When the heart of the darkness is hunger-starven,
    And the throats of the gulfs are agape for thirst,
And stars are as flowers that the wind bids wither,
    And dawn is as hope struck dead by fear,
The rage of the ravenous night sets hither,
        And the crown of her work is here.

All shores about and afar lie lonely,
    But lonelier are these than the heart of grief,
These loose-linked rivets of rock, whence only
    Strange life scarce gleams from the sheer main reef,

With a blind wan face in the wild wan morning,
  With a live lit flame on its brows by night,
That the lost may lose not its word's mute warning
  And the blind by its grace have sight.

Here, walled in with the wide waste water,
  Grew the grace of a girl's lone life,
The sea's and the sea-wind's foster-daughter,
  And peace was hers in the main mid strife.
For her were the rocks clothed round with thunder,
  And the crests of them carved by the storm-smith's
    craft :
For her was the mid storm rent in sunder
  As with passion that wailed and laughed.

For her the sunrise kindled and scattered
  The red rose-leaflets of countless cloud :
For her the blasts of the springtide shattered
  The strengths reluctant of waves back-bowed.
For her would winds in the mid sky levy
  Bright wars that hardly the night bade cease :
At noon, when sleep on the sea lies heavy,
  For her would the sun make peace.

Peace rose crowned with the dawn on golden
  Lit leagues of triumph that flamed and smiled :
Peace lay lulled in the moon-beholden
  Warm darkness making the world's heart mild
For all the wide waves' troubles and treasons,
  One word only her soul's ear heard
Speak from stormless and storm-rent seasons,
  And nought save peace was the word.

All her life waxed large with the light of it,
    All her heart fed full on the sound :
Spirit and sense were exalted in sight of it,
    Compassed and girdled and clothed with it round
Sense was none but a strong still rapture,
    Spirit was none but a joy sublime,
Of strength to curb and of craft to capture
    The craft and the strength of Time.

Time lay bound as in painless prison
    There, closed in with a strait small space.
Never thereon as a strange light risen
    Change had unveiled for her grief's far face.
Three white walls flung out from the basement
    Girt the width of the world whereon
Gazing at night from her flame-lit casement
    She saw where the dark sea shone.

Hardly the breadth of a few brief paces,
    Hardly the length of a strong man's stride,
The small court flower-lit with children's faces
    Scarce held scope for a bird to hide.
Yet here was a man's brood reared and hidden
    Between the rocks and the towers and the foam,
Where peril and pity and peace were bidden
    As guests to the same sure home.

Here would pity keep watch for peril,
    And surety comfort his heart with peace.
No flower save one, where the reefs lie sterile,
    Gave of the seed of its heart's increase.

Pity and surety and peace most lowly
   Were the root and the stem and the bloom of the
       flower :
And the light and the breath of the buds kept holy
    That maid's else blossomless bower.

With never a leaf but the seaweed's tangle,
   Never a bird's but the seamew's note,
It heard all round it the strong storms wrangle,
   Watched far past it the waste wrecks float.
But her soul was stilled by the sky's endurance,
   And her heart made glad with the sea's content ;
And he faith waxed more in the sun's assurance
    For the winds that came and went.

Sweetness was brought for her forth of the bitter
   Sea's strength, and light of the deep sea's dark,
From where green lawns on Alderney glitter
   To the bastioned crags of the steeps of Sark.
These she knew from afar beholden,
   And marvelled haply what life would be
On moors that sunset and dawn leave golden,
    In dells that smile on the sea.

And forth she fared as a stout-souled rover,
   For a brief blithe raid on the bounding brine :
And light winds ferried her light bark over
   To the lone soft island of fair-limbed kine.
But the league-long length of its wild green border,
   And the small bright streets of serene St. Anne,
Perplexed her sense with a strange disorder
·   At sight of the works of man.

The world was here, and the world's confusion,
   And the dust of the wheels of revolving life,
Pain, labour, change, and the fierce illusion
   Of strife more vain than the sea's old strife.
And her heart within her was vexed, and dizzy
   The sense of her soul as a wheel that whirled :
She might not endure for a space that busy
      Loud coil of the troublous world.

Too full, she said, was the world of trouble,
   Too dense with noise of contentious things,
And shows less bright than the blithe foam's bubble
   As home she fared on the smooth wind's wings.
For joy grows loftier in air more lonely,
   Where only the sea's brood fain would be ;
Where only the heart may receive in it only
      The love of the heart of the sea.

A BALLAD OF SARK.

HIGH beyond the granite portal arched across
  Like the gateway of some godlike giant's hold
Sweep and swell the billowy breasts of moor and moss
  East and westward, and the dell their slopes enfold
  Basks in purple, glows in green, exults in gold.
Glens that know the dove and fells that hear the lark
Fill with joy the rapturous island, as an ark
    Full of spicery wrought from herb and flower and
      tree.
None would dream that grief even here may disembark
  On the wrathful woful marge of earth and sea.

Rocks emblazoned like the mid shield's royal boss
  Take the sun with all their blossom broad and
      bold.
None would dream that all this moorland's glow and
      gloss
  Could be dark as tombs that strike the spirit acold
  Even in eyes that opened here, and here behold
Now no sun relume from hope's belated spark
Any comfort, nor may ears of mourners hark
    Though the ripe woods ring with golden-throated
      glee,
While the soul lies shattered, like a stranded bark
  On the wrathful woful marge of earth and sea.

Death and doom are they whose crested triumphs
toss
  On the proud plumed waves whence mourning
    notes are tolled.
Wail of perfect woe and moan for utter loss
  Raise the bride-song through the graveyard on the
    wold
  Where the bride-bed keeps the bridegroom fast in
    mould,
Where the bride, with death for priest and doom for
  clerk,
Hears for choir the throats of waves like wolves that
  bark,
  Sore anhungered, off the drear Eperquerie.
Fain to spoil the strongholds of the strength of Sark
  On the wrathful woful marge of earth and sea.

Prince of storm and tempest, lord whose ways are
  dark,
Wind whose wings are spread for flight that none
  may mark,
  Lightly dies the joy that lives by grace of thee.
Love through thee lies bleeding, hope lies cold and
  stark,
  On the wrathful woful marge of earth and sea.

NINE YEARS OLD

February 4, 1883

I

Lord of light, whose shrine no hands destroy,
   God of song, whose hymn no tongue refuses,
Now, though spring far hence be cold and coy,
   Bid the golden mouths of all the Muses
Ring forth gold of strains without alloy,
   Till the ninefold rapture that suffuses
Heaven with song bid earth exult for joy,
   Since the child whose head this dawn bedews is
Sweet as once thy violet-cradled boy.

II

Even as he lay lapped about with flowers,
   Lies the life now nine years old before us
Lapped about with love in all its hours ;
   Hailed of many loves that chant in chorus
Loud or low from lush or leafless bowers,
   Some from hearts exultant born sonorous,
Some scarce louder-voiced than soft-tongued
     showers
   Two months hence, when spring's light wings
     poised o'er us
High shall hover, and her heart be ours.

III

Even as he, though man-forsaken, smiled
  On the soft kind snakes divinely bidden
There to feed him in the green mid wild
  Full with hurtless honey, till the hidden
Birth should prosper, finding fate more mild,
  So full-fed with pleasures unforbidden,
So by love's lures blamelessly beguiled,
  Laughs the nursling of our hearts unchidden
Yet by change that mars not yet the child.

IV

Ah, not yet !   Thou, lord of night and day,
  Time, sweet father of such blameless pleasure,
Time, false friend who tak'st thy gifts away,
  Spare us yet some scantlings of the treasure,
Leave us yet some rapture of delay,
  Yet some bliss of blind and fearless leisure
Unprophetic of delight's decay,
  Yet some nights and days wherein to measure
All the joys that bless us while they may.

V

Not the waste Arcadian woodland, wet
  Still with dawn and vocal with Alpheus,
Reared a nursling worthier love's regret,
  Lord, than this, whose eyes beholden free us
Straight from bonds the soul would fain forget,
  Fain cast off, that night and day might see us
Clear once more of life's vain fume and fret :
  Leave us, then, whate'er thy doom decree us,
Yet some days wherein to love him yet.

VI

Yet some days wherein the child is ours,
  Ours, not thine, O lord whose hand is o'er us
Always, as the sky with suns and showers
  Dense and radiant, soundless or sonorous ;
Yet some days for love's sake, ere the bowers
  Fade wherein his fair first years kept chorus
Night and day with Graces robed like hours,
  Ere this worshipped childhood wane before us,
Change, and bring forth fruit—but no more flowers.

VII

Love we may the thing that is to be,
  Love we must : but how forego this olden
Joy, this flower of childish love, that we
  Held more dear than aught of Time is holden—
Time, whose laugh is like as Death's to see—
  Time, who heeds not aught of all beholden,
Heard, or touched in passing—flower or tree,
  Tares or grain of leaden days or golden—
More than wind has heed of ships at sea ?

VIII

First the babe, a very rose of joy,
  Sweet as hope's first note of jubilation,
Passes : then must growth and change destroy
  Next the child, and mar the consecration
Hallowing yet, ere thought or sense annoy,
  Childhood's yet half heavenlike habitation,
Bright as truth and frailer than a toy ;
  Whence its guest with eager gratulation
Springs, and life grows larger round the boy.

IX

Yet, ere sunrise wholly cease to shine,
  Ere change come to chide our hearts, and scatter
Memories marked for love's sake with a sign,
  Let the light of dawn beholden flatter
Yet some while our eyes that feed on thine,
  Child, with love that change nor time can shatter,
Love, whose silent song says more than mine
  Now, though charged with elder loves and latter
Here it hails a lord whose years are nine.

AFTER A READING

For the seven times seventh time love would renew
    the delight without end or alloy
That it takes in the praise as it takes in the presence
    of eyes that fulfil it with joy ;
But how shall it praise them and rest unrebuked by
    the presence and pride of the boy ?

Praise meet for a child is unmeet for an elder whose
    winters and springs are nine :
What song may have strength in its wings to expand
    them, or light in its eyes to shine,
That shall seem not as weakness and darkness if
    matched with the theme I would fain make mine ?

The round little flower of a face that exults in the
    sunshine of shadowless days
Defies the delight it enkindles to sing of it aught not
    unfit for the praise
Of the sweetest of all things that eyes may rejoice in
    and tremble with love as they gaze.

Such tricks and such meanings abound on the lips
    and the brows that are brighter than light,
The demure little chin, the sedate little nose, and the
    forehead of sun-stained white,
That love overflows into laughter and laughter sub-
    sides into love at the sight.

Each limb and each feature has action in tune with
    the meaning that smiles as it speaks
From the fervour of eyes and the fluttering of hands
    in a foretaste of fancies and freaks,
When the thought of them deepens the dimples that
    laugh in the corners and curves of his cheeks.

As a bird when the music within her is yet too intense
    to be spoken in song,
That pauses a little for pleasure to feel how the notes
    from withinwards throng,
·So pauses the laugh at his lips for a little, and waxes
    within more strong.

As the music elate and triumphal that bids all things
    of the dawn bear part
With the tune that prevails when her passion has
    risen into rapture of passionate art,
So lightens the laughter made perfect that leaps from
    its nest in the heaven of his heart.

Deep, grave and sedate is the gaze of expectant
    intensity bent for awhile
And absorbed on its aim as the tale that enthralls him
    uncovers the weft of its wile,
Till the goal of attention is touched, and expectancy
    kisses delight in a smile.

And it seems to us here that in Paradise hardly the
    spirit of Lamb or of Blake
May hear or behold aught sweeter than lightens and
    rings when his bright thoughts break
In laughter that well might lure them to look, and to
    smile as of old for his sake.

O singers that best loved children, and best for their
  sakes are beloved of us here,
In the world of your life everlasting, where love has
  no thorn and desire has no fear,
All else may be sweeter than aught is on earth,
  nought dearer than these are dear.

MAYTIME IN MIDWINTER

A NEW year gleams on us, tearful
   And troubled and smiling dim
As the smile on a lip still fearful,
   As glances of eyes that swim :
But the bird of my heart makes cheerful
   The days that are bright for him.

Child, how may a man's love merit
   The grace you shed as you stand,
The gift that is yours to inherit ?
   Through you are the bleak days bland ;
Your voice is a light to my spirit ;
   You bring the sun in your hand.

The year's wing shows not a feather
   As yet of the plumes to be ;
Yet here in the shrill grey weather
   The spring's self stands at my knee,
And laughs as we commune together,
   And lightens the world we see.

The rains are as dews for the christening
   Of dawns that the nights benumb :
The spring's voice answers me listening
   For speech of a child to come,
While promise of music is glistening
   On lips that delight keeps dumb.

The mists and the storms receding
  At sight of you smile and die :
Your eyes held wide on me reading
  Shed summer across the sky :
Your heart shines clear for me, heeding
  No more of the world than I.

The world, what is it to you, dear,
  And me, if its face be grey,
And the new-born year be a shrewd year
  For flowers that the fierce winds fray ?
You smile, and the sky seems blue, dear ;
  You laugh, and the month turns May.

Love cares not for care, he has daffed her
  Aside as a mate for guile :
The sight that my soul yearns after
  Feeds full my sense for awhile ;
Your sweet little sun-faced laughter,
  Your good little glad grave smile.

Your hands through the bookshelves flutter ;
  Scott, Shakespeare, Dickens, are caught ;
Blake's visions, that lighten and mutter ;
  Molière—and his smile has nought
Left on it of sorrow, to utter
  The secret things of his thought.

No grim thing written or graven
  But grows, if you gaze on it, bright ;
A lark's note rings from the raven,
  And tragedy's robe turns white ;
And shipwrecks drift into haven ;
  And darkness laughs, and is light.

Grief seems but a vision of madness ;
Life's key-note peals from above
With nought in it more of sadness
Than broods on the heart of a dove :
At sight of you, thought grows gladness,
And life, through love of you, love.

A DOUBLE BALLAD OF AUGUST

(1884)

ALL Afric, winged with death and fire,
Pants in our pleasant English air.
Each blade of grass is tense as wire,
And all the wood's loose trembling hair
Stark in the broad and breathless glare
Of hours whose touch wastes herb and tree.
This bright sharp death shines everywhere ;
Life yearns for solace toward the sea.

Earth seems a corpse upon the pyre ;
The sun, a scourge for slaves to bear.
All power to fear, all keen desire,
Lies dead as dreams of days that were
Before the new-born world lay bare
In heaven's wide eye, whereunder we
Lie breathless till the season spare :
Life yearns for solace toward the sea.

Fierce hours, with ravening fangs that tire
On spirit and sense, divide and share
The throbs of thoughts that scarce respire,
The throes of dreams that scarce forbear

II.

One mute immitigable prayer
For cold perpetual sleep to be
Shed snowlike on the sense of care.
Life yearns for solace toward the sea.

The dust of ways where men suspire
Seems even the dust of death's dim lair.
But though the feverish days be dire
The sea-wind rears and cheers its fair
Blithe broods of babes that here and there
Make the sands laugh and glow for glee
With gladder flowers than gardens wear.
Life yearns for solace toward the sea.

The music dies not off the lyre
That lets no soul alive despair.
Sleep strikes not dumb the breathless choir
Of waves whose note bids sorrow spare.
As glad they sound, as fast they fare,
As when fate's word first set them free
And gave them light and night to wear.
Life yearns for solace toward the sea.

For there, though night and day conspire
To compass round with toil and snare
And changeless whirl of change, whose gyre
Draws all things deathwards unaware,
The spirit of life they scourge and scare,
Wild waves that follow on waves that flee
Laugh, knowing that yet, though earth despair,
Life yearns for solace toward the sea.

HEARTSEASE COUNTRY

TO ISABEL SWINBURNE

THE far green westward heavens are bland,
   The far green Wiltshire downs are clear
As these deep meadows hard at hand :
   The sight knows hardly far from near,
   Nor morning joy from evening cheer.
In cottage garden-plots their bees
Find many a fervent flower to seize
   And strain and drain the heart away
From ripe sweet-williams and sweet-peas
   At every turn on every way.

But gladliest seems one flower to expand
   Its whole sweet heart all round us here ;
'Tis Heartsease Country, Pansy Land.
   Nor sounds nor savours harsh and drear
   Where engines yell and halt and veer
Can vex the sense of him who sees
One flower-plot midway, that for trees
   Has poles, and sheds all grimed or grey
For bowers like those that take the breeze
   At every turn on every way.

Content even there they smile and stand,
   Sweet thought's heart-easing flowers, nor fear,
With reek and roaring steam though fanned,
   Nor shrink nor perish as they peer.
   The heart's eye holds not those more dear
That glow between the lanes and leas
Where'er the homeliest hand may please
   To bid them blossom as they may
Where light approves and wind agrees
   At every turn on every way.

Sister, the word of winds and seas
Endures not as the word of these
   Your wayside flowers whose breath would say
How hearts that love may find heart's ease
   At every turn on every way.

A BALLAD OF APPEAL

TO CHRISTINA G. ROSSETTI

SONG wakes with every wakening year
  From hearts of birds that only feel
Brief spring's deciduous flower-time near :
  And song more strong to help or heal
  Shall silence worse than winter seal ?
From love-lit thought's remurmuring cave
The notes that rippled, wave on wave,
  Were clear as love, as faith were strong ;
And all souls blessed the soul that gave
  Sweet water from the well of song.

All hearts bore fruit of joy to hear,
  All eyes felt mist upon them steal
For joy's sake, trembling toward a tear,
  When, loud as marriage-bells that peal,
  Or flutelike soft, or keen like steel,
Sprang the sheer music ; sharp or grave,
We heard the drift of winds that drave,
  And saw, swept round by ghosts in throng,
Dark rocks, that yielded, where they clave,
  Sweet water from the well of song.

Blithe verse made all the dim sense clear
   That smiles of babbling babes conceal :
Prayer's perfect heart spake here : and here
   Rose notes of blameless woe and weal,
   More soft than this poor song's appeal.
Where orchards bask, where cornfields wave,
They dropped like rains that cleanse and lave,
   And scattered all the year along,
Like dewfall on an April grave,
   Sweet water from the well of song.

Ballad, go bear our prayer, and crave
Pardon, because thy lowlier stave
   Can do this plea no right, but wrong.
Ask nought beside thy pardon, save
   Sweet water from the well of song.

CRADLE SONGS

(TO A TUNE OF BLAKE'S)

I

BABY, baby bright,
Sleep can steal from sight
Little of your light :

Soft as fire in dew,
Still the life in you
Lights your slumber through.

Four white eyelids keep
Fast the seal of sleep
Deep as love is deep :

Yet, though closed it lies.
Love behind them spies
Heaven in two blue eyes.

II

Baby, baby dear,
Earth and heaven are near
Now, for heaven is here.

Heaven is every place
Where your flower-sweet face
Fills our eyes with grace.

Till your own eyes deign
Earth a glance again,
Earth and heaven are twain.

Now your sleep is done,
Shine, and show the sun
Earth and heaven are one.

III

Baby, baby sweet,
Love's own lips are meet
Scarce to kiss your feet.

Hardly love's own ear,
When your laugh crows clear,
Quite deserves to hear.

Hardly love's own wile,
Though it please awhile,
Quite deserves your smile.

Baby full of grace,
Bless us yet a space :
Sleep will come apace.

IV

Baby, baby true,
Man, whate'er he do,
May deceive not you.

Smiles whose love is guile,
Worn a flattering while,
Win from you no smile.

One, the smile alone
Out of love's heart grown,
Ever wins your own.

Man, a dunce uncouth,
Errs in age and youth :
Babies know the truth.

V

Baby, baby fair,
Love is fain to dare
Bless your haughtiest air.

Baby blithe and bland,
Reach but forth a hand
None may dare withstand ;

Love, though wellnigh cowed,
Yet would praise aloud
Pride so sweetly proud.

No ! the fitting word
Even from breeze or bird
Never yet was heard.

VI

Baby, baby kind,
Though no word we find,
Bear us yet in mind.

Half a little hour,
Baby bright in bower,
Keep this thought aflower —

Love it is, I see,
Here with heart and knee
Bows and worships me.

What can baby do,
Then, for love so true?—
Let it worship you.

VII

Baby, baby wise,
Love's divine surmise
Lights your constant eyes.

Day and night and day
One mute word would they,
As the soul saith, say.

Trouble comes and goes;
Wonder ebbs and flows;
Love remains and glows.

As the fledgeling dove
Feels the breast above,
So your heart feels love.

PELAGIUS

I

THE sea shall praise him and the shores bear part
   That reared him when the bright south world was
      black
   With fume of creeds more foul than hell's own
      rack,
Still darkening more love's face with loveless art
Since Paul, faith's fervent Antichrist, of heart
   Heroic, haled the world vehemently back
   From Christ's pure path on dire Jehovah's track,
And said to dark Elisha's Lord, " Thou art."
But one whose soul had put the raiment on
Of love that Jesus left with James and John
   Withstood that Lord whose seals of love were
     lies,
Seeing what we see—how, touched by Truth's bright
     rod,
The fiend whom Jews and Africans called God
   Feels his own hell take hold on him, and dies.

II

The world has no such flower in any land,
   And no such pearl in any gulf the sea,
   As any babe on any mother's knee.
But all things blessed of men by saints are banned :

God gives them grace to read and understand
   The palimpsest of evil, writ where we,
   Poor fools and lovers but of love, can see
Nought save a blessing signed by Love's own hand.
The smile that opens heaven on us for them
   Hath sin's transmitted birthmark hid therein :
      The kiss it craves calls down from heaven a rod.
If innocence be sin that Gods condemn,
   Praise we the men who so being born in sin
      First dared the doom and broke the bonds of
        God.

III

Man's heel is on the Almighty's neck who said,
   Let there be hell, and there was hell—on earth.
   But not for that may men forget their worth—
Nay, but much more remember them—who led
The living first from dwellings of the dead,
   And rent the cerecloths that were wont to engirth
   Souls wrapped and swathed and swaddled from
      their birth
With lies that bound them fast from heel to head.
Among the tombs when wise men all their lives
Dwelt, and cried out, and cut themselves with
      knives,
These men, being foolish, and of saints abhorred
   Beheld in heaven the sun by saints reviled,
Love, and on earth one everlasting Lord
   In every likeness of a little child.

LOUIS BLANC

THREE SONNETS TO HIS MEMORY

I

THE stainless soul that smiled through glorious eyes ;
  The bright grave brow whereon dark fortune's
    blast
  Might blow, but might not bend it, nor o'ercast,
Save for one fierce fleet hour of shame, the skies
Thrilled with warm dreams of worthier days to rise
  And end the whole world's winter ; here at last,
  If death be death, have passed into the past ;
If death be life, live, though their semblance dies.
Hope and high faith inviolate of distrust
  Shone strong as life inviolate of the grave
    Through each bright word and lineament serene.
Most loving righteousness and love most just
  Crowned, as day crowns the dawn-enkindled wave,
    With visible aureole thine unfaltering mien.

II

Strong time and fire-swift change, with lightnings
    clad
  And shod with thunders of reverberate years,
  Have filled with light and sound of hopes and fears
The space of many a season, since I had

Grace of good hap to make my spirit glad,
   Once communing with thine : and memory hears
   The bright voice yet that then rejoiced mine ears,
Sees yet the light of eyes that spake, and bade
Fear not, but hope, though then time's heart were
    weak
   And heaven by hell shade-stricken, and the range
   Of high-born hope made questionable and strange
As twilight trembling till the sunlight speak.
   Thou sawest the sunrise and the storm in one
   Break : seest thou now the storm-compelling sun ?

III

Surely thou seest, O spirit of light and fire,
   Surely thou canst not choose, O soul, but see
   The days whose dayspring was beheld of thee
Ere eyes less pure might have their hope's desire.
Beholding life in heaven again respire
   Where men saw nought that was or was to be,
   Save only death imperial.   Thou and he
Who has the heart of all men's hearts for lyre,
Ye twain, being great of spirit as time is great,
   And sure of sight as truth's own heavenward eye,
   Beheld the forms of forces passing by
And certitude of equal-balanced fate,
Whose breath forefelt makes darkness palpitate,
   And knew that light should live and darkness die.

VOS DEOS LAUDAMUS:

THE CONSERVATIVE JOURNALIST'S ANTHEM

"As a matter of fact, no man living, or who ever lived—not CÆSAR or PERICLES, not SHAKESPEARE or MICHAEL ANGELO — could confer honour more than he took on entering the House of Lords."—*Saturday Review*, December 15, 1883.

"Clumsy and shallow snobbery—can do no hurt."—*Ibid.*

I

O LORDS our Gods, beneficent, sublime,
  In the evening, and before the morning flames,
  We praise, we bless, we magnify your names.
The slave is he that serves not ; his the crime
And shame, who hails not as the crown of Time
  That House wherein the all-envious world acclaims
  Such glory that the reflex of it shames
All crowns bestowed of men for prose or rhyme.
The serf, the cur, the sycophant is he
Who feels no cringing motion twitch his knee
  When from a height too high for Shakespeare nods
The wearer of a higher than Milton's crown.
Stoop, Chaucer, stoop: Keats, Shelley, Burns, bow
      down :
  These have no part with you, O Lords our Gods.

II

O Lords our Gods, it is not that ye sit
    Serene above the thunder, and exempt
    From strife of tongues and casualties that tempt
Men merely found by proof of manhood fit
For service of their fellows : this is it
    Which sets you past the reach of Time's attempt,
    Which gives us right of justified contempt
For commonwealths built up by mere men's wit :
That gold unlocks not, nor may flatteries ope,
The portals of your heaven ; that none may hope
    With you to watch how life beneath you plods,
Save for high service given, high duty done ;
That never was your rank ignobly won :
    For this we give you praise, O Lords our Gods.

III

O Lords our Gods, the times are evil : you
    Redeem the time, because of evil days.
    While abject souls in servitude of praise
Bow down to heads untitled, and the crew
Whose honour dwells but in the deeds they do,
    From loftier hearts your nobler servants raise
    More manful salutation : yours are bays
That not the dawn's plebeian pearls bedew ;
Yours, laurels plucked not of such hands as wove
Old age its chaplet in Colonos' grove.
    Our time, with heaven and with itself at odds,
Makes all lands else as seas that seethe and boil ;
But yours are yet the corn and wine and oil,
    And yours our worship yet, O Lords our Gods.

December 15. 1883.

ON THE BICENTENARY OF CORNEILLE

CELEBRATED UNDER THE PRESIDENCY OF
VICTOR HUGO

SCARCE two hundred years are gone, and the world
    is past away
As a noise of brawling wind, as a flash of breaking
    foam,
    That beheld the singer born who raised up the
      dead of Rome ;
And a mightier now than he bids him too rise up
    to-day.
All the dim great age is dust, and its king is tombless
    clay,
    But its loftier laurel green as in living eyes it
      clomb,
    And his memory whom it crowned hath his people's
      heart for home,
And the shade across it falls of a lordlier-flowering
    bay.

Stately shapes about the tomb of their mighty maker
    pace,
Heads of high-plumed Spaniards shine, souls revive
    of Roman race,

BICENTENARY OF CORNEILLE

Sound of arms and words of wail through the glowing
darkness rise,
Speech of hearts heroic rings forth of lips that know
not breath,
And the light of thoughts august fills the pride of
kindling eyes
Whence of yore the spell of song drove the shadow
of darkling death.

IN SEPULCRETIS

" Vidistis ipso rapere de rogo cœnam."— CATULLUS, LIX. 3.

" To publish even one line of an author which he himself has not intended for the public at large—especially letters which are addressed to private persons—is to commit a despicable act of felony."—HEINE.

I

IT is not then enough that men who give
  The best gifts given of man to man should feel,
  Alive, a snake's head ever at their heel :
Small hurt the worms may do them while they live—
Such hurt as scorn for scorn's sake may forgive.
  But now, when death and fame have set one seal
  On tombs whereat Love, Grief, and Glory kneel,
Men sift all secrets, in their critic sieve,
Of graves wherein the dust of death might shrink
  To know what tongues defile the dead man's name
  With loathsome love, and praise that stings like
      shame.
Rest once was theirs, who had crossed the mortal
      brink :
  No rest, no reverence now : dull fools undress
  Death's holiest shrine, life's veriest nakedness.

II

A man was born, sang, suffered, loved, and died.
  Men scorned him living : let us praise him dead.
  His life was brief and bitter, gently led
And proudly, but with pure and blameless pride.
He wrought no wrong toward any ; satisfied
  With love and labour, whence our souls are fed
  With largesse yet of living wine and bread.
Come, let us praise him : here is nought to hide.
Make bare the poor dead secrets of his heart,
  Strip the stark-naked soul, that all may peer,
  Spy, smirk, sniff, snap, snort, snivel, snarl, and
      sneer :
Let none so sad, let none so sacred part
  Lie still for pity, rest unstirred for shame,
  But all be scanned of all men.   This is fame.

III

" Now, what a thing it is to be an ass ! " [1]
  If one, that strutted up the brawling streets
  As foreman of the flock whose concourse greets
Men's ears with bray more dissonant than brass,
Would change from blame to praise as coarse and crass
  His natural note, and learn the fawning feats
  Of lapdogs, who but knows what luck he meets ?
But all in vain old fable holds her glass.

Mocked and reviled by men of poisonous breath,
  A great man dies : but one thing worst was spared ;
  Not all his heart by their base hands lay bared.

[1] *Titus Andronicus*, Act iv., Scene 2.

One comes to crown with praise the dust of death ;
  And lo, through him this worst is brought to pass.
  Now, what a thing it is to be an ass !

IV

Shame, such as never yet dealt heavier stroke
  On heads more shameful, fall on theirs through
    whom
  Dead men may keep inviolate not their tomb,
But all its depths these ravenous grave-worms choke.
And yet what waste of wrath were this, to invoke
  Shame on the shameless ? Even their twin-born
    doom,
  Their native air of life, a carrion fume,
Their natural breath of love, a noisome smoke,
The bread they break, the cup whereof they drink,
  The record whose remembrance damns their name,
  Smells, tastes, and sounds of nothing but of shame.
If thankfulness nor pity bids them think
  What work is this of theirs, and pause betimes,
  Not Shakespeare's grave would scare them off with
    rhymes.

LOVE AND SCORN

I

Love, loyallest and lordliest born of things,
  Immortal that shouldst be, though all else end,
  In plighted hearts of fearless friend with friend,
Whose hand may curb or clip thy plume-plucked
      wings?
Not grief's nor time's: though these be lords and kings
  Crowned, and their yoke bid vassal passions bend,
  They may not pierce the spirit of sense, or blend
Quick poison with the soul's live watersprings.
The true clear heart whose core is manful trust
Fears not that very death may turn to dust
  Love lit therein as toward a brother born,
If one touch make not all its fine gold rust,
  If one breath blight not all its glad ripe corn,
  And all its fire be turned to fire of scorn.

II

Scorn only, scorn begot of bitter proof
  By keen experience of a trustless heart,
  Bears burning in her new-born hand the dart
Wherewith love dies heart-stricken, and the roof

Falls of his palace, and the storied woof
  Long woven of many a year with life's whole art
  Is rent like any rotten weed apart,
And hardly with reluctant eyes aloof
Cold memory guards one relic scarce exempt
Yet from the fierce corrosion of contempt,
  And hardly saved by pity.   Woe are we
That once we loved, and love not ; but we know
The ghost of love, surviving yet in show,
  Where scorn has passed, is vain as grief must be.

III

O sacred, just, inevitable scorn,
  Strong child of righteous judgment, whom with
     grief
  The rent heart bears, and wins not yet relief,
Seeing of its pain so dire a portent born,
Must thou not spare one sheaf of all the corn,
  One doit of all the treasure ? not one sheaf,
  Not one poor doit of all ? not one dead leaf
Of all that fell and left behind a thorn ?
Is man so strong that one should scorn another ?
Is any as God, not made of mortal mother,
  That love should turn in him to gall and flame ?
Nay : but the true is not the false heart's brother :
  Love cannot love disloyalty : the name
  That else it wears is love no more, but shame.

ON THE DEATH OF RICHARD DOYLE

A LIGHT of blameless laughter, fancy-bred,
   Soft-souled and glad and kind as love or sleep,
   Fades, and sweet mirth's own eyes are fain to weep
Because her blithe and gentlest bird is dead.
Weep, elves and fairies all, that never shed
   Tear yet for mortal mourning : you that keep
   The doors of dreams whence nought of ill may
      creep,
Mourn once for one whose lips your honey fed.
Let waters of the Golden River steep
   The rose-roots whence his grave blooms rosy red,
And murmuring of Hyblæan hives be deep
   About the summer silence of its bed,
And nought less gracious than a violet peep
   Between the grass grown greener round his head.

IN MEMORY OF HENRY A. BRIGHT

YET again another, ere his crowning year,
  Gone from friends that here may look for him no
    more.
  Never now for him shall hope set wide the door,
Hope that hailed him hither, fain to greet him here.
All the gracious garden-flowers he held so dear,
  Oldworld English blossoms, all his homestead
    store,
  Oldworld grief had strewn them round his bier of
    yore,
Bidding each drop leaf by leaf as tear by tear ;
Rarer lutes than mine had borne more tuneful token,
  Touched by subtler hands than echoing time can
    wrong,
  Sweet as flowers had strewn his graveward path
    along.
Now may no such old sweet dirges more be spoken,
Now the flowers whose breath was very song are
    broken,
  Nor may sorrow find again so sweet a song.

A SOLITUDE

Sea beyond sea, sand after sweep of sand,
  Here ivory smooth, here cloven and ridged with flow
  Of channelled waters soft as rain or snow,
Stretch their lone length at ease beneath the bland
Grey gleam of skies whose smile on wave and strand
  Shines weary like a man's who smiles to know
  That now no dream can mock his faith with show,
Nor cloud for him seem living sea or land.

Is there an end at all of all this waste,
These crumbling cliffs defeatured and defaced,
These ruinous heights of sea-sapped walls that slide
  Seaward with all their banks of bleak blown flowers
Glad yet of life, ere yet their hope subside
  Beneath the coil of dull dense waves and hours?

VICTOR HUGO:
L'ARCHIPEL DE LA MANCHE

Sea and land are fairer now, nor aught is all the same,
  Since a mightier hand than Time's hath woven
    their votive wreath.
  Rocks as swords half drawn from out the smooth
    wave's jewelled sheath,
Fields whose flowers a tongue divine hath numbered
    name by name,
Shores whereby the midnight or the noon clothed
    round with flame
  Hears the clamour jar and grind which utters from
    beneath
  Cries of hungering waves like beasts fast bound
    that gnash their teeth,
All of these the sun that lights them lights not like
    his fame ;
None of these is but the thing it was before he came.
  Where the darkling overfalls like dens of torment
    seethe,
High on tameless moorlands, down in meadows
    bland and tame,
  Where the garden hides, and where the wind
    uproots the heath,
Glory now henceforth for ever, while the world shall
    be,
Shines, a star that keeps not time with change on
    earth and sea.

THE TWILIGHT OF THE LORDS

I

Is the sound a trumpet blown, or a bell for burial
    tolled,
  Whence the whole air vibrates now to the clash of
    words like swords—
    " Let us break their bonds in sunder, and cast away
      their cords ;
Long enough the world has mocked us, and marvelled
    to behold
How the grown man bears the curb whence his boy-
    hood was controlled " ?
  Nay, but hearken : surer counsel more sober speech
    affords :
    " Is the past not all inscribed with the praises of
      our Lords ?
Is the memory dead of deeds done of yore, the love
    grown cold
That should bind our hearts to trust in their counsels
    wise and bold ?
  These that stand against you now, senseless crowds
    and heartless hordes,
Are not these the sons of men that withstood your
    kings of old ?
  Theirs it is to bind and loose ; theirs the key that
    knows the wards,

Theirs the staff to lead or smite ; yours, the spades and
     ploughs and hods :
Theirs to hear and yours to cry, Power is yours,
     O Lords our Gods."

II

Hear, O England : these are they that would counsel
     thee aright.
  Wouldst thou fain have all thy sons sons of thine
      indeed, and free ?
  Nay, but then no more at all as thou hast been shalt
      thou be :
Needs must many dwell in darkness, that some may
     look on light ;
Needs must poor men brook the wrong that ensures
     the rich man's right.
  How shall kings and lords be worshipped, if no man
      bow the knee ?
  How, if no man worship these, may thy praise
      endure with thee ?
  How, except thou trust in these, shall thy name not
      lose its might ?
These have had their will of thee since the Norman
     came to smite :
  Sires on grandsires, even as wave after wave along
      the sea,
Sons on sires have followed, steadfast as clouds or
     hours in flight.
  Time alone hath power to say, time alone hath
      eyes to see,
If your walls of rule be built but of clay-compacted
     sods,
If your place of old shall know you no more, O Lords
     our Gods.

III

Through the stalls wherein ye sit sounds a sentence
 while we wait,
 Set your house in order : is it not builded on the
  sand ?
 Set your house in order, seeing the night is hard at
  hand.
As the twilight of the Gods in the northern dream of
 fate
Is this hour that comes against you, albeit this hour
 come late.
 Ye whom Time and Truth bade heed, and ye would
  not understand,
 Now an axe draws nigh the tree overshadowing all
  the land,
And its edge of doom is set to the root of all your
 state.
Light is more than darkness now, faith than fear and
 hope than hate ;
 And what morning wills, behold, all the night shall
  not withstand.
Rods of office, helms of rule, staffs of wise men,
 crowns of great,
 While the people willed, ye bare ; now their hopes
  and hearts expand,
Time with silent foot makes dust of your broken
 crowns and rods,
And the lordship of your godhead is gone, O Lords
 our Gods.

CLEAR THE WAY!

CLEAR the way, my lords and lackeys ! you have had
 your day.
Here you have your answer—England's yea against
 your nay :
Long enough your house has held you : up, and clear
 the way !

Lust and falsehood, craft and traffic, precedent and
 gold,
Tongue of courtier, kiss of harlot, promise bought
 and sold,
Gave you heritage of empire over thralls of old.

Now that all these things are rotten, all their gold is
 rust,
Quenched the pride they lived by, dead the faith and
 cold the lust,
Shall their heritage not also turn again to dust ?

By the grace of these they reigned, who left their sons
 their sway :
By the grace of these, what England says her lords
 unsay :
Till at last her cry go forth against them—Clear the
 way !

By the grace of trust in treason knaves have lived and
lied :
By the force of fear and folly fools have fed their pride :
By the strength of sloth and custom reason stands
defied.

Lest perchance your reckoning on some latter day be
worse,
Halt and hearken, lords of land and princes of the
purse,
Ere the tide be full that comes with blessing and with
curse.

Where we stand, as where you sit, scarce falls a
sprinkling spray ;
But the wind that swells, the wave that follows, none
shall stay :
Spread no more of sail for shipwreck : out, and clear
the way !

A WORD FOR THE COUNTRY

MEN, born of the land that for ages
  Has been honoured where freedom was dear,
Till your labour wax fat on its wages
  You shall never be peers of a peer.
      Where might is, the right is :
        Long purses make strong swords.
      Let weakness learn meekness :
        God save the House of Lords !

You are free to consume in stagnation :
  You are equal in right to obey :
You are brothers in bonds, and the nation
  Is your mother—whose sons are her prey.
      Those others your brothers,
        Who toil not, weave, nor till,
      Refuse you and use you
        As waiters on their will.

But your fathers bowed down to their masters
  And obeyed them and served and adored.
 Shall the sheep not give thanks to their pastors ?
  Shall the serf not give praise to his lord ?
      Time, waning and gaining,
        Grown other now than then,
      Needs pastors and masters
        For sheep, and not for men.

II.   2 G 2

If his grandsire did service in battle,
  If his grandam was kissed by a king,
Must men to my lord be as cattle
  Or as apes that he leads in a string?
    To deem so, to dream so,
      Would bid the world proclaim
    The dastards for bastards,
      Not heirs of England's fame.

Not in spite but in right of dishonour,
  There are actors who trample your boards
Till the earth that endures you upon her
  Grows weary to bear you, my lords.
    Your token is broken,
      It will not pass for gold ·
    Your glory looks hoary,
      Your sun in heaven turns cold.

They are worthy to reign on their brothers,
  To contemn them as clods and as carles,
Who are Graces by grace of such mothers
  As brightened the bed of King Charles.
    What manner of banner,
      What fame is this they flaunt,
    That Britain, soul-smitten,
      Should shrink before their vaunt?

Bright sons of sublime prostitution,
  You are made of the mire of the street
Where your grandmothers walked in pollution
  Till a coronet shone at their feet.
    Your Graces, whose faces
      Bear high the bastard's brand,
    Seem stronger no longer
      Than all this honest land.

But the sons of her soldiers and seamen,
  They are worthy forsooth of their hire.
If the father won praise from all free men,
  Shall the sons not exult in their sire ?
      Let money make sunny
        And power make proud their lives,
      And feed them and breed them
        Like drones in drowsiest hives

But if haply the name be a burden
  And the souls be no kindred of theirs,
Should wise men rejoice in such guerdon
  Or brave men exult in such heirs ?
      Or rather the father
        Frown, shamefaced, on the son,
      And no men but foemen,
        Deriding, cry " Well done " ?

Let the gold and the land they inherit
  Pass ever from hand into hand :
In right of the forefather's merit
  Let the gold be the son's, and the land.
      Soft raiment, rich payment,
        High place, the state affords ;
      Full measure of pleasure ;
        But now no more, my lords.

Is the future beleaguered with dangers
  If the poor be far other than slaves ?
Shall the sons of the land be as strangers
  In the land of their forefathers' graves ?
      Shame were it to bear it,
        And shame it were to see :
      If free men you be, men,
        Let proof proclaim you free.

" But democracy means dissolution :
    See, laden with clamour and crime,
  How the darkness of dim revolution
    Comes deepening the twilight of time !
      Ah, better the fetter
        That holds the poor man's hand
      Than peril of sterile
        Blind change that wastes the land.

" Gaze forward through clouds that environ ;
    It shall be as it was in the past :
  Not with dreams, but with blood and with iron,
    Shall a nation be moulded to last."
      So teach they, so preach they,
        Who dream themselves the dream
      That hallows the gallows
        And bids the scaffold stream.

" With a hero at head, and a nation
    Well gagged and well drilled and well cowed,
  And a gospel of war and damnation,
    Has not empire a right to be proud ?
      Fools prattle and tattle
        Of freedom, reason, right,
      The beauty of duty,
        The loveliness of light.

" But we know, we believe it, we see it,
    Force only has power upon earth."
  So be it ! and ever so be it
    For souls that are bestial by birth !
      Let Prussian with Russian
        Exchange the kiss of slaves :
      But sea-folk are free folk
        By grace of winds and waves.

Has the past from the sepulchres beckoned?
  Let answer from Englishmen be—
No man shall be lord of us reckoned
  Who is baser, not better, than we.
      No coward, empowered
        To soil a brave man's name :
      For shame's sake and fame's sake,
        Enough of fame and shame.

Fame needs not the golden addition ;
  Shame bears it abroad as a brand.
Let the deed, and no more the tradition,
  Speak out and be heard through the land.
      Pride, rootless and fruitless,
        No longer takes and gives ·
      But surer and purer
        The soul of England lives.

He is master and lord of his brothers
  Who is worthier and wiser than they.
Him only, him surely, shall others,
  Else equal, observe and obey.
      Truth, flawless and awless,
        Do falsehood what it can,
      Makes royal the loyal
        And simple heart of man.

Who are these, then, that England should hearken,
  Who rage and wax wroth and grow pale
If she turn from the sunsets that darken
  And her ship for the morning set sail ?
      Let strangers fear dangers :
        All know, that hold her dear,
      Dishonour upon her
        Can only fall through fear.

Men, born of the landsmen and seamen
Who served her with souls and with swords,
She bids you be brothers, and free men,
And lordless, and fearless of lords.
She cares not, she dares not
Care now for gold or steel :
Light lead her, truth speed her,
God save the Commonweal !

A WORD FOR THE NATION

I

A WORD across the water
  Against our ears is borne,
Of threatenings and of slaughter,
  Of rage and spite and scorn :
We have not, alack, an ally to befriend us,
And the season is ripe to extirpate and end us :
Let the German touch hands with the Gaul,
And the fortress of England must fall ;
And the sea shall be swept of her seamen,
  And the waters they ruled be their graves,
And Dutchmen and Frenchmen be free men,
        And Englishmen slaves.

II

Our time once more is over,
  Once more our end is near :
A bull without a drover,
  The Briton reels to rear,
And the van of the nations is held by his betters,
And the seas of the world shall be loosed from
  his fetters,
And his glory shall pass as a breath,
And the life that is in him be death ;

And the sepulchre sealed on his glory
  For a sign to the nations shall be
As of Tyre and of Carthage in story,
    Once lords of the sea.

III

The lips are wise and loyal,
  The hearts are brave and true,
Imperial thoughts and royal
  Make strong the clamorous crew,
Whence louder and prouder the noise of defiance
Rings rage from the grave of a trustless alliance,
And bids us beware and be warned,
As abhorred of all nations and scorned,
As a swordless and spiritless nation,
  A wreck on the waste of the waves.
So foams the released indignation
    Of masterless slaves.

IV

Brute throats that miss the collar,
  Bowed backs that ask the whip,
Stretched hands that lack the dollar,
  And many a lie-seared lip,
Forefeel and foreshow for us signs as funereal
As the signs that were regal of yore and imperial;
We shall pass as the princes they served,
We shall reap what our fathers deserved,
And the place that was England's be taken
  By one that is worthier than she,
And the yoke of her empire be shaken
    Like spray from the sea.

V

French hounds, whose necks are aching
   Still from the chain they crave,
In dog-day madness breaking
   The dog-leash, thus may rave :
But the seas that for ages have fostered and fenced
     her
Laugh, echoing the yell of their kennel against her
And their moan if destruction draw near them
And the roar of her laughter to hear them ;
For she knows that if Englishmen be men
   Their England has all that she craves ;
All love and all honour from free men,
      All hatred from slaves.

VI

All love that rests upon her
   Like sunshine and sweet air,
All light of perfect honour
   And praise that ends in prayer,
She wins not more surely, she wears not more
    proudly,
Than the token of tribute that clatters thus loudly,
The tribute of foes when they meet
That rattles and rings at her feet,
The tribute of rage and of rancour,
   The tribute of slaves to the free,
To the people whose hope hath its anchor
   ·   Made fast in the sea.

VII

No fool that bows the back he
   Feels fit for scourge or brand,
No scurril scribes that lackey
   The lords of Lackeyland,
No penman that yearns, as he turns on his pallet,
For the place or the pence of a peer or a valet,
No whelp of as currish a pack
As the litter whose yelp it gives back,
Though he answer the cry of his brother
   As echoes might answer from caves,
Shall be witness as though for a mother
      Whose children were slaves.

VIII

But those found fit to love her,
   Whose love has root in faith,
Who hear, though darkness cover
   Time's face, what memory saith,
Who seek not the service of great men or small men
But the weal that is common for comfort of all men,
Those yet that in trust have beholden
Truth's dawn over England grow golden
And quicken the darkness that stagnates
   And scatter the shadows that flee,
Shall reply for her meanest as magnates
      And masters by sea.

IX

And all shall mark her station,
   Her message all shall hear,
When, equal-eyed, the nation
   Bids all her sons draw near,

And freedom be more than tradition or faction,
And thought be no swifter to serve her than action,
And justice alone be above her,
That love may be prouder to love her,
And time on the crest of her story
    Inscribe, as remembrance engraves,
The sign that subdues with its glory
        Kings, princes, and slaves.

A WORD FROM THE PSALMIST

Ps. xciv. 8

I

"TAKE heed, ye unwise among the people :
   O ye fools, when will ye understand ? "
From pulpit or choir beneath the steeple,
   Though the words be fierce, the tones are
      bland.
But a louder than the Church's echo thunders
   In the ears of men who may not choose but hear ;
And the heart in him that hears it leaps and wonders,
   With triumphant hope astonished, or with fear.
   For the names whose sound was power awaken
      Neither love nor reverence now nor dread ;
   Their strongholds and shrines are stormed and
      taken,
      Their kingdom and all its works are dead.

II

Take heed : for the tide of time is risen :
   It is full not yet, though now so high
That spirits and hopes long pent in prison
   Feel round them a sense of freedom nigh,

And a savour keen and sweet of brine and billow,
  And a murmur deep and strong of deepening
      strength.
Though the watchman dream, with sloth or pride for
      pillow,
  And the night be long, not endless is its length.
    From the springs of dawn, from clouds that sever,
      From the equal heavens and the eastward sea,
    The witness comes that endures for ever,
      Till men be brethren and thralls be free.

III

  But the wind of the wings of dawn expanding
    Strikes chill on your hearts as change and
        death.
  Ye are old, but ye have not understanding ;
    And proud, but your pride is a dead man's
        breath.
And your wise men, toward whose words and signs
      ye hearken,
  And your strong men, in whose hands ye put your
      trust,
Strain eyes to behold but clouds and dreams that
      darken,
  Stretch hands that can find but weapons red with
      rust.
    Their watchword rings, and the night rejoices,
      But the lark's note laughs at the night-bird's
          notes—
    " Is virtue verily found in voices ?
      Or is wisdom won when all win votes ?

IV

" Take heed, ye unwise indeed, who listen
    When the wind's wings beat and shift and
        change ;
    Whose hearts are uplift, whose eyeballs glisten,
    With desire of new things great and strange.
Let not dreams misguide nor any visions wrong you :
    That which has been, it is now as it was then.
Is not Compromise of old a god among you ?
    Is not Precedent indeed a king of men ?
    But the windy hopes that lead mislead you,
        And the sounds ye hear are void and vain,
    Is a vote a coat ? will franchise feed you,
        Or words be a roof against the rain ?

V

" Eight ages are gone since kingship entered,
    With knights and peers at its harnessed back,
    And the land, no more in its own strength centred,
    Was cast for a prey to the princely pack.
But we pared the fangs and clipped the ravening
        claws of it,
    And good was in time brought forth of an evil
        thing,
And the land's high name waxed lordlier in war
        because of it,
    When chartered Right had bridled and curbed the
        king.
    And what so fair has the world beholden,
        And what so firm has withstood the years,
    As Monarchy bound in chains all golden,
        And Freedom guarded about with peers ?

VI

" How think ye ? know not your lords and masters
   What collars are meet for brawling throats ?
  Is change not mother of strange disasters ?
   Shall plague or peril be stayed by votes ?
Out of precedent and privilege and order
  Have we plucked the flower of compromise, whose
     root
Bears blossoms that shine from border again to
     border,
  And the mouths of many are fed with its temperate
     fruit.
    Your masters are wiser than ye, their henchmen :
     Your lords know surely whereof ye have need.
    Equality ?   Fools, would you fain be Frenchmen?
     Is equity more than a word indeed ?

VII

" Your voices, forsooth, your most sweet voices,
   Your worthy voices, your love, your hate,
  Your choice, who know not whereof your choice is,
   What stays are these for a stable state ?
Inconstancy, blind and deaf with its own fierce babble,
  Swells ever your throats with storm of uncertain
     cheers :
He leans on straws who leans on a light-souled
     rabble ;
  His trust is frail who puts not his trust in peers."
    So shrills the message whose word convinces
     Of righteousness knaves, of wisdom fools ;
    That serfs may boast them because of princes,
     And the weak rejoice that the strong man rules.

VIII

True friends, ye people, are these, the faction
    Full-mouthed that flatters and snarls and bays,
That fawns and foams with alternate action,
    And mocks the names that it soils with praise.
As from fraud and force their power had first begin-
    ning,
So by righteousness and peace it may not stand,
But by craft of state and nets of secret spinning,
    Words that weave and unweave wiles like ropes of
        sand,
    Form, custom, and gold, and laws grown hoary,
        And strong tradition that guards the gate :
    To these, O people, to these give glory,
        That your name among nations may be great.

IX

How long—for haply not now much longer—
    Shall fear put faith in a faithless creed,
And shapes and shadows of truths be stronger
    In strong men's eyes than the truth indeed ?
If freedom be not a word that dies when spoken,
    If justice be not a dream whence men must wake,
How shall not the bonds of the thraldom of old be
    broken,
    And right put might in the hands of them that
        break ?
    For clear as a tocsin from the steeple
        Is the cry gone forth along the land,
    Take heed, ye unwise among the people :
        O ye fools, when will ye understand ?

A BALLAD AT PARTING

SEA to sea that clasps and fosters England, uttering
    evermore
Song eterne and praise immortal of the indomitable
    shore,
    Lifts aloud her constant heart up, south to north
        and east to west,
Here in speech that shames all music, there in thunder-
    throated roar,
    Chiming concord out of discord, waking rapture
        out of rest.
All her ways are lovely, all her works and symbols
    are divine,
    Yet shall man love best what first bade leap his
        heart and bend his knee ;
Yet where first his whole soul worshipped shall his
    soul set up her shrine :
    Nor may love not know the lovelier, fair as both
        beheld may be,
    Here the limitless north-eastern, there the strait
        south-western sea.

Though their chant bear all one burden, as ere man
    was born it bore ;
Though the burden be diviner than the songs all
    souls adore ;

Yet may love not choose but choose between them
    which to love the best.
Me the sea my nursing-mother, me the Channel
    green and hoar,
  Holds at heart more fast than all things, bares for
    me the goodlier breast,
Lifts for me the lordlier love-song, bids for me more
    sunlight shine,
  Sounds for me the stormier trumpet of the
    sweeter strain to me.
So the broad pale Thames is loved not like the tawny
    springs of Tyne :
  Choice is clear between them for the soul whose
    vision holds in fee
  Here the limitless north-eastern, there the strait
    south-western sea.

Choice is clear, but dear is either ; nor has either not
    in store
Many a likeness, many a written sign of spirit-
    searching lore,
  Whence the soul takes fire of sweet remembrance,
    magnified and blest.
Thought of songs whose flame-winged feet have trod
    the unfooted water-floor
  When the lord of all the living lords of souls bade
    speed their quest ;
Soft live sound like children's babble down the
    rippling sand's incline,
  Or the lovely song that loves them, hailed with
    thankful prayer and plea ;
These are parcels of the harvest here whose gathered
    sheaves are mine,

Garnered now, but sown and reaped where winds
    make wild with wrath or glee
Here the limitless north-eastern, there the strait
    south-western sea.

Song, thy name is freedom, seeing thy strength was
    born of breeze and brine.
  Fare now forth and fear no fortune : such a seal is
    set on thee.
Joy begat and memory bare thee, seeing in spirit a
    twofold sign,
  Even the sign of those thy fosters, each as thou
    from all time free,
  Here the limitless north-eastern, there the strait
    south-western sea.

ASTROPHEL

AND OTHER POEMS

TO WILLIAM MORRIS

ASTROPHEL

AFTER READING SIR PHILIP SIDNEY'S ARCADIA IN THE
GARDEN OF AN OLD ENGLISH MANOR HOUSE

1

A STAR in the silence that follows
  The song of the death of the sun
Speaks music in heaven, and the hollows
  And heights of the world are as one ;
One lyre that outsings and outlightens
  The rapture of sunset, and thrills
Mute night till the sense of it brightens
  The soul that it fills.

The flowers of the sun that is sunken
  Hang heavy of heart as of head ;
The bees that have eaten and drunken
  The soul of their sweetness are fled ;
But a sunflower of song, on whose honey
  My spirit has fed as a bee,
Makes sunnier than morning was sunny
  The twilight for me.

The letters and lines on the pages
  That sundered mine eyes and the flowers

Wax faint as the shadows of ages
   That sunder their season and ours ;
As the ghosts of the centuries that sever
   A season of colourless time
From the days whose remembrance is ever,
     As they were, sublime.

The season that bred and that cherished
   The soul that I commune with yet,
Had it utterly withered and perished
   To rise not again as it set,
Shame were it that Englishmen living
   Should read as their forefathers read
The books of the praise and thanksgiving
     Of Englishmen dead

O light of the land that adored thee
   And kindled thy soul with her breath,
Whose life, such as fate would afford thee,
   Was lovelier than aught but thy death,
By what name, could thy lovers but know it,
   Might love of thee hail thee afar,
Philisides, Astrophel, poet
     Whose love was thy star ?

A star in the moondawn of Maytime,
   A star in the cloudland of change ;
Too splendid and sad for the daytime
   To cheer or eclipse or estrange ;
Too sweet for tradition or vision
   To see but through shadows of tears
Rise deathless across the division
     Of measureless years.

The twilight may deepen and harden
    As nightward the stream of it runs
Till starshine transfigure a garden
    Whose radiance responds to the sun's :
The light of the love of thee darkens
    The lights that arise and that set :
The love that forgets thee not hearkens
        If England forget.

II

Bright and brief in the sight of grief and love the light
    of thy lifetime shone,
Seen and felt by the gifts it dealt, the grace it gave,
    and again was gone :
Ay, but now it is death, not thou, whom time has
    conquered as years pass on.

Ay, not yet may the land forget that bore and loved
    thee and praised and wept,
Sidney, lord of the stainless sword, the name of
    names that her heart's love kept
Fast as thine did her own, a sign to light thy life till
    it sank and slept.

Bright as then for the souls of men thy brave Arcadia
    resounds and shines,
Lit with love that beholds above all joys and sorrows
    the steadfast signs,
Faith, a splendour that hope makes tender, and truth,
    whose presage the soul divines.

All the glory that girds the story of all thy life as
    with sunlight round,

All the spell that on all souls fell who saw thy spirit,
    and held them bound,
Lives for all that have heard the call and cadence yet
    of its music sound.

Music bright as the soul of light, for wings an eagle,
    for notes a dove,
Leaps and shines from the lustrous lines where-
    through thy soul from afar above
Shone and sang till the darkness rang with light
    whose fire is the fount of love.

Love that led thee alive, and fed thy soul with
    sorrows and joys and fears,
Love that sped thee, alive and dead, to fame's fair
    goal with thy peerless peers,
Feeds the flame of thy quenchless name with light
    that lightens the rayless years.

Dark as sorrow though night and morrow may lower
    with presage of clouded fame,
How may she that of old bare thee, may Sidney's
    England, be brought to shame ?
How should this be, while England is ? What need
    of answer beyond thy name ?

III

From the love that transfigures thy glory,
    From the light of the dawn of thy death,
The life of thy song and thy story
    Took subtler and fierier breath.

And we, though the day and the morrow
  Set fear and thanksgiving at strife,
Hail yet in the star of thy sorrow
  The sun of thy life.

Shame and fear may beset men here, and bid thanksgiving and pride be dumb :
Faith, discrowned of her praise, and wound about
  with toils till her life wax numb,
Scarce may see if the sundawn be, if darkness die
  not and dayrise come.

But England, enmeshed and benetted
  With spiritless villainies round,
With counsels of cowardice fretted,
  With trammels of treason enwound,
Is yet, though the season be other
  Than wept and rejoiced over thee,
Thine England, thy lover, thy mother,
    Sublime as the sea.

Hers wast thou : if her face be now less bright, or
  seem for an hour less brave,
Let but thine on her darkness shine, thy saviour
  spirit revive and save,
Time shall see, as the shadows flee, her shame
  entombed in a shameful grave.

If death and not life were the portal
  That opens on life at the last,
If the spirit of Sidney were mortal
  And the past of it utterly past,

Fear stronger than honour was ever,
  Forgetfulness mightier than fame,
Faith knows not if England should never
  Subside into shame.

Yea, but yet is thy sun not set, thy sunbright spirit
  of trust withdrawn :
England's love of thee burns above all hopes that
  darken or fears that fawn :
Hers thou art : and the faithful heart that hopes
  begets upon darkness dawn.

The sunset that sunrise will follow
  Is less than the dream of a dream :
The starshine on height and on hollow
  Sheds promise that dawn shall redeem :
The night, if the daytime would hide it,
  Shows lovelier, aflame and afar,
Thy soul and thy Stella's beside it,
  A star by a star.

A NYMPHOLEPT

SUMMER, and noon, and a splendour of silence, felt,
  Seen, and heard of the spirit within the sense.
Soft through the frondage the shades of the sun-
    beams melt,
    Sharp through the foliage the shafts of them, keen
      and dense,
    Cleave, as discharged from the string of the God's
      bow, tense
As a war-steed's girth, and bright as a warrior's belt.
  Ah, why should an hour that is heaven for an hour
    pass hence ?

I dare not sleep for delight of the perfect hour,
  Lest God be wroth that his gift should be scorned
    of man.
The face of the warm bright world is the face of a
    flower,
    The word of the wind and the leaves that the light
      winds fan
    As the word that quickened at first into flame, and
      ran,
Creative and subtle and fierce with invasive power,
  Through darkness and cloud, from the breath of
    the one God, Pan.

The perfume of earth possessed by the sun pervades
　The chaster air that he soothes but with sense of
　　sleep.
Soft, imminent, strong as desire that prevails and
　　fades,
　The passing noon that beholds not a cloudlet weep
　Imbues and impregnates life with delight more
　　deep
Than dawn or sunset or moonrise on lawns or glades
　Can shed from the skies that receive it and may
　　not keep.

The skies may hold not the splendour of sundown
　　fast ;
　It wanes into twilight as dawn dies down into
　　day.
And the moon, triumphant when twilight is overpast,
　Takes pride but awhile in the hours of her stately
　　sway.
　But the might of the noon, though the light of it
　　pass away,
Leaves earth fulfilled of desires and of dreams that
　　last ;
　But if any there be that hath sense of them none
　　can say.

For if any there be that hath sight of them, sense, or
　　trust
　Made strong by the might of a vision, the strength
　　of a dream,
His lips shall straiten and close as a dead man's
　　must,
　His heart shall be sealed as the voice of a frost-
　　bound stream.

For the deep mid mystery of light and of heat that
  seem
To clasp and pierce dark earth, and enkindle dust,
  Shall a man's faith say what it is ? or a man's
    guess deem ?

Sleep lies not heavier on eyes that have watched all
    night
  Than hangs the heat of the noon on the hills and
    trees.
Why now should the haze not open, and yield to
    sight
  A fairer secret than hope or than slumber sees ?
  I seek not heaven with submission of lips and knees,
With worship and prayer for a sign till it leap to
    light :
  I gaze on the gods about me, and call on these.

I call on the gods hard by, the divine dim powers
  Whose likeness is here at hand, in the breathless
    air,
In the pulseless peace of the fervid and silent flowers,
  In the faint sweet speech of the waters that whisper
    there.
  Ah, what should darkness do in a world so fair ?
The bent-grass heaves not, the couch-grass quails
    not or cowers ;
  The wind's kiss frets not the rowan's or aspen's
    hair.

But the silence trembles with passion of sound sup-
    pressed,
  And the twilight quivers and yearns to the sun-
    ward, wrung

With love as with pain ; and the wide wood's mo-
  tionless breast
  Is thrilled with a dumb desire that would fain find
    tongue
    And palpitates, tongueless as she whom a man-
      snake stung,
Whose heart now heaves in the nightingale, never at
  rest
  Nor satiated ever with song till her last be sung.

Is it rapture or terror that circles me round, and
  invades
  Each vein of my life with hope—if it be not fear ?
Each pulse that awakens my blood into rapture
  fades,
  Each pulse that subsides into dread of a strange
    thing near
  Requickens with sense of a terror less dread than
    dear.
Is peace not one with light in the deep green glades
  Where summer at noonday slumbers ? Is peace not
    here ?

The tall thin stems of the firs, and the roof sublime
  That screens from the sun the floor of the steep
    still wood,
Deep, silent, splendid, and perfect and calm as time,
  Stand fast as ever in sight of the night they stood,
  When night gave all that moonlight and dewfall
    could.
The dense ferns deepen, the moss glows warm as the
  thyme :
  The wild heath quivers about me : the world is
    good.

Is it Pan's breath, fierce in the tremulous maidenhair,
  That bids fear creep as a snake through the wood-
      lands, felt
In the leaves that it stirs not yet, in the mute bright air,
  In the stress of the sun? For here has the great
      God dwelt :
  For hence were the shafts of his love or his anger
      dealt.
For here has his wrath been fierce as his love was fair,
  When each was as fire to the darkness its breath
      bade melt.

Is it love, is it dread, that enkindles the trembling
      noon,
  That yearns, reluctant in rapture that fear has fed,
As man for woman, as woman for man? Full soon,
  If I live, and the life that may look on him drop
      not dead,
  Shall the ear that hears not a leaf quake hear his
      tread,
The sense that knows not the sound of the deep day's
      tune
  Receive the God, be it love that he brings or dread.

The naked noon is upon me : the fierce dumb spell,
  The fearful charm of the strong sun's imminent
      might,
Unmerciful, steadfast, deeper than seas that swell,
  Pervades, invades, appals me with loveless light,
  With harsher awe than breathes in the breath of
      night.
Have mercy, God who art all ! For I know thee well,
  How sharp is thine eye to lighten, thine hand to
      smite.

II.   2 H 2

The whole wood feels thee, the whole air fears thee :
    but fear
  So deep, so dim, so sacred, is wellnigh sweet.
For the light that hangs and broods on the wood-
    lands here,
  Intense, invasive, intolerant, imperious, and meet
  To lighten the works of thine hands and the ways
    of thy feet,
Is hot with the fire of the breath of thy life, and dear
  As hope that shrivels or shrinks not for frost or
    heat.

Thee, thee the supreme dim godhead, approved afar,
  Perceived of the soul and conceived of the sense of
    man,
We scarce dare love, and we dare not fear : the star
  We call the sun, that lit us when life began
  To brood on the world that is thine by his grace
    for a span,
Conceals and reveals in the semblance of things that
    are
  Thine immanent presence, the pulse of thy heart's
    life, Pan.

The fierce mid noon that wakens and warms the
    snake
  Conceals thy mercy, reveals thy wrath : and again
The dew-bright hour that assuages the twilight
    brake
  Conceals thy wrath and reveals thy mercy : then
  Thou art fearful only for evil souls of men
That feel with nightfall the serpent within them
    wake,
  And hate the holy darkness on glade and glen.

Yea, then we know not and dream not if ill things be,
Or if aught of the work of the wrong of the world
be thine.
We hear not the footfall of terror that treads the
sea,
We hear not the moan of winds that assail the
pine :
We see not if shipwreck reign in the storm's dim
shrine ;
If death do service and doom bear witness to thee
We see not,—know not if blood for thy lips be
wine.

But in all things evil and fearful that fear may scan,
As in all things good, as in all things fair that fall,
We know thee present and latent, the lord of man ;
In the murmuring of doves, in the clamouring of
winds that call
And wolves that howl for their prey ; in the mid-
night's pall,
In the naked and nymph-like feet of the dawn, O
Pan,
And in each life living, O thou the God who art all.

Smiling and singing, wailing and wringing of hands,
Laughing and weeping, watching and sleeping, still
Proclaim but and prove but thee, as the shifted sands
Speak forth and show but the strength of the sea's
wild will
That sifts and grinds them as grain in the storm-
wind's mill.
In thee is the doom that falls and the doom that
stands :
The tempests utter thy word, and the stars fulfil.

Where Etna shudders with passion and pain volcanic
    That rend her heart as with anguish that rends a
        man's,
Where Typho labours, and finds not his thews Titanic,
    In breathless torment that ever the flame's breath
        fans,
    Men felt and feared thee of old, whose pastoral
        clans
Were given to the charge of thy keeping ; and
        soundless panic
    Held fast the woodland whose depths and whose
        heights were Pan's.

And here, though fear be less than delight, and awe
    Be one with desire and with worship of earth and
        thee,
So mild seems now thy secret and speechless law,
    So fair and fearless and faithful and godlike she,
    So soft the spell of thy whisper on stream and sea,
Yet man should fear lest he see what of old men
        saw
    And withered : yet shall I quail if thy breath smite
        me.

Lord God of life and of light and of all things fair,
    Lord God of ravin and ruin and all things dim,
Death seals up life, and darkness the sunbright air,
    And the stars that watch blind earth in the deep
        night swim
    Laugh, saying, " What God is your God, that ye
        call on him ?
What is man, that the God who is guide of our way
        should care
    If day for a man be golden, or night be grim ? "

But thou, dost thou hear ?   Stars too but abide for a
    span,
  Gods too but endure for a season; but thou, if
    thou be
God, more than shadows conceived and adored of man,
  Kind Gods and fierce, that bound him or made him
    free,
  The skies that scorn us are less in thy sight than
    we,
Whose souls have strength to conceive and perceive
    thee, Pan,
  With sense more subtle than senses that hear and
    see.

Yet may not it say, though it seek thee and think to
    find
  One soul of sense in the fire and the frost-bound
    clod,
What heart is this, what spirit alive or blind,
  That moves thee : only we know that the ways we
    trod
  We tread, with hands unguided, with feet unshod,
With eyes unlightened ; and yet, if with steadfast
    mind,
  Perchance may we find thee and know thee at last
    for God.

Yet then should God be dark as the dawn is bright,
  And bright as the night is dark on the world—no
    more.
Light slays not darkness, and darkness absorbs not
    light ;
  And the labour of evil and good from the years of
    yore

Is even as the labour of waves on a sunless shore.
And he who is first and last, who is depth and height,
  Keeps silence now, as the sun when the woods
    wax hoar.

The dark dumb godhead innate in the fair world's life
  Imbues the rapture of dawn and of noon with
    dread,
Infects the peace of the star-shod night with strife,
  Informs with terror the sorrow that guards the
    dead.
  No service of bended knee or of humbled head
May soothe or subdue the God who has change to
    wife :
  And life with death is as morning with evening wed.

And yet, if the light and the life in the light that here
  Seem soft and splendid and fervid as sleep may
    seem
Be more than the shine of a smile or the flash of a tear,
  Sleep, change, and death are less than a spell-
    struck dream,
  And fear than the fall of a leaf on a starlit stream.
And yet, if the hope that hath said it absorb not fear,
  What helps it man that the stars and the waters
    gleam ?

What helps it man, that the noon be indeed intense,
  The night be indeed worth worship ? Fear and
    pain
Were lords and masters yet of the secret sense,
  Which now dares deem not that light is as dark-
    ness, fain
  Though dark dreams be to declare it, crying in vain.

For whence, thou God of the light and the darkness,
    whence
  Dawns now this vision that bids not the sunbeams
    wane?

What light, what shadow, diviner than dawn or
    night,
  Draws near, makes pause, and again—or I dream—
    draws near?
More soft than shadow, more strong than the strong
    sun's light,
  More pure than moonbeams—yea, but the rays
    run sheer
  As fire from the sun through the dusk of the pine-
    wood, clear
And constant; yea, but the shadow itself is bright
  That the light clothes round with love that is one
    with fear.

Above and behind it the noon and the woodland lie,
  Terrible, radiant with mystery, superb and subdued,
Triumphant in silence; and hardly the sacred sky
  Seems free from the tyrannous weight of the dumb
    fierce mood
  Which rules as with fire and invasion of beams
    that brood
The breathless rapture of earth till its hour pass by
  And leave her spirit released and her peace renewed.

I sleep not: never in sleep has a man beholden
  This. From the shadow that trembles and yearns
    with light
Suppressed and elate and reluctant—obscure and
    golden

As water kindled with presage of dawn or night—
A form, a face, a wonder to sense and sight,
Grows great as the moon through the month ; and
 her eyes embolden
 Fear, till it change to desire, and desire to delight.

I sleep not : sleep would die of a dream so strange ;
 A dream so sweet would die as a rainbow dies,
As a sunbow laughs and is lost on the waves that
  range
 And reck not of light that flickers or spray that flies.
 But the sun withdraws not, the woodland shrinks
  not or sighs,
No sweet thing sickens with sense or with fear of
 change ;
 Light wounds not, darkness blinds not, my stead-
  fast eyes.

Only the soul in my sense that receives the soul
 Whence now my spirit is kindled with breathless
  bliss
Knows well if the light that wounds it with love
 makes whole,
 If hopes that carol be louder than fears that hiss,
 If truth be spoken of flowers and of waves that kiss,
Of clouds and stars that contend for a sunbright goal.
 And yet may I dream that I dream not indeed of
  this ?

An earth-born dreamer, constrained by the bonds of
 birth,
 Held fast by the flesh, compelled by his veins that
  beat
And kindle to rapture or wrath. to desire or to mirth,

May hear not surely the fall of immortal feet,
May feel not surely if heaven upon earth be sweet ;
And here is my sense fulfilled of the joys of earth,
 Light, silence, bloom, shade, murmur of leaves
  that meet.

Bloom, fervour, and perfume of grasses and flowers
 aglow,
 Breathe and brighten about me : the darkness
  gleams,
The sweet light shivers and laughs on the slopes
 below,
 Made soft by leaves that lighten and change like
  dreams ;
The silence thrills with the whisper of secret streams
That well from the heart of the woodland : these I
 know :
 Earth bore them, heaven sustained them with
  showers and beams.

I lean my face to the heather, and drink the sun
 Whose flame-lit odour satiates the flowers : mine
  eyes
Close, and the goal of delight and of life is one :
 No more I crave of earth or her kindred skies.
 No more? But the joy that springs from them
  smiles and flies :
The sweet work wrought of them surely, the good
 work done,
 If the mind and the face of the season be loveless,
  dies.

Thee, therefore, thee would I come to, cleave to,
 cling,
 If haply thy heart be kind and thy gifts be good,

Unknown sweet spirit, whose vesture is soft in spring,
    In summer splendid, in autumn pale as the wood
    That shudders and wanes and shrinks as a shamed
            thing should,
In winter bright as the mail of a war-worn king
    Who stands where foes fled far from the face of
        him stood.

My spirit or thine is it, breath of thy life or of mine,
    Which fills my sense with a rapture that casts out
        fear?
Pan's dim frown wanes, and his wild eyes brighten
        as thine,
    Transformed as night or as day by the kindling
        year.
    Earth-born, or mine eye were withered that sees,
        mine ear
That hears were stricken to death by the sense divine,
    Earth-born I know thee : but heaven is about me
        here.

The terror that whispers in darkness and flames in
        light,
    The doubt that speaks in the silence of earth and
        sea,
The sense, more fearful at noon than in midmost
        night,
    Of wrath scarce hushed and of imminent ill to be,
    Where are they?   Heaven is as earth, and as
        heaven to me
Earth : for the shadows that sundered them here
        take flight ;
    And nought is all, as am I, but a dream of thee.

ON THE SOUTH COAST

To Theodore Watts

Hills and valleys where April rallies his radiant
  squadron of flowers and birds,
Steep strange beaches and lustrous reaches of
  fluctuant sea that the land engirds,
Fields and downs that the sunrise crowns with life
  diviner than lives in words,

Day by day of resurgent May salute the sun with
  sublime acclaim,
Change and brighten with hours that lighten and
  darken, girdled with cloud or flame ;
Earth's fair face in alternate grace beams, blooms,
  and lowers, and is yet the same.

Twice each day the divine sea's play makes glad with
  glory that comes and goes
Field and street that her waves keep sweet, when
  past the bounds of their old repose,
Fast and fierce in renewed reverse, the foam-flecked
  estuary ebbs and flows.

Broad and bold through the stays of old staked fast
    with trunks of the wildwood tree,
Up from shoreward, impelled far forward, by marsh
    and meadow, by lawn and lea,
Inland still at her own wild will swells, rolls, and
    revels the surging sea.

Strong as time, and as faith sublime,—clothed round
    with shadows of hopes and fears,
Nights and morrows, and joys and sorrows, alive
    with passion of prayers and tears,—
Stands the shrine that has seen decline eight hundred
    waxing and waning years.

Tower set square to the storms of air and change of
    season that glooms and glows,
Wall and roof of it tempest-proof, and equal ever to
    suns and snows,
Bright with riches of radiant niches and pillars
    smooth as a straight stem grows.

Aisle and nave that the whelming wave of time has
    whelmed not or touched or neared,
Arch and vault without stain or fault, by hands of
    craftsmen we know not reared,
Time beheld them, and time was quelled ; and
    change passed by them as one that feared.

Time that flies as a dream, and dies as dreams that
    die with the sleep they feed,
Here alone in a garb of stone incarnate stands as a
    god indeed,
Stern and fair, and of strength to bear all burdens
    mortal to man's frail seed.

Men and years are as leaves or tears that storm or
    sorrow is fain to shed :
These go by as the winds that sigh, and none takes
    note of them quick or dead :
Time, whose breath is their birth and death, folds
    here his pinions, and bows his head.

Still the sun that beheld begun the work wrought
    here of unwearied hands
Sees, as then, though the Red King's men held
    ruthless rule over lawless lands,
Stand their massive design, impassive, pure and
    proud as a virgin stands.

Statelier still as the years fulfil their count, subserving
    her sacred state,
Grows the hoary grey church whose story silence
    utters and age makes great :
Statelier seems it than shines in dreams the face un-
    veiled of unvanquished fate.

Fate, more high than the star-shown sky, more deep
    than waters unsounded, shines
Keen and far as the final star on souls that seek not
    for charms or signs ;
Yet more bright is the love-shown light of men's
    hands lighted in songs or shrines.

Love and trust that the grave's deep dust can soil
    not, neither may fear put out,
Witness yet that their record set stands fast, though
    years be as hosts in rout,
Spent and slain ; but the signs remain that beat
    back darkness and cast forth doubt.

Men that wrought by the grace of thought and toil
    things goodlier than praise dare trace,
Fair as all that the world may call most fair, save
    only the sea's own face,
Shrines or songs that the world's change wrongs not,
    live by grace of their own gift's grace.

Dead, their names that the night reclaims—alive,
    their works that the day relumes—
Sink and stand, as in stone and sand engraven ; none
    may behold their tombs :
Nights and days shall record their praise while here
    this flower of their grafting blooms.

Flower more fair than the sun-thrilled air bids laugh
    and lighten and wax and rise,
Fruit more bright than the fervent light sustains
    with strength from the kindled skies,
Flower and fruit that the deathless root of man's
    love rears though the man's name dies.

Stately stands it, the work of hands unknown of :
    statelier, afar and near,
Rise around it the heights that bound our landward
    gaze from the seaboard here ;
Downs that swerve and aspire, in curve and change
    of heights that the dawn holds dear.

Dawn falls fair on the grey walls there confronting
    dawn, on the low green lea,
Lone and sweet as for fairies' feet held sacred, silent
    and strange and free,
Wild and wet with its rills ; but yet more fair falls
    dawn on the fairer sea.

Eastward, round by the high green bound of hills
    that fold the remote fields in,
Strive and shine on the low sea-line fleet waves and
    beams when the days begin ;
Westward glow, when the days burn low, the sun
    that yields and the stars that win.

Rose-red eve on the seas that heave sinks fair as
    dawn when the first ray peers ;
Winds are glancing from sunbright Lancing to
    Shoreham, crowned with the grace of years ;
Shoreham, clad with the sunset, glad and grave with
    glory that death reveres.

Death, more proud than the kings' heads bowed
    before him, stronger than all things, bows
Here his head : as if death were dead, and kingship
    plucked from his crownless brows,
Life hath here such a face of cheer as change appals
    not and time avows.

Skies fulfilled with the sundown, stilled and splendid,
    spread as a flower that spreads,
Pave with rarer device and fairer than heaven's the
    luminous oyster-beds,
Grass-embanked, and in square plots ranked, inlaid
    with gems that the sundown sheds.

Squares more bright and with lovelier light than
    heaven that kindled it shines with shine
Warm and soft as the dome aloft, but heavenlier yet
    than the sun's own shrine :
Heaven is high, but the water-sky lit here seems
    deeper and more divine.

Flowers on flowers, that the whole world's bowers
    may show not, here may the sunset show,
Lightly graven in the waters paven with ghostly gold
    by the clouds aglow :
Bright as love is the vault above, but lovelier lightens
    the wave below.

Rosy grey, or as fiery spray full-plumed, or greener
    than emerald, gleams
Plot by plot as the skies allot for each its glory,
    divine as dreams
Lit with fire of appeased desire which sounds the
    secret of all that seems ;

Dreams that show what we fain would know, and
    know not save by the grace of sleep,
Sleep whose hands have removed the bands that eyes
    long waking and fain to weep
Feel fast bound on them—light around them strange,
    and darkness above them steep.

Yet no vision that heals division of love from love,
    and renews awhile
Life and breath in the lips where death has quenched
    the spirit of speech and smile,
Shows on earth, or in heaven's mid mirth, where no
    fears enter or doubts defile,

Aught more fair than the radiant air and water here
    by the twilight wed,
Here made one by the waning sun whose last love
    quickens to rosebright red
Half the crown of the soft high down that rears to
    northward its wood-girt head.

There, when day is at height of sway, men's eyes
　　who stand, as we oft have stood,
High where towers with its world of flowers the
　　golden spinny that flanks the wood,
See before and around them shore and seaboard glad
　　as their gifts are good.

Higher and higher to the north aspire the green
　　smooth-swelling unending downs ;
East and west on the brave earth's breast glow
　　girdle-jewels of gleaming towns ;
Southward shining, the lands declining subside in
　　peace that the sea's light crowns.

Westward wide in its fruitful pride the plain lies
　　lordly with plenteous grace ;
Fair as dawn's when the fields and lawns desire her
　　glitters the glad land's face :
Eastward yet is the sole sign set of elder days and a
　　lordlier race.

Down beneath us afar, where seethe in wilder weather
　　the tides aflow,
Hurled up hither and drawn down thither in quest of
　　rest that they may not know,
Still as dew on a flower the blue broad stream now
　　sleeps in the fields below.

Mild and bland in the fair green land it smiles, and
　　takes to its heart the sky ;
Scarce the meads and the fens, the reeds and grasses,
　　still as they stand or lie,
Wear the palm of a statelier calm than rests on waters
　　that pass them by.

Yet shall these, when the winds and seas of equal
    days and coequal nights
Rage, rejoice, and uplift a voice whose sound is even
    as a sword that smites,
Felt and heard as a doomsman's word from seaward
    reaches to landward heights,

Lift their heart up, and take their part of triumph,
    swollen and strong with rage,
Rage elate with desire and great with pride that
    tempest and storm assuage ;
So their chime in the ear of time has rung from age
    to rekindled age.

Fair and dear is the land's face here, and fair man's
    work as a man's may be :
Dear and fair as the sunbright air is here the record
    that speaks him free ;
Free by birth of a sacred earth, and regent ever of all
    the sea.

AN AUTUMN VISION

OCTOBER 31, 1889

Ζεφύρου γίγαντος αὔρᾳ

I

Is it Midsummer here in the heavens that illumine
    October on earth ?
Can the year, when his heart is fulfilled with desire
    of the days of his mirth,
      Redeem them, recall, or remember ?
For a memory recalling the rapture of earth, and
    redeeming the sky,
Shines down from the heights to the depths : will the
    watchword of dawn be July
      When to-morrow acclaims November ?
The stern salutation of sorrow to death or repentance
    to shame
Was all that the season was wont to accord her of
    grace or acclaim ;
      No lightnings of love and of laughter.
But here, in the laugh of the loud west wind from
    around and above,
In the flash of the waters beneath him, what sound
    or what light but of love
      Rings round him or leaps forth after ?

II

Wind beloved of earth and sky and sea beyond all
          winds that blow,
  Wind whose might in fight was England's on her
          mightiest warrior day,
South-west wind, whose breath for her was life, and
          fire to scourge her foe,
  Steel to smite and death to drive him down an
          unreturning way,
Well-beloved and welcome, sounding all the clarions
          of the sky,
  Rolling all the marshalled waters toward the charge
          that storms the shore,
We receive, acclaim, salute thee, we who live and
          dream and die,
  As the mightiest mouth of song that ever spake
          acclaimed of yore.
We that live as they that pe. 'sh praise thee, lord of
          cloud and wave,
  Wind of winds, clothed on with darkness whence
          as lightning light comes forth,
We that know thee strong to guard and smite, to
          scatter and to save,
  We to whom the south-west wind is dear as Athens
          held the north.
He for her waged war as thou for us against all
          powers defiant,
  Fleets full-fraught with storm from Persia, laden
          deep with death from Spain:
Thee the giant god of song and battle hailed as god
          and giant,
  Yet not his but ours the land is whence thy praise
          should ring and rain ;

Rain as rapture shed from song, and ring as trumpets
    blown for battle,
  Sound and sing before thee, loud and glad as leaps
    and sinks the sea :
Yea, the sea's white steeds are curbed and spurred
    of thee, and pent as cattle,
  Yet they laugh with love and pride to live, subdued
    not save of thee.
Ears that hear thee hear in heaven the sound of
    widening wings gigantic,
  Eyes that see the cloud-lift westward see thy
    darkening brows divine ;
Wings whose measure is the limit of the limitless
    Atlantic,
  Brows that bend, and bid the sovereign sea submit
    her soul to thine.

III

    Twelve days since is it—twelve days gone,
    Lord of storm, that a storm-bow shone
    Higher than sweeps thy sublime dark wing,
    Fair as dawn is and sweet like spring ?

    Never dawn in the deep wide east
    Spread so splendid and strange a feast,
    Whence the soul as it drank and fed
    Felt such rapture of wonder shed.

    Never spring in the wild wood's heart
    Felt such flowers at her footfall start,
    Born of earth, as arose on sight
    Born of heaven and of storm and light.

Stern and sullen, the grey grim sea
Swelled and strove as in toils, though free,
Free as heaven, and as heaven sublime,
Clear as heaven of the toils of time.

IV

Suddenly, sheer from the heights to the depths of the
    sky and the sea,
Sprang from the darkness alive as a vision of life
    to be
Glory triune and transcendent of colour afar and afire,
Arching and darkening the darkness with light as of
    dream or desire.
Heaven, in the depth of its height, shone wistful and
    wan from above :
Earth from beneath, and the sea, shone stricken and
    breathless with love.
As a shadow may shine, so shone they ; as ghosts of
    the viewless blest,
That sleep hath sight of alive in a rapture of sun-
    bright rest,
The green earth glowed and the grey sky gleamed for
    a wondrous while ;
And the storm's full frown was crossed by the light
    of its own deep smile.
As the darkness of thought and of passion is touched
    by the light that gives
Life deathless as love from the depth of a spirit that
    sees and lives,
From the soul of a seer and a singer, wherein as a
    scroll unfurled
Lies open the scripture of light and of darkness, the
    word of the world,

So, shapeless and measureless, lurid as anguish and
    haggard as crime,
Pale as the front of oblivion and dark as the heart of
    time,
The wild wan heaven at its height was assailed and
    subdued and made
More fair than the skies that know not of storm and
    endure not shade.
The grim sea-swell, grey, sleepless, and sad as a soul
    estranged,
Shone, smiled, took heart, and was glad of its wrath :
    and the world's face changed.

v

Up from moorlands northward gleaming
    Even to heaven's transcendent height,
Clothed with massive cloud, and seeming
    All one fortress reared of night,
Down to where the deep sea, dreaming
    Angry dreams, lay dark and white,
White as death and dark as fate,
Heaving with the strong wind's weight,
Sad with stormy pride of state,
One full rainbow shone elate.

Up from inmost memory's dwelling
    Where the light of life abides,
Where the past finds tongue, foretelling
    Time that comes and grace that guides,
Power that saves and sways, compelling
    Souls that ebb and flow like tides,
Shone or seemed to shine and swim
Through the cloud-surf great and grim,
Thought's live surge, the soul of him
By whose light the sun looks dim.

In what synod were they sitting,
    All the gods and lords of time,
Whence they watched as fen-fires flitting
    Years and names of men sublime,
When their counsels found it fitting
    One should stand where none might climb—
None of man begotten, none
Born of men beneath the sun
Till the race of time be run,
Save this heaven-enfranchised one?

With what rapture of creation
    Was the soul supernal thrilled,
With what pride of adoration
    Was the world's heart fired and filled,
Heaved in heavenward exaltation
    Higher than hopes or dreams might build,
Grave with awe not known while he
Was not, mad with glorious glee
As the sun-saluted sea,
When his hour bade Shakespeare be?

VI

There, clear as night beholds her crowning seven,
The sea beheld his likeness set in heaven.
The shadow of his spirit full in sight
Shone : for the shadow of that soul is light.
Nor heaven alone bore witness : earth avowed
Him present, and acclaimed of storm aloud.
From the arching sky to the ageless hills and sea
The whole world, visible, audible, was he :
Each part of all that wove that wondrous whole
The raiment of the presence of his soul.
The sun that smote and kissed the dark to death
Spake, smiled, and strove, like song's triumphant
    breath ;

The soundless cloud whose thunderous heart was
    dumb
Swelled, lowered, and shrank to feel its conqueror
    come.
Yet high from heaven its empire vast and vain
Frowned, and renounced not night's reluctant reign.
The serpentine swift sounds and shapes wherein
The stainless sea mocks earth and death and sin,
Crawls dark as craft, or flashes keen as hate,
Subdued and insubmissive, strong like fate
And weak like man, bore wrathful witness yet
That storms and sins are more than suns that set ;
That evil everlasting, girt for strife
Eternal, wars with hope as death with life.
The dark sharp shifting wind that bade the waves
Falter, lose heart, bow down like foes made slaves,
And waxed within more bitter as they bowed,
Baffling the sea, swallowing the sun with cloud,
Devouring fast as fire on earth devours
And hungering hard as frost that feeds on flowers,
Clothed round with fog that reeked as fume from hell,
And darkening with its miscreative spell
Light, glad and keen and splendid as the sword
Whose heft had known Othello's hand its lord,
Spake all the soul that hell drew back to greet
And felt its fire shrink shuddering from his feet.
Far off the darkness darkened, and recoiled,
And neared again, and triumphed : and the coiled
Colourless cloud and sea discoloured grew
Conscious of horror huge as heaven, and knew
Where Goneril's soul made chill and foul the mist,
And all the leprous life in Regan hissed.
Fierce homeless ghosts, rejected of the pit,
From hell to hell of storm fear watched them flit.

About them and before, the dull grey gloom
Shuddered, and heaven seemed hateful as the tomb
That shrinks from resurrection ; and from out
That sullen hell which girt their shades about
The nether soul that lurks and lowers within
Man, made of dust and fire and shame and sin, ·
Breathed : all the cloud that felt it breathe and blight
Was blue as plague or black as thunderous night.
Elect of hell, the children of his hate
Thronged, as to storm sweet heaven's triumphal
        gate.
The terror of his giving rose and shone
Imminent : life had put its likeness on.
But higher than all its horrent height of shade
Shone sovereign, seen by light itself had made,
Above the woes of all the world, above
Life, sin, and death, his myriad-minded love.
From landward heights whereon the radiance leant
Full-fraught from heaven, intense and imminent,
To depths wherein the seething strengths of cloud
Scarce matched the wrath of waves whereon they
        bowed,
From homeborn pride and kindling love of home
To the outer skies and seas of fire and foam,
From splendour soft as dew that sundawn thrills
To gloom that shudders round the world it fills,
From midnights murmuring round Titania's ear
To midnights maddening round the rage of Lear,
The wonder woven of storm and sun became
One with the light that lightens from his name.
The music moving on the sea that felt
The storm-wind even as snows of springtide melt
Was blithe as Ariel's hand or voice might make
And bid all grief die gladly for its sake.

And there the soul alive in ear and eye
That watched the wonders of an hour pass by
Saw brighter than all stars that heaven inspheres
The silent splendour of Cordelia's tears,
Felt in the whispers of the quickening wind
The radiance of the laugh of Rosalind,
And heard, in sounds that melt the souls of men
With love of love, the tune of Imogen.

VII

For the strong north-east is not strong to subdue
    and to slay the divine south-west,
And the darkness is less than the light that it
    darkens, and dies in reluctant rest.
It hovers and hangs on the labouring and trembling
    ascent of the dawn from the deep,
Till the sun's eye quicken the world and the waters,
    and smite it again into sleep.
Night, holy and starry, the fostress of souls, with the
    fragrance of heaven in her breath,
Subdues with the sense of her godhead the forces and
    mysteries of sorrow and death.
Eternal as dawn's is the comfort she gives : but the
    mist that beleaguers and slays
Comes, passes, and is not : the strength of it withers,
    appalled or assuaged by the day's.
Faith, haggard as Fear that had borne her, and dark
    as the sire that begat her, Despair,
Held rule on the soul of the world and the song of it
    saddening through ages that were ;
Dim centuries that darkened and brightened and
    darkened again, and the soul of their song
Was great as their grief, and sublime as their suffer-
    ing, and strong as their sorrows were strong.

It knew not, it saw not, but shadows triune, and
    evoked by the strength of their spell

Dark hell, and the mountain of anguish, and heaven
    that was hollower and harder than hell.

These are not : the womb of the darkness that bare
    them rejects them, and knows them no more :

Thought, fettered in misery and iron, revives in the
    light that it lived in of yore.

For the soul that is wisdom and freedom, the spirit
    of England redeemed from her past,

Speaks life through the lips of the master and
    lord of her children, the first and the last.

Thought, touched by his hand and redeemed by his
    breath, sees, hears, and accepts from above

The limitless lightnings of vision and passion, the
    measureless music of love.

A SWIMMER'S DREAM

NOVEMBER 4, 1889

Somno mollior unda

I

DAWN is dim on the dark soft water,
  Soft and passionate, dark and sweet.
Love's own self was the deep sea's daughter,
  Fair and flawless from face to feet,
Hailed of all when the world was golden,
Loved of lovers whose names beholden
Thrill men's eyes as with light of olden
  Days more glad than their flight was fleet.

So they sang : but for men that love her,
  Souls that hear not her word in vain,
Earth beside her and heaven above her
  Seem but shadows that wax and wane.
Softer than sleep's are the sea's caresses,
Kinder than love's that betrays and blesses,
Blither than spring's when her flowerful tresses
  Shake forth sunlight and shine with rain.

All the strength of the waves that perish
    Swells beneath me and laughs and sighs,
Sighs for love of the life they cherish,
    Laughs to know that it lives and dies,
Dies for joy of its life, and lives
Thrilled with joy that its brief death gives—
Death whose laugh or whose breath forgives
    Change that bids it subside and rise.

II

Hard and heavy, remote but nearing,
    Sunless hangs the severe sky's weight,
Cloud on cloud, though the wind be veering
    Heaped on high to the sundawn's gate.
Dawn and even and noon are one,
Veiled with vapour and void of sun ;
Nought in sight or in fancied hearing
    Now less mighty than time or fate.

The grey sky gleams and the grey seas glimmer,
    Pale and sweet as a dream's delight,
As a dream's where darkness and light seem dimmer,
    Touched by dawn or subdued by night.
The dark wind, stern and sublime and sad,
Swings the rollers to westward, clad
With lustrous shadow that lures the swimmer,
    Lures and lulls him with dreams of light.

Light, and sleep, and delight, and wonder,
    Change, and rest, and a charm of cloud,
Fill the world of the skies whereunder
    Heaves and quivers and pants aloud

A SWIMMER'S DREAM

All the world of the waters, hoary
Now, but clothed with its own live glory,
That mates the lightning and mocks the thunder
  With light more living and word more proud.

III

Far off westward, whither sets the sounding strife,
  Strife more sweet than peace, of shoreless waves
      whose glee
  Scorns the shore and loves the wind that leaves
    them free,
 Strange as sleep and pale as death and fair as life,
  Shifts the moonlight-coloured sunshine on the sea.

Toward the sunset's goal the sunless waters crowd,
  Fast as autumn days toward winter : yet it seems
  Here that autumn wanes not, here that woods and
    streams
Lose not heart and change not likeness, chilled and
  bowed,
  Warped and wrinkled : here the days are fair as
    dreams.

IV

O russet-robed November,
  What ails thee so to smile ?
Chill August, pale September,
  Endured a woful while,
And fell as falls an ember
  From forth a flameless pile :
But golden-girt November
  Bids all she looks on smile.

The lustrous foliage, waning
  As wanes the morning moon,
Here falling, here refraining,
  Outbraves the pride of June
With statelier semblance, feigning
  No fear lest death be soon :
As though the woods thus waning
  Should wax to meet the moon.

As though, when fields lie stricken
  By grey December's breath,
These lordlier growths that sicken
  And die for fear of death
Should feel the sense requicken
  That hears what springtide saith
And thrills for love, spring-stricken
  And pierced with April's breath.

The keen white-winged north-easter
  That stings and spurs thy sea
Doth yet but feed and feast her
  With glowing sense of glee :
Calm chained her, storm released her,
  And storm's glad voice was he :
South-wester or north-easter,
  Thy winds rejoice the sea.

v

A dream, a dream is it all—the season,
  The sky, the water, the wind, the shore ?
A day-born dream of divine unreason,
  A marvel moulded of sleep—no more ?

For the cloudlike wave that my limbs while cleaving
Feel as in slumber beneath them heaving
Soothes the sense as to slumber, leaving
   Sense of nought that was known of yore.

A purer passion, a lordlier leisure,
   A peace more happy than lives on land,
Fulfils with pulse of diviner pleasure
   The dreaming head and the steering hand.
I lean my cheek to the cold grey pillow,
The deep soft swell of the full broad billow,
And close mine eyes for delight past measure,
   And wish the wheel of the world would stand.

The wild-winged hour that we fain would capture
   Falls as from heaven that its light feet clomb,
So brief, so soft, and so full the rapture
   Was felt that soothed me with sense of home.
To sleep, to swim, and to dream, for ever—
Such joy the vision of man saw never ;
For here too soon will a dark day sever
   The sea-bird's wing from the sea-wave's foam.

A dream, and more than a dream, and dimmer
   At once and brighter than dreams that flee,
The moment's joy of the seaward swimmer
   Abides, remembered as truth may be.
Not all the joy and not all the glory
Must fade as leaves when the woods wax hoary ;
For there the downs and the sea-banks glimmer,
   And here to south of them swells the sea.

GRACE DARLING

Take, O star of all our seas, from not an alien
hand,
  Homage paid of song bowed down before thy
  glory's face,
Thou the living light of all our lovely stormy strand,
  Thou the brave north-country's very glory of
  glories, Grace.

Loud and dark about the lighthouse rings and glares
the night ;
  Glares with foam-lit gloom and darkling fire of
  storm and spray,
Rings with roar of winds in chase and rage of waves
in flight,
  Howls and hisses as with mouths of snakes and
  wolves at bay.
Scarce the cliffs of the islets, scarce the walls of
Joyous Gard,
  Flash to sight between the deadlier lightnings of
  the sea :
Storm is lord and master of a midnight evil-starred,
  Nor may sight or fear discern what evil stars may
  be.

Dark as death and white as snow the sea-swell
    scowls and shines,
  Heaves and yearns and pants for prey, from raven-
    ing lip to lip,
Strong in rage of rapturous anguish, lines on hurt-
    ling lines,
  Ranks on charging ranks, that break and rend the
    battling ship.
All the night is mad and murderous : who shall front
    the night ?
  Not the prow that labours, helpless as a storm-
    blown leaf,
Where the rocks and waters, darkling depth and
    beetling height,
  Rage with wave on shattering wave and thundering
    reef on reef.
Death is fallen upon the prisoners there of darkness,
    bound
  Like as thralls with links of iron fast in bonds of
    doom ;
How shall any way to break the bands of death be
    found,
  Any hand avail to pluck them from that raging
    tomb ?
All the night is great with child of death : no stars
    above
  Show them hope in heaven, no lights from shores
    ward help on earth.
Is there help or hope to seaward, is there help in
    love,
  Hope in pity, where the ravening hounds of storm
    make mirth ?
Where the light but shows the naked eyeless face of
    Death

Nearer, laughing dumb and grim across the loud
    live storm?
Not in human heart or hand or speech of human
       breath,
    Surely, nor in saviours found of mortal face or
       form.
Yet below the light, between the reefs, a skiff shot
    out
    Seems a sea-bird fain to breast and brave the strait
    fierce pass
Whence the channelled roar of waters driven in
    raging rout,
    Pent and pressed and maddened, speaks their mon-
    strous might and mass.
Thunder heaves and howls about them, lightning
    leaps and flashes,
    Hard at hand, not high in heaven, but close
    between the walls
Heaped and hollowed of the storms of old, whence
    reels and crashes
    All the rage of all the unbaffled wave that breaks
    and falls.
Who shall thwart the madness and the gladness of
    it, laden
    Full with heavy fate, and joyous as the birds that
    whirl?
Nought in heaven or earth, if not one mortal-moulded
    maiden,
    Nought if not the soul that glorifies a northland
    girl.
Not the rocks that break may baffle, not the reefs that
    thwart
    Stay the ravenous rapture of the waves that crowd
    and leap ;

Scarce their flashing laughter shows the hunger of
    their heart,
  Scarce their lion-throated roar the wrath at heart
    they keep.
Child and man and woman in the grasp of death
    clenched fast
  Tremble, clothed with darkness round about, and
    scarce draw breath,
Scarce lift eyes up toward the light that saves not,
    scarce may cast
  Thought or prayer up, caught and trammelled in
    the snare of death.
Not as sea-mews cling and laugh or sun their plumes
    and sleep
  Cling and cower the wild night's waifs of shipwreck,
    blind with fear,
Where the fierce reef scarce yields foothold that a bird
    might keep,
  And the clamorous darkness deadens eye and
    deafens ear.
Yet beyond their helpless hearing, out of hopeless
    sight,
  Saviours, armed and girt upon with strength of
    heart, fare forth,
Sire and daughter, hand on oar and face against the
    night,
  Maid and man whose names are beacons ever to
    the North.
Nearer now; but all the madness of the storming
    surf
  Hounds and roars them back; but roars and hounds
    them back in vain:
As a pleasure-skiff may graze the lake-embanking
    turf,

So the boat that bears them grates the rock where-
toward they strain.
Dawn as fierce and haggard as the face of night
scarce guides
Toward the cries that rent and clove the darkness,
crying for aid,
Hours on hours, across the engorged reluctance of the
tides,
Sire and daughter, high-souled man and mightier-
hearted maid.
Not the bravest land that ever breasted war's grim
sea,
Hurled her foes back harried on the lowlands whence
they came,
Held her own and smote her smiters down, while such
durst be,
Shining northward, shining southward, as the
aurorean flame,
Not our mother, not Northumberland, brought ever
forth,
Though no southern shore may match the sons that
kiss her mouth,
Children worthier all the birthright given of the ardent
north
Where the fire of hearts outburns the suns that fire
the south.
Even such fire was this that lit them, not from lowering skies
Where the darkling dawn flagged, stricken in the
sun's own shrine,
Down the gulf of storm subsiding, till their earnest
eyes
Find the relics of the ravening night that spared
but nine.

Life by life the man redeems them, head by storm-
    worn head,
  While the girl's hand stays the boat whereof the
    waves are fain :
Ah, but woe for one, the mother clasping fast her
   · dead !
  Happier, had the surges slain her with her children
    slain.
Back they bear, and bring between them safe the
    woful nine,
  Where above the ravenous Hawkers fixed at watch
    for prey
Storm and calm behold the Longstone's towering
    signal shine
  Now as when that labouring night brought forth a
    shuddering day.
Now as then, though like the hounds of storm against
    her snarling
  All the clamorous years between us storm down
    many a fame,
As our sires beheld before us we behold Grace
    Darling
  Crowned and throned our queen, and as they hailed
    we hail her name.
Nay, not ours alone, her kinsfolk born, though
    chiefliest ours,
  East and west and south acclaim her queen of
    England's maids,
Star more sweet than all their stars and flower than
    all their flowers,
  Higher in heaven and earth than star than sets or
    flower that fades.
How should land or sea that nurtured her forget, or
    love

Hold not fast her fame for us while aught is borne
    in mind ?
Land and sea beneath us, sun and moon and stars
    above,
    Bear the bright soul witness, seen of all but souls
      born blind.
Stars and moon and sun may wax and wane, subside
    and rise,
    Age on age as flake on flake of showering snows be
      shed :
Not till earth be sunless, not till death strike blind
    the skies,
    May the deathless love that waits on deathless
      deeds be dead.

Years on years have withered since beside the hearth
    once thine
    I, too young to have seen thee, touched thy father's
      hallowed hand :
Thee and him shall all men see for ever, stars that
    shine
    While the sea that spared thee girds and glorifies
      the land.

LOCH TORRIDON

To E. H.

THE dawn of night more fair than morning rose,
Stars hurrying forth on stars, as snows on snows
Haste when the wind and winter bid them speed.
Vague miles of moorland road behind us lay
Scarce traversed ere the day
Sank, and the sun forsook us at our need,
Belated.   Where we thought to have rested, rest
Was none ; for soft Maree's dim quivering breast,
Bound round with gracious inland girth of green
And fearless of the wild wave-wandering West,
Shone shelterless for strangers ; and unseen
The goal before us lay
Of all our blithe and strange and strenuous day.

For when the northering road faced westward—when
The dark sharp sudden gorge dropped seaward—
    then,
Beneath the stars, between the steeps, the track
We followed, lighted not of moon or sun,
And plunging whither none

Might guess, while heaven and earth were hoar and
    black,
Seemed even the dim still pass whence none turns
    back :
And through the twilight leftward of the way,
And down the dark, with many a laugh and leap,
The light blithe hill-streams shone from scaur to
    steep
In glittering pride of play ;
And ever while the night grew great and deep
We felt but saw not what the hills would keep
Sacred awhile from sense of moon or star ;
And full and far
Beneath us, sweet and strange as heaven may be,
The sea.

The very sea : no mountain-moulded lake
Whose fluctuant shapeliness is fain to take
Shape from the steadfast shore that rules it round,
And only from the storms a casual sound :
The sea, that harbours in her heart sublime
The supreme heart of music deep as time,
And in her spirit strong
The spirit of all imaginable song.

Not a whisper or lisp from the waters : the skies
    were not silenter.   Peace
Was between them ; a passionless rapture of respite
    as soft as release.
Not a sound, but a sense that possessed and per-
    vaded with patient delight
The soul and the body, clothed round with the com-
    fort of limitless night.

Night infinite, living, adorable, loved of the land and
    the sea :
Night, mother of mercies, who saith to the spirits in
    prison, Be free.
And softer than dewfall, and kindlier than starlight,
    and keener than wine,
Came round us the fragrance of waters, the life of
    the breath of the brine.
We saw not, we heard not, the face or the voice of
    the waters : we knew
By the darkling delight of the wind as the sense of
    the sea in it grew,
By the pulse of the darkness about us enkindled and
    quickened, that here,
Unseen and unheard of us, surely the goal we had
    faith in was near.
A silence diviner than music, a darkness diviner than
    light,
Fulfilled as from heaven with a measureless comfort
    the measure of night.

    But never a roof for shelter
      And never a sign for guide
        Rose doubtful or visible : only
          And hardly and gladly we heard
    The soft waves whisper and welter,
      Subdued, and allured to subside,
        By the mild night's magic : the lonely
          Sweet silence was soothed, not stirred,
    By the noiseless noise of the gleaming
      Glad ripples, that played and sighed,
        Kissed, laughed, recoiled, and relented,
          Whispered, flickered, and fled.

No season was this for dreaming
    How oft, with a stormier tide,
        Had the wrath of the winds been vented
        On sons of the tribes long dead :
The tribes whom time, and the changes
    Of things, and the stress of doom,
        Have erased and effaced ; forgotten
        As wrecks or weeds of the shore
In sight of the stern hill-ranges
    That hardly may change their gloom
        When the fruits of the years wax rotten
        And the seed of them springs no more.
For the dim strait footway dividing
    The waters that breathed below
        Led safe to the kindliest of shelters
        That ever awoke into light :
And still in remembrance abiding
    Broods over the stars that glow
        And the water that eddies and welters
        The passionate peace of the night.

All night long, in the world of sleep,
Skies and waters were soft and deep :
Shadow clothed them, and silence made
Soundless music of dream and shade :
All above us, the livelong night,
Shadow, kindled with sense of light ;
All around us, the brief night long,
Silence, laden with sense of song.
Stars and mountains without, we knew,
Watched and waited, the soft night through :
All unseen, but divined and dear,
Thrilled the touch of the sea's breath near :

All unheard, but alive like sound,
Throbbed the sense of the sea's life round :
Round us, near us, in depth and height,
Soft as darkness and keen as light.

And the dawn leapt in at my casement : and there,
as I rose, at my feet
No waves of the landlocked waters, no lake submissive and sweet,
Soft slave of the lordly seasons, whose breath may
loose it or freeze ;
But to left and to right and ahead was the ripple
whose pulse is the sea's.
From the gorge we had travelled by starlight the
sunrise, winged and aflame,
Shone large on the live wide wavelets that shuddered
with joy as it came ;
As it came and caressed and possessed them, till
panting and laughing with light
From mountain to mountain the water was kindled
and stung to delight.
And the grey gaunt heights that embraced and constrained and compelled it were glad,
And the rampart of rock, stark naked, that thwarted
and barred it, was clad
With a stern grey splendour of sunrise : and scarce
had I sprung to the sea
When the dawn and the water were wedded, the hills
and the sky set free.
The chain of the night was broken : the waves that
embraced me and smiled
And flickered and fawned in the sunlight, alive, un-
afraid, undefiled,

Were sweeter to swim in than air, though fulfilled
    with the mounting morn,
Could be for the birds whose triumph rejoiced that a
    day was born.

And a day was arisen indeed for us.   Years and the
    changes of years
Clothed round with their joys and their sorrows, and
    dead as their hopes and their fears,
Lie noteless and nameless, unlit by remembrance or
    record of days
Worth wonder or memory, or cursing or blessing, or
    passion or praise,
Between us who live and forget not, but yearn with
    delight in it yet,
And the day we forget not, and never may live and
    may think to forget.
And the years that were kindlier and fairer, and
    kindled with pleasures as keen,
Have eclipsed not with lights or with shadows the
    light on the face of it seen.
For softly and surely, as nearer the boat that we
    gazed from drew,
The face of the precipice opened and bade us as birds
    pass through,
And the bark shot sheer to the sea through the strait
    of the sharp steep cleft,
The portal that opens with imminent rampires to
    right and to left,
Sublime as the sky they darken and strange as a
    spell-struck dream,
On the world unconfined of the mountains, the reign
    of the sea supreme,

The kingdom of westward waters, wherein when we
    swam we knew
The waves that we clove were boundless, the wind
    on our brows that blew
Had swept no land and no lake, and had warred not
    on tower or on tree,
But came on us hard out of heaven, and alive with
    the soul of the sea.

THE PALACE OF PAN

INSCRIBED TO MY MOTHER

SEPTEMBER, all glorious with gold, as a king
  In the radiance of triumph attired,
Outlightening the summer, outsweetening the spring,
Broods wide on the woodlands with limitless wing,
  A presence of all men desired.

Far eastward and westward the sun-coloured lands
  Smile warm as the light on them smiles ;
And statelier than temples upbuilded with hands,
Tall column by column, the sanctuary stands
  Of the pine-forest's infinite aisles.

Mute worship, too fervent for praise or for prayer,
  Possesses the spirit with peace,
Fulfilled with the breath of the luminous air,
The fragrance, the silence, the shadows as fair
  As the rays that recede or increase.

Ridged pillars that redden aloft and aloof,
  With never a branch for a nest,
Sustain the sublime indivisible roof,
To the storm and the sun in his majesty proof,
  And awful as waters at rest.

Man's hand hath not measured the height of them;
    thought
  May measure not, awe may not know;
In its shadow the woofs of the woodland are
    wrought;
As a bird is the sun in the toils of them caught,
  And the flakes of it scattered as snow.

As the shreds of a plumage of gold on the ground
  The sun-flakes by multitudes lie,
Shed loose as the petals of roses discrowned
On the floors of the forest engilt and embrowned
  And reddened afar and anigh.

Dim centuries with darkling inscrutable hands
  Have reared and secluded the shrine
For gods that we know not, and kindled as brands
On the altar the years that are dust, and their sands
  Time's glass has forgotten for sign.

A temple whose transepts are measured by miles,
  Whose chancel has morning for priest,
Whose floor-work the foot of no spoiler defiles,
Whose musical silence no music beguiles,
  No festivals limit its feast.

The noon's ministration, the night's and the dawn's,
  Conceals not, reveals not for man,
On the slopes of the herbless and blossomless lawns,
Some track of a nymph's or some trail of a faun's
  To the place of the slumber of Pan.

Thought, kindled and quickened by worship and
    wonder
  To rapture too sacred for fear

On the ways that unite or divide them in sunder,
Alone may discern if about them or under
   Be token or trace of him here.

With passionate awe that is deeper than panic
   The spirit subdued and unshaken
Takes heed of the godhead terrene and Titanic
Whose footfall is felt on the breach of volcanic
   Sharp steeps that their fire has forsaken.

By a spell more serene than the dim necromantic
   Dead charms of the past and the night,
Or the terror that lurked in the noon to make frantic
Where Etna takes shape from the limbs of gigantic
   Dead gods disanointed of might,

The spirit made one with the spirit whose breath
   Makes noon in the woodland sublime
Abides as entranced in a presence that saith
Things loftier than life and serener than death,
   Triumphant and silent as time.

PINE RIDGE : *September* 1893

A YEAR'S CAROLS

JANUARY

Hail, January, that bearest here
On snowbright breasts the babe-faced year
   That weeps and trembles to be born.
Hail, maid and mother, strong and bright,
Hooded and cloaked and shod with white,
   Whose eyes are stars that match the morn.
Thy forehead braves the storm's bent bow,
Thy feet enkindle stars of snow.

FEBRUARY

Wan February with weeping cheer,
Whose cold hand guides the youngling year
   Down misty roads of mire and rime,
Before thy pale and fitful face
The shrill wind shifts the clouds apace
   Through skies the morning scarce may climb.
Thine eyes are thick with heavy tears,
But lit with hopes that light the year's

MARCH

Hail, happy March, whose foot on earth
Rings as the blast of martial mirth
   When trumpets fire men's hearts for fray.
No race of wild things winged or finned
May match the might that wings thy wind
   Through air and sea, through scud and spray.
Strong joy and thou were powers twin-born
Of tempest and the towering morn.

APRIL

Crowned April, king whose kiss bade earth
Bring forth to time her lordliest birth
   When Shakespeare from thy lips drew breath
And laughed to hold in one soft hand
A spell that bade the world's wheel stand,
   And power on life, and power on death,
With quiring suns and sunbright showers
Praise him, the flower of all thy flowers.

MAY

Hail, May, whose bark puts forth full-sailed
For summer ; May, whom Chaucer hailed
   With all his happy might of heart,
And gave thy rosebright daisy-tips
Strange fragrance from his amorous lips
   That still thine own breath seems to part
And sweeten till each word they say
Is even a flower of flowering May.

JUNE

Strong June, superb, serene, elate
With conscience of thy sovereign state
    Untouched of thunder, though the storm
Scathe here and there thy shuddering skies
And bid its lightning cross thine eyes
    With fire, thy golden hours inform
Earth and the souls of men with life
That brings forth peace from shining strife.

JULY

Hail, proud July, whose fervent mouth
Bids even be morn and north be south
    By grace and gospel of thy word,
Whence all the splendour of the sea
. Lies breathless with delight in thee
    And marvel at the music heard
From the ardent silent lips of noon
And midnight's rapturous plenilune.

AUGUST

Great August, lord of golden lands,
Whose lordly joy through seas and strands
    And all the red-ripe heart of earth
Strikes passion deep as life, and stills
The folded vales and folding hills
    With gladness too divine for mirth,
The gracious glories of thine eyes
Make night a noon where darkness dies.

SEPTEMBER

Hail, kind September, friend whose grace
Renews the bland year's bounteous face
    With largess given of corn and wine
Through many a land that laughs with love
Of thee and all the heaven above,
    More fruitful found than all save thine
Whose skies fulfil with strenuous cheer
The fervent fields that knew thee near.

OCTOBER

October of the tawny crown,
Whose heavy-laden hands drop down
    Blessing, the bounties of thy breath
And mildness of thy mellowing might
Fill earth and heaven with love and light
    Too sweet for fear to dream of death
Or memory, while thy joy lives yet,
To know what joy would fain forget.

NOVEMBER

Hail, soft November, though thy pale
Sad smile rebuke the words that hail
    Thy sorrow with no sorrowing words
Or gratulate thy grief with song
Less bitter than the winds that wrong
    Thy withering woodlands, where the birds
Keep hardly heart to sing or see
How fair thy faint wan face may be.

DECEMBER

December, thou whose hallowing hands
On shuddering seas and hardening lands
   Set as a sacramental sign
The seal of Christmas felt on earth
As witness toward a new year's birth
   Whose promise makes thy death divine,
The crowning joy that comes of thee
Makes glad all grief on land or sea.

ENGLAND: AN ODE

1

Sea and strand, and a lordlier land than sea-tides
   rolling and rising sun
Clasp and lighten in climes that brighten with day
   when day that was here is done,
Call aloud on their children, proud with trust that
   future and past are one.

Far and near from the swan's nest here the storm-
   birds bred of her fair white breast,
Sons whose home was the sea-wave's foam, have
   borne the fame of her east and west;
North and south has the storm-wind's mouth rung
   praise of England and England's quest.

Fame, wherever her flag flew, never forbore to fly
   with an equal wing:
France and Spain with their warrior train bowed
   down before her as thrall to king;
India knelt at her feet, and felt her sway more fruitful of life than spring.

Darkness round them as iron bound fell off from
   races of elder name.

Slain at sight of her eyes, whose light bids freedom
    lighten and burn as flame ;
Night endures not the touch that cures of kingship
    tyrants, and slaves of shame.

All the terror of time, where error and fear were lords
    of a world of slaves,
Age on age in resurgent rage and anguish darkening
    as waves on waves,
Fell or fled from a face that shed such grace as
    quickens the dust of graves.

Things of night at her glance took flight : the
    strengths of darkness recoiled and sank :
Sank the fires of the murderous pyres whereon wild
    agony writhed and shrank :
Rose the light of the reign of right from gulfs of
    years that the darkness drank.

Yet the might of her wings in flight, whence glory
    lightens and music rings,
Loud and bright as the dawn's, shall smite and still
    the discord of evil things,
Yet not slain by her radiant reign, but darkened now
    by her sail-stretched wings.

II

Music made of change and conquest, glory born of
    evil slain,
Stilled the discord, slew the darkness, bade the lights
    of tempest wane,
Where the deathless dawn of England rose in sign
    that right should reign.

Mercy, where the tiger wallowed mad and blind with
　　blood and lust,
Justice, where the jackal yelped and fed, and slaves
　　allowed it just,
Rose as England's light on Asia rose, and smote
　　them down to dust.

Justice bright as mercy, mercy girt by justice with
　　her sword,
Smote and saved and raised and ruined, till the
　　tyrant-ridden horde
Saw the lightning fade from heaven and knew the sun
　　for God and lord.

Where the footfall sounds of England, where the
　　smile of England shines,
Rings the tread and laughs the face of freedom, fair
　　as hope divines
Days to be, more brave than ours and lit by lordlier
　　stars for signs.

All our past acclaims our future : Shakespeare's
　　voice and Nelson's hand,
Milton's faith and Wordsworth's trust in this our
　　chosen and chainless land,
Bear us witness : come the world against her,
　　England yet shall stand.

Earth and sea bear England witness if he lied who
　　said it ; he
Whom the winds that ward her, waves that clasp,
　　and herb and flower and tree
Fed with English dews and sunbeams, hail as more
　　than man may be.

No man ever spake as he that bade our England be
    but true,
Keep but faith with England fast and firm, and none
    should bid her rue ;
None may speak as he : but all may know the sign
    that Shakespeare knew.

III

From the springs of the dawn, from the depths of the
    noon, from the heights of the night that shine,
Hope, faith, and remembrance of glory that found
    but in England her throne and her shrine,
Speak louder than song may proclaim them, that here
    is the seal of them set for a sign.

And loud as the sea's voice thunders applause of the
    land that is one with the sea
Speaks Time in the ear of the people that never at
    heart was not inly free
The word of command that assures us of life, if we
    will but that life shall be ;

If the race that is first of the races of men who behold
    unashamed the sun
Stand fast and forget not the sign that is given of
    the years and the wars that are done,
The token that all who are born of its blood should
    in heart as in blood be one.

The word of remembrance that lightens as fire from
    the steeps of the storm-lit past

Bids only the faith of our fathers endure in us, firm
as they held it fast :
That the glory which was from the first upon England
alone may endure to the last.

That the love and the hate may change not, the faith
may not fade, nor the wrath nor scorn,
That shines for her sons and that burns for her foemen as fire of the night or the morn :
That the births of her womb may forget not the sign
of the glory wherein they were born.

A light that is more than the sunlight, an air that is
brighter than morning's breath,
Clothes England about as the strong sea clasps her,
and answers the word that it saith ;
The word that assures her of life if she change not,
and choose not the ways of death.

Change darkens and lightens around her, alternate
in hope and in fear to be :
Hope knows not if fear speak truth, nor fear whether
hope be not blind as she :
But the sun is in heaven that beholds her immortal,
and girdled with life by the sea.

ETON : AN ODE

FOR THE FOUR HUNDRED AND FIFTIETH ANNIVERSARY
OF THE FOUNDATION OF THE COLLEGE

I

FOUR hundred summers and fifty have shone on the
    meadows of Thames and died
Since Eton arose in an age that was darkness, and
    shone by his radiant side
As a star that the spell of a wise man's word bade
    live and ascend and abide.

And ever as time's flow brightened, a river more dark
    than the storm-clothed sea,
And age upon age rose fairer and larger in promise of
    hope set free,
With England Eton her child kept pace as a fostress
    of men to be.

And ever as earth waxed wiser, and softer the beat-
    ing of time's wide wings,
Since fate fell dark on her father, most hapless and
    gentlest of star-crossed kings,
Her praise has increased as the chant of the dawn
    that the choir of the noon outsings.

II

Storm and cloud in the skies were loud, and light-
    ning mocked at the blind sun's light ;
War and woe on the land below shed heavier shadow
    than falls from night ;
Dark was earth at her dawn of birth as here her
    record of praise is bright.

Clear and fair through her morning air the light first
    laugh of the sunlit stage
Rose and rang as a fount that sprang from depths
    yet dark with a spent storm's rage,
Loud and glad as a boy's, and bade the sunrise open
    on Shakespeare's age.

Lords of state and of war, whom fate found strong in
    battle, in counsel strong,
Here, ere fate had approved them great, abode their
    season, and thought not long :
Here too first was the lark's note nursed that filled
    and flooded the skies with song.

III

Shelley, lyric lord of England's lordliest singers, here
    first heard
Ring from lips of poets crowned and dead the Pro-
    methean word
Whence his soul took fire, and power to outsoar the
    sunward-soaring bird.

ETON : AN ODE

Still the reaches of the river, still the light on field
and hill,
Still the memories held aloft as lamps for hope's
young fire to fill,
Shine, and while the light of England lives shall
shine for England still.

When four hundred more and fifty years have risen
and shone and set,
Bright with names that men remember, loud with
names that men forget,
Haply here shall Eton's record be what England
finds it yet.

THE UNION

I

THREE in one, but one in three,
God, who girt her with the sea,
Bade our Commonweal to be :
    Nought, if now not one.
Though fraud and fear would sever
The bond assured for ever,
Their shameful strength shall never
    Undo what heaven has done.

II

South and North and West and East
Watch the ravens flock to feast,
Dense as round some death-struck beast,
    Black as night is black.
Stand fast as faith together
In stress of treacherous weather
When hounds and wolves break tether
    And Treason guides the pack.

III

Lovelier than thy seas are strong,
Glorious Ireland, sword and song
Gird and crown thee : none may wrong,
    Save thy sons alone.

The sea that laughs around us
Hath sundered not but bound us :
The sun's first rising found us
    Throned on its equal throne.

IV

North and South and East and West,
All true hearts that wish thee best
Beat one tune and own one quest,
    Staunch and sure as steel.
God guard from dark disunion
Our threefold State's communion,
God save the loyal Union,
    The royal Commonweal !

EAST TO WEST

Sunset smiles on sunrise : east and west are one,
Face to face in heaven before the sovereign sun.
From the springs of the dawn everlasting a glory
renews and transfigures the west,
From the depths of the sunset a light as of morning
enkindles the broad sea's breast,
And the lands and the skies and the waters are glad
of the day's and the night's work done.

Child of dawn, and regent on the world-wide sea,
England smiles on Europe, fair as dawn and free.
Not the waters that gird her are purer, nor mightier
the winds that her waters know.
But America, daughter and sister of England, is
praised of them, far as they flow :
Atlantic responds to Pacific the praise of her days
that have been and shall be.

So from England westward let the watchword fly,
So for England eastward let the seas reply ;
Praise, honour, and love everlasting be sent on the
wind's wings, westward and east,
That the pride of the past and the pride of the future
may mingle as friends at feast,
And the sons of the lords of the world-wide seas be
one till the world's life die.

INSCRIPTIONS

FOR THE FOUR SIDES OF A PEDESTAL

I

MARLOWE, the father of the sons of song
  Whose praise is England's crowning praise, above
All glories else that crown her, sweet and strong
  As England, clothed with light and fire of love,
And girt with might of passion, thought, and trust,
Stands here in spirit, sleeps not here in dust.

II

Marlowe, a star too sovereign, too superb,
  To fade when heaven took fire from Shakespeare's
     light,
A soul that knew but song's triumphal curb
  And love's triumphant bondage, holds of right
His pride of place, who first in place and time
Made England's voice as England's heart sublime.

III

Marlowe bade England live in living song :
  The light he lifted up lit Shakespeare's way :
He spake, and life sprang forth in music, strong
  As fire or lightning, sweet as dawn of day.
Song was a dream where day took night to wife :
" Let there be life," he said : and there was life.

IV

Marlowe of all our fathers first beheld
  Beyond the tidal ebb and flow of things
The tideless depth and height of souls, impelled
  By thought or passion, borne on waves or wings,
Beyond all flight or sight but song's : and he
First gave our song a sound that matched our sea.

ON THE DEATH OF RICHARD BURTON

NIGHT or light is it now, wherein
Sleeps, shut out from the wild world's din,
    Wakes, alive with a life more clear,
One who found not on earth his kin?

Sleep were sweet for awhile, were dear
Surely to souls that were heartless here,
    Souls that faltered and flagged and fell,
Soft of spirit and faint of cheer.

A living soul that had strength to quell
Hope the spectre and fear the spell,
    Clear-eyed, content with a scorn sublime
And a faith superb, can it fare not well?

Life, the shadow of wide-winged time,
Cast from the wings that change as they climb,
    Life may vanish in death, and seem
Less than the promise of last year's prime.

But not for us is the past a dream
Wherefrom, as light from a clouded stream,
    Faith fades and shivers and ebbs away,
Faint as the moon if the sundawn gleam.

Faith, whose eyes in the low last ray
Watch the fire that renews the day,
 Faith which lives in the living past,
Rock-rooted, swerves not as weeds that sway.

As trees that stand in the storm-wind fast
She stands, unsmitten of death's keen blast,
 With strong remembrance of sunbright spring
Alive at heart to the lifeless last.

Night, she knows, may in no wise cling
To a soul that sinks not and droops not wing,
 A sun that sets not in death's false night
Whose kingdom finds him not thrall but king.

Souls there are that for soul's affright
Bow down and cower in the sun's glad sight,
 Clothed round with faith that is one with fear,
And dark with doubt of the live world's light.

But him we hailed from afar or near
As boldest born of the bravest here
 And loved as brightest of souls that eyed
Life, time, and death with unchangeful cheer,

A wider soul than the world was wide,
Whose praise made love of him one with pride,
 What part has death or has time in him,
Who rode life's lists as a god might ride?

While England sees not her old praise dim,
While still her stars through the world's night swim,
 A fame outshining her Raleigh's fame,
A light that lightens her loud sea's rim,

Shall shine and sound as her sons proclaim
The pride that kindles at Burton's name.
　　And joy shall exalt their pride to be
The same in birth if in soul the same.

But we that yearn for a friend's face—we
Who lack the light that on earth was he—
　　Mourn, though the light be a quenchless flame
That shines as dawn on a tideless sea.

ELEGY

1869–1891

Auvergne, Auvergne, O wild and woful land,
  O glorious land and gracious, white as gleam
The stairs of heaven, black as a flameless brand,
  Strange even as life, and stranger than a dream,

Could earth remember man, whose eyes made bright
  The splendour of her beauty, lit by day
Or soothed and softened and redeemed by night,
  Wouldst thou not know what light has passed
    away?

Wouldst thou not know whom England, whom the
    world,
  Mourns? For the world whose wildest ways he trod,
And smiled their dangers down that coiled and curled
  Against him, knows him now less man than god.

Our demigod of daring, keenest-eyed
  To read and deepest read in earth's dim things,
A spirit now whose body of death has died
  And left it mightier yet in eyes and wings,

The sovereign seeker of the world, who now
   Hath sought what world the light of death may
      show,
Hailed once with me the crowns that load thy brow,
   Crags dark as midnight, columns bright as snow.

Thy steep small Siena, splendid and content
   As shines the mightier city's Tuscan pride
Which here its face reflects in radiance, pent
   By narrower bounds from towering side to side,

Set fast between the ridged and foamless waves
   Of earth more fierce and fluctuant than the sea,
The fearless town of towers that hails and braves
   The heights that gird, the sun that brands Le Puy;

The huddled churches clinging on the cliffs
   As birds alighting might for storm's sake cling,
Moored to the rocks as tempest-harried skiffs
   To perilous refuge from the loud wind's wing;

The stairs on stairs that wind and change and climb
   Even up to the utmost crag's edge curved and curled,
More bright than vision, more than faith sublime,
   Strange as the light and darkness of the world;

Strange as are night and morning, stars and sun,
   And washed from west and east by day's deep tide.
Shine yet less fair, when all their heights are won,
   Than sundawn shows thy pillared mountain-side.

Even so the dawn of death, whose light makes dim
   The starry fires that life sees rise and set,
Shows higher than here he shone before us him
   Whom faith forgets not, nor shall fame forget.

Even so those else unfooted heights we clomb
  Through scudding mist and eddying whirls of cloud,
Blind as a pilot beaten blind with foam,
  And shrouded as a corpse with storm's grey shroud,

Foot following foot along the sheer strait ledge
  Where space was none to bear the wild goat's feet
Till blind we sat on the outer footless edge
  Where darkling death seemed fain to share the
    seat,

The abyss before us, viewless even as time's,
  The abyss to left of us, the abyss to right,
Bid thought now dream how high the freed soul
    climbs
  That death sets free from change of day and night.

The might of raging mist and wind whose wrath
  Shut from our eyes the narrowing rock we trod,
The wondrous world it darkened, made our path
  Like theirs who take the shadow of death for God.

Yet eastward, veiled in vapour white as snow,
  The grim black herbless heights that scorn the
    sun
And mock the face of morning rose to show
  The work of earth-born fire and earthquake done.

And half the world was haggard night, wherein
  We strove our blind way through : but far above
Was light that watched the wild mists whirl and
    spin,
  And far beneath a land worth light and love.

Deep down the Valley of the Curse, undaunted
By shadow and whisper of winds with sins for
wings
And ghosts of crime wherethrough the heights live
haunted
By present sense of past and monstrous things,

The glimmering water holds its gracious way
Full forth, and keeps one happier hand's-breadth
green
Of all that storm-scathed world whereon the sway
Sits dark as death of deadlier things unseen.

But on the soundless and the viewless river
That bears through night perchance again to day
The dead whom death and twin-born fame deliver
From life that dies, and time's inveterate sway,

No shadow save of falsehood and of fear
That brands the future with the past, and bids
The spirit wither and the soul grow sere,
Hovers or hangs to cloud life's opening lids,

If life have eyes to lift again and see,
Beyond the bounds of sensual sight or breath,
What life incognisable of ours may be
That turns our light to darkness deep as death.

Priests and the soulless serfs of priests may swarm
With vulturous acclamation, loud in lies,
About his dust while yet his dust is warm
Who mocked as sunlight mocks their base blind
eyes,

Their godless ghost of godhead, false and foul
  As fear his dam or hell his throne : but we,
Scarce hearing, heed no carrion church-wolf's howl :
  The corpse be theirs to mock ; the soul is free.

Free as ere yet its earthly day was done
  It lived above the coil about us curled :
A soul whose eyes were keener than the sun,
  A soul whose wings were wider than the world.

We, sons of east and west, ringed round with
    dreams,
  Bound fast with visions, girt about with fears,
Live, trust, and think by chance, while shadow
    seems
  Light, and the wind that wrecks a hand that
    steers.

He, whose full soul held east and west in poise,
  Weighed man with man, and creed of man's with
    creed,
And age with age, their triumphs and their toys,
  And found what faith may read not and may read.

Scorn deep and strong as death and life, that lit
  With fire the smile at lies and dreams outworn
Wherewith he smote them, showed sublime in it
  The splendour and the steadfastness of scorn.

What loftier heaven, what lordlier air, what space
  Illimitable, insuperable, infinite,
Now to that strong-winged soul yields ampler place
  Than passing darkness yields to passing light,

No dream, no faith can tell us : hope and fear,
  Whose tongues were loud of old as children's, now
From babbling fall to silence : change is here,
    And death ; dark furrows drawn by time's dark
      plough.

Still sunward here on earth its flight was bent,
  Even since the man within the child began
To yearn and kindle with superb intent
  And trust in time to magnify the man.

Still toward the old garden of the Sun, whose fruit
  The honey-heavy lips of Sophocles
Desired and sang, wherein the unwithering root
    Sprang of all growths that thought brings forth
      and sees

Incarnate, bright with bloom or dense with leaf
  Far-shadowing, deep as depth of dawn or night :
And all were parcel of the garnered sheaf
  His strenuous spirit bound and stored aright.

And eastward now, and ever toward the dawn,
  If death's deep veil by life's bright hand be rent,
We see, as through the shadow of death withdrawn,
  The imperious soul's indomitable ascent.

But not the soul whose labour knew not end—
  But not the swordsman's hand, the crested head—
The royal heart we mourn, the faultless friend,
  Burton—a name that lives till fame be dead.

A SEQUENCE OF SONNETS
ON THE DEATH OF ROBERT BROWNING

I

THE clearest eyes in all the world they read
  With sense more keen and spirit of sight more
    true
  Than burns and thrills in sunrise, when the dew
Flames, and absorbs the glory round it shed,
As they the light of ages quick and dead,
  Closed now, forsake us : yet the shaft that slew
  Can slay not one of all the works we knew,
Nor death discrown that many-laurelled head.

The works of words whose life seems lightning
    wrought,
And moulded of unconquerable thought,
  And quickened with imperishable flame,
Stand fast and shine and smile, assured that nought
  May fade of all their myriad-moulded fame,
  Nor England's memory clasp not Browning's
    name.

December 13, 1889.

II

Death, what hast thou to do with one for whom
   Time is not lord, but servant? What least part
   Of all the fire that fed his living heart,
Of all the light more keen than sundawn's bloom
That lit and led his spirit, strong as doom
   And bright as hope, can aught thy breath may dart
   Quench? Nay, thou knowest he knew thee what
      thou art,
A shadow born of terror's barren womb,
That brings not forth save shadows. What art thou,
To dream, albeit thou breathe upon his brow,
   That power on him is given thee,—that thy breath
Can make him less than love acclaims him now,
   And hears all time sound back the word it saith?
   What part hast thou then in his glory, Death?

III

A graceless doom it seems that bids us grieve:
   Venice and winter, hand in deadly hand,
   Have slain the lover of her sunbright strand
And singer of a stormbright Christmas Eve.
A graceless guerdon we that loved receive
   For all our love, from that the dearest land
   Love worshipped ever. Blithe and soft and bland,
Too fair for storm to scathe or fire to cleave,
Shone on our dreams and memories evermore
The domes, the towers, the mountains and the shore
   That gird or guard thee, Venice: cold and black
Seems now the face we loved as he of yore.
   We have given thee love—no stint, no stay, no lack:
   What gift, what gift is this thou hast given us back?

IV

But he—to him, who knows what gift is thine,
  Death? Hardly may we think or hope, when we
  Pass likewise thither where to-night is he,
Beyond the irremeable outer seas that shine
And darken round such dreams as half divine
  Some sunlit harbour in that starless sea
  Where gleams no ship to windward or to lee,
To read with him the secret of thy shrine.

There too, as here, may song, delight, and love,
The nightingale, the sea-bird, and the dove,
  Fulfil with joy the splendour of the sky
Till all beneath wax bright as all above :
  But none of all that search the heavens, and try
  The sun, may match the sovereign eagle's eye.

December 14.

V

Among the wondrous ways of men and time
  He went as one that ever found and sought
  And bore in hand the lamplike spirit of thought
To illume with instance of its fire sublime
The dusk of many a cloudlike age and clime.
  No spirit in shape of light and darkness wrought,
  No faith, no fear, no dream, no rapture, nought
That blooms in wisdom, nought that burns in crime,
No virtue girt and armed and helmed with light,
No love more lovely than the snows are white,
  No serpent sleeping in some dead soul's tomb,
No song-bird singing from some live soul's height,
  But he might hear, interpret, or illume
  With sense invasive as the dawn of doom.

VI

What secret thing of splendour or of shade
  Surmised in all those wandering ways wherein
  Man, led of love and life and death and sin,
Strays, climbs, or cowers, allured, absorbed, afraid,
Might not the strong and sunlike sense invade
  Of that full soul that had for aim to win
  Light, silent over time's dark toil and din,
Life, at whose touch death fades as dead things fade?
O spirit of man, what mystery moves in thee
That he might know not of in spirit, and see
  The heart within the heart that seems to strive,
The life within the life that seems to be,
    And hear, through all thy storms that whirl and
      drive,
    The living sound of all men's souls alive?

VII

He held no dream worth waking : so he said,
  He who stands now on death's triumphal steep,
  Awakened out of life wherein we sleep
And dream of what he knows and sees, being dead.
But never death for him was dark or dread :
  "Look forth" he bade the soul, and fear not. Weep,
  All ye that trust not in his truth, and keep
Vain memory's vision of a vanished head
As all that lives of all that once was he
Save that which lightens from his word : but we,
  Who, seeing the sunset-coloured waters roll,
Yet know the sun subdued not of the sea,
    Nor weep nor doubt that still the spirit is whole,
    And life and death but shadows of the soul.

  December 15.

SUNSET AND MOONRISE

NEW YEAR'S EVE, 1889

ALL the west, whereon the sunset sealed the dead
    year's glorious grave
  Fast with seals of light and fire and cloud that
    light and fire illume,
  Glows at heart and kindles earth and heaven with
    joyous blush and bloom,
Warm and wide as life, and glad of death that only
    slays to save.
As a tide-reconquered sea-rock lies aflush with the
    influent wave
  Lies the light aflush with darkness, lapped about
    by lustrous gloom,
  Even as life with death, and fame with time, and
    memory with the tomb
Where a dead man hath for vassals Fame the serf
    and Time the slave.

Far from earth as heaven, the steadfast light with-
    drawn, superb, suspense,
  Burns in dumb divine expansion of illimitable
    flower :

Moonrise whets the shadow's edges keen as noon-
    tide : hence and thence
  Glows the presence from us passing, shines and
    passes not the power.
Souls arise whose word remembered is as spirit
    within the sense :
  All the hours are theirs of all the seasons : death
    has but his hour.

BIRTHDAY ODE

August 6, 1891

I

Love and praise, and a length of days whose shadow
    cast upon time is light,
Days whose sound was a spell shed round from
    wheeling wings as of doves in flight,
Meet in one, that the mounting sun to-day may
    triumph, and cast out night.

Two years more than the full fourscore lay hallowing
    hands on a sacred head—
Scarce one score of the perfect four uncrowned of
    fame as they smiled and fled :
Still and soft and alive aloft their sunlight stays
    though the suns be dead.

Ere we were or were thought on, ere the love that
    gave us to life began,
Fame grew strong with his crescent song, to greet
    the goal of the race they ran,
Song with fame, and the lustrous name with years
    whose changes acclaimed the man.

II

Soon, ere time in the rounding rhyme of choral seasons
    had hailed us men,
We too heard and acclaimed the word whose breath
    was life upon England then—
Life more bright than the breathless light of soundless
    noon in a songless glen.

Ah, the joy of the heartstruck boy whose ear was
    opened of love to hear !
Ah, the bliss of the burning kiss of song and spirit,
    the mounting cheer
Lit with fire of divine desire and love that knew not
    if love were fear !

Fear and love as of heaven above and earth enkindled
    of heaven were one ;
One white flame, that around his name grew keen and
    strong as the worldwide sun ;
Awe made bright with implied delight, as weft with
    weft of the rainbow spun.

III

He that fears not the voice he hears and loves shall
    never have heart to sing :
All the grace of the sun-god's face that bids the soul
    as a fountain spring
Bids the brow that receives it bow, and hail his like-
    ness on earth as king.

We that knew when the sun's shaft flew beheld and
    worshipped, adored and heard :
Light rang round it of shining sound, whence all
    men's hearts were subdued and stirred :
Joy, love, sorrow, the day, the morrow, took life upon
    them in one man's word.

Not for him can the years wax dim, nor downward
    swerve on a darkening way :
Upward wind they, and leave behind such light as
    lightens the front of May :
Fair as youth and sublime as truth we find the fame
    that we hail to-day.

THRENODY

OCTOBER 6, 1892

I

LIFE, sublime and serene when time had power upon
it and ruled its breath,
Changed it, bade it be glad or sad, and hear what
change in the world's ear saith,
Shines more fair in the starrier air whose glory
lightens the dusk of death.

Suns that sink on the wan sea's brink, and moons
that kindle and flame and fade,
Leave more clear for the darkness here the stars that
set not and see not shade
Rise and rise on the lowlier skies by rule of sunlight
and moonlight swayed.

So, when night for his eyes grew bright, his proud
head pillowed on Shakespeare's breast,
Hand in hand with him, soon to stand where shine
the glories that death loves best,
Passed the light of his face from sight, and sank
sublimely to radiant rest.

II

Far above us and all our love, beyond all reach of
its voiceless praise,
Shines for ever the name that never shall feel the
shade of the changeful days
Fall and chill the delight that still sees winter's light
on it shine like May's.

Strong as death is the dark day's breath whose blast
has withered the life we see
Here where light is the child of night, and less than
visions or dreams are we :
Strong as death ; but a word, a breath, a dream is
stronger than death can be.

Strong as truth and superb in youth eternal, fair as
the sundawn's flame
Seen when May on her first-born day bids earth exult
in her radiant name,
Lives, clothed round with its praise and crowned
with love that dies not, his love-lit fame.

III

Fairer far than the morning star, and sweet for us as
the songs that rang
Loud through heaven from the choral Seven when all
the stars of the morning sang,
Shines the song that we loved so long—since first
such love in us flamed and sprang.

England glows as a sunlit rose from mead to mountain, from sea to sea,
Bright with love and with pride above all taint of
sorrow that needs must be,
Needs must live for an hour, and give its rainbow's
glory to lawn and lea.

Not through tears shall the new-born years behold
him, crowned with applause of men,
Pass at last from a lustrous past to life that lightens
beyond their ken,
Glad and dead, and from earthward led to sunward,
guided of Imogen.

THE BALLAD OF MELICERTES

In Memory of Théodore de Banville

Death, a light outshining life, bids heaven resume
   Star by star the souls whose light made earth divine.
Death, a night outshining day, sees burn and bloom
    Flower by flower, and sun by sun, the fames that shine
     Deathless, higher than life beheld their sovereign sign.
Dead Simonides of Ceos, late restored,
Given again of God, again by man deplored,
   Shone but yestereve, a glory frail as breath.
Frail? But fame's breath quickens, kindles, keeps in ward,
   Life so sweet as this that dies and casts off death.

Mother's love, and rapture of the sea, whose womb
   Breeds eternal life of joy that stings like brine,
Pride of song, and joy to dare the singer's doom,
    Sorrow soft as sleep and laughter bright as wine,
    Flushed and filled with fragrant fire his lyric line.
As the sea-shell utters, like a stricken chord,
Music uttering all the sea's within it stored,
   Poet well-beloved, whose praise our sorrow saith,
So thy songs retain thy soul, and so record
   Life so sweet as this that dies and casts off death.

Side by side we mourned at Gautier's golden tomb :
  Here in spirit now I stand and mourn at thine.
Yet no breath of death strikes thence, no shadow of
      gloom,
    Only light more bright than gold of the inmost
      mine,
    Only steam of incense warm from love's own
      shrine.
Not the darkling stream, the sundering Stygian ford,
Not the hour that smites and severs as a sword,
  Not the night subduing light that perisheth,
Smite, subdue, divide from us by doom abhorred,
  Life so sweet as this that dies and casts off death.

Prince of song more sweet than honey, lyric lord,
Not thy France here only mourns a light adored,
  One whose love-lit fame the world inheriteth.
Strangers too, now brethren, hail with heart's accord
  Life so sweet as this that dies and casts off death.

AU TOMBEAU DE BANVILLE

La plus douce des voix qui vibraient sous le ciel
Se tait : les rossignols ailés pleurent le frère
Qui s'envole au-dessus de l'âpre et sombre terre,
Ne lui laissant plus voir que l'être essentiel,

Esprit qui chante et rit, fleur d'une âme sans fiel.
L'ombre élyséenne, où la nuit n'est que lumière,
Revoit, tout revêtu de splendeur douce et fière,
Mélicerte, poète à la bouche de miel.

Dieux exilés, passants célestes de ce monde,
Dont on entend parfois dans notre nuit profonde
Vibrer la voix, frémir les ailes, vous savez
S'il vous aima, s'il vous pleura, lui dont la vie
Et le chant rappelaient les vôtres.   Recevez
L'âme de Mélicerte affranchie et ravie.

LIGHT: AN EPICEDE

To Philip Bourke Marston

Love will not weep because the seal is broken
  That sealed upon a life beloved and brief
Darkness, and let but song break through for token
  How deep, too far for even thy song's relief,
  Slept in thy soul the secret springs of grief.

Thy song may soothe full many a soul hereafter,
  As tears, if tears will come, dissolve despair ;
As here but late, with smile more bright than
    laughter,
  Thy sweet strange yearning eyes would seem to
    bear
  Witness that joy might cleave the clouds of care.

Two days agone, and love was one with pity
  When love gave thought wings toward the glim-
    mering goal
Where, as a shrine lit in some darkling city,
  Shone soft the shrouded image of thy soul :
  And now thou art healed of life ; thou art healed,
    and whole.

Yea, two days since, all we that loved thee pitied :
  And now with wondering love, with shame of face,
We think how foolish now, how far unfitted,
    Should be from us, toward thee who hast run thy
      race,
    Pity—toward thee, who hast won the painless
      place ;

The painless world of death, yet unbeholden
  Of eyes that dream what light now lightens thine
And will not weep.   Thought, yearning toward those
    olden
    Dear hours that sorrow sees and sees not shine,
    Bows tearless down before a flameless shrine :

A flameless altar here of life and sorrow
  Quenched and consumed together.   These were
    one,
One thing for thee, as night was one with morrow
  And utter darkness with the sovereign sun :
  And now thou seest life, sorrow, and darkness
    done.

And yet love yearns again to win thee hither ;
  Blind love, and loveless, and unworthy thee :
Here where I watch the hours of darkness wither,
  Here where mine eyes were glad and sad to see
  Thine that could see not mine, though turned on me.

But now, if aught beyond sweet sleep lie hidden,
  And sleep be sealed not fast on dead men's sight
For ever, thine hath grace for ours forbidden,
    And sees us compassed round with change and
      night :
    Yet light like thine is ours, if love be light.

THRENODY

Watching here alone by the fire whereat last year
Sat with me the friend that a week since yet was
near,
  That a week has borne so far and hid so deep,
  Woe am I that I may not weep,
  May not yearn to behold him here.

Shame were mine, and little the love I bore him
were,
Now to mourn that better he fares than love may
fare
  Which desires, and would not have indeed, its
will,
  Would not love him so worse than ill,
  Would not clothe him again with care.

Yet can love not choose but remember, hearts but
ache,
Eyes but darken, only for one vain thought's poor
sake,
  For the thought that by this hearth's now lonely
side
  Two fast friends, on the day he died,
  Looked once more for his hand to take.

Let thy soul forgive them, and pardon heal the sin,
Though their hearts be heavy to think what then had
       been,
   The delight that never while they live may be—
   Love's communion of speech with thee,
   Soul and speech with the soul therein.

O my friend, O brother, a glory veiled and marred !
Never love made moan for a life more evil-starred.
   Was it envy, chance, or chance-compelling fate,
   Whence thy spirit was bruised so late,
   Bowed so heavily, bound so hard ?

Now released, it may be,—if only love might
       know—
Filled and fired with sight, it beholds us blind and
       low
   With a pity keener yet, if that may be,
   Even than ever was this that we
   Felt, when love of thee wrought us woe.

None may tell the depths and the heights of life and
       death.
What we may we give thee : a word that sorrow
       saith,
   And that none will heed save sorrow : scarce a
       song.
   All we may, who have loved thee long,
   Take : the best we can give is breath.

A DIRGE

A BELL tolls on in my heart
　As though in my ears a knell
　Had ceased for awhile to swell,
But the sense of it would not part
From the spirit that bears its part
　In the chime of the soundless bell.

Ah dear dead singer of sorrow,
　The burden is now not thine
　That grief bade sound for a sign
Through the songs of the night whose morrow
Has risen, and I may not borrow
　A beam from its radiant shrine.

The burden has dropped from thee
　That grief on thy life bound fast ;
　The winter is over and past
Whose end thou wast fain to see.
Shall sorrow not comfort me
　That is thine no longer—at last ?

II.

Good day, good night, and good morrow,
   Men living and mourning say.
   For thee we could only pray
That night of the day might borrow
Such comfort as dreams lend sorrow :
   Death gives thee at last good day.

A REMINISCENCE

THE rose to the wind has yielded : all its leaves
  Lie strewn on the graveyard grass, and all their
     light
  And colour and fragrance leave our sense and
     sight
Bereft as a man whom bitter time bereaves
Of blossom at once and hope of garnered sheaves,
  Of April at once and August. Day to night
  Calls wailing, and life to death, and depth to
     height,
And soul upon soul of man that hears and grieves.

Who knows, though he see the snow-cold blossom
     shed,
  If haply the heart that burned within the rose,
The spirit in sense, the life of life be dead ?
  If haply the wind that slays with storming snows
Be one with the wind that quickens ? Bow thine
     head,
  O Sorrow, and commune with thine heart : who
     knows ?

VIA DOLOROSA

THE days of a man are threescore years and ten.
  The days of his life were half a man's, whom we
  Lament, and would yet not bid him back, to be
Partaker of all the woes and ways of men.
Life sent him enough of sorrow : not again
  Would anguish of love, beholding him set free,
  Bring back the beloved to suffer life and see
No light but the fire of grief that scathed him then.

We know not at all : we hope, and do not fear.
We shall not again behold him, late so near,
  Who now from afar above, with eyes alight
And spirit enkindled, haply toward us here
  Looks down unforgetful yet of days like night
  And love that has yet his sightless face in sight.

February 15, 1887.

I

TRANSFIGURATION

But half a man's days—and his days were nights.
   What hearts were ours who loved him, should we
      pray
   That night would yield him back to darkling day,
Sweet death that soothes, to life that spoils and
      smites ?
For now, perchance, life lovelier than the light's
   That shed no comfort on his weary way
   Shows him what none may dream to see or say
Ere yet the soul may scale those topless heights
Where death lies dead, and triumph.   Haply there
   Already may his kindling eyesight find
Faces of friends—no face than his more fair—
   And first among them found of all his kind
Milton, with crowns from Eden on his hair,
   And eyes that meet a brother's now not blind.

II

DELIVERANCE

O DEATH, fair Death, sole comforter and sweet,
  Nor Love nor Hope can give such gifts as thine.
  Sleep hardly shows us round thy shadowy shrine
What roses hang, what music floats, what feet
Pass and what wings of angels. We repeat
  Wild words or mild, disastrous or divine,
  Blind prayer, blind imprecation, seeing no sign
Nor hearing aught of thee not faint and fleet
As words of men or snowflakes on the wind.
But if we chide thee, saying " Thou hast sinned,
        thou hast sinned,
Dark Death, to take so sweet a light away
  As shone but late, though shadowed, in our skies,"
We hear thine answer—" Night has given what day
  Denied him : darkness hath unsealed his eyes."

III

THANKSGIVING

COULD love give strength to thank thee ! Love can
    give
  Strong sorrow heart to suffer : what we bear
  We would not put away, albeit this were
A burden love might cast aside and live.
Love chooses rather pain than palliative,
  Sharp thought than soft oblivion. May we dare
  So trample down our passion and our prayer
That fain would cling round feet now fugitive
And stay them—so remember, so forget,
What joy we had who had his presence yet,
What griefs were his while joy in him was ours
  And grief made weary music of his breath,
As even to hail his best and last of hours
  With love grown strong enough to thank thee,
    Death ?

IV

LIBITINA VERTICORDIA

Sister of sleep, healer of life, divine
  As rest and strong as very love may be,
  To set the soul that love could set not free,
To bid the skies that day could bid not shine,
To give the gift that life withheld was thine.
  With all my heart I loved one borne from me :
  And all my heart bows down and praises thee,
Death, that hast now made grief not his but mine.

O Changer of men's hearts, we would not bid thee
  Turn back our hearts from sorrow : this alone
  We bid, we pray thee, from thy sovereign throne
And sanctuary sublime where heaven has hid thee,
  Give : grace to know of those for whom we weep
  That if they wake their life is sweet as sleep.

V

THE ORDER OF RELEASE

THOU canst not give it.   Grace enough is ours
  To know that pain for him has fallen on rest.
  The worst we know was his on earth : the best,
We fain would think,—a thought no fear deflowers—
Is his, released from bonds of rayless hours.
  Ah, turn our hearts from longing ; bid our quest
  Cease, as content with failure.   This thy guest
Sleeps, vexed no more of time's imperious powers,
The spirit of hope, the spirit of change and loss,
The spirit of love bowed down beneath his cross,
  Nor now needs comfort from the strength of song.
Love, should he wake, bears now no cross for him :
Dead hope, whose living eyes like his were dim,
  Has brought forth better comfort, strength more
      strong.

VI

PSYCHAGOGOS

As Greece of old acclaimed thee God and man,
  So, Death, our tongue acclaims thee : yet wast thou
  Hailed of old Rome as Romans hail thee now,
Goddess and woman.   Since the sands first ran
That told when first man's life and death began,
  The shadows round thy blind ambiguous brow
  Have mocked the votive plea, the pleading vow
That sought thee sorrowing, fain to bless or ban.

But stronger than a father's love is thine,
  And gentler than a mother's.   Lord and God,
  Thy staff is surer than the wizard rod
That Hermes bare as priest before thy shrine
  And herald of thy mercies.   We could give
  Nought, when we would have given : thou bidst
      him live

VII

THE LAST WORD

So many a dream and hope that went and came,
　So many and sweet, that love thought like to be,
　Of hours as bright and soft as those for me
That made our hearts for song's sweet love the same,
Lie now struck dead, that hope seems one with
　　　shame.
　O Death, thy name is Love : we know it, and see
　The witness : yet for very love's sake we
Can hardly bear to mix with thine his name.

Philip, how hard it is to bid thee part
Thou knowest, if aught thou knowest where now
　　　thou art
　Of us that loved and love thee.　None may tell
What none but knows—how hard it is to say
The word that seals up sorrow, darkens day,
　And bids fare forth the soul it bids farewell.

IN MEMORY OF AURELIO SAFFI

THE wider world of men that is not ours
   Receives a soul whose life on earth was light.
Though darkness close the date of human hours,
   Love holds the spirit and sense of life in sight,
   That may not, even though death bid fly, take flight.
Faith, love, and hope fulfilled with memory, see
As clear and dear as life could bid it be
The present soul that is and is not he.

He, who held up the shield and sword of Rome
   Against the ravening brood of recreant France,
Beside the man of men whom heaven took home
   When earth beheld the spring's first eyebeams
      glance
   And life and winter seemed alike a trance
Eighteen years since, in sight of heaven and spring
That saw the soul above all souls take wing,
He too now hears the heaven we hear not sing.

He too now dwells where death is dead, and stands
   Where souls like stars exult in life to be :
Whence all who linked heroic hearts and hands
   Shine on our sight, and give it strength to see
   What hope makes fair for all whom faith makes
      free :

Free with such freedom as we find in sleep,
The light sweet shadow of death, when dreams are
      deep
And high as heaven whence light and lightning leap.

And scarce a month yet gone, his living hand
    Writ loving words that sealed me friend of his.
Are heaven and earth as near as sea to strand?
    May life and death as bride and bridegroom kiss?
    His last month's written word abides, and is;
Clear as the sun that lit through storm and strife
And darkling days when hope took fear to wife
The faith whose fire was light of all his life.

A life so fair, so pure of earthlier leaven,
    That none hath won through higher and harder
      ways
The deathless life of death which earth calls heaven;
    Heaven, and the light of love on earth, and praise
    Of silent memory through subsiding days
Wherein the light subsides not whence the past
Feeds full with life the future.   Time holds fast
Their names whom faith forgets not, first and last.

Forget?   The dark forgets not dawn, nor we
    The suns that sink to rise again, and shine
Lords of live years and ages.   Earth and sea
    Forget not heaven that makes them seem divine,
    Though night put out their fires and bid their
      shrine
Be dark and pale as storm and twilight.   Day,
Not night, is everlasting: life's full sway
Bids death bow down as dead, and pass away.

What part has death in souls that past all fear
  Win heavenward their supernal way, and smite
With scorn sublime as heaven such dreams as here
  Plague and perplex with cloud and fire the light
    That leads men's waking souls from glimmering
      night
To the awless heights of day, whereon man's awe,
Transfigured, dies in rapture, seeing the law
Sealed of the sun that earth arising saw?

Faith, justice, mercy, love, and heaven-born hate
  That sets them all on fire and bids them be
More than soft words and dreams that wake too late,
  Shone living through the lordly life that we
  Beheld, revered, and loved on earth, while he
Dwelt here, and bade our eyes take light thereof;
Light as from heaven that flamed or smiled above
In light or fire whose very hate was love.

No hate of man, but hate of hate whose foam
  Sheds poison forth from tongues of snakes and
    priests,
And stains the sickening air with steams whence Rome
  Now feeds not full the God that slays and feasts;
  For now the fangs of all the ravenous beasts
That ramped about him, fain of prayer and prey,
Fulfil their lust no more: the tide of day
Swells, and compels him down the deathward way.

Night sucks the Church its creature down, and hell
  Yawns, heaves, and yearns to clasp its loathliest
    child
Close to the breasts that bore it. All the spell
  Whence darkness saw the dawn in heaven defiled
  Is dumb as death: the lips that lied and smiled

Wax white for fear as ashes.   She that bore
The banner up of darkness now no more
Sheds night and fear and shame from shore to shore.

When they that cast her kingdom down were born,
  North cried on south and east made moan to west
For hopes that love had hardly heart to mourn,
  For Italy that was not.   Kings on quest,
  By priests whose blessings burn as curses blest,
Made spoil of souls and bodies bowed and bound,
Hunted and harried, leashed as horse or hound,
And hopeless of the hope that died unfound.

And now that faith has brought forth fruit to time,
  How should not memory praise their names, and
      hold
Their record even as Dante's life sublime,
  Who bade his dream, found fair and false of old,
  Live ?   Not till earth and heaven be dead and cold
May man forget whose work and will made one
Italy, fair as heaven or freedom won,
And left their fame to shine beside her sun.

April 1890.

THE FESTIVAL OF BEATRICE

DANTE, sole standing on the heavenward height,
  Beheld and heard one saying, " Behold me well :
  I am, I am Beatrice."   Heaven and hell
Kept silence, and the illimitable light
Of all the stars was darkness in his sight
  Whose eyes beheld her eyes again, and fell
  Shame-stricken.   Since her soul took flight to dwell
In heaven, six hundred years have taken flight.

And now that heavenliest part of earth whereon
Shines yet their shadow as once their presence shone
  To her bears witness for his sake, as he
For hers bare witness when her face was gone :
  No slave, no hospice now for grief—but free
  From shore to mountain and from Alp to sea.

THE MONUMENT OF GIORDANO BRUNO

I

Not from without us, only from within,
   Comes or can ever come upon us light
   Whereby the soul keeps ever truth in sight.
No truth, no strength, no comfort man may win,
No grace for guidance, no release from sin,
   Save of his own soul's giving.   Deep and bright
   As fire enkindled in the core of night
Burns in the soul where once its fire has been
The light that leads and quickens thought, inspired
   To doubt and trust and conquer.   So he said
   Whom Sidney, flower of England, lordliest head
Of all we love, loved : but the fates required
   A sacrifice to hate and hell, ere fame
   Should set with his in heaven Giordano's name.

II

Cover thine eyes and weep, O child of hell,
   Grey spouse of Satan, Church of name abhorred.
   Weep, withered harlot, with thy weeping lord,
Now none will buy the heaven thou hast to sell
At price of prostituted souls, and swell
   Thy loveless list of lovers.   Fire and sword
   No more are thine : the steel, the wheel, the cord,
The flames that rose round living limbs, and fell

In lifeless ash and ember, now no more
   Approve thee godlike.   Rome, redeemed at last
   From all the red pollution of thy past,
Acclaims the grave bright face that smiled of yore
   Even on the fire that caught it round and clomb
   To cast its ashes on the face of Rome.

June 9, 1889.

LIFE IN DEATH

He should have followed who goes forth before us,
  Last born of us in life, in death first-born :
  The last to lift up eyes against the morn,
The first to see the sunset.   Life, that bore us
Perchance for death to comfort and restore us,
  Of him hath left us here awhile forlorn,
  For him is as a garment overworn,
And time and change, with suns and stars in chorus,
Silent.   But if, beyond all change or time,
A law more just, more equal, more sublime
  Than sways the surge of life's loud sterile sea
Sways that still world whose peace environs him,
Where death lies dead as night when stars wax dim,
  Above all thought or hope of ours is he.

  August 2, 1891.

EPICEDE

As a vesture shalt thou change them, said the
    prophet,
  And the raiment that was flesh is turned to dust ;
Dust and flesh and dust again the likeness of it,
  And the fine gold woven and worn of youth is rust.
Hours that wax and wane salute the shade and scoff it,
  That it knows not aught it doth nor aught it must :
Day by day the speeding soul makes haste to doff it,
  Night by night the pride of life resigns its trust.

Sleep, whose silent notes of song loud life's derange
    not,
  Takes the trust in hand awhile as angels may :
Joy with wings that rest not, grief with wings that
    range not,
  Guard the gates of sleep and waking, gold or grey.
Joys that joys estrange, and griefs that griefs estrange
    not,
  Day that yearns for night, and night that yearns for
    day,
As a vesture shalt thou change them, and they change
    not,
  Seeing that change may never change or pass
    away.

Life of death makes question, " What art thou that
    changest ?
  What am I, that fear should trust or faith should
    doubt ?
I that lighten, thou that darkenest and estrangest,
    Is it night or day that girds us round about ?
Light and darkness on the ways wherein thou
    rangest
  Seem as one, and beams as clouds they put to
    rout.
Strange is hope, but fear of all things born were
    strangest,
  Seeing that none may strive with change to cast it
    out.

" Change alone stands fast, thou sayest, O death :
    I know not :
  What art thou, my brother death, that thou
    shouldst know ?
Men may reap no fruits of fields wherein they sow
    not ;
  Hope or fear is all the seed we have to sow.
Winter seals the sacred springs up that they flow
    not :
  Wind and sun and change unbind them, and they
    flow.
Am I thou or art thou I ?   The years that show not
  Pass, and leave no sign when time shall be to
    show."

Hope makes suit to faith lest fear give ear to sorrow :
  Doubt strews dust upon his head, and goes his way.
All the golden hope that life of death would borrow,
  How, if death require again, may life repay ?

Earth endures no darkness whence no light yearns
    thorough ;
  God in man as light in darkness lives, they say :
Yet, would midnight take assurance of the morrow,
    Who shall pledge the faith or seal the bond of day ?

Darkness, mute or loud with music or with mourn-
      ing,
  Starry darkness, winged with wind or clothed with
    calm,
Dreams no dream of grief or fear or wrath or warn-
      ing,
  Bears no sign of race or goal or strife or palm.
Word of blessing, word of mocking or of scorning,
  Knows it none, nor whence its breath sheds blight
    or balm.
Yet a little while, and hark, the psalm of morning :
  Yet a little while, and silence takes the psalm.

All the comfort, all the worship, all the wonder,
  All the light of love that darkness holds in fee,
All the song that silence keeps or keeps not under,
  Night, the soul that knows gives thanks for all to
    thee.
Far beyond the gates that morning strikes in sunder,
  Hopes that grief makes holy, dreams that fear sets
    free,
Far above the throne of thought, the lair of thunder,
  Silent shines the word whose utterance fills the
    sea.

MEMORIAL VERSES ON THE
DEATH OF WILLIAM BELL SCOTT

A LIFE more bright than the sun's face, bowed
Through stress of season and coil of cloud,
    Sets : and the sorrow that casts out fear
Scarce deems him dead in his chill still shroud,

Dead on the breast of the dying year,
Poet and painter and friend, thrice dear
    For love of the suns long set, for love
Of song that sets not with sunset here,

For love of the fervent heart, above
Their sense who saw not the swift light move
    That filled with sense of the loud sun's lyre
The thoughts that passion was fain to prove

In fervent labour of high desire
And faith that leapt from its own quenched pyre
    Alive and strong as the sun, and caught
From darkness light, and from twilight fire.

Passion, deep as the depths unsought
Whence faith's own hope may redeem us nought,
    Filled full with ardour of pain sublime
His mourning song and his mounting thought.

Elate with sense of a sterner time,
His hand's flight clomb as a bird's might climb
    Calvary : dark in the darkling air
That shrank for fear of the crowning crime,

Three crosses rose on the hillside bare,
Shown scarce by grace of the lightning's glare
    That clove the veil of the temple through
And smote the priests on the threshold there.

The soul that saw it, the hand that drew,
Whence light as thought's or as faith's glance flew,
    And stung to life the sepulchral past,
And bade the stars of it burn anew,

Held no less than the dead world fast
The light live shadows about them cast,
    The likeness living of dawn and night,
The days that pass and the dreams that last.

Thought, clothed round with sorrow as light,
Dark as a cloud that the moon turns bright,
    Moved, as a wind on the striving sea,
That yearns and quickens and flags in flight,

Through forms of colour and song that he
Who fain would have set its wide wings free
    Cast round it, clothing or chaining hope
With lights that last not and shades that flee.

Scarce in song could his soul find scope,
Scarce the strength of his hand might ope
    Art's inmost gate of her sovereign shrine,
To cope with heaven as a man may cope.

But high as the hope of a man may shine
The faith, the fervour, the life divine
    That thrills our life and transfigures, rose
And shone resurgent, a sunbright sign,

Through shapes whereunder the strong soul glows
And fills them full as a sunlit rose
    With sense and fervour of life, whose light
The fool's eye knows not, the man's eye knows.

None that can read or divine aright
The scriptures writ of the soul may slight
    The strife of a strenuous soul to show
More than the craft of the hand may write.

None may slight it, and none may know
How high the flames that aspire and glow
    From heart and spirit and soul may climb
And triumph ; higher than the souls lie low

Whose hearing hears not the livelong rhyme,
Whose eyesight sees not the light sublime,
    That shines, that sounds, that ascends and lives
Unquenched of change, unobscured of time.

A long life's length, as a man's life gives
Space for the spirit that soars and strives
    To strive and soar, has the soul shone through
That heeds not whither the world's wind drives

Now that the days and the ways it knew
Are strange, are dead as the dawn's grey dew
    At high midnoon of the mounting day
That mocks the might of the dawn it slew.

Yet haply may not—and haply may—
No sense abide of the dead sun's ray
    Wherein the soul that outsoars us now
Rejoiced with ours in its radiant sway.

Hope may hover, and doubt may bow,
Dreaming.   Haply—they dream not how—
    Not life but death may indeed be dead
When silence darkens the dead man's brow.

Hope, whose name is remembrance, fed
With love that lightens from seasons fled,
    Dreams, and craves not indeed to know,
That death and life are as souls that wed.

But change that falls on the heart like snow
Can chill not memory nor hope, that show
    The soul, the spirit, the heart and head,
Alive above us who strive below.

AN OLD SAYING

MANY waters cannot quench love,
  Neither can the floods drown it.
Who shall snare or slay the white dove
  Faith, whose very dreams crown it,
Gird it round with grace and peace, deep,
Warm, and pure, and soft as sweet sleep ?
Many waters cannot quench love,
  Neither can the floods drown it.

Set me as a seal upon thine heart,
  As a seal upon thine arm.
How should we behold the days depart
  And the nights resign their charm ?
Love is as the soul : though hate and fear
Waste and overthrow, they strike not here.
Set me as a seal upon thine heart,
  As a seal upon thine arm.

A MOSS-ROSE

If the rose of all flowers be the rarest
   That heaven may adore from above,
And the fervent moss-rose be the fairest
   That sweetens the summer with love,

Can it be that a fairer than any
   Should blossom afar from the tree ?
Yet one, and a symbol of many,
   Shone sudden for eyes that could see.

In the grime and the gloom of November
   The bliss and the bloom of July
Bade autumn rejoice and remember
   The balm of the blossoms gone by.

Would you know what moss-rose now it may be
   That puts all the rest to the blush,
The flower was the face of a baby,
   The moss was a bonnet of plush.

TO A CAT

I

Stately, kindly, lordly friend,
      Condescend
Here to sit by me, and turn
Glorious eyes that smile and burn,
Golden eyes, love's lustrous meed,
On the golden page I read.

All your wondrous wealth of hair,
      Dark and fair,
Silken-shaggy, soft and bright
As the clouds and beams of night,
'Pays my reverent hand's caress
Back with friendlier gentleness.

Dogs may fawn on all and some
      As they come ;
You, a friend of loftier mind,
Answer friends alone in kind.
Just your foot upon my hand
Softly bids it understand.

Morning round this silent sweet
    Garden-seat
Sheds its wealth of gathering light,
Thrills the gradual clouds with might,
Changes woodland, orchard, heath.
Lawn, and garden there beneath.

Fair and dim they gleamed below :
    Now they glow
Deep as even your sunbright eyes,
Fair as even the wakening skies.
Can it not or can it be
Now that you give thanks to see ?

May not you rejoice as I,
    Seeing the sky
Change to heaven revealed, and bid
Earth reveal the heaven it hid
All night long from stars and moon,
Now the sun sets all in tune ?

What within you wakes with day
    Who can say ?
All too little may we tell,
Friends who like each other well,
What might haply, if we might,
Bid us read our lives aright.

II

Wild on woodland ways your sires
    Flashed like fires :

Fair as flame and fierce and fleet
As with wings on wingless feet
Shone and sprang your mother, free,
Bright and brave as wind or sea.

Free and proud and glad as they,
          Here to-day
Rests or roams their radiant child,
Vanquished not, but reconciled,
Free from curb of aught above
Save the lovely curb of love.

Love through dreams of souls divine
          Fain would shine
Round a dawn whose light and song
Then should right our mutual wrong—
Speak, and seal the love-lit law
Sweet Assisi's seer foresaw.

Dreams were theirs; yet haply may
          Dawn a day
When such friends and fellows born,
Seeing our earth as fair at morn,
May for wiser love's sake see
More of heaven's deep heart than we.

HAWTHORN DYKE

ALL the golden air is full of balm and bloom
  Where the hawthorns line the shelving dyke with
    flowers.
  Joyous children born of April's happiest hours,
High and low they laugh and lighten, knowing their
    doom
Bright as brief—to bless and cheer they know not
    whom,
  Heed not how, but washed and warmed with suns
    and showers
  Smile, and bid the sweet soft gradual banks and
    bowers
Thrill with love of sunlit fire or starry gloom.
All our moors and lawns all round rejoice ; but here
All the rapturous resurrection of the year
  Finds the radiant utterance perfect, sees the word
Spoken, hears the light that speaks it. Far and
    near,
  All the world is heaven : and man and flower and
    bird
  Here are one at heart with all things seen and
    heard.

THE BROTHERS

There were twa brethren fell on strife;
　Sweet fruits are sair to gather:
The tane has reft his brother of life;
　And the wind wears owre the heather.

There were twa brethren fell to fray;
　Sweet fruits are sair to gather:
The tane is clad in a cloak of clay;
　And the wind wears owre the heather.

O loud and loud was the live man's cry,
　(Sweet fruits are sair to gather)
" Would God the dead and the slain were I ! "
　And the wind wears owre the heather.

" O sair was the wrang and sair the fray,"
　(Sweet fruits are sair to gather)
" But liefer had love be slain than slay."
　And the wind wears owre the heather.

" O sweet is the life that sleeps at hame,"
　(Sweet fruits are sair to gather)
" But I maun wake on a far sea's faem."
　And the wind wears owre the heather.

II.

" And women are fairest of a' things fair,"
  (Sweet fruits are sair to gather)
" But never shall I kiss woman mair."
  And the wind wears owre the heather.

Between the birk and the aik and the thorn
  (Sweet fruits are sair to gather)
He's laid his brother to lie forlorn :
  And the wind wears owre the heather.

Between the bent and the burn and the broom
  (Sweet fruits are sair to gather)
He's laid him to sleep till dawn of doom :
  And the wind wears owre the heather.

He's tane him owre the waters wide,
  (Sweet fruits are sair to gather)
Afar to fleet and afar to bide :
  And the wind wears owre the heather.

His hair was yellow, his cheek was red,
  (Sweet fruits are sair to gather)
When he set his face to the wind and fled :
  And the wind wears owre the heather.

His banes were stark and his een were bright
  (Sweet fruits are sair to gather)
When he set his face to the sea by night :
  And the wind wears owre the heather.

His cheek was wan and his hair was grey
  (Sweet fruits are sair to gather)
When he came back hame frae the wide world's way :
  And the wind wears owre the heather.

His banes were weary, his een were dim,
  (Sweet fruits are sair to gather)
And nae man lived and had mind of him :
  And the wind wears owre the heather.

" O whatten a wreck wad they seek on land "
  (Sweet fruits are sair to gather)
" That they houk the turf to the seaward hand? "
  And the wind wears owre the heather.

" O whatten a prey wad they think to take "
  (Sweet fruits are sair to gather)
" That they delve the dykes for a dead man's sake ? "
  And the wind wears owre the heather.

A bane of the dead in his hand he's tane ;
  Sweet fruits are sair to gather :
And the red blood brak frae the dead white bane.
  And the wind wears owre the heather.

He's cast it forth of his auld faint hand ;
  Sweet fruits are sair to gather :
And the red blood ran on the wan wet sand.
  And the wind wears owre the heather.

" O whatten a slayer is this," they said,
  (Sweet fruits are sair to gather)
" That the straik of his hand should raise his dead ? "
  And the wind wears owre the heather.

" O weel is me for the sign I take "
  (Sweet fruits are sair to gather)
" That now I may die for my auld sin's sake."
  And the wind wears owre the heather.

"For the dead was in wait now fifty year,"
  (Sweet fruits are sair to gather)
"And now shall I die for his blood's sake here."
  And the wind wears owre the heather.

JACOBITE SONG

Now who will speak, and lie not,
   And pledge not life, but give?
Slaves herd with herded cattle :
The dawn grows bright for battle
And if we die, we die not ;
   And if we live, we live.

The faith our fathers fought for,
   The kings our fathers knew,
We fight but as they fought for :
We seek the goal they sought for,
   The chance they hailed and knew,
The praise they strove and wrought for,
   To leave their blood as dew
   On fields that flower anew.

Men live that serve the stranger ;
   Hounds live that huntsmen tame :
These life-days of our living
Are days of God's good giving
Where death smiles soft on danger
   And life scowls dark on shame.

And what would you do other,
   Sweet wife, if you were I ?
And how should you be other,
My sister, than your brother,
   If you were man as I,
Born of our sire and mother,
   With choice to cower and fly,
   And chance to strike and die ?

No churl's our oldworld name is,
   The lands we leave are fair :
But fairer far than these are,
But wide as all the seas are,
But high as heaven the fame is
   That if we die we share.

Our name the night may swallow,
   Our lands the churl may take :
But night nor death may swallow,
Nor hell's nor heaven's dim hollow,
   The star whose height we take,
The star whose light we follow
   For faith's unfaltering sake
   Till hope that sleeps awake.

Soft hope's light lure we serve not,
   Nor follow, fain to find :
Dark time's last word may smite her
Dead, ere man's falsehood blight her :
But though she die, we swerve not,
   Who cast not eye behind.

Faith speaks when hope dissembles :
   Faith lives when hope lies dead :

If death as life dissembles,
And all that night assembles
   Of stars at dawn lie dead,
Faint hope that smiles and trembles
   May tell not well for dread:
   But faith has heard it said.

Now who will fight, and fly not,
   And grudge not life to give?
And who will strike beside us,
If life's or death's light guide us?
For if we live, we die not,
   And if we die, we live.

THE BALLAD OF DEAD MEN'S BAY

THE sea swings owre the slants of sand,
  All white with winds that drive ;
The sea swirls up to the still dim strand,
  Where nae man comes alive.

At the grey soft edge of the fruitless surf
  A light flame sinks and springs ;
At the grey soft rim of the flowerless turf
  A low flame leaps and clings.

What light is this on a sunless shore,
  What gleam on a starless sea ?
Was it earth's or hell's waste womb that bore
  Such births as should not be ?

As lithe snakes turning, as bright stars burning,
  They bicker and beckon and call ;
As wild waves churning, as wild winds yearning,
  They flicker and climb and fall.

A soft strange cry from the landward rings—
  " What ails the sea to shine ? "
A keen sweet note from the spray's rim springs—
  " What fires are these of thine ? "

A soul am I that was born on earth
  For ae day's waesome span :
Death bound me fast on the bourn of birth
  Ere I were christened man.

" A light by night, I fleet and fare
  Till the day of wrath and woe ;
On the hems of earth and the skirts of air
  Winds hurl me to and fro."

" O well is thee, though the weird be strange
  That bids thee flit and flee ;
For hope is child of the womb of change,
  And hope keeps watch with thee.

" When the years are gone, and the time is come,
  God's grace may give thee grace ;
And thy soul may sing, though thy soul were dumb,
  And shine before God's face.

" But I, that lighten and revel and roll
  With the foam of the plunging sea,
No sign is mine of a breathing soul
  That God should pity me.

" Nor death, nor heaven, nor hell, nor birth
  Hath part in me nor mine :
Strong lords are these of the living earth
  And loveless lords of thine.

" But I that know nor lord nor life
  More sure than storm or spray,
Whose breath is made of sport and strife,
  Whereon shall I find stay ? "

" And wouldst thou change thy doom with me,
  Full fain with thee would I :
For the life that lightens and lifts the sea
  Is more than earth or sky.

" And what if the day of doubt and doom
  Shall save nor smite not me ?
I would not rise from the slain world's tomb
  If there be no more sea.

" Take he my soul that gave my soul,
  And give it thee to keep ;
And me, while seàs and stars shall roll
  Thy life that falls on sleep."

That word went up through the mirk mid sky,
  And even to God's own ear :
And the Lord was ware of the keen twin cry,
  And wroth was he to hear.

He 's tane the soul of the unsained child
  That fled to death from birth ;
He 's tane the light of the wan sea wild,
  And bid it burn on earth.

He 's given the ghaist of the babe new-born
  The gift of the water-sprite,
To ride on revel from morn to morn
  And roll from night to night

He 's given the sprite of the wild wan sea
  The gift of the new-born man,
A soul for ever to bide and be
  When the years have filled their span.

When a year was gone and a year was come,
  O loud and loud cried they—
" For the lee-lang year thou hast held us dumb
  Take now thy gifts away ! "

O loud and lang they cried on him,
  And sair and sair they prayed :
" Is the face of thy grace as the night's face grim
  For those thy wrath has made ?

A cry more bitter than tears of men
  From the rim of the dim grey sea ;—
" Give me my living soul again,
  The soul thou gavest me,
The doom and the dole of kindly men,
  To bide my weird and be ! "

A cry more keen from the wild low land
  Than the wail of waves that roll ;—
" Take back the gift of a loveless hand,
  Thy gift of doom and dole,
The weird of men that bide on land ;
  Take from me, take my soul ! "

The hands that smite are the hands that spare ;
  They build and break the tomb ;
They turn to darkness and dust and air
  The fruits of the waste earth's womb ;
But never the gift of a granted prayer,
  The dole of a spoken doom.

Winds may change at a word unheard,
  But none may change the tides :
The prayer once heard is as God's own word ;
  The doom once dealt abides.

And ever a cry goes up by day,
   And ever a wail by night ;
And nae ship comes by the weary bay
But her shipmen hear them wail and pray,
   And see with earthly sight
The twofold flames of the twin lights play
Where the sea-banks green and the sea-floods grey
Are proud of peril and fain of prey,
And the sand quakes ever ; and ill fare they
   That look upon that light.

DEDICATION

1893

THE sea of the years that endure not
　Whose tide shall endure till we die
And know what the seasons assure not,
　If death be or life be a lie,
Sways hither the spirit and thither,
　A waif in the swing of the sea
Whose wrecks are of memories that wither
　　As leaves of a tree.

We hear not and hail not with greeting
　The sound of the wings of the years,
The storm of the sound of them beating,
　That none till it pass from him hears :
But tempest nor calm can imperil
　The treasures that fade not or fly ;
Change bids them not change and be sterile,
　　Death bids them not die.

Hearts plighted in youth to the royal
　High service of hope and of song,
Sealed fast for endurance as loyal,
　And proved of the years as they throng,

Conceive not, believe not, and fear not
    That age may be other than youth ;
That faith and that friendship may hear not
    And utter not truth.

Not yesterday's light nor to-morrow's
    Gleams nearer or clearer than gleams,
Though joys be forgotten and sorrows
    Forgotten as changes of dreams,
The dawn of the days unforgotten
    That noon could eclipse not or slay,
Whose fruits were as children begotten
    Of dawn upon day.

The years that were flowerful and fruitless,
    The years that were fruitful and dark,
The hopes that were radiant and rootless,
    The hopes that were winged for their mark,
Lie soft in the sepulchres fashioned
    Of hours that arise and subside,
Absorbed and subdued and impassioned,
    In pain or in pride.

But far in the night that entombs them
    The starshine as sunshine is strong,
And clear through the cloud that resumes them
    Remembrance, a light and a song,
Rings lustrous as music and hovers
    As birds that impend on the sea,
And thoughts that their prison-house covers
    Arise and are free.

Forgetfulness deep as a prison
    Holds days that are dead for us fast

Till the sepulchre sees rearisen
  The spirit whose reign is the past,
Disentrammelled of darkness, and kindled
  With life that is mightier than death,
When the life that obscured it has dwindled
      And passed as a breath.

But time nor oblivion may darken
  Remembrance whose name will be joy
While memory forgets not to hearken,
  While manhood forgets not the boy
Who heard and exulted in hearing
  The songs of the sunrise of youth
Ring radiant above him, unfearing
      And joyous as truth.

Truth, winged and enkindled with rapture
  And sense of the radiance of yore,
Fulfilled you with power to recapture
  What never might singer before—
The life, the delight, and the sorrow
  Of troublous and chivalrous years
That knew not of night or of morrow,
      Of hopes or of fears.

But wider the wing and the vision
  That quicken the spirit have spread
Since memory beheld with derision
  Man's hope to be more than his dead.
From the mists and the snows and the thunders
  Your spirit has brought for us forth
Light, music, and joy in the wonders
      And charms of the north.

The wars and the woes and the glories
   That quicken and lighten and rain
From the clouds of its chronicled stories,
   The passion, the pride, and the pain,
Whose echoes were mute and the token
   Was lost of the spells that they spake,
Rise bright at your bidding, unbroken
     Of ages that break.

For you, and for none of us other,
   Time is not : the dead that must live
Hold commune with you as a brother
   By grace of the life that you give.
The heart that was in them is in you,
   Their soul in your spirit endures :
The strength of their song is the sinew
     Of this that is yours.

Hence is it that life, everlasting
   As light and as music, abides
In the sound of the surge of it, casting
   Sound back to the surge of the tides,
Till sons of the sons of the Norsemen
   Watch, hurtling to windward and lee,
Round England, unbacked of her horsemen,
     The steeds of the sea.

A CHANNEL PASSAGE

AND OTHER POEMS

A CHANNEL PASSAGE

1855

FORTH from Calais, at dawn of night, when sunset
summer on autumn shone,
Fared the steamer alert and loud through seas whence
only the sun was gone :
Soft and sweet as the sky they smiled, and bade man
welcome : a dim sweet hour
Gleamed and whispered in wind and sea, and heaven
was fair as a field in flower
Stars fulfilled the desire of the darkling world as with
music : the starbright air
Made the face of the sea, if aught may make the face
of the sea, more fair.

Whence came change ? Was the sweet night weary
of rest ? What anguish awoke in the dark ?
Sudden, sublime, the strong storm spake : we heard
the thunders as hounds that bark.
Lovelier if aught may be lovelier than stars, we saw
the lightnings exalt the sky,
Living and lustrous and rapturous as love that is born
but to quicken and lighten and die.

Heaven's own heart at its highest of delight found
  utterance in music and semblance in fire :
Thunder on thunder exulted, rejoicing to live and to
  satiate the night's desire.

And the night was alive and anhungered of life as a
  tiger from toils cast free :
And a rapture of rage made joyous the spirit and
  strength of the soul of the sea.
All the weight of the wind bore down on it, freighted
  ·   with death for fraught :
And the keen waves kindled and quickened as things
  transfigured or things distraught.
And madness fell on them laughing and leaping ; and
  madness came on the wind :
And the might and the light and the darkness of
  storm were as storm in the heart of Ind.
Such glory, such terror, such passion, as lighten and
  harrow the far fierce East,
Rang, shone, spake, shuddered around us : the night
  was an altar with death for priest.
The channel that sunders England from shores where
  never was man born free
Was clothed with the likeness and thrilled with the
  strength and the wrath of a tropic sea.
As a wild steed ramps in rebellion, and rears till it
  swerves from a backward fall,
The strong ship struggled and reared, and her deck
  was upright as a sheer cliff's wall.
Stern and prow plunged under, alternate : a glimpse,
  a recoil, a breath,
And she sprang as the life in a god made man would
  spring at the throat of death.
Three glad hours, and it seemed not an hour of
  supreme and supernal joy,

Filled full with delight that revives in remembrance
    a sea-bird's heart in a boy.

For the central crest of the night was cloud that
    thundered and flamed, sublime

As the splendour and song of the soul everlasting
    that quickens the pulse of time.

The glory beholden of man in a vision, the music of
    light overheard,

The rapture and radiance of battle, the life that
    abides in the fire of a word,

In the midmost heaven enkindled, was manifest far
    on the face of the sea,

And the rage in the roar of the voice of the waters
    was heard but when heaven breathed free.

Far eastward, clear of the covering of cloud, the sky
    laughed out into light

From the rims of the storm to the sea's dark edge
    with flames that were flowerlike and white.

The leaping and luminous blossoms of live sheet
    lightning that laugh as they fade

From the cloud's black base to the black wave's brim
    rejoiced in the light they made.

Far westward, throned in a silent sky, where life was
    in lustrous tune,

Shone, sweeter and surer than morning or evening,
    the steadfast smile of the moon.

The limitless heaven that enshrined them was lovelier
    than dreams may behold, and deep

As life or as death, revealed and transfigured, may
    shine on the soul through sleep.

All glories of toil and of triumph and passion and
    pride that it yearns to know

Bore witness there to the soul of its likeness and
    kinship, above and below.

The joys of the lightnings, the songs of the thunders,
    the strong sea's labour and rage,
Were tokens and signs of the war that is life and is
    joy for the soul to wage.
No thought strikes deeper or higher than the heights
    and the depths that the night made bare,
Illimitable, infinite, awful and joyful, alive in the
    summit of air—
Air stilled and thrilled by the tempest that thundered
    between its reign and the sea's,
Rebellious, rapturous, and transient as faith or as
    terror that bows men's knees.
No love sees loftier and fairer the form of its godlike
    vision in dreams
Than the world shone then, when the sky and the
    sea were as love for a breath's length seems—
One utterly, mingled and mastering and mastered
    and laughing with love that subsides
As the glad mad night sank panting and satiate with
    storm, and released the tides.
In the dense mid channel the steam-souled ship hung
    hovering, assailed and withheld
As a soul born royal, if life or if death be against it,
    is thwarted and quelled.
As the glories of myriads of glowworms in lustrous
    grass on a boundless lawn
Were the glories of flames phosphoric that made of
    the water a light like dawn.
A thousand Phosphors, a thousand Hespers, awoke
    in the churning sea,
And the swift soft hiss of them living and dying was
    clear as a tune could be ;
As a tune that is played by the fingers of death on
    the keys of life or of sleep,

Audible alway alive in the storm, too fleet for a dream
    to keep :

Too fleet, too sweet for a dream to recover and
    thought to remember awake :

Light subtler and swifter than lightning, that whis-
    pers and laughs in the live storm's wake,

In the wild bright wake of the storm, in the dense
    loud heart of the labouring hour,

A harvest of stars by the storm's hand reaped, each
    fair as a star-shaped flower.

And sudden and soft as the passing of sleep is the
    passing of tempest seemed

When the light and the sound of it sank, and the
    glory was gone as a dream half dreamed.

The glory, the terror, the passion that made of the
    midnight a miracle, died,

Not slain at a stroke, nor in gradual reluctance abated
    of power and of pride ;

With strong swift subsidence, awful as power that is
    wearied of power upon earth,

As a God that were wearied of power upon heaven,
    and were fain of a new God's birth,

The might of the night subsided : the tyranny kindled
    in darkness fell :

And the sea and the sky put off them the rapture and
    radiance of heaven and of hell.

The waters, heaving and hungering at heart, made
    way, and were wellnigh fain,

For the ship that had fought them, and wrestled, and
    revelled in labour, to cease from her pain.

And an end was made of it : only remembrance en-
    dures of the glad loud strife ;

And the sense that a rapture so royal may come not
    again in the passage of life.

THE LAKE OF GAUBE

THE sun is lord and god, sublime, serene,
   And sovereign on the mountains : earth and air
Lie prone in passion, blind with bliss unseen
   By force of sight and might of rapture, fair
   As dreams that die and know not what they were.
The lawns, the gorges, and the peaks, are one
Glad glory, thrilled with sense of unison
In strong compulsive silence of the sun.

Flowers dense and keen as midnight stars aflame
   And living things of light like flames in flower
That glance and flash as though no hand might tame
   Lightnings whose life outshone their stormlit hour
   And played and laughed on earth, with all their
      power
Gone, and with all their joy of life made long
And harmless as the lightning life of song,
Shine sweet like stars when darkness feels them
      strong.

The deep mild purple flaked with moonbright gold
   That makes the scales seem flowers of hardened
      light,

The flamelike tongue, the feet that noon leaves cold,
  The kindly trust in man, when once the sight
  Grew less than strange, and faith bade fear take
      flight,
Outlive the little harmless life that shone
And gladdened eyes that loved it, and was gone
Ere love might fear that fear had looked thereon.

Fear held the bright thing hateful, even as fear,
  Whose name is one with hate and horror, saith
That heaven, the dark deep heaven of water near,
  Is deadly deep as hell and dark as death.
  The rapturous plunge that quickens blood and
      breath
With pause more sweet than passion, ere they strive
To raise again the limbs that yet would dive
Deeper, should there have slain the soul alive.

As the bright salamander in fire of the noonshine
      exults and is glad of his day,
The spirit that quickens my body rejoices to pass
      from the sunlight away,
To pass from the glow of the mountainous flowerage,
      the high multitudinous bloom,
Far down through the fathomless night of the water,
      the gladness of silence and gloom.
Death-dark and delicious as death in the dream of a
      lover and dreamer may be,
It clasps and encompasses body and soul with delight
      to be living and free :
Free utterly now, though the freedom endure but the
      space of a perilous breath,
And living, though girdled about with the darkness
      and coldness and strangeness of death :

Each limb and each pulse of the body rejoicing, each
    nerve of the spirit at rest,
All sense of the soul's life rapture, a passionate peace
    in its blindness blest.
So plunges the downward swimmer, embraced of the
    water unfathomed of man,
The darkness unplummeted, icier than seas in mid-
    winter, for blessing or ban ;
And swiftly and sweetly, when strength and breath
    fall short, and the dive is done,
Shoots up as a shaft from the dark depth shot, sped
    straight into sight of the sun ;
And sheer through the snow-soft water, more dark
    than the roof of the pines above,
Strikes forth, and is glad as a bird whose flight is
    impelled and sustained of love.
As a sea-mew's love of the sea-wind breasted and
    ridden for rapture's sake
Is the love of his body and soul for the darkling
    delight of the soundless lake :
As the silent speed of a dream too living to live for a
    thought's space more
Is the flight of his limbs through the still strong chill
    of the darkness from shore to shore.
Might life be as this is and death be as life that casts
    off time as a robe,
The likeness of infinite heaven were a symbol revealed
    of the lake of Gaube.

    Whose thought has fathomed and measured
        The darkness of life and of death,
    The secret within them treasured,
        The spirit that is not breath ?

Whose vision has yet beholden
   The splendour of death and of life ?
Though sunset as dawn be golden,
   Is the word of them peace, not strife ?
Deep silence answers : the glory
   We dream of may be but a dream,
And the sun of the soul wax hoary
   As ashes that show not a gleam.
But well shall it be with us ever
   Who drive through the darkness here,
If the soul that we live by never,
   For aught that a lie saith, fear.

THE PROMISE OF THE HAWTHORN

SPRING sleeps and stirs and trembles with desire
   Pure as a babe's that nestles toward the breast.
The world, as yet an all unstricken lyre,
   With all its chords alive and all at rest,
Feels not the sun's hand yet, but feels his breath
   And yearns for love made perfect.   Man and bird,
Thrilled through with hope of life that casts out death,
   Wait with a rapturous patience till his word
Speak heaven, and flower by flower and tree by tree
   Give back the silent strenuous utterance.   Earth,
Alive awhile and joyful as the sea,
   Laughs not aloud in joy too deep for mirth,
Presageful of perfection of delight,
Till all the unborn green buds be born in white.

HAWTHORN TIDE

I

DAWN is alive in the world, and the darkness of
    heaven and of earth
Subsides in the light of a smile more sweet than the
    loud noon's mirth,
Spring lives as a babe lives, glad and divine as the
    sun, and unsure
If aught so divine and so glad may be worshipped
    and loved and endure.
A soft green glory suffuses the love-lit earth with
    delight,
And the face of the noon is fair as the face of the star-
    clothed night.
Earth knows not and doubts not at heart of the
    glories again to be :
Sleep doubts not and dreams not how sweet shall the
    waking beyond her be.
A whole white world of revival awaits May's whisper
    awhile,
Abides and exults in the bud as a soft hushed laugh
    in a smile.
As a maid's mouth laughing with love and subdued
    for the love's sake, May
Shines and withholds for a little the word she revives
    to say.

When the clouds and the winds and the sunbeams
            are warring and strengthening with joy that
            they live,
    Spring, from reluctance enkindled to rapture, from
            slumber to strife,
Stirs, and repents, and is winter, and weeps, and
            awakes as the frosts forgive,
    And the dark chill death of the woodland is
            troubled, and dies into life.
And the honey of heaven, of the hives whence night
            feeds full on the springtide's breath,
    Fills fuller the lips of the lustrous air with delight
            in the dawn :
Each blossom enkindling with love that is life and
            subsides with a smile into death
    Arises and lightens and sets as a star from her
            sphere withdrawn.
Not sleep, in the rapture of radiant dreams, when
            sundawn smiles on the night,
    Shows earth so sweet with a splendour and fra-
            grance of life that is love :
Each blade of the glad live grass, each bud that
            receives or rejects the light,
    Salutes and responds to the marvel of Maytime
            around and above.

Joy gives thanks for the sight and the savour of
            heaven, and is humbled
    With awe that exults in thanksgiving : the towers
            of the flowers of the trees
Shine sweeter than snows that the hand of the season
            has melted and crumbled,
    And fair as the foam that is lesser of life than the
            loveliest of these.

But the sense of a life more lustrous with joy and
enkindled of glory
Than man's was ever or may be, and briefer than
joys most brief,
Bids man's heart bend and adore, be the man's head
golden or hoary,
As it leapt but a breath's time since and saluted
the flower and the leaf.
The rapture that springs into love at the sight of the
world's exultation
Takes not a sense of rebuke from the sense of
triumphant awe :
But the spirit that quickens the body fulfils it with
mute adoration,
And the knees would fain bow down as the eyes that
rejoiced and saw.

II

Fair and sublime as the face of the dawn is the
splendour of May,
But the sky's and the sea's joy fades not as earth's
pride passes away.
Yet hardly the sun's first lightning or laughter of
love on the sea
So humbles the heart into worship that knows not or
doubts if it be
As the first full glory beholden again of the life new-
born
That hails and applauds with inaudible music the
season of morn
A day's length since, and it was not : a night's length
more, and the sun
Salutes and enkindles a world of delight as a strange
world won.

A new life answers and thrills to the kiss of the young
  strong year,
And the glory we see is as music we hear not, and
  dream that we hear.
From blossom to blossom the live tune kindles, from
  tree to tree,
And we know not indeed if we hear not the song of
  the life we see.

For the first blithe day that beholds it and worships
    and cherishes cannot but sing
  With a louder and lustier delight in the sun and
    the sunlit earth
Than the joy of the days that beheld but the soft
    green dawn of the slow faint spring
  Glad and afraid to be glad, and subdued in a shame-
    fast mirth.
When the first bright knoll of the woodland world
    laughs out into fragrant light,
  The year's heart changes and quickens with sense
    of delight in desire,
And the kindling desire is one with thanksgiving for
    utter fruition of sight,
  For sight and for sense of a world that the sun
    finds meet for his lyre.
Music made of the morning that smites from the
    chords of the mute world song
  Trembles and quickens and lightens, unfelt, un-
    beholden, unheard,
From blossom on blossom that climbs and exults in
    the strength of the sun grown strong,
  And answers the word of the wind of the spring
    with the sun's own word.

Hard on the skirt of the deep soft copses that spring
    refashions,
  Triumphs and towers to the height of the crown of
    a wildwood tree
One royal hawthorn, sublime and serene as the joy
    that impassions
  Awe that exults in thanksgiving for sight of the
    grace we see,
The grace that is given of a god that abides for a
    season, mysterious
  And merciful, fervent and fugitive, seen and un-
    known and adored :
His presence is felt in the light and the fragrance,
    elate and imperious,
  His laugh and his breath in the blossom are love's,
    the beloved soul's lord.
For surely the soul if it loves is beloved of the god as
    a lover
  Whose love is not all unaccepted, a worship not
    utterly vain :
So full, so deep is the joy that revives for the soul
    to recover
  Yearly, beholden of hope and of memory in sun-
    shine and rain.

III

Wonder and love stand silent, stricken at heart and
    stilled.
But yet is the cup of delight and of worship un-
    pledged and unfilled.
A handsbreadth hence leaps up, laughs out as an
    angel crowned,
A strong full fountain of flowers overflowing above
    and around.

The boughs and the blossoms in triumph salute with
    adoring mirth
The womb that bare them, the glad green mother,
    the sunbright earth.
Downward sweeping, as song subsides into silence,
    none
May hear what sound is the word's they speak to the
    brooding sun.
None that hearken may hear : man may but pass and
    adore,
And humble his heart in thanksgiving for joy that is
    now no more.
And sudden, afront and ahead of him, joy is alive
    and aflame
On the shrine whose incense is given of the godhead,
    again the same

Pale and pure as a maiden secluded in secret and
    cherished with fear,
    One sweet glad hawthorn smiles as it shrinks
        under shelter, screened
By two strong brethren whose bounteous blossom
    outsoars it, year after year,
    While earth still cleaves to the live spring's breast
        as a babe unweaned.
Never was amaranth fairer in fields where heroes of
    old found rest,
    Never was asphodel sweeter : but here they endure
        not long,
Though ever the sight that salutes them again and
    adores them awhile is blest,
    And the heart is a hymn, and the sense is a soul,
        and the soul is a song.

Alone on a dyke's trenched edge, and afar from the
  blossoming wildwood's verge,
  Laughs and lightens a sister, triumphal in love-lit
    pride ;
Clothed round with the sun, and inviolate : her
  blossoms exult as the springtide surge,
  When the wind and the dawn enkindle the snows
    of the shoreward tide.

Hardly the worship of old that rejoiced as it knelt in
  the vision
  Shown of the God new-born whose breath is the
    spirit of spring
Hailed ever with love more strong and defiant of
  death's derision
  A joy more perfect than here we mourn for as May
    takes wing.
Time gives it and takes it again and restores it : the
  glory, the wonder,
  The triumph of lustrous blossom that makes of the
    steep sweet bank
One visible marvel of music inaudible, over and
  under,
  Attuned as in heaven, pass hence and return for the
    sun to thank.
The stars and the sun give thanks for the glory
  bestowed and beholden,
  For the gladness they give and rejoice in, the
    night and the dawn and the day :
But nought they behold when the world is aflower
  and the season is golden
  · Makes answer as meet and as sweet as the flower
    that itself is May.

THE PASSING OF THE HAWTHORN

THE coming of the hawthorn brings on earth
   Heaven : all the spring speaks out in one sweet
     word,
   And heaven grows gladder, knowing that earth
     has heard.
Ere half the flowers are jubilant in birth,
The splendour of the laughter of their mirth
   Dazzles delight with wonder : man and bird
   Rejoice and worship, stilled at heart and stirred
With rapture girt about with awe for girth.

The passing of the hawthorn takes away
   Heaven : all the spring falls dumb, and all the soul
Sinks down in man for sorrow.   Night and day
   Forego the joy that made them one and whole.
The change that falls on every starry spray
   Bids, flower by flower, the knell of springtime toll.

TO A BABY KINSWOMAN

Love, whose light thrills heaven and earth,
Smiles and weeps upon thy birth,
Child, whose mother's love-lit eyes
Watch thee but from Paradise.
Sweetest sight that earth can give,
Sweetest light of eyes that live,
Ours must needs, for hope withdrawn,
Hail with tears thy soft spring dawn.
Light of hope whose star hath set,
Light of love whose sun lives yet,
Holier, happier, heavenlier love
Breathes about thee, burns above,
Surely, sweet, than ours can be,
Shed from eyes we may not see,
Though thine own may see them shine
Night and day, perchance, on thine.
Sun and moon that lighten earth
Seem not fit to bless thy birth :
Scarce the very stars we know
Here seem bright enough to show
Whence in unimagined skies
Glows the vigil of such eyes.
Theirs whose heart is as a sea
Swoln with sorrowing love of thee
Fain would share with thine the sight
Seen alone of babes aright,

Watched of eyes more sweet than flowers
Sleeping or awake : but ours
Can but deem or dream or guess
Thee not wholly motherless.
Might they see or might they know
What nor faith nor hope may show,
We whose hearts yearn toward thee now
Then were blest and wise as thou.
Had we half thy knowledge,—had
Love such wisdom,—grief were glad,
Surely, lit by grace of thee ;
Life were sweet as death may be.
Now the law that lies on men
Bids us mourn our dead : but then
Heaven and life and earth and death,
Quickened as by God's own breath,
All were turned from sorrow and strife ;
Earth and death were heaven and life
All too far are then and now
Sundered : none may be as thou.
Yet this grace is ours—a sign
Of that goodlier grace of thine,
Sweet, and thine alone—to see
Heaven, and heaven's own love, in thee.
Bless them, then, whose eyes caress
Thee, as only thou canst bless.
Comfort, faith, assurance, love,
Shine around us, brood above,
Fear grows hope, and hope grows wise,
Thrilled and lit by children's eyes.
Yet in ours the tears unshed,
Child, for hope that death leaves dead,
Needs must burn and tremble ; thou
Knowest not, seest not, why nor how,

More than we know whence or why
Comes on babes that laugh and lie
Half asleep, in sweet-lipped scorn,
Light of smiles outlightening morn,
Whence enkindled as is earth
By the dawn's less radiant birth
All the body soft and sweet
Smiles on us from face to feet
When the rose-red hands would fain
Reach the rose-red feet in vain.
Eyes and hands that worship thee
Watch and tend, adore and see
All these heavenly sights, and give
Thanks to see and love and live.
Yet, of all that hold thee dear,
Sweet, the dearest smiles not here.
Thine alone is now the grace,
Haply, still to see her face ;
Thine, thine only now the sight
Whence we dream thine own takes light.
Yet, though faith and hope live blind,
Yet they live in heart and mind
Strong and keen as truth may be :
Yet, though blind as grief were we
Inly for a weeping-while,
Sorrow's self before thy smile
Smiles and softens, knowing that yet,
Far from us though heaven be set,
Love, bowed down for thee to bless,
Dares not call thee motherless.

May 1894.

THE ALTAR OF RIGHTEOUSNESS

ἐς τὸ πᾶν δέ σοι λέγω,
βωμὸν αἴδεσαι δίκας·
μηδέ νιν
κέρδος ἰδὼν ἀθέῳ ποδὶ λὰξ ἀτίσῃς·
ποινὰ γὰρ ἐπέσται.
κύριον μένει τέλος.

ÆSCH. Eum. 538–544

πάρα τὸ φῶς ἰδεῖν.

ÆSCH. Cho. 972

THE ALTAR OF RIGHTEOUSNESS

I

Light and night, whose clouds and glories change
and mingle and divide,
Veil the truth whereof they witness, show the truth
of things they hide.
Through the darkness and the splendour of the
centuries, loud or dumb,
Shines and wanes and shines the spirit, lit with love
of life to come.
Man, the soul made flesh, that knows not death from
life, and fain would know,
Sees the face of time change colour as its tides recoil
and flow.
All his hope and fear and faith and doubt, if aught at
all they be,
Live the life of clouds and sunbeams, born of heaven
or earth or sea.
All are buoyed and blown and brightened by their
hour's evasive breath :
All subside and quail and darken when their hour is
done to death.
Yet, ere faith, a wandering water, froze and curdled
into creeds,
Earth, elate as heaven, adored the light that quickens
dreams to deeds.

Invisible : eye hath not seen it, and ear hath not
    heard as the spirit hath heard
From the shrine that is lit not of sunlight or starlight
    the sound of a limitless word.
And visible : none that hath eyes to behold what the
    spirit must perish or see
Can choose but behold it and worship : a shrine that
    if light were as darkness would be.
Of cloud and of change is the form of the fashion that
    man may behold of it wrought :
Of iron and truth is the mystic mid altar, where
    worship is none but of thought.
No prayer may go up to it, climbing as incense of
    gladness or sorrow may climb :
No rapture of music may ruffle the silence that guards
    it, and hears not of time.
As the winds of the wild blind ages alternate in
    passion of light and of cloud,
So changes the shape of the veil that enshrouds it
    with darkness and light for a shroud.
And the winds and the clouds and the suns fall silent,
    and fade out of hearing or sight,
And the shrine stands fast and is changed not, whose
    likeness was changed as a cloud in the night.

    All the storms of time, and wrath of many winds,
        may carve no trace
    On the viewless altar, though the veil bear many a
        name and face :
    Many a live God's likeness woven, many a scripture
        dark with awe,
    Bids the veil seem verier iron than the word of life's
        own law.

Till the might of change hath rent it with a rushing
    wind in twain,
Stone or steel it seems, whereon the wrath of chance
    is wreaked in vain :
Stone or steel, and all behind it or beyond its lifted
    sign
Cloud and vapour, no subsistence of a change-
    unstricken shrine.
God by god flits past in thunder, till his glories turn
    to shades :
God to god bears wondering witness how his gospel
    flames and fades.
More was each of these, while yet they were, than
    man their servant seemed :
Dead are all of these, and man survives who made
    them while he dreamed.

Yet haply or surely, if vision were surer than theirs
    who rejoiced that they saw,
Man might not but see, through the darkness of
    godhead, the light that is surety and law.
On the stone that the close-drawn cloud which veils
    it awhile makes cloudlike stands
The word of the truth everlasting, unspoken of
    tongues and unwritten of hands.
By the sunbeams and storms of the centuries engraven,
    and approved of the soul as it reads,
It endures as a token dividing the light from the
    darkness of dreams and of deeds.
The faces of gods on the face of it carven, or gleam-
    ing behind and above,
Star-glorified Uranus, thunderous Jehovah, for terror
    or worship or love,

Change, wither, and brighten as flowers that the wind
    of eternity sheds upon time,
All radiant and transient and awful and mortal, and
    leave it unmarred and sublime.
As the tides that return and recede are the fears and
    the hopes of the centuries that roll,
Requenched and rekindled : but strong as the sun is
    the sense of it shrined in the soul.

II

In the days when time was not, in the time when days
    were none,
Ere sorrow had life to lot, ere earth gave thanks for
    the sun,
Ere man in his darkness waking adored what the
    soul in him could,
And the manifold God of his making was manifest
    evil and good,
One law from the dim beginning abode and abides in
    the end,
In sight of him sorrowing and sinning with none but
    his faith for friend.
Dark were the shadows around him, and darker the
    glories above,
Ere light from beyond them found him, and bade him
    for love's sake love.
About him was darkness, and under and over him
    darkness : the night
That conceived him and bore him had thunder for
    utterance and lightning for light.
The dust of death was the dust of the ways that the
    tribes of him trod :

And he knew not if just or unjust were the might of
the mystery of God.

Strange horror and hope, strange faith and unfaith,
were his boon and his bane :

And the God of his trust was the wraith of the soul
or the ghost of it slain.

A curse was on death as on birth, and a Presence
that shone as a sword

Shed menace from heaven upon earth that beheld
him, and hailed him her Lord.

Sublime and triumphant as fire or as lightning, he
kindled the skies,

And withered with dread the desire that would look
on the light of his eyes.

Earth shuddered with worship, and knew not if hell
were not hot in her breath ;

If birth were not sin, and the dew of the morning
the sweat of her death.

The watchwords of evil and good were unspoken of
men and unheard :

They were shadows that willed as he would, that
were made and unmade by his word.

His word was darkness and light, and a wisdom that
makes men mad

Sent blindness upon them for sight, that they saw but
and heard as he bade.

Cast forth and corrupt from the birth by the crime of
creation, they stood

Convicted of evil on earth by the grace of a God found
good.

The grace that enkindled and quickened the darkness
of hell with flame

Bade man, though the soul in him sickened, obey,
and give praise to his name.

The still small voice of the spirit whose life is as·
    plague's hot breath
Bade man shed blood, and inherit the life of the
    kingdom of death.

" Bring now for blood-offering thy son to mine altar,
    and bind him and slay,
That the sin of my bidding be done " : and the soul
    in the slave said, " Yea."
Yea, not nay, was the word : and the sacrifice offered
    withal
Was neither of beast nor of bird, but the soul of a
    man, God's thrall.
And the word of his servant spoken was fire, and the
    light of a sword,
When the bondage of Israel was broken, and Sinai
    shrank from the Lord.
With splendour of slaughter and thunder of song as
    the sound of the sea
Were the foes of him stricken in sunder and silenced
    as storms that flee.
Terror and trust and the pride of the chosen, approved
    of his choice,
Saw God in the whirlwind ride, and rejoiced as the
    winds rejoice.
Subdued and exalted and kindled and quenched by
    the sense of his might,
Faith flamed and exulted and dwindled, and saw
    not, and clung to the sight.
The wastes of the wilderness brightened and trembled
    with rapture and dread
When the word of him thundered and lightened and
    spake through the quick and the dead.

The chant of the prophetess, louder and loftier than
    tempest and wave,
Rang triumph more ruthless and prouder than death,
    and profound as the grave.
And sweet as the moon's word spoken in smiles that
    the blown clouds mar
The psalmist's witness in token arose as the speech
    of a star.
Starlight supreme, and the tender desire of the moon,
    were as one
To rebuke with compassion the splendour and strength
    of the godlike sun.
God softened and changed : and the word of his
    chosen, a fire at the first,
Bade man, as a beast or a bird, now slake at the
    springs his thirst.
The souls that were sealed unto death as the bones
    of the dead lie sealed
Rose thrilled and redeemed by the breath of the dawn
    on the flame-lit field.
The glories of darkness, cloven with music of thunder,
    shrank
As the web of the word was unwoven that spake, and
    the soul's tide sank.
And the starshine of midnight that covered Arabia
    with light as a robe
Waxed fiery with utterance that hovered and flamed
    through the whirlwind on Job.
And prophet to prophet and vision to vision made
    answer sublime,
Till the valley of doom and decision was merged in
    the tides of time.

III

Then, soft as the dews of night,
As the star of the sundawn bright,
    As the heart of the sea's hymn deep,
    And sweet as the balm of sleep,
Arose on the world a light
    Too pure for the skies to keep.

With music sweeter and stranger than heaven had
    heard
When the dark east thrilled with light from a saviour's
    word
And a God grew man to endure as a man and abide
The doom of the will of the Lord of the loud world's
    tide,
Whom thunders utter, and tempest and darkness
    hide,
With larger light than flamed from the peak whereon
Prometheus, bound as the sun to the world's wheel,
    shone,
A presence passed and abode but on earth a span,
And love's own light as a river before him ran,
And the name of God for awhile upon earth was man.

O star that wast not and wast for the world a sun,
O light that was quenched of priests, and its work
    undone,
O Word that wast not as man's or as God's, if God
Be Lord but of hosts whose tread was as death's that
    trod
On souls that felt but his wrath as an unseen rod,

What word, what praise, what passion of hopeless
    prayer,
May now rise up to thee, loud as in years that were,
From years that gaze on the works of thy servants
    wrought
While strength was in them to satiate the lust of
    thought
That craved in thy name for blood as the quest it
    sought ?

> From the dark high places of Rome
> Far over the westward foam
>   God's heaven and the sun saw swell
>   The fires of the high priest's hell,
> And shrank as they curled and clomb
> And revelled and ravaged and fell.

IV

Yet was not the work of thy word all withered with
    wasting flame
By the sons of the priests that had slain thee, whose
    evil was wrought in thy name.
From the blood-sodden soil that was blasted with
    fires of the Church and her creed
Sprang rarely but surely, by grace of thy spirit,
    a flower for a weed.
Thy spirit, unfelt of thy priests who blasphemed
    thee, enthralled and enticed
To deathward a child that was even as the child we
    behold in Christ.
The Moors, they told her, beyond bright Spain and
    the strait brief sea,
Dwelt blind in the light that for them was as darkness,
    and knew not thee.

But the blood of the martyrs whose mission was
    witness for God, they said,
Might raise to redemption the souls that were here,
    in the sun's sight, dead.
And the child rose up in the night, when the stars
    were as friends that smiled,
And sought her brother, and wakened the younger
    and tenderer child.
From the heaven of a child's glad sleep to the heaven
    of the sight of her eyes
He woke, and brightened and hearkened, and kindled
    as stars that rise.
And forth they fared together to die for the stranger's
    sake,
For the souls of the slayers that should slay them,
    and turn from their sins, and wake.
And the light of the love that lit them awhile on
    a brief blind quest
Shines yet on the tear-lit smile that salutes them,
    belated and blest.

And the girl, full-grown to the stature of godhead in
    womanhood, spake
The word that sweetens and lightens her creed for
    her great love's sake.
From the godlike heart of Theresa the prayer above
    all prayers heard,
The cry as of God made woman, a sweet blind
    wonderful word,
Sprang sudden as flame, and kindled the darkness of
    faith with love,
And the hollow of hell from beneath shone, quickened
    of heaven from above.

Yea, hell at her word grew heaven, as she prayed
    that if God thought well
She there might stand in the gateway, that none
    might pass into hell.
Not Hermes, guardian and guide, God, herald, and
    comforter, shed
Such lustre of hope from the life of his light on the
    night of the dead.
Not Pallas, wiser and mightier in mercy than Rome's
    God shone,
Wore ever such raiment of love as the soul of a saint
    put on.
So blooms as a flower of the darkness a star of the
    midnight born,
Of the midnight's womb and the blackness of dark-
    ness, and flames like morn.
Nor yet may the dawn extinguish or hide it, when
    churches and creeds
Are withered and blasted with sunlight as poisonous
    and blossomless weeds.
So springs and strives through the soil that the
    legions of darkness have trod,
From the root that is man, from the soul in the body,
    the flower that is God.

v

Ages and creeds that drift
Through change and cloud uplift
The soul that soars and seeks her sovereign shrine,
Her faith's veiled altar, there
To find, when praise and prayer
Fall baffled, if the darkness be divine.

Lights change and shift through star and sun :
Night, clothed with might of immemorial years, is one.

Day, born and slain of night,
Hath hardly life in sight
As she that bears and slays him and survives,
And gives us back for one
Cloud-thwarted fiery sun
The myriad mysteries of the lambent lives
Whose starry soundless music saith
That light and life wax perfect even through night
and death.

In vain had darkness heard
Light speak the lustrous word
That cast out faith in all save truth and love :
In vain death's quickening rod
Bade man rise up as God,
Touched as with life unknown in heaven above :
Fear turned his light of love to fire
That wasted earth, yet might not slay the soul's
desire.

Though death seem life, and night
Bid fear call darkness light,
Time, faith, and hope keep trust, through sorrow
and shame,
Till Christ, by Paul cast out,
Return, and all the rout
Of raging slaves whose prayer defiles his name
Rush headlong to the deep, and die,
And leave no sign to say that faith once heard them
lie.

VI

Since man, with a child's pride proud, and abashed
    as a child and afraid,
Made God in his likeness, and bowed him to worship
    the Maker he made,
No faith more dire hath enticed man's trust than the
    saint's whose creed
Made Caiaphas one with Christ, that worms on the
    cross might feed.
Priests gazed upon God in the eyes of a babe new-
    born, and therein
Beheld not heaven, and the wise glad secret of love,
    but sin.
Accursed of heaven, and baptized with the baptism
    of hatred and hell,
They spat on the name they despised and adored as a
    sign and a spell.
" Lord Christ, thou art God, and a liar : they were
    children of wrath, not of grace,
Unbaptized, unredeemed from the fire they were born
    for, who smiled in thy face."
Of such is the kingdom—he said it—of heaven : and
    the heavenly word
Shall live when religion is dead, and when falsehood
    is dumb shall be heard.
And the message of James and of John was as Christ's
    and as love's own call :
But wrath passed sentence thereon when Annas
    replied in Paul.
The dark old God who had slain him grew one with
    the Christ he slew,
And poison was rank in the grain that with growth
    of his gospel grew.

And the blackness of darkness brightened : and red
    in the heart of the flame
Shone down, as a blessing that lightened, the curse
    of a new God's name.
Through centuries of burning and trembling belief as
    a signal it shone,
Till man, soul-sick of dissembling, bade fear and her
    frauds begone.
God Cerberus yelps from his throats triune : but his
    day, which was night,
Is quenched, with its stars and the notes of its night-
    birds, in silence and light.
The flames of its fires and the psalms of their
    psalmists are darkened and dumb :
Strong winter has withered the palms of his angels,
    and stricken them numb.
God, father of lies, God, son of perdition, God, spirit
    of ill,
Thy will that for ages was done is undone as a dead
    God's will.
Not Mahomet's sword could slay thee, nor Borgia's
    or Calvin's praise :
But the scales of the spirit that weigh thee are
    weighted with truth, and it slays.
The song of the day of thy fury, when nature and
    death shall quail,
Rings now as the thunders of Jewry, the ghost of a
    dead world's tale.
That day and its doom foreseen and foreshadowed on
    earth, when thou,
Lord God, wast lord of the keen dark season, are
    sport for us now.
Thy claws were clipped and thy fangs plucked out by
    the hands that slew

Men, lovers of man, whose pangs bore witness if
truth were true.

Man crucified rose again from the sepulchre builded
to be

No grave for the souls of the men who denied thee,
but, Lord, for thee.

When Bruno's spirit aspired from the flames that thy
servants fed,

The spirit of faith was fired to consume thee and
leave thee dead.

When the light of the sunlike eyes whence laughter
lightened and flamed

Bade France and the world be wise, faith saw thee
naked and shamed.

When wisdom deeper and sweeter than Rabelais
veiled and revealed

Found utterance diviner and meeter for truth whence
anguish is healed,

Whence fear and hate and belief in thee, fed by thy
grace from above,

Fall stricken, and utmost grief takes light from the
lustre of love,

When Shakespeare shone into birth, and the world he
beheld grew bright,

Thy kingdom was ended on earth, and the darkness
it shed was light.

In him all truth and the glory thereof and the power
and the pride,

The song of the soul and her story, bore witness that
fear had lied.

All hope, all wonder, all trust, all doubt that knows
not of fear,

The love of the body, the lust of the spirit to see and
to hear,

All womanhood, fairer than love could conceive or
    desire or adore,
All manhood, radiant above all heights that it held
    of yore,
Lived by the life of his breath, with the speech of his
    soul's will spake,
And the light lit darkness to death whence never the
    dead shall wake.
For the light that lived in the sound of the song of
    his speech was one
With the light of the wisdom that found earth's tune
    in the song of the sun;
His word with the word of the lord most high of us
    all on earth,
Whose soul was a lyre and a sword, whose death
    was a deathless birth.
Him too we praise as we praise our own who as he
    stand strong;
Him, Æschylus, ancient of days, whose word is the
    perfect song.
When Caucasus showed to the sun and the sea what
    a God could endure,
When wisdom and light were one, and the hands of
    the matricide pure,
A song too subtle for psalmist or prophet of Jewry to
    know.
Elate and profound as the calmest or stormiest of
    waters that flow,
A word whose echoes were wonder and music of fears
    overcome,
Bade Sinai bow, and the thunder of godhead on
    Horeb be dumb.
The childless children of night, strong daughters of
    doom and dread,

The thoughts and the fears that smite the soul, and
  its life lies dead,
Stood still and were quelled by the sound of his word
  and the light of his thought,
And the God that in man lay bound was unbound
  from the bonds he had wrought.
Dark fear of a lord more dark than the dreams of
  his worshippers knew
Fell dead, and the corpse lay stark in the sunlight of
  truth shown true.

VII

Time, and truth his child, though terror set earth
  and heaven at odds,
See the light of manhood rise on the twilight of the
  Gods.
Light is here for souls to see, though the stars of
  faith be dead :
All the sea that yearned and trembled receives the
  sun instead.
All the shadows on the spirit when fears and dreams
  were strong,
All perdition, all redemption, blind rain-stars watched
  so long,
Love whose root was fear, thanksgiving that cowered
  beneath the rod,
Feel the light that heals and withers : night weeps
  upon her God.
All the names wherein the incarnate Lord lived his
  day and died
Fade from suns to stars, from stars into darkness un-
  descried.

Christ the man lives yet, remembered of man as
    dreams that leave
Light on eyes that wake and know not if memory
    bid them grieve.
Fire sublime as lightning shines, and exults in thunder
    yet,
Where the battle wields the name and the sword of
    Mahomet.
Far above all wars and gospels, all ebb and flow of
    time,
Lives the soul that speaks in silence, and makes mute
    earth sublime.
Still for her, though years and ages be blinded and
    bedinned,
Mazed with lightnings, crazed with thunders, life
    rides and guides the wind.
Death may live or death may die, and the truth be
    light or night:
Not for gain of heaven may man put away the rule
    of right.

A NEW YEAR'S EVE

CHRISTINA ROSSETTI DIED DECEMBER 29, 1894

THE stars are strong in the deeps of the lustrous
    night,
Cold and splendid as death if his dawn be bright ;
    Cold as the cast-off garb that is cold as clay,
Splendid and strong as a spirit intense as light.

A soul more sweet than the morning of new-born May
Has passed with the year that has passed from the
        world away.
    A song more sweet than the morning's first-born
        song
Again will hymn not among us a new year's day.

Not here, not here shall the carol of joy grown strong
Ring rapture now, and uplift us, a spell-struck
        throng,
    From dream to vision of life that the soul may see
By death's grace only, if death do its trust no wrong.

Scarce yet the days and the starry nights are three
Since here among us a spirit abode as we,
    Girt round with life that is fettered in bonds of
        time,
And clasped with darkness about as is earth with sea.

And now, more high than the vision of souls may
　　climb,
The soul whose song was as music of stars that
　　chime,
　Clothed round with life as of dawn and the
　　mounting sun,
Sings, and we know not here of the song sublime.

No word is ours of it now that the songs are done
Whence here we drank of delight as in freedom won,
　In deep deliverance given from the bonds we bore.
There is none to sing as she sang upon earth, not
　one.

We heard awhile : and for us who shall hear no more
The sound as of waves of light on a starry shore
　Awhile bade brighten and yearn as a father's face
The face of death, divine as in days of yore.

The grey gloom quickened and quivered : the sunless
　place
Thrilled, and the silence deeper than time or space
　Seemed now not all everlasting.　Hope grew
　strong,
And love took comfort, given of the sweet song's
　grace.

Love that finds not on earth, where it finds but
　wrong,
Love that bears not the bondage of years in throng
　Shone to show for her, higher than the years that
　mar,
The life she looked and longed for as love must
　long.

Who knows? We know not. Afar, if the dead be
 far,
Alive, if the dead be alive as the soul's works are,
  The soul whose breath was among us a heavenward
    song
Sings, loves, and shines as it shines for us here a
    star.

...

IN A ROSARY

THROUGH the low grey archway children's feet that
    pass
Quicken, glad to find the sweetest haunt of all.
Brightest wildflowers gleaming deep in lustiest grass,
Glorious weeds that glisten through the green sea's
    glass,
Match not now this marvel, born to fade and fall.

Roses like a rainbow wrought of roses rise
Right and left and forward, shining toward the sun.
Nay, the rainbow lit of sunshine droops and dies
Ere we dream it hallows earth and seas and skies ;
Ere delight may dream it lives, its life is done.

Round the border hemmed with high deep hedges
    round
Go the children, peering over or between
Where the dense bright oval wall of box inwound,
Reared about the roses fast within it bound,
Gives them grace to glance at glories else unseen.

Flower outlightening flower and tree outflowering tree
Feed and fill the sense and spirit full with joy.
Nought awhile they know of outer earth and sea :
Here enough of joy it is to breathe and be :
Here the sense of life is one for girl and boy.

Heaven above them, bright as children's eyes or
    dreams,
Earth about them, sweet as glad soft sleep can show
Earth and sky and sea, a world that scarcely seems
Even in children's eyes less fair than life that gleams
Through the sleep that none but sinless eyes may
    know.

Near beneath, and near above, the terraced ways
Wind or stretch and bask or blink against the sun.
Hidden here from sight on soft or stormy days
Lies and laughs with love toward heaven, at silent
    gaze,
All the radiant rosary—all its flowers made one.

All the multitude of roses towering round
Dawn and noon and night behold as one full flower,
Fain of heaven and loved of heaven, curbed and
    crowned,
Raised and reared to make this plot of earthly ground
Heavenly, could but heaven endure on earth an hour.

Swept away, made nothing now for ever, dead,
Still the rosary lives and shines on memory, free
Now from fear of death or change as childhood, fled
Years on years before its last live leaves were shed:
None may mar it now, as none may stain the sea.

THE HIGH OAKS

Barking Hall, July 19th, 1896

Fourscore years and seven
Light and dew from heaven
Have fallen with dawn on these glad woods each
day
Since here was born, even here,
A birth more bright and dear
Than ever a younger year
Hath seen or shall till all these pass away,
Even all the imperious pride of these,
The woodland ways majestic now with towers of
trees.

Love itself hath nought
Touched of tenderest thought
With holiest hallowing of memorial grace
For memory, blind with bliss,
To love, to clasp, to kiss,
So sweetly strange as this,
The sense that here the sun first hailed her face,
A babe at Her glad mother's breast,
And here again beholds it more beloved and blest.

Love's own heart, a living
Spring of strong thanksgiving,
Can bid no strength of welling song find way
When all the soul would seek
One word for joy to speak,
And even its strength makes weak
The too strong yearning of the soul to say
What may not be conceived or said
While darkness makes division of the quick and dead.

Haply, where the sun
Wanes, and death is none,
The word known here of silence only, held
Too dear for speech to wrong,
May leap in living song
Forth, and the speech be strong
As here the silence whence it yearned and welled
From hearts whose utterance love sealed fast
Till death perchance might give it grace to live at
last.

Here we have our earth
Yet, with all the mirth
Of all the summers since the world began,
All strengths of rest and strife
And love-lit love of life
Where death has birth to wife,
And where the sun speaks, and is heard of man :
Yea, half the sun's bright speech is heard,
And like the sea the soul of man gives back his word.

Earth's enkindled heart
Bears benignant part
In the ardent heaven's auroral pride of prime :

If ever home on earth
Were found of heaven's grace worth
So God-beloved a birth
As here makes bright the fostering face of time,
Here, heaven bears witness, might such grace
Fall fragrant as the dewfall on that brightening face.

Here, for mine and me,
All that eyes may see
Hath more than all the wide world else of good,
All nature else of fair :
Here as none otherwhere
Heaven is the circling air,
Heaven is the homestead, heaven the wold, the
wood :
The fragrance with the shadow spread
From broadening wings of cedars breathes of dawn's
bright bed.

Once a dawn rose here
More divine and dear,
Rose on a birth-bed brighter far than dawn's,
Whence all the summer grew
Sweet as when earth was new
And pure as Eden's dew :
And yet its light lives on these lustrous lawns,
Clings round these wildwood ways, and cleaves
To the aisles of shadow and sun that wind unweaves
and weaves.

Thoughts that smile and weep,
Dreams that hallow sleep,
Brood in the branching shadows of the trees,

Tall trees at agelong rest
Wherein the centuries nest,
Whence, blest as these are blest,
We part, and part not frcm delight in these ;
Whose comfort, sleeping as awake,
We bear about within us as when first it spake.

Comtort as of song
Grown with time more strong,
Made perfect and prophetic as the sea,
Whose message, when it lies
Far off our hungering eyes,
Within us prophesies
Of life not ours, yet ours as theirs may be
Whose souls far off us shine and sing
As ere they sprang back sunward, swift as fire might
spring.

All this oldworld pleasance
Hails a hallowing presence,
And thrills with sense of more than summer near,
And lifts toward heaven more high
The song-surpassing cry
Of rapture that July
Lives, for her love who makes it loveliest here ;
For joy that she who here first drew
The breath of life she gave me breathes it here
anew.

Never birthday born
Highest in height of morn
Whereout the star looks forth that leads the sun

Shone higher in love's account,
Still seeing the mid noon mount
From the eager dayspring's fount
Each year more lustrous, each like all in one ;
Whose light around us and above
We could not see so lovely save by grace of love.

BARKING HALL : A YEAR AFTER

STILL the sovereign trees
Make the sundawn's breeze
More bright, more sweet, more heavenly than it
    rose,
As wind and sun fulfil
Their living rapture : still
Noon, dawn, and evening thrill
With radiant change the immeasurable repose
Wherewith the woodland wilds lie blest
And feel how storms and centuries rock them still to
    rest.

Still the love-lit place
Given of God such grace
That here was born on earth a birth divine
Gives thanks with all its flowers
Through all their lustrous hours,
From all its birds and bowers
Gives thanks that here they felt her sunset shine
Where once her sunrise laughed, and bade
The life of all the living things it lit be glad.

Soft as light and strong
Rises yet their song
And thrills with pride the cedar-crested lawn

And every brooding dove.
But she, beloved above
All utterance known of love,
Abides no more the change of night and dawn,
Beholds no more with earth-born eye
These woods that watched her waking here where all
                    things die.

Not the light that shone
When she looked thereon
Shines on them or shall shine for ever here.
We know not, save when sleep
Slays death, who fain would keep
His mystery dense and deep,
Where shines the smile we held and hold so dear.
Dreams only, thrilled and filled with love,
Bring back its light ere dawn leave nought alive
                    above.

Nought alive awake
Sees the strong dawn break
On all the dreams that dying night bade live.
Yet scarce the intolerant sense
Of day's harsh evidence
How came their word and whence
Strikes dumb the song of thanks it bids them give,
The joy that answers as it heard
And lightens as it saw the light that spake the word.

Night and sleep and dawn
Pass with dreams withdrawn :
But higher above them far than noon may climb

BARKING HALL: A YEAR AFTER 1171

Love lives and turns to light
The deadly noon of night.
His fiery spirit of sight
Endures no curb of change or darkling time.
Even earth and transient things of earth
Even here to him bear witness not of death but birth.

MUSIC: AN ODE

Was it light that spake from the darkness, or music
  that shone from the word,
When the night was enkindled with sound of the
  sun or the first-born bird?
Souls enthralled and entrammelled in bondage of
  seasons that fall and rise,
Bound fast round with the fetters of flesh, and blinded
  with light that dies,
Lived not surely till music spake, and the spirit of
  life was heard.

II

Music, sister of sunrise, and herald of life to be,
  Smiled as dawn on the spirit of man, and the thrall
    was free.
Slave of nature and serf of time, the bondman of life
  and death,
Dumb with passionless patience that breathed but
  forlorn and reluctant breath,
Heard, beheld, and his soul made answer, and com-
  muned aloud with the sea.

III

Morning spake, and he heard : and the passionate
  silent noon
Kept for him not silence : and soft from the mounting moon
Fell the sound of her splendour, heard as dawn's in
  the breathless night,
Not of men but of birds whose note bade man's soul
  quicken and leap to light :
And the song of it spake, and the light and the darkness of earth were as chords in tune.

THE CENTENARY OF THE BATTLE OF THE NILE

AUGUST 1898

' Horatio Nelson—Honor est a Nilo '

A HUNDRED years have lightened and have waned
Since ancient Nile by grace of Nelson gained
   A glory higher in story now than time
Saw when his kings were gods that raged and reigned.

The day that left even England more sublime
And higher on heights that none but she may climb
   Abides above all shock of change-born chance
Where hope and memory hear the stars keep chime.

The strong and sunbright lie whose name was France
Arose against the sun of truth, whose glance
   Laughed large from the eyes of England, fierce as
      fire
Whence eyes wax blind that gaze on truth askance.

A name above all names of heroes, higher
Than song may sound or heart of man aspire,
   Rings as the very voice that speaks the sea
To-day from all the sea's enkindling lyre.

The sound that bids the soul of silence be
Fire, and a rapturous music, speaks, and we
   Hear what the sea's heart utters, wide and far :
" This was his day, and this day's light was he."

O sea, our sea that hadst him for thy star,
A hundred years that fall upon thee are
   Even as a hundred flakes of rain or snow :
No storm of battle signs thee with a scar.

But never more may ship that sails thee show,
But never may the sun that loves thee know,
   But never may thine England give thee more,
A man whose life and death shall praise thee so.

The Nile, the sea, the battle, and the shore,
Heard as we hear one word arise and soar,
   Beheld one name above them tower and glow—
Nelson : a light that time bows down before.

TRAFALGAR DAY

Sea, that art ours as we are thine, whose name
Is one with England's even as light with flame,
    Dost thou as we, thy chosen of all men, know
This day of days when death gave life to fame?

Dost thou not kindle above and thrill below
With rapturous record, with memorial glow,
    Remembering this thy festal day of fight,
And all the joy it gave, and all the woe?

Never since day broke flowerlike forth of night
Broke such a dawn of battle.   Death in sight
    Made of the man whose life was like the sun
A man more godlike than the lord of light.

There is none like him, and there shall be none.
When England bears again as great a son,
    He can but follow fame where Nelson led.
There is not and there cannot be but one.

As earth has but one England, crown and head
Of all her glories till the sun be dead,
    Supreme in peace and war, supreme in song,
Supreme in freedom, since her rede was read,

Since first the soul that gave her speech grew strong
To help the right and heal the wild world's wrong,
    So she hath but one royal Nelson, born
To reign on time above the years that throng.

The music of his name puts fear to scorn,
And thrills our twilight through with sense of morn :
    As England was, how should not England be ?
No tempest yet has left her banner torn.

No year has yet put out the day when he
Who lived and died to keep our kingship free
    Wherever seas by warring winds are worn
Died, and was one with England and the sea.

October 21, 1895.

CROMWELL'S STATUE[1]

WHAT needs our Cromwell stone or bronze to say
His was the light that lit on England's way
   The sundawn of her time-compelling power,
The noontide of her most imperial day?

His hand won back the sea for England's dower;
His footfall bade the Moor change heart and cower;
   His word on Milton's tongue spake law to France
When Piedmont felt the she-wolf Rome devour.

From Cromwell's eyes the light of England's glance
Flashed, and bowed down the kings by grace of
      chance,
   The priest-anointed princes; one alone
By grace of England held their hosts in trance.

The enthroned Republic from her kinglier throne
Spake, and her speech was Cromwell's. Earth has
      known
   No lordlier presence. How should Cromwell stand
With kinglets and with queenlings hewn in stone?

  [1] Refused by the party of reaction and disunion in the House of
Commons on the 17th of June, 1895.

Incarnate England in his warrior hand
Smote, and as fire devours the blackening brand
    Made ashes of their strengths who wrought her
        wrong,
And turned the strongholds of her foes to sand.

His praise is in the sea's and Milton's song ;
What praise could reach him from the weakling
        throng
    That rules by leave of tongues whose praise is
        shame—
Him, who made England out of weakness strong ?

There needs no clarion's blast of broad-blown fame
To bid the world bear witness whence he came
    Who bade fierce Europe fawn at England's heel
And purged the plague of lineal rule with flame.

There needs no witness graven on stone or steel
For one whose work bids fame bow down and kneel ;
    Our man of men, whose time-commanding name
Speaks England, and proclaims her Commonweal.

June 20, 1895

A WORD FOR THE NAVY

I

Queen born of the sea, that hast borne her
  The mightiest of seamen on earth,
Bright England, whose glories adorn her
  And bid her rejoice in thy birth
    As others made mothers
      Rejoice in births sublime,
    She names thee, she claims thee
      The lordliest child of time.

II

All hers is the praise of thy story,
  All thine is the love of her choice
The light of her waves is thy glory,
  The sound of thy soul is her voice
    They fear it who hear it
      And love not truth nor thee :
    They sicken, heart-stricken,
      Who see and would not see.

III

The lords of thy fate, and thy keepers
  Whose charge is the strength of thy ships,
If now they be dreamers and sleepers,
  Or sluggards with lies at their lips,

Thy haters and traitors,
    False friends or foes descried,
Might scatter and shatter
    Too soon thy princely pride.

IV

Dark Muscovy, reptile in rancour,
    Base Germany, blatant in guile,
Lay wait for thee riding at anchor
    On waters that whisper and smile.
    They deem thee or dream thee
        Less living now than dead,
    Deep sunken and drunken
        With sleep whence fear has fled.

V

And what though thy song as thine action
    Wax faint, and thy place be not known,
While faction is grappling with faction,
    Twin curs with thy corpse for a bone?
    They care not, who spare not
        The noise of pens or throats ;
    Who bluster and muster
        Blind ranks and bellowing votes.

VI

Let populace jangle with peerage
    And ministers shuffle their mobs ;
Mad pilots who reck not of steerage
    Though tempest ahead of them throbs.
    That throbbing and sobbing
        Of wind and gradual wave
    They hear not and fear not
        Who guide thee toward thy grave.

VII

No clamour of cries or of parties
  Is worth but a whisper from thee,
While only the trust of thy heart is
  At one with the soul of the sea.
    In justice her trust is
      Whose time her tidestreams keep :
    They sink not, they shrink not,
      Time casts them not on sleep.

VIII

Sleep thou : for thy past was so royal,
  Love hardly would bid thee take heed
Were Russia not faithful and loyal
  Nor Germany guiltless of greed.
    No nation, in station
      Of story less than thou,
    Re-risen from prison,
      Can stand against thee now.

IX

Sleep on : is the time not a season
  For strong men to slumber and sleep,
And wise men to palter with treason ?
  And that they sow tares, shall they reap ?
    The wages of ages
      Wherein men smiled and slept,
    Fame fails them, shame veils them,
      Their record is not kept.

X

Nay, whence is it then that we know it,
  What wages were theirs, and what fame?
Deep voices of prophet and poet
  Bear record against them of shame.
    Death, starker and darker
      Than seals the graveyard grate,
    Entombs them and dooms them
      To darkness deep as fate.

XI

But thou, though the world should misdoubt thee,
  Be strong as the seas at thy side;
Bind on but thine armour about thee,
  That girds thee with power and with pride.
    Where Drake stood, where Blake stood,
      Where fame sees Nelson stand,
    Stand thou too, and now too
      Take thou thy fate in hand.

XII

At the gate of the sea, in the gateway,
  They stood as the guards of thy gate;
Take now but thy strengths to thee straightway,
  Though late, we will deem it not late
    Thy story, thy glory,
      The very soul of thee,
    It rose not, it grows not,
      It comes not save by sea.

NORTHUMBERLAND

BETWEEN our eastward and our westward sea
  The narrowing strand
Clasps close the noblest shore fame holds in fee
Even here where English birth seals all men free—
  Northumberland.

The sea-mists meet across it when the snow
  Clothes moor and fell,
And bid their true-born hearts who love it glow
For joy that none less nobly born may know
  What love knows well.

The splendour and the strength of storm and fight
  Sustain the song
That filled our fathers' hearts with joy to smite,
To live, to love, to lay down life that right
  Might tread down wrong.

They warred, they sang, they triumphed, and they
    passed,
  And left us glad
Here to be born, their sons, whose hearts hold fast
The proud old love no change can overcast,
  No chance leave sad.

None save our northmen ever, none but we,
    Met, pledged, or fought
Such foes and friends as Scotland and the sea
With heart so high and equal, strong in glee
    And stern in thought.

Thought, fed from time's memorial springs with pride,
    Made strong as fire
Their hearts who hurled the foe down Flodden side,
And hers who rode the waves none else durst ride—
    None save her sire.

O land beloved, where nought of legend's dream
    Outshines the truth,
Where Joyous Gard, closed round with clouds that
        gleam
For them that know thee not, can scarce but seem
    Too sweet for sooth,

Thy sons forget not, nor shall fame forget,
    The deed there done
Before the walls whose fabled fame is yet
A light too sweet and strong to rise and set
    With moon and sun.

Song bright as flash of swords or oars that shine
    Through fight or foam
Stirs yet the blood thou hast given thy sons like
        wine
To hail in each bright ballad hailed as thine
    One heart, one home.

Our Collingwood, though Nelson be not ours,
    By him shall stand
Immortal, till those waifs of oldworld hours,
Forgotten, leave uncrowned with bays and flowers
    Northumberland.

STRATFORD-ON-AVON

June 27, 1901

Be glad in heaven above all souls insphered,
Most royal and most loyal born of men,
Shakespeare, of all on earth beloved or feared
Or worshipped, highest in sight of human ken.
The homestead hallowed by thy sovereign birth,
Whose name, being one with thine, stands higher
     than Rome,
Forgets not how of all on English earth
Their trust is holiest, there who have their home.
Stratford is thine and England's.　None that hate
The commonweal whose empire sets men free
Find comfort there, where once by grace of fate
A soul was born as boundless as the sea.
    If life, if love, if memory now be thine,
      Rejoice that still thy Stratford bears thy sign.

BURNS: AN ODE

A FIRE of fierce and laughing light
That clove the shuddering heart of night
Leapt earthward, and the thunder's might
    That pants and yearns
Made fitful music round its flight:
    And earth saw Burns.

The joyous lightning found its voice
And bade the heart of wrath rejoice
And scorn uplift a song to voice
    The imperial hate
That smote the God of base men's choice
    At God's own gate.

Before the shrine of dawn, wherethrough
The lark rang rapture as she flew,
It flashed and fired the darkling dew:
    And all that heard
With love or loathing hailed anew
    A new day's word.

The servants of the lord of hell,
As though their lord had blessed them, fell
Foaming at mouth for fear, so well
    They knew the lie
Wherewith they sought to scan and spell
    The unsounded sky.

And Calvin, night's prophetic bird,
Out of his home in hell was heard
Shrieking ; and all the fens were stirred
    Whence plague is bred ;
Can God endure the scoffer's word ?
    But God was dead.

The God they made them in despite
Of man and woman, love and light,
Strong sundawn and the starry night,
    The lie supreme,
Shot through with song, stood forth to sight
    A devil's dream.

And he that bent the lyric bow
And laid the lord of darkness low
And bade the fire of laughter glow
    Across his grave,
And bade the tides above it flow,
    Wave hurtling wave,

Shall he not win from latter days
More than his own could yield of praise ?
Ay, could the sovereign singer's bays
    Forsake his brow,
The warrior's, won on stormier ways,
    Still clasp it now.

He loved, and sang of love : he laughed,
And bade the cup whereout he quaffed
Shine as a planet, fore and aft,
    And left and right,
And keen as shoots the sun's first shaft
    Against the night.

But love and wine were moon and sun
For many a fame long since undone,
And sorrow and joy have lost and won
    By stormy turns
As many a singer's soul, if none
    More bright than Burns.

And sweeter far in grief or mirth
Have songs as glad and sad of birth
Found voice to speak of wealth or dearth
    In joy of life :
But never song took fire from earth
    More strong for strife.

The daisy by his ploughshare cleft,
The lips of women loved and left,
The griefs and joys that weave the weft
    Of human time,
With craftsman's cunning, keen and deft,
    He carved in rhyme.

But Chaucer's daisy shines a star
Above his ploughshare's reach to mar,
And mightier vision gave Dunbar
    More strenuous wing
To hear around all sins that are
    Hell dance and sing.

And when such pride and power of trust
In song's high gift to arouse from dust
Death, and transfigure love or lust
    Through smiles or tears
In golden speech that takes no rust
    From cankering years,

As never spake but once in one
Strong star-crossed child of earth and sun,
Villon, made music such as none
    May praise or blame,
A crown of starrier flower was won
    Than Burns may claim.

But never, since bright earth was born
In rapture of the enkindling morn,
Might godlike wrath and sunlike scorn
    That was and is
And shall be while false weeds are worn
    Find word like his.

Above the rude and radiant earth
That heaves and glows from firth to firth
In vale and mountain, bright in dearth
    And warm in wealth,
Which gave his fiery glory birth
    By chance and stealth,

Above the storms of praise and blame
That blur with mist his lustrous name,
His thunderous laughter went and came,
    And lives and flies ;
The roar that follows on the flame
    When lightning dies.

Earth, and the snow-dimmed heights of air,
And water winding soft and fair
Through still sweet places, bright and bare,
    By bent and byre,
Taught him what hearts within them were ·
    But his was fire.

THE COMMONWEAL

A Song for Unionists

Men, whose fathers braved the world in arms against
	our isles in union,
	Men, whose brothers met rebellion face to face,
Show the hearts ye have, if worthy long descent and
	high communion,
	Show the spirits, if unbroken, of your race.

What are these that howl and hiss across the strait
	of westward water?
	What is he who floods our ears with speech in
	flood?
See the long tongue lick the dripping hand that
	smokes and reeks of slaughter !
	See the man of words embrace the man of blood !

Hear the plea whereby the tonguester mocks and
	charms the gazing gaper—
	" We are they whose works are works of love and
	peace ;
Till disunion bring forth union, what is union, sirs,
	but paper ?
	Break and rend it, then shall trust and strength
	increase."

II.   2 P 2

Who would fear to trust a double-faced but single
 hearted dreamer,
  Pure of purpose, clean of hand, and clear of guile?
" Life is well-nigh spent," he sighs ; " you call me
 shuffler, trickster, schemer?
  I am old—when young men yell at me, I smile."

Many a year that priceless light of life has trembled,
 we remember,
  On the platform of extinction—unextinct ;
Many a month has been for him the long year's last—
 life's calm December :
  Can it be that he who said so, saying so, winked?

No ; the lust of life, the thirst for work and days with
 work to do in,
  Drove and drives him down the road of splendid
  shame ;
All is well, if o'er the monument recording England's
 ruin
  Time shall read, inscribed in triumph, Gladstone's
  name.

Thieves and murderers, hands yet red with blood and
 tongues yet black with lies,
  Clap and clamour—" Parnell spurs his Gladstone
  well ! "
Truth, unscared and undeluded by their praise or
 blame, replies—
  " Is the goal of fraud and bloodshed heaven or
  hell ? "

Old men eloquent, who truckle to the traitors of the
 time,
  Love not office—power is no desire of theirs :

What if yesterday their hearts recoiled from blood
      and fraud and crime?
  Conscience erred—an error which to-day repairs.

Conscience only now convinces them of strange
      though transient error:
  Only now they see how fair is treason's face;
See how true the falsehood, just the theft, and
      blameless is the terror,
  Which replaces just and blameless men in place.

Place and time decide the right and wrong of thought
      and word and action;
  Crime is black as hell, till virtue gain its vote;
Then—but ah, to think or say so smacks of fraud or
      smells of faction!—
  Mercy holds the door while Murder hacks the throat.

Murder? Treason? Theft? Poor brothers who
      succumb to such temptations,
  Shall we lay on you or take on us the blame?
Reason answers, and religion echoes round to
      wondering nations,
  " Not with Ireland, but with England rests the
      shame."

Reason speaks through mild religion's organ, loud
      and long and lusty—
  Profit speaks through lips of patriots pure and
      true—
" English friends, whose trust we ask for, has not
      England found us trusty?
  Not for us we seek advancement, but for you.

" Far and near the world bears witness of our
    wisdom, courage, honour ;
  Egypt knows if there our fame burns bright or dim.
Let but England trust as Gordon trusted, soon shall
    come upon her
  Such deliverance as our daring brought on him.

" Far and wide the world rings record of our faith,
    our constant dealing,
  Love of country, truth to friends, contempt for foes.
Sign once more the bond of trust in us that here
    awaits but sealing,
  We will give yet more than all our record shows.

" Perfect ruin, shame eternal, everlasting degrada-
    tion,
  Freedom bought and sold, truth bound and treason
    free."
Yet an hour is here for answer ; now, if here be yet
    a nation,
  Answer, England, man by man from sea to sea !

June 30, 1886.

THE QUESTION

1887

SHALL England consummate the crime
  That binds the murderer's hand, and leaves
  No surety for the trust of thieves?
Time pleads against it—truth and time—
  And pity frowns and grieves.

The hoary henchman of the gang
  Lifts hands that never dew nor rain
  May cleanse from Gordon's blood again,
Appealing : pity's tenderest pang
  Thrills his pure heart with pain.

Grand helmsman of the clamorous crew,
  The good grey recreant quakes and weeps
  To think that crime no longer creeps
Safe toward its end : that murderers too
  May die when mercy sleeps.

While all the lives were innocent
  That slaughter drank, and laughed with rage,
  Bland virtue sighed, " A former age
Taught murder : souls long discontent
  Can aught save blood assuage?

" You blame not Russian hands that smite
  By fierce and secret ways the power
  That leaves not life one chainless hour ;
Have these than they less natural right
  To claim life's natural dower ?

" The dower that freedom brings the slave
  She weds, is vengeance : why should we,
  Whom equal laws acclaim as free,
Think shame, if men too blindly brave
  Steal, murder, skulk, and flee ?

" At kings they strike in Russia : there
  Men take their life in hand who slay
  Kings : these, that have not heart to lay
Hand save on girls whose ravaged hair
  Is made the patriot's prey,

" These, whom the sight of old men slain
  Makes bold to bid their children die,
  Starved, if they hold not peace, nor lie,
Claim loftier praise : could others deign
  To stand in shame so high ?

" Could others deign to dare such deeds
  As holiest Ireland hallows ? Nay,
  But justice then makes plain our way :
Be laws burnt up like burning weeds
  That vex the face of day.

" Shall bloodmongers be held of us
  Blood-guilty ? Hands reached out for gold
  Whereon blood rusts not yet, we hold
Bloodless and blameless : ever thus
  Have good men held of old.

" Fair Freedom, fledged and imped with lies,
    Takes flight by night where murder lurks,
    And broods on murderous ways and works,
Yet seems not hideous in our eyes
    As Austrians or as Turks.

" Be it ours to undo a woful past,
    To bid the bells of concord chime,
    To break the bonds of suffering crime,
Slack now, that some would make more fast :
    Such teaching comes of time."

So pleads the gentlest heart that lives,
    Whose pity, pitiless for all
    Whom darkling terror holds in thrall,
Toward none save miscreants yearns, and gives
    Alms of warm tears—and gall.

Hear, England, and obey : for he
    Who claims thy trust again to-day
    Is he who left thy sons a prey
To shame whence only death sets free :
    Hear, England, and obey.

Thy spoils he gave to deck the Dutch ;
    Thy noblest pride, most pure, most brave,
    To death forlorn and sure he gave ;
Nor now requires he overmuch
    Who bids thee dig thy grave.

Dig deep the grave of shame, wherein
    Thy fame, thy commonweal, must lie ,
    Put thought of aught save terror by ;
To strike and slay the slayer is sin ;
    And Murder must not die.

Bind fast the true man ; loose the thief ;
  Shamed were the land, the laws accursed,
  Were guilt, not innocence, amerced ;
And dark the wrong and sore the grief,
  Were tyrants too coerced.

The fiercest cowards that ever skulked,
  The cowardliest hounds that ever lapped
  Blood, if their horde be tracked and trapped,
And justice claim their lives for mulct,
  Gnash teeth that flashed and snapped.

Bow down for fear, then, England : bow,
  Lest worse befall thee yet ; and swear
  That nought save pity, conscience, care
For truth and mercy, moves thee now
  To call foul falsehood fair.

So shalt thou live in shame, and hear
  The lips of all men laugh thee dead ;
  The wide world's mockery round thy head
Shriek like a storm-wind : and a bier
  Shall be thine honour's bed.

APOSTASY

Et Judas m'a dit : Traître !—VICTOR HUGO

I

TRUTHS change with time, and terms with truth.
    To-day
  A statesman worships union, and to-night
  Disunion. Shame to have sinned against the
    light
Confounds not but impels his tongue to unsay
What yestereve he swore. Should fear make way
  For treason ? honour change her livery ? fright
  Clasp hands with interest? wrong pledge faith
    with right ?
Religion, mercy, conscience, answer—Yea.

To veer is not to veer : when votes are weighed,
The numerous tongue approves him renegade
  Who cannot change his banner : he that can
Sits crowned with wreaths of praise too pure to fade.
  Truth smiles applause on treason's poisonous
    plan :
And Cleon is an honourable man.

II

Pure faith, fond hope, sweet love, with God for guide,
  Move now the men whose blameless error cast
  In prison (ah, but love condones the past !)
Their subject knaves that were—their lords that ride

Now laughing on their necks, and now bestride
    Their vassal backs in triumph. Faith stands fast
    Though fear haul down the flag that crowned her
        mast
And hope and love proclaim that truth has lied.

Turn, turn, and turn—so bids the still small voice,
    The changeless voice of honour. He that stands
    Where all his life he stood, with bribeless hands,
With tongue unhired to mourn, reprove, rejoice,
    Curse, bless, forswear, and swear again, and lie,
    Stands proven apostate in the apostate's eye

III

Fraud shrinks from faith : at sight of swans, the raven
    Chides blackness, and the snake recoils aghast
    In fear of poison when a bird flies past.
Thersites brands Achilles as a craven ;
The shoal fed full with shipwreck blames the haven
    For murderous lust of lives devoured, and vast
    Desire of doom whose feast is mercy's fast :
And Bacon sees the traitor's mark engraven
Full on the front of Essex. Grief and shame
    Obscure the chaste and sunlike spirit of Oates
At thought of Russell's treason ; and the name
Of Milton sickens with superb disgust
    The heaving heart of Waller. Wisdom dotes,
If wisdom turns not tail and licks not dust.

IV

The sole sweet land found fit to wed the sea,
    With reptile rebels at her heel of old,
    Set hard her heel upon them, and controlled
The cowering poisonous peril. How should she

Cower, and resign her trust of empire? Free
    As winds and waters live the loyal-souled
    And true-born sons that love her : nay, the bold
Base knaves who curse her name have leave to be
The loud-tongued liars they are. For she, beyond
All woful years that bid men's hearts despond,
    Sees yet the likeness of her ancient fame
Burn from the heavenward heights of history, hears
Not Leicester's name but Sidney's—faith's, not
        fear's—
    Not Gladstone's now but only Gordon's name.

RUSSIA: AN ODE

1890

I

Out of hell a word comes hissing, dark as doom,
Fierce as fire, and foul as plague-polluted gloom ;
Out of hell wherein the sinless damned endure
More than ever sin conceived of pains impure ;
More than ever ground men's living souls to dust ;
Worse than madness ever dreamed of murderous lust.
Since the world's wail first went up from lands and
  seas
Ears have heard not, tongues have told not things
  like these.
Dante, led by love's and hate's accordant spell
Down the deepest and the loathliest ways of hell,
Where beyond the brook of blood the rain was fire,
Where the scalps were masked with dung more deep
  than mire,
Saw not, where the filth was foulest, and the night
Darkest, depths whose fiends could match the
  Muscovite.
Set beside this truth, his deadliest vision seems
Pale and pure and painless as a virgin's dreams.

Maidens dead beneath the clasping lash, and wives
Rent with deadlier pangs than death—for shame
    survives,
Naked, mad, starved, scourged, spurned, frozen,
    fallen, deflowered,
Souls and bodies as by fangs of beasts devoured,
Sounds that hell would hear not, sights no thought
    could shape,
Limbs that feel as flame the ravenous grasp of rape,
Filth of raging crime and shame that crime enjoys,
Age made one with youth in torture, girls with boys,
These, and worse if aught be worse than these things
    are,
Prove thee regent, Russia—praise thy mercy, Czar.

II

Sons of man, men born of women, may we dare
Say they sin who dare be slain and dare not spare ?
They who take their lives in hand and smile on death,
Holding life as less than sleep's most fitful breath,
So their life perchance or death may serve and speed
Faith and hope, that die if dream become not deed ?
Nought is death and nought is life and nought is fate
Save for souls that love has clothed with fire of hate.
These behold them, weigh them, prove them, find
    them nought,
Save by light of hope and fire of burning thought.
What though sun be less than storm where these
    aspire,
Dawn than lightning, song than thunder, light than
    fire ?
Help is none in heaven : hope sees no gentler star :
Earth is hell, and hell bows down before the Czar.

All its monstrous, murderous, lecherous births acclaim
Him whose empire lives to match its fiery fame.
Nay, perchance at sight or sense of deeds here done,
Here where men may lift up eyes to greet the sun,
Hell recoils heart-stricken : horror worse than hell
Darkens earth and sickens heaven ; life knows the
    spell,
Shudders, quails, and sinks—or, filled with fierier
    breath,
Rises red in arms devised of darkling death.
Pity mad with passion, anguish mad with shame,
Call aloud on justice by her darker name ;
Love grows hate for love's sake · life takes death for
    guide.
Night hath none but one red star—Tyrannicide.

III

" God or man, be swift ; hope sickens with delay :
Smite, and send him howling down his father's
    way !
Fall, O fire of heaven, and smite as fire from hell
Halls wherein men's torturers, crowned and cowering,
    dwell !
These that crouch and shrink and shudder, girt with
    power—
These that reign, and dare not trust one trembling
    hour—
These omnipotent, whom terror curbs and drives—
These whose life reflects in fear their victims' lives—
These whose breath sheds poison worse than plague's
    thick breath—
These whose reign is ruin, these whose word is death,

These whose will turns heaven to hell, and day to
    night,
These, if God's hand smite not, how shall man's not
    smite ? "
So from hearts by horror withered as by fire
Surge the strains of unappeasable desire ;
Sounds that bid the darkness lighten, lit for death ;
Bid the lips whose breath was doom yield up their
    breath :
Down the way of Czars, awhile in vain deferred,
Bid the Second Alexander light the Third.
How for shame shall men rebuke them ? how may we
Blame, whose fathers died, and slew, to leave us free ?
We, though all the world cry out upon them, know,
Were our strife as theirs, we could not strike but so ;
Could not cower, and could not kiss the hands that
    smite ;
Could not meet them armed in sunlit battle's light.
Dark as fear and red as hate though morning rise,
Life it is that conquers ; death it is that dies.

FOR GREECE AND CRETE

Storm and shame and fraud and darkness fill the
    nations full with night :
Hope and fear whose eyes yearn eastward have but
    fire and sword in sight :
One alone, whose name is one with glory, sees and
    seeks the light.

Hellas, mother of the spirit, sole supreme in war and
    peace,
Land of light, whose word remembered bids all fear
    and sorrow cease,
Lives again, while freedom lightens eastward yet for
    sons of Greece.

Greece, where only men whose manhood was as god
    head ever trod,
Bears the blind world witness yet of light wherewith
    her feet are shod :
Freedom, armed of Greece was always very man and
    very God.

Now the winds of old that filled her sails with triumph,
    when the fleet
Bound for death from Asia fled before them stricken,
    wake to greet
Ships full-winged again for freedom toward the sacred
    shores of Crete.

There was God born man, the song that spake of
    old time said : and there
Man, made even as God by trust that shows him
    nought too dire to dare,
Now may light again the beacon lit when those we
    worship were.

Sharp the concert wrought of discord shrills the tune
    of shame and death,
Turk by Christian fenced and fostered, Mecca backed
    by Nazareth :
All the powerless powers, tongue-valiant, breathe but
    greed's or terror's breath.

Though the tide that feels the west wind lift it wave
    by widening wave
Wax not yet to height and fullness of the storm that
    smites to save,
None shall bid the flood back seaward till no bar be
    left to brave.

DELPHIC HYMN TO APOLLO

(B.C. 280)

DONE INTO ENGLISH

I

THEE, the son of God most high,
Famed for harping song, will I
Proclaim, and the deathless oracular word
From the snow-topped rock that we gaze on heard,
  Counsels of thy glorious giving
  Manifest for all men living,
How thou madest the tripod of prophecy thine
Which the wrath of the dragon kept guard on, a shrine
  Voiceless till thy shafts could smite
  All his live coiled glittering might.

II

  Ye that hold of right alone
  All deep woods on Helicon,
Fair daughters of thunder-girt God, with your bright
White arms uplift as to lighten the light,
  Come to chant your brother's praise,
  Gold-haired Phœbus, loud in lays,
Even his, who afar up the twin-topped seat
Of the rock Parnassian whereon we meet

Risen with glorious Delphic maids
Seeks the soft spring-sweetened shades
Castalian, fain of the Delphian peak
Prophetic, sublime as the feet that seek.
Glorious Athens, highest of state,
Come, with praise and prayer elate,
O thou that art queen of the plain unscarred
That the warrior Tritonid hath alway in guard,
Where on many a sacred shrine
Young bulls' thigh-bones burn and shine
As the god that is fire overtakes them, and fast
The smoke of Arabia to heavenward is cast,
Scattering wide its balm : and shrill
Now with nimble notes that thrill
The flute strikes up for the song, and the harp of gold
Strikes up to the song sweet answer . and all behold,
All, aswarm as bees, give ear,
Who by birth hold Athens dear.

A NEW CENTURY

An age too great for thought of ours to scan,
  A wave upon the sleepless sea of time
  That sinks and sleeps for ever, ere the chime
Pass that salutes with blessing, not with ban,
The dark year dead, the bright year born for man,
  Dies: all its days that watched man cower and climb,
  Frail as the foam, and as the sun sublime,
Sleep sound as they that slept ere these began.

Our mother earth, whose ages none may tell,
  Puts on no change : time bids not her wax pale
Or kindle, quenched or quickened, when the knell
  Sounds, and we cry across the veering gale
Farewell—and midnight answers us, Farewell ;
  Hail—and the heaven of morning answers, Hail.

AN EVENING AT VICHY

SEPTEMBER 1896

WRITTEN ON THE NEWS OF THE DEATH OF LORD LEIGHTON

A LIGHT has passed that never shall pass away,
  A sun has set whose rays are unquelled of night.
The loyal grace, the courtesy bright as day,
    The strong sweet radiant spirit of life and light
    That shone and smiled and lightened on all men's
      sight,
The kindly life whose tune was the tune of May,
  For us now dark, for love and for fame is bright.

Nay, not for us that live as the fen-fires live,
  As stars that shoot and shudder with life and die,
Can death make dark that lustre of life, or give
    The grievous gift of trust in oblivion's lie.
    Days dear and far death touches, and draws them
      nigh,
And bids the grief that broods on their graves forgive
  The day that seems to mock them as clouds that fly.

If life be life more faithful than shines on sleep
  When dreams take wing and lighten and fade like
    flame,
Then haply death may be not a death so deep

That all things past are past for it wholly—fame,
Love, loving-kindness, seasons that went and came,
And left their light on life as a seal to keep
  Winged memory fast and heedful of time's dead
    claim.

Death gives back life and light to the sunless years
  Whose suns long sunken set not for ever. Time,
Blind, fierce, and deaf as tempest, relents, and hears
  And sees how bright the days and how sweet their
    chime
  Rang, shone, and passed in music that matched
    the clime
Wherein we met rejoicing—a joy that cheers
  Sorrow, to see the night as the dawn sublime.

The days that were outlighten the days that are,
  And eyes now darkened shine as the stars we see .
And hear not sing, impassionate star to star,
  As once we heard the music that haply he
  Hears, high in heaven if ever a voice may be
The same in heaven, the same as on earth, afar
  From pain and earth as heaven from the heaving
    sea.

A woman's voice, divine as a bird's by dawn
  Kindled and stirred to sunward, arose and held
Our souls that heard, from earth as from sleep with-
    drawn,
  And filled with light as stars, and as stars com-
    pelled
  To move by might of music, elate while quelled,
Subdued by rapture, lit as a mountain lawn
  By morning whence all heaven in the sunrise welled.

And her the shadow of death as a robe clasped round
  Then : and as morning's music she passed away.
And he then with us, warrior and wanderer, crowned
    With fame that shone from eastern on western
      day,
      More strong, more kind, than praise or than grief
        might say,
Has passed now forth of shadow by sunlight bound,
    Of night shot through with light that is frail as
      May.

May dies, and light grows darkness, and life grows
      death :
    Hope fades and shrinks and falls as a changing leaf:
Remembrance, touched and kindled by love's live
        breath,
      Shines, and subdues the shadow of time called grief,
      The shade whose length of life is as life's date brief,
With joy that broods on the sunlight past, and saith
    That thought and love hold sorrow and change in
      fief.

Sweet, glad, bright spirit, kind as the sun seems kind
    When earth and sea rejoice in his gentler spell,
Thy face that was we see not ; bereft and blind,
    We see but yet, rejoicing to see, and dwell
    Awhile in days that heard not the death-day's
        knell,
A light so bright that scarcely may sorrow find
    One old sweet word that hails thee and mourns—
        Farewell.

TO GEORGE FREDERICK WATTS

On the Eightieth Anniversary of his Birth,
February 23 1897

High thought and hallowed love, by faith made one,
Begat and bare the sweet strong-hearted child,
Art, nursed of Nature ; earth and sea and sun
Saw Nature then more godlike as she smiled.
Life smiled on death, and death on life : the Soul
Between them shone, and soared above their strife,
And left on Time's unclosed and starry scroll
A sign that quickened death to deathless life.
Peace rose like Hope, a patient queen, and bade
Hell's firstborn, Faith, abjure her creed and die ;
And Love, by life and death made sad and glad,
Gave Conscience ease, and watched Good Will
pass by.
All these make music now of one man's name,
Whose life and age are one with love and fame.

ON THE DEATH OF MRS. LYNN LINTON

KIND, wise, and true as truth's own heart,
    A soul that here
Chose and held fast the better part
    And cast out fear,

Has left us ere we dreamed of death
    For life so strong,
Clear as the sundawn's light and breath,
    And sweet as song.

We see no more what here awhile
    Shed light on men :
Has Landor seen that brave bright smile
    Alive again ?

If death and life and love be one
    And hope no lie
And night no stronger than the sun,
    These cannot die.

The father-spirit whence her soul
    Took strength, and gave
Back love, is perfect yet and whole,
    As hope might crave.

His word is living light and fire :
    And hers shall live
By grace of all good gifts the sire
    Gave power to give.

The sire and daughter, twain and one
    In quest and goal,
Stand face to face beyond the sun,
    And soul to soul.

Not we, who loved them well, may dream
    What joy sublime
Is theirs, if dawn through darkness gleam,
    And life through time.

Time seems but here the mask of death,
    That falls and shows
A void where hope may draw not breath :
    Night only knows.

Love knows not : all that love may keep
    Glad memory gives :
The spirit of the days that sleep
    Still wakes and lives.

But not the spirit's self, though song
    Would lend it speech,
May touch the goal that hope might long
    In vain to reach.

How dear that high true heart, how sweet
    Those keen kind eyes,
Love knows, who knows how fiery fleet
    Is life that flies.

> If life there be that flies not, fair
> > The life must be
> That thrills her sovereign spirit there
> > And sets it free.

ON THE DEATH OF LYNN LYTTON

If life there be that dies not, this
The life must be
That thrills her sovereign spirit there
And sets it free.

IN MEMORY OF AURELIO SAFFI

BELOVED above all nations, land adored,
Sovereign in spirit and charm, by song and sword,
   Sovereign whose life is love, whose name is light,
Italia, queen that hast the sun for lord,

Bride that hast heaven for bridegroom, how should
     night
Veil or withhold from faith's and memory's sight
   A man beloved and crowned of thee and fame,
Hide for an hour his name's memorial might?

Thy sons may never speak or hear the name
Saffi, and feel not love's regenerate flame
   Thrill all the quickening heart with faith and pride
In one whose life makes death and life the same.

They die indeed whose souls before them died :
Not he, for whom death flung life's portal wide,
   Who stands where Dante's soul in vision came,
In Dante's presence, by Mazzini's side.

    March 26, 1896.

CARNOT

DEATH, winged with fire of hate from deathless hell
  Wherein the souls of anarchs hiss and die,
  With stroke as dire has cloven a heart as high
As twice beyond the wide sea's westward swell
The living lust of death had power to quell
  Through ministry of murderous hands whereby
  Dark fate bade Lincoln's head and Garfield's lie
Low even as his who bids his France farewell.

France, now no heart that would not weep with thee
  Loved ever faith or freedom.   From thy hand
  The staff of state is broken : hope, unmanned
With anguish, doubts if freedom's self be free.
  The snake-souled anarch's fang strikes all the land
Cold, and all hearts unsundered by the sea.

  June 25, 1894.

AFTER THE VERDICT

FRANCE, cloven in twain by fire of hell and hate,
  Shamed with the shame of men her meanest born,
  Soldier and judge whose names, inscribed for scorn,
Stand vilest on the record writ of fate,
Lies yet not wholly vile who stood so great,
  Sees yet not all her praise of old outworn.
  Not yet is all her scroll of glory torn,
Or left for utter shame to desecrate.
High souls and constant hearts of faithful men
Sustain her perfect praise with tongue and pen
Indomitable as honour.   Storms may toss
  And soil her standard ere her bark win home :
But shame falls full upon the Christless cross
  Whose brandmark signs the holy hounds of Rome.

September 1899.

THE TRANSVAAL

PATIENCE, long sick to death, is dead.   Too long
  Have sloth and doubt and treason bidden us be
  What Cromwell's England was not, when the sea
To him bore witness given of Blake how strong
She stood, a commonweal that brooked no wrong
  From foes less vile than men like wolves set free
  Whose war is waged where none may fight or flee—
With women and with weanlings.   Speech and song
Lack utterance now for loathing.   Scarce we hear
  Foul tongues that blacken God's dishonoured name
  With prayers turned curses and with praise found
     shame
Defy the truth whose witness now draws near
  To scourge these dogs, agape with jaws afoam,
  Down out of life.   Strike, England, and strike
     home.

    October 9, 1899.

REVERSE

THE wave that breaks against a forward stroke
   Beats not the swimmer back, but thrills him through
   With joyous trust to win his way anew
Through stronger seas than first upon him broke
And triumphed. England's iron-tempered oak
   Shrank not when Europe's might against her grew
   Full, and her sun drank up her foes like dew,
And lion-like from sleep her strength awoke.

As bold in fight as bold in breach of trust
   We find our foes, and wonder not to find,
   Nor grudge them praise whom honour may not
      bind :
But loathing more intense than speaks disgust
   Heaves England's heart, when scorn is bound to
      greet
   Hunters and hounds whose tongues would lick
      their feet.

     November 1, 1899.

THE TURNING OF THE TIDE

Storm, strong with all the bitter heart of hate,
  Smote England, now nineteen dark years ago,
  As when the tide's full wrath in seaward flow
Smites and bears back the swimmer. Fraud and fate
Were leagued against her : fear was fain to prate
  Of honour in dishonour, pride brought low,
  And humbleness whence holiness must grow,
And greatness born of shame to be so great.

The winter day that withered hope and pride
Shines now triumphal on the turning tide
  That sets once more our trust in freedom free,
That leaves a ruthless and a truthless foe
And all base hopes that hailed his cause laid low,
  And England's name a light on land and sea.

    February 27, 1900.

ON THE DEATH OF COLONEL BENSON

NORTHUMBERLAND, so proud and sad to-day,
  Weep and rejoice, our mother, whom no son
  More glorious than this dead and deathless one
Brought ever fame whereon no time shall prey.
Nor heed we more than he what liars dare say
  Of mercy's holiest duties left undone
  Toward whelps and dams of murderous foes, whom
      none
Save we had spared or feared to starve and slay.

Alone as Milton and as Wordsworth found
And hailed their England, when from all around
  Howled all the recreant hate of envious knaves,
Sublime she stands : while, stifled in the sound,
  Each lie that falls from German boors and slaves
  Falls but as filth dropt in the wandering waves.

November 4, 1901.

ASTRÆA VICTRIX

ENGLAND, elect of time,
By freedom sealed sublime,
And constant as the sun that saw thy dawn
Outshine upon the sea
His own in heaven, to be
A light that night nor day should see withdrawn,
If song may speak not now thy praise,
Fame writes it higher than song may soar or faith
may gaze.

Dark months on months beheld
Hope thwarted, crossed, and quelled,
And heard the heartless hounds of hatred bay
Aloud against thee, glad
As now their souls are sad
Who see their hope in hatred pass away
And wither into shame and fear
And shudder down to darkness, loth to see or hear.

Nought now they hear or see
That speaks or shows not thee
Triumphant ; not as empires reared of yore,
The imperial commonweal
That bears thy sovereign seal

And signs thine orient as thy natural shore
　　Free, as no sons but thine may stand,
Steers lifeward ever, guided of thy pilot hand.

　　　　Fear, masked and veiled by fraud,
　　　　Found shameful time to applaud
　　Shame, and bow down thy banner towards the
　　　　　dust.
　　　　And call on godly shame
　　　　To desecrate thy name
　　And bid false penitence abjure thy trust :
　　　　Till England's heart took thought at last,
And felt her future kindle from her fiery past.

　　　　Then sprang the sunbright fire
　　　　High as the sun, and higher
　　Than strange men's eyes might watch it undis-
　　　　　mayed :
　　　　But winds athwart it blew
　　　　Storm, and the twilight grew
　　Darkness awhile, an unenduring shade :
　　　　And all base birds and beasts of night
Saw no more England now to fear, no loathsome light

　　　　All knaves and slaves at heart
　　　　Who, knowing thee what thou art,
　　Abhor thee, seeing what none save here may see
　　　　Strong freedom, taintless truth,
　　　　Supreme in ageless youth,
　　Howled all their hate and hope aloud at thee
　　　　While yet the wavering wind of strife
Bore hard against her sail whose freight is hope and
　　life.

And now the quickening tide
That brings back power and pride
To faith and love whose ensign is thy name
Bears down the recreant lie
That doomed thy name to die,
Sons, friends, and foes behold thy star the same
As when it stood in heaven a sun
And Europe saw no glory left her sky save one.

And now, as then she saw,
She sees with shamefast awe
How all unlike all slaves and tyrants born
Where bondmen champ the bit
And anarchs foam and flit,
And day mocks day, and year puts year to scorn,
Our mother bore us, English men,
Ashamed of shame and strong in mercy, now as then.

We loosed not on these knaves
Their scourge-tormented slaves :
We held the hand that fain had risen to smite
The torturer fast, and made
Justice awhile afraid,
And righteousness forego her ruthless right :
We warred not even with these as they ;
We bade not them they preyed on make of them their
prey.

All murderous fraud that lurks
In hearts where hell's craft 'works
Fought, crawled, and slew in darkness : they that
died
Dreamed not of foes too base
For scorn to grant them grace :

Men wounded, women, children at their side,
　Had found what faith in fiends may live :
And yet we gave not back what righteous doom would
　give.

　　No false white flag that fawns
　　On faith till murder dawns
Blood-red from hell-black treason's heart of hate
　　Left ever shame's foul brand
　　Seared on an English hand :
And yet our pride vouchsafes them grace too great
　For other pride to dream of : scorn
Strikes retribution silent as the stars at morn.

　　And now the living breath
　　Whose life puts death to death,
Freedom, whose name is England, stirs and
　　thrills
　　The burning darkness through
　　Whence fraud and slavery grew,
We scarce may mourn our dead whose fame fulfils
　The record where her foes have read
That earth shall see none like her born ere earth be
　dead.

THE FIRST OF JUNE

PEACE and war are one in proof of England's deathless praise.
  One divine day saw her foemen scattered on the
sea
Far and fast as storm could speed : the same strong
day of days
  Sees the imperial commonweal set friends and foemen free.
Save where freedom reigns, whose name is England,
fraud and fear
  Grind and blind the face of men who look on her
and lie :
Now may truth and pride in truth, whose seat of old
was here,
  See them shamed and stricken blind and dumb as
worms that die.
Even before our hallowed hawthorn-blossom pass and
cease,
  Even as England shines and smiles at last upon
the sun,

Comes the word that means for England more than
      passing peace,
  Peace with honour, peace with pride in righteous
      work well done.
Crowned with flowers the first of all the world and
      all the year,
Peace, whose name is one with honour born of war,
      is here.

ROUNDEL

FROM THE FRENCH OF VILLON

DEATH, I would plead against thy wrong,
  Who hast reft me of my love, my wife,
  And art not satiate yet with strife,
But needs wilt hold me lingering long.
No strength since then has kept me strong :
  But what could hurt thee in her life,
      Death ?

Twain we were, and our hearts one song,
  One heart : if that be dead, thy knife
  Hath cut me off alive from life,
Dead as the carver's figured throng,
      Death !

A ROUNDEL OF RABELAIS

THELEME is afar on the waters, adrift and afar,
Afar and afloat on the waters that flicker and gleam,
And we feel but her fragrance and see but the
    shadows that mar
        Theleme.

In the sun-coloured mists of the sunrise and sunset
    that steam
As incense from urns of the twilight, her portals ajar
Let pass as a shadow the light of the sound of a
    dream.

But the laughter that rings from her cloisters that
    know not a bar
So kindles delight in desire that the souls in us deem
He erred not, the seer who discerned on the seas as
    a star
        Theleme.

LUCIFER

Écrasez l'infâme.—VOLTAIRE

Les prêtres ont raison de l'appeler Lucifer.—VICTOR HUGO

VOLTAIRE, our England's lover, man divine
  Beyond all Gods that ever fear adored
  By right and might, by sceptre and by sword,
By godlike love of sunlike truth, made thine
Through godlike hate of falsehood's marshlight shine
  And all the fume of creeds and deeds abhorred
  Whose light was darkness, till the dawn-star
     soared,
Truth, reason, mercy, justice, keep thy shrine
Sacred in memory's temple, seeing that none
Of all souls born to strive before the sun
  Loved ever good or hated evil more.
The snake that felt thy heel upon her head,
Night's first-born, writhes as though she were not
    dead,
  But strikes not, stings not, slays not as before

THE CENTENARY OF ALEXANDRE DUMAS

SOUND of trumpets blowing down the merriest winds
  of morn,
  Flash of hurtless lightnings, laugh of thunders
    loud and glad,
Here should hail the summer day whereon a light
    was born
  Whence the sun grew brighter, seeing the world
    less dark and sad.
Man of men by right divine of boyhood everlasting,
  France incarnate, France immortal in her deathless
    boy,
Brighter birthday never shone than thine on earth,
    forecasting
  More of strenuous mirth in manhood, more of
    manful joy.
Child of warriors, friend of warriors, Garibaldi's
    friend,
  Even thy name is as the splendour of a sunbright
    sword :
While the boy's heart beats in man, thy fame shall
    find not end :
  Time and dark oblivion bow before thee as their
    lord.

Youth acclaims thee gladdest of the gods that gild
    his days :
Age gives thanks for thee, and death lacks heart to
    quench thy praise.

AT A DOG'S GRAVE

I

GOOD NIGHT, we say, when comes the time to win
The daily death divine that shuts up sight,
Sleep, that assures for all who dwell therein
      Good night.

The shadow shed round those we love shines bright
As love's own face, when death, sleep's gentler twin,
From them divides us even as night from light.

Shall friends born lower in life, though pure of sin,
Though clothed with love and faith to usward plight,
Perish and pass unbidden of us, their kin,
      Good night?

II

To die a dog's death once was held for shame.
Not all men so beloved and mourned shall lie
As many of these, whose time untimely came
      To die.

His years were full : his years were joyous : why
Must love be sorrow, when his gracious name
Recalls his lovely life of limb and eye?

If aught of blameless life on earth may claim
Life higher than death, though death's dark wave
        rise high,
Such life as this among us never came
                To die.

III

White violets, there by hands more sweet than they
Planted, shall sweeten April's flowerful air
About a grave that shows to night and day
                White violets there.

A child's light hands, whose touch makes flowers
        more fair,
Keep fair as these for many a March and May
The light of days that are because they were.

It shall not like a blossom pass away ;
It broods and brightens with the days that bear
Fresh fruits of love, but leave, as love might pray,
                White violets there.

THREE WEEKS OLD

THREE weeks since tnere was no such rose in being ;
  Now may eyes made dim with deep delight
See how fair it is, laugh with love, and seeing
  Praise the chance that bids us bless the sight.

Three weeks old, and a very rose of roses,
  Bright and sweet as love is sweet and bright.
Heaven and earth, till a man's life wanes and closes,
  Show not life or love a lovelier sight.

Three weeks past have renewed the rosebright
      creature
  Day by day with life, and night by night.
Love, though fain of its every faultless feature,
  Finds not words to match the silent sight.

A CLASP OF HANDS

I

Soft, small, and sweet as sunniest flowers
    That bask in heavenly heat
When bud by bud breaks, breathes, and cowers,
    Soft, small, and sweet.

A babe's hands open as to greet
    The tender touch of ours
And mock with motion faint and fleet

The minutes of the new strange hours
    That earth, not heaven, must mete ;
Buds fragrant still from heaven's own bowers,
    Soft, small, and sweet.

II

A velvet vice with springs of steel
    That fasten in a trice
And clench the fingers fast that feel
    A velvet vice—

What man would risk the danger twice,
    Nor quake from head to heel ?
Whom would not one such test suffice ?

Well may we tremble as we kneel
    In sight of Paradise,
If both a babe's closed fists conceal
    A velvet vice.

III

Two flower-soft fists of conquering clutch,
    Two creased and dimpled wrists,
That match, if mottled overmuch,
    Two flower-soft fists—

What heart of man dare hold the lists
    Against such odds and such
Sweet vantage as no strength resists?

Our strength is all a broken crutch,
    Our eyes are dim with mists,
Our hearts are prisoners as we touch
    Two flower-soft fists.

PROLOGUE TO ARDEN OF FEVERSHAM

Love dark as death and fierce as fire on wing
Sustains in sin the soul that feels it cling
Like flame whose tongues are serpents : hope and fear
Die when a love more dire than hate draws near,
And stings to death the heart it cleaves in twain,
And leaves in ashes all but fear and pain.
Our lustrous England rose to life and light
From Rome's and hell's immitigable night,
And music laughed and quickened from her breath,
When first her sons acclaimed Elizabeth.
Her soul became a lyre that all men heard
Who felt their souls give back her lyric word.
Yet now not all at once her perfect power
Spake : man's deep heart abode awhile its hour,
Abode its hour of utterance ; not to wake
Till Marlowe's thought in thunderous music spake.
But yet not yet was passion's tragic breath
Thrilled through with sense of instant life and death,
Life actual even as theirs who watched the strife,
Death dark and keen and terrible as life.
Here first was truth in song made perfect : here
Woke first the war of love and hate and fear.
A man too vile for thought's or shame's control
Holds empire on a woman's loftier soul,

And withers it to wickedness : in vain
Shame quickens thought with penitential pain :
In vain dark chance's fitful providence
Withholds the crime, and chills the spirit of sense :
It wakes again in fire that burns away
Repentance, weak as night devoured of day.
Remorse, and ravenous thirst of sin and crime,
Rend and consume the soul in strife sublime,
And passion cries on pity till it hear
And tremble as with love that casts out fear.
Dark as the deed and doom he gave to fame
For ever lies the sovereign singer's name.
Sovereign and regent on the soul he lives
While thought gives thanks for aught remembrance
    gives,
And mystery sees the imperial shadow stand
By Marlowe's side alone at Shakespeare's hand.

PROLOGUE TO OLD FORTUNATUS

THE golden bells of fairyland, that ring
Perpetual chime for childhood's flower-sweet spring,
Sang soft memorial music in his ear
Whose answering music shines about us here.
Soft laughter as of light that stirs the sea
With darkling sense of dawn ere dawn may be,
Kind sorrow, pity touched with gentler scorn,
Keen wit whose shafts were sunshafts of the morn,
Love winged with fancy, fancy thrilled with love,
An eagle's aim and ardour in a dove,
A man's delight and passion in a child,
Inform it as when first they wept and smiled.
Life, soiled and rent and ringed about with pain
Whose touch lent action less of spur than chain,
Left half the happiness his birth designed,
And half the power, unquenched in heart and mind.
Comrade and comforter, sublime in shame,
A poor man bound in prison whence he came
Poor, and took up the burden of his life
Smiling, and strong to strive with sorrow and strife,
He spake in England's ear the poor man's word,
Manful and mournful, deathless and unheard.
His kind great heart was fire, and love's own fire,
Compassion, strong as flesh may feel desire,

To enkindle pity and mercy toward a soul
Sunk down in shame too deep for shame's control.
His kind keen eye was light to lighten hope
Where no man else might see life's darkness ope
And pity's touch bring forth from evil good,
Sweet as forgiveness, strong as fatherhood.
Names higher than his outshine it and outsoar,
But none save one should memory cherish more :
Praise and thanksgiving crown the names above,
But him we give the gift he gave us, love.

PROLOGUE TO THE DUCHESS OF MALFY

WHEN Shakespeare soared from life to death, above
All praise, all adoration, save of love,
As here on earth above all men he stood
That were or are or shall be—great, and good,
Past thank or thought of England or of man—
Light from the sunset quickened as it ran.
His word, who sang as never man may sing
And spake as never voice of man may ring,
Not fruitless fell, as seed on sterile ways,
But brought forth increase even to Shakespeare's
 praise.
Our skies were thrilled and filled, from sea to sea,
With stars outshining all their suns to be.
No later light of tragic song they knew
Like his whose lightning clove the sunset through.
Half Shakespeare's glory, when his hand sublime
Bade all the change of tragic life and time
Live, and outlive all date of quick and dead,
Fell, rested, and shall rest on Webster's head.
Round him the shadows cast on earth by light
Rose, changed, and shone, transfiguring death and
 night.
Where evil only crawled and hissed and slew
On ways where nought save shame and bloodshed
 grew,

He bade the loyal light of honour live,
And love, when stricken through the heart, forgive.
Deep down the midnight of the soul of sin
He lit the star of mercy throned therein.
High up the darkness of sublime despair
He set the sun of love to triumph there.
Things foul or frail his touch made strong and pure,
And bade things transient like to stars endure.
Terror, on wings whose flight made night in heaven,
Pity, with hands whence life took love for leaven,
Breathed round him music whence his mortal breath
Drew life that bade forgetfulness and death
Die : life that bids his light of fiery fame
Endure with England's, yea, with Shakespeare's
    name.

PROLOGUE TO THE REVENGER'S TRAGEDY

FIRE, and behind the breathless flight of fire
Thunder that quickens fear and quells desire,
Make bright and loud the terror of the night
Wherein the soul sees only wrath for light.
Wrath winged by love and sheathed by grief in steel
Sets on the front of crime death's withering seal.
The heaving horror of the storms of sin
Brings forth in fear the lightning hid therein,
And flashes back to darkness : truth, found pure
And perfect, asks not heaven if shame endure.
What life and death were his whose raging song
Bore heaven such witness of the wild world's wrong,
What hand was this that grasped such thunder, none
Knows: night and storm seclude him from the sun.
By daytime none discerns the fire of Mars :
Deep darkness bares to sight the sterner stars,
The lights whose dawn seems doomsday.   None may
    tell
Whence rose a world so lit from heaven and hell.
Life-wasting love, hate born of raging lust,
Fierce retribution, fed with death's own dust
And sorrow's pampering poison, cross and meet,
And wind the world in passion's winding-sheet.
So, when dark faith in faith's dark ages heard
Falsehood, and drank the poison of the Word,

Two shades misshapen came to monstrous birth,
A father fiend in heaven, a thrall on earth :
Man, meanest born of beasts that press the sod,
And die : the vilest of his creatures, God.
A judge unjust, a slave that praised his name,
Made life and death one fire of sin and shame.
And thence reverberate even on Shakespeare's age
A light like darkness crossed his sunbright stage.
Music, sublime as storm or sorrow, sang
Before it : tempest like a harpstring rang.
The fiery shadow of a name unknown
Rose, and in song's high heaven abides alone.

PROLOGUE TO THE BROKEN HEART

THE mightiest choir of song that memory hears
Gave England voice for fifty lustrous years.
Sunrise and thunder fired and shook the skies
That saw the sun-god Marlowe's opening eyes.
The morn's own music, answered of the sea,
Spake, when his living lips bade Shakespeare be,
And England, made by Shakespeare's quickening
    breath
Divine and deathless even till life be death,
Brought forth to time such godlike sons of men
That shamefaced love grows pride, and now seems
    then.
Shame that their day so shone, so sang, so died,
Remembering, finds remembrance one with pride.
That day was clouding toward a stormlit close
When Ford's red sphere upon the twilight rose.
Sublime with stars and sunset fire, the sky
Glowed as though day, nigh dead, should never die.
Sorrow supreme and strange as chance or doom
Shone, spake, and shuddered through the lustrous
    gloom.
Tears lit with love made all the darkening air
Bright as though death's dim sunrise thrilled it there
And life re-risen took comfort. Stern and still
As hours and years that change and anguish fill,

The strong secluded spirit, ere it woke,
Dwelt dumb till power possessed it, and it spoke.
Strange, calm, and sure as sense of beast or bird,
Came forth from night the thought that breathed the
    word ;
That chilled and thrilled with passion-stricken breath
Halls where Calantha trod the dance of death.
A strength of soul too passionately pure
To change for aught that horror bids endure,
To quail and wail and weep faint life away
Ere sovereign sorrow smite, relent, and slay,
Sustained her silent, till her bridal bloom
Changed, smiled, and waned in rapture toward the
    tomb.
Terror twin-born with pity kissed and thrilled
The lips that Shakespeare's word or Webster's filled :
Here both, cast out, fell silent : pity shrank,
Rebuked, and terror, spirit-stricken, sank :
The soul assailed arose afar above
All reach of all but only death and love.

PROLOGUE TO A VERY WOMAN

SWIFT music made of passion's changeful power,
Sweet as the change that leaves the world in flower
When spring laughs winter down to deathward, rang
From grave and gracious lips that smiled and sang
When Massinger, too wise for kings to hear
And learn of him truth, wisdom, faith, or fear,
Gave all his gentler heart to love's light lore,
That grief might brood and scorn breed wrath no
    more.
Soft, bright, fierce, tender, fitful, truthful, sweet,
A shrine where faith and change might smile and
    meet,
A soul whose music could but shift its tune
As when the lustrous year turns May to June
And spring subsides in summer, so makes good
Its perfect claim to very womanhood.
The heart that hate of wrong made fire, the hand
Whose touch was fire as keen as shame's own brand
When fraud and treason, swift to smile and sting,
Crowned and discrowned a tyrant, knave or king,
False each and ravenous as the fitful sea,
Grew gently glad as love that fear sets free.
Like eddying ripples that the wind restrains,
The bright words whisper music ere it wanes.

Ere fades the sovereign sound of song that rang
As though the sun to match the sea's tune sang,
When noon from dawn took life and light, and time
Shone, seeing how Shakespeare made the world
    sublime,
Ere sinks the wind whose breath was heaven's and
    day's,
The sunset's witness gives the sundawn praise.

PROLOGUE TO THE SPANISH GIPSY

THE wind that brings us from the springtide south
Strange music as from love's or life's own mouth
Blew hither, when the blast of battle ceased
That swept back southward Spanish prince and priest,
A sound more sweet than April's flower-sweet rain,
And bade bright England smile on pardoned Spain.
The land that cast out Philip and his God
Grew gladly subject where Cervantes trod.
Even he whose name above all names on earth
Crowns England queen by grace of Shakespeare's birth
Might scarce have scorned to smile in God's wise down
And gild with praise from heaven an earthlier crown.
And he whose hand bade live down lengthening years
Quixote, a name lit up with smiles and tears,
Gave the glad watchword of the gipsies' life,
Where fear took hope and grief took joy to wife.
Times change, and fame is fitful as the sea :
But sunset bids not darkness always be,
And still some light from Shakespeare and the sun
Burns back the cloud that masks not Middleton.
With strong swift strokes of love and wrath he drew
Shakespearean London's loud and lusty crew :
No plainer might the likeness rise and stand
When Hogarth took his living world in hand.

II.

No surer then his fire-fledged shafts could hit,
Winged with as forceful and as faithful wit :
No truer a tragic depth and heat of heart
Glowed through the painter's than the poet's art.
He lit and hung in heaven the wan fierce moon
Whose glance kept time with witchcraft's air-struck
    tune :
He watched the doors where loveless love let in
The pageant hailed and crowned by death and sin
He bared the souls where love, twin-born with hate,
Made wide the way for passion-fostered fate.
All English-hearted, all his heart arose
To scourge with scorn his England's cowering foes :
And Rome and Spain, who bade their scorner be
Their prisoner, left his heart as England's free.
Now give we all we may of all his due
To one long since thus tried and found thus true.

PROLOGUE TO THE TWO NOBLE KINSMEN

Sweet as the dewfall, splendid as the south,
Love touched with speech Boccaccio's golden mouth,
Joy thrilled and filled its utterance full with song,
And sorrow smiled on doom that wrought no wrong.
A starrier lustre of lordlier music rose
Beyond the sundering bar of seas and snows
When Chaucer's thought took life and light from his
And England's crown was one with Italy's.
Loftiest and last, by grace of Shakespeare's word,
Arose above their quiring spheres a third,
Arose, and flashed, and faltered : song's deep sky
Saw Shakespeare pass in light, in music die.
No light like his, no music, man might give
To bid the darkened sphere, left songless, live.
Soft though the sound of Fletcher's rose and rang
And lit the lunar darkness as it sang,
Below the singing stars the cloud-crossed moon
Gave back the sunken sun's a trembling tune.
As when at highest high tide the sovereign sea
Pauses, and patience doubts if passion be,
Till gradual ripples ebb, recede, recoil,
Shine, smile, and whisper, laughing as they toil,
Stark silence fell, at turn of fate's high tide,
Upon his broken song when Shakespeare died,

Till Fletcher's light sweet speech took heart to say
What evening, should it speak for morning, may.
And fourfold now the gradual glory shines
That shows once more in heaven two twinborn signs,
Two brethren stars whose light no cloud may fret,
No soul whereon their story dawns forget.

THE AFTERGLOW OF SHAKESPEARE

LET there be light, said Time : and England heard :
And manhood grew to godhead at the word.
No light had shone, since earth arose from sleep,
So far ; no fire of thought had cloven so deep.
A day beyond all days bade life acclaim
Shakespeare : and man put on his crowning name.
All secrets once through darkling ages kept
Shone, sang, and smiled to think how long they slept.
Man rose past fear of lies whereon he trod :
And Dante's ghost saw hell devour his God.
Bright Marlowe, brave as winds that brave the sea
When sundawn bids their bliss in battle be,
Lit England first along the ways whereon
Song brighter far than sunlight soared and shone.
He died ere half his life had earned his right
To lighten time with song's triumphant light.
Hope shrank, and felt the stroke at heart : but one
She knew not rose, a man to match the sun.
And England's hope and time's and man's became
Joy, deep as music's heart and keen as flame.
Not long, for heaven on earth may live not long,
Light sang, and darkness died before the song.
He passed, the man above all men, whose breath
Transfigured life with speech that lightens death.
He passed : but yet for many a lustrous year
His light of song bade England shine and hear.

As plague and fire and faith in falsehood spread,
So from the man of men, divine and dead,
Contagious godhead, seen, unknown, and heard,
Fulfilled and quickened England ; thought and word,
When men would fain set life to music, grew
More sweet than years which knew not Shakespeare
    knew.
The simplest soul that set itself to song
Sang, and may fear not time's or change's wrong.
The lightest eye that glanced on life could see
Through grief and joy the God that man might be.
All passion whence the living soul takes fire
Till death fulfil despair and quench desire,
All love that lightens through the cloud of chance,
All hate that lurks in hope and smites askance,
All holiness of sorrow, all divine
Pity, whose tears are stars that save and shine,
All sunbright strength of laughter like the sea's
When spring and autumn loose their lustrous breeze,
All sweet, all strange, all sad, all glorious things,
Lived on his lips, and hailed him king of kings.
All thought, all strife, all anguish, all delight,
Spake all he bade, and speak till day be night.
No soul that heard, no spirit that beheld,
Knew not the God that lured them and compelled.
On Beaumont's brow the sun arisen afar
Shed fire which lit through heaven the younger star
That sank before the sunset : one dark spring
Slew first the kinglike subject, then the king.
The glory left above their graves made strong
The heart of Fletcher, till the flower-sweet song
That Shakespeare culled from Chaucer's field, and
    died,
Found ending on his lips that smiled and sighed.

From Dekker's eyes the light of tear-touched mirth
Shone as from Shakespeare's, mingling heaven and
    earth.
Wild witchcraft's lure and England's love made one
With Shakespeare's heart the heart of Middleton.
Harsh, homely, true, and tragic, Rowley told
His heart's debt down in rough and radiant gold.
The skies that Tourneur's lightning clove and rent
Flamed through the clouds where Shakespeare's
    thunder went.
Wise Massinger bade kings be wise in vain
Ere war bade song, storm-stricken, cower and wane.
Kind Heywood, simple-souled and single-eyed,
Found voice for England's home-born praise and
    pride.
Strange grief, strange love, strange terror, bared the
    sword
That smote the soul by grace and will of Ford.
The stern grim strength of Chapman's thought found
    speech
Loud as when storm at ebb-tide rends the beach :
And all the honey brewed from flowers in May
Made sweet the lips and bright the dreams of Day.
But even as Shakespeare caught from Marlowe's word
Fire, so from his the thunder-bearing third,
Webster, took light and might whence none but he
Hath since made song that sounded so the sea
Whose waves are lives of men—whose tidestream rolls
From year to darkening year the freight of souls.
Alone above it, sweet, supreme, sublime,
Shakespeare attunes the jarring chords of time
Alone of all whose doom is death and birth,
Shakespeare is lord of souls alive on earth.

CLEOPATRA

" Her beauty might outface the jealous hours,
Turn shame to love and pain to a tender sleep,
And the strong nerve of hate to sloth and tears ;
Make spring rebellious in the sides of frost,
Thrust out lank winter with hot August growths,
Compel sweet blood into the husks of death,
And from strange beasts enforce harsh courtesy."

T. HAYMAN, *Fall of Antony*, 1655.

CLEOPATRA

I

HER mouth is fragrant as a vine,
  A vine with birds in all its boughs ;
Serpent and scarab for a sign
  Between the beauty of her brows
And the amorous deep lids divine.

II

Her great curled hair makes luminous
  Her cheeks, her lifted throat and chin
Shall she not have the hearts of us
  To shatter, and the loves therein
To shred between her fingers thus ?

III

Small ruined broken strays of light,
  Pearl after pearl she shreds them through
Her long sweet sleepy fingers, white
  As any pearl's heart veined with blue,
And soft as dew on a soft night.

IV

As if the very eyes of love
   Shone through her shutting lids, and stole
The slow looks of a snake or dove ;
   As if her lips absorbed the whole
Of love, her soul the soul thereof.

V

Lost, all the lordly pearls that were
   Wrung from the sea's heart, from the green
Coasts of the Indian gulf-river ;
   Lost, all the loves of the world—so keen
Towards this queen for love of her.

VI

You see against her throat the small
   Sharp glittering shadows of them shake ;
And through her hair the imperial
   Curled likeness of the river snake,
Whose bite shall make an end of all.

VII

Through the scales sheathing him like wings,
   Through hieroglyphs of gold and gem,
The strong sense of her beauty stings,
   Like a keen pulse of love in them,
A running flame through all his rings.

VIII

Under those low large lids of hers
  She hath the histories of all time ;
The fruit of foliage-stricken years ;
  The old seasons with their heavy chime
That leaves its rhyme in the world's ears.

IX

She sees the hand of death made bare,
  The ravelled riddle of the skies,
The faces faded that were fair,
  The mouths made speechless that were wise,
The hollow eyes and dusty hair ;

X

The shape and shadow of mystic things,
  Things that fate fashions or forbids ;
The staff of time-forgotten Kings
  Whose name falls off the Pyramids,
Their coffin-lids and grave-clothings ;

XI

Dank dregs, the scum of pool or clod,
  God-spawn of lizard-footed clans,
And those dog-headed hulks that trod
  Swart necks of the old Egyptians,
Raw draughts of man's beginning God ;

XII

The poised hawk, quivering ere he smote,
  With plume-like gems on breast and back ;
The asps and water-worms afloat
  Between the rush-flowers moist and slack ;
The cat's warm black bright rising throat.

XIII

The purple days of drouth expand
  Like a scroll opened out again ;
The molten heaven drier than sand,
  The hot red heaven without rain,
Sheds iron pain on the empty land.

XIV

All Egypt aches in the sun's sight ;
  The lips of men are harsh for drouth,
The fierce air leaves their cheeks burnt white,
  Charred by the bitter blowing south,
Whose dusty mouth is sharp to bite.

XV

All this she dreams of, and her eyes
  Are wrought after the sense hereof.
There is no heart in her for sighs ;
  The face of her is more than love—
A name above the Ptolemies.

XVI

Her great grave beauty covers her
 As that sleek spoil beneath her feet
Clothed once the anointed soothsayer ;
 The hallowing is gone forth from it
Now, made unmeet for priests to wear.

XVII

She treads on gods and god-like things,
 On fate and fear and life and death,
On hate that cleaves and love that clings,
 All that is brought forth of man's breath
And perisheth with what it brings.

XVIII

She holds her future close, her lips
 Hold fast the face of things to be ;
Actium, and sound of war that dips
 Down the blown valleys of the sea,
Far sails that flee, and storms of ships ;

XIX

The laughing red sweet mouth of wine
 At ending of life's festival ;
That spice of cerecloths, and the fine
 White bitter dust funereal
Sprinkled on all things for a sign ;

XX

His face, who was and was not he,
  In whom, alive, her life abode ;
The end, when she gained heart to see
  Those ways of death wherein she trod,
Goddess by god, with Antony

DEDICATION

DEDICATION

The sea that is life everlasting
   And death everlasting as life
Abides not a pilot's forecasting,
   Foretells not of peace or of strife.
The might of the night that was hidden
   Arises and darkens the day,
A glory rebuked and forbidden,
   Time's crown, and his prey.

No sweeter, no kindlier, no fairer,
   No lovelier a soul from its birth
Wore ever a brighter and rarer
   Life's raiment for life upon earth
Than his who enkindled and cherished
   Art's vestal and luminous flame,
That dies not when kingdoms have perished
   In storm or in shame.

No braver, no trustier, no purer,
   No stronger and clearer a soul
Bore witness more splendid and surer
   For manhood found perfect and whole
Since man was a warrior and dreamer
   Than his who in hatred of wrong
Would fain have arisen a redeemer
   By sword or by song.

Twin brethren in spirit, immortal
  As art and as love, which were one
For you from the birthday whose portal
  First gave you to sight of the sun,
To-day nor to-night nor to-morrow
  May bring you again from above,
Drawn down by the spell of the sorrow
  Whose anguish is love.

No light rearising hereafter
  Shall lighten us here as of old
When seasons were lustrous as laughter
  Of waves that are snowshine and gold.
The dawn that imbues and enkindles
  Life's fluctuant and fugitive sea
Dies down as the starshine that dwindles
  And cares not to be.

Men, mightier than death which divides us,
  Friends, dearer than sorrow can say,
The light that is darkness and hides us
  Awhile from each other away
Abides but awhile and endures not,
  We know, though the day be as night,
For souls that forgetfulness lures not
  Till sleep be in sight.

The sleep that enfolds you, the slumber
  Supreme and eternal on earth,
Whence ages of numberless number
  Shall bring us not back into birth,
We know not indeed if it be not
  What no man hath known if it be,
Life, quickened with light that we see not
  If spirits may see.

The love that would see and would know it
    Is even as the love of a child.
But the fire of the fame of the poet
    Who gazed on the past, and it smiled,
But the light of the fame of the painter
    Whose hand was as morning's in May,
Death bids not be darker or fainter,
    Time casts not away.

We, left of them loveless and lonely,
    Who lived in the light of their love,
Whose darkness desires it, we only,
    Who see them afar and above,
So far, if we die not, above us,
    So lately no dearer than near,
May know not of death if they love us,
    Of night if they hear.

We, stricken and darkling and living,
    Who loved them and love them, abide
A day, and the gift of its giving,
    An hour, and the turn of its tide,
When twilight and midnight and morrow
    Shall pass from the sight of the sun,
And death be forgotten, and sorrow
    Discrowned and undone.

For us as for these will the breathless
    Brief minute arise and pass by :
And if death be not utterly deathless,
    If love do not utterly die,
From the life that is quenched as an ember
    The soul that aspires as a flame
Can choose not but wholly remember
    Love, lovelier than fame.

Though sure be the seal of their glory
  And fairer no fame upon earth,
Though never a leaf shall grow hoary
  Of the crowns that were given them at birth,
While time as a vassal doth duty
  To names that he towers not above,
More perfect in price and in beauty
  For ever is love.

The night is upon us, and anguish
  Of longing that yearns for the dead.
But mourners that faint not or languish,
  That veil not and bow not the head,
Take comfort to heart if a token
  Be given them of comfort to be :
While darkness on earth is unbroken,
  Light lives on the sea.

INDEX OF FIRST LINES